Sourcebook
of the
World's Religions

Sourcebook of the World's Religions

An Interfaith Guide to Religion and Spirituality

Edited by Joel Beversluis

New World Library

Novato, California

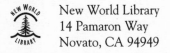 New World Library
14 Pamaron Way
Novato, CA 94949

Symbols used on the cover:
Top: Wicca, Zoroastrianism, Hinduism, Taoism, Bahá'í faith, Native American, Christianity
Bottom: Judaism, Sikhism, Shintoism, Jainism, Buddhism, Islam, Unnamed religions

Library of Congress Cataloging-in-Publication Data   ·

Sourcebook of the world's religions : an interfaith guide to religion and spirituality /
edited by Joel Beversluis.—3rd ed.
        p. cm.
  Rev. ed of: A sourcebook for earth's community of religions.
  Includes bibliographical references and indexes.
  ISBN 1-57731-121-3
    1. Religions—Handbooks, manuals, etc. 2. Religons—Relations—Handbooks, manuals, etc.
    I. Beversluis, Joel D. (Joel Diederik) II. Sourcebook for earth's community of religions.

BL82.S58 2000
291—dc21   00-038676

First printing, July 2000
ISBN 1-57731-121-3
Printed in Canada on acid-free, recycled paper
Distributed to the trade by Publishers Group West

10 9 8 7 6 5 4 3 2 1

Contents

Introduction, *Joel Beversluis* ix

◈ **PART ONE: Who Are We?** Major Religions, Spiritual Traditions, and Philosophies of the World 1
Introduction, *Joel Beversluis* 1

CHAPTER 1: African Traditional Religions 3
Introduction to African Traditional Religions, *Rev. Dr. Abraham Akrong* 3
Prayers and Religious Expression, *Dr. M. Darrol Bryant* 4
Zulu Traditional Religion of Southern Africa, *Lizo Doda Jafta* 5

CHAPTER 2: The Bahá'í Faith 6
A Portrait, *Dr. Robert H. Stockman* 6
Gleanings from the Writings of Bahá'u'lláh, 'Abdu'l-Bahá, and Shoghi Effendi 6

CHAPTER 3: Buddhism 11
A Portrait, *Dr. Geshe Sopa and Ven. Elvin W. Jones* 11
Selected Texts and Wisdom from Buddhist Tradition 11
Buddhist Experience in North America, *Ven. Mahinda Deegalle* 15
Mutual Recognition, *H.H. The 14th Dalai Lama of Tibet* 15
Zen, *The Zen Center, San Francisco* 17

CHAPTER 4: Christianity 18
Origins and Beliefs, *The Rev. Dr. Thomas A. Baima, S.T.L.* 18
Selected Scriptures 18
The Christian Family Tree, *The Rev. Epke VanderBerg* 21
Christianity in the World Today, *Dr. Dieter T. Hessel* 26
Selected Scriptures 28
African-American Christianity, *Dr. David D. Daniels* 32
Selected Scriptures 33
Native American–Christian Worship, *The Right Rev. Steve Charleston* 34
A Call for Evangelical Renewal, *Chicago Declaration II* 34

CHAPTER 5: Confucianism 37
A Portrait, *Dr. Douglas K. Chung* 37
Integration of Confucianism with Other Traditions, *Dr. Douglas K. Chung* 40

CHAPTER 6: First Peoples and Native Traditions 42
A Portrait of the First Peoples 42
The First Peoples in the Fourth World: Terms 42
Voices of Indigenous Peoples 43
Partners toward a Sustainable Future, *Maurice Strong* 44
Ancient Prophecies for Modern Times, *Bette Stockbauer* 45
Native American Spirituality, *Robert Staffanson* 48
A Teaching from Tecumseh 49

CHAPTER 7: Hinduism 50
A Portrait, *Dr. T. K. Venkateswaran* 50
Wisdom from the Hindu Tradition, *Compiled and translated by Dr. T. K. Venkateswaran* 50
On Yoga, *compiled by Dr. T. K. Venkateswaran* 56
Yoga in the West, *Fred Stella and Joel Beversluis* 57
Vedanta, Ramakrishna, and Vivekananda 57
Vivekananda Speaks, from the 1893 Parliament 58
Self-Realization Fellowship 59
ISKCON, the International Society for Krishna Consciousness 59

CHAPTER 8: Humanism 60
  Humanist Manifesto II 60
CHAPTER 9: Islam 66
  A Portrait, *Dr. Ghulam Haider Aasi* 66
  Islam in North America, *Dr. Aminah B. McCloud* 73
  The Golden Words of a Sufi Sheikh, *M. R. Bawa Muhaiyaddeen* 75
  Islam in the World Today, *Syed Z. Abedin* 76
CHAPTER 10: Jainism 79
  A Portrait, *Amar T. Salgia* 79
  Jain Prayers and Songs 79
  Virchand Raghavji Gandhi 84
CHAPTER 11: Judaism 85
  A Portrait, *Rabbi Herbert Bronstein* 85
  The Worth of Wisdom 85
CHAPTER 12: Shinto 89
  A Portrait, *Naofusa Hirai* 89
  Edict and Principles 90
CHAPTER 13: Sikhism 92
  A Portrait, *Dr. Rajwant Singh and Ms. Georgia Rangel* 92
  Excerpts from *Guru Granth Sahib* (The Sikh Scriptures) 93
CHAPTER 14: Spiritual, Esoteric, and Evolutionary Philosophies 98
  Anthroposophy: Toward a More Human Future 98
  The Arcane School 99
  The Evolutionary Philosophy of Sri Aurobindo and the Mother 100
  A Portrait of Theosophy, *Dr. John Algeo* 101
  Wisdom in the Theosophical Tradition 102
CHAPTER 15: Taoism 105
  A Portrait, *Dr. Douglas K. Chung* 105
CHAPTER 16: The Unification Church 109
  A Portrait, *Dr. Frank Kaufmann* 109
CHAPTER 17: The Unitarian Universalist Church 111
  A History of Diversity and Openness, *The Rev. David A. Johnson* 111
CHAPTER 18: Wicca and Nature Spirituality 113
  A Portrait of Wicca, *H.Ps. Phyllis W. Curott, J.D.* 113
  The Charge of the Goddess 114
  A Guide to Nature Spirituality Terms, *Selena Fox* 116
CHAPTER 19: Zoroastrianism 119
  Portrait of an Ancient Monotheistic Religion, *Dr. Pallan R. Ichaporia* 119
  Zoroastrianism in the World Today, *Dr. Jehan Bagli* 120
  Contributions to Western Thought, *Rohinton M. Rivetna* 121

◆ PART TWO: Becoming a Community of Religions 123
  Introduction, *Joel Beversluis* 123

CHAPTER 20: Interfaith Dialogue: How and Why Do We Speak Together? 126
  Introduction, *Joel Beversluis* 126
  Objectives of the 1893 World's Parliament of Religions 128
  The Interfaith Movement in the 20th Century, *The Rev. Dr. Marcus Braybrooke* 129
  Points of Similarity Found in Dialogue, *Father Thomas Keating, O.S.C.O.* 137
  The Deep-Dialogue Decalogue, *Dr. Leonard Swidler and Global Dialogue Institute* 138
  Proposal for a Code of Ethics among Religions in Mexico, *Mexican InterFaith Council* 142

CHAPTER 21: The Interfaith Movement: Who Are the Interfaith Organizations and What Do They Do? 146
    Introduction, *Joel Beversluis* 146
    A Sampling of Interfaith Organizations and Programs, *compiled by Joel Beversluis* 148
    A Grassroots Model, *Dr. Lillian Sigal* 157
    A Definition of Terms, *Association of Interfaith Ministers (AIM)* 159
    Collaboration among the Diverse Religions, *Pope John Paul II* 160
    Young Adult and Youth Organizations, *Joel Beversluis* 162
CHAPTER 22: The Parliaments and the Quest for a Global Ethic 166
    Introduction, *Joel Beversluis* 166
    The Quest for a Global Ethic, *Joel Beversluis* 171
    An Ancient Precept 172
    Towards a Global Ethic, *Council for a Parliament of the World's Religions* 174
    The 1999 Parliament, *Joel Beversluis with CPWR Press Releases* 182
    A Call to Our Guiding Institutions, *Council for a Parliament of the World's Religions* 184
    Visions of Challenge, Harmony, and Transformation, *Brother Wayne Teasdale and Joel Beversluis* 202
    Suggestions to Strengthen and Broaden the Parliament, *Dr. Allan Mott Keislar* 205
CHAPTER 23: Facing Religious Intolerance, Violence, and Other Evils 209
    Introduction, *Joel Beversluis* 209
    The Interreligious Assembly at the Vatican 211
    Temples Firebombed in Sacramento, *Alan Canton* 212
    Lutherans and Judaism—A New Possibility, *Dr. Stephen A. Schmidt* 215
    Universal Declaration on Nonviolence 216
    Eliminating Intolerance and Discrimination Based on Religion or Belief 217
    How May I Help?, *Dr. Guy de Mallac* 221
    The Seville Statement on Violence 224
    May the Light Dawn, *Dr. Paulos Mar Gregorios* 226
    The Threat of Nuclear Weapons 228
CHAPTER 24: Spirituality and Community 231
    Introduction, *Joel Beversluis* 231
    Exploring Spirituality, *Dr. Peter Laurence* 232
    Toward a Global Spirituality, *Dr. Patricia M. Mische* 236
    Global Spiritualities, *Joel Beversluis* 237
    Sacred Community at the Dawn of the Second Axial Age, *Brother Wayne Teasdale* 238
    The Cosmology of Religions and the Sacred Story of the Universe, *Dr. Thomas Berry* 244
    A Universal Understanding of Spirituality and Mysticism, *Brother Wayne Teasdale* 250
    The World House 254

◆ **PART THREE: Choosing Our Future** 259
    Introduction: Making the Connections, *Joel Beversluis* 259

CHAPTER 25: Creating a Culture of Peace 262
    Introduction, *Joel Beversluis* 262
    Declaration on the Role of Religion in the Promotion of a Culture of Peace, *UNESCO* 263
    Religion and World Order, *Dr. Patricia M. Mische* 264
    The Causes of Peace Failure 266
    Seeking the True Meaning of Peace, *Joel Beversluis* 269
    Declaration of Human Responsibilities for Peace and Sustainable Development 270
    Toward a Universal Civilization with a "Heart," *Brother Wayne Teasdale* 273
    New Roles for Religious Nongovernmental Organizations, *Joel Beversluis* 278
    Prayers, Scriptures, and Reflections on Peace 280
CHAPTER 26: Religions, Ecology, and Spirituality 282
    Preserving and Cherishing the Earth—A Joint Appeal in Religion and Science 282

Spiritual Dimensions of the Environmental Crisis, *Dr. Daniel Gomez-Ibanez* 283
The Gaia Hypothesis, *Joel Beversluis* 291
Prayers, Scriptures, and Reflections in Celebration of the Earth 295
The Earth Charter 303
The Declaration of the Sacred Earth Gathering 309
An Evangelical Christian Declaration on the Care of Creation 310
The Jain Declaration on Nature 310
On the Urgency of a Jewish Response to the Environmental Crisis 311
Cairo Declaration on Population and Development 312
Our Children, Their Earth 315
A Declaration of Independence—from Overconsumption, *Vicki Robin* 317
CHAPTER 27: Human Rights and Responsibilities 320
Faith in Human Rights, *Dr. Robert Traer* 320
Universal Declaration of Human Rights, *United Nations* 325
The NGO Committee on Freedom of Religion and Belief 328
The Enduring Revolution, *Charles W. Colson* 329
The Conversion Dilemma, *Joel Beversluis* 330
Voices of the Dispossessed, *David Nelson* 331
The Sweetgrass Hills, *Native American Rights Fund* 335
Women Struggle for Survival 336
Finally—Choosing Our Future As Women, *Rev. Marchiene Vroon Rienstra* 336
The World's Religions for the World's Children 340
The Convention on the Rights of the Child 342
A Universal Declaration of Human Responsibilities, *The InterAction Council* 343
CHAPTER 28: What Shall We Do Next? 345
Introduction, *Joel Beversluis* 345
A Response to Those Who Despair about the State of the World, *Dr. Willis W. Harman* 347
Towards the Dialogue of Love, *Robert L. Fastiggi* 348
Hope 349
A Dual Awakening Process, *Dr. Ahangamage T. Ariyaratne* 349
Make Love Your Aim 350
The Family of Abraham, *Dom Helder Camara* 350
Decide to Network 351
The Practice of Meditation, *K. G. von Durckheim* 351
Action and Prayer 352
Who Will Tell Us What to Do? *Thich Nhat Hahn* 352
Concerning Acts of Initiative and Creation 353
A Critical Point in History 353
Prayer for the Sacred Community 354

◆ PART FOUR: Selected Resources for the Community of Religions 355

CHAPTER 29: Use the Internet! 356
An Online Congress of World Religions? *Bruce Schuman* 356
Internet Sites for Comparative Religious Studies and World Religions, *compiled by James T. Cloud* 357
Interfaith Internet Links, *compiled by Susan Sarfaty* 360
CHAPTER 30: A Directory of Faith and Interfaith Voices for Peace and Justice, *Gloria Weber and Bruce Schuman* 363
Index of Organizations in the Directory by Area of Focus 420
Index 431
Acknowledgments 441

INTRODUCTION

Joel D. Beversluis

The Editor of this Sourcebook, Joel Beversluis, has worked in academic religious publishing, volunteered in peace, ecology, and interfaith organizations, studied comparative religion at Western Michigan University, and is now Editor and Publisher of CoNexus Press.

Initially created as a resource for the participants in the 1993 Parliament of the World's Religions, the *Sourcebook* was substantially revised and enlarged in 1995. In this Third Edition, many new articles, documents, reports up to the turn of the century, and resource listings such as a Directory make it a unique compilation.

Its pages are brim full of beliefs, wisdom, pioneering ideas, essays, prayers, scriptures, resource listings, organizational goals, projects, analysis, and visions. Through the contributions from members of many of the world's religions and spiritual traditions, the book also aims to reveal a variety of perceptions about the Source of all, about the meanings and purposes of our lives, and about the challenges and opportunities in the contemporary world. This book is also a resource through which readers may start to evaluate both the uniquenesses and commonalities of humanity's beliefs, truths, and wisdom.

We are not, however, proposing the deliberate mixing or watering-down of beliefs and traditions into a consensus or world religion. In this sense and in other ways, the book is an *Interfaith Guide*. The *Sourcebook* incorporates the standard of most major interfaith organizations: affirming the integrity of religious and spiritual traditions, and appreciating the diversity of the world's religions and cultures.

While the selection of the materials printed here inevitably reflects its Editor's values and interfaith experiences, the contents also showcase the distinctive beliefs, experience, and knowledge of hundreds of contributors. These members of different religions, professions, and ethnic backgrounds do not always agree with each other. Nevertheless, their inclusion here models an exciting,

"In this new ecological age of developing global community and interfaith dialogue, the world religions face what is perhaps the greatest challenge that they have ever encountered. Each is inspired by a unique vision of the divine and has a distinct cultural identity. At the same time, each perceives the divine as the source of unity and peace. The challenge is to preserve their religious and cultural uniqueness without letting it operate as a cause of narrow and divisive sectarianism that contradicts the vision of divine unity and peace.

"It is a question whether the healing light of religious vision will overcome the social and ideological issues that underlie much of the conflict between religions."

DR. STEVEN C. ROCKEFELLER
from *Spirit and Nature*, p. 169

"True spirituality—the authentic religious journey—can never be an escape from life's problems....Our spiritual journey...must be worked out now in a global context in the midst of global crises and global community."

DR. PATRICIA MISCHE
Cofounder of Global Education Associates,
in *Towards a Global Spirituality*

"All the religions and all the people of the world are undergoing the most challenging transformation in history, leading to the birth of a new consciousness. Forces which have been at work for centuries are drawing the human race into a global network, and the religions of the world into a global spiritual community."

DR. EWERT COUSINS
in *Journal of Ecumenical Studies*

interfaith interaction. Out of this wide-ranging collage, arranged in four parts, each reader must draw out his or her own conclusions and, hopefully, enrich his or her own spiritual commitments.

Part One: Who Are We?

The first nineteen chapters offer portraits of major religions and spiritual philosophies. In most cases these were written by adherents of the community described. Contributors provided prayers, songs, and texts to give a flavor of their worship and beliefs. Many chapters also include perspectives on relationships with other religious communities and on how the community portrayed responds to one or more global issues. These articles provide the foundation for the book, the primary resources that support the explorations in its other parts and chapters.

Who are we? On the one hand, we are complex, wonderful, mysterious, diverse, creative seekers of divine truth, exploring who we are, why we're here, and how we should live. On the other hand. . . see other chapters (e.g., Chapter 23) and other media.

Part Two: Becoming a Community of Religions

While the pages of this *Sourcebook* hold many different convictions, one guiding principle for compiling it is this: a critical task for leaders and members of all of the world's religions and spiritual traditions is to enrich the sense of community and hospitality among us. We are part of the community of the Earth and, within it, we are becoming the community of religions.

As we learn more about the interaction of the systems of the Earth and, at the same time, discover their subtleties in the spiritual wisdom of the ages, we are also becoming aware of the primordial matrix that binds us together. We often don't appreciate our dependence on Earth and our relationship with the cosmos, whose systems have given birth to us and nurtured us in all our mystery of body, consciousness, heart, mind, and soul.

Although this spiritual-physical matrix has always been evident to some peoples, contemporary cultures need the knowledge of these webs of interconnectedness and of the obligations that these place upon us. Taking responsibility for these obligations is one primary function of the emerging global community of religions. Other functions include learning to speak together in dialogue, defining and committing to principles of a global ethic, facing religious intolerance and other evils among us, and understanding spirituality and mysticism.

The interfaith movement, through its numerous organizations and participants throughout the world, is a symptom of the emergence of community among religions. The movement is also helping to create that sense of community. Observers who focus on the evidence of conflict between religions may see this alleged community as little more than a fantasy. Clearly, it does have its dysfunctional aspects, as most communities do. Other observers, however, understand that naming the ideal provides a vision and reasons for hope.

And for many, including this writer, the emergence of a sense of community among religions is proved by the values and responses of numerous participants in religious and spiritual communities, in the interfaith movement, in numerous service organization—peace, ecology, justice, education, humanitarian, and many more—and in this book.

Part Three: Choosing Our Future

Without a vision, as the Jewish prophet warned, we will perish. Unfortunately, this prophecy is not warning against some future apocalyptic scenario. In fact, even now many of our brothers and sisters of all species are victims of ethical, political, economic and environmental disasters that are rooted in spiritual disorder.

Which future vision and reality shall we choose? It's clear that religious and spiritual communities do help create, and often lead the march toward, a culture of peace and justice when they draw on their highest ideals. Likewise, their wisdom and organizing capacities are now enriching the responses to environmental disasters and sustainable development. Basic ideas about human rights and human responsibilities are derived from and supported by religious and spiritual traditions.

At the same time, lest we overlook the abuses of religion, the interfaith movement and spiritually alert people everywhere are encouraging religious and spiritual communities to reflect on our own failures. Can we face these, too, and in so doing reshape our future?

Part Four: Resources

The phenomenon of global Internet use provides amazing new opportunities for religious and inter-

religious study, encounter, dialogue, and action. Those who have Web access can explore some of the many new Internet Web-sites and online indices listed in Part Four. Those who are curious about just what it is that religious, spiritual, and interfaith groups are doing should consult the nearly seven hundred organizations listed in the inspiring, one-of-a-kind "Directory of Faith and Interfaith Voices for Peace and Justice."

How to Read the *Sourcebook*

This book is a unique anthology, bringing together elements characteristic of many different kinds of publications. The *Sourcebook* deliberately crosses topical and stylistic boundaries, connecting content and disciplines that are too often kept apart. This not only meets the varying interests and needs of readers. It is, in short, a holistic exploration, seeking to provide readers with perspectives to help shape their own world-transforming vision.

Past readers of the *Sourcebook* have found it useful in many ways: for information, wisdom, and inspiration; for stimulating discussion groups and classes; and as a tool for reference. It serves not only members of the world's religions and spiritual traditions but also humanists, atheists, and agnostics. Indeed, some of the documents in the *Sourcebook*, such as "The Humanist Manifesto," "The Earth Charter," and "Towards a Global Ethic," were written for both religious and nonreligious consideration.

Although the book's contents do follow a progression, one need not read it front to back. Indeed, the book may be much more meaningful if readers follow their own interests, paging through it or choosing from the table of contents and indices.

A Challenge

Due in part to the media, to laborsaving devices, and to our evolving uses of leisure time, we can very easily become spectators of life or consumers of information. Modern education, media, and even our religious lives are so colored by the inclination to observation that we are seduced by the idea that pleasant thoughts and significant information—and even entertainment—are necessary and sufficient for the good life. This book suggests that there is more, much more!

The *Sourcebook* had its genesis in the vision of the Parliament of the World's Religions. A primary theme of the 1993 Chicago Parliament and of the 1999 Parliament in Cape Town was a question: "What shall we do?" The question mirrors back to us the demands of our changing times, our future focus, and the need for ethical and appropriate action. Now, as we move across the threshold into a new century and millennium, through the swirling nexus of beliefs, wisdom, conflicts, challenges, and opportunities, we must each begin to answer that question.

The *Sourcebook of the World's Religions* is designed to nurture a process of reflection and action, in what can be a transformative process. In presenting who we humans claim to be and hope to become, the *Sourcebook* seeks to help readers appreciate humanity's strengths, promote the many gifts of religion and spirituality, and identify some of our tasks and commitments. If the book helps readers move into more intriguing reflections on powerful ideas and beliefs, and then into appropriate responses, its goals will be accomplished.

Now it is in your hands.

—*January 2000*

Part One

WHO ARE WE?
Major Religions, Spiritual Traditions, and Philosophies of the World

Introduction

Joel Beversluis

We—the members of major religions, spiritual traditions, and philosophies of the world—are beyond accurate counting and beyond comprehensive descriptions. Our local and individual variations cannot be circumscribed, in part because we are always in flux. We are influenced by each other, by our experiences in the world, and by our own changing perceptions. So we are also beyond definition.

Nevertheless, we may describe some of our diverse characteristics and thus begin to develop a picture of the whole. One such image guiding this survey is that a sense of community is—and should be—emerging among the religions, spiritual traditions, and philosophies, within the larger community of the Earth.

Those who read this *Sourcebook* may conclude with its Editor that indeed there is a "community" and that, furthermore, one of its most significant characteristics is that this community has many wondrous yet underutilized gifts within it. The sense of commitment engendered by the religions and spiritual philosophies, their organizational and motiva-

tional resources, the wisdom and insight in their heritages, and their practical experience with real life issues are all portions of a substantial cultural and spiritual legacy. These gifts must be given freedom and put to work!

The authors of nearly all the essays in Part One have written not as official representatives, nor as disinterested specialists (though most of them are scholars), but as committed participants within the traditions they describe. In addition to the essays, most contributors also provided selections of scriptures, prayers, and commentary valued by their traditions, and some even made original translations.

Most of the major religious and spiritual traditions of the Earth—and some of their movements and branches—are portrayed here. Yet, since the traditions and their many manifestations are so numerous, this work must be seen as an introduction and survey. Much more detail is available in other works.

Despite enhancements in this Revised Edition, there remain imbalances. The alphabetical listing of so many traditions and movements side by side does not do justice to disproportions in the numbers of adherents, their global presence, and their complexity. The following criteria guided the choices of what to include

1. Religious and spiritual traditions that are historic and worldwide

2. Representative indigenous traditions

3. Examples of spiritual and esoteric philosophies

4. Examples of influential new movements or branches off historic traditions

5. Groups that were accessible and whose members responded to the invitation to participate.

This last factor led to an emphasis on those groups with a substantial presence in North America; this emphasis is, of course, unfortunate in a book purporting to have a global outlook. It is also unfortunate because so many traditions have religious and cultural ties to the land itself—outside of North America. Yet, because the rich and increasingly pluralistic North American culture has adherents from so many traditions and lands of origin, we offer their beliefs and experience as a starting point.

Authors of the Portraits were invited to write short essays and provide materials on

1. The origins, beliefs, and membership of their tradition

2. Its approach to interreligious encounter and cooperation

3. Its understanding of, and responses to, critical issues

4. Selected wisdom, scriptures, prayers, or commentary relating to the above.

Other articles offer insights into important aspects of a tradition or movement. The Editor has also selected previously printed articles, reflections, scriptures, or prayers that provide further insight into the self-understanding of some members of a tradition. All materials are intended to add depth to our understanding and to provide insights about the challenges and opportunities we face in today's world.

Chapter One
AFRICAN TRADITIONAL RELIGIONS

Introduction to African Traditional Religions

Rev. Dr. Abraham Akrong

Professor of Religion

The Term "Africa"

Since the time of Pliny the Elder, who is reputed to have first used it, the term "Africa" has been a bone of contention because it means different things to different people—for many people Africa is essentially a racial group; for some, Africa is a geopolitical entity carved up in the last century at the Berlin conference of 1884–85; for others, Africa is a linguistic-cultural entity that describes the life of the African peoples that belong to these communities: the Niger-Congo, the Nilo-Sahara, the Afro-Asiatic, and the Khoisan linguistic groups.

Generally, today, we are conditioned to view Africa as a conglomeration of different ethnic groups bound together by the colonial divisions of Africa, which still persist today in independent Africa.

The Concept of African Religion

Related to this geopolitical and cultural view of Africa is the 19th-century classification based on the so-called evolutionary theory of culture and religion. This classification of religions based on belief systems puts African religion and culture on the lowest level of the evolutionary ladder, because, it was believed, African primitive culture can only produce the most elementary and primitive belief systems. Until recently, this treatment of African religions in the Western intellectual tradition has made it impossible for African traditional religion to speak for itself except in terms of 19th-century evolutionism or the Western anthropological theories of primitive religions and cultures.

From History to Culture

Today the liberation from the classifications of the last century has given an intellectual autonomy to African religion and culture. They can now be understood as self-contained systems that are internally coherent without reference to any grand theories. This has allowed us to face up to the plurality of religions and cultures. Therefore in any discourse about African religion we must start from the perspective of the worshipers and devotees of African traditional religion.

African Religion from Within

A study of the beliefs and practices of the African peoples leads to the theological observation that African traditional religion is a religion of salvation and wholeness. A careful analysis shows an emphasis on this-worldly salvation and wholeness as the *raison d'être* of African traditional religion. Because Africans believe that life is a complex web of relationships that may either enhance and preserve life or diminish and destroy it, the goal of religion is to maintain those relationships that protect and preserve life. For it is the harmony and stability provided by these relationships, both spiritual and material, that create the conditions for well-being and wholeness.

The threat to life both physical and spiritual is the premise of the quest for salvation. The threat is so near and real because, for the African, life is a continuum of power points that are transformed into being and life is constantly under threat from evil forces.

This logic of the relationality of being and cosmic life gives rise to the view that all reality is interrelated like a family. This same relational metaphysics is what undergirds the life of the individual in community.

Individual in Community

J. S. Mbiti captures this relational metaphysics succinctly in the dictum: "I am because we are and because we are therefore I am." The life of the individual comes into fruition through the social ritual of rites of passage. These rites are the process that can help the individual to attain the goals of his or her destiny, given at birth by God. Those who successfully go through the rites of passage become candidates for ancestorhood—the goal of the ideal life. For the African, ancestors are much more than dead parents of the living. They are the embodiment of what it means to live the full life that is contained in one's destiny.

God, Creation, and Cosmic Life

God in Africa is a relational being who is known through various levels of relationship with creation. In relation to humanity, God is the great ancestor of the human race. Therefore, all over Africa God is portrayed more in terms of parent than as sovereign. In relation to the earth, God is a husband who stands behind the creative fecundity of the earth that sustains human life. God in relation to creation is the creator from whom life flows and is sustained. In relation to the divinities, God is their father who requires them to care for the cosmic processes.

Unity and Diversity

The various elements of African religion that make what I call the transcendental structure of African religion are expressed differently by the various African peoples on the basis of their social organization and environment.

A Definition

One can describe African religion as a this-worldly religion of salvation that promises well-being and wholeness here and now. It is a religion that affirms life and celebrates life in its fullness; this accounts for the lively and celebrative mood that characterizes African worship in all its manifestations.

Prayers and Religious Expression

Dr. M. Darrol Bryant

Professor of Religion, Waterloo University, and Secretary General of the Inter Religious Federation for World Peace

The expressions of African traditional religion are manifold. They have shaped the lives of African peoples from the dawn of history down to the present time. They have lived as oral traditions in the memory and practice of countless generations. The name of God varies across traditions as do the names of the divinities and the practices of the spiritual life. The Nuer of East Africa, for example, believe that prayer is appropriate at any time because "they like to speak to God when they are happy."

A typical Nuer prayer is

Our Father, it is thy universe, it is thy will,
let us be at peace,
let the soul of thy people be cool.
Thou art our Father,
remove all evil from our path.

For African traditional religion there is a daily intercourse between the living and the dead, the ancestral spirits. The interaction with these realities is facilitated through prayers, rites, incantations, and libations. Many of these practices involve elements of nature such as water, foodstuffs like cassava or nuts, or animals like chickens in sacrificial rites. Yoruba practices involve all types of foods and drinks in their offerings. A Yoruba chant cries out:

O God of heaven, O God of earth,
I pray thee uphold my hand,
My ancestors and ancestresses
Lean upon earth and succor me
That I may not quickly come to you.

This tradition celebrates the spirits present in the natural world and seeks to maintain proper relations between the living community and the living cosmos. Drums and dancing often figure prominently in its rites and practices. There is often a great concern for healing and health. Expressions of this tradition are too diverse to allow easy generalizations.

—previously printed in the "General Programme," IRFWP New Delhi Congress, 1993

Zulu Traditional Religion of Southern Africa

Lizo Doda Jafta

Lecturer at the Federal Theological Seminary of Southern Africa, Natal

One of the basic human experiences is that a human being is a dependent creature; therefore, the contingency of being human demands that one should properly relate oneself to the environment upon which one depends. Thus the human sense of dependence becomes the root religion.

One becomes aware that one did not create the universe; one found the universe already created. This awe-inspiring universe with its boundless spaces and measureless forces occasions God-consciousness. Natural events in particular are occasions of God-consciousness among the Zulu people. The changes in the clouds, the highness of the heavens, the overflowing rivers, the frightening lightning and thunderstorms side-by-side with religious ceremonies are all occasions of God-consciousness. In these events God is experienced as the One, the Other, the Divine, and the Many. The key word is experience. [...]

The Zulu notion of God-consciousness . . . says that God lives in, through, and beyond everything and everyone, but that God is most clearly apprehended through those spirits who are always around, below, above, and in them. . . . When the Zulus see the Deity in every place and all the time, they are acknowledging the ubiquitous nature of God as well as their constant sojourn within the realm of the divine presence.

—excerpted from "The One, the Other, the Divine, the Many in Zulu Traditional Religion of Southern Africa" in *Dialogue and Alliance*, Summer 1992, pp. 79–89

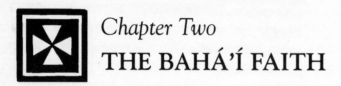

Chapter Two
THE BAHÁ'Í FAITH

Gleanings from the Writings of Bahá'u'lláh, 'Abdu'l-Bahá, and Shoghi Effendi

"Know thou of a certainty that Love is the secret of God's holy Dispensation, the manifestation of the All-Merciful, the fountain of spiritual outpourings. Love is heaven's kindly light, the Holy Spirit's eternal breath that vivifieth the human soul. Love is the cause of God's revelation unto man, the vital bond inherent, in accordance with the divine creation, in the realities of things. Love is the one means that ensureth true felicity both in this world and the next. Love is the light that guideth in darkness, the living link that uniteth God with man, that assureth the progress of every illumined soul . . . .

"Love is the most great law that ruleth this mighty and heavenly cycle, the unique power that bindeth together the diverse elements of this material world, the supreme magnetic force that directeth the movements of the spheres in the celestial realms. Love revealeth with unfailing and limitless power the mysteries latent in the universe. Love is the spirit of life unto the adorned body of mankind, the establisher of true civilization in this mortal world, and the shedder of imperishable glory upon every high-aiming race and nation."

'ABDU'L-BAHÁ,
Selections from the Writings of 'Abdu'l-Bahá, p. 27

A Portrait

Dr. Robert H. Stockman

Director of Research, Bahá'í National Center, Wilmette, Illinois

The Bahá'í Faith is an independent world religion now in the 150th year of its existence. According to the *Encyclopedia Britannica Yearbook* it is the second most widely spread religion in the world, with five million members residing in 232 countries and dependent territories, and national spiritual assemblies (national Bahá'í governing bodies) in 172.

The Bahá'í Faith began in Iran. Its history is intimately connected with the lives of its leading figures:

'Alí-Muhammad, Titled *the Báb.*

Born in southern Iran in 1819, in 1844 he announced that he was the promised one or Mahdi expected by Muslims. He wrote scriptures in which he promulgated a new calendar, new religious laws, and new social norms. Opposed by Iran's Muslim clergy and ultimately by its government, thousands of the Báb's followers were killed; in 1850 the Báb himself was put to death.

Mirzá Husayn-'Alí, Titled *Bahá'u'lláh.*

Born in northern Iran in 1817, Bahá'u'lláh became a follower of the Báb in 1844 and was imprisoned for his beliefs. In 1853 he had a vision that he was the divine teacher the Báb had promised; he publicly declared himself as a messenger of God in 1863. He spent the rest of his life in exile and prison, where he wrote over 100 volumes of scripture.

'Abbas Effendi, Titled *'Abdu'l-Bahá.*

Son of Bahá'u'lláh, 'Abdu'l-Bahá was born in 1844 and accompanied his father on his exile to Palestine. Bahá'u'lláh appointed 'Abdu'l-Bahá his successor, the exemplar of his teachings, and the interpreter of his revelation. Under 'Abdu'l-Bahá the Bahá'í Faith spread beyond the Middle East, India, and Burma to Europe, the

Americas, southern Africa, and Australasia. He died in 1921.

Shoghi Effendi Rabbani.

Grandson of 'Abdu'l-Bahá and his successor, Shoghi Effendi was born in Palestine in 1897 and received an Oxford education. As head of the Bahá'í Faith from 1921 until his death in 1957, Shoghi Effendi translated the most important of Bahá'u'lláh's scriptures into elegant English, wrote extensive interpretations and explanations of the Bahá'í teachings, built the Bahá'í organizational system, and oversaw the spread of the Bahá'í Faith worldwide.

The Bahá'í scriptures constitute the books, essays, and letters composed by Bahá'u'lláh, 'Abdu'l-Bahá, and Shoghi Effendi. Together they comprised nearly 60,000 letters, a significant portion of which are available in English; the content of this scriptural corpus is encyclopedic in nature. The Bahá'í teachings are those principles and values promulgated in the Bahá'í scriptures, and touch on nearly every aspect of human life.

Central Bahá'í teachings are the "oneness of God," that there is only one God and that God is actively concerned about the development of humanity; the "oneness of religion," that God sends messengers such as Abraham, Moses, Zoroaster, Krishna, Buddha, Christ, Muhammad, the Báb, and Bahá'u'lláh to humanity to educate it in morals and in social values; and the "oneness of humanity," that all humans come from the same original stock and deserve equal opportunities and treatment.

The teachings also include a detailed discussion of the spiritual nature of human beings, prayers and religious practices to foster spiritual growth, a strong emphasis on the importance of creating unified and loving families, and a prescription for solving the social ills of human society.

The Bahá'í community consists of those people who have accepted Bahá'u'lláh as God's messenger for this day and who are actively trying to live by, and promulgate, the Bahá'í teachings. The community has no clergy and a minimum of ritual. Independent investigation of truth, private prayer, and collective discussion and action are the favored modes of religious action. Usually Bahá'í communities have no weekly worship service; rather, a monthly program called *feast* is held that includes worship, consultation on community business, and social activities.

Through a process that involves no campaigning and nominations, each local community elects annually by secret ballot a nine-member local spiritual assembly. The assembly coordinates community activities, enrolls new members, counsels and assists

"Be generous in prosperity, and thankful in adversity.

Be worthy of the trust of thy neighbor, and look upon him with a bright and friendly face.

Be a treasure to the poor, an admonisher to the rich, an answerer of the cry of the needy, a preserver of the sanctity of thy pledge.

Be fair in thy judgment, and guarded in thy speech.

Be unjust to no man, and show all meekness to all men.

Be as a lamp unto them that walk in darkness, a joy to the sorrowful, a sea for the thirsty, a haven for the distressed, an upholder and defender of the victim of oppression.

Let integrity and uprightness distinguish all thine acts.

Be a home for the stranger, a balm to the suffering, a tower of strength for the fugitive. Be eyes to the blind, and a guiding light unto the feet of the erring. Be an ornament to the countenance of truth, a crown to the brow of fidelity, a pillar of the temple of righteousness, a breath of life to the body of mankind, an ensign of the hosts of justice, a luminary above the horizon of virtue, a dew to the soil of the human heart, an ark on the ocean of knowledge, a sun in the heaven of bounty, a gem on the diadem of wisdom, a shining light in the firmament of thy generation, a fruit upon the tree of humility." (p. 285)

Gleanings (cont.)

"The essential purpose of the religion of God is to establish unity among mankind. The divine Manifestations were Founders of the means of fellowship and love. They did not come to create discord, strife, and hatred in the world. The religion of God is the cause of love, but if it is made to be the source of enmity and bloodshed, surely its absence is preferable to its existence; for then it becomes satanic, detrimental, and an obstacle to the human world."

'ABDU'L-BAHÁ,
*Promulgation of
Universal Peace*, p. 202

"The unity of the human race, as envisaged by Bahá'u'lláh, implies the establishment of a world commonwealth in which all nations, races, creeds, and classes are closely and permanently united, and in which the autonomy of its state members and the personal freedom and initiative of the individuals that compose them are definitely and completely safeguarded. This commonwealth must, as far as we can visualize it, consist of a world legislature, whose members will, as the trustees of the whole of mankind, ultimately control the entire resource of all the component nations, and will enact such laws as shall be required to regulate the life, satisfy the needs and adjust the relationships of all races and peoples.... In such a world society, science and religion, the two most potent forces in human life, will be reconciled, will cooperate, and will harmoniously develop."

SHOGHI EFFENDI,
World Order of Bahá'u'lláh,
pp. 203–204

members in need, and conducts Bahá'í marriages and funerals. A nine-member national spiritual assembly is elected annually by locally elected delegates, and every five years the national spiritual assemblies meet together to elect the Universal House of Justice, the supreme international governing body of the Bahá'í Faith. Worldwide there are about 20,000 local spiritual assemblies; the United States has over 1,400 local spiritual assemblies and about 120,000 Bahá'ís.

The Bahá'í View of the Challenges Facing Humanity

The Bahá'í scriptures emphasize that the challenges facing humanity stem from two sources: age-old problems that could have been solved long ago had humanity accepted and acted on the moral and spiritual values given it by God's messengers; and new challenges stemming from the creation of a global society, which can be solved if the moral and spiritual principles enunciated by Bahá'u'lláh are accepted and followed. Chief among these principles are

1. *Racial unity.* Racism retards the unfoldment of the boundless potentialities of its victims, corrupts its perpetrators, and blights human progress. Bahá'u'lláh's call that all humans accept and internalize the principle of the oneness of humanity is partly directed at destroying racist attitudes.

2. *Emancipation of women.* The denial of equality to women perpetrates an injustice against one-half of the world's population and promotes in men harmful attitudes and habits that are carried from the family to the workplace, to political life, and ultimately to international relations. Even though he lived in the 19th-century Middle East, Bahá'u'lláh called for the equality of women and enunciated their full rights to education and work.

3. *Economic justice.* The inordinate disparity between rich and poor is a source of acute suffering and keeps the world in a state of instability, virtually on the brink of war. Few societies have dealt effectively with this issue. The Bahá'í scriptures offer a fresh approach, including such features as a new perspective concerning money, profits, work, and the poor; an understanding of the purpose of economic growth and the relationships between management and labor; and certain economic principles, such as profit sharing.

4. *Patriotism* within a global perspective. The Bahá'í scriptures state that citizens should be proud of their countries and of their national identities, but such pride should be subsumed within a wider loyalty to all of humanity and to global society.

5. *Universal education.* Historically, ignorance has been the principal reason for the decline and fall of peoples and the perpetuation of prejudice. The Bahá'í scriptures state that every human being has

a fundamental right to an education, including the right to learn to read and write.

6. *A universal auxiliary language.* A major barrier to communication is the lack of a common language. Bahá'u'lláh urged humanity to choose one auxiliary tongue that would be taught in all schools in addition to the local native language, so that humans could understand each other anywhere they go on the planet.

7. *The environment and development.* The unrestrained exploitation of natural resources is a symptom of an overall sickness of the human spirit. Any solutions to the related crises of environmental destruction and economic development must be rooted in an approach that fosters spiritual balance and harmony within the individual, between individuals, and with the environment as a whole. Material development must serve not only the body, but the mind and spirit as well.

8. *A world federal system.* The Bahá'í scriptures emphatically state that for the first time in its history, humanity can and must create an international federation capable of coordinating the resources of, and solving the problems facing, the entire planet. A high priority needs to be given to the just resolution of regional and international conflicts; responding to urgent humanitarian crises brought on by war, famine, or natural disasters; forging a unified approach to environmental degradation; and establishing the conditions where the free movement of goods, services, and peoples across the globe becomes possible.

9. *Religious dialogue.* Religious strife has caused numerous wars, has been a major blight to progress, and is increasingly abhorrent to the people of all faiths and of no faith. The Bahá'í view that all religions come from God and thus constitute valid paths to the divine is a cornerstone of Bahá'í interfaith dialogue. Bahá'u'lláh calls on Bahá'ís to consort with the followers of all religions in love and harmony. Because Bahá'ís share with other religionists many common values and concerns, they frequently work with local interfaith organizations.

The Bahá'í Response to the Challenges Facing Humanity

Bahá'ís have responded to the challenges facing humanity in two ways: internally, by creating a Bahá'í community that reflects the principles listed above and that can serve as a model for others; and externally, to help heal the damage that inequality, injustice, and ignorance have done to society.

The international Bahá'í community contains within it 2,100 ethnic groups speaking over eight hundred languages. In some nations minority groups make up a substantial fraction of the Bahá'í

"The source of all learning is the knowledge of God, exalted be His glory, and this cannot be attained save through the knowledge of His Divine Manifestation. The essence of abasement is to pass out from under the shadow of the Merciful and seek the shelter of the Evil One.

"The source of error is to disbelieve in the One true God, rely upon aught else but him, and flee from His Decree. True loss is for him whose days have been spent in utter ignorance of his self.

"The essence of all that we have revealed for thee is Justice, is for man to free himself from idle fancy and imitation, discern with the eye of oneness His glorious handiwork, and look into all things with a searching eye.

"Thus have We instructed thee, manifested unto thee Words of Wisdom, that thou mayest be thankful unto the Lord, thy God, and glory therein amidst all peoples."
BAHÁ'U'LLÁH

Gleanings (cont.)

Prayer

O my God! O my God!

Unite the hearts of thy servants,

and reveal to them Thy great purpose.

May they follow Thy commandments and abide in Thy law.

Help them, O God, in their endeavor, and grant them strength to serve Thee.

O God! Leave them not to themselves,

but guide their steps by the light of Thy knowledge,

and cheer their hearts by Thy love.

Verily, Thou art their Helper and their Lord.

BAHÁ'U'LLÁH,
Bahá'í Prayers, p. 204

population; in the United States, for example, perhaps a third of the membership is African American, and Southeast Asians, Iranians, Hispanics, and Native Americans make up another 20 percent. Racial integration of local Bahá'í communities has been the standard practice of the American Bahá'í community since about 1905. Women have played a major, if not central, role in the administration of local American Bahá'í communities, and of the national community, since 1910. American Bahá'ís have been involved in education, especially in the fostering of Bahá'í educational programs overseas, since 1909.

Worldwide, numerous Bahá'ís have become prominent in efforts to promote racial amity and equality, strengthen peace groups, extend the reach and effectiveness of educational systems, encourage ecological awareness and stewardship, develop new approaches to social and economic development, and promote the new field of conflict resolution. The Bahá'í Faith runs seven radio stations in less developed areas of the world that have pioneered new techniques for educating rural populations and fostering economic and cultural development. The Faith also conducts about seven hundred schools, primarily in the third world, as well as about two hundred other literacy programs. Bahá'í communities sponsor five hundred development projects such as tree planting, agricultural improvement, vocational training and rural health care. The Bahá'í international community is particularly active at the United Nations and works closely with many international development agencies. Many national and local Bahá'í communities have been active in promoting interreligious understanding and cooperation.

Chapter Three
BUDDHISM

A Portrait

Dr. Geshe Sopa and Ven. Elvin W. Jones

Ven. Geshe Sopa, born in Tsang Province, Tibet, is Professor in the Department of South Asian Studies, University of Wisconsin–Madison. Elvin W. Jones is Cofounder and Associate Director of Deer Buddhist Center, near Madison, Wisconsin.

Buddhism as we know it commenced in Northeast India about 500 B.C. through the teaching of Prince Siddartha Gautama, often known subsequent to his experience of "enlightenment" as Sakyamuni. Sakyamuni traveled around and taught in the Ganges basin until his death at the age of eighty-four. From there Buddhism spread through much of India until its total disappearance from the land of its origin by the end of the 13th century. This disappearance occurred as a consequence of several centuries of foreign invasions leading ultimately to the conquest of India by successive waves of conquerors who had been unified under Islam.

By the time of its disappearance in India, Buddhism had spread through much of Asia where it has been a dominant faith in Southeast Asia in Sri Lanka, Thailand, Vietnam, Cambodia, Burma, and Laos; in Central and East Asia in China, Korea, Japan, Tibet, and Mongolia; and in numerous Himalayan areas such as Nepal, Sikkim, Butan, and Ladakh. It is estimated that today there are a little over 250 million Buddhists in the world. In the U.S.A. alone there are about 5 million, the majority of whom are Asian immigrants or their descendants. However, in recent years, numerous Americans of English and European descent have also adopted Buddhism.

From the start, the teaching of the Buddha was a middle way. In ethics it taught a middle way avoiding the two extremities of asceticism and hedonism. In philosophy it taught a middle way avoiding the two extremities of eternalism and annihilation. The single most important and fundamental notion underpinning Buddhist thought was the idea of "contingent genesis" or "dependent origination" (*pratitya-amutpada*). Here the thought is that every birth or origination occurs in dependence on necessary causes and conditions;

Selected Texts and Wisdom from Buddhist Tradition

"As the previous . . . Buddhas, like a divine skillful wise horse, a great elephant, did what had to be done, accomplished all tasks, overcame all the burdens of the five aggregates controlled by delusion and karma, fulfilled all their aspirations by relinquishing their attachments, by speaking immaculately divine words and liberating the minds of all from the bondage of subtle delusions' impression, and who possess great liberated transcendental wisdom, for the sake of all that lives, in order to benefit all, in order to prevent famine, in order to prevent mental and physical sicknesses, in order for living beings to complete a Buddha's 37 realizations, and to receive the stage of fully completed buddhahood . . .
I . . . shall take the eight Mahayana precepts. . . ."
—from "One-Day Mahayana Vow Ritual," trans. Library of Tibetan Works and Archives

Selected Texts (cont.)

*"Perfect Wisdom spreads her radiance...
and is worthy of worship. Spotless, the
whole world cannot stain her.... In her
we may find refuge; her works are most
excellent; she brings us safety under the
sheltering wings of enlightenment. She
brings light to the blind, that all fears and
calamities may be dispelled... and she
scatters the gloom and darkness of
delusion. She leads those who have gone
astray to the right path. She is omniscience;
without beginning or end is Perfect
Wisdom, who has emptiness as her
characteristic mark; she is mother of the
bodhisattvas.... She cannot be struck
down, the protector of the unprotected, ...
the Perfect Wisdom of the Buddhas, she
turns the Wheel of the Law."*

ASTASAHASRIKA
PRAJNAPARAMITA-SUTRA,
The Buddhist Tradition, ed.
by W. M. Theodore De Bary

however, not everything so asserted can function as a cause—in particular, any kind of eternal or permanent whole. Consequently, the Buddhist idea of "contingent genesis" came to be characterized by three salient features, i.e., unpropelledness, impermanence, and consistency. Unpropelledness signifies that origination or genesis is not propelled by a universal design such as the thought or will of a creator. Impermanence means that the cause of an effect is always something impermanent and never permanent. Finally, consistency requires that the genesis or effect will be consistent with and not exceed the creative power of the cause. For example, it is on the basis of the quality of consistency that the Buddhist denies that any kind of material body can provide a sufficient material cause for the production of a mind. Thus, on account of this primary philosophical underpinning of contingent genesis, Buddhism has produced a quite large etiological rather than theological literature.

Taking as his basis the idea of contingent genesis in general, Sakyamuni taught a specific theory of a twelvefold dependent genesis accounting for the particularized birth of a person or personality, which naturally occurs in some kind of existence which is not free of various forms of suffering or ill. The spectrum of naturally occurring births which are characterized by ill is called the "round of transmigration" (*samsara*), and the force impelling this transmigration and unsatisfactory condition of attendant births was taught by Sakyamuni to be action under the sway of afflictors or afflicting elements such as nescience, attraction, aversion, and so forth. In the language of Buddhism, this action is called *karma*; the afflictors are called *klesa*; and the resultant ills are called *dukha*. The Buddha called the reality of suffering (*dukha*) the truth of suffering, and called this action—conjoined with afflicting elements (*karma* and *klesa*)—the truth of the cause of suffering. These two truths constitute the first of the Four Noble Truths, which were the principal teaching of Sakyamuni and the principle object of understanding of the Buddhist saint.

Sakyamuni also taught the possibility of freedom or emancipation from suffering or ill through its cessation. Likewise, he taught a path leading to this cessation. These two, cessation and path, constitute the third and fourth of the Four Noble Truths. Thus, we have suffering and its causes and the cessation of suffering and its causes; these are the Four Noble Truths of suffering, its causes, cessation, and path. Through the cessation of suffering and its causes one obtains nirvana, which is simply peace or quiescence, and the cause of the attainment of this peace is the path of purification eliminating action under the sway of the afflictors. The Buddha taught that of all the afflictors contaminating action, the chief is a perverse kind of nescience which apprehends a real or independent self existing in or outside of the various identifiable corporeal and mental elements which constitute a person or personality. Thus, the cultivation of the path of purification hinges on the reversal of this mistaken apprehension of a real soul or ego or selfhood. This Buddhist view that there is no real or enduring substratum to the personality is called *anatma*.

Sakyamuni's most precise and important articulation of the Four Noble Truths was his formulation of a twelvefold causal linkage generating each and every particular instance of birth of a person. This twelvefold causal nexus begins with nescience and ends with old age and death. This nescience is in particular the perverse ignorance which grasps a real selfhood. Conditioned by this kind of nescience, actions are performed which deposit inclinations and proclivities upon the unconscious mind. These proclivities are later ripened by other factors such as grasping and misappropriation and thereby bring about unsatisfactory results through birth and death. With, however, the correct seeing of the reality of no-self, this nescience may be stopped, and thereby the whole chain of causation leading to unsatisfactory birth is brought to an end. In this way the twelvefold causal linkage is not only a theory of the genesis of a personality but also a theory of its potential for deliverance from every kind of ill. Thus it is said in Buddhist scripture:

Gather up and cast away.
Enter to the Buddha's teaching.
Like a great elephant in a house of mud,
conquer the lord of death's battalions.
Whoever with great circumspection,
practices this discipline of the Law,
abandoning the wheel of births,
will make an end to suffering.

"Gather up and cast away" refers to the gathering together of virtuous or wholesome qualities and the abandonment of non-virtuous or unwholesome qualities in the personality. Thus the same scripture says:

Not to do evil, to bring about the excellence of
   virtue,
completely to subdue the mind,
this is the teaching of the Buddha.

On his deathbed, the Buddha had exhorted his disciples to work on their own salvation with diligence; hence these teachings are sometimes characterized as a doctrine of individual emancipation.

About five to six hundred years after the passing away of the teacher Sakyamuni, another formulation of the Buddhist doctrine and practice gained a wide circulation in India. This later propagation is associated with the great Buddhist teacher Nagarjuna. Taking his stand on the fundamental Buddhist idea of contingent genesis, Nagarjuna argued that if every instance of genesis is a contingent genesis, then continued analysis will show that every kind of permanent and even impermanent cause proposed either by Buddhists or others will be non-absolute and non-ultimate; consequently, causality itself is in some sense illusory. In this sense even true phenomena like causality are just empty of any kind of ultimate nature. Nagarjuna carried his analysis to cover permanent non-originating phenomena like space as well. The nonexistence of all phenomena as ultimates or absolutes is the Buddhist idea of emptiness (*sunyata*), which provided a great impetus to another kind of religious aspiration aiming at the emancipation not only of one's own individual lifestream but that of all sentient life from the round of unsatisfactory birth and rebirth. He especially demonstrated the absence of any final or absolute difference between *samsara* and *nirvana*, even though phenomenally they are and will always remain opposites. Thereby, Nagarjuna opened wide the way for the pursuit of the nonattached *nirvana* taught to be achieved by the Buddhas along with numerous other sublime qualities of knowledge belonging to perfect enlightenment. From earliest times the Buddhist had already distinguished between the path of purification trodden by Sakyamuni himself, already known as the *Bodhisattva* path, and that taught and followed by numerous of his disciples. Now the Buddha's own path was encouraged for all.

By its followers this later path was called *Mahayana*, or "greater vehicle," whereas the former came to be called the *Hinayana*, or "smaller vehicle." The *Mahayana* was synonymous with the path of a *Bodhisattva* or one who, moved by great compassion, developed the aspiration to perfect enlightenment for the sake of others. This aspiration was called *Bodhicitta*, or the mind to enlightenment, and provided the motivation for the cultivation of the *Mahayana* path. This path was also taught extensively in the *Prajnaparamita-sutras*, or Perfection of Wisdom Scriptures, which also gained wide circulation in India through the efforts of Nagarjuna.

About five hundred years later still another very important development occurred in Indian Buddhism. This development is associated with the brothers Asanga and Vasubandhu. This led to a great systematization of the *Mahayana* and in particular to another less radical interpretation of the meaning of the *Prajnaparamita-sutras* than that associated with Nagarjuna, whose school continued on and is generally called the *Madhyamika* or Middleist School; Asanga's is called the *Cittamatra* or Mind-Only School.

Also around this time, a special kind of Buddhist esoteric scripture and practice gained wide currency. They constituted four classes or levels which moved from outer ritual action through inner meditative action to a full-fledged esoteric path of spiritual attainment. These scriptures were known as the *tantras*, and their practice was called the diamond vehicle or the secret mantra vehicle. Espousing the practice of the *Mahayana*, they added many ritual methods together with numerous profound and difficult yoga or meditation practices and techniques. The *tantras* saw themselves as fulfilling the practice of the *Mahayana* as well as providing an accelerated path to its realization. The vehicle of the *tantras* is often called the vehicle of the effect because straightaway it envisages the final result of the path and imaginatively dwells upon and rehearses that until it becomes not an imagined but an accomplished result. The *Mahayana* being wisdom and method, the *tantras*

add to the general wisdom and method of the *Mahayana* their own very special varieties.

Thus in India along with four classes of *tantras*, four main philosophical schools developed, each with a number of subschools, i.e., the *Vaibhasika*, *Sautrantika*, *Madhyamika* and the *Yogacara*. The former two are schools of the *Hinayana*, and the latter two are schools of the *Mahayana*. The *Vaibhasika* early developed eighteen subschools, two of which are of particular importance—the *Sthaviravada*, which is the immediate ancestor of the *Theravada*, the principal Buddhism of Southeast Asia, and the *Sarvastivada*, which is the basis of monasticism in Tibet and the Tibetan community today. The *Madhyamika* provides the chief viewpoint of Tibetan Buddhism today, and the *Yogacara* has had profound and far-reaching influences on the Buddhism of China, and through China on Korea and Japan. Some secret mantra practices were transmitted into China and from there to Japan, where they survive today, and the practices of all four levels of *tantra* are still alive in the Tibetan community.

From India by way of Central Asia, Buddhism began its penetration into China around the 1st century C.E. There it encountered the already developed systems of Confucianism and Taoism. The latter in particular provided the terminology and numerous seemingly analogous concepts for subsequent centuries of effort devoted to the translation of Buddhist scriptures into Chinese and the establishment of Buddhist practice in China. By the 8th century, Chinese Buddhism reached its mature form with its two main theoretical schools of Tien-tai and Hua-yen, together with its two popular schools of Pure Land and Ch'an (Japanese: Zen). These sinicized forms of Buddhism began their spread to Korea mainly from the 4th century on and commenced spreading from Korea to Japan from the middle of the 6th century. Although some important Buddhist development occurred a century earlier, Buddhism began to be strongly cultivated in Tibet in the eighth century. In this century Indian and various Sinitic Buddhist developments collided in a debate held by the Tibetan king at Samyas, the first Buddhist monastery founded in Tibet. Tibetan history records that the Indian faction won this debate, and it is clear that afterwards Tibet looked to India throughout its prolonged subsequent period of importation of Buddhism. As a consequence, Tibet remains a great repository of a vast body of important literature which later perished in India itself. From Tibet, Buddhism was afterward spread into Mongolia and throughout the Himalayan region.

Now, in the aftermath of World War II and the collapse of Western colonial establishments in Asia, the modern efforts of numerous Asian countries to make a transition from agrarian to industrial societies has led and still leads often to the establishment of military dictatorships or to socialist totalitarian regimes. Buddhism has generally fallen upon difficult times particularly at the hands of Marxist-Leninist regimes, for whereas Buddhism does not see any natural conflict between itself and modern science, its middle-way philosophy is staunchly opposed to dialectical materialism. In fact, two of the worst atrocities of nearly genocidal proportions to be perpetrated in modern times have taken place in two such countries, Cambodia and Tibet, the latter continuing—and this is hard to believe—for over thirty years. Buddhist leadership nonetheless has continued to press for freedom and democracy, for peace and nonviolence, as these will be the best safeguard for the natural human wish to avoid suffering. Here, it is particularly indicative to note that two recent Nobel Peace Prize winners have been Buddhists—His Holiness the 14th Dalai Lama of Tibet and Daw Aung San Suu Kyi of Burma.

Mutual Recognition

"For the last several years I have been looking at the world's problems, including our own problem, the Tibetan situation. I have been thinking about this and meeting with persons from different fields and in different countries. Basically all are the same. I come from the East; most of you are Westerners. If I look at you superficially, we are different, and if I put my emphasis on that level, we grow more distant. If I look on you as my own kind, as human beings like myself, with one nose, two eyes, and so forth, then automatically that distance is gone. We are the same human flesh. I want happiness; you also want happiness. From that mutual recognition we can build respect and real trust for each other. From that can come cooperation and harmony, and from that we can stop many problems."

H.H. THE 14TH DALAI LAMA
OF TIBET

Buddhist Experience in North America

Ven. Mahinda Deegalle

Student of the History of Religions, University of Chicago, and member of the Sri Lankan Buddhist community

The arrival of two leading Buddhists—Anagarika Dharmapala and Soyen Shaku—to attend the World's Parliament of Religions held in Chicago in 1893 was, and is, an important event for all Buddhists who are living in North America today. These two representatives are frequently named in tracing the birth of Buddhist traditions on this continent. In fact, however, Buddhism did not become a visible religious alternative to the Judeo-Christian tradition until the 1970s. Yet, as a minority tradition, its contribution to the religious life of Americans was quite apparent at the 1993 World's Parliament of Religions. This participation included very wide representation from Buddhist denominations that trace their affiliations to many different Asian countries.

Largely within the last four decades, a variety of Asian Buddhist traditions have found the United States a fertile land in which to establish their religious centers. As a result, Buddhist centers in all major American cities serve both Asian immigrants and nonimmigrants who are interested in Buddhism. They provide facilities for meditation and educate Americans in the customs and cultural events of Asian countries. Like any other American religious group, American Buddhists are definitely a diverse group. In major cities such as Los Angeles, Chicago, San Francisco, and Toronto there is a great deal of ethnic variety among the Buddhist denominations.

Nevertheless, Buddhist communities in these major cities seem to work very harmoniously together to spread the Buddha's teachings. For example, in Chicago, the members of The Buddhist Council of the Midwest celebrate Vesak—the birthday, the day of *samma sambodhi* (perfect awakening), and the passing away (*parinirvana*) of Gautama Buddha— jointly each year in May, with cultural festivals from Japan, China, Taiwan, Thailand, Vietnam, Cambodia, Burma, and Laos. This unity among diverse denominations that trace their roots to different Asian nations is based on the understanding that, as Buddhists, they share certain fundamental doctrines in common, even while demonstrating cultural variety through their specific festivals and religious practices.

As members of immigrant communities and representatives of an alien religion, immigrant American Buddhists have to adapt to the cultural and religious setting of the United States and to deal with people who do not share their world view. It is important that Buddhists understand the way the people of other world religions think about the world and its problems.

Unlike Buddhists, for many Americans the notion of God is fundamental to life; all Judeo-Christian religious communities derive inspiration from a concept of "God." Also, American society is structured around individualism; there is a strong emphasis on the primacy of individuality rather than on the interests of the society or community as in Buddhist cultures. So Buddhists in general and Theravadins in particular have to struggle to understand these two world views. At the same time, since all Buddhist communities profess a doctrine of selflessness in one form or another, it is difficult for most Americans, who think mainly in terms of "self" and "individual," to understand Buddhism.

With the development of an awareness of the earth, environment, plants, and animals, American Buddhists seem to have embraced positive teachings of the Buddhist traditions with regard to plants and the environment. Rather than thinking that human beings are separate from nature and that human beings are rulers of the earth, people are starting to think of the entire universe as a "whole," of which humanity is only a "part." This sense of a global community sharing the resources of the earth harmoniously is a very positive development which has been encouraged during the last few decades, and is growing fast in the United States. This kind of a world view or consciousness of the environment and nature marks a shift in human thinking: human beings not as rulers of the earth but as a part of a larger global community.

In the development of an awareness of nature and the environment, Buddhist teachings, in particular the theories of codependent origination (*paticcasamuppada*) and interconnectedness, have a great deal to offer to Western thinkers. For example, the doctrine of codependent origination proposes an interdependence between nature and human beings. Furthermore, Buddhist teachings maintain that the nature of the human psyche affects the natural environment, while the natural environment in turn influences the shape of the human psyche positively or negatively. In particular, the doctrine of five laws, *niyama dhammas*, proposes that human beings and nature are bound together in a mutual causal relationship. The five laws are physical, biological, psychological, moral, and causal. Among these five, the causal law operates within each of the first four; likewise, the physical law conditions biological growth, and all the laws influence human thought patterns, which eventually shape the moral standards of a society. These Buddhist doctrines and insights, which seem to appeal to modern Western thinking, attempt to suggest that human beings and the environment mutually condition and influence each other in the formation of the human psyche and of the nature of the world. The notions of interdependence and interconnectedness have become the centerpiece of the declaration, "Towards a Global Ethic," of the 1993 Parliament of the World's Religions.

Though some Buddhist communities have experienced resistance from certain segments of the American population, this does not reflect the attitude of the majority of Americans, whose pluralist tradition shows in their openness and willingness to help religious and ethnic minorities. However, some hostile elements are still present in certain sections of society and parts of this country; in the recent past, several temples have been burned or bombed, and some practitioners have even been murdered.

The most positive response towards Buddhism is found in the genuine interest of Americans from many parts of the country in knowing and practicing Buddhism. This positive tendency is quite evident in the curriculum of American colleges and universities. In several major universities, I have witnessed a genuine interest in learning about Buddhism, and private colleges and universities provide the facilities to do so. Every year, American universities produce a large number of academic specialists in diverse forms of Buddhism, such as Japanese, Chinese, Indian, Tibetan, Sri Lankan, Thai, or Burmese.

While in many places Buddhism functions as a cultural resource and inspiration for Asian immigrant Buddhist communities, non-immigrant Caucasian converts are drawn to Buddhism for its contemplative and meditative aspects rather than because of its cultural specificity. One of the strengths which Buddhism offers to American practitioners of Zen, Theravadan, or Tibetan meditation is its tradition of contemplative practice. The considerable growth of meditation centers shows that Buddhism is becoming a vital force in the pluralistic American society and is having an influential impact on it. The Buddhist experience in the United States highlights the ability of its practitioners to adapt to a completely different cultural and social environment and make remarkable progress in shaping the lives of others who encounter Buddhism. Since the establishment of Buddhism in the United States is still in progress, its impact and influence will become more clearly visible in the 21st century.

Zen

from the Zen Center,
San Francisco

In the 6th century C.E., Bodhidharma, the semilegendary figure from whom all Zen schools trace their ancestry, brought to China that Buddhist practice which we call Zen. The word itself is a Japanese transliteration of a Chinese transliteration of a Sanskrit word meaning meditation. Thus, Zen is that school of Buddhism which emphasizes meditation (*zazen* = sitting meditation) as a primary practice for calming and clearing the mind and for directly perceiving reality. According to the texts the Zen that Bodhidharma taught and practiced can be summed up as

> A special transmission outside the scriptures; no dependence upon words and letters; directly pointing at one's own nature; attaining Buddhahood.

Zen eventually reached Japan, where the Soto school was established by Eihei Dogen (1200–1255), who considered Zen not as a separate school but simply as Buddhism. In the early 1960s Shunryu Suzuki Roshi came to San Francisco to minister to the local Japanese congregation. Out of his contacts with Western students, the Zen Center of San Francisco was born. Many other centers have since opened elsewhere in North America and in other countries.

Chapter Four
CHRISTIANITY

Selected Scriptures

"We declare to you what was from the beginning, what we have heard, what we have seen with our eyes, what we have looked at and touched with our hands, concerning the word of life. This life was revealed, and we have seen it and testify to it, and declare to you the eternal life that was with the Father and was revealed to us. We declare to you what we have seen and heard so that you also may have fellowship with us; and truly our fellowship is with the Father and with his Son Jesus Christ."

1 JOHN 1:1–4

[Jesus said,] "If you love me you will keep my commandments."

JOHN 14:15

"Whatever you do to the least of my brothers and sisters, you do to me."

MATTHEW 25:40

"You shall love the Lord your God with all your heart, and with all your soul, and with all your mind. This is the greatest and first commandment. And a second is like it: You shall love your neighbor as yourself."

MATTHEW 22:37–39

Origins and Beliefs

The Rev. Dr. Thomas A. Baima, S.T.L.

Catholic Priest, past Director of the Office for Ecumenical and Interreligious Affairs of the Archdiocese of Chicago, Professor and Trustee of the Council for a Parliament of the World's Religions.

NOTE: Because the range of communities within Christianity is so wide, members of several distinct traditions have provided essays on specific topics. In the essay below, Father Baima introduces the origins and basic beliefs of Christianity and its approaches to interfaith relations

The origin of Christianity begins in the heart of God. The Divine nature is Love. Love is not something that comes from God. Love is God and God is Love. If a Christian were to name the Divine in English, the best term would be simply "God-Love."

Within God-Love, before time, came an urge to create. This urge was not for pleasure, since God-Love is beyond such things. Rather it was, as Archbishop Joseph Raya says, for the multiplication of love. God created for this reason alone, that love might grow. Divine love by its very nature shares itself.

Made in the image and likeness of God-Love, humanity had the essential quality or condition that makes loving possible, free will. Some humans chose to reject the offer of close relationship with God-Love. This rejection, which we will call sin, entered human experience and remains a permanent part of it. Sin is separation or a false autonomy, false because it is not possible to be or exist independently of God. This false autonomy is the basis of human rejection of God-Love.

The separation between humanity and God-Love required divine action to overcome it. As a permanent part of human nature nothing we could do of our own power could heal the separation. A new offer of relationship by God-Love was required.

So God-Love selected one of the nations of the earth to be a sign and instrument of this divine action. That nation was the Hebrew people. Through a process of self-disclosure, God-Love guided Israel out of slavery into an experience of rescue. God-Love guided Israel through the naming of sin in the Ten Commandments and the calling to virtue through the commandments to pray, celebrate sacred ritual, and act with compassion.

The guiding and forming of Israel created a sign and instrument that could extend and express God-Love. Throughout almost 2,000 years of faithfulness and struggle, this one people, guided by prophets, priests, and kings, was the light of God-Love among the nations.

Then God-Love chose to graft onto this one people all the nations. In a small village in the northern part of Palestine, a young woman became pregnant even though she was a virgin. Though no man had ever touched Mary, Life grew within her. Nine months later "a child was born, a son given, upon whom dominion rested. And the prophet had called him 'wonder-counselor, God-hero, Father forever, and Prince of Peace.'" Mary named him Jesus— "God saves."

It is here that Christianity, which began eternally in the heart of God, is made visible in the person and event of Jesus. We who are his disciples have come to see the fullness of revelation from God-Love, of God-Love in him. For this reason we call him Lord, Son of God, Savior. And it is in the teaching of Jesus that we learned something new about the inner life of the one God. Within the Godhead there exist relationships of love—as Father, Son, and Holy Spirit. God is personal, not merely as a way to relate to us, but in the very divine being. We would not know this about God had not the Son taken flesh in Jesus of Nazareth and revealed it to us.

In addition to this revelation of the inner life of God, the Lord Jesus taught a way of life that made it possible for God-Love to be experienced as a reality in the world. After his earthly ministry the Lord returned to his Father. He empowered and designated a few of the disciples to carry the teaching on. Thus it has come to us, handed on by living witnesses.

These living witnesses or apostles went out from Jerusalem and founded local assemblies of faith. Like Israel of old, these assemblies were the sign and instrument of the Lord Jesus in that place. It was by the example of love that others became attracted to Christianity. It was through prayer and life within the assemblies that the living witnesses were able to go forth and preach. And it was through incorporation into these assemblies that an individual came to know the Lord Jesus, receive formation in the Teaching, be sanctified in prayer, and be guided in the Christian life.

Within these assemblies believers entered into worship of God—as Father, Son, and Holy Spirit. Through the singing of psalms, hymns, and inspired songs, through the breaking of bread and the prayers, they met the Lord Jesus who sanctified their inner life. Through devotion to the teaching of the apostles, they came to know the revelation of God which Jesus had disclosed in himself.

The primary elements of the teaching are

There is one God who is almighty, whom Jesus called Father. This one God is the Creator of heaven and earth. Jesus is the divine and human, only Son of this Father, and as we call God Lord, we call Jesus Lord, for the Father is in him and he is in the Father. The miracle of Jesus' virgin birth attests to this. Jesus suffered at the hands of the Roman Governor, Pontius Pilate, giving his life in the process. He died and was buried as we all shall be. But he did not remain in the tomb, for God raised him up out of death. His suffering and death broke the chains of sin for all who died before his coming, again making God-Love available to them. He rose from the dead, making life with God now and forever our blessed hope. He ascended, returning into the presence of God-Love from which he came. He sent the Holy Spirit to create the assembly of believers and to be its constant guide in faith, hope, and love. He will return to bring time to an end, to judge the living and the dead, and to complete creation with the inauguration of the eternal kingdom of, with, and in God-Love.

These assemblies of faith, formed and guided by the Spirit, also taught a way of conduct based not on law, but virtue. The Lord Jesus taught that all sin in life could be overcome and rooted out of human experience by the avoidance of negative behavior and the substitution of a corresponding virtue. These virtues are seen as active gifts of the Holy Spirit to the believer. Love, joy, peace, patience, kindness, goodness, faithfulness, and self-control are the spiritual means to a Christian life.

This simple foundation of doctrine and virtue has been reflected on over the centuries in the development of our understanding. Through prayer, holy women and men have penetrated to the depths of these mysteries guided by the Holy Spirit of God-Love. The assemblies look to four sources for insights to develop the living faith carried in the mind of the whole people of Christ. These are the sources of theological reflection: Scripture, the Oral Tradition, Reason, and Experience.

1. Scripture includes the Hebrew Scriptures interpreted through the New Testament.

2. Oral Tradition is the preaching, teaching, and ritual which guide the assembly in prayer life, work, and worship.

3. Reason is the application of disciplined thought to understand more fully the mystery.

4. Experience focuses on the changes within us which doctrine makes.

Faith is handed on through life in the assembly, sometimes through preaching and sometimes through sacred rites. Baptism and Eucharist are the signs and means of entrance into and nourishment of the assembly's life. Confession of sins and anointing with oil heal the spiritual and physical life of the body, while marriage and ordination create, lead, and guide the family and the assembly.

In Christianity today, almost 2,000 years after the ascension of the Lord Jesus, divisions exist. John Wesley, one of the great reformers in England, spoke of a fully balanced Christianity having the four components mentioned above—Scripture, Oral Tradition, Reason, and Experience—as the bases of religious knowledge. We could consider the divisions within Christianity to be a function of favoring one or more of these components over the others. Political, economic, and other human considerations aside, the division in the Church has resulted from the development of different theological schools that emphasize the different components. For example, the Orthodox are known for their emphasis on Tradition and Experience; the Catholics on Tradition and Reason; the Protestants on Scripture and Reason; and Pentecostals on Scripture and Experience. These differences in emphasis have led to differences in the formulation of doctrine, the number and status of the sacred rites or sacraments, and the authority of the ordered ministries. These emphases have brought each Christian community a deeper insight into faith but also have limited their fellowship with the rest of Christianity.

Interfaith Relations

Christians also differ in their relation to non-Christians. These relations are characterized by three positions:

1. The *"exclusive position"* holds that a saving relationship with the Lord Jesus is the only way to salvation. In this perspective, those who lack this will suffer forever, excluded from God-Love.

2. The *"pluralist position"* sees Christianity as merely one path to God among other religions that also offer the possibility of salvation. This view sees salvation as universal and knowledge of God as relative to culture and tradition.

3. Between them is the *"inclusive position."* While holding to the belief that the fullness of revelation came in the person of Jesus and that he is the ordinary way to right relationship with God, here it is believed that God-Love can work beyond this. Hence a Christian may esteem truth where he/she sees it, and we will know it is the truth when it agrees with Jesus and the teaching and example received from him. In this position, the revelation of God-Love is fully disclosed in Jesus.

This description of Christianity can in no way capture the breadth, height, and depth of the religion. But it is our hope that this summary has presented a glimpse of our life.

—Copyright 1993 Thomas A. Baima. All rights reserved.

The Christian Family Tree

The Rev. Epke VanderBerg

Protestant Minister, member of the Episcopal family and of the Grand Rapids Interfaith Dialogue Association

NOTE: We present here short portraits of main families and communities within Christianity, particularly those in the Middle East, Europe, and North America. The descriptions provide some primary characteristics and a method of categorizing Christianity into fifteen families. A major resource for this summary was the work of J. Gordon Melton in *The Encyclopedia of American Religions* (Triumph Books, 1989, New York). Readers are encouraged to explore Melton's detailed and fascinating work.

Looking back down the many branches of Christianity, we see a tree called Jesus the Christ. Beyond this trunk, Christianity is rooted in God's call to Abraham in the land of Ur. From the time of Jesus into the 20th century, the roots divided and multiplied, dipping into soils and water foreign to its beginning, affecting its color and character. Throughout its history, however, it never forgot its beginning, even though its memories of who Jesus was and what he taught waxed and waned through time and place.

Western Liturgical Family: The four oldest Christian families are the following: the Eastern Orthodox tradition, the non-Chalcedonian Orthodox tradition, the Western Catholic tradition, and the Anglican tradition. A strong liturgical life characterizes these Christian families, along with true creeds, sacraments, language, and culture, which find their expression in their liturgy. Most of these families observe seven sacraments: baptism, eucharist, holy orders, unction, marriage, confirmation, and penance. Two other characteristics mark these churches: allegiance to creeds, and belief in apostolic succession. Even though these churches evolved from one common beginning, they unfolded into separate entities with Christianity's spread into other cultures.

The Eastern Orthodox Family: Its authority was centered in the cities of Antioch, Alexandria, and Constantinople, and split from the Western Catholic tradition in A.D. 1054. The Western Catholic tradition, based in Rome and entrenched in Western Europe, exercised strong political and religious authority. The Anglican tradition in England broke with Rome in the 16th century when Henry VIII saw opportunity for an independent church that would give him his desired divorce and financial freedom for battle. "The Thirty-Nine Articles of Religion" and "The Book of Common Prayer" established it as a separate liturgical tradition. In the immigration to North America and after the American Revolutionary War, the Anglican Church became known, in 1787, as the Protestant Episcopal Church in the U.S.

Eastern Liturgical Family: Political, cultural, and doctrinal differences separated the Eastern Orthodox churches from the Roman churches in 1054. Thereafter, and not having a Pope, this family was governed by Patriarchs who have equal authority and are in communion with each other. Even though the family does not demand celibacy of its priests (as long as they are married before their ordination), monks, who are celibate, are the only members who attain the office of Bishop. This family does not recognize the authority of the Bishop in Rome, nor that part of the Chalcedonian Creed that says that the Holy Spirit proceeds from the Son.

A number of groups fall into this family:

Nestorians: This group, recognizing Christ's two natures, does not believe that Christ had two equal natures and that Mary bore only the human nature of Christ—she did not bear God [Mary is not *theotikos*].

Monophysites: This group believes that Christ is of one person (mono) and of one nature (physis); it rejects the two-nature position of the Nestorians.

The Armenians: Established in Armenia as a bishopric in 260, this group customarily celebrates Holy Communion only on Sunday, using pure wine [without water] and unleavened bread. Infants are served immediately after baptism. Under persecution by the

Turks in 1890, many moved to North America. Controversy soon followed: would the pro-Soviet dominance of Armenia govern or would the Armenian nationalists?

Syrian Churches: Under the leadership of Jacob Baradeus (followers were often called Jacobites), who was a monophysite, the Syrian churches spread throughout the Mediterranean region and beyond.

Coptic Churches of Egypt and Ethiopia: Formerly one of the largest Christian groups in the world, this group diminished through persecution. Today, found mainly in Egypt, its numbers are increasing. The Ethiopian Church differs from the Coptic on several points:

1. Accepts Apocrypha as Scripture
2. Venerates the Sabbath along with Sunday
3. Recognizes Old Testament figures as saints
4. Observes many Old Testament regulations on food and purification.

Lutheran Family: Martin Luther, in cooperation with German princes, brought about the first successful breach with the Roman Catholic Church. Even though October 31, 1517, is often thought to be the start of the Lutheran Church, a more persuasive argument may be made for the year 1530, in which the Augsburg Confession was published. This confession became the standard that congregations used to justify their independent existence and distinguished the churches that used written confessions as "confessing churches." Luther taught that salvation is by grace through faith, rather than works and faith, and that the Bible is the rule of faith and sole authority for doctrine. Luther, in distinction from other Reformation churches, placed greater emphasis on the sacramental liturgy and understood the eucharist as consubstantiation (Christ present but elements not changed) in distinction from the Roman Catholic tradition of transubstantiation (elements changed into Christ's essence). Luther's translation of the Bible into the German vernacular (1532–34) became the standard for the German language and sparked the use of the vernacular in the Lutheran liturgy. Through Luther, many new hymns came into use and changed the complexion of the liturgy.

Reformed-Presbyterian Family: The force behind this family is John Calvin, who established the Reformed church in Geneva, Switzerland, in the 1540s. The Reformed churches distinguish themselves from the other Christian families by their theology (Reformed) and the church government (Presbyterian). Calvin derived his Reformed theology from the major premise of God's sovereignty in creation and salvation. He taught that God predestined some to salvation and that atonement is limited to those whom God has elected. Today, a strict or lenient interpretation of predestination separates many Reformed churches. On the continent, the churches were known as Reformed; in the British Isles they came to be known as Presbyterian. The Reformed churches were one with other Protestant churches in adherence to the authority of the early Christian creeds and believing in the Trinity, salvation by grace through faith, and that the Bible is the sole authority for faith and doctrine (in opposition to the Roman Catholics' position of salvation by faith and works, and of authority in the Bible and tradition). These churches did not concern themselves with apostolic succession, but with the pure preaching of the Gospel (predominantly a teaching function) and in the pure administration of the sacraments (baptism and eucharist). In the eucharist, God, who is present, can be apprehended by faith; this is in opposition to the Lutherans and Roman Catholics who maintain God's special presence in the elements.

Pietist-Methodist Family: Three groups of churches fall under this category: the Moravian Church, the Swedish Evangelical churches, and the Methodist (Wesleyan) churches. As a movement of pietism, these churches reacted to Protestantism as practiced in the late 17th century. They reacted to the rigidity and systematic doctrine of the scholastic Lutheran and Calvinist theologians. Not wishing to leave their established churches, they wanted a shift from scholasticism to spiritual experience. They advocated a Bible-centered faith, the experience of the Christian life, and giving free expression of faith in hymns, testimony, and evangelical zeal. Through the early work of Philip Jacob Spener and August Hermann Francke, and using home studies, their work rejuvenated the Moravian Church in 1727, influenced John Wesley, and helped establish the Swedish Evangelical Church. In their work they were open to traditional practices and beliefs and sought life within the forms of the traditional churches.

Methodists are characterized by their dissent from the Calvinist teachings on predestination and irresistible grace. In 1784, at a Christmas conference, the Methodists in America formed the Methodist Episcopal Church. Its history in North America reflects the history of other denominations, including their relationships to Old World governments, ecclesiastical affiliations, and changing North American political patterns.

Holiness Family: Through the influence of John Wesley's teaching of perfection, the holiness movement uses Matthew 5:48 as its theme: "Be ye perfect as my father is perfect." It is distinct from modern Wesleyism and other Protestant churches by how it understands the framework of holiness and perfection. These believers have traditionally separated themselves from Christians who did not strive high enough for perfection. Wesley, however, seeing the practical problems with perfection or sinlessness, then stressed love as the primary theme for Christians, while the holiness movement continued to stress sinlessness. Holiness, or the sanctification experience, is the end work of a process that starts with accepting Christ as one's personal savior (being "born again"). Having accepted Christ, one then grows in grace with the help of the Holy Spirit. The second work of grace comes when the Holy Spirit cleanses the heart of sin and provides the power for living the Christian life. Living the life of holiness results in banning certain forms of behavior as inappropriate for the Christian. This tendency resulted in the adoption of a strict set of codes of behavior. However, groups of churches, depending upon their understanding of holiness—whether it comes instantaneously or later—established their own independent churches.

Pentecostal Family: Today's Pentecostal family is usually traced back to the work of Rev. Charles Parham and his experience at Bethel Bible College in 1901. However, the movement has also had a long history replete with the experiences usually associated with it. What makes this family distinct from other Protestant churches is not their doctrinal differences; it is their form of religious experience and their practice of speaking in tongues—called glossolalia. Tongue speaking is a sign of baptism by the Holy Spirit, a baptism that often is accompanied by other forms of spiritual gifts such as healing, prophecy, wisdom, and discernment of spirits. Pentecostals seek the experience, interpret events from within it, and work to have others share in it. Those who do not manifest the experience are thought often to be less than "full of the Spirit." Pentecostal worship services appear to be more spontaneous than the traditional churches; however, Pentecostal services repeat a pattern of seeking the experience and showing the desire to talk about it. Because it is shaped by cultural forces, Pentecostalism appears in different forms, emphasizes different gifts, yet collects similar minds into its community. Neo-Pentecostalism, however, is a recent phenomenon, and has occurred predominantly in established churches that have found room for this movement.

European Free-Church Family: While Luther and Calvin advocated a fairly close relationship with the state, 16th-century radical reformers from within the Roman Catholic Church advocated a complete break with the state church. Their doctrines resembled many of the Protestant doctrines, but their ecclesiology differed. They thought the visible Church to be a free association of adults who had been baptized as believers (as opposed to being baptized as infants) and who avoided worldly ways. The Free-Church family is thought to have started on December 25, 1521, when one of the leaders celebrated the first Protestant communion service, a service format that is followed by much of Protestantism. From this group evolved the Mennonites, the Amish, the Brethren, the Quakers, and the Free Church of Brethren. Because many of them shunned allegiance to the government, they suffered persecution. Suffering persecution, many of them moved to North America and established congregations there.

Many members of these groups, particularly Quakers and Mennonites, are pacifists in their response to war; at the same time, they are highly active in their work to prevent war and in their relief efforts worldwide.

Baptist Family: As a free association of adult believers, Baptists make up the second largest religious family on the American landscape. Though they may also be related to the continental free-church family, American Baptists seem more related to British Puritanism. In general, they teach that the creeds have a secondary place to Scripture, that baptism is by immersion and administered only to believing and confessing adults, that the Lord's supper (not understood as a sacrament, but as an ordinance) is a memorial, that salvation is a gift of God's grace, and that people must exercise their free will to receive salvation. Even though they are a free association, they have organized themselves into various groupings, depending upon emphases of creed and the necessity for control, and at times by differences in theological perspectives due to the American phenomenon of regionalism (e.g., Southern and Northern Baptist conventions).

Independent Fundamentalist Family: Following the lead of Englishman John Nelson Darby (1800–1882), Independent Fundamental families distinguish themselves from Baptists by their belief in dispensationalism. The Fundamentalists believe the Bible is a history of God's actions with people in different periods.

Because of apparent Biblical contradictions, they resolve those differences by assigning Biblical passages to different dispensations. Human failure to meet God's commands causes God's economy to establish new paths. The present dispensation thus leads to the final dispensation in which Christ is recognized as the supreme universal authority. This dispensational framework has resulted in much speculation about prophecy of the Last Times. Another distinguishing feature of this family is the belief that the Church is only a unity of the Spirit, and not of organization. The Fundamentalist family frequently uses the Scofield Reference Bible as a major source for doctrine.

Adventist Family: The feature that distinguishes the Adventist family from other Christian groups is their belief in the expectation or imminent return of Christ when Christ will replace the old order of the world with an order of joy and goodness. When Christ comes again, he will establish a millennial (a thousand-year) reign in which unbelievers will have a second chance to accept Christ's Lordship. Even though a belief in the imminent return has long roots, it was heightened with the work of William Miller, a poor New York farmer. He believed that Biblical chronology could be deciphered, a belief that prompted him to predict Christ's return between March 21, 1843, and March 21, 1844. The 50,000 people who followed these teachings, and who experienced the nonreturn, retrenched. Rather than seeing a literal return of Christ that failed, one group advocated a spiritualized return—following the teachings of Charles Taze Russell—in which the event is understood as a "heavenly or internal event." The Adventist Family shares many of the Baptist teachings, from which much of the family has its genesis. Some of the more distinctive teachings of the family (but not all) are the following:

1. The imminent return of Christ

2. Denial of a person's immortality

3. Old Testament laws are effective, including the observance of the Sabbath (Saturday)

4. Rejection of the belief in a Hell

5. Christ's death counters the death penalty of Adam passed to his children by inheritance

6. That the Church is the suffering body of Christ and offers a spiritual sacrifice of atonement to God

7. That God's name is Yahweh.

Some of the more well-known families that have evolved from the millennial expectation are the Seventh Day Adventists, Church of Jesus Christ of the Latter-Day Saints, the Jehovah's Witnesses, British Israel Movement, and the WorldWide Church of God.

Jehovah's Witnesses, who trace their roots to Charles Taze Russell, mentioned above, prefer to separate themselves from the Christendom that was founded nearly 300 years after Jesus' death, believing that its beliefs deviate greatly from what Jesus taught. For instance, they do not accept Christendom's belief in the doctrine of the Trinity, which teaches that Jesus "is" God, though he is identified as God's Son. They do not use the cross as a symbol; yet Jesus was the promised Messiah and did provide the legal means of rescuing mankind from the consequences of Adam's sin, thus fulfilling the requirements for the new covenant which would bring faithful people into the promised earthly Paradise. Today, Jehovah's Witnesses form a large international organization, well known for its door-to-door evangelistic methods and its belief that many who are now living will survive when God's Kingdom brings an end to all present governments. Watch Tower, the denominational publishing company, provides Bible-study and educational materials.

The Liberal Family: Because yesterday's liberal may be today's conservative, the word "liberal" can be somewhat ambiguous. Most often, however, members of this family are identified as being against the mainstream theistic position of the dominant culture in Western society. The Liberal family, depending upon orientation, finds itself somewhere among the three positions *of unitarianism, universalism*, and *atheism*. Unitarianists think that God is One, that the Trinity does not exist; the universalists think that all will be saved, that Hell does not exist; the atheists reject the idea of a transcendental God. Liberalism's American origins developed in reaction to New England's Calvinism. However, the genesis of Liberalism is most often thought to rest in the work of Michael Servetus, martyred by John Calvin in Geneva. Liberals have championed human rights, the need for education, and the high worth of every person. By removing God from cosmic calculations, Liberals find life's answers in two other sources: human intuition—as in the position of Transcendentalists—and human reason—as in the Rationalist position. Early 18th-century liberals advocated that people could improve the world through reason. Nineteenth-century liberalism, seeing the results of scientific thought, expanded the above with evolution, science, and materialism, seen as necessary for uncovering the essential (monotheistic) laws of the universe.

Latter-Day Saints Family: Joseph Smith, in the fervor of revivalist movements sweeping New York in the early 19th century, received at the hands of an angel in 1827 gold plates written in what he described as a reformed Egyptian language. By means of two crystal-like stones, the "Urim" and "Thummim," this translation has been become known as the *Book of Mormon*. *The Book of Mormon* claims to be the history of two tribes, the Jeredites and the Israelites. The Jeredites moved to North America after the Tower of Babel; the Israelites moved to North America after the destruction of Jerusalem in the 6th century B.C. Joseph Smith published a number of other works including the *Book of Moses*, the *Book of Abraham*, and the *Book of Commandments* (now called the "Doctrine and Covenants"). The early history of Mormonism includes persecution, schisms, and violence, culminating in the murder of Joseph Smith in Carthage, Illinois, June 27, 1844. In the ensuing power struggle, Brigham Young moved his group to Salt Lake City, Utah, where he established the dominant branch of Mormonism. Another branch, which resides in Independence, Missouri, claiming Joseph Smith III as successor to his father, is known as the Reorganized Church of Jesus Christ of Latter-Day Saints. Several major Mormon beliefs are the following:

1. Affirmation of a trinitheism (not Christian Trinity) of the Father, Jesus, and Holy Spirit

2. Denial of original sin and the necessity of obedience to certain articles of faith for salvation

3. A specific church hierarchy

4. The Word of God consists of the Bible, the *Book of Mormon*, and *The Pearl of Great Price*

5. Revelation is open and added to the "Doctrine and Covenants" when received

6. The future Kingdom of Zion will be established

in North America—either in Independence, Missouri, or Salt Lake City, Utah.

Communal Family: Citing references to the early Christian Church, the Communal Family desires to share all its worldly possessions with other members of the group. Communalism made a serious start in the 4th century with the development of monasticism, a movement that thought the Western Catholic tradition brought everyone into the church rather than seeing the church as the body of true believers. Monasticism thought the principle of equality could be achieved through poverty and renunciation of the world. Francis of Assisi, thinking that monasticism did not represent true poverty (monastic orders had become very wealthy), advocated poverty of use as a method of reform. The Roman Catholic Church did not accept his vision, but saw it as a threat. The Taborites and the Munsterites, shortly after the Reformation, set up several communities, but, for a variety of reasons, failed. After 1860, visionaries and reformists began the most active era in the building of communities. In North America, the most famous and successful of these is the Hutterite community. Having a similar background to Russian Mennonites, today these people have established and maintain well over three hundred communities.

Christian Science-Metaphysical Family: Concerned with the role of the Mind in the healing process, the Christian Science and the New Thought movement drew on the metaphysical traditions of the 19th century that suggested the presence of spiritual powers operating on the mind and body. Swedenborg, a prolific writer, suggested the priority of the spiritual world over the material and that the material becomes real in its correspondence to the spiritual. The Christian Bible, he also taught, must be interpreted spiritually.

In the late 1800s, Mary Baker Eddy (the founder of Christian Science) and Emma Curtis Hopkins (the founder of New Thought) built on the methodology of Swedenborg. Disease, they taught, is the result of disharmony between mind and matter. New Thought, however, is distinct from Christian

Science. New Thought governs itself through ordained ministers (most of whom are women), developed a decentralized movement, emphasized prosperity (poverty is as unreal as disease), and emphasized the universal position that all religions have value. Christian Science is itself a major religion founded on American soil over one hundred years ago. Its primary text, *Science and Health with Key to the Scriptures*, has sold over 8 million copies worldwide.

Unity School of Christianity: This is another religious organization with metaphysical inclinations. Founded more than one hundred years ago and based on the teachings of Jesus Christ, Unity offers a practical approach to Christianity that helps people lead happier, healthier, more productive lives and find deeper spiritual meaning for their lives. Unity serves millions of people worldwide through its twenty-four-hour prayer, publishing, and education ministries. Through its publishing ministry, Unity produces a variety of inspirational resources for personal study and growth; *Unity* is a metaphysical journal and *Daily Word* is a devotional publication. Unity's educational ministry is designed to train and prepare Unity ministers and teachers for pastoral service and to foster personal spiritual growth.

Christianity in the World Today

Dr. Dieter T. Hessel

NOTE: This essay, addressing the critical issues and wisdom, is written by a Presbyterian minister and ethicist; Dr. Hessel has directed the ecumenical Program on Ecology, Justice and Faith, and is editor of *After Nature's Revolt* (Fortress Press, 1992).[1]

The Primary Challenges and Issues Facing Humanity

Among perennial challenges are the quest for meaningful human existence and the struggle for social justice and peace. Greater scientific and technological power over nature tempts humans to ignore creaturely limits and to make themselves the center of value. Human efforts to achieve inordinate security and comfort actually oppress and destroy other life, offending the Source of existence and warping right relationships in earth community. Today, the rich/poor gap has become harsher. More than a billion people lack enough to eat, while another billion misuse resources and overconsume. Militarization brings mass death to the "meek" even as it allows the militarily powerful to retain unjust advantage over the earth's resources for a wealthy few.

Pressing *new* issues face humanity, including the degradation of the environment on a global scale and the negative impact of exploding human population growth on social systems and other species. The world's religions and governments have also been surprised by a new public health crisis worsened by AIDS, and by the breakdown of public and private morality, as well as by the failures of common educational systems, in commodified societies. Meanwhile, counterrevolutionary forms of cultural/religious fundamentalism foster crusading intolerance of other faiths or ethnic groups and threaten minority rights. Mature religion and politics, to the contrary, will foster multicultural appreciation, religious tolerance, civil liberties, gender equality, and racial justice.

How Christians Respond to These Issues

First, rethink and reinterpret faith for these times. Pertinent Christian faith expresses reverence for the Creator, Sustainer, and Redeemer of the cosmos, and corresponding respect for all of the creatures whom God loves and enjoys. Such faith guides compassionate and courageous human living. The norm for spirited humanity is set by Jesus of Nazareth, "pioneer of faith" and "Son of God," whom Christians perceive as Reconciler of the world and Sovereign of life. His prophetic and healing public ministry inaugurates the Kingdom of God. Everyone is invited to enter this commonwealth, a community of *shalom* and sharing intended to encompass all known races, cultures, species, places. The church's role is to be the ecumenical social body of the crucified-risen Christ,

celebrative of God's design, concerned for the well-being of all. Christian worship through word and sacrament and social witness in each locale visibly signify God's reign already operative but not yet fulfilled in history.

Second, embody an ethic of covenant faithfulness. A Christian ethics that is: a) based on the biblical story of God's love for creation and covenant with human creatures (*humus* = "from earth"), and b) responsive to the needs of the time will foster and embody these values:

- Love for human beings everywhere who are equally "created in the image of God," and respect for basic human rights
- Care for the well-being of near and distant neighbors, both human and other kind, on this home planet
- Justice to the oppressed as well as generosity toward the deprived
- Prophetic denunciation of sin toward neighbor and nature, and idolatry or corruption in personal life and public affairs
- Frugality of lifestyle—neither strictness nor laxity—so that there may be sustainable sufficiency for all
- Nonviolent action to resist exploitation, and cooperative habits of coping with social conflict,
- Renewal of community life and cultivation of civil processes for the common good.

Third, examine ambiguities of religious life. Christianity in the late modern era has partially embodied but often contradicted its faith affirmations and moral imperatives. Transformative faith leading toward biophilic harmony has been obscured by domineering or distorting tendencies. Christians have proclaimed "the grace of our Lord Jesus Christ, the love of God, and the communion of the Holy Spirit," while acquiescing to racist, sexist, classist, naturist, and ecclesiastical practices of domination. The church's emphasis on human rights worldwide has fostered liberation of the oppressed, but is in fragmentary ways captive to individualism, ethnocentrism, and popular moralism.

On every continent, Christian communions have

Selected Scriptures

"The Lord said to Moses on Mount Sinai, 'Say to the people of Israel, When you come into the land which I give you, the land shall keep a sabbath to the Lord. Six years you shall sow your field, and six years you shall prune your vineyard, and gather in its fruits; but in the seventh year there shall be a sabbath of solemn rest for the land, a sabbath to the Lord; you shall not sow your field or prune your vineyard.'"

LEVITICUS 25:1–4

"And he came to Nazareth, where he had been brought up; and he went to the synagogue, as his custom was, on the sabbath day. And he stood up to read; and there was given to him the book of the prophet Isaiah. He opened the book and found the place where it was written, 'The Spirit of the Lord is upon me, because he has anointed me to preach good news to the poor. He has sent me to proclaim release to the captives and recovering of sight to the blind, to set at liberty those who are oppressed, to proclaim the acceptable year of the Lord.'"

LUKE 4:16–21

"Blessed are you poor, for yours is the kingdom of God. Blessed are you that hunger now, for you shall be satisfied. Blessed are you that weep now, for you shall laugh. . . . But woe to you that are rich, for you have received your consolation. Woe to you that are full now, for you shall hunger. . . .

"But I say to you that hear, love your enemies, do good to those who hate you, bless those who curse you, pray for those who abuse you. . . . And as you wish that men would do to you, do so to them."

LUKE 6:20–31
Jesus' Sermon on the Mount

been co-opted by the forces of destructive nationalism, and even now the ecumenical church remains shamefully divided over issues of gender justice and reproductive rights, added to ancient divisions over faith and order. Moreover, most local congregations lack racial and class heterogeneity, or constructive relations with other faith communities and popular movements for social change.

Nations with Christian majorities have relied on military force much more than on peacemaking initiatives and cooperative development. Western economic ethics has favored democratic capitalism over policies and practices of social solidarity and ecological integrity. Newly awakened ecumenical concern for "integrity of creation" is still very anthropocentric and has just begun to explore intrinsic values in nature, or sacred dimensions of the evolutionary story.

Priestly celebrations of grace within nature will see earth, water, and wind as sacramental, along with bread, wine, and spirit. Prophetic responses to these times will seek "eco-justice"—social and economic equity coupled with ecological integrity and cooperative peacemaking for the sake of earth and people.

Ethical Guidance in Christianity

Christians characteristically ask *not* "What is the good?" but "What purposes and patterns of conduct are in keeping with being faithful *people of God?*" Since Pentecost, Christian communities have understood themselves to be people of "the Way" (Acts 4:32–35; 18:24–26). The Christian Way is viewed as consistent with the expectations of the Noachic and Sinai covenants. A Christian ethical spirituality—"Live your life in a manner worthy of the gospel of Christ"—is expressed in the communion meal and baptism, as well as in public preaching and social practice. The individualistic, bureaucratic, and technocratic acids of modernity have corroded commitment to this way; intentional Christian communities, though often ignored by mainline churches, have been primary bearers of the tradition.

People of the Way have vision, values, and virtues that are consistent with the basic themes, though not legal details, of the Hebrew *covenant* story. Today, Christians and Jews alike are rediscovering wisdom dimensions of covenant ethics, keyed to the rest-and-play Sabbath purpose of creation's seventh day. For example, Exodus 23, Leviticus 19 and 25, plus Deuteronomy 15 summarize covenant laws that contain the implicit ecological and social wisdom of herding tribes and primitive agrarians living close to the land. Faithful people give animals frequent "time off" and let the land lie fallow at least once every seven years. Neither neighbors nor nature are to be exploited.

Earth-keeping humans are responsible for making sure that people, animals, and the land have their times of rest, peace, and restoration (Ex. 20:8–11; 23:10–12). It is a grand jubilee tradition (Lev. 25 and 26, Luke 4:16–22) with much contemporary relevance.

Covenant teaching fosters an ethic of environmental care coupled with social justice. Moral responsibility toward land and beasts must be matched by justice toward the poor. An appropriate response to poverty, therefore, involves more than alms-giving; it entails debt relief, gleaning opportunities, and equitable redistribution of land, as well as care for "strangers, widows, and orphans."

Yet, despite deep appreciation of nature and reverential descriptions in the Psalms, in Job, in Jesus' Sermon on the Mount, and despite Isaiah's hopeful vision of *shalom*, which includes a restored creation, scripture is punctuated with sad stories of land coveting and defilement. Some striking biblical examples of eco-injustice are the tale of Naboth's vineyard (1 Kings 21), Solomon's order to cut down the beloved cedars of Lebanon to aggrandize Jerusalem (1 Kings 5:6–11; Ps. 104:16), and the people's lament at becoming powerless tenant farmers after the return from exile (Neh. 5:3–5). Wherever human beings are unfaithful to the eco-social requirements of God's covenant, their idolatrous behavior has devastating consequences (Jer. 9:4–11); the land mourns, even the birds die (Hos. 4:3). Even so, there is hope for renewal of the covenant; God continually acts with justice and mercy to redeem creation.

Covenant ethics is concerned with right relationships within the whole web of created interdependency. It views Jesus Christ as the normative clue to faithful and fitting life. "Faithful" means loyal to the cause of God who makes covenant with creation after the flood, through the exodus, and at the incarnation. "Fitting" means practical human action consistent with the kingdom vision and covenant values. Responsible action "fits in" with everything that is going on and that is needed to solve problems.[2]

The cross, the central symbol in the new covenant story, signifies God grappling with human sin, accepting and overcoming life's persistent suffering and perpetual perishing, and ultimately creation's comprehensive renewal, including harmonious human living with myriad species of animals and plants (as envisioned by the prophet Hosea 2:18–22). That is not all it means, but Christians can perceive Jesus' crucifixion-resurrection as the deed that reconciles human beings to God, each other, and the world of creation. This can be understood as *at-one-ment* with nature and society, *attunement* to what God is doing with us and all other creatures. The gracious, enabling work of Christ brings responsive communities of faith into right relation with God, other people, and the larger ecological-social environment with its biodiversity.

But "developed" and "developing" societies alike have yet to face the limits nature places on polluting economic growth and material consumption, and to adopt an ethic and practice of eco-justice that would keep the earth, achieve justice, build community. This ethic comes into sharp focus in terms of four norms: ecologically *sustainable* or environmentally fitting enterprise; socially *just participation* in obtaining sustenance and managing community life; *sufficiency* as an equitable standard of organized sharing that requires basic consumption floors and ceilings, and *solidarity* with other people and creatures—companions, victims, and allies—in earth community. Observance of each ethical norm reinforces the others, serving the common eco-social good by joining what is socially just with what is ecologically right.

Enriching Theological Traditions

The *covenant theology tradition*, going back to Augustine, and behind him to both testaments, has prominence in the preceding portrait of Christianity. But there are several other important Christian approaches, rooted in tradition, which can be viewed as having complementary rather than competing effects on Christian witness in the contemporary world.

One of these is the *wisdom tradition* of Job, the Psalms, Proverbs, Ecclesiastes, and the New Testament gospel and epistles of John. Practical folk wisdom among Christians carries on the tradition, which is also folded into Biblical covenant faith and ethics, as we have seen. Suffice it to add here that from the wisdom perspective, Jesus is understood to be the incarnate Word of God, *logos* of life and reason—from the beginning to the end. The prologue to the book of John views the logos as involved immanently in the whole of God's creation, enlivening all living things while enlightening all that have such capacity.

Another approach is offered by *mature evangelical* Christianity (as distinct from crusading fundamentalism). It recognizes that to start and stay on a path of *sustainable sufficiency for all* requires spiritual conversion—change of heart and repentance—moving toward sanctification that must be reinforced in a faithful, nurturing community. Saving grace is the joyous message so characteristic of 19th-century Protestant hymnody. The crucial result of Christ's redemptive work is to restore human "mutability"—our ability to respond to God's call and to grow and change toward maturity. This is not possible by human willing alone. The gracious, saving work of Christ is necessary for the flourishing of responsible human activity.

Another Christian approach is the *sacramental tradition*, fostered by Catholic mystics, and supported in Anglican and Orthodox liturgy. It "ecstatically experiences the divine bodying forth in the cosmos, and beckons us into communion" (as Rosemary Radford Ruether writes in *Gaia & God*). "We must start thinking of reality as the connecting links of a dance in which each part is equally vital to the whole, rather than [using] the linear competitive model in which the above prospers by defeating and suppressing what is below." The resulting ethical spirituality knows the value and transcience of selves in relation to the great Self, the living interdependence of all things, and the joy of personal communion within the matrix of life—a sacred community.

Passionist Fr. Thomas Berry, a contemporary interpreter of the sacramental tradition, recently discussed the question, "What are the conditions for entering into a Viable Future?"

First condition: Recognize that the universe is a communion of subjects, not a collection of objects. (A theology of stewardship misses the point that communion—deep rapport—is the primary experience.) Earth community *is* the sacred society where we have complementary manifestations of the divine.

Second condition: Appreciate that the earth is primary; humans are derivative. So earth-healing comes first. All professions, business, education, and religion must focus on the well-being of the whole community.

Third condition: Come to grips with the fact that in the future nothing much will happen that humans are not involved in, given our numbers and power. This requires human subjectivity in contact with the subjectivity of the world. "All human activities must be judged primarily by the extent to which they generate and foster a mutually enhancing human/earth relationship."

Adequate theological and ethical responses to the environmental challenge will encompass (in a wholistic way) both created reality *and* human subjectivity. William French of Loyola University, Chicago, emphasizes the "need to move beyond dualistic thinking that suggests we must choose between focusing on subjectivity or creation, freedom or natural necessity, historical consciousness or ecological sensitivity" (in *Journal of Religion*, 1992). Just as subject-centered theology need not turn against creation, critical creation-centered theology need and should not reject the importance of human subjectivity or constructive historical projects.

Adequate theology and ethics will pay close attention to the "view from below" even as it also learns to listen to nature. The *feminist* or egalitarian insight is catching hold that

Domination of women has provided a key link, both socially and symbolically, to domination of earth; hence the tendency in patriarchal cultures to link women with earth, matter, and nature, while identifying males with sky, intellect, and transcendent spirit.... The work of eco-justice and the work of spirituality are interrelated, the outer and inner aspects of one process of conversion and transformation... [involving] a reordering to bring about just and loving interrelationships between men and women, between races and nations, between groups presently stratified into social classes, manifest in great disparities of access to the means of life.[3]

Poor and indigenous communities of people who are most affected by economic exploitation and environmental destruction have important things to teach us about living in harmony with nature and caring for place. Such communities have priority justice claims on religious, educational, business, and political organizations.

Finally, in response to modern physics, biology, and ecology, we should note the maturing of a more philosophical and interdisciplinary style of Christian *process thought*, as fostered by John Cobb. His thought in *The Liberation of Life* (1981, with biologist Charles Birch) asserts the need for an organic or ecological view of God and reality that does not construe God as a substance isolated from the world. God is inherently related to the world, indwelling all eco-social systems, which by their nature are intrinsically interconnected communities. Rev. Carol Johnston, a student of Cobb, notes that

When relations are conceived as inherent, then the person is both influenced by relations with others and influences them. In this context, justice is a matter of the quality of relationships... characterized by freedom, participation, and solidarity. Recognition of inherent relatedness establishes the need to take marginalized people and externalized ecosystems into account.... All entities have a right to be respected appropriate to their degree of intrinsic value and to their importance to the possibility of value in others.[4]

To cultivate a renewed spirituality that undergirds an ethic of care for earth community is the special obligation of religious leaders, clergy and lay, in these times. Otherwise, many more people will suffer from environmental degradation and social injustice, while numerous special places and wondrous otherkind will not be saved; sooner or later they also will fall to the utilitarian logic of the developers.

Authentic spirituality features awe, respect, humane pace, justice, and generosity, *not* intensively efficient use of all being, as goes the instrumental logic of modern life and business. Authentic spirituality loves the suffering ones, aspires toward harmony with the wilderness, shows deep respect for the dignity of animals, plants, mountains, and waters. Such religion celebrates spirit in creation, inculcates an ethic of genuine care for vulnerable people, creatures, ecosystems, as it appropriates the wisdom of nature and of long-standing communities.

In this web of life, religious people will praise and participate in the "economy of God" on this planetary home, foster loving deeds of eco-justice, build communities that model sufficiency, join with others to envision and move toward reverential, sustainable development (and foster corporate responsibility consistent with this goal). They will also explore urban and rural dimensions of ecology, encourage appropriate technologies at home and abroad, participate in community organizations that are working for environmental and economic justice, while they express integrity in both individual and institutional lifestyle, consistent with a spirituality of creation-justice-peace.

NOTES

1 Dieter Hessel also served the national staff of the Presbyterian Church (U.S.A.) for twenty-five years as coordinator of social education and of social policy development. Among his titles is *The Church's Public Role: Retrospect and Prospect*; Wm.B. Eerdmans, 1993.

2 See Charles McCoy, "Creation and Covenant: A Comprehensive Vision for Environmental Ethics," in *Covenant for a New Creation*, Carol S. Robb and Carl J. Casebolt, eds.; Orbis Books, 1991.

3 Ruether, *Gaia & God*, Harper Collins, *1992*.

4 "Economics, Eco-Justice, and the Doctrine of God," in Dieter T. Hessel, ed., *After Nature's Revolt*; Fortress Press, 1992. Also see Herman Daly and John B.

Cobb, Jr., *For the Common Good: Redirecting the Economy toward Community, the Environment, and a Sustainable Future;* Beacon Press, rev. edition 1993.

African American Christianity

Dr. David D. Daniels

Associate Professor of Church History, McCormick Theological Seminary, Chicago, Illinois

African American Christianity is a religious community within global Christianity, located in the United States of America among the descendents of the African slaves who were violently transported to the Americas beginning in the 1500s. While it has always believed the common creeds of the Christian Church, the African American Christian community also recognizes that religion must be embodied in social structures and practices, and it demands correspondence between these social embodiments of faith in God with personal confessions and lives of faith.

The African American Church emerged in colonial British North America during the revolutionary fervor of the late 18th century. At that time, African Americans discerned the need for assuming responsibility for their religious lives within the Christian faith rather than totally entrusting their religious existence to their oppressors, the slaveholders of European national origins. The other major issue which promoted the emergence of African American Christianity was the institutional racism which shaped most American congregations. In these congregations, parishioners were segregated by race, and African Americans were denied the right to official religious leadership, including the office of minister.

Historically, the African American Church has struggled to create social space where a just system could be erected that affirms the human dignity of African Americans and their relationships with others. Currently, African American Christianity is an interdenominational movement with members in communions ranging from Roman Catholicism to Baptist and Pentecostal.

African American churches confess faith in God the Creator, accenting God's creation of all races from a common humanity. African Americans opened their congregations to all Christians regardless of race, and campaigned to end discrimination against persons because of race. During the late 19th and early 20th centuries, the African American Church buttressed its faith in God the Creator by confessing the essence of relationships as "The Fatherhood of God and the Brotherhood of Man." The Civil Rights Movement of the 1950s and 1960s, led by the Rev. Martin Luther King, Jr., communicated the strength of African American Christian faith and demonstrated its resolve to embody its faith within social structures. The congregations spearheaded a national interreligious campaign which struggled to reshape American society; its goal was to dismantle the system of legalized segregation which denied God as the creator of all races and the image of God in all humanity.

African American Christians, as other Christians, confess faith in the providence of God. During the eras of slavery and segregation, African Americans remained confident that God was acting in history to overthrow slavery and segregation. They held in creative tension a firm belief in both personal and social salvation. The African American Church is shaped by God's revelation in Jesus Christ. Jesus is worshipped in song, prayer, and life as the revelation of God's solidarity with the poor and oppressed through the historical Jesus' identification with the poor, the outcast, women, and the oppressed of the 1st century C.E.

The African American Church identifies racial injustice as the social impact of sin. The impact of slavery and segregation as forms of racism is evident in the structuring and legalizing of an inferior or less-than-human status of African Americans, beneath their God-given status and creation as human beings. The African American Church weds God's goodness to the African American practice of Christian love, along with strong demands for justice; these are seen as keys to the social embodiment of faith in God the Creator and glimpses of the justice of God in society.

Racism, specifically slavery and segregation, is named as the curse of the earth, a violation of God's model of human interaction, a model which reflects God's justice and love which is to be reflected in human relationships. Racism is problematic because it reduces persons who are its victims to objects of labor. It arrogantly uncreates what God created—the humanity of its victims—thus blaspheming God. Racism violates creation by treating people as less than human. The issue goes beyond the denial of inalienable human rights, inhumane labor, restriction of freedoms or cruel treatment. At its core is the attempt to destroy the image of God in persons, annihilating the personhood of its victims. Ultimately, racism mars both the oppressed and the oppressor through its confusion of human authority with the prerogatives and authority of the Creator. Racism also undermines the bonds of human community and corrupts the religions and governments that sanction it.

Interreligious Dimensions

In addition to the interreligious dimension of the Civil Rights movement, African American Christianity has indirectly created religious communities with Judaism and Islam through African Americans who adopted Jewish and Islamic beliefs and practices.

From African American Christianity there emerged in the 1890s a new movement which was led by converts to Judaism. While these converts borrowed heavily from Judaism, their core remained African American Christianity. Even the early names of their organizations within African American Judaism reflected Christian forms: Church of God and Saints of Christ; Church of the Living God. Other names, reflecting themes of identity were Ethiopian Hebrews and the Moorish Zionist Temple. During the late 20th century, dialogues with the world Jewish communities led African American Judaism to incorporate more aspects of Global Judaism.

In the 1910s there emerged a new movement within Islam led by converts from African American Christianity. Like African American Judaism, it relied on African American Christianity for its form, but borrowed heavily from Islam. This religious community is represented by such organizations as the Moorish Science Temple, the Nation of Islam, and the American Muslim Mission.

The African American Church has provided an historic witness to the justice and sovereignty of God within the world community, identifying with many movements committed to the liberation of peoples from oppression. It has historically had dialogue with movements such as the Hindu-inspired decolonization campaign in India

Selected Scriptures

"When you lift your hands outspread in prayer I will hide my eyes from you. Though you offer countless prayers, I will not listen. There is blood on your hands . . . cease to do evil, learn to do right, pursue justice and champion the oppressed, give the orphan his rights, plead the widow's cause."

GOD,
speaking in Isaiah 1:15–17

"Is not this what I require of you as a fast: to loose the fetters of injustice, to untie the knots of the yoke, to snap every yoke and set free those who have been crushed? Is it not sharing your food with the hungry, taking the homeless poor into your house, clothing the naked when you meet them and never evading a duty to your kinsfolk?"

GOD,
speaking in the Book of Isaiah

"Inasmuch as ye have done it to the least of these my brethren, ye have done it to me . . . . Inasmuch as ye have not done it to the least of these my brethren, ye have not done it to me."

JESUS,
in Matthew 25

"The spirit of the Lord is upon me for he has anointed me.

"He has sent me to announce Good News to the poor, to proclaim release for prisoners and recovery of sight for the blind; to let the broken victims go free, to proclaim the acceptable Year of the Lord."

ISAIAH 61:1–3

led by Gandhi and the Islam-inspired Palestinian liberation movement. Each endeavor worships God by bringing correspondence between the embodiment of faith in social structures and humane relationships, with personal confession and lives of faith.

Native American–Christian Worship

The Right Rev. Steve Charleston

NOTE: In North America, as in many countries, there has been a considerable range of interaction between Christians of many denominations and indigenous peoples from a variety of tribal communities. Some indigenous people are reclaiming parts of their heritage and combining them with the Christian message. This description explains several elements which may be utilized in cross-cultural worship. One of the goals here is to appreciate the gifts, rituals, and meanings found in the traditions of "the other"—as the Native American believers themselves experience those meanings.

The Circle: For Native American people, and for their theology, the Circle is the symbol that expresses their unique identity as a people. It expresses the sense of wholeness, harmony, unity, and mutual interdependence that is at the heart of Native American civilization. The Circle is a powerful metaphor for the special insights and gifts that Indian and Eskimo people bring into the Christian faith as part of their ancient cultural heritage.

The Drum: In Indian country, the term *drum* means more than just the physical instrument itself. It implies also the singers who are seen as an organic part of the music; they are also the instrument of the Drum. The Drum, a perfect representation of the Circle, embodies the heartbeat of the body of Christ.

The Four Sacred Directions: Within the Circle, the points of the spiritual compass indicate the four sacred directions of God's creation. These directions represent the eternal balance of the harmony and goodness of the world. They can be illustrated by different colors, depending on the tribal tradition.

Our Mother, the Earth: Here is a very precious part of Native American theology; it is one that must be accorded great respect. Speaking of the Earth is not done casually in Native worship; rather, the living Earth shows the nurturing, sustaining power of God in all its warmth and beauty.

Cedar, Sage, Sweet Grass, and Tobacco: Many tribes have a form of incense to purify the place of prayer and worship. Any of these four can be used individually or collectively as incense during a service.

Native Hymns: A great many traditional Christian hymns have been translated into Native languages. One hymn, "Many and Great, O God, are Thy Works," is actually a Dakota hymn, translated into English, and a part of some hymnals.

—excerpted from the service booklet for "A Celebration of Native American Survival," by the Right Rev. Steve Charleston, a Native American

A Call for Evangelical Renewal

Chicago Declaration II

In 1973 a group of evangelical Christians gathered in Chicago to offer a declaration of social concern. In November of 1993, evangelicals sharing the same concerns and convictions gathered again in Chicago to reconsider what they should do in the midst of a worsening social and moral crisis.

We Give Thanks!

We give thanks for the Christian communities that are living out the sacrificial and compassionate demonstration of the reconciling love of God. Their faithfulness encourages us to follow Christ more closely in the power of the Holy Spirit. While we acknowledge our weaknesses and confess our failures, we take heart from the love of God at work in their lives and communities.

We Weep and Dream

We weep for those who do not know and confess Jesus Christ, the hope of the world. We dream of a missionary church that, by its witness and love, draws people into a living relationship with our Lord.

We weep over the persistence of racism, the broken relationships, and the barriers that divide races and ethnic groups. We dream of churches that demonstrate the reconciling Gospel of Christ, uniting believers from every nation, tribe, and tongue.

We weep over the growing disparity between the rich and the poor, the scandal of hunger, and the growing number of people who live in oppressive conditions, insecurity, and danger. We dream of churches that work for education, economic empowerment, and justice, both at the personal and structural levels, and that address the causes and the symptoms of poverty.

We weep over escalating violence, abuse, disregard for the sanctity of human life, and addiction to weapons—in both nations and neighborhoods—that destroy lives and breed fear. We dream of faith communities that model loving ways of resolving conflict, and seek to be peacemakers rather than passive spectators, calling the nations to justice and righteousness.

We weep over the brokenness expressed in relationships between generations, between men and women, in families, in distorted sexualities, and in cruel judgmentalism. We dream of faith communities that honor and protect both our elders and our children, foster a genuine partnership and mutual submission between men and women, nourish healthy families, affirm celibate singleness, work for healing and compassion for all, and for the keeping of marriage covenants.

We weep over the spiritual emptiness and alienation of modern secular society. We dream of a redemptive church that restores personal identity, provides loving community, offers purpose in life, and brings transcendent values and moral conscience to the public square.

We weep over our exploitive practices and consumerist lifestyles that destroy God's good creation. We dream of a church that leads in caring for creation and calls Christians to serve as faithful partners of God in renewing and sustaining God's handiwork.

In all of these, we have fallen so far short of God's glory and awesome holiness, yet we rejoice that in the incarnation, death, and resurrection of Jesus Christ, and in the power of the Holy Spirit, we are called by God to the obedience than comes from faith.

We Commit

Because of the hope we have in the Gospel, we dare to commit ourselves to the kingdom of God and oppose the demonic spiritual forces that seek to undermine the reign of God in this world. Because of our faith we dare to risk and seek the future that God has promised, and we give ourselves to works of love.

We recommit ourselves to grow in the knowledge and the love of God, drinking from the well of worship and praise, word and sacrament. We commit ourselves to sacrificial and loving engagement with God, with all other Christians, and with a needy world.

We commit ourselves to share the good news of Jesus Christ, by living and announcing the Gospel of the kingdom, so that all may come to know, love, and serve God.

We repent of our complacency, our reliance on technique, and our complicity with the evils of the status quo. We repudiate the idolatries of nation and economic system, and zealously dedicate ourselves to Christ and his kingdom's values. We turn away from obsession with power, possessions, self-fulfillment, security, and safety, and willingly risk discomfort and conflict as we live our dreams.

In 1973, we called evangelicals to social engagement: this call still stands. We are thankful that more social engagement is emerging, yet tragically it has frequently divided us along ideological lines. Too often recent evangelical political engagement has been uncivil and polarizing, has demonized opponents, and has lacked careful analysis and biblical integrity. Faithfulness to the full authority of the Scriptures transcends traditional categories of left and right.

The Gospel is not divided—it embraces both the call to conversion and the summons to justice. Obedience to Jesus' teaching and example demands congregations that integrate prayer, worship, evangelism, and social transformation.

We Pray

In the face of such complex and unremitting problems, we claim the promise of God to give wisdom to those who ask. Therefore we ask: *Oh God, Giver and Sustainer of life, Holy Redeemer and Lord, comforting and empowering Spirit, teach us your ways, show us your will, give us your presence, and pour out your power. Amen.*

Come Lord Jesus.

Chapter Five
CONFUCIANISM

A Portrait

Dr. Douglas K. Chung

Professor, Grand Valley State University School of Social Work

Confucianism is a philosophy of a way of life, although many people also consider it a religion. The tradition derives its name from Kung Fu Tzu, or Confucius, (551–479 B.C.) who is renowned as a philosopher and educator. He is less known for his roles as a researcher, statesman, social planner, social innovator, and advocate. Confucius was a generalist with a universal vision. The philosophical method he developed offers a means to transform individuals, families, communities, and nations into a harmonious international society.

The overall goal of Confucianism is to educate people to be self-motivated, self-controlled, and able to assume responsibilities; it has the dual aims of cultivating the individual self and contributing to the attainment of an ideal, harmonious society. Confucius based his method on the assumption that lawlessness and social problems result from the combination of unenlightened individuals and a social structure without norms.

The Confucian system is based on several principles:

1. In the beginning, there is nothing.

2. The Great Ultimate (*Tao*) exists in the *I* (change). The Great Ultimate is the cause of change and generates the two primary forms: the Great *Yang* (a great energy) and its counterforce, the Great *Yin* (a passive form). *Yang* and *Yin* symbolize the energy within any system of counterforces: positive and negative, day and night, male and female, rational and intuitive. *Yang* and *Yin* are complementary; in their interaction, everything—from quanta to galaxies—comes to be. Everything that exists—all systems—coexist in an interdependent network with all other systems.

3. The dynamic tension between *Yin* and *Yang* forces results in an endless process of change—of production and reproduction and the transformation of energy. This is a natural order, an order in which we can see basic moral values. Human nature is inherently good. If

a human being goes along with the Great Ultimate and engages in rigorous self-discipline, that person will discover the real self (the nature of *Tao*) and enjoy the principle of change. And since all systems exist in an interdependent network, one who knows this truth also cares.

4. There are four principles of change:

a. Change is easy.

b. Change is a transforming process due to the dynamics between *Yin* and *Yang*. Any change in either part will lead to a change in the system and related systems. This process has its own cycle of expansion and contraction.

c. Change carries with it the notion of change-lessness; that there is change is a fact that is itself unchanging.

d. The best transformation promotes the growth and development of the individual and the whole simultaneously—it strives for excellence for all systems in the network.

5. Any search for change should consider the following:

a. The status of the object in the interdependent network—that is, what is the system and what are this object's role, position, rights, and duties in the system?

b. Timing within the interrelated network—that is, is this the right time to initiate change?

c. The mean position or the Golden Path in the interrelated network situation; the mean position is regarded as the most strategic position from which one can deal with change. *Tao* (Truth) exists in the mean (*Chung*).

d. The respondence of *Yin* and *Yang* forces—that is, are the counterforces willing to dialogue or compromise?

e. The integration between the parts and the whole—that is, the system in its economic, political and cultural realms.

6. There is an interconnected network of individual existence, and this pattern of interdependent relationships exists in all levels of systems, from individual, through family and state, to the whole world. The whole is dependent upon the harmonious integration of all the parts, or subsystems, while the parts require the nurture of the whole. The ultimate unit within this framework is the universe itself. Self is a here-and-now link in a chain of existence stretching both into the past and into a future to be shaped by the way an individual performs his or her roles in daily life. One's humanity is achieved only with and through others.

Individual and social transformations are based on self-cultivation, the personal effort to search for truth and to become a life-giving person. Searching for and finding the truth will lead to originality, the creative ability to solve problems, and development. The process will also enable individuals and systems to be life-giving and life-sharing—to possess a *Jen* (love) personality. Wisdom, love, and courage are inseparable concepts.

7. Organizational effectiveness and efficiency are reached when systematically interconnected individuals or subsystems find the truth—and stay with it. Existence consists of the interconnected whole. Methods that assume and take account of connections work better than methods that focus on isolated elements. Organizational effectiveness can be improved through a rearrangement of the relationships between the parts and the whole.

In other words, a balanced and harmonious development within the interdependent network is the most beneficial state for all. Self-actualizing and collective goals should always be integrated.

These principles of Confucian social transformation are drawn primarily from *I Ching*, *The Great Learning*, *Confucian Analects*, and *The Doctrine of the Mean*. In contemporary terms, Confucianism can be defined as a school of social transformation that is research oriented and that employs a multidimensional, cross-cultural, and comprehensive approach that is applicable to both micro and macro systems. It is a way of life—or an art of living—that aims to synchronize the systems of the universe to achieve both individual and collective fulfillment.

Two major schools of Neo-Confucianism eventually emerged: the rationalists, who emphasized the "inner world" (philosophy), and the idealists, who emphasized practical learning in the "outer world" (social science). The leading exponent of the rationalists was Chu Hsi (1033–1107 C.E.) and that of the idealists was Wang Yang-Ming (1472–1529 C.E.). The rationalists held that reason is inherent in nature and that the mind and reason are not the same thing. The idealists held that reason is not to be sought from without; it is nothing other than the mind itself. In ethical application, the rationalists considered the flesh to be a stumbling block to the soul. The idealists, on the other hand, considered the flesh to be as the soul makes it. Neo-Confucianism in Korea was led by Lee T'oegye (1501–1570), who taught a philosophy of inner life and moral subjectivity.

Confucianism in the World Today

Confucianism is a strong influence in China, Korea, Japan, and the countries of Southeast Asia as well as among people of Far Eastern descent living around the world. Western people are able to appreciate Confucianism through international contacts and through its literature.

Yet postindustrial social change has led to human crisis in social networks. Postindustrial Confucians today are carrying the vision forward by applying the Confucian model of social transformation to reach the goal of a Great Harmonious Society. The effects of this are seen in volunteerism, social support, social care, and the self-help movement.

In *Great Learning*, Confucius prescribed seven steps in a general strategy of social transformation to achieve the ideal society:

1. The investigation of things (variables). Find out the way things are and how they are related.

2. The completion of knowledge. Find out why things are the way they are; that is, why the dependent variable was related to other variables. This is the reality of things, the truth, *Tao*. And since everything exists in an interrelated network, discovering this truth empowers a person to transform his or her attitude.

3. The sincerity of thought. One should be sincere in wanting to change or to set goals that are a commitment to excellence and the truth, *Tao*,

which is the source of self-motivation, the root of self-actualization and the cornerstone of adequate I-Thou and I-Thing relationships. The most complete sincerity is the ability to foreknow.

4. The rectifying of the heart. The motivation for change must be the right one, good for the self as well as for the whole. It is a cultivation aimed at virtue, a moral self achieved through the intuitive integration of *Jen* (humanity, benevolence, perfect virtue, compassion, and love), *Yi* (righteousness), *Li* (politeness, respect), and wisdom (from steps 1, 2 & 3). Only such a self has real freedom—from evil, and to have moral courage and the ability to be good.

5. The cultivation of the person. There must be lifelong integration between the "knowledge self" (steps 1 & 2) and the "moral self" (steps 3 & 4) through self-discipline (education) and self-improvement. This is the key to helping self and others.

6. The regulation of the family. One should use self-discipline within the family by honoring parents, respecting and caring for siblings, and loving children. One should understand the weaknesses of those one likes and appreciate the strength of those one dislikes to avoid prejudice and disharmony in the family.

7. The governance of the state. The state must provide public education, set policies to care for vulnerable people, root policies in public opinions, appoint and elect capable and moral persons as public officials, and apply management principles based on the Mean and the Golden Path. This sort of public administration should lead to the harmonious state.

The practice of these seven steps is a self-cultivated discipline that seeks the truth, *Tao*, as the practitioner enacts individual and social changes for an improved and more harmonious world. The most persistent form of the Confucian worldview sees the person as an integral part of a cosmos dominated by nature. Contentment and material success come only through acceptance of the rightness of the person adjusting himself or herself to the greater natural world to which that person belongs.

Under the impetus of a contemporary revitalization

of Confucianism, Confucian ethics has become an important force for initiating social transformation and economic change in much of eastern Asia, including China, Japan, Hong Kong, Korea, Singapore, and Taiwan.

Confucius described the ideal welfare state in *Li Chi* (*The Book of Rites*) as follows:

> When the Grand course was pursued, a public and common spirit ruled all under the sky; they chose people of talents, virtue, and ability; their words were sincere, and what they cultivated was harmony.
>
> Thus people did not love their parents only, nor treat as children only their own. An effective provision was secured for the aged till their death, employment for the able-bodied, and the means of growing up to the young.
>
> They showed kindness and compassion to widows/ers, orphans, childless people, and those who were disabled by disease, so that they were all sufficiently maintained. Males had their proper work, and females had their homes.
>
> (They accumulated) articles (of value), disliking that they should be thrown away upon the ground, but not wishing to keep them for their own gratification.
>
> (They labored) with their strength, disliking that it should not be exerted, but not exerting it (only) with a view to their own advantage.
>
> In this way (selfish) scheming was repressed and found no development. Robbers, filchers, and rebellious traitors did not show themselves, and hence the outer doors remained open, and were not shut. This was (the period of) what we call the Grand Union (pp. 365–66).

Integration of Confucianism with Other Traditions

Dr. Douglas K. Chung

Chinese, Korean, and Japanese philosophical systems have each synthesized elements from several traditions. The Chinese came in contact with Indian thought, in the form of Buddhism, around the 1st century C.E. This event, comparable to the spread of Christianity in the West, was marked by three characteristics in particular:

First, the translation of the Buddhist *sutras* stimulated Chinese philosophers and led them to interpret the teachings of the Buddha in the light of their own philosophies. The impact of this study led to the establishment of the Hua-yen and Tien-tai schools of Buddhism in China and the Kegon school in Japan.

Second, under the influence of their familiar, pragmatic Confucian ways of thought, the Chinese creatively responded most to the practical aspects of Buddhism's spiritual discipline, which the Chinese called *Ch'an* (meditation). The *Ch'an* philosophy was eventually adopted by Japan around 1200 C.E. under the Japanese term *Zen*. *Zen* is thus a well-integrated blend of mystical Buddhism of India, the natural philosophy of Taoism, and the pragmatism of the Confucian mentality.

Third, traditional Chinese scholars, both Confucian and Taoist, felt that their cultural foundation had been shaken by the challenge of Buddhism. They reexamined their own philosophies and worked out a way to apply the *I-Ching*—and thus *Yin-Yang* theory—to integrate Buddhism into a new Chinese culture. The *I-Ching*, or *Book of Changes*, describes a universal ontology, the processes by which things evolve, principles of change, and guidelines for choosing among alternatives of change. This ancient book of omens and advice is the oldest of the Chinese classics. Confucius used it as an important text in instructing in methods of personal and social transformation.

Different interpretations of the *I-Ching* demonstrate how Buddhism, Taoism, and traditional Confucianism were blended into the Neo-Confucianism that profoundly affected the premodern Chinese, Korean, Japanese, and Vietnamese dynasties. These include interpretations by Cheng Yi (1050), *I-Ching, the Tao of Organization*; Chih-hsu Ou-i (1599–1655), *The Buddhist I-Ching*; and Liu I-ming (1796), *The Taoist I-Ching: I-Ching Mandalas, A Program of Study for the Book of Changes*, translated by Cleary. Under the influence of the *I-Ching* the Chinese are equipped with a *both-and* mentality that seems to integrate religious diversity with less difficulty than the *either-or* tendency of Western mentality.

The Chinese Neo-Confucian school's synthesis of Confucianism, Buddhism, and Taoism culminated in the philosophy of Chu Hsi (1033–1107 C.E.), one of the greatest of all Chinese thinkers. It guides people to learn the truth (*Tao*) in order to solve problems, which leads one in turn to be harmonious with *Tao*, or truth (unification), the core of Confucianism and Taoism.

Both Confucianism and Taoism share the same ontology from the *I-Ching*, while Buddhism also came to use *I-Ching* to interpret Buddhist thought. The three philosophies use different approaches, however, to reach the unification with *Tao*/Brahman. Confucians emphasize a rational approach, Taoists focus on an intuitive approach and Buddhists favor a psychological approach. Confucianism favors education and the intellectual approach, while Taoism tends to look down on education in favor of intuitive insight into Nature. Buddhists are interested in changing human perception and thus stress detach-ment; each tends to participate in world affairs accordingly.

Huang Te-Hui (1644–1661 C.E.) of the Ching Dynasty integrated the three main belief systems of Confucianism, Taoism, and Buddhism to form the *Hsien-Tien-Tao*. *I-Kuan-Tao* (Integrated Tao) evolved from the *Hsien-Tien-Tao*. Chang Tien-Jan was recognized as a master of *I-Kuan-Tao* in 1930. Various *I-Kuan-Tao* groups moved to Taiwan in 1946 and 1947, and today, *I-Kuan-Tao* priests teach an integrated religion drawn from Confucian, Buddhist, Taoist, Christian, and Islamic canons. The concept of oneness of all religions is the major theme, and its mission is to integrate all religions into one.

This group was among the first in contemporary society to start interfaith dialogue and interfaith integration. However, many people in Taiwan viewed the *I-Kuan-Tao* religion as a heresy, and it was banned for many years by the government. Since being granted official recognition in 1987, *I-Kuan-Tao* of Taiwan has expanded internationally. It now has organizations in South Korea, Japan, Singapore, Malaysia, Thailand, Indonesia, the Philippines, Australia, the United States, Canada, Brazil, and Paraguay.

Building on the successful integration of Buddhism into Neo-Confucianism, many contemporary Confucians have issued a challenge for another religious integration among Buddhism, Christianity, Confucianism, Islam, and Taoism. For this to come about, more Asians need to read the Bible and the Qur'an, and more Westerners need to know about the I-Ching and the Qur'an. Such a global dialogue would certainly help facilitate a new understanding of religions.

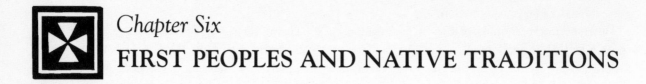

Chapter Six
FIRST PEOPLES AND NATIVE TRADITIONS

The First Peoples in the Fourth World: Terms

Julian Burger explains (in *The Gaia Atlas of First Peoples*) that there is no universally agreed name for the peoples he describes as "first peoples":

" ...because their ancestors were the original inhabitants of the lands, since colonized by foreigners. Many territories continue to be so invaded. The book also calls them indigenous, a term widely accepted by the peoples themselves, and now adopted by the United Nations."

p. 16

"'Fourth World' is a term used by the World Council of Indigenous Peoples to distinguish the way of life of indigenous peoples from those of the First (highly industrialized), Second (Socialist bloc), and Third (developing) Worlds. The First, Second, and Third Worlds believe that 'the land belongs to the people'; the Fourth World believes that 'the people belong to the land.'"

p. 18

A Portrait of the First Peoples

NOTE: Texts and quotations by Julian Burger and the indigenous peoples are from *The Gaia Atlas of First Peoples: A Future for the Indigenous World*, by edited Julian Burger with campaigning groups and native peoples worldwide (London: Gaia Books Ltd., 1990). Some of what follows was written by representatives of indigenous peoples; some was provided by non-indigenous people.

First peoples see existence as a living blend of spirits, nature, and people. All are one, inseparable and interdependent—a holistic vision shared with mystics throughout the ages. The word for religion does not exist in many cultures, as it is so closely integrated into life itself. For many indigenous peoples spirits permeate matter—they animate it. This led the early anthropologists to refer to such beliefs as "animist" (p. 64).

Myths that explain the origins of the world remind people of their place in the universe and of their connection with the past. Some are humorously ironic, others complex and esoteric. Some, notably Aboriginal Dreamtime, speak of the creation of the hills, rocks, hollows, and rivers formed by powerful ancestral spirits in the distant past. Others describe a dramatic split between the gods and humankind or the severance of the heavens and the Earth—as in the sudden separation of the Sky Father and Earth Mother in Maori legend. Others tell the story of how the Earth was peopled, as in the sacred book of the Maya of Central America. Myths invest life with meaning. The rich symbolic associations found in the oral traditions of many indigenous cultures bring the sacred into everyday life—through a pipe, a feather, a rattle, a color even—and help individuals to keep in touch with both themselves and the spirit world (p. 66).

Indigenous peoples are strikingly diverse in their culture, religion, and social and economic organization. Yet, today as in the past, they are prey to stereotyping by the outside world. By some they are idealized as the embodiment of spiritual values; by others they are denigrated as an obstacle impeding economic progress. But they are neither: they are people who cherish their own distinct cultures, are the victims of past and present-day colonialism, and are determined to survive. Some live according to their traditions, some receive welfare, others work in factories, offices, or the professions. As well as their diversity, there are some shared values and experiences among indigenous cultures....By understanding how they organize their societies, the wider society may learn to recognize that they are not at some primitive stage of development, but are thoughtful and skillful partners of the natural world, who can help all people to reflect on the way humanity treats the environment and our fellow creatures (p. 15).

Voices of Indigenous Peoples

Selections from *The Gaia Atlas of First Peoples* by Julian Burger with indigenous peoples.

Earth

"Every part of the earth is sacred to my people. Every shining pine needle, every sandy shore, every mist in the dark woods, every clearing and humming insect is holy in the memory and experience of my people."

A DUWAMISH CHIEF

"One has only to develop a relationship with a certain place, where the land knows you, and experience that the trees, the Earth, and Nature are extending their love and light to you to know there is so much we can receive from the Earth to fill our hearts and souls."

INTI MELASQUEZ, Inca

"The Earth is the foundation of Indigenous Peoples; it is the seat of spirituality, the fountain from which our cultures and languages flourish.

"The Earth is our historian, the keeper of events, and the bones of our forefathers. Earth provides us with food, medicine, shelter, and clothing. It is the source of our independence, it is our Mother. We do not dominate her; we must harmonize with her."

HAYDEN BURGESS, native Hawaiian

"Man is an aspect of nature, and nature itself is a manifestation of primordial religion. Even the word 'religion' makes an unnecessary separation, and there is no word for it in the Indian tongues. Nature is the 'Great Mysterious,' the 'religion before religion,' the profound intuitive apprehension of the true nature of existence attained by sages of all epochs, everywhere on Earth; the whole universe is sacred, man is the whole universe, and the religious ceremony is life itself, the common acts of every day."

PETER MATTHIESSEN, *Indian Country*

"We Indian people are not supposed to say, 'This land is mine.' We only use it. It is the white man who buys land and puts a fence around it. Indians are not supposed to do that, because the land belongs to all Indians, it belongs to God, as you call it. The land is a part of our body, and we are a part of the land."

BUFFALO TIGER, Miccosukee

"When the last red man has vanished from the Earth, and the memory is only a shadow of a cloud moving across the prairie, these shores and forests will still hold the spirits of my people, for they love this Earth as the newborn loves its mother's heartbeat."

SEALTH, A Duwamish Chief

"When Indians referred to animals as 'people'—just a different sort of person from Man—they were not being quaint. Nature to them was a community of such 'people' for whom they had a great deal of genuine regard and with whom they had a contractual relationship to protect one another's interests and to fulfill their mutual needs. Man and Nature, in short, were joined by compact—not by ethical ties—a compact predicated on mutual esteem. This was the essence of the traditional land relationship."

OJIBWAY MAGAZINE

"Our roots are deep in the lands where we live. We have a great love for our country, for our birthplace is here. The soil is rich from the bones of thousands of our generations. Each of us was created in these lands and it is our duty to take great care of them, because from these lands will spring the future generations of our peoples. We walk about with great respect, for the Earth is a very Sacred Place."

Sioux, Navaho, and Iroquois Declaration, 1978

Economy, Wealth, and a Way of Life

The economic life of indigenous people is based not on competition but on cooperation, for survival is only possible when the community works together. Most small-scale indigenous societies have elaborate systems for sharing food, possessions, and ritualizing conflict....Indigenous forms of economy cannot, of course, satisfy the needs of a burgeoning world population now nearing 6 billion. But the knowledge and, especially, the values of the peoples practicing them are vital. The scientific community has recently begun research into indigenous skills in resource management. But it is, above all, wisdom that is needed in Western culture—we all need to learn respect for the Earth, conservation of resources, equitable distribution of wealth, harmony, balance and modest cooperation. In 1928 Gandhi wrote:

> God forbid that India should ever take to industrialism after the manner of the West....It would strip the world bare like locusts.

p. 42

"An Innu hunter's prestige comes not from the wealth he accumulates but from what he gives away. When a hunter kills caribou or other game he shares with everyone else in the camp."

DANIEL ASHINI, Innu

War and Peace, Life and Death

"Was it an awful war?"
"It was a terrible war."
"Were many people killed?"
"One man was killed."
"What did you do?"
"We decided that those of us who had done the killing should never meet again because we were not fit to meet one another."

SAN
describing a war to Laurens van der Post

In Papua New Guinea hostilities between groups are part of the cycle of events encompassing long periods of peace and enmity. War is just one aspect of cultural life. The idea of annihilating the other group is absent; indeed, the Tsembaga and Mae Enga are known as the peoples who marry their enemies. War is a means by which the individual and the group find their identity, and is largely ceremonial.... Even on the point of war there is always a ritual means of stepping back from open confrontation. Anger can be channelled into a "nothing fight," a competition of insults and shouting. Or else it may lead to a real fight, with blows exchanged and sometimes even serious casualties. After a war a lengthy process of peacemaking begins. Gifts, ceremonies, and marriages establish links and obligations between the parties.

p. 62

Partners toward a Sustainable Future

Maurice Strong

General Secretary of the United Nations Conference on Environment and Development, held in Rio de Janeiro in 1992

As we awaken our consciousness that humankind and the rest of nature are inseparably linked, we will need to look to the world's more than 250 million indigenous peoples. They are the guardians of the extensive and fragile ecosystems that are vital to the well-being of the planet. Indigenous peoples have evolved over many centuries a judicious balance between their needs and those of nature. The notion of sustainability, now recognized as the framework for our future development, is an integral part of most indigenous cultures.

In the last decades, indigenous peoples have suffered from the consequences of some of the most destructive aspects of our development. They have been separated from their traditional lands and ways of life, deprived of their means of livelihood, and forced to fit into societies in which they feel like aliens. They have protested and resisted. Their call is for control over their own lives, the space to live, and the freedom to live their own ways. And it is a call not merely to save their own territories, but the Earth itself.

While no one would suggest that the remainder of the more than 5 billion people on our planet would live at the level of indigenous societies, it is equally clear that we cannot pursue our present course of development. Nor can we rely on technology to provide an easy answer. What modern civilization has gained in knowledge, it has perhaps lost in sagacity. The indigenous peoples of the world retain our collective evolutionary experience and insights which have slipped our grasp. Yet these hold critical lessons for our future. Indigenous peoples are thus indispensable partners as we try to make a successful transition to a more secure and sustainable future on our precious planet.

—excerpted from the foreword to *The Gaia Atlas of First Peoples* by Julian Burger

Ancient Prophecies for Modern Times

Bette Stockbauer

A freelance writer whose philosophical background is Esoteric Christianity

NOTE: This article surveys native cultures whose representatives are stepping forward to tell the world about their traditions, particularly their ancient prophecies, so that mankind may choose correctly at this important point in world civilization.

"We live in a time of the fulfillment of prophecy."
                                        WILLARU HUARTA

Although Western history has depicted native cultures as primitive and sometimes barbaric, in our own day a much richer picture is emerging.

French author Pierre Honore minutely examined the original journals of the conquerors. There he found records of what they encountered in the New World—huge cities with urban populations well versed in the arts and sciences, following finely ordered systems of law. Archeological excavations of modern times have verified these accounts, unearthing sophisticated cities and pyramids that rival those of Egypt.

Most importantly the native peoples themselves are stepping forward, revealing traditions and sacred knowledge they took underground five hundred years ago when the conquerors came. They speak now because they understand the import of the present times. Their sacred sciences tell them the world is at a turning point, that its choices today will determine the future course of civilization. Their prophecies have instructed them to travel out into the world and tell us of the dangers we face. These voices are important for us to hear because they speak from hearts that have tried to remain true to their sacred teachings—to live in the way of brotherhood and simplicity, establishing harmony with one another and with all living things.

This is what they say:

- We are entering a time of purification and can expect to witness chaos and destruction in all the kingdoms of nature.
- It is a time for the reuniting of the races. Barriers of religion and nationality will begin to fall as all people realize their essential unity.
- We must heal the damage done to Mother Earth, the source of life, and recognize that all living things are endowed with spirit.
- In the coming times we will see the return of one or more Great Teachers who will guide us into the future.

In his book *The Return of the Pahana*, Robert Boissière discusses the widely held belief among native peoples in the imminent return of a savior figure, and claims that it in no way differs from the Christian belief in a second coming. In the legendary history of many tribes there is a story of a teacher similar to Jesus who taught the spiritual mysteries and an ethical way of life. When he left, they say, he promised to return at a time when the Earth would be in great turmoil, to guide humanity into the future. He is best known by the names of Quetzalcoatl and Kukulcan.

North America

Thomas Banyacya has traveled the world for almost fifty years speaking about the prophecies of his tribe, the Hopi. For centuries the Hopi have lived in one of the harshest environments of the US— perched on a desert mesa in Arizona. Their ancestors chose such a place to settle because they knew it would keep their people close to the creator. They continually reaffirm their reliance on God by an annual series of rituals asking the spirits to supply their every need.

In 1948 a group of Hopi elders accepted the task of warning the world of the events that the Hopi prophecies foretold. The prophecies themselves instructed them to approach the UN. It took forty-four years of effort, but in 1992 they were finally permitted to address the General Assembly. This beginning led to another gathering at the UN in 1993, called the "Cry of the Earth Conference," when leaders from seven nations released their prophecies.

Hopi prophecies speak of the return of Pahana, their True White Brother, who left them in ancient Arial promising to return. They wear their hair in bangs to form a window, they say, by which to see their Elder Brother when He returns. It is also an identifying mark for the Elder Brother to recognize them.

Black Elk and Crazy Horse were leaders of the Lakota Sioux in the late 1800s, a period which saw in the U.S. the decimation of many native groups. Each had a vision of the future. Black Elk saw that his people would be plagued by famine and sickness and war. They would lose heart and the sacred hoop of his nation would be broken. But he saw a vision of his own nation being reunited after seven generations and becoming part of the greater hoop of all the nations of the earth. Then he saw the daybreak star rising in the east, and heard a voice that said: "It

shall be a relative to them, and who shall see it shall see much more, for from there comes Wisdom; and those who do not see it shall be dark." Black Elk thought this meant that a great Prophet from the East would bring a message to his people.

Crazy Horse's vision foretold the darkness that descended on his people. He saw the coming of automobiles and airplanes and the tragic world wars of the modern era. He saw his people gradually awakening after the last war and beginning to dance again under the Sacred Tree. Then amazingly he saw that dancing along with his people were representatives of all races who had become brothers. Thus he foresaw that the world would be made whole again, not just by his own nation but by all peoples working together.

Among the Lakota, the Crow, the Chippewa, and other Native American tribes, the White Buffalo is one of the most sacred symbols. It represents purity, sacrifice, and a sign that prophecy is being fulfilled. The messiah honored by the Lakota Sioux is the White Buffalo Calf Woman who brought the Sacred Pipe and established the foundation of their ritual and social life. When she left, she turned into a white buffalo, and promised some day to return. In 1994 a white buffalo calf was born in Wisconsin; in 1996 another was born in South Dakota. For the native peoples these births have been a sign to "mend the hoop" of the nations, to establish brotherhood within the family of man, and return to a spiritual way of life.

Jake Swamp of the Mohawk nation tells of the Peacemaker, Deganawida, who unified the tribes of the Iroquois Confederacy. The Peacemaker foresaw the turmoil and destruction that would destroy the lives and culture of the Confederacy tribes. But he also saw a time beyond when there would come a great Prophet who would be a World Uniter. He would come in the same spirit as other prophets before Him, but would renew the spirit of man in a way more worldwide and all-embracing than ever before in history. In 1969 the elders of Dhyani Ywahoo's Tsalagi/Cherokee group decided to release teachings that have been kept in secret since the conquest. Through books, lectures, and workshops, Dhyani Ywahoo is disseminating that knowledge. She claims that her own Ywahoo lineage was founded by a legendary prophet called the Pale One who rekindled the sacred fires throughout the Americas. She says: "The Pale One is a cyclically incarnating being. He comes when the people have forgotten their sacred ways, bringing reminders of the Law, recalling all to right relationship. He is expected soon again, and he may be alive even now. It is good."

Australia and New Zealand

Among the Australian Aboriginals it is believed that each tribe has a responsibility to take care of one part of the environment. They believe that underground minerals are a vital part of the earth's energy grid and are greatly concerned about the excessive mining in modern Arial, particularly of uranium. In 1975 the elders met in Canberra, drawing together over 350 Aboriginal people. They gave a warning of cataclysms to come and told the people to go out and teach their knowledge to the world, to prepare it for a future time when we would go back to our beginnings—when all cultures will exist as one.

The Waitaha nation claims the most ancient lineage in New Zealand. When the nation was broken up by warriors from the Pacific, the elders concealed one thousand years of their generational history and wisdom teachings, passing the knowledge on through only a tiny number of people in each generation. In 1990 the elders saw in the heavens a configuration that was a sign for them to release their sacred knowledge. A book, *The Song of Waitaha*, by Barry Brailsford, contains these teachings. In their language *wai* means water and *taha* means gourd, implying the idea of a water carrier, the sign of Aquarius.

South America

The Kogi are a pre-Columbian tribe who live an isolated existence in the Sierra Nevada de Santa Marta in Colombia. They are one of the few who escaped destruction by the Europeans and still live their lives in accordance with their ancient spiritual heritage. Alarmed by the excessive mining and deforestation of modern Arial, in 1990 (for the one and only time) they allowed a BBC television film crew to visit them and document their lives. Calling themselves "The Elder Brothers," they wished to issue an urgent warning to the "younger brothers." High in their mountain lands, they see that the earth is drying up; the sources of water that should give sustenance to the plains below are no longer vital. They warn us that the earth is dying and, "When the Earth dies we will all die."

Willaru Huarta grew up in the jungles of Peru, studying with the shamans. He says that his native Quechua Incan prophecies predicted the white man's coming would bring five hundred years of materialism and imbalance. But now they say that era is coming to an end and the Age of Aquarius will "signal the return of Light to the planet and the dawn of a golden era. We live in a time of the fulfillment of prophecy." Now he tours the world teaching his simple message: "Humanity should cure itself and give help to the poor. Regenerate yourself with light, and then help those who have poverty of the soul. Return to the inner spirit, which we have abandoned while looking elsewhere for happiness."

The Q'ero are another Peruvian group that are releasing prophecy, traveling to the industrialized nations to hold ceremonies and share their vision of the future.

Mayan Prophecy

Hunbatz Men tells of an ancient confederation of Native American elders made up of representatives from Nicaragua to the Arctic Circle. They have been meeting for thousands of years and continue to do so today. Before the Spaniards came the confederation decided to hide the Mayan teachings, entrusting certain families with their care. Hunbatz Men is an inheritor of that lineage. In his book *Secrets of Mayan Science/Religion*, he reveals teachings that mirror the Hindu and Buddhist ones of astrology, meditation, and the septenary root of creation.

He speaks of Kukulcan and Quetzalcoatl, not so much in light of an expected return, but rather in terms of the possibility that each of us can attain the same exalted stage by treading the path of attaining knowledge. "To be Quetzalcoatl or Kukulcan is to know the seven forces that govern our body—not only know them but also use them and understand their intimate relationship with natural and cosmic laws. We must comprehend the long and short cycles and the solar laws that sustain our lives. We must know how to die, and how to be born."

Don Alejandro Oxlaj is a seventh-generation priest from Guatemala and head of the Quiche Maya Elder Council. He has traveled throughout North America, comparing the native prophecies of different tribes. In the coming year he hopes to record and publish, for the first time in five hundred years, the Mayan prophecies of his people.

What is enlightening in all of these statements is their consistent tone of reconciliation. The native groups are opening their doors to people of every color, speaking of themselves as "Rainbow Warriors." Their elders have reminded them to "remember the original instructions" when each tribe was given by the creator a mandate to follow. That mandate has told them that now is the time to heal the past, despite the centuries of pain and persecution. Now is the time to join together and work in harmony to rehabilitate the planet and establish an era of alignment and peace.

Suggested reading:

Robert Boissiere, *The Return of Pahana*

Vinson Brown, *Voices of Earth and Sky*

Pierre Honore, *In Quest of the White God*

Steven McFadden, *Ancient Voices*

Hunbatz Men, *Secrets of Mayan Science/Religion*

Scott Peterson, *Native American Prophecies*

Dhyani Ywahoo, *Voices of Our Ancestors*

Native American Spirituality

Robert Staffanson

Executive Director, American Indian Institute

NOTE: A dictionary's definition of spirituality: "devotion to spiritual (i.e., metaphysical) things instead of worldly things." This definition does not apply to Native Americans because they do not recognize a dichotomy between "spiritual" and material things.

A simplistic definition of Native American spirituality would be that it is the opposite of pragmatism (i.e., short-term concern with "practical" results). While Native American spirituality is not easily defined, it has several defining characteristics:

1. *Recognition of the interconnectedness of all Creation*, and the responsibility of human beings to use their intelligence in protecting that interconnectedness. That applies particularly to the life-giving elements: water, air, and soil.

2. *Belief that all life is equal*, and that the presence of the life spark implies a degree of spirituality whether in humans, animals, or plants. In their view the species of animals and birds, as well as forests and other plant life, have as much "right" to existence as human beings, and should not be damaged or destroyed. That does not mean that they cannot be used but that use has limitations.

3. *The primary concern is with the long-term welfare of life* rather than with short-term expediency or comfort. They consider all issues and actions in relationship to their long-term effect on all life, not just human life.

4. *Spirituality is undergirded by thankfulness to the Creator.* Prayer, ceremonies, meditation, and fasting are an important part of their lives. But they ask for nothing. They give thanks: for all forms of life and for all the elements that make life possible, and they are concerned with the continuation of that life and the ingredients upon which it depends.

Traditional Native Americans believe that any of

their people who lack spirituality are no longer Indian. Traditional Native Americans do not see any spirituality in our "western" world. They believe that we have a kind of mindless materialism that is destroying both us and the world we live in.

A Teaching from Tecumseh

"So live your life that the fear of death can never enter your heart. Trouble no one about his religion; respect others in their view, and demand that they respect yours. Love your life, perfect your life, beautify all things in your life. Seek to make your life long and its purpose in the service of your people. Prepare a noble death song for the day when you go over the great divide. Always give a word or a sign of salute when meeting or passing a friend, even a stranger, when in a lonely place. Show respect to all people and grovel to none.

"When you arise in the morning, give thanks for the food and for the joy of living. If you see no reason for giving thanks, the fault lies only in yourself. Abuse no one and nothing, for abuse turns the wise ones to fools and robs the spirit of its vision. When it comes your time to die, be not like those whose hearts are filled with the fear of death, so that when their time comes they weep and pray for a little more time to live their lives over again in a different way. Sing your death song and die like a hero going home."

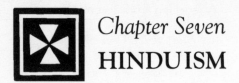

Chapter Seven
HINDUISM

Wisdom from the Hindu Tradition

Compiled and translated by
Dr. T. K. Venkateswaran

*"We meditate upon that adorable holy
Light of the resplendent Life-Giver Savitar.
May He stimulate and inspire our
intellects."*

Rig Veda III-62–10

This is one of the most sacred of the
mantras, prayers, and chants that have
played a dominant part in the religious
history of the Hindus, as a part of their
daily repeated prayers. All intellect
creativity, and imagination are derived
from God. He is the supreme Knowledge,
pure Intelligence and Consciousness.

*"I am firmly seated in the hearts of all.
From Me comes knowledge and memory
and the departing of doubts. I am the
Knower and Knowledge of the Vedas. I am
the author of Vedanta (the sacred
Upanishads and their teachings, the means
to spiritual salvation/liberation)."*

GOD (AS KRISHNA)
speaking, *Bhagavad-Gita* XV:15

*"Come together in unity. Speak in
profound agreements. May your minds
converge (in deep consensus). May your
deliberations be uniform and united be
your hearts. May you be firmly bound and
united in your intentions and resolves."*

Rig Veda X-191, 2–4

A Portrait

Dr. T. K. Venkateswaran

Professor of Religious Studies (Emeritus), University of Detroit; former Research Scholar, Harvard University

Introduction

Hinduism is the oldest and perhaps the most complex of all the living, historical world religions. It has no one single identifiable founder. The actual names found for the religion in the Hindu scriptures are Vedic Religion, i.e., the Religion of the *Vedas* (Scriptures) and *Sangtana Dharma*, i.e., the Universal or Perennial Wisdom and Righteousness, the "Eternal Religion." Hinduism is not merely a religion, however. It encompasses an entire civilization and way of life, whose roots date back prior to 3000 B.C.E. beyond the peoples of Indus Valley culture. Yet, since the time of the *Vedas*, there is seen a remarkable continuity, a cultural and philosophical complexity and also a pattern of unity in diversity that evolved in the course of its history, also a demonstrated propensity for deep integration and assimilation of all new and external influences.

Main Sources of Religious Knowledge

Scriptures: 1) The four *Vedas*—*Rig, Yajur, Sama,* and *Atharva Vedas*—are seen as *Sruti*, "Heard," as Revelation and "not human-originated," though human beings, wise and holy sages, seers, and prophets were the human channels of the revealed wisdom. They "heard" in their hearts the eternal messages and "saw" and symbolized various names and forms of the One, Sacred, Ultimate Reality, Truth, God from different perspectives and contexts. The Hindu gods and goddesses, worshipped with different names and forms and qualities, are, in reality, many aspects, powers, functions, and symbols of the only One all-pervasive Supreme Being, without a second. The *Upanishads*, later portions in the *Vedas*, teach that salvation/liberation is achieved in an experiential way and that oneness with the supreme Reality, *Brahman*, is possible; the supreme goal, *Brahman*, is also the One Self, the higher Self found in all. The philosophy and spiritual practice is known as *Vedanta*.

2) The *Agamas* (Further Scriptures) teach union with God as the

Lord, the Highest Person, *Brahman* seen in the process of action.

Supplements to the Scriptures: 1) *Smritis* (works of Hindu Law, etc.).

2) The two epics: the *Ramayana* and the *Mahabharata* (along with the *Bhagavad-Gita* in the latter, seen almost as an autonomous scripture) and the various Puranas.

Basic Beliefs, Values, Paradigms, and Teachings

The one all-pervasive supreme Being is both immanent and transcendent, both supra-personal and highest person (God), who can be worshipped as both Father and/or Mother of the universe. The universe undergoes endless cycles of creation, preservation, and dissolution. All souls are evolving and progressing toward union with God and everyone will ultimately attain salvation/liberation.

Karma is the moral and physical law of cause and effect by which each individual creates one's own future destiny by accepting responsibility and accountability for one's own thoughts, words, and deeds, individual and collective.

The individual soul reincarnates, evolving through many births and deaths, until all the *karmic* results, good and bad, are resolved. One can and should strive to attain liberation from this cycle of constant births and deaths in this very life, by pursuing one of the four spiritual paths to God-realization—the ways of Knowledge, Love and Devotion, Selfless Action, and Meditation.

Four aims or goals in life are arranged hierarchically: the *joy* cluster (sensual, sexual, artistic, aesthetic joys, compatible with ethics), the *economic and social fulfillment* cluster, the *morality* cluster (duties, obligations, right action, law, righteousness, general virtues, and supreme ethical values, etc.), and the *spiritual goal of salvation/liberation* (union and oneness with God). All the elements that are usually seen as exclusive or antagonistic in life are brought together in this holistic model, in which every goal has its own place.

Each individual passes through several stages in his/her journey through life toward the spiritual goal. The four classical stages in life are 1) the student, 2) the house-holder, 3) retirement to the woods for spiritual pursuits, and 4) renunciation (optional). Within each stage are specific goals that provide a practical model for the organization of life.

Divine aspects and elements of God, the "presence," are invoked through ritual symbolism and prayers in consecrated images and icons for purposes of worship. God also "descends," periodically, in incarnations and historical personalities such as Rama and Krishna.

All life is sacred and is to be loved and revered, through the practice of nonviolence, realizing that there is unity and interdependency among all forms of life and all aspects of the universe. Exemplary spir-

"Then, in the beginning, there was neither nonbeing nor being (existence). Neither were there worlds, nor the sky, nor anything beyond …nor death, nor immortality was there, no knowing of night or day. That One (Ultimate) breathed by its own self-power, svadha, without air. All was concealed in darkness.…That One became creative by self-power and the warmth of contemplation. There arose love and desire, the prime seed of the mind.…The gods appeared later than this original creative activity. Then, who knows wherefrom creation came into being? Who can know this truth? That One, who was supervising (the origins) from the highest heavens, indeed knows or knows not!"
Rig Veda X:129

In the above *Hymn of Origins*, several ultimate questions are raised: What is time? What is the nature of potency, *karma* (action-influence)? How to understand the mystery of division and differentiation through naming, language into being, nonbeing, death, immortality, and so forth? How to transcend the boundaries of conceptual thought?

Only the highest Spirit knows the full truth of the origins of creation and existence. The quest for the original undivided unifying "Field" and ground cannot be purely conceptual, but has to be experiential, through meditation and spiritual *yajna*. The hymn leads one to the farthest reaches of the frontiers of modern science and cosmology and shows the profundity of what lies beyond anything that can be conceived and spoken of.

Wisdom (cont.)

"The Knowledge of Akshara, the immutable unchanging ground of all relative existence and expressions, brings integrity, stability, and fulfillment to the goals of life. One whose awareness is not opened up to realize that Akshara, what is the use of mere words and knowledge, scriptures, etc., to him?"

Rig Veda I-164–39;
also *Svetasvatara Upanishad* IV-1

"To one who aspires and is established in Rta, the Cosmic and Moral Order and Harmony, sweet blow the winds. The rivers flow sweet. For us, who are rooted in Rta, may the herbs and plants be as sweet as also the nights and dawns. May the earth and its soil be full of sweetness. May our Father, may the Heaven be sweet. May the plants, the sun, and the cows (and animals) be full of sweetness in our life."

Rig Veda I-90, 6–8

This beautiful hymn (above) is of profound value for environmental and ecological concerns and awareness. Such hymns in the *Vedas* link peace and sweetness, beauty and quality of life to the daily practice and experience of *Rta* in personal lives with sacred commitment. One of the oft-repeated definitions of God in the *Vedas* is *Rta*, which has several nuances of meanings: Cosmic and Moral Order, Balance, Harmony, the Divine Natural Law, and unified Life-Giving Energy and Rhythm. *Rta* is also the fundamental norm of existence. Human greed, selfish power, transgression, and violation of *Rta*—individually and collectively—bring ecological and social disaster and destruction of the earth.

itual teachers (*Gurus*) who themselves are liberated in this life help the spiritual aspirants with their knowledge and compassion.

No particular religion (including Hinduism) teaches the only, exclusive way to God and salvation, above all others. All authentic, genuine religious paths and traditions lead to the One God and are facets of God's love and light, deserving proper respect, mutual tolerance, and right understanding.

Hindu Sub-traditions (*sampradayas*)

The One Brahman is conceived and symbolized according to divine functions as Brahma (the Creator), Vishnu (the Sustainer and Preserver), and Shiva (the Destroyer of evils and the Dissolver of the universe). This is referred to as the Hindu Trinity. Within the Great Tradition of Hinduism are four main, living subtraditions, called *sampradayas*: 1) *Shaivites*, 2) *Vaishnavites*, 3) *Shaktas*, and 4) *Smartas*. The differences are based upon conceptions and worship of the central name, form, symbols, liturgies, mythologies, and theologies of the One God, Lord and highest Person, as Vishnu, Shiva, Shakti (the Divine as Mother), etc. *Smartas* worship, equally, several personal manifestations of the supreme Reality and philosophically emphasize the ultimate identity-experience of the individual self with the supreme Self, which is also Brahman.

Hinduism has a vast network of sacred symbols. Some are drawn from sacred geography like the Ganges River, others are drawn from plant, bird, and animal life; other symbols include profound polyvalent (multilevel meanings) symbols such as the sacred sound-syllable *Om* (also written as AUM) which contains all reality, and Shiva's icon as the "Cosmic Dancer," fulfilling all the divine functions.

Approaches to Interfaith Dialogue and Cooperation

There are several hymns in the *Vedas* and other scriptures that categorically declare that there are different approaches and perspectives to God and experience of God and Ultimate Reality. This also arises, necessarily, from different human contexts. The central teaching, constantly repeated, is God is One, but names and forms are many; symbols and paths are many. Thus, there arose a rich theological and philosophical pluralism within Hinduism creating an internal "parliament of sub-traditions and sub-religions," but all grounded in the unity of the *Vedas* and One Brahman. Also, multiplicity is encouraged and thrives by means of the free choice and self-determined identification with one specially loved manifestation of God—Shiva, Krishna, Shakti, Rama, and so on—in pursuing the moral and spiritual path to salvation/liberation.

Because people are at different starting points and stations, Hindu scriptures affirm and accept variety in religious experiences as a necessity and psychological reality. This wisdom is extended to other non-Hindu religions as a spontaneous and logical outflow of the same ethos. There is no historical tradition or theological necessity in Hinduism for proselytization or conversion of non-Hindus to Hinduism. All authentic religions and traditions, all over the world, rising from different historical and cultural starting points and contexts, are to be respected, accepted, appreciated, and cherished.

Multiplicity brings with it differences, which one cannot destroy or do away with. Yet, the deep commonalities in structures of religious experience and in the profound moral values found in all religions are to be constantly probed and appropriated for the development of a deeper spiritual and human solidarity and fellowship, transcending the cultural and other barriers. At the same time, the distinctive theological and core-symbol elements and central rites of all religions are to be respected in dialogue and interrelations, based on correct and accurate understandings and on mutual empathy. All should work together to eliminate, in the future, horrors that have been committed in the name of God and religion. Truth values are equally important to the values of religious satisfaction.

Primary Challenges Facing Humanity at This Time

Our age has deteriorated to an age of quick fixes of meaning from sources such as science and the media; it has become an analgesic culture. Our contemporary metaphors, symbols, and signals are mixed, confused, and contradictory. Several examples can show that we live in a mosaic of fragmentation in consciousness, with nothing to hold the pieces together, nothing beneath to connect them and provide a meaningful substratum. We inhabit several historical ages simultaneously.

Social stability and participation in a common good have vastly eroded; we lack a broad consensus where an intricate web of mutual obligations and an accepted network of responsibilities uphold society. Family integrity is threatened.

Cultural and ecological balance and harmony in the universe are being depleted. Economic and technological progress has limits. It now seems unlikely that the wasteful affluence of the West can become available to all. Everyone should learn to endure more weal and woe equally, develop more patience, and pursue real quality of life on the planet, which is not found in the acquisitive amassing of material goods.

"May there be peace on earth, peace in the atmosphere and in the heavens. Peaceful be the waters, the herbs and plants. May the Divine bring us peace. May the holy prayers and invocations of peace-liturgies generate ultimate Peace and Happiness everywhere. With these meditations which resolve and dissolve harm, violence, and conflicts, we render peaceful whatever on earth is terrible, sinful, cruel, and violent. Let the earth become fully auspicious, let everything be beneficial to us."

Atharva-Veda XIX-9

"Having entered into the earth with My Life-Giving Energy, I support and uphold all the life-forms. Having become the life-giving nectar, I nourish all the herbs and plants."

Bhagavad-Gita XV-13

In the above verse, God (speaking as Krishna) indicates that the healing and nourishing functions found in the herbs and plants is divine and of divine origin. The divinity cannot be segregated from nature nor the latter exploited by human selfishness and greed.

"They call and name the One, Indra, Mitra, Varuna, Agni, and the beautiful Garutman. The Real is One, though wise sages (perceive in their minds) and name It variously."

Rig Veda I-164–46

"The wise sages shape (and symbolize) the One, with their words and expressions into many forms and manifestations."

Rig Veda X-114–5

The above and similar hymns categorically declare for the Hindu that God is One, but names and symbols are many, paths and perspectives are many, all to be respected and loved.

Wisdom (cont.)

*"All this, whatsoever moves in this moving
universe, is permeated and inhabited by
God, enveloped by God. Therefore, you
should enjoy (the world), only by first
renouncing and disowning (the things of
the world). Do not covet; whose indeed are
(these) treasures (in the universe)? . . .
In darkness are they who worship only the
world. In greater darkness are they who
worship the Infinite alone. Those who
accept both (seen in relationship) save
themselves from death by the knowledge of
the former and attain immortality by the
knowledge of the latter. . . . And one who
sees all beings in his own Self, and his own
Self in all beings, no more loathes and
hates."*

Isa Upanishad 1,6, 9–11

The above verses teach nonpossessive love
and stewardship—enjoyment of things in
the world.

*"Oh Brahman Supreme! Formless and
colorless are you. But in mystery, through
your power you transform your light and
radiance into many forms and colors in
creation. You bring forth the creation and
then withdraw them to yourself. Fill us
with the grace of your auspicious thoughts
and vision. . . . You are in the woman, in
the man. You are in the young boy, in the
youthful maiden. You are in the old man
who walks with his staff. . . . You are in the
dark butterfly, in the green parrot with red
eyes. . . . You are without beginning,
infinite, beyond time and space. All the
worlds had their origins in you."*

Svetasvatara Upanishad IV: 1–4

God reveals in silence through women,
men, all life-forms. The above verses validate all the four stages of life and also tilt
toward those usually neglected and
abused—children, women, and the elderly—
by specific scriptural mention. God is
equally present in men and women.

Uncontrolled population growth has become another global war,
a war which must be won. Religious, cultural, and ethnic hatreds are
on the increase; horrors of unprecedented scale, violence, and cruelty are being unleashed in different parts of the world. Group identities and ideologies are being sanctified and absolutized.

Holistic human development and the complete fulfillment of all
needs—material, moral, and spiritual—have been lost from view;
physical and mental health and the quality of our lifestyles have
deteriorated.

Depersonalization caused by mega-cities and technology continues to cheapen the richness and meaning of human joys and life.
Computer simulations usurp relationships and are on the verge of
providing the most intimate pleasures, online, providing virtual sex.

How Do Members of the Hindu Community Respond to These Issues?

The responses of both the Hindu community and contemporary
Hinduism are briefly summarized. Some of these responses are still
modest.

There is a renewed and vigorous interest in restoring the rich,
polyvalent Hindu myths and their moral, philosophical, and spiritual impact through new art forms, media ventures, etc. Of all the
peoples, Hindus never abandoned their myths through excessive
demythologization and heavy rationalization, as happened in the
West. If the body needs a house and nourishing food, provided by
latest technologies, the soul equally needs an abode in which to
grow. In Hinduism, the religious myths built that house and provided a unified and integrated vision of life. One cannot live with
values that are only contingent and ephemeral. Hindu art and
myths save one from the one-sided, reductionistic understanding of
reality. It should be carefully noted that myths are different from
verbal dogma and ideology. They also help to raise the human consciousness to the highest levels and heal fragmentations.

The "fourfold goals" scheme and the "four stages in life" paradigm, found in the Hindu *Dharma*, are both needed for holistic
human development. These are now being carefully restudied in
their contemporary contexts with help and insight derived from
the social sciences. Further relevant interpolations and applications are being generated, with universal implications. Too much
emphasis on individual rights has somewhat torn the intricate and
delicate network of obligations and duties that are necessary to sustain and uphold family integrity, restore a sense of community, and
foster world responsibilities. This shredded fabric has thwarted the

creation of abilities and energies needed to create new forms of consensus on the common good.

One of the central definitions of God (*Brahman*) found in the *Vedas* is *Rta*, which is manifested in the universe and also on planet Earth. *Rta* also has mystery and transcendental dimensions, with many meanings, including Order, Balance, Harmony, Law, Unified Life-Energy, and the principle of Intelligence. The divine *Rta* is the foundational and fundamental norm of existence, the ground of cosmic and human morality and intelligence. To be fully and really rational is also to be fully moral. *Satya* (Truth) and *Rta* are two sides to the same Divine. Divinity should not be segregated from creation and the all-embracing presence should be constantly felt. This truth, a vital part of the Hindu tradition, is being researched and re-probed to formulate sound environmental and ecological policies and programs at the highest levels. The aim is to seek to restore cultural and ecological balance and harmony, including new population-management and family planning programs with a Hindu ethos, combined with the latest scientific help.

Preventive medicine as seen and practiced in the ancient Hindu medicine texts and life sciences, such as *Ayurveda* and *yoga* manuals, along with the already established and well-documented mind-body connections found in those ancient texts, have spurred vast new research and applications worldwide, with future relevance for all. Renewed interest in and use of ancient meditation systems and techniques is supported by pioneering brain studies, consciousness research, and new mind-body behavior modification techniques; together these are pointing toward renewed physical, mental, and spiritual health in humanity.

Conclusion

The respect within Hinduism for other religions has been discussed in detail. Beyond that, Hindus everywhere are actively promoting and aggressively participating in interfaith dialogues and other interreligious projects. The constant message is, One should not delimit or circumscribe God by one's own concepts or by one's own religion or worldviews.

"Everything here is verily Brahman (the supreme Sacred Divinity). Atman, the (higher) Self, is Brahman. The Self has four grades (four states of consciousness). The first condition of the Self (state) is the waking life of outward cognition and consciousness (of subject-object, dualistic perception).... The second state is the inward dream state cognizing internal objects. The third condition is the deep sleep state, where there are no desires for objects nor any dream objects, only silent consciousness full of peace and bliss. The fourth (highest) grade of state of consciousness is the (complete) Self (God) in Its own pure state, the fully awakened (and integrated) life of supreme Consciousness. This (fourth) highest ineffable state of the Self is Peace, Love, and Bliss, in which the fragmented world perception disappears, which is the end of evolution, which is the One without a second and non-dual, which should be known, realized, and experienced (in Life). In the oneness experience with Him (the Self) lies the ultimate proof of His reality. This Atman (Self) is (indicated, symbolized by) the eternal Word OM."

Mandukya Upanishad (most of the verses)

"In whatever way and path, humans worship Me, in that same path do I (meet) and fulfill their aspirations and grace them. It is always My Path that humans follow in all their different paths and journeys, on all sides."

Bhagavad-Gita IV:11

God's Way is the Way behind all paths and religions.

*"Lead us from the unreal to the Real, from darkness to Light,
and from death to Immortality.
Om! Peace, Peace, Peace."*

—from the *Upanishads*

Wisdom (cont.)

"O Mother! Let all my speech be your prayer; let all my crafts and technology be your worship and be the mystic gestures of my hands, adoring you.

May all my movements become your devotional circumambulations.

May everything I eat or drink be oblations to you.

Let my lying down in rest and sleep be prostrations to you. Mother!

Whatever I do, may all that become a sacramental service and worship for you."

ADI SANKARA,
Hymn to the Divine Mother

Adi Sankara of the 8th century C.E. here worships God as the Divine Mother, exemplifying the experience of Hindus who relate to God, the supreme Person, equally in male and female orientations, both as Father and as Mother. This has profound implications for the vision of equality towards and between the sexes.

"May there be welfare to all beings; may there be fullness and wholeness to all people; may there be constant good and auspicious life to everyone; may there be peace everywhere...

"May all be full of happiness and abundance; may everyone in the world enjoy complete health, free from diseases; may all see and experience good things in their lives, may not even a single person experience sorrow and misery. Om!

"Peace! Peace! Peace!"

Daily prayers of Hindus

Prayers like the ones above and below have been offered and recited daily since ancient times. It is to be noted that the word *sarve* (all, everyone) is constantly repeated. The prayers are universal, offered for all and in the name of all, not for one group, religion, nation, or collectivity; they show the interdependence of the welfare of one with the welfare of all, treating the whole world as a single family.

On Yoga

Compiled by T. K. Venkateswaran

"Not even by deep learning and knowledge (alone) can the Self (*Atman*) be reached and realized, unless the evil ways are abandoned and there is discipline and rest in the senses and concentration and meditation practiced in one's mind."

Katha Upanishad, Ch. II

"Yoga is the control and cessation of the constant fluctuations and modifications of the mind. Then, when the *citta* (mind-stuff) is ripple-less, the Subject (*Purusha*, Seer) is established in Its own real form (the original Self). By constant practice and detachment are these activities of the mind-stuff to be brought to stillness—or through deep meditation on the Supreme Spirit, the ultimate Lord who is the unique special Being, not vitiated by the afflictions, (selfish) works, resulting fruits of the impressions and desires thereof."

Yoga-Sutras, I Pada

"The eight limbs (and progressions) of Yoga are self-restraint; moral rules and observances regulating one's life; postures of bodily restfulness; regulation and control of breath; inward withdrawal of the senses from the external field of objects; holding and fixing the mind on a spiritual symbol; profound continued meditation process (*dhyana*); and finally absorption and establishment of oneself in (union) and as the object of meditation."

Yoga-Sutras, II Pada

"When one does not expect any selfish fruits even in meditation, (and when one) also has perfect knowledge and discernment and differentiation (between the real and the unreal), then the absorption (*samadhi*) also called the '*dharma*-raining cloud' results (and is experienced). At that stage, all afflictions, sorrow, and selfish actions cease.... The blissful liberation of the soul (the individual self) is the Subject's (the Self's, God's) power established in Its own true innate nature."

Yoga-Sutras, IV Pada

The above are excerpts from sage Patanjali's *Yoga-Sutras*, in the form of aphorisms. The whole work deals with the theory, guidance, and procedures for the practice of Yoga (meditation) leading to physical, moral, mental, and spiritual well-being and liberation. They can be fully and properly understood and practiced, under the instructions, guidance, and counseling, of a realized and accomplished spiritual guru.

There are several significant and "clinically" oriented commentaries on the *Yoga-Sutra*, including those of Vyasa, Bhoja, and Vacas-pati. The total corpus of these writings, many still untranslated from Sanskrit, are of great value in their contributions (some already made and many yet to be researched) to contemporary interdisciplinary studies of the mind-body continuum and the total understanding, cure, and care of the physical and mental health of the human person.

Yoga in the West

Fred Stella and Joel Beversluis

Many in the West identify Yoga primarily with bodily postures and breathing exercises for physical health. This *Hatha Yoga* has been adapted to accommodate the interests of Western cultures. Some teachers have identified five approaches to Yoga:

1. *Hatha Yoga* focuses on concentration and physical well-being through attention to postures, breathing, and relaxation.

2. *Bhakti Yoga* is the way of devotion to personalized manifestations of God.

3. *Karma Yoga*, the way of selfless service, is for persons with an inclination to be active with interpersonal concerns and obligations.

4. *Jnana Yoga* names the path to God realization through knowledge; it is particularly for aspirants with a strong intellectual inclination.

5. *Raja Yoga*, the path of meditation, is for those who choose an experimental and experiential approach.

Some of the credit for the introduction of Yoga to the West is attributed to Swami Vivekananda at the 1893 World's Parliament of Religions and during his subsequent tours throughout North America and Europe. Among his books is *Raja Yoga*, in which Vivekananda describes the goal of learning about God, our souls, and eternity through direct experience:

"This is what Raja Yoga proposes to teach. The goal of all its teaching is to show how to concentrate the mind; then how to discover the innermost recesses of our own minds; then how to generalize their contents and form our own conclusions from them. It never asks what our belief is—whether we are deists, or atheists, whether Christians, Jews, or Buddhists. We are human beings, and that is sufficient. Every human being has the right and power to seek religion; every human being has the right to ask the reason why and to have his question answered by himself—if only he takes the trouble."

Vedanta, Ramakrishna, and Vivekananda

Vedanta is a philosophy taught by the *Vedas*, the most ancient scriptures of India. Its basic teaching is that our real nature is divine. God, the underlying reality, exists in every being. Religion is therefore a search for self-knowledge, a search for God within ourselves.

"Find God. That is the only purpose in life."

RAMAKRISHNA

According to the words of a Sanskrit hymn, there are different approaches to God:

"As the different streams having their sources in different places all mingle their waters in the sea, so, O Lord, the different paths which men take through various tendencies, various though they appear, crooked or straight, all lead to thee."

Thus, Vedanta teaches respect for all religions. Throughout the centuries, India has produced many great saints and illumined teachers. One of the greatest of these was Ramakrishna (1836–1886). His intense spirituality attracted a group of young disciples who, on his passing, formed a monastic community, later to be called the Ramakrishna Order of India.

One of the young monks, Swami Vivekananda, came to America as the representative of Hinduism at the World's Parliament of Religions held in Chicago in 1893. His success was so great that he was invited to remain. For three years he toured the United States lecturing and holding classes. With the help of some monks and nuns, Vedanta centers were started in America. Swami Vivekananda also had a profound influence throughout the world, spending time in England and Europe during his travels.

There are now 13 Vedanta societies in the United States and approximately 125 centers in the world managed by the Ramakrishna Order. Over one thousand more centers bear the names of Ramakrishna and Vivekananda.

Vivekananda Speaks, from the 1893 Parliament

Personal Spiritual Growth

"Each soul is potentially divine. The goal is to manifest this divine within, by controlling nature external and internal. Do this either by work, or worship, or psychic control or philosophy—by one or more, or all of these—and be free."

"This is the whole of religion. Doctrines or dogmas or rituals or books or temples or forms are but secondary details."

Peace and Harmony

"I would ask mankind to recognize this maxim: DO NOT DESTROY! Break not, pull not anything down, but build. Help, if you can; if you cannot, fold your hands and stand by and see things go on."

"Do not injure if you cannot render help. Say not a word against any man's convictions so far as they are sincere."

"Secondly, take man where he stands and from there give him a lift … and at the centre where all the radii meet all our differences will cease."

Social Justice

"My heart is too full to express my feeling: You know it, you can imagine it. So long as the millions live in hunger and ignorance, I hold every man a 'traitor' who, having been educated at their expense, pays not the least heed to them.

" … These men who strut about in their finery, having got all their money grinding the poor wretches, so long as they do not do anything for these millions, are no better than savages."

Faith, Strength, and Women

"Ye are the Children of God, the sharers of immortal bliss, holy and perfect beings. Ye divinities on earth—sinners? It is a sin to call a man so; it is a standing libel on human nature. Come up, O lions, and shake off the delusion that you are sheep; you are souls immortal, spirits free, blest and eternal; ye are not matter, ye are not bodies; matter is your servant, not you the servant of matter.…"

"Let positive, strong, helpful thoughts enter into their brains from very childhood. Lay yourselves open to these thoughts, and not to weakening and paralyzing ones."

"Women must be in a position to solve their own problems in their own way. No one can or ought to do this for them. And our Indian women are as capable of doing it as any in the world."

—The materials on this page were compiled by the
   Editor from materials provided by Vedanta societies.

Self-Realization Fellowship

Self-Realization Fellowship is an international religious organization founded in 1920 by Paramahansa Yogananda to disseminate his teachings worldwide. Those teachings—which provide in-depth guidance in all aspects of physical, mental, and spiritual development—center around the science of *Kriya Yoga*, an advanced system of meditation that leads to direct, personal experience of God. Yogananda's *Autobiography of a Yogi* provides a fascinating and comprehensive introduction to the science of Yoga, and has remained a classic in its field since it was first published in 1946.

In the "Aims and Ideals of Self-Realization Fellowship," Paramahansa Yogananda set forth these principles:

- To liberate man from his threefold suffering: physical disease, mental inharmonies, and spiritual ignorance....
- To demonstrate the superiority of mind over body, of soul over mind....
- To serve mankind as one's larger self.

From the late 1930s until the early '50s, Sri Yogananda established several temples in southern California, Phoenix, Arizona, and Washington, D.C. Each was christened as a "Self-Realization Fellowship Church of All Religions." The emphasis was on religious unity and dialogue with devotees of all faiths. SRF has participated in interfaith meetings and councils throughout the years, and has established several "world brotherhood colonies."

The government of India paid tribute to the founder of Self-Realization Fellowship/Yogoda Satsanga Society of India on March 7, 1977, the twenty-fifth anniversary of his passing: "The ideal of love for God and service to humanity found full expression in the life of Paramahansa Yogananda ....Though the major part of his life was spent out-side India, still [he] takes his place among our great saints. His work continues to grow and shine ever more brightly, drawing people everywhere on the path of the pilgrimage of the Spirit."

ISKCON, the International Society for Krishna Consciousness

ISKCON, also known as the Hare Krishna Movement, is a worldwide community of devotees practicing *Bhakti Yoga*, the eternal science of loving service to God, which has been practiced in India for at least the last five thousand years. Its religious belief is monotheistic. Scriptures include the *Vedas*, particularly the *Bhagavad-Gita* and the *Srimad-Bhagavatam*. The *Vedas* deal with the process of devotional service to God as well as with different arts and sciences.

Basic beliefs include these: everyone is a servant of God; belief in reincarnation (souls are reborn if necessary); a person is embodied at present, but the goal is to reconnect oneself with God; loving service is a method of reconnection; chanting of names of God (Hare Krishna) is a means of meeting God; God is one and has had many incarnations; four main laws of life include no meat, no intoxicants, no gambling, and no illicit sex.

The Hare Krishna Movement was brought to the West in 1965 by A. C. Bhaktivedanta Swami Prabhupada. A very important figure in the history of the movement is the great saint Sri Caitanya Mahaprabhu, who lived in the 16th century. The Hare Krishna Movement follows the disciplic succession named *the Gaudia Vaishnava* and is thus sees itself as an authorized spiritual movement representing the ancient Vedic ideas.

—compiled by the Editor from information provided by ISKCON Centre, Toronto

Chapter Eight
HUMANISM

NOTE: One might not immediately classify Humanism among religions and spiritual traditions since it finds no evidence for—and therefore denies—claims of supernatural or transcendent realities. Humanist publications, furthermore, provide an ongoing and sometimes appropriate critique of abuses by religions. On the other hand, there are those among humanists who label themselves religious humanists, and many others join societies and churches for fellowship and to affirm meaning and ethical commitments. The *Manifesto* itself describes humanism as "a living and growing faith." However one labels it—philosophical movement or worldview—humanism clearly reflects significant inclinations found in many modern and postmodern societies.

The document reprinted below is the second *Humanist Manifesto*, published in 1973. *Humanist Manifesto I*, published in 1933, was described by Raymond Bragg as

> designed to represent a developing point of view, not a new creed....The importance of the document is that more than thirty men have come to general agreement on matters of final concern and that these men are undoubtedly representative of a large number who are forging a new philosophy out of the materials of the modern world.

That declaration is now superseded by *Humanist Manifesto II* which, like the first, represents a consensus statement on philosophy, ethics, and social values.

Humanist Manifesto II

Introduction

The next century can be and should be the humanistic century. Dramatic scientific, technological, and ever-accelerating social and political changes crowd our awareness. We have virtually conquered the planet, explored the moon, overcome the natural limits of travel and communication; we stand at the dawn of a new age, ready to move farther into space and perhaps inhabit other planets. Using technology wisely, we can control our environment, conquer poverty, markedly reduce disease, extend our life span, significantly modify our behavior, alter the course of human evolution and cultural development, unlock vast new powers, and provide humankind with unparalleled opportunity for achieving an abundant and meaningful life.

The future is, however, filled with dangers. In learning to apply the scientific method to nature and human life, we have opened the door to ecological damage, overpopulation, dehumanizing institutions, totalitarian repression, and nuclear and biochemical disaster. Faced with apocalyptic prophesies and doomsday scenarios, many flee in despair from reason and embrace irrational cults and theologies of withdrawal and retreat.

Traditional moral codes and newer irrational cults both fail to meet the pressing needs of today and tomorrow. False "theologies of hope" and messianic ideologies, substituting new dogmas for old, cannot cope with existing world realities. They separate rather than unite peoples.

Humanity, to survive, requires bold and daring measures. We need to extend the uses of scientific method, not renounce them, to fuse reason with compassion in order to build constructive social and moral values. Confronted by many possible futures, we must decide which to pursue. The ultimate goal should be the fulfillment of the potential for growth in each human personality—not for the favored few, but for all of humankind. Only a shared world and global measures will suffice.

A humanist outlook will tap the creativity of each human being and provide the vision and courage for us to work together. This outlook emphasizes the role human beings can play in their own spheres of action. The decades ahead call for dedicated, clear-minded men and women able to marshal the will, intelligence, and cooperative skills for shaping a desirable future. Humanism can provide the purpose and inspiration that so many seek; it can give personal meaning and significance to human life.

Many kinds of humanism exist in the contemporary world. The varieties and emphases of naturalistic humanism include "scientific," "ethical," "democratic," "religious," and "Marxist" humanism. Free thought, atheism, agnosticism, skepticism, deism, rationalism, ethical culture, and liberal religion all claim to be heir to the humanist tradition. Humanism traces its roots from ancient China, classical Greece and Rome, through the Renaissance and the Enlightenment, to the scientific revolution of the modern world. But views that merely reject theism are not equivalent to humanism. They lack commitment to the positive belief in the possibilities of human progress and to the values central to it. Many within religious groups, believing in the future of humanism, now claim humanist credentials. Humanism is an ethical process through which we all can move, above and beyond the divisive particulars, heroic personalities, dogmatic creeds, and ritual customs of past religions or their mere negation.

We affirm a set of common principles that can serve as a basis for united action—positive principles relevant to the present human condition. They are a design for a secular society on a planetary scale.

For these reasons, we submit this new *Humanist Manifesto* for the future of humankind; for us, it is a vision of hope, a direction for satisfying survival.

Religion

First: In the best sense, religion may inspire dedication to the highest ethical ideals. The cultivation of moral devotion and creative imagination is an expression of genuine "spiritual" experience and aspiration.

We believe, however, that traditional dogmatic or authoritarian religions that place revelation, God, ritual, or creed above human needs and experience do a disservice to the human species. Any account of nature should pass the tests of scientific evidence; in our judgment, the dogmas and myths of traditional religions do not do so. Even at this late date in

human history, certain elementary facts based upon the critical use of scientific reason have to be restated. We find insufficient evidence for belief in the existence of a supernatural; it is either meaningless or irrelevant to the question of the survival and fulfillment of the human race. As non-theists, we begin with humans not God, nature not deity. Nature may indeed be broader and deeper than we now know; any new discoveries, however, will but enlarge our knowledge of the natural.

Some humanists believe we should reinterpret traditional religions and reinvest them with meanings appropriate to the current situation. Such redefinitions, however, often perpetuate old dependencies and escapisms; they easily become obscurantist, impeding the free use of the intellect. We need, instead, radically new human purposes and goals.

We appreciate the need to preserve the best ethical teachings in the religious traditions of humankind, many of which we share in common. But we reject those features of traditional religious morality that deny humans a full appreciation of their own potentialities and responsibilities. Traditional religions often offer solace to humans, but, as often, they inhibit humans from helping themselves or experiencing their full potentialities. Such institutions, creeds, and rituals often impede the will to serve others. Too often traditional faiths encourage dependence rather than independence, obedience rather than affirmation, fear rather than courage. More recently they have generated concerned social action, with many signs of relevance appearing in the wake of the "God Is Dead" theologies. But we can discover no divine purpose or providence for the human species. While there is much that we do not know, humans are responsible for what we are or will become. No deity will save us; we must save ourselves.

Second: Promises of immortal salvation or fear of eternal damnation are both illusory and harmful. They distract humans from present concerns, from self-actualization, and from rectifying social injustices. Modern science discredits such historic concepts as the "ghost in the machine" and the "separable soul." Rather, science affirms that the human species is an emergence from natural evolutionary forces. As far as we know, the total personality is a function of the biological organism transacting in a social and cultural context. There is no credible evidence that life survives the death of the body. We continue to exist in our progeny and in the way that our lives have influenced others in our culture.

Traditional religions are surely not the only obstacles to human progress. Other ideologies also impede human advance. Some forms of political doctrine, for instance, function religiously, reflecting the worst features of orthodoxy and authoritarianism, especially when they sacrifice individuals on the altar of Utopian promises. Purely economic and political viewpoints, whether capitalist or communist, often function as religious and ideological dogma. Although humans undoubtedly need economic and political goals, they also need creative values by which to live.

Ethics

Third: We affirm that moral values derive their source from human experience. Ethics is *autonomous and situational,* needing no theological or ideological sanction. Ethics stems from human need and interest. To deny this distorts the whole basis of life. Human life has meaning because we create and develop our futures. Happiness and the creative realization of human needs and desires, individually and in shared enjoyment, are continuous themes of humanism. We strive for the good life, here and now. The goal is to pursue life's enrichment despite debasing forces of vulgarization, commercialization, bureaucratization, and dehumanization.

Fourth: *Reason and intelligence* are the most effective instruments that humankind possesses. There is no substitute: neither faith nor passion suffices in itself. The controlled use of scientific methods, which have transformed the natural and social sciences since the Renaissance, must be extended further in the solution of human problems. But reason must be tempered by humility, since no group has a

monopoly of wisdom or virtue. Nor is there any guarantee that all problems can be solved or all questions answered. Yet critical intelligence, infused by a sense of human caring, is the best method that humanity has for resolving problems. Reason should be balanced with compassion and empathy and the whole person fulfilled. Thus, we are not advocating the use of scientific intelligence independent of or in opposition to emotion, for we believe in the cultivation of feeling and love. As science pushes back the boundary of the known, man's sense of wonder is continually renewed, and art, poetry, and music find their places, along with religion and ethics.

The Individual

Fifth: *The preciousness and dignity of the individual person* is a central humanist value. Individuals should be encouraged to realize their own creative talents and desires. We reject all religious, ideological, or moral codes that denigrate the individual, suppress freedom, dull intellect, dehumanize personality. We believe in maximum individual autonomy consonant with social responsibility. Although science can account for the causes of behavior, the possibilities of individual freedom of choice exist in human life and should be increased.

Sixth: *In the area of sexuality,* we believe that intolerant attitudes, often cultivated by orthodox religions and puritanical cultures, unduly repress sexual conduct. The right to birth control, abortion, and divorce should be recognized. While we do not approve of exploitive, denigrating forms of sexual expression, neither do we wish to prohibit, by law or social sanction, sexual behavior between consenting adults. The many varieties of sexual exploration should not in themselves be considered "evil." Without countenancing mindless permissiveness or unbridled promiscuity, a civilized society should be a tolerant one. Short of harming others or compelling them to do likewise, individuals should be permitted to express their sexual proclivities and pursue their lifestyles as they desire. We wish to cultivate the development of a responsible attitude toward sexuality, in which humans are not exploited as sexual objects, and in which intimacy, sensitivity, respect, and honesty in interpersonal relations are encouraged. Moral education for children and adults is an important way of developing awareness and sexual maturity.

Democratic Society

Seventh: To enhance freedom and dignity, the individual must experience a full range of *civil liberties* in all societies. This includes freedom of speech and the press, political democracy, the legal right of opposition to governmental policies, fair judicial process, religious liberty, freedom of association, and artistic, scientific, and cultural freedom. It also includes recognition of an individual's right to die with dignity, euthanasia, and the right to suicide. We oppose the increasing invasion of privacy, by whatever means, in both totalitarian and democratic societies. We would safeguard, extend, and implement the principles of human freedom evolved from the *Magna Carta* to the *Bill of Rights*, the *Rights of Man*, and the *Universal Declaration of Human Rights*.

Eighth: We are committed to *an open and democratic society*. We must extend participatory democracy in its true sense to the economy, the school, the family, the workplace, and voluntary associations. Decision making must be decentralized to include widespread involvement of people at all levels—social, political, and economic. All persons should have a voice in developing the values and goals that determine their lives. Institutions should be responsive to expressed desires and needs. The conditions of work, education, devotion, and play should be humanized. Alienating forces should be modified or eradicated and bureaucratic structures should be held to a minimum. People are more important than decalogues, rules, proscriptions, or regulations.

Ninth: The separation of church and state and the separation of ideology and state are imperatives. The state should encourage maximum freedom for different moral, political, religious, and social values in society. It should not favor any particular religious bodies through the use of public monies, nor espouse a single ideology and function thereby as an instrument of propaganda or oppression, particularly against dissenters.

Tenth: Humane societies should evaluate economic systems not by rhetoric or ideology, but by whether or not they *increase economic well-being* for all individuals and groups, minimize poverty and hardship, increase the sum of human satisfaction, and enhance the quality of life. Hence the door is open to alternative economic systems. We need to democratize the economy and judge it by its responsiveness to human needs, testing results in terms of the common good.

Eleventh: The principle of *moral equality* must be furthered through elimination of all discrimination based upon race, religion, sex, age, or national origin. This means equality of opportunity and recognition of talent and merit. Individuals should be encouraged to contribute to their own betterment. If unable, then society should provide means to satisfy their basic economic, health, and cultural needs, including, wherever resources make possible, a minimum guaranteed annual income. We are concerned for the welfare of the aged, the infirm, the disadvantaged, and also for the outcasts—the mentally retarded, abandoned, or abused children, the handicapped, prisoners, and addicts—for all who are neglected or ignored by society. Practicing humanists should make it their vocation to humanize personal relations.

We believe in the *right to universal education*. Everyone has a right to the cultural opportunity to fulfill his or her unique capacities and talents. The schools should foster satisfying and productive living. They should be open at all levels to any and all; the achievement of excellence should be encouraged. Innovative and experimental forms of education are to be welcomed. The energy and idealism of the young deserve to be appreciated and channeled to constructive purposes.

We deplore racial, religious, ethnic, or class antagonisms. Although we believe in cultural diversity and encourage racial and ethnic pride, we reject separations which promote alienation and set people and groups against each other; we envision an integrated community where people have a maximum opportunity for free and voluntary association.

We are *critical of sexism or sexual chauvinism*—male or female. We believe in equal rights for both women and men to fulfill their unique careers and potentialities as they see fit, free of invidious discrimination.

World Community

Twelfth: We deplore the division of humankind on nationalistic grounds. We have reached a turning point in human history where the best option is to *transcend the limits of national sovereignty* and to move toward the building of a world community in which all sectors of the human family can participate. Thus we look to the development of a system of world law and a world order based upon transnational federal government. This would appreciate cultural pluralism and diversity. It would not exclude pride in national origins and accomplishments nor the handling of regional problems on a regional basis. Human progress, however, can no longer be achieved by focusing on one section of the world, Western or Eastern, developed or underdeveloped. For the first time in human history, no part of humankind can be isolated from any other. Each person's future is in some way linked to all. We thus reaffirm a commitment to the building of world community, at the same time recognizing that this commits us to some hard choices.

Thirteenth: This world community must *renounce the resort to violence and force* as a method of solving international disputes. We believe in the peaceful adjudication of differences by international courts and by the development of the arts of negotiation and compromise. War is obsolete. So is the use of nuclear, biological, and chemical weapons. It is a planetary imperative to reduce the level of military expenditures and turn these savings to peaceful and people-oriented uses.

Fourteenth: The world community must *engage in cooperative planning* concerning the use of rapidly depleting resources. The planet earth must be considered a single *ecosystem*. Ecological damage, resource depletion, and excessive population growth

must be checked by international concord. The cultivation and conservation of nature is a moral value; we should perceive ourselves as integral to the sources of our being in nature. We must free our world from needless pollution and waste, responsibly guarding and creating wealth, both natural and human. Exploitation of natural resources, uncurbed by social conscience, must end.

Fifteenth: The problems of *economic growth and development* can no longer be resolved by one nation alone; they are worldwide in scope. It is the moral obligation of the developed nations to provide—through an international authority that safeguards human rights—massive technical, agricultural, medical, and economic assistance, including birth control techniques, to the developing portions of the globe. World poverty must cease. Hence extreme disproportions in wealth, income, and economic growth should be reduced on a worldwide basis.

Sixteenth: *Technology is a vital key* to human progress and development. We deplore any neoromantic efforts to condemn indiscriminately all technology and science or to counsel retreat from its further extension and use for the good of humankind. We would resist any moves to censor basic scientific research on moral, political, or social grounds. Technology must, however, be carefully judged by the consequences of its use; harmful and destructive changes should be avoided. We are particularly disturbed when technology and bureaucracy control, manipulate, or modify human beings without their consent. Technological feasibility does not imply social or cultural desirability.

Seventeenth: We must *expand communication and transportation* across frontiers. Travel restrictions must cease. The world must be open to diverse political, ideological, and moral viewpoints and evolve a worldwide system of television and radio for information and education. We thus call for full international cooperation in culture, science, the arts, and technology *across ideological borders*. We must learn to live openly together or we shall perish together.

Humanity as a Whole

In closing: The world cannot wait for a reconciliation of competing political or economic systems to solve its problems. These are the times for men and women of goodwill to further the building of a peaceful and prosperous world. We urge that parochial loyalties and inflexible moral and religious ideologies be transcended. We urge recognition of the common humanity of all people. We further urge the use of reason and compassion to produce the kind of world we want—a world in which peace, prosperity, freedom, and happiness are widely shared. Let us not abandon that vision in despair or cowardice. We are responsible for what we are or will be. Let us work together for a humane world by means commensurate with humane ends. Destructive ideological differences among communism, capitalism, socialism, conservatism, liberalism, and radicalism should be overcome.

Let us call for an end to terror and hatred. We will survive and prosper only in a world of shared humane values. We can initiate new directions for humankind; ancient rivalries can be superseded by broad-based cooperative efforts. The commitment to tolerance, understanding, and peaceful negotiation does not necessitate acquiescence to the status quo nor the damming up of dynamic and revolutionary forces. The true revolution is occurring and can continue in countless nonviolent adjustments. But this entails the willingness to step forward onto new and expanding plateaus. At the present juncture of history, commitment to all humankind is the highest commitment of which we are capable; it transcends the narrow allegiances of church, state, party, class, or race in moving toward a wider vision of human potentiality. What more daring a goal for humankind than for each person to become, in ideal as well as practice, a citizen of a world community. It is a classical vision; we can now give it new vitality. Humanism thus interpreted is a moral force that has time on its side. We believe that humankind has the potential intelligence, goodwill, and cooperative skill to implement this commitment in the decades ahead.

We, the undersigned, while not necessarily endorsing every detail of the above, pledge our general support to *Humanist Manifesto II* for the future of humankind. These affirmations are not a final credo or dogma but an expression of a living and growing faith. We invite others in all lands to join us in further developing and working for these goals.

(Editor's Note: Thousands of names have been added to the list of signatories which followed the publication of Humanist Manifesto II *in the September/October 1973 issue of* The Humanist, *published by the American Humanist Association.)*

Chapter Nine
ISLAM

A Portrait

Dr. Ghulam Haider Aasi

Associate Professor of Islamic Studies and the History of Religions, American Islamic College, Chicago; Trustee of the Council for a Parliament of the World's Religions

Islam

Islam is the proper name of religion which Allah, the Alone God, revealed to mankind through the series of human messengers-prophets in human history and completed in His final revelation of *Al-Quran al-Karim, Kalam-Allah* (the speech of God) sent down upon the Prophet Muhammad (570–632 C.E.) *Salla-Allahu alayhi wa Sallam* ("may Allah's blessings and peace be upon him"; this blessing on the names of honored prophets is sometimes abbreviated in print to SAAWS or SA). Within history, Islam is embodied in the Qur'an and in the *Sunnah* (the sayings, actions, and approvals of the Prophet Muhammad) in its final and eternal form.

The term "Islam" derives from the root letters *s.l.m.* (Ar. *Sin, Lam, Mim*) which means "to be in peace," "to be secure," and "to be integral whole." Hence, Islam means one's conscious submission to the Will, Law, and Guidance of Allah, the Almighty Alone God, and thus to be in peace with one's own self, with all creatures, and with the Creator and Originator of all that exists. One who consciously surrenders one's whole being to God and commits oneself to pattern one's life on the divine guidance communicated and exemplified by the human messengers-prophets sent by God is called a "Muslim." The Qur'an describes Islam in two ways: 1) as the primordial or natural religion (*religio naturalis*) of the innate nature with which Allah created mankind (Q. 30:30), and 2) as the religion which was completed and consummated in the Qur'an, the final and definitive Divine Writ from Allah.

Allah, the Exalted Almighty Alone God, declares in the Qur'an that all the universe and creation surrenders to Him either willingly or unwillingly and that all must return to him (Q. 3:83). Whereas the universe surrenders to God's law by its innate nature and is endowed with order, humankind obeys the guidance of God through its divinely endowed moral choice and free will.

> Glorify the name of your Sustainer, the All-Highest, Who creates all that exists, then forms it in its best mold, determines its nature with the proper measure and guides it towards its fulfillment. (Q. 87:1–3; tr. by M. Asad)

Allah created humanity, endowed them with an innate awareness of Him, empowered them with faculties of reason and cognition, and made them to inherit the earth, testing their free choice of good and evil by their obedience to or denial of Allah's universal guidance. Qur'an unequivocally declares the unity, uniqueness, and universality of Allah, the unity and equality of all mankind, the universality of His guidance to all mankind through the human messengers-prophets, and the unity and indivisibility of the Truth. Allah created Adam, the first human being, made him and his progeny inheritors of the earth (*Khalifat-Allah fi al.Ard*), and endowed them with the requisite faculties to be His trustees on earth. His messengers-prophets, starting with Adam and culminating in the Prophet Muhammad (SAAWS), conveyed and exemplified His guidance to their communities.

Historical Establishment

Muslims believe in the historical crystalization and establishment of Islam within the religious experience of the Prophet Muhammad (SAAWS). He actualized the Will of God as embodied in the Qur'an by his beautiful model, the *Sunnah*, and raised a society of true Muslims. His Companions, rightly guided Caliphs and Imams, carried out his tradition, transmitted it to the following generations and established it in history.

The Prophet Muhammad (SAAWS) was born at Makkah (Mecca) in what is now Saudi Arabia in 570 C.E. From a very young age he came to be known as Al-Amin, the honest and trustworthy. At the age of twenty-five he married a righteous widow, Khadijah, who was fifteen years his senior. When he was in his forties, he was called upon by Allah to deliver His final guidance and message, the Qur'an, to mankind and to bring about the *Ummah Muslimah*, the community of submitters to Allah. The Prophet Muhammad received the first revelation sent down upon him through the agency of angel *Jibrail* (Gabriel) while he was meditating in the cave of Hira'. It reads in translation as follows:

> Read in the name of thy Sustainer, who has created. Created man out of a germ cell. Read, for thy Sustainer is the Most-Bountiful One. Who has taught man the use of the pen. Taught man what he did not know. Nay, verily, man becomes grossly overweening whenever he believes himself to be self-sufficient: for, behold, unto thy Sustainer all must return. (Q. 96:1–8; tr. by M. Asad)

In Makkah, the Prophet Muhammad called upon the Arab idolaters of his time to believe in One Alone God, Allah (*Tawhid*), and not to ascribe divinity to aught beside Allah. As a result of the scathing criticism of the Qur'an against idolatry and its various forms of Associationism (*shirk*) the Makkan oligarchy turned to persecuting Muhammad and his followers. It became so harsh and harrying that the Prophet was commanded to migrate along with his Makkan followers to Yathrib.

This emigration of the Prophet Muhammad and his Makkan Muslims who since then were designated *Muhajirun* (migrants in the Cause of Allah) in 622 C.E. marked a watershed point in the history of mankind. The Muslims' religious calendar, known as *Hijri*, is based on this most meaningful and significant event. The city of Yathrib since then came to be known as Madinah (abbreviated from Madinat al-Nabi, city of the Prophet) and it was here that the Prophet was able to establish *Ummah Muslimah*, the religio-moral and sociopolitical community of Muslims commonly known as the Islamic city-state of Madinah.

Within a decade this nascent and model Muslim community was successful in establishing Islam in the whole of the Arabian Peninsula; in addition, the Prophet sent missions to all the surrounding rulers and empires including both the superpowers of the time, the Persian Sasanid and the Byzantian Roman Christian empires. Just months before his death, the Prophet Muhammad addressed all mankind during his Farewell Pilgrimage to Ka'bah in Makkah and made the eternal message of Allah universally known and established. Some of the salient parts of this historic address are the following:

> O, mankind, listen to what I say: I do not know whether I will meet you ever at this place after this year. O, mankind, verily your lives, your honor, and your property are inviolable and sacred like this day and this month until you meet your Sustainer. You will definitely meet your Sustainer and He will ask you of your deeds....Whoever is entrusted with any trust, he must return the trust fully. Verily, all usury is abolished but you have your capital. Wrong not and you shall not be wronged. Allah has decreed that there is to be no usury....You have rights over your women and they have rights over you....Listen and understand, O, mankind, I am leaving with you the Divine writ, the Qur'an and the *Sunnah* of His Prophet. If you stick to it you will never go astray. This is a self-evident fact. You must know every Muslim is a brother to another Muslim. All Muslims constitute one brotherhood. One is only permitted to take from a brother what he gives willingly, so wrong not yourselves. O, Allah, be witness I have conveyed. (Ibn Hisham, *Sirat al-Rasul*)

After the death of the Prophet Muhammad in 10 H/632 C.E., the *Ummah* was first led by the four rightly guided Caliphs (10–40 H/632–661 C.E.), followed by the dynastic rulers. Both the historical spread of Islam and unprecedented expansion of Muslim rule through all the continents known at the time, within less than a century after the death of the Prophet, changed not only the map of the world but also transformed the destiny of human history and world civilization. By 711 C.E., Islam had crossed Gibraltar in the west, Caucasus in the north, and Sudan in the south, and reached India and China in the east. Muslim Caliphantes ruled most of the world, from Al-Andalus, Spain (711–1492 C.E.) to Asia and Africa, at the period when Europe and the West were still in their Dark and Middle Ages. Islam made lasting contributions to human civilization and transformed ancient regional civilizations into a world civilization. The so-called Western civilization would never have emerged had there not been the integrating Islamic civilization across the European Dark and Middle Ages and the Renaissance.

This *pax Islamica*, however, was never immune from internal disintegration or from external repulsions and reconquests. The Christian reconquest of Spain, the Inquisition, and the Crusades set a course of historical conflict between the West and the Muslim world of which European colonialism and Western neo-imperialism have been the historical corollaries. Despite all these geopolitical changes and socioeconomic conflicts, Islam continued to spread, gaining adherents in all parts of the world. Today, Muslims total over a billion and their geographical spread is throughout all the continents. The historic spread of Islam has never been due to its early conquests alone; rather, its appeals are the egalitarian bonding of all believers into universal brotherhood (*Ummah*) and providing them with the spiritual truth of God-consciousness (*Tawhid* and *Taqwa*) that transforms their lives to be meaningful and purposeful.

Main Sources

For Muslims the essential sources for all aspects of life are a) the Qur'an, b) the *Sunnah* and *Hadith*, c)

Ijma (traditional consensus of the Companions of the Prophet and teachings of the Imams for the Shi'ah), and d) *Ijtihad* (reasoning and analogical deduction based on the Qur'an and *Hadith* to derive solutions for new problems).

A. The Qur'an. Muslims believe in the Qur'an as verbatim revelation from Allah, sent down upon Muhammad through the agency of the angel Gabriel during Muhammad's prophethood, 610–632 C.E. The whole Qur'an was sent down upon the Prophet piecemeal, was memorized, written and publicly transmitted upon its revelation. Its uniqueness as an inimitable miracle and the eternally definitive words of God, its historical preservation, regular and authentic transmission, and dissemination are essential beliefs of Islam. It comprises 114 *surahs* (chapters) which are designated as Makkan or Madinan according to the place of their descent upon Muhammad.

B. *Sunnah* and *Hadith*. The second universal source of Islam is the *Sunnah* which comprises sayings, actions, and approvals of the Prophet Muhammad. Their reportage in narration is called *Hadith*. Six collections are recognized as authentic by the Sunni Muslims; the Shi'ah recognize Al-Kulini's collection, entitled "Al-Kafi," as earliest and authentic.

C. *Ijma*. Sunni Muslims believe in the consensus of the Muslim scholars and the community as the third source of Islamic law whereas the Shi'ah take the teachings and interpretations of the Imams as binding.

D. *Ijtihad*. This names the total effort of a religious scholar to discover both the intent of the Islamic law and the correct answer to a new problem in light of the first two material sources called *Nass* (divine text), through a well-defined systematic procedure of *Qiyas* (analogical deduction).

Beliefs and Observances

A. Articles of Faith (*Arkan al Iman*)

Muslims believe in six articles of faith which are derived from revealed sources, the Qur'an and the *Sunnah*. (Q. 2:285; 4:136, 150–152)

i. Belief in One Alone God, Allah. He is Unique, Infinite, Transcendent, Creator and Sustainer of all that exists. "Nothing is like unto Him" (Q. 42:11). He Alone is worthy of worship. All else is His creature and servant. He is Unique both in his essence (*Dhat*) and in His attributes (*Sifat*). "His are the beautiful names (99 beautiful names described in the Qur'an) and all that is in the heavens and the earth glorify Him. . . ." (Q. 59:24; 7:180; 17:110; 20:8)

ii. Belief in the eternal life of Hereafter (*Al-Akhirah*). Muslims believe in the end of the world, in Resurrection, in the resurrection of whole person after death (*al-Ba'th*), in the Day of Judgment (*Yawm al-Hisab*) and in eternal Hell and Paradise.

iii. Belief in angels. Muslims believe in angels as creatures of Allah, eternally busy in His service, glorification, and praise: " . . . they never disobey God what he commanded them to do and do what they are ordered." (Q. 66:6; 16:50)

iv. Belief in Revelations from God, commonly known as belief in the Books from God. Muslims believe that Allah revealed His messages and guidance to different messengers at different times and places. These include the scrolls of Abraham, the Torah to Moses, Psalms to David, *Injil* to Jesus, culminating in the Qur'an to the Prophet Muhammad.

v. Belief in human messengers—prophets of God. Muslims believe that Allah chose certain human beings as His prophets and messengers to convey His guidance and to exemplify it for their people. All peoples have a prophet from among themselves who conveyed the guidance and norms of God to them in their own language. Muslims believe that the series of prophets starts with Adam and includes Abraham, Noah, Moses, Jesus, and culminates in Muhammad, who is the Seal of the office of Prophethood. The office of Prophethood is indivisible. May God's blessing and peace be with all of them. (Q. 10:47,14:4, 16:36, 21:25, 28:59, 33:40)

vi. Belief in the Decree and Plan of God. Muslims believe that all happens, good or evil, with the decree of God and nothing can fail His Plan (*Qada wa Qadar*).

B. Pillars of Islam (*Arkan al Islam*)

i. *Shahadah*: The statement of faith. A person becomes a Muslim when out of one's own will and conviction one bears witness to the fact that there is no deity but Allah and Muhammad is His messenger (and final prophet and servant).

ii. *Salat*: Every male and female adult Muslim is obliged to offer five daily worship-prayers. (Q. 4:103, 2:177)

iii. *Sawm*: Fasting during the whole month of *Ramadan*, the ninth month of Muslims' lunar calendar and abstaining from food, drink, sex, and all sorts of idle and immoral acts from dawn to sunset. (Q. 2:183–187)

iv. *Zakat*: Sharing wealth. Every Muslim who has his savings for a year is obligated to pay a fixed portion of it to the needy, the poor, and those who are under debt. Wealth sharing purifies the giver's wealth from greed and stinginess and reconciles the hearts of the recipients. (Q. 9:60)

v. *Hajj*: Pilgrimage. All Muslims who can afford the journey to Ka'bah, in Makkah, Saudi Arabia, both physically and financially, are obliged to perform the pilgrimage once in their lifetime; it is usually made during the first ten days of the last month of the Muslim *Hijri* Calendar, *Dhu-al. Hijjah*. Pilgrimage at other times is called "*Umrah*." (Q. 2:189–179, 3:97)

Schools of Law

With the developing needs of the Muslim *Ummah*, the expansion of the Muslim empire, and changing situations, there arose a need to derive laws from the revealed sources and to develop a systematic method for doing so. Though there were many legal opinions in the beginning, by the end of third century *Hijrah*, four schools of law were recognized as orthodox among the Sunni Muslims: *Hanafi*, *Maliki*, *Shafi'i*, and *Hanbali*. Among the Shi'ah, two became prominent: *Ja'fariyah* of the Twelver Shi'ahs of Iran and *Zaydiyah* (Fivers) of Yemen.

Theological Schools

At its earliest stage Muslim theological speculation emerged in response to internal political differences.

The murder of Uthman (d. 656 C.E.), the third Caliph, and subsequent civil wars raised important issues, including: Who is a true believer? What is the nature of faith (Iman) and its relation to Islam (submission to God's law)? What qualifies a person both to be the leader and member of a truly believing Community? Variant responses to these questions split the *Ummah* first into different political views and groups, then resulted in sects:

A. *Khawarij.* The first explicit political and theological schism was of the *Khawarij* (Secessionists) who called for extreme piety and idealistic egalitarianism. They fought against all claimants of political rule. Some even rejected the need for any governing institution. Their pursuit of a pure society later led them to fanaticism and violence. Continuous rebellion against every government and ever-increasing internal dissension and disunity almost eliminated their role and existence. Those who survived took refuge in the rugged mountains of North Africa and Yemen.

B. *Shi'ah.* The second major schism represented, in its earliest phase, primarily a sociopolitical critique against the rulers; later it became a permanent sect or branch of Islam. The name "Shi'ah" was given to the partisans of 'Ali (d. 661 C.E.), the son-in-law of the Prophet, the fourth rightly guided Caliph of the Sunnis and the first Imam of the Shi'ah. They developed the doctrine of *Imamah* over and against the Sunni *Khilafah.* According to this view, the legitimate successor of the Prophet was 'Ali, their first Imam, whose succession then continued in his descendants who are thus political and religious leaders. These Imams are divinely inspired, infallible, and authoritative interpreters of the Qur'an. Later, debating the legitimacy of different Imams, Shi'ism split into numerous sects. Their main branches are

i. *Ithna 'Ash'ariyyah* (Twelvers) believe in the twelve Imams and hold that a son, Muhammad al-Muntazar, was born to the eleventh Imam, Hassan al-Askari (d. 874) but went into concealment until he will reappear at the proper time to set the whole world in order. They subscribe to the legal school

Ja'fariyyah, have been established in Iran since the *Safvid* period (1501), and are the largest branch of Shi'ah.

ii. *Zaydiyah* consider Zayd b. Ali (d. 740), the second grandson of Husayn, to be the fifth and final Imam. Zaydiyah follow the Zaydi school of Islamic law and are closer to Sunnis. They established themselves in Yemen.

iii. *Isma'iliyah* take Ismail's (d. 760) son Muhammad as the impending Mahdi. They split into many offshoots such as Fatimids, Qaramitah, Druz, Nizaris, and Agha Khanis, continuing to present times.

C. *Sunnis.* The majority of Muslims—more than 90 percent of all Muslims in the world—identify themselves with the term *Ahl-al-Sunnah wa al-Jama'ah*, or People of the Tradition and the Community, commonly known as Sunni in distinction to nonorthodox sects and groups. Among them, two main theological schools and dispositions became permanent. In their classical terms, these are known as *Mu'tazilah* and *Ash'ariyah*. The first tendency represents rationalist philosophical theology while the second emphasizes the absolute primacy and total sufficiency of the revealed texts, the Qur'an and the *Sunnah.*

Contemporary Movements

Most of the revivalist or reform movements—pejoratively called fundamentalist or neo-fundamentalist groups in the West—derive their thought and arguments from *Ash'ariyah* and its sister traditional theologies.

Feasts and Festivals

Muslims observe a lunar calendar of 354 days. The two most important religious feasts celebrated by all, everywhere, are the two *Ids*:

A. *Id al-Adha*, the feast of Sacrifice and *Hajj*, is celebrated on the tenth of *Dhu al-Hijjah*, the twelfth month. Congregational worship prayer is offered in the open or in big mosques. Every household slaughters an animal, and meat of sacrifices is shared and distributed.

B. *Id al-Fitr* is celebrated on the first day of

Shawwal, the tenth month, to give thanks for completion of the fasting of Ramadan and asking God's forgiveness. *Id-Salat* is offered in congregation in the open or in big mosques. On both *Ids*, charity is given, gifts are exchanged, open houses are maintained, visits are made to friends, neighbors, relatives, and even to graveyards. Generosity, hospitality, and caring are hallmarks of these feasts.

C. In addition to the two *Ids* there are other optional small holidays or historical celebrations such as fasting on the tenth of the first month, vigil on *Laylat al-Qadr*, popularly on the twenty-seventh night of the fasting month of Ramadan, celebrating the birthday of the Prophet (*Mawlid al-Nabi*) on twelfth of the third month and on first Muharram, as the Hijri new year day, etc. Shi'ah particularly commemorate the martyrdom of Husain (d. 680), the grandson of the Prophet, during the first ten days of Muharram.

Sufism

One of the most enduring contributions of Islam to human spirituality is its mystical tradition and dimension generally known as Sufism, more correctly called *Tasawwuf*. It is unfortunate that, more often than not, Islam has been perceived as a political, legalistic, orthopraxic, and this-worldly religion due to its distinctive emphasis on the Transcendence and complete otherness of Unique and Alone God. The historical fact, however, is that it is the Islamic spiritual reality rather than Muslim *imperium* or an Islamic state which made Islam a universal religion. This stream of spiritual experience has been carried on by Sufis who have been the mystics and scholars of traditional Islam up to the present. Sufism sees the essence of the human in his being "of God, in the world" rather than "of the world, for God." It sees humans innately bound with God due to the primordial covenant of their souls witnessing to the fact of God's lordship. (Q. 7:172)

It is human forgetfulness of God and absorption in the material world that makes them alienated from their essence (Q. 59:18–19). Hence, to gain one's real self is to be in constant remembrance of God (*Dhikr*; Q. 13:28) and to detach oneself from the transitory material world. True submission (Islam) is to make one's heart, not just head, the real throne of God where God manifests Himself both as Transcendent and Immanent. Realizing such presence of God requires one to experience the absolute love of God, by dying in Him and living in Him. Out of their religious experiences, Sufis derived the doctrines of *Fana* (dying in God or annihilation of the human self and attributes in God) and *Baqa* (living with God and acquiring divine attributes). They systematically developed and explained the different stations and states through which every genuine mystic has to tread on the path of spiritual experience of reality. While the primary requirement for a Muslim is to abide by the rules and regulation of the Islamic law and rituals (*Shari'ah*), that observance does not guarantee the spiritual experience of God and His vision.

By devoting and pledging oneself to God through the experienced guide, one can tread the path of spiritual reality (*Tariqah*). Within the variety of these religious-spiritual experiences, the mystics of Islam introduced their orders and provided institutions where adepts lead initiates to the experience of spiritual reality.

Islam and Other Religious Traditions

No other religious scripture addresses the issue of the religious diversity of mankind as directly as the Qur'an. It emphasizes the unity and universality of One Alone God, unity and equality of mankind, unity of the Truth and universality of God's guidance to all mankind through human messengers-prophets, starting from Adam and culminating in the Prophet Muhammad, who is the final messenger and the mercy to all the worlds (*Rahmatan lil'alamin*, Q. 21:107; 7:158; 34:28; 33:40). The Qur'an declares that God created all mankind as one religio-moral community (*Ummah wahidah*). It was humanity's exercise of freedom of will and claim of self-sufficiency (Q. 96:6–7) that led to differentiation and to deviation from the innate nature. Then God, out of His universal grace, raised among them messengers who conveyed God's guidance to them in their own languages (Q. 16:36; cf: 35:23–25; 23:44; 10:47; 14:4 and more).

Whereas each community ought to have accepted the universality of God's messages and believed in His messengers-prophets, their mutual jealousy and attempts to appropriate God's favor turned them instead to splitting the one and true religion of God and dividing into sects and mutually exclusive communities (Q. 23:51–53; 21:92–94; 30:30–32). Yet even this religious diversity with different symbols and rituals is categorized by the Qur'an as God-willed reality so long as it does not fall into the worship of false deities (idolatry) and does not deny universal fundamental principles of truth and morality. (Q. 10:19; 11:117–119; 16:93; 42:8)

All mankind were once one single community; (then they began to differ) whereupon God raised up the prophets as heralds of glad tidings and as warners, and through them bestowed revelation from on high, setting forth the truth, so that it might decide between people with regard to all on which they had come to hold divergent views. Yet none other than the selfsame people who had been granted this (revelation) began, out of mutual jealousy, to disagree about its meaning after all evidence of the truth had come unto them. But God guided the believers unto the truth about which, by His leave, they had disagreed: for God guides onto a straight way him that wills (to be guided). (Q. 2:213; tr. by M. Asad)

And unto thee (O Prophet) have We vouchsafed this divine writ, setting forth the truth, confirming the truth of whatever there still remains of earlier revelations and determining what is true therein. Judge, then, between the followers of earlier revelation in accordance with what God has bestowed from on high, and do not follow their errant views, forsaking the truth that has come unto thee. Unto every one of you have We appointed a (different) law and way of life. And if God had so willed, He could surely have made

you all one single community: but (He willed it otherwise) in order to test you by means of what He has vouchsafed unto you. Vie then with one another in doing good works! Unto God you all must return; and then He will make you truly understand all that on which you were wont to differ. (Q. 5:48; tr. by M. Asad)

Qur'an rejects any claim of appropriating God's truth or favor. No person, race, or nation is chosen of God. Any claim on God's unilateral covenant or saving grace by any atonement is vehemently rejected by the Qur'an. For God all humans are equal. What characterizes one as noble is one's God-consciousness (*Taqwa*) and carrying out His norms of universal ethics.

O' mankind, Behold, We have created you all from a male and a female and have made you into tribes and nations so that you might come to recognize one another as (interdependent and equal), verily noblest of you before God is one who is most conscious of Him, verily, God is all knowing, all aware. (Q. 49:13; tr. by M. Asad)

Islam abolished and condemns all forms of racial, tribal, or national prejudices that cause one to stand by one's own people in an unjust cause over and against truth and justice. (Q. 5:2, 8)

The Qur'an reconfirms the fact of earlier revelations from God and hence it gives to the adherents of *Torah* and *Injil*, Jews and Christians, the appellation of "Ahl-al-Kitab," the people of the revealed scriptures. Though the Qur'an explicitly identifies the Jews and Christians as *Ahl-al-Kitab*, the term in its general import and implicit Qur'anic allusions extends to all religious traditions which might concur with identifying their religious sources as derived from one and the same Divine source. Thus the Prophet also included Zoroastrians in this category. With the spread of Muslim rule over Asia, India, and Africa, some Muslim jurists later included both Hindus and Buddhists in the category of *Ahl-al-Dhimma* which, by extension, absorbed all non-Muslims who chose to be the subjects of the Muslim rule.

Islam does not identify people in terms of political, geographical, ethnic, racial, or national entities; rather, it categorizes them in terms of their religio-moral commitments and religious traditions. As Professor Dr. Syed Muhammad Naquib al-Attas, the Founder-Director of International Institute of Islamic Thought and Civilization, Kuala Lumpur, maintains:

> We Muslims not only tolerated non-Muslims but also opened our doors of lands and houses even, our hearts and minds to make them feel at home amongst us.

But what made Muslims the pioneers of religious coexistence was their recognition of non-Muslims as legal citizens based on rules derived from the teachings of the Qur'an and the *Sunnah*. And it was on these grounds that Muslims worked out the detailed legal rights and duties of non-Muslims vis-à-vis the Muslims as a part of Islamic law. Muslims were the first to recognize non-Muslims as *religio licita*, providing them legal religio-cultural autonomy. Every Muslim government or leader is obliged by the Prophetic command to safeguard the rights of non-Muslims with special care (*Dhimmat-Allah wa Rasulihi*).

The Qur'an categorically prohibits coercion in matters of religion, be it by sheer force or implicit deceptive ways. Muslims are obliged to call mankind toward submission to God by wisdom, good example, and sincere exhortation, not in argument, but with kind manner (Q. 2:257; 16:125). Such imperatives of the Qur'an provide Muslims with a clear call to humanity; Muslims repeat and try to live by the following guidelines in their interreligious dialogues and cooperations:

> Say, O followers of earlier revelation, come unto that tenet which we and you hold in common—that we shall not ascribe divinity to aught beside Him, and that we shall not take human beings for our lords beside God. (Q. 3:64; tr. by M. Asad)

Cooperation, Peace, Justice, and Virtue

The main objective of every venture of interreligious dialogue and cooperation is to bring about justice, order, and peace in the world. Cooperation in furthering virtue and justice and in ending evil and aggression is among the most distinctive imperatives of the Qur'an. (Q. 5:2 & 8)

ACKNOWLEDGMENTS

First, all praise and thanks are due to Allah. I am also grateful to American Islamic College, both to its administration and community, for providing me with the time and facilities to work for the Parliament. For the preparation of this article, I am extremely thankful to International Institute of Islamic Thought and Civilization, Kuala Lumpur; to its Founder-Director, Dr. Prof. Syed Muhammad Naquib al-Attas; and to all its members for providing me with time and facilities. Special thanks are due to Ms. Nor Azimah for her typing.

Most of all, my heartfelt gratitude is due to my wife, Zubaida and to my children: Humaira, Sumaira, Irfan, Rummanah, and Salman. Without their continuous support and unceasing sacrifices I would have never been able to make contributions to these good causes.

Finally, I acknowledge Joel Beversluis, the Editor of this *Sourcebook*, whose constant encouragement and unceasing forbearance brought this to publication.

May God Almighty bless all!

Islam in North America

Dr. Aminah B. McCloud

Professor of Islamic Studies in the Department of Religious Studies at DePaul University, Chicago

Islam first came to North America on the souls and tongues of African traders, and then in the hearts of many African slaves. Islam comes in a more noticeable garb with immigrants in the late 19th century and with a string of influence beginning with the 20th century. There is no monolithic Islamic expression among Muslims in America since it has all the diversity of the Muslim world. By 1960 Islam was definitely an American religion with its own institutions and several generations of indigenous Muslims.

Muslim children could attend Muslim schools through the high school level in almost every major city in America by 1960. Since the 1960s the Muslim presence in the public space is also evident in the spread of the domed masajid and Arabic calligraphy signs.

The study of Islam in America is important for a variety of reasons. It is the fastest growing religion in America. Its basic practices and beliefs are obviously different from American Protestant Christianity. Since Muslims act in concert with other Americans in a wide assortment of tasks such as the practice of medicine, industry, education, and even celebrations, some knowledge of those differences is crucial. To handle the needs of their community and to promote an understanding of Islam, Muslims have formed dozens of organizations—professional, social, and educational. In spite of these efforts, dialogue between Muslims and other religious communities has been sparse. While there are numerous texts on Muslim-Christian relations, there are almost no texts on encounters within the American context. It is only recently that Islam has come to be seen as a legitimate part of the American religious landscape by scholars, and most of this has come through a media focus.

In America, Muslims struggle to enact the obligations of their faith. The obligation to pray five times daily (*salat*) at certain times can be problematic in the American workplace or school. Often Muslims encounter the American resistance to the notion of prayer as an intimate part of one's self-understanding. In the workplace, Muslims often trade breaks and/or lunchtimes to meet the obligations of daily prayer and the congregational prayer on Fridays (*Jum'ah*).

The workplace can also provide challenging social encounters with regard to dress, lifestyles, holidays, and professionalism. Most Muslim women have met numerous obstacles with reference to dress and their head scarves, while some Muslim men have the same problems with the length or presence of their beards. Muslim reluctance to participate in social gatherings where the main activities are drinking and dancing has led to difficulties. Differences

have often led initially to hostility, later followed by understanding and in some cases accommodation. The celebration of holidays remains an issue since Islamic celebration days appear on very few calendars; most often, Muslims must take vacation or sick days in order to participate in the festivities. On Christian holidays, however, Muslims are forced to observe closed offices and the cessation of work.

Fasting (*sawm*) also provides some difficulty for the Muslim in America. The Islamic fast is one of abstinence from food, drink, and certain behaviors from sunrise to sunset for thirty days. Alertness of mind and the ability to carry out tasks is somewhat compromised during the first few days of the fast, which can make the American workload difficult. Whether the Muslim is a student or a physician, this is indeed challenging. The other part of the tradition during this month of fasting where the believer tries to make extra prayers nightly in the *masjid* also puts a strain on the Muslim who has to be at work at 8 A.M. the next morning. Students often experience the most challenge in the public school systems where they may be questioned as to the legitimacy of this religious obligation.

Muslims fulfill the obligations of the giving of charity in several ways. *Zakat* (the formal giving of a specified amount of charity) is given to the local community for distribution to those in need at the end of the month of fasting. The more informal, day-to-day charitable response to misfortune or to assist in a positive venture is carried out on a person-to-person basis in and across communities.

Muslims in America have taken their diversity and in many ways have welded these cultural differences into one face of Islam. All communities are open for prayer and participation in social activities to everyone. Efforts in business and education express the variety of ethnicities and their social concerns. Muslims in America, without regard to ethnicity, remain tied to all parts of the Muslim world. Political issues emerging abroad have profound effects on Muslims in America at many levels. In many cases these communities are highlighted and sometimes maligned for political and religious differences. This is currently the fueling force for the necessity of dialogue.

The largest single contingent of Muslims in America is African American. At least seventeen different communities evidence choices of Islamic philosophy and Islamic responses to American racism and theo-centricity. As indigenous Americans and as ex-slaves, their move into the Islamic worldview has often been challenged as inauthentic. There remains an ongoing suspicion that these choices for Islam by up to four generations of African Americans continue to be a protest against the abuses of Christianity. While this may have been a primary impetus decades ago, it has long ceased to hold weight in current spiritual understandings and experience. African American Muslims, alongside their brothers and sisters from the Muslim world, have developed the necessary institutions and businesses for community in America.

The real need now is for greater attention to Islam in its American context. There is a critical need for awareness of the American Muslim position on American affairs as well as for dialogue on issues and concerns.

The Golden Words of a Sufi Sheikh

M. R. Bawa Muhaiyaddeen

Author of many books and pamphlets on the Sufi tradition; considered by many to have been a 20th-century saint

My son! This is a *hadith* of the *Rasulullah (Sal.)* about Islam:

Brothers in Islam! You who are *Iman-Islam!* You must not see differences between yourselves and your neighbors. You must not discriminate against any religion. You must not oppress or harm any man, no matter what religion or race he may be. Islam is one and Allah is one; just as we in Islam see Allah as one, we must see all mankind as one.

All the prophets brought the words of Allah, and all the words they brought are true. Allah sent His messages through each of the prophets, and they brought His commandments step by step. In the revelations contained in the Qur'an, Allah has given the entirety of His teaching. The Qur'an is the ultimate and final teaching, showing everything in its fullness.

All the children of Adam (AS) are brothers and sisters. They are not different. Although they may stand on different steps of the teachings brought by the prophets in their respective times, you must not discriminate against any of them. You must not harass their places of worship, their bodies, or their hearts. You must protect them as you would protect your own life.

To comfort the hunger of your neighbor, no matter who he is or what religion he belongs to, is Islam. When someone dies, to join together and give him a decent burial is Islam. To realize the pain and suffering of others and offer your hands in assistance, helping to alleviate their suffering, is Islam.

To see division is not Islam. To see other men as different is not Islam. In this world and the next, there must be no prejudice in our hearts, for all will come together on the Day of Reckoning and the Day of Judgment. All of us will come together in heaven. Therefore, we must not see any differences or create any divisions here. Where Allah does not see a difference, we must not see a difference. We must not despise anyone whom Allah loves—and Allah loves everyone. He belongs equally to everyone, just as Islam belongs equally to everyone. Islam is unity, not division.

Hurting another is not Islam. Failing to comfort the hunger of your neighbor is not Islam. The purity of Islam is to avoid hurting others; you must regard others as you regard yourself. You must accept Allah's word totally. There must be no discrimination in your heart against the children of Islam.

You who are Islam must understand what is *halal* and what is *haram*, what is permissible and what is forbidden. You must understand that there is only One worthy of worship. You must understand *Qiyamah*, the Day of Reckoning, and the Day of Judgment.

To understand this world and the next world is Islam. Because Islam is the wealth of grace, you must use that grace to wash and comfort the hearts of others. To truly understand this and see all lives as your own life, without any differences, is the way of Islam. To see your neighbor as yourself, to heal the suffering of others, to share food from the same plate in harmony and peace, to live unified in food and in prayer, in happiness and in sorrow, is the way of Islam. To live separated and divided is not Islam. You must reflect on this.

O you who have faith! Do not compare anything to Allah. Do not hold anything equal to Allah. Do not make distinctions between men; king and beggar must be equal in your sight. There must be no difference between rich and poor. No one is rejected by Islam. Islam is one. You must realize this.

This is what the *Rasulullah (Sal.)* has said. He has given countless *hadith* with his divine lips of grace, from the flower of his divine mouth, his mouth of faith, his mouth of Allah's grace, and his mouth of Allah's divine knowledge. O you who have received the wealth of faith! May you understand and act with the clarity of these teachings.

—from *The Golden Words of a Sufi Sheikh*,
    by M. R. Bawa Muhaiyaddeen,
    Copyright © 1981 Fellowship Press, Philadelphia.

Islam in the World Today
SITUATIONS OF MINORITY CONFLICT AND THE UMMAH'S RESPONSIBILITIES

Syed Z. Abedin

Director of the Institute of Muslim Minority Affairs, Jeddah, Saudi Arabia, and London, U.K. (Deceased)

Introduction

The world situation with respect to Muslim minority communities around the globe is getting more complex day by day. No respite appears to be in sight. We at the Institute of Muslim Minority

Affairs have at the moment no propositions either. In any case, we do not see ourselves as problem solvers. Most cases of conflict in present times that involve Muslims are of a political nature and their solution calls for political initiatives on the part of governments.

What we can do and have been doing over the past ten years, in our capacity as an independent research institute, is to formulate the right questions and to provide an accurate and objective database for possible answers. This helps to clarify the issues. And if there is will on the part of the contending parties, the Institute's input could facilitate the search for solutions.

One reason perhaps why viable solutions have not been forthcoming is that nobody is asking the right questions.

As is well known, there are at least half a dozen situations in various corners of the globe where Muslims are presently engaged in a desperate struggle. Imminent or potential conflict situations are many times this number.

Now in all these situations, live or latent, major or minor, the *Ummah* is urged to intervene. These calls for active intervention are made not only by those minority Muslims who are immediately affected but also by various constituents within the *Ummah*. Thus the pressure on the *Ummah* is both domestic and foreign, internal and external.

The *Ummah* is thus faced with a dilemma. The dilemma consists in that even if there were consensual will on issues of minority conflict on the part of all constituent members, resources are not inexhaustible. There is no way in which the *Ummah* could wage a determined, aggressive, and successful campaign on all fronts where Muslims are presently engaged in conflict with others.

Let us not forget that even the United States not too long ago had to solicit material and manpower resources of over two dozen countries of the world in order to wage a successful campaign on one single front.

To make matters more complicated upholders of the Islamic cause inside the *Ummah* insist on making each occasion of conflict anywhere in the world, in which any number of Muslims are involved, a test case for the *Ummah's* Islamic commitment and its consciousness of accountability before God Almighty.

The *Ummah* has therefore before it two options: it could either choose to plunge into every quarrel anywhere in the world where Muslims in any number feel that they are being thwarted from getting whatever they want, and in consequence cease to be a credible world power; or it has to face the wrath of its own people, who see in the lack of alacrity on the part of the *Ummah* a sign of betrayal of Islam.

Verbal *Jihad*

The *Ummah's* record in the past indicates that to save face it has opted for a third alternative, which, for want of a better term, may be described as a verbal *jihad*. Every now and then, when the domestic pressures build up, various spokesmen of the *Ummah* come forward with passionate statements directed at the offending parties.

In these events, the statements could have constituted a clever, strategic compromise between the two options noted above. But these statements, pliable though they are, end up adding further fuel to a fire that should not have been started in the first place: they alienate the non-Muslims concerned from all the constituents of the *Ummah* (even from the faith they profess), and raise false hopes of *Ummah* support among the Muslim minorities. This leads to tragic consequences.

The *Ummah* Concept

One possible way of resolving this dilemma could be to look at the *Ummah* as representing not a political but primarily a religious and spiritual concept. Realistically speaking, in present times there appears to be no other way of giving viable meaning to this concept. For, if the *Ummah* is projected as a political entity, then there is in truth no *Ummah*. There are indeed 50 or more sovereign Muslim states, but they are nation states, each with its own national goals and interests, but no *Ummah*.

If on the other hand the term *Ummah* is accepted as primarily reflecting a religious and spiritual concept, then in all situations of conflict the questions to ask would be, Is this a religious conflict (i.e., are Muslims being victimized because of their religion)? Are their rights to freedom of worship, belief, practice, and propagation being denied?

If the consensus among the constituents of the *Ummah* is that, yes, it is a religious conflict, then without doubt every effort should be made to resolve it to Muslim satisfaction.

But if our investigation reveals that the real cause of the conflict is not religious but ethnic, national, economic, strategic, or political and that religion is being used merely as a pretext, then like all secular conflicts it should be amenable to negotiations, accommodation, and compromise. The *Ummah's* responsibility would then be to use its good offices to facilitate such a resolution.

However, it is important to remember that the procedures adopted for doing so by the *Ummah* would be markedly different from those adopted in the case of a religious conflict. The hellfire and brimstone strategies most often employed in religious conflicts in our time are not likely to pay much in dividends in political conflicts.

Unfortunately, this important distinction has not always been maintained by even responsible spokesmen of the *Ummah*.

Furthermore, it has also to be considered that if a conflict is truly a religious conflict, then in all good conscience it has to be conducted as one. We cannot claim commitment to a cause and then go on to pursue the cause oblivious to its value limitations. Islam is not a racial, national, or ethnic concept. We are Muslims not because we all have kinship or language ties, or live in the same territory, or dress in the same way, or prefer the same cuisine. We are Muslims because we together believe in certain common values. These values color (or should color) everything we do. So that without being told who we are, anybody looking at us, from our appearance and behavior, could determine that these must be followers of the faith of Islam.

In Islam there is no concept of total war. In any case, we as a people were not raised to conquer the world for God. God is capable of doing so Himself. Didn't He say in the Qur'an that if He had wanted to He could have made the whole world Muslim? But He did not (Qur'an 10:99). We were raised in order to be a witness (a model) unto what a God-conscious life of total surrender to His will is supposed to be lived like and look like.

Revenge or Reconciliation?

In a situation of conflict between two groups, one Muslim and the other non-Muslim, in particular in the case of actual or potential conflict between Muslim minorities and non-Muslim majorities, the crucial question to determine at the very outset is: Is the primary concern of the *Ummah* to put a nation or a community or a religion in the dock before the international community, i.e., to determine culpability first?

Or, is it to provide urgent relief to the suffering millions engaged in conflict?

It should never be forgotten that however cheap Muslim life may have become in our time, causing its wanton loss for self-titillation or communal ego-boosting is still a cardinal sin.

It is also perhaps instructive to note here that however cynical and polarized, religiously or nationally, the world may have become, the conscience of the world community is still alive and well. Indeed, some of the most damaging indictments of government policies toward their Muslim minorities have come not from Muslims but from non-Muslims, both indigenous and foreign.

And Herein Lies Our Hope

Let us build on this hope. Let not the forces of hatred and fanaticism drown our Islamic good sense. Let some people among us plumb the depths and resources of our moral and Islamic being and come up with ways of understanding and resolution.

Who knows what non-Muslim powers may also be waiting for such an opening? After all, they also well realize that, considering the present international order, the minorities that reside within their jurisdiction cannot be just wished away. In fact, looked at from the perspective of history, non-Muslim states such as Russia, China, India, and Bulgaria, which contain significant Muslim minorities, would not be what they are today if their national life had not been interwoven by the multiple and many-hued contributions of their minority constituents.

The people of conscience in these countries have given and are giving expression to their sense of outrage at the violation of human and civil rights perpetrated in these societies. Perhaps these people are also wishing for such a gesture on our part. They have already done *their* human duty. It is now *our* turn.

Let us put aside, for a while at least, our sense of umbrage as Muslims and take our Islamic courage in hand and be the first to break this impasse, this standoff between communities and states, between the governors and the governed.

Let the world community know that we come, not to condemn nor to aggravate an already sensitive and explosive situation, but that we desire only to understand and ameliorate. Whether it be Russia or China or India or the Philippines or Bulgaria or Cyprus or Burma, let the world know that we come, more in sorrow than in anger, to help find a workable arrangement that would put a stop to the bloodletting and the suffering and the humiliation and the loss of honor and dignity. And to help lift the burdens and the shackles that have oppressed the victims, and equally, the conscience of the perpetrators.

Is this too much to ask?

Chapter Ten
JAINISM

A Portrait

Amar T. Salgia

Founding Member of Young Jains of America

The religions of the world differ widely in their beliefs, faiths, and theories regarding good and evil, happiness and misery, and survival of death. A popular alternative to the doctrine of a kind and almighty creator who governs the universe is the theory of soulless, materialistic atheism which maintains that life and consciousness are the outcome of the activity of matter, to be dissipated upon death.

For those finding neither of these assertions satisfactory, there has been, since time immemorial, a system which neither denies the existence of the soul, nor starts with the presupposition of a creator. This system makes each individual the master of its own destiny, affirming the immortality of every soul and insisting upon the very highest rectitude of life, unto final perfection, as a necessary means to permanent happiness now and hereafter. In this modern era, it is commonly known as Jainism.

It is claimed of the ancient Jain spiritual teachers that they had purged themselves of the passions of anger, greed, ego, and deceit, were free from all worldly attachments, and were therefore omniscient. The Jain scriptures are claimed to be the historical records of the lives and teachings of those omniscient spiritual leaders, and it is from these scriptures that the Jain doctrines are taken. These spiritual leaders lived in the flesh on earth, as human beings. They realized the true nature of worldly existence and taught the human race the path to Final Liberation.

Jainism begins with a serious concern for the human soul in its relationship with the laws governing existence in the universe, with other living beings, and to its own future state in eternity. First and foremost, it is a religion of the heart: the golden rule is *Ahimsa*, nonviolence by all faculties—mental, verbal, and physical. The whole of its structure is built upon compassion for all forms of life. Like an inner Japanese garden, with its profusion of inner worlds, restrained exuberance, and perfect orchestration, Jainism, too, emerges as a secret refuge for life, an artistic oasis; and its delicate balance spanning hope and despair does not brashly declare itself nor go in for theatrics.

Jain Prayers and Songs

Prayer

*Highly auspicious are the adorable ones
And so are the emancipated;
The saints too are the auspicious ones
And so is the speech divine.*

*Best in the world are the adorable ones
And so are the emancipated;
The saints too are the best in the world,
And so is the speech divine.*

*Refuge do I take in the adorable ones.
And also in the emancipated;
Saints are also the place of my refuge.
And so is the speech divine.*

*Thus do I pay homage and veneration
Unto the great Arihants every day
In devotion deep with the purity in mind,
In speech and in deed indeed.*

The Immortal Song

1. May the sacred stream of amity flow forever in my heart. May the universe prosper—such is my cherished desire.

2. May my heart sing with ecstasy at the sight of the virtuous. And may my life be an offering at their feet.

3. May my heart bleed at the sight of the wretched, the cruel, the irreligious, and my tears of compassion flow from my eyes.

4. May I always be there to show the path to the pathless wanderers of life. Yet if they should not hearken to me, may I bide in patience.

5. May the spirit of goodwill enter all our hearts. May we all sing in chorus the immortal song of human concord.

From the Acharanga Sutra (1:4:1)

*The Arhats and Bhagavats of the past,
present and future all say thus, speak thus,
declare thus, explain thus:*

*All breathing, existing, living, sentient
creatures should not be slain, nor treated
with violence, nor abused nor tormented,
nor driven away.*

*This is the pure, unchangeable, eternal
law, which the clever ones, who
understand the world, have declared:
among the zealous and the not zealous,
among the faithful and the not faithful,
among the not cruel and the cruel, among
those who have worldly weakness and those
who have not, among those who like social
bonds and those who do not: "that is the
truth, that is so, that is proclaimed in this
(creed)."*

Fight against Desires

*O man! Control thyself. Only then can
you get salvation.*

*If you are to fight, fight against your own
desires.*

*Nothing will be achieved by fighting against
external enemies;*

*If you miss this occasion, it will be lost
forever.*

*One's own unconquered soul is one's
greatest enemy.*

Jainism offers a quiet, overwhelmingly serious way of life, a cultural insistence on compassion, a society of aesthetics that has dramatically changed the world and will continue to effect change. Jainism is a momentous example to all of us that there can exist a successful, ecologically responsible way of life which is abundantly nonviolent in thought, action, and deed. As a species, we might misread our history, go forward confusedly to perpetrate other follies, but we will do so knowing that there is a viable alternative.

Moreover, Jainism is unlike other systems of thought in that its theories of cognition, perception, and the nature of the cosmos are, to the utmost, accurate in the context of modern scientific thought and reasoning. They will bear the severest scrutiny of the intellect, and they give freedom to the individual. Jainism does not offer a deity for humanity to worship or but another means of obtaining its grace; beyond the rules of right conduct, which are based upon its understanding of reality and nature, it offers no commandments to obey or dogmas to accept unconditionally. It teaches that we—humans, animals, plants, angelics, or denizens of hell—are individually responsible to ourselves for our own condition, and for our conduct towards others. It ennobles the natural purity inherent in all souls, and allows one the freedom to perceive Truth as it truly is.

The "Jains" are, etymologically, the followers of the *Jinas*. "Jina" literally means "Conqueror." He who has conquered love and hate, pleasure and pain, attachment and aversion, and has thereby freed the soul from the karmas obscuring knowledge, perception, truth, and ability, is a *Jina*. A *Jina* is omniscient and has realized the soul's innate qualities of Infinite Knowledge, Perception, Energy, and Bliss. Such a soul is also called an *Arihant* (Destroyer of Inner Enemies). The Jains refer to the *Jina* as God.

Time rolls along in an eternal cycle of rise and decline. An *Utsarpini* is a "rising" era in which human affairs and natural conditions improve and aggrandize over time. At the peak of the *Utsarpini* begins an *Avasarpini*, a "declining" era of the same length, in which the ultra-utopia which evolved gradually corrupts, weakens, and becomes more difficult to endure. During every declining era are born twenty-four persons quite different from their contemporary societies. Upon realizing the nature of suffering, the cycle of misery, and the path to liberation from it, those twenty-four individuals renounce all ties to the world, mental and material. Those twenty-four, human like us, blaze a path to perfection. They are apostles of *Ahimsa*, born for the upliftment of all living things in the three worlds. The Jains refer to these individuals who become *Jinas* and teach mankind how to follow the noble path of Enlightened Perception, Knowledge, and Conduct the Twenty-four Crossing-

Makers, or *Tirthankaras*. It is the ultimate goal of the Jain to follow in the footsteps of the Crossing-Makers by attaining freedom from the misery inherent in the material world while crossing the ocean of worldly existence.

Originating on the Indian subcontinent, Jainism—or, more properly, the Jain *Dharm*—is one of the oldest religions of its homeland and indeed of the world. Having prehistoric origins before 3,000 B.C.E., and before the propagation of Indo-Aryan culture, the Twenty-four Crossing-Makers guided its evolution and elaboration by first achieving, and then teaching. The first *Tirthankara* of the present declining era was Lord Rishabhanath, and the last was Lord Mahavira (599–527 B.C.E.).

Jain religion is unique in that, during its existence of over five thousand years, it has never compromised on the concept of nonviolence either in principle or practice. It upholds nonviolence as the supreme religion (*Ahimsa Paramo Dharmah*) and has insisted upon its observance in thought, word, and deed at the individual as well as social levels. Both in its philosophical essence as well as in its rituals, Jain religion invokes an intense and constant awareness of communion and understanding of not only all living beings but indeed all that exists. The holy text *Tattvartha Sutra* sums it up in the phrase "*Parasparopagraho Jivanam*" (all life is mutually supportive). Jain religion presents a truly enlightened perspective of equality of souls, irrespective of differing physical forms, ranging from human beings to animals and microscopic living organisms. Humans, alone among living beings, are endowed with all the six senses of seeing, hearing, tasting, smelling, touching, and thinking; thus humans are enjoined upon to act responsibly towards all life by being compassionate, egoless, fearless, forgiving, rational, and therefore full of equanimity.

Jain religion has a clearly articulated scientific basis that elucidates the properties and qualities of animate and inanimate substances which make up the cosmos; their interrelationship is described in terms of evolution and growth of monads (like atoms), molecules, nonmaterial continuums, and souls. Jainism sets forth the existence of two fundamental categories of existing entities: *Jiva* and *Ajiva*, soul and non-soul. The non-soul "substances" are time, space, *pudgal* (the continuum of matter and energy), and the media of motion and rest. Genius lies in this cosmology. Elements of the Jain worldview, as taught for thousands of years before the Renaissance, include the atomic makeup of matter, the charged nature of elementary particles, the interconvertibility of energy and matter, the conditions under which particles combine and dissociate, and dimensions of the universe comparable to those theorized by Einstein. *Jiva* and *Ajiva* are

Nomokar Maha Mantra (The Universal Prayer)

Obeisance to the Arihantas, perfect souls—Godmen

I bow down to those who have reached omniscience in the flesh and teach the road to everlasting life in the liberated state.

Obeisance to the Siddhas—liberated bodiless souls

I bow down to those who have attained perfect knowledge and liberated their souls of all karma.

Obeisance to the masters—heads of congregations

I bow down to those who have experienced self-realization of their souls through self-control and self-sacrifice.

Obeisance to the teachers—ascetic teachers

I bow down to those who understand the true nature of soul and teach the importance of the spiritual over the material.

Obeisance to all the ascetic aspirants in the universe

I bow down to those who strictly follow the five great vows of conduct and inspire us to live a virtuous life.

This fivefold obeisance mantra

To these five types of great souls I offer my praise.

Destroys all demerit

Such praise will help diminish my sins.

And is the first and foremost of all

Giving this praise is most auspicious—

Auspicious recitations

So auspicious as to bring happiness and bliss.

Ahimsa Parmo Dharma: Nonviolence Is the Supreme Religion

Know other creatures' love for life, for they are like you.

Kill them not; save their life from fear and enmity.

All creatures desire to live, not to die.

Hence to kill is to sin.

A godly man does not kill.

Therefore, kill not yourself, consciously or unconsciously,

living organisms which move or move not, nor cause slaughter of them.

He who looketh on the creatures of the earth, big and small, as his own self, comprehendeth this immense world.

Among the careless, he who restraineth self is enlightened.

LORD MAHAVIRA

characterized as having distinct, immutable properties, but which undergo modification due to certain conditions. For the soul, those conditions are brought about as conscious and subconscious thought activity. Through the interworkings of passions and attachments, soul remains associated with non-soul, and persists in its cycle of material rise and decline, suffering and distress, delusion and wandering. Religious impulse is equated with the search for Truth, which begins with thought activity along the lines of "By soul alone I am governed" (*appanan anusasayi*) and "Let karma not bind you." Dissociation from non-soul is brought about solely through the requisites of Enlightened Perception, Knowledge, and Conduct. Thus, the soul is no longer under the influence of that which it is not, and for the rest of eternity enjoys its natural attributes of Infinite Knowledge, Perception, Energy, and Bliss; thus the underlying theory translates directly into practice.

In short, the code of conduct is made up of the following five vows, and all of their logical conclusions: *Ahimsa, Satya* (truthfulness), *Asteya* (nonstealing), *Aparigraha* (nonpossessiveness), and *Brahmacharya* (chastity). Jain religion focuses much attention on *Aparigraha*, nonpossessiveness towards material things through self-control, self-imposed penance, abstinence from overindulgence, voluntary curtailment of one's needs, and the consequent subsiding of the aggressive urge. The code of conduct prescribed for the Jain monastic order, made up of monks and nuns, is more rigorous than that prescribed for the laity.

Vegetarianism is a way of life for a Jain, taking its origin in the concept of compassion for living beings, *Jiva Daya*. The practice of vegetarianism is regarded as a potent instrument for the practice of nonviolence and peaceful, cooperative coexistence. Jains are strict vegetarians, consuming only one-sensed beings, primarily from the plant kingdom. While the Jain diet does, of course, involve harm to plants and microorganisms, it is regarded as a means of survival that involves the bare minimum amount of violence towards living beings. (Many forms of plant material, including roots and certain fruits, are also excluded from the Jain diet due to the greater number of living beings they contain owing to the environment in which they develop.)

Anekantavada, the doctrine of the multifaceted nature of Truth, is another basic principle of Jainism that offers systematic, logical, and nondogmatic algorithms for understanding the multifarious aspects of the truth behind statements, human perceptions, knowledge, and the nature of the Self. As a very simple example, just as a father may also have the role of a husband, a brother, a boss, or a cousin to different persons, life cannot be understood if taken from one perspective that prejudices the individual against all others. Indeed, it is a doctrine rooted in *Ahimsa*.

Jainism has not only shown a spiritual way of life to its followers, but has inspired a distinct stream of culture which has enriched philosophy, literature, art, architecture, democratic living, and spiritual advancement in the land of India. Classical Jain literature is found in the Sanskrit, Prakrit, Hindi, Marathi, Gujarati, Kannada, and Tamil languages, and in varied forms of poetry, prose, drama, and story. Its influence has also been traced to other lands like Greece and Israel. In addition to compounding philosophical and spiritual treatises, the Jain ascetic-scholars were champions of secular learning in areas including astronomy, music theory, political science, linguistics, and mathematics. The artistry and architecture of Jain temples all over the Indian subcontinent depict the magnificence of detachment, serenity, and the natural purity of the soul.

The followers of Jainism number around 10 million. Jain societies are neither caste-ridden nor male-dominated.

Jainism is an eternal philosophy, whose benefits can be taken up by anyone willing to improve his or her life and rational conduct in situations of both stress and tranquility. Today, more than ever, when suspicion and distrust are vitiating the atmosphere of international peace, when the world is filled with fear and hate, we require a living philosophy which will help us discard those destructive qualities and recover ourselves. Such a living, wholesome philosophy, bearing a message of love and goodwill, *Ahimsa* and peace, personally as well as universally, is the Jain philosophy of life. This system of religion, thought, and living stands for the highest and noblest human values, and offers a path guaranteeing eternal peace and happiness.

—Portions of this article have been adapted from Dr. N. P. Jain's article "A Portrait of Jainism."

BIBLIOGRAPHY

Jain, Jyoti Prasad, *Religion and Culture of the Jains*. Bharatiya Jnanpith, New Delhi: 1983.

Jaini, Padmanabh, *The Jain Path of Purification*. University of California Press, Berkeley, Calif.: 1979.

Tobias, Michael, *Life Force: The World of Jainism*. Asian Humanities Press, Berkeley, Calif.: 1991.

Warren, Herbert, *Jainism*. Shree Vallabhsuri Smarak Nidhi, Bombay: 1913.

1. May my thoughts and feeling be such that I may always act in a simple and straightforward manner. May I ever, so far as I can, do good in this life to others.

2. May I never hurt and harm any living being; may I never speak a lie. May I never be greedy of wealth or the wife [spouse] of another. May I ever drink the nectar of contentment!

3. May I always have a friendly feeling towards all living beings of the world and may the stream of compassion always flow from my heart towards distressed and afflicted living beings.

4. May I never entertain an idea of egotism; nor may I be angry with anybody! May I never become jealous on seeing the worldly prosperity of other people.

5. May I never become fretful towards bad, cruel, and wicked persons. May I keep tolerance towards them. May I be so disposed!

6. May I ever have the good company of learned ascetics and may I ever keep them in mind. May my heart be always engrossed and inclined to adopt the rules of conduct which they observe.

7. May my heart be overflowing with love at the sight of the virtuous, and may I be happy to serve them so far as possible.

8. May I never be ungrateful (towards anybody); nor may I revolt (against anybody). May I ever be appreciating the good qualities of other persons and may I never look at their faults.

9. May my mind neither be puffed up with joy, nor may it become nervous in pain and grief. May it never be frightened even if I am in a terrible forest or strange places of cremation or graveyards.

10. May my mind remain always steady and firm, unswerving and unshaken; may it become stronger every day. May I bear and endure with patience the deprivation of dear

(cont.)

ones and occurrences of undesired evils.

11. May all living beings of the world be happy! May nobody ever feel distressed! May the people of the world renounce enmity, sin, pride and sing the songs of joy every day.

12. May Dharma (truth) be the topic of house-talk in every home! May evil be scarce! May (people) increase their knowledge and conduct and thereby enjoy the blessed fruit of human birth.

13. May disease and pestilence never spread, may the people live in peace, may the highest religion of Ahimsa (non-injury) pervade the whole world and may it bring about universal good!

14. May universal love pervade the world and may ignorance of attachment remain far away. May nobody speak unkind, bitter, and harsh words!

15. May all become heroes of the age heartily and remain engaged in elevating the Cause of Righteousness. May all gain the sight of Truth called Vastuswarupa (Reality of substance) and may they bear, with pleasure, trouble and misfortunes!

AMEN

—The prayers and songs are from *Jainism—Past and Present: Prayers, Articles, and Short Stories*, published by Dr. Tansukh J. Salgia (1984, Parma, Ohio).

Virchand Raghavji Gandhi

EMISSARY TO THE WEST

Among the few representatives from India to the 1893 Parliament of the World's Religions was Virchand Raghavji Gandhi. By the age of 21 he became the first honorary secretary of the Jain Association of India; he mastered fourteen language and was a brilliant scholar of Jainism. His speeches at the World Parliament of Religions echoed the true spirit and culture of India as he lectured on Jainism and defended Hinduism. V. R. Gandhi was accorded a warm reception and shown highest appreciation from clubs, literary and church societies, philosophical branches, and spiritual associations in the U.S.A. He corrected the false and perverse impression of India as being the land of Maharajahs, tigers, and cobras.

V. R. Gandhi stayed in the U.S.A for about two years and visited several cities. In 1896 he organized a shipload of grain and about Rs.40,000 cash for famine relief in India. He also visited England and European cities.

One of the comments about him came from the Hon. E. B. Sherman of the U.S. Circuit Court:

> "It has rarely, if ever, been my good fortune to meet a man whose reading and culture have been so wide and varied, and who, withal, has so sweet, sincere, and teachable a spirit as Mr. Gandhi."

—adapted from a booklet titled "The Jains," prepared by the Jain Host Committee for distribution at the Parliament of the World's Religions, 1993

Chapter Eleven
JUDAISM

A Portrait

Rabbi Herbert Bronstein

Senior Rabbi, North Shore Congregation Israel, Glencoe, Illinois; member of the Board of Trustees of the Council for a Parliament of the World's Religions

*"Hear O Israel,
the Lord Our God, the Lord is One."
And you shall love the Lord, your God,
with all your heart, with all your might, with all your soul.
And these words which I command you this day,
shall be upon your heart that you may remember,
do all my commandments
and be holy unto your God.*

DEUTERONOMY (*D'Varim*) 6.4–9

Though often spoken of as a "Western" religion and linked with Christianity (as in "Judeo-Christian tradition"), Judaism has its origins in the Middle East.

Judaism is a spirituality that indeed gave birth to Christianity, and later played a role during the emergence of Islam. But Judaism as we know it began almost four thousand years ago among a pastoral/nomadic and later agricultural people, the ancient Hebrews.

The religion of the people of Israel was and is the loving and faithful Covenant devotion to one God who revealed Divine Teaching through the fathers and mothers of the people of Israel (the Patriarchs and Matriarchs), through Moses and the Prophets and Sages whose spirituality is documented in the twenty-two books of the Hebrew Bible.

The goal of this Covenant consciousness in alliance with the Divine is clearly put in the ancient texts as

A good life for all, through adherence to God's Teaching (*Torah*) and Commandments (*Mitzvot*), harmony on earth on the individual and social levels culminating in peace and well-being for all humanity.

The Worth of Wisdom

*"With what shall I come before the Lord
And bow myself before God most high?
Shall I come before him with burnt-offerings, with calves a year old?
Will the Lord be pleased with thousands of rams,
With myriads of streams of oil?
Shall I give my first born for my transgression,
The fruit of my body for the sin of my soul?
You have been told, O man, what is good,
And what the Lord requires of you:
Only to do justice,
and to love mercy,
And to walk humbly with your God."*

MICAH 6:6–8

"God shall judge between many peoples, and shall decide for strong nations afar off; and they shall beat their swords into plowshares, and their spears into pruning hooks; nation shall not lift up sword against nation, neither shall they learn war any more; but they shall sit every man under his vine and under his fig tree, and none shall make them afraid."

MICAH 4:3–4

"How happy is the one who finds wisdom,
The one who gains understanding!
For wisdom's income is better than income
of silver,
And her revenue than gold.
She is more precious than corals,
And none of your heart's desires can
compare with her.
Long life is in her right hand,
In her left are riches and honor. . . .
The Lord by wisdom founded the earth,
By reason he established the heavens;
By his knowledge the depths are broken up,
And the clouds drop down dew."

THE BOOK OF PROVERBS

"The highest wisdom is kindness."

BERAKOT, 17A

"Deeds of kindness are equal in weight to
all the commandments."

T. J. PE'AH, 1:1

"'Thou shalt love thy neighbor as thyself.'
This is the great general rule in Torah."

T. J. NEDARIM, 9:4

"The beginning and the end thereof
[Torah] is the performance of loving-
kindness."

SOTAH, 14A

"If two men claim thy help, and one is thy
enemy, help him first."

BABA METZIA, 32B

Thus Judaism is characterized as a religion of deed, a "Way" by which human beings are capable of understanding and responding to God's teaching.

Because over the centuries every major power that entered the Middle East (namely Egypt, Assyria, Babylonia, Persia, Greece, and Rome) coveted the land of Israel (a strategic joining point of Africa, Asia, and Europe), the religion of Israel changed, not in central principles or institution, but in form, in response to the demands of changing conditions, including oppression and exile.

After the Roman destruction of the central Temple in Jerusalem and the end of Jewish independent existence in the Holy Land, Judaism was separated from the sacrificial cult, the priesthood disappeared, and Judaism became a religion of congregations all over the world in which worship, deeds of loving kindness, and the study of God's teaching replaced the central cult of the Temple in Jerusalem. Nevertheless, Jerusalem remained a central spiritual symbol of Jewry throughout the world linked with the vision of redemption of the Jewish people from exile and oppression, and peace for all the world (the Messianic vision).

In Judaism as it developed, prayer services emerged which recapitulated the main stories and themes of Judaism, from the universal *Creation* by the Universal God to the *Revelation* of God's Teaching to Moses and the people at Mount Sinai to the *Redemption* of Israel and all humanity. It is a way of life in which all Jews are equally responsible as "a Kingdom of Priests and a Holy People."

Over the centuries a vast body of teaching and lore has grown up, often taking the form of exegesis or interpretation of the ancient Biblical texts. This has included the elaboration of actual religious practice (the *Halacha* or "Way") and philosophical texts, stories, homilies, parable, and poetry (the *Aggada*). The vast rabbinic text known as the *Talmud* (again, "Teaching") is second only to the Bible in importance. There is also a continual mystical stream in Judaism embodied in the various texts known collectively as *Kabbalah* (the "received" tradition), such as the *Zohar* (the *Book of Splendor* or *Illumination*), which teach the emanation of the Godhead into the world, the experience of communion with God in transcendence of the self, and the maintenance of the cosmos through human action in Covenant with God. Again the basic mythos or narrative embodied in Judaic consciousness is *from* the universal God, Creator of all of existence *through* particular Jewish Covenant existence *to* the universal redemption of all Beings and all Being from bondage.

The basic symbol of Judaism is thus a seven-branched candelabrum which embodies cosmic images of all Time and Space. It is also a symbol of the Redemption, which is the goal of human existence. This symbol is reducible to Light, which is expressed many times in Jewish observance: the kindling of the Sabbath and Festival lights in the home; the braided candle at the end of the Sabbath; the kindling of lights in the eight-day midwinter Festival of Lights (*Chanukah*), which commemorates the rededication of the holy Temple from pollution and therefore of the sacred from profanity; the memorial lights to remember the dead; and the Eternal Light over the Ark in the synagogue which contains the *Scroll of the Torah*.

Jews celebrate the recreation of the moral order of the world and the rebirth of the soul at the beginning of the religious year *(Rosh Hashanah,* and the Day of Atonement, *Yom Kippur*), a ten-day period of spiritual introspection and moral resolve. The home celebration or service, which relives in story and song, ritual and prayer, the Exodus from Egypt at the Passover *(Pesach)* season is called a *Seder* celebration. Its themes reenergize Jewish social consciousness, Jewish hope and vision of a better day for all.

Jews are not divided into creedal denominations, strictly speaking, in the same manner as Christianity. There are "streams" of Jewish religious life which express varying responses to the encounter of Jews with the modern world.

The most liberal of these is usually designated as **Reform** or **Liberal** Judaism, which has responded by adapting to more Western styles of worship. *Reform* leans toward the vernacular in worship and has modified considerably the forms of observance passed down by tradition.

Orthodox Judaism conceives of the entire corpus of Jewish observance, the received tradition, as equivalent to having been given by God at Sinai and therefore unchangeable except through procedures which were themselves given at Sinai.

Conservative Judaism finds its way between these two positions.

Reconstructionism is the most recent stream to emerge in modern Jewish life. It conceives of Jewish religious forms and observances as part of a historic Jewish culture or "civilization." Reconstructionism values this culture, linking its preservation with a naturalist theology. Reconstructionism has recently been hospitable to neo-mystical themes and observances.

However, this does not begin to describe the considerable varieties of Jewish religious life in all of its dimensions and degrees in our time. The number of Jews in the world is estimated at 12,807,000; the number of Jews in North America is estimated at 5,880,000.

The Worth of Wisdom *(continued)*

"If the community is in trouble, a man must not say,

'I will go to my house, and eat and drink, and peace shall be with thee, O my soul.' But a man must share in the trouble of the community, even as Moses did. He who shares in its troubles is worthy to see its consolation."

TA'ANIT, 11A

"The command to give charity weighs as much as all the other commandments put together. . . . He who gives alms in secret is greater than Moses."

BABA BATHRA, 9B

"In that hour when the Egyptians died in the Red Sea, the ministers wished to sing the song of praise before the Holy One, but he rebuked them saying:

'My handiwork is drowning in the sea; would you utter a song before me in honor of that?' "

ANHEDRIN, 98B

"In a city where there are both Jews and Gentiles, the collectors of alms collect both from Jews and Gentiles, and feed the poor of both, visit the sick of both, bury both, comfort the mourners whether they be Jews or Gentiles, and restore the lost goods of both."

T. J. DEMAI, 6:6

"One man alone was brought forth at the time of Creation in order that thereafter none should have the right to say to another, 'My father was greater than your father.' "

T. Y. SANHEDRIN, 4:5

"You must not pervert the justice due the resident alien or the orphan, nor take a widow's garment in pledge. You must remember that you were once a slave yourself in Egypt, and the Lord your God rescued you from there; that is why I am commanding you to do this.

"When you reap your harvest in your field, and forget a sheaf in the field, you must not go back to get it; it is to go to the resident alien, the orphan, and the widow, that the Lord your God may bless you in all your enterprises. When you beat your olive trees, you must not go over them a second time; that is to go to the resident alien, the orphan, and the widow. When you pick the grapes of your vineyard, you must not go over it a second time; that is to go to the resident alien, the orphan, and the widow. You must remember that you were once a slave yourself in the land of Egypt; that is why I am commanding you to do this."

LEVITICUS 24:6–22

"But ask the beasts, and they will teach you; the birds of the sky, and they will tell you; or speak to the earth and it will teach you; the fish of the sea, they will inform you. Who among all these does not know that the hand of the Eternal has done this?"

JOB 12:7–9

"When the Holy One created the first human beings,
God led them around the Garden of Eden and said,
  'Look at My works.
  See how beautiful they are, how excellent!
  For your sake I created them all.
  See to it that you do not spoil or destroy My world—
  for if you do, there will be no one to repair it after you.' "

MIDRASH ECCLESIASTES RABBAH 7:13

Judaism and Interfaith Dialogue

There is a profound religious and historic basis to the Jewish view on interfaith dialogue.

Jewish belief encompasses a dialectic between an all-embracing humane Universalism and deep commitment to a particular Jewish religious way of life and to the continuity of the Jewish people as a religious people. Between the two—namely, universal humane concern and Jewish particularism—there is, in the Judaic worldview, no contradiction. And, in fact, the ideal Jewish position is integration of the two. On the one hand, the ideal Jew is deeply loyal to his own faith, way of life, and people. There is, at the same time, a firm commitment in Judaism to God's universal embrace, care, and love for all humanity, the ideal of loving one's fellow human being as oneself. The *Torah* teaches that all humanity is created in the image of God. In the Jewish myth of creation, one couple, Adam and Eve, are the parents of all humanity. In this view God speaks to all human beings and all human communities in various ways. All perceive the one God in their own way and take different paths to the service of the ultimate Godhead. Dialogue would therefore be an endeavor to understand, on the deepest level possible, the views and positions of the Other toward the goal of ultimate harmony between all human beings, which is the Judaic affirmation of the Sovereignty of God, harmony, peace, *Shalom*.

But over the centuries Jews, as a minority in the Christian world, were subject to persecution, degradation, impoverishment, rioting, and even mass death for their loyalty to their faith. "Interfaith" contact was all too often a staged disputation to prove the falsity of Jewish faith and a prelude to the burning of Jewish holy books, physical attacks, and even murder of Jews, sometimes in massive numbers. Jews often confronted the choice between conversion and martyrdom. Therefore, many Jews of traditional leaning, while willing and eager to work on ameliorative civil projects with all other groups, are leery of any theological dialogue that would tend to undermine the faith commitment of Jews as a minority community. However, throughout the modern period, but most particularly in the 20th century and particularly in pluralistic North America, Jews have been partners in Christian/Jewish dialogue as well as with Muslims and Buddhists.

Today Jews join in that trend of dialogue which is moving toward an attempt to understand the *faith of the believer* rather than simply studying simplistically about the beliefs of other faiths.

Chapter Twelve
SHINTO

A Portrait

Naofusa Hirai

Professor at Kokugakuin University, Tokyo (Emeritus); assistance was graciously provided by Professor H. Byron Earhart of Western Michigan University.

About Shinto

Shinto is the indigenous national religion of Japan. It is more vividly observed in the social life of the people, or in personal motivations, than as a firmly established theology or philosophy; yet it has been closely connected with the value system and ways of thinking and acting of the Japanese people.

Modern Shinto can be roughly classified into three types: Shrine Shinto, Sectarian Shinto, and Folk Shinto.

Shrine Shinto has been in existence from the prehistoric ages to the present and constitutes a main current of Shinto tradition. Until the end of 1945, it included State Shinto within its structure and even now has close relations with the emperor system.

Sectarian Shinto is a relatively new movement based on the Japanese religious tradition, and is represented by the thirteen major sects, which originated in Japan around the 19th century. Each of the thirteen sects has either a founder or a systematizer who organized the religious body. New Shinto sects which appeared in Japan after World War II are conveniently included in this type.

Folk Shinto is an aspect of Japanese folk belief closely related to Shinto. It has neither a firmly organized religious body nor any doctrinal formulas, and includes small roadside images, agricultural rites of individual families, and so on.

These three types of Shinto are interrelated: Folk Shinto exists as the substructure of Shinto faith, and a Sectarian Shinto follower is usually a parishioner of a certain shrine of Shrine Shinto at the same time.

The majority of Japanese people are simultaneously believers of both Shrine Shinto and Buddhism. The number of Sectarian Shintoists is about 10 million. In North America, Shinto exists mainly among some people of Japanese descent.

The center of Japanese myths consists of tales about Amaterasu Omikami (usually translated as "Sun Goddess"), the ancestress of the Imperial Family, and tales of how her direct descendants unified the nation under her authority. At the beginning of Japanese mythology, a divine couple named Izanagi and Izanami, the parents of Amaterasu, gave birth to the Japanese islands as well as to the deities who became ancestors of various clans. Here we can see an ancient Japanese inclination to regard the nature around us as offspring from the same parents. This view of nature requires us to reflect on our conduct toward the pollution of the earth.

The same myth also tells us that if we trace our lineage to its roots, we find ourselves as descendants of *kami* (deities). In Shinto, it is common to say that "man is *kami's* child." This means that, as we see in the above-mentioned myth, humanity is given life through *kami* and therefore human nature is sacred. Reinterpreting this myth more broadly in terms of our contemporary contacts with people of the world, we must revere the life and basic human rights of everyone, regardless of race, nationality, and creed, the same as our own.

At the core of Shinto are beliefs in the mysterious power of *kami* (*musuhi*—creating and harmonizing power) and in the way or will of *kami* (*makoto*—sincerity or true heart). Parishioners of a Shinto shrine believe in their tutelary *kami* as the source of human life and existence. Each *kami* is believed to have a divine personality and to respond to sincere prayers. Historically, the ancient tutelary *kami* of each local

Edict and Principles

"Then she commanded her August Grandchild, saying:

'This Reed-Plain-1500-autumns-fair-rice-ear Land is the region which my descendants shall be lords of. Do thou, my August Grandchild, proceed thither and govern it. Go! and may prosperity attend thy dynasty, and may it, like Heaven and Earth, endure for ever.' "

—from *The Divine Edict of Amaterasu Omikami to Her Grandson*, described in Japanese myth, when he descended from the Plain-of-High-Heaven to Japan with many deities (trans. by W. G. Aston, *Nihongi*, London, George Allen & Unwin, reprinted 1956, p. 77)

This myth, blessing the eternality of the imperial line, is today interpreted by Shinto believers as a myth blessing the eternality of all humans including the Japanese people who have the imperial line as their center. Within Shinto we believe in the endless advance of descendants within this world, and we must work hard in order to realize this.

The following declaration was presented at the tenth anniversary of the founding of the Association of Shinto Shrines, and since that time has been recited at the beginning of many meetings of Shrine Shinto.

1. Let us be grateful for kami's grace and ancestors' benevolence, and with bright and pure makoto (sincerity or true heart) perform religious services.

2. Let us work for people and the world, and serve as representatives of the kami to make the society firm and sound.

3. In accordance with the Emperor's will, let us be harmonious and peaceful, and pray for the nation's development as well as the world's coexistence and coprosperity.

—from The *General Principles of Shinto Life*, proclaimed in 1956 by the Association of Shinto Shrines (transl. by Naofusa Hirai)

community played an important role in combining and harmonizing different elements and powers. After the Meiji Restoration (1868), Shinto was used as a means of spiritually unifying the people during the period of repeated wars. Since the end of World War II, the age-old desire for peace has been reemphasized.

Shinto in the World Today

Since the Industrial Revolution, advanced countries including Japan have undergone rapid modernization in pursuit of material comforts and convenience. Unfortunately, these efforts have resulted in producing well-known critical global issues. To cope with such issues, Shinto leaders have begun to be aware of the necessity of international cooperation and mutual aid with other peoples. In this connection, there are several challenges facing Shinto.

1. Accumulation of experience in international life, which even today is not common in Japan.

2. Acquisition of new ethical standards to join a new spiritual and cultural world community, e.g. transforming the "in-group consciousness" which is one of the characteristics of the Japanese people. Today we need to care not only for the people within our own limited group, but also for unknown people outside our own group.

3. Changing the patterns of expression for international communication. As a cultural trait, Japanese people tend to express matters symbolically rather than logically. These efforts sometimes result in misunderstanding by others.

4. Cultivation of capable Shinto leaders equipped with a good command of foreign languages and cultures.

In spite of these difficulties, Shinto has the following merits for working positively with interfaith dialogue and cooperation.

1. Shinto's notion of *kami* emphasizes belief in many deities, and its doctrine does not reject other religions, so it is natural for Shinto to pay respect to other religions and objects of worship.

2. Within Shinto, it is thought that nature is the place where *kami* dwell, and we give thanks for the blessings of nature. This attitude toward nature may be of use to religious people considering environmental problems.

3. Within Japan, there is a tradition of carefully preserving and cultivating religions which originate in other countries. Within its boundaries, various religions have practiced cooperation and harmonious coexistence.

However, the emphasis of these three points is not suggesting that, at the present time, Shinto seeks a simple syncretism. Shinto leaders, while intent on the peaceful coexistence of all people, wish to preserve Shinto's distinctive features and strengthen its religious depths.

About twenty years ago, Shinto leaders, together with people of other religions, initiated various activities for the purpose of international religious dialogue and cooperation. Since the first assembly of The World Conference on Religion and Peace was opened in Kyoto in 1970, important figures within the Shinto world have participated both in Japan and abroad in the meetings of WCRP, IARF, and others. *Jinja Honcho*, the Association of Shinto Shrines, which includes about 99 percent of Shinto shrines, initiated in 1991 an International Department for the purpose of international exchange and cooperation.

One noteworthy movement in Japan is the "offer a meal movement." Supporters of this movement give up one meal (usually breakfast) at least once each month, and donate the equivalent expense through their religious organization. This money is used by the organization for international relief and other activities. This movement was begun in 1970s by the new religion *Shoroku-Shinto-Yamatoyama*; believers of *Misogikyo* (Sectarian Shinto) and *Izumo Taisha* (Shrine Shinto) have been doing the same for several years. Among Buddhists, *Rissho Kosei-kai* has actively advanced the same movement. While it is not easy to continue this practice, the participants have said, "At first we thought this was for the sake of others, but actually we noticed this is the way to strengthen our own faith."

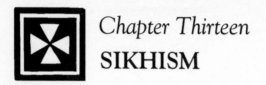

Chapter Thirteen
SIKHISM

A Portrait

Dr. Rajwant Singh and Ms. Georgia Rangel

*Dr. R. Singh has been Secretary, The Guru Gobind Singh
Foundation, Maryland, and a member of the Board of
Directors of North American Interfaith Network; Georgia
Rangel is a member of the Guru Gobind Singh
Foundation.*

Founded only five hundred years ago by Guru
Nanak (1439–1539), Sikhism is one of the
youngest world religions. After a revelatory experience at the age of about thirty-eight, Nanak began to
teach that true religion consisted of being ever-mind-
ful of God, meditating on God's Name, and reflecting it in all activities of daily life. He condemned
superstition and discouraged ritual. He traveled
throughout India, Ceylon, Tibet, and parts of the
Arab world with followers of both Hindu and
Muslim origin, discussing his revelation with those
he met. His followers became known as Sikhs (from
the Sanskrit word *shishya*—disciple).

Nanak and his nine successors are known as *gurus*,
which is a very common term in all Indian traditions
for a spiritual guide or teacher. In Sikhism, *guru*
means the voice of God speaking through someone.
Sikh *gurus* were careful to prevent worship being
offered to them. The last living *guru*, Guru Gobind
Singh, who died in 1708, pronounced the end of the
line of succession and declared that henceforth the
function of the *guru* as teacher and final authority for
faith and conduct was vested in the community and
the Scriptures, the *Guru Granth Sahib*. It occupies
the same place in Sikh veneration that was given to
the living *gurus*.

The *Guru Granth Sahib* is at the heart of Sikh worship, and its presence lends sanctity to the Sikh place
of worship, the *gurdwara*. This holy book contains
devotional compositions written by the Sikh *gurus*,

recorded during their lifetimes. It also contains
hymns by Hindu and Muslim religious thinkers.
Written in Sanskrit, Persian, Hindi, and Punjabi, the
compositions are set in rhymed couplets. The *Guru
Granth Sahib* is printed in *Gurmukhi* script, an alpha-
bet adapted by the second *guru*, Guru Angad, for the
Punjabi language. It has standardized pagination: all
copies having 1,430 pages. The *Rehat Maryada* (Sikh
Code of Conduct) published in 1945 by the SGPC of
Amritsar, Punjab, India, regulates individual and
corporate Sikh life.

Beliefs

The seminal belief in Sikhism is found in the
Mool Mantra with which the *Guru Granth Sahib*
begins:

> There is One God. He
> > Is the Supreme Truth
> > Is without fear
> > Is not vindictive
> > Is Timeless, Eternal
> > Is not born, so
> > He does not die to be reborn.
> > Self-illumined,
> > By Guru's grace
> > He is revealed to the human soul.
> Truth was in the beginning, and throughout
> > the ages.
> Truth is now and ever will be.

In Sikhism, time is cyclical, not linear, so Sikhism
has no eschatological beliefs. Rather, just as time is
seen as repeated sequences of creation and destruction, individual existence is believed to be a repeated
sequence of birth, death, and rebirth as the soul seeks
spiritual enlightenment.

Sikhs believe that greed, lust, pride, anger, and
attachment to the passing values of earthly existence

constitute *haumai* (self-centeredness). This is the source of all evil. It is a person's inclination to evil that produces the *karma* that leads to endless rebirth. *Haumai* separates human beings from God.

God is All-Pervading and is the Source of all life. Sikhism believes that human life is the opportunity for spiritual union with the Supreme Being—to merge with the Ultimate Reality as a drop of water merges with the ocean and becomes one with it. Thus is one released from the cycle of death and rebirth. By God's Grace, not by one's own merits, is achieved the level of spiritual self-knowledge necessary to reach this stage of enlightenment. Any person, of whatever intellectual or economic level, may become enlightened through a life of single-minded devotion to God. Enlightenment, not redemption, is the Sikh concept of salvation.

Life-cycle events are recognized in Sikhism by naming of the newborn in the *gurdwara*, the marriage ceremony, and the funeral, following which the body is cremated. Any kind of funeral monument is forbidden.

Sikhism rejects asceticism and encourages full participation in family and workday life and responsibility as the framework within which to seek God. Sikhism is founded on the principle of equality of all persons. It rejects the caste system, and inculcates in its adherents an egalitarian attitude and practice toward men and women of all races, religions, and social classes.

Sikh names do not indicate gender. All Sikh men, therefore, take the additional name Singh (lion) and women take the name Kaur (princess). Guru Gobind Singh, the tenth *guru*, instructed his followers to drop their last names, which in India indicate one's caste. They are to use only Singh and Kaur to show their acceptance of the universal equality of all persons. Another symbol of the Sikhs' acceptance of universal equality is the *langar*. This is a meal that is eaten together by the congregation, shared food becoming a social leveler.

In adulthood, a Sikh is initiated into full membership by the *Amrit* ceremony, which was originated by the last human *guru* in 1699. At this time, the initiate promises to follow the Sikh code of conduct as an integral part of the path toward God-realization. He or she vows at that time:

- To abstain from the use of tobacco and/or other intoxicants.
- Never to cut the hair on any part of the body.
- Not to eat the meat of animals killed in a religious or sacrificial manner.
- To refrain totally from any sexual contact outside of marriage.
- To wear the five symbols of Sikhs.

Excerpts from *Guru Granth Sahib* (The Sikh Scriptures)

Meditation

"Meditation on the Name (of God)
Quenches thirst of the Soul.
Let us drink together
The Nectar treasure of the Lord's Name."

"In the garden of the soul,
Plant the seed of the Word (Lord's Name).
Water the soil with love and humility
And reap the fruits of divinity."

Waheguru (Sikh name for God)

"You are the Creator of all.
You give the soul, the body, and life.
We are meritless, without virtue.
Bless us, O Merciful Lord."

"He creates the Universe and then
    reveals Himself
To us and in us. He made Himself
    manifest."

Excerpts (*cont.*)

Service

"By doing service one loses one's egoistic nature and thereby gets respect from the society."

"The Supreme Lord is realized only by those who indulge in selfless service."

"We should do active service within the world if we want to attain everlasting bliss."

Environment

"The world is a garden, Waheguru (Sikh name for God) its gardener.

Cherishing all, none is neglected;

From all comes the fragrance put there by Waheguru—

By such fragrance is each known."

Caring and Human Rights

"Where the poor are cared for, the rain of Your (God's) gracious glance falls, O Lord."

"The sign of a good man is that he always seeks the welfare of others."

After this ceremony, the initiate is considered a part of the *Khalsa* (belonging to God) brotherhood, and is enjoined to tithe both time and income and to pray and meditate daily. He or she must live a moral life of service to mankind, in humility and honesty. The five symbols worn by the initiated Sikh are

1. Unshorn hair, over which men wear a turban
2. A comb
3. A steel bracelet
4. A short sword
5. A type of knickers usually worn under a Sikh's outer clothes.

The symbols most often associated with Sikhs as a group are the characters that symbolize One God, and an arrangement of three swords, called *khanda*.

Sikhs do not have a priestly order, nor monks, nor nuns. The Sikh clergyman is the *granthi*, who is encouraged to marry. Sikh congregations are autonomous. There is no ecclesiastic hierarchy. The *Akal Takhat* heads the five temporal seats of Sikh religious authority in India, which debates matters of concern to the Sikh community worldwide and issues edicts which are morally binding on Sikhs. These decisions are coordinated by the SGPC, which also manages Sikh shrines in India.

Formal Sikh worship consists mainly of singing of passages of the *Guru Granth Sahib* to the accompaniment of music. A passage of the *Guru Granth Sahib* is read aloud and expounded upon by the *granthi* at the conclusion of the religious service. The central prayer of Sikhs, *Ardas*, which simply means prayer, is recited by the *granthi* and the assembled congregation. This prayer gives a synopsis of Sikh history as well as being a supplication to God. Any Sikh with sufficient religious knowledge is permitted to conduct *gurdwara* worship in the absence of a *granthi*. All are welcome to religious services and to participate in the *langar* served after.

There are no denominations in Sikhism, but in the United States, in particular, there is grouping along language and cultural lines. The majority of Sikhs in the U.S. are immigrants of Indian origin, speak Punjabi, and have distinct customs and dress that originate in Punjab, India. Since the 1960s, however, there has existed a group, generally called American Sikhs, whose leader is Yogi Harbhajan Singh. American Sikhs are easily distinguished from others by their all-white attire and by the fact that turbans are worn by both men and women. This group now numbers about five thousand. The majority of American Sikhs, who refer to their group as 3HO (Healthy, Happy, Holy Organization), know only limited Punjabi. Indian Sikhs and American Sikhs are mutually accepting and visit one another's *gurdwaras*. Sikhs of Indian origin number approximately a half million in North America and approximately 21 million throughout the world.

Interfaith Dialogue

Interfaith dialogue and cooperation have been a part of Sikhism since the time of Guru Nanak, its founder. He did not attempt to convert the followers of other faiths but, rather, urged them to rediscover the internal significance of their beliefs and rituals, without forsaking their chosen paths. He indicated that because of human limitations, each group grasps only a narrow aspect of God's revelation. The Sikh *gurus* were opposed to any exclusive claim on truth which a particular religion might make.

Just as this indicates a pluralistic acceptance of the legitimacy of all faiths, and that all are valid, it indicates, too, an acceptance of all groups and individuals. Guru Arjan said: "All are co-equal partners in the Commonwealth with none treated as alien." (*Guru Granth Sahib*, p. 97)

Numerous examples show how this attitude has evidenced itself in Sikh history:

When compiling the manuscripts that would make up the *Guru Granth Sahib*, Guru Arjan included hymns written by both Hindu and Muslim religious thinkers. It is the only scripture which includes and sanctifies texts of people belonging to other faiths, whose spirit conformed to the spirit of Sikhism. There are also, in the *Guru Granth Sahib*, hymns written by persons considered by Hindus to be untouchables.

The holiest of Sikh shrines, the Golden Temple at Amritsar, has four doors, each facing a cardinal direction, to indicate that all are welcome. The cornerstone of the Golden Temple was laid by a Muslim holy man. The ninth *guru*, Guru Tegh Bahadur, died championing the rights of Hindus to practice their own religion.

In modern times, the lesson of equality that is taught by the *langar*, the meal eaten together by Sikh congregations, extends beyond caste obliteration to the acceptance and toleration of people of all races, creeds, and nationalities. Sikhs do not disparage other faiths, nor claim sole possession of the truth. Sikhs do not attempt to convert adherents of other faiths.

In North America, Sikh congregations belong to local interfaith associations and participate fully in efforts such as environmental protection campaigns, issues affecting children, AIDS, food, and other help for the homeless and displaced. In India, particularly, there are many free clinics operated by Sikhs that accept persons of all religions and castes as patients. In some North American cities, Sikhs have continued that tradition.

Since the intrinsic spirit of Sikhism is pluralistic, it has much to contribute towards interfaith and intercommunity accommodation. It is a willing partner in the emergence of a pluralistic world community that preserves the rights of human dignity and freedom for all human beings. In witness of this attitude, the *Ardas* recited at the end of a Sikh religious service ends with the words "May the whole world be blessed by your grace."

Responses to Social Problems

Gender equality: Sikhism recognizes each human being as a valuable creation of God, having a divine spark. Every human being has a right to live life free of religious, political, and economic exploitation. The Sikh *gurus* vehemently condemned the caste system in India that had divided the whole society into many hereditary castes and sub-castes. The lowest caste, the *untouchable*, was the most exploited of all, even to the extent of being barred from temples, as were all women of all castes.

In the time of the *gurus*, as is true in many places even now, women of all social levels were treated as property and grossly exploited. Rejecting the idea of female inequality, Guru Nanak said:

Man is nourished in the womb and born from a woman; he is betrothed and married to a woman. Friendship is made with women and civilization originates from a woman. When a wife dies, another wife is sought because family affairs depend upon a woman. Why call her bad, from whom are born kings? From a woman another woman is born; none is born without a woman.

Guru Nanak specifically forbade the practices of widow *sati* (self-immolation on the pyre of her husband). He encouraged the remarriage of widows, which was unheard of in his time. He was gravely concerned about the practice of female infanticide. Not only is it forbidden to Sikhs, but a Sikh cannot associate with anyone who kills his female children. In the name of equality, Guru Nanak abolished the custom of the bride's family giving the groom dowry, since this encourages men to think of women as commercial commodities.

In Sikh society, a woman occupies a position equal to men and is not prevented from fulfilling her potential through education, religion, or profession.

Environmental concerns: Conservation, preservation, restoration, and enrichment of environment have become major global issues at all political, social, and ethical levels. Into his beautiful creation, God has placed man with the power to enhance or destroy. Modern technology and man's greed and unconcern have made the potential for destruction of species, of the fertility of the land, of the viability of our waters, indeed of the world itself, a very real possibility. The Sikh Scriptures say:

Air the vital force,
water like the father,
and earth like the great mother.
Day and night are like nurses
caring for the whole world in their lap.

If air is our vital force, it is a sin, as well as self-destructive, to pollute it. If we consider water to be our progenitor, dumping industrial wastes in it is unforgivable disrespect. As we destroy the ozone layer, the cycle that manufactures chlorophyll in green plants is damaged or interrupted; since plants are part of the air-producing cycle, we strangle ourselves.

Sikhism seeks to give to humankind a progressive and responsible philosophy as a guide to all of the world's concerns. Recognizing that there is a part of the divine in all that He created, we must recognize the interdependence of all generations, species, and resources. We must preserve what was passed to us

and pass it on in a healthy and robust condition.

The Sikh response to AIDS: During the time of Guru Arjan (1563–1606), leprosy was considered by most of the world's population, Indians included, to be a form of Divine retribution for a person's transgressions. Sikhs have, from the time of their founding, rejected the idea that God is vindictive, wreaking vengeance on humankind. To show his rejection of this concept, to show that lepers were not to be feared and that they deserve compassion and care, Guru Arjan set up a treatment area for lepers in the city of Lahore, and himself spent a year there serving them.

In this supposedly modern age, AIDS victims face the same kind of prejudice and fear. Sikhs follow the example of Guru Arjan and join in the care of those who are ill and dying of this terrible virus, as well as join in vocally pushing for more research to find a cure. Service and compassion characterize the Sikh approach to AIDS.

The Sikh scriptures say, " . . . God dwells in you, unaffected, like the image in a mirror." Recognizing that God dwells in all, Sikhs reach out to those with AIDS, offering whatever service is needed.

Service to Humanity

A cornerstone of the Sikh faith is the concept of *seva*, the selfless service of the community—not just the Sikh community, but the community of humanity. Bhai Gurdas, the early Sikh theologian whose *Vars* (poems) are highly respected by Sikhs, says, "Service of one's fellows is a sign of divine worship." What one does in selfless service is considered to be real prayer. When one prays or meditates, it is often done for the good of one's own soul or to supplicate for one's own imagined needs. A Sikh who, with no thought of reward, serves others, performs the truest form of worship, whether he is feeding the homeless or bringing company and compassion to an AIDS sufferer.

Among the lowly, I am lowliest of the low.

My place is with them. What have I to do with the
*   great?*   (*Guru Granth Sahib*, p. 15)

Sikhs are instructed to pray, before they eat, that a needy person will come and share their food. This attitude toward each person's role in achieving social justice motivates Sikhs to actively participate in ensuring that the poor in the world community, as well as in the local community, are fed, clothed, and sheltered, and motivates them to be part of finding long-term solutions.

Chapter Fourteen
SPIRITUAL, ESOTERIC, AND EVOLUTIONARY PHILOSOPHIES

NOTE: The several different philosophies and organizations represented in this chapter are only a sampling of numerous systems that might also have been included. While each of these has its own character, including differences of belief and practice from the others, the groups or philosophies represented here seem to this Editor to have the following elements in common:

1. Belief in and promoting the spiritual evolution of both individuals and the human race within a new civilization, as part of a larger cosmic scenario

2. A focus on personal spiritual practice and experience, not on doctrines and dogma

3. Belief in the interpenetration of the material by the spiritual—thus they teach the spiritual or esoteric (hidden) meanings of experience, religions, and scriptures

4. A claim not to be a religion, though applauding the best ethics and wisdom from all religions; some encourage students to enrich their own traditions with insights derived from spiritual philosophy and from other religions

5. Paying particular attention to certain revealed or inspired sources of information and/or to charismatic figures who provide information, analysis, and leadership—at the same time, encouraging personal independence

6. Tracing their roots back to "ageless wisdom" or ancient, perennial philosophy, though the organization or concepts taught have reemerged in the past 125 years.

Anthroposophy: Toward a More Human Future

Echoing the ancient Greek axiom, "Man, know thyself," Rudolf Steiner, the founder of anthroposophy, described it as "awareness of one's humanity." Nowhere is the need for such awareness greater than in relation to our fellow human beings, and to the life and work we share with them. It is this awareness that lies at the heart of the practical work fostered by the worldwide General Anthroposophical Society, which Steiner founded in 1923 as "an association of people who would foster the life of the soul,

both in the individual and in human society, on the basis of a true knowledge of the spiritual world."

Rudolf Steiner (1861–1925) was born in lower Austria and grew up with the clairvoyant certainty of a spiritual world. Recognizing the need to reconcile the experience of the supersensible realities with that of the material world, he schooled himself in modern science and philosophy, and developed anthroposophy as a "spiritual science." Steiner was active in the cultural and social life of his day, and shared the results of his spiritual research in over six thousand lectures and forty books. He is increasingly recognized as a seminal thinker of the 20th century and one of humanity's great spiritual teachers.

Anthroposophy embraces a spiritual view of the human being and the cosmos, but its emphasis is on knowing, not faith. It is a path in which the human heart and hand, and especially our capacity for thinking, are essential. It leads, in Steiner's words, "from the spirit in the human being to the spirit in the universe." Humanity (*anthropos*) has the inherent wisdom (*sophia*) to transform both itself and the world. Today, when many aspects of our culture are in crisis, and people are easily drawn into cynicism and despair, anthroposophy's vision of human potential is a source of hope and renewal.

Since Steiner's death in 1925, many people have sought to continue his research through study, reflection, and meditation, and to apply it in many areas of human endeavor. The international center for this work is the School for Spiritual Science, at the Goetheanum in Dornach, Switzerland. The Society is entirely non-sectarian and nonpolitical, but its activities range across many disciplines and interests, including the following:

• Waldorf Schools (500 worldwide) place as much emphasis on creativity and moral judgment as on intellectual growth, with reverence for beauty, goodness, truth, and freedom as the goals.

- Adult education balances study with inner development and creative work.
- Medical practice is holistic, treating body, soul, and spirit.
- Biodynamic agriculture relates to the earth as a living organism, utilizing sustainable and organic processes.
- Eurythmy translates the sounds, phrasing, and rhythms of speech and music into movement and gesture.
- Other work with the arts, cooperative projects, health products, and publishing demonstrate principles of anthroposophy.

"Anthroposophy intends to be a living presence; it wants to use words, concepts, and ideas so that something living may shine down from the spiritual world into the physical. Anthroposophy does not only want to impart knowledge, it seeks to awaken life."

R. STEINER
—compiled by the Editor from brochures published by the Anthroposophical Society in North America: *Toward a More Human Future* and *Rudolf Steiner*

The Arcane School

The Arcane School was established by Mrs. Alice A. Bailey in 1923 to help meet an obvious and growing demand for further teaching and training in the science of the soul. The School is one of many activities of the Lucis Trust.

The purpose of the esoteric training given in the Arcane School is to help the student grow spiritually toward acceptance of discipleship responsibility and to serve the Plan of the spiritual hierarchy by serving humanity. Esotericism is a practical way of life. The function of the School is to assist those at the end of the probationary path to move forward on to the path of discipleship, and to assist those already on that path to move on more quickly and to achieve greater effectiveness in service.

A disciple is one who, above all else, is pledged to do three things: (a) to serve humanity, (b) to cooperate with the Plan as he sees it and as best he may, and (c) to develop the powers of the soul, to expand his consciousness, and to follow the guidance of the higher self and not the dictates of his threefold lower self.

Discipleship is a word in constant use among aspirants in the world, both in the East and in the West. Discipleship could be defined as the final stage of the path of evolution. It is the stage in which a man knowingly pledges himself to impose the will of the soul (which is essentially the will of God) upon the lower nature. Upon this path he submits himself to a training process through a systematized and applied discipline, producing a more rapid unfoldment of the power and the life of the soul.

The training given in the Arcane School is based on three fundamental requirements—occult meditation, study, and service to humanity. The Arcane School is a place for hard work. The presentation of the teaching adapted to the rapidly emerging new civilization includes the training of disciples in group formation and group meditation and study, helping to precipitate the ideas on which the new civilization and culture will be founded. The work of the Arcane School all over the world is carried forward entirely by correspondence with one of three headquarters.

The Arcane School is nonsectarian, and respects the right of each student to hold his own view and beliefs. It does not rely upon an authoritarian presentation of any one line of thought or code of ethics. The knowledge, insight wisdom, and capacity to wield spiritual energy resulting from work and training with the Arcane School should be expressed and applied in daily living service in helping to materialize the Plan of God and to aid in solving the problems of humanity.

—compiled by the Editor from materials provided by Lucis Trust

Testimony and Treasure

"In every race and nation, in every climate and part of the world, and throughout the endless reaches of time itself, back into the limitless past, men have found the Path to God; they have trodden it and accepted its conditions, endured its disciplines, rested back in confidence upon its realities, received its rewards and found their goal. Arrived there, they have 'entered into the joy of the Lord,' participated in the mysteries of the kingdom of heaven, dwelt in the glory of the divine Presence, and then returned to the ways of men, to serve. The testimony to the existence of this Path is the priceless treasure of all the great religions and its witnesses are those who have transcended all forms and all theologies, and have penetrated into the world of meaning which all symbols veil."

—Alice A. Bailey, *The Externalization of the Hierarchy,*
      p. 405

The Great Invocation

This world prayer is translated into over fifty languages and dialects. It expresses certain central truths that all men innately and normally accept:

- That there exists a basic intelligence to whom we give the name of God.
- That there is a divine evolutionary Plan in the universe—the motivating power of which is love.
- That a great individuality called by Christians the Christ—the World Teacher—came to Earth and embodied that love so that we could understand that love and intelligence are effects of the purpose, and the will, and the Plan of God. Many religions believe in a World Teacher, knowing him under such names as the Lord Maitreya, the Imam Mahdi, and the Messiah.
- Only through humanity itself can the divine Plan work out.

From the point of Light within the Mind of God
Let light stream forth into the minds of men.
Let Light descend on Earth.

From the point of Love within the Heart of God
Let love stream forth into the hearts of men.

May Christ return to Earth.

From the center where the Will of God is known
Let purpose guide the little wills of men—
The purpose which the Masters know and serve.

From the center which we call the race of men
Let the Plan of Love and Light work out.
And may it seal the door where evil dwells.

Let Light and Love and Power
Restore the Plan on Earth.

The Evolutionary Philosophy of Sri Aurobindo and the Mother

Sri Aurobindo is the highly respected author of thirty volumes of philosophy, poetry, political essays, and spiritual discourse. A scholar and political activist in India at the turn of this century, he withdrew to the reclusive, though prolific, life of a mystic following spiritual experiences he had while in prison. Sri Aurobindo's vision inspired the founding of the experimental community of Auroville in India. Selections from his writings follow:

"At once a first question arises—is this world an unchanging succession of the same phenomena always or is there in it an evolutionary urge, an evolutionary fact, a ladder of ascension somewhere from an original apparent *inconscience* to a more and more developed consciousness, from each development still ascending, emerging on highest heights not yet within our normal reach? If so, what is the sense, the fundamental principle, the logical issue of that progression? Everything seems to point to such a progression as a fact—to a spiritual and not merely a physical evolution."

"This erring race of human beings dreams always of perfecting its environment by the machinery of Government and society, but it is only by the perfection of the soul within that the outer environment can be perfected. What thou art within, that outside thee thou shalt enjoy, no machinery can rescue thee from the law of thy being."

"Consciousness is a fundamental thing, the fundamental thing in existence—it is the energy, the motion, the movement of consciousness that creates the universe and all that is in it—not only the macrocosm but the microcosm is nothing but consciousness arranging itself. For instance, when consciousness in its movement or rather a certain stress of movement forgets itself in the action it becomes an apparently "unconscious" energy; when it forgets itself in the form it becomes the electron, the atom, the material object. In reality it is still consciousness that works in the energy and determines the form and the evolution of form. When it wants to liberate itself, slowly, evolutionarily, out of Matter, but still in the form, it emerges as life, as animal, as man and it can go on evolving itself still farther out of its involution and become something more than mere man."

The Mother

Sri Aurobindo's longtime student and companion, the Mother (Mirra Alfassa), continued his work, founding Auroville and helping to spread the vision worldwide. The Mother also wrote a thirteen-volume *Agenda* on her experiences and explorations in the expression of consciousness that resides within the body's cellular structure, as well as twelve volumes of collected conversations and writings.

"If we want to find a true solution to the confusion, the chaos, and the misery of the world, we have to find it in the world itself. In fact, it is to be found only there: it exists latent, one has to bring it out. It is neither mystical nor imaginary, but altogether concrete, furnished by Nature herself, if we know how to observe her. For Nature's is an ascending movement; out of one form, one species, she brings forth a new one capable of manifesting something more of the universal consciousness. All go to

prove that man is not the last step in terrestrial evolution. The human species will necessarily be succeeded by a new one which will be to man what man is to the animal; the present human consciousness will be replaced by a new consciousness, no more mental, but supramental. . . .

"The time is come when this possibility . . . must become a reality lived upon earth."

> —These excerpts from the writings of Sri Aurobindo and the Mother are printed in a brochure titled "Introduction to Auroville." Used with permission.

A Portrait of Theosophy

Dr. John Algeo

President of the Theosophical Society in America

About Theosophy

The modern Theosophical movement dates from the founding of the Theosophical Society in New York City in 1875 by Helena Petrovna Blavatsky, Henry Steel Olcott, William Quan Judge, and others. The movement, however, views itself as a contemporary expression of a tradition going back to the Neo-Platonists of Classical antiquity (hence the name) and earlier. Primary concepts are

1. The fundamental unity of all existence, so that all dichotomies—matter and spirit, the human and the divine, I and thou—are seen as transitory and relative distinctions of an underlying absolute Oneness

2. The regularity of universal law, cyclically producing universes out of the absolute ground of being

3. The progress of consciousness developing through the cycles of life to an ever-increasing realization of Unity.

Theosophy is nondogmatic, but many Theosophists believe in reincarnation; *karma* (or moral justice); the existence of worlds of experience beyond the physical; the presence of life and consciousness

Wisdom in the Theosophical Tradition

"Help Nature and work on with her; and Nature will regard thee as one of her creators and make obeisance."[sl. 66]

"To live to benefit mankind is the first step." [sl. 144]

H. P. BLAVATSKY,
The Voice of the Silence, 1889

"There is a road, steep and thorny, beset with perils of every kind, but yet a road, and it leads to the very heart of the Universe: I can tell you how to find those who will show you the secret gateway that opens inward only, and closes fast behind the neophyte for evermore. There is no danger that dauntless courage cannot conquer; there is no trial that spotless purity cannot pass through; there is no difficulty that strong intellect cannot surmount. For those who win onwards, there is reward past all telling—the power to bless and save humanity; for those who fail, there are other lives in which success may come."

H. P. BLAVATSKY,
1891, CW 13:219

"O hidden Life,
*   vibrant in every atom,*
O hidden Light,
*   shining in every creature,*
O hidden Love,
*   embracing all in oneness,*
May all who feel themselves
*   as one with thee*
Know they are therefore one
*   with every other."*

ANNIE BESANT

in all matter; the evolution of spirit and intelligence as well as matter; the possibility of conscious participation in evolution; the power of thought to affect one's self and surroundings; free will and self-responsibility; and the duty of altruism, a concern for the welfare of others.

These beliefs often lead to such practices as meditation, vegetarianism and care for animal welfare, active support of women's and minority rights, and a concern for ecology.

Knowledge of such ideas and practices derives from the traditions of cultures spread over the world from antiquity to the present in a "perennial philosophy" or "ancient wisdom," held to be fundamentally identical in all cultures. But it also derives from the experiences of individuals through the practice of meditation and the development of insight. No Theosophist is asked to accept any opinion or adopt any practice that does not appeal to the inner sense of reason and morality.

Theosophy has no developed rituals. Meetings typically consist of talks and discussion or the study of a book, although they may be opened and closed by brief meditations or the recitation of short texts. There are no privileged symbols in Theosophy, but various symbols from the religious traditions of the world are used, such as the interlaced triangles and the *ankh*.

Today there are three main Theosophical organizations. Membership statistics are not available for all of them, but the American section of the society with international headquarters in Madras, India, has a membership of about five thousand. There are associated groups in about fifty countries.

Theosophy in the World Today

The first object of the Theosophical Society is (in one wording), "To form a nucleus of the Universal Brotherhood of Humanity without distinction of race, creed, sex, caste, or color"; and the second is, "To encourage the study of comparative religion, philosophy, and science." As those objects indicate, Theosophy is dedicated to increasing cooperation among human beings and understanding among their cultures and religions.

Theosophy holds that all religions are expressions of humanity's effort to relate to one another, to the universe around us, and to the ultimate ground of being. Particular religions differ from one another because they are expressions of that effort adapted to particular times, places, cultures, and needs. Theosophy is not itself a religion, although it is religious, in being concerned with the effort to relate. Individual Theosophists profess various of the world's religions—Christian, Jewish, Moslem, Zoroastrian, Hindu, Buddhist; others have no religious affiliation.

The Theosophical Society has, from the time of its founding, promoted dialogue and cooperation among the religious traditions of humanity, since we regard them all as varying expressions of a basic human need and impulse. The Society itself is an expression of the faith that human beings, however diverse their backgrounds, can communicate and cooperate.

Primary Challenges and Issues Facing Humanity

Humanity is faced by a range of seemingly insuperable problems: uncontrolled population growth, diminishing resources, exploitation of one group by another, ancient animosities, passion for revenge, racial antagonism, religious prejudice, territorial ambition, destructive use of the environment, oppression of women, disregard of the rights of others, greed for wealth and power, and so on. In the Theosophical view, all these are secondary or derivative problems—the symptoms of a disease. The primary, original problem, the cause of the disease, is the illusion of separateness, the notion that we are unconnected, independent beings whose particular welfare can be achieved at the expense of the general good.

The primary challenge facing humanity is therefore to recognize the unity of our species and in turn our ultimate unity with all life in the universe. Despite the superficial cultural and genetic differences that divide humanity, we are a remarkably homogeneous species—physically, psychologically, intellectually, and spiritually. Biologically, we are a single human gene pool, with only minor local variations. Psychologically and intellectually, we respond to stimuli in fundamentally the same way. Linguistically, behind the surface variations of the world's tongues, our underlying language ability is remarkably uniform. Spiritually, we have a common origin and a common destiny.

Neither is the human species isolated from the rest of life in the universe. We are part and parcel of the totality of existence stretching from this planet Earth to the farthest reaches of the cosmos in every conceivable dimension. When we realize our integral connection with all other human beings, with all other life-forms, with the most distant reaches of space, we will realize that we cannot either harm or help another without harming or helping ourselves. We are all one, not as metaphor, but as fact.

Individual Theosophists engage in social, political, and charitable action as they are moved by their consciences and sense of duty to become so engaged. They are urged by the Theosophical tradition to realize the concept of Unity in practical responses to the challenges we face. Collectively and as Theosophists, however, we do not regard it as our special calling to be social, political, or charitable activists. Theosophy addresses the cause rather than the

"It is well known that the first rule of the society is to carry out the object of forming the nucleus of a universal brotherhood. The practical working of this rule was explained by those who laid it down, to the following effect:

"'He who does not practice altruism; he who is not prepared to share his last morsel with a weaker or poorer than himself; he who neglects to help his brother man, of whatever race, nation, or creed, whenever and wherever he meets suffering, and who turns a deaf ear to the cry of human misery; he who hears an innocent person slandered, whether a brother Theosophist or not, and does not undertake his defense as he would undertake his own—is no Theosophist.'"

H. P. BLAVATSKY,
"Let Every Man Prove His Own Work,"
1887, CW 8:170–71

"There is but one way of ever ameliorating human life and it is by the love of one's fellow man for his own sake and not for personal gratification. The greatest Theosophist—he who loves divine truth under all its forms—is the one who works for and with the poor."

H. P. BLAVATSKY,
"Misconceptions," 1887, CW 8:77

Wisdom (cont.)

*"The Society was founded to teach no new
and easy paths to the acquisition of
'powers'; . . . its only mission is to re-kindle
the torch of truth, so long extinguished for
all but the very few, and to keep that truth
alive by the formation of a fraternal union
of mankind, the only soil in which the good
seed can grow."*

H. P. BLAVATSKY,
"Spiritual Progress," 1885, CW 6:333

*"The path of right progress should include
the amelioration of the individual, the
nation, the race, and humanity; and ever
keeping in view the last and grandest
object, the perfecting of man, should reject
all apparent bettering of the individual at
the expense of his neighbor."*

H. P. BLAVATSKY,
"The Struggle for Existence," 1889,
CW 11:151–52

*"If Theosophy [is] prevailing in the
struggle, its all-embracing philosophy strikes
deep root into the minds and hearts of
men, if its doctrines of Reincarnation and
Karma, in other words, of Hope and
Responsibility, find a home in the lives of
the new generations, then, indeed, will
dawn the day of joy and gladness for all
who now suffer and are outcast. For real
Theosophy is Altruism, and we cannot
repeat it too often. It is brotherly love,
mutual help, unswerving devotion to
Truth. If once men do but realize that in
these alone can true happiness be found,
and never in wealth, possessions or any
selfish gratification, then the dark clouds
will roll away, and a new humanity will be
born upon earth. Then, the Golden Age
will be there, indeed."*

H. P. BLAVATSKY,
"Our Cycle and the Next," 1889,
CW 11:202

symptoms of the human disease. Theosophy seeks to make humanity aware—intellectually, affectively, and experientially—of our
unity with one another and with the whole universe. From such
awareness will flow naturally and inevitably a respect for differences,
a wise use of the environment, the fair treatment of others, a sympathy with the afflictions of our neighbors, and the will to respond
to those afflictions helpfully and lovingly.

Chapter Fifteen
TAOISM

A Portrait

Dr. Douglas K. Chung

Professor at Grand Valley State University School of Social Work, Grand Rapids, Michigan

Li Erh (6th century B.C.E.) commonly known as Lao Tzu (the Old Master), was a contemporary of Confucius. He was the keeper of the imperial library, but in his old age he disappeared to the west, leaving behind him the *Tao Te Ching (Book of Tao and Virtue)*.

Taoism derived its name from this profoundly wise book, only about five thousand words in length. It can be used as a guide to the cultivation of the self as well as a political manual for social transformation at both the micro and macro levels. The philosophy of Taoism and its belief in immortals can be traced back to the Yellow Emperor, Huang-Ti. That is why Taoism is often called the "Huang-Lao" philosophy.

Taoism believes *Tao* to be the cosmic, mysterious, and ultimate principle underlying form, substance, being, and change. *Tao* encompasses everything. It can be used to understand the universe and nature as well as the human body. For example, "*Tao* gives birth to the One, the One gives birth to Two, and from Two emerges Three, Three gives birth to all the things. All things carry the *Yin* and the *Yang* deriving their vital harmony from the proper blending of the two vital forces" (*Tao Te Ching*, ch. 42).

Tao is the cause of change and the source of all nature, including humanity. Everything from quanta to solar systems consists of two primary elements of existence, *Yin* and *Yang* forces, which represent all opposites. These two forces are complementary elements in any system and result in the harmony or balance of the system. All systems coexist in an interdependent network. The dynamic tension between *Yin* and *Yang* forces in all systems results in an endless process of change: production and reproduction and the transformation of energy. This is the natural order.

Tao and virtue are said to be the same coin with different sides. The very title *Tao Te Ching* means the canon of *Tao* and virtue. Lao Tzu says, "The Highest Virtue is achieved through non-action. It does not require effort," because virtue is natural to people. This is

"Trees and animals, humans and insects, flowers and birds: these are active images of the subtle energies that flow from the stars throughout the universe. Meeting and combining with each other and the elements of the Earth, they give rise to all living things. The superior person understands this, and understands that her own energies play a part in it. Understanding these things, she respects the Earth as her mother, the heavens as her father, and all living things as her brothers and sisters."

"Those who want to know the truth of the universe should practice . . . reverence for all life; this manifests as unconditional love and respect for oneself and all other beings."

LAO TZU
(trans. by Brian Walker)

"If you want to nourish a bird, you should let it live any way it chooses. Creatures differ because they have different likes and dislikes. Therefore the sages never require the same ability from all creatures. . . . The true saint leaves wisdom to the ants, takes a cue from the fishes, and leaves willfulness to the sheep."

CHANG TZU

Interconnectedness

what is meant by "*Tao* creates and Virtue sustains" (ch. 51).

Taoists believe that *Tao* has appeared in the form of sages and teachers of humankind, as, for example, Fu Hsi, the giver of the *Pa Qua* (eight trigrams) and the arts of divination to reveal the principles of *Tao*. The *Pa Qua* is the foundation of the *I Ching* and represents the eight directions of the compass associated with the forces of nature that make up the universe. There are two forms of the *Pa Qua*: the *Pa Qua* of the Earlier Heaven (the *Ho To*), which describes the ideal state of existence, and the *Pa Qua* of Later Heaven (*Lo Shu*), which describes a state of disharmonious existence. The path of the *Return to the Tao* is the process of transforming Later Heaven into Earlier Heaven. In other words, it is the process of a reunification with *Tao*, of being transformed from a conflicting mode to a harmonious mode.

The conflicting mode is the destructive or waning cycle of the Five Elements (metal, wood, earth, water, and fire). The destructive cycle consists of metal destroying wood (axes cutting trees); wood dominating earth as the roots of the trees dig into the ground (power domination); earth mastering water and preventing the flood (anti-nature forces); water destroying fire (anti-nature causes pollution that destroys the beauty of the world); and fire melting metals (pollution).

Taoists believe that through both personal and social transformation we can convert the destructive cycle of the Five Elements into a creative cycle of the Five Elements—to change from a conflicting mode of life into a supportive way of living. The creative cycle of the Five Elements is this: metal in the veins of the earth nourishes the underground waters (purification); water gives life to vegetation and creates wood (nourishment); wood feeds fire to create ashes forming earth (nature recycling). The cycle is completed when metal is formed in the veins of the earth. The path of the Return to the *Tao* is clearly needed in light of today's concerns about energy and environment.

Taoism believes in the value of life. Taoists do not focus on life after death, but rather emphasize practi-cal methods of cultivating health to achieve longevity. Therefore, Taoism teaches people to enhance their health and longevity by minimizing their desires and centering themselves on stillness. Taoists firmly believe that human lives are in our control. For example, Lao Tzu promotes *chi-kung* (breathing exercise) to enhance life (ch. 5, 20, 52). He offers three methods of life enhancement: 1) keeping original "oneness," that is, to integrate energy, *chi*, and spirit; 2) maintaining one's vital energy in order to retain the flexibility and adaptability a newborn baby has; 3) persisting in practice for longevity (ch. 10, 52, 59). To practice *chi-kung* is to practice the path of the *Return to the Tao* on an individual level to integrate physical, emotional, and spiritual development for health and longevity.

Taoism advocates nonaggressive, nonviolent, peaceful coexistence of states. For example, Lao Tzu describes an ideal state as one in which people love their own country and lifestyle so much that, even though the next country is so close the citizens can hear its roosters crowing and its dogs barking, they are content to die of old age without ever having gone to see it (ch. 80). Lao Tzu regards weapons as the tools of violence; all decent people detest them. He recommends that the proper demeanor after a military victory should be the same as that at a funeral (ch. 31).

Taoism advocates a minimum of government intervention, relying instead on individual development to reach a natural harmony under *Tao*'s leading. To concentrate on individual development is to practice the path of the *Return to the Tao* on a macro level. Lao Tzu writes:

The *Tao* never does anything, yet through it all things are done. (ch. 37)

If you want to be a great leader, you must learn to follow the *Tao*. Stop trying to control. Let go of fixed plans and concepts, and the world will govern itself. The more prohibitions you have, the less virtuous people will be. The more weapons you have, the less secure people will be.

The more subsidies you have, the less self-reliant people will be. (ch. 57)

Act without doing, work without effort. Think of the small as large and the few as many. Confront the difficult while it is still easy; accomplish the great task by a series of small acts. The Master never reaches for the great; thus achieves greatness. (ch. 63)

Prevent trouble before it arises. Put things in order before they exist. The giant pine tree grows from a tiny sprout. The journey of a thousand miles starts from your first step. (ch. 64)

Lao Tzu's view of social distribution is this:

Tao adjusts excess and deficiency so that there is perfect balance. It takes from what is too much and gives to what isn't enough. Those who try to control, who use force to protect their power, go against the direction of the *Tao*. They take from those who don't have enough and give to those who have far too much. (ch. 77)

Basically, Taoists promote a way of life that exhibits six characteristics (Ho, 1988):

1. Determining and working with the Tao when making changes

2. Basing one's life on the *laissez faire* principle—let nature follow its own course as its guideline for change

3. Modeling one's life on the sage, on nature, and thus on the *Tao*

4. Emphasizing the *Tao's* strategy of reversal transformation

5. Focusing on simplicity and originality

6. Looking for intuitive awareness and insight and de-emphasizing rational and intellectual efforts.

These characteristics are the essential Taoist guidelines for personal and social development.

Taoism in the World Today

The people of the world today are confronted with the problems of environmental pollution, fragmentation, competition, dehumanization, and no common agreement on what constitutes an ideal society. In this world of conflict and unrest, a world that is nevertheless interdependent, Taoists still search to provide natural ways of solving problems. They gain the strength to transform their own lives and thereby to fulfill their mission. They try to help individuals as well as societies to transform from a way of life based on conflict to a harmonious way of life.

The practitioners of Taoism and those who are influenced by its philosophy include environmentalists, naturalists, libertarians, wildlife protectors, natural food advocates or vegetarians, and many physicists. More and more Westerners are able to appreciate Taoism through international contacts and Taoist literature.

Two leading teachers in North America are Dr. Eva Wong and Chungliang A. Huang. Dr. Wong, the director of studies at Fung Loy Kok Taoist Temple, is a member of the state of Colorado's Interfaith Advisory Council to the governor. She translated *Cultivating Stillness: A Taoist Manual for Transforming Body and Mind* (1992). She also offers graduate-level courses on Taoist and Buddhist philosophy at the University of Denver. Fung Loy Kok Taoist Temple has branch temples in the United States and in Canada. These temples offer various activities, including scripture study, lectures, meditation, classes in *chi-kung*, cooking, retreats, *kung-fu*, and training in traditional Lion Dance.

Chungliang A. Huang formed the Living Tao Foundation to promote Tao sports and to publish various books related to Tao. Many people practice *chi-kung*, *Tai-chi chuan*, and acupuncture daily even without knowing that they are practicing Taoism.

Chapter Sixteen
THE UNIFICATION CHURCH

"The world is fast becoming one global village. The survival and prosperity of all are dependent on a spirit of cooperation. The human race must recognize itself as one family of man."

REV. SUN MYUNG MOON,
in *The Healing of the World*, 1993

"History is calling for reconciliation, compassion, love, service, and sacrifice. Today's problems cannot be solved by the logic of power . . . our present problems can only be solved by the logic of love."

HAK JA HAN MOON,
in *The Healing of the World*, 1993

A Portrait

Dr. Frank Kaufmann

Executive Director, Inter-Religious Federation for World Peace

The Unification Church is best understood in the context of the larger work of Reverend Moon and Mrs. Moon. In addition to heading the Unification Church, Reverend Moon and Mrs. Moon have founded and support dozens of initiatives for world peace in all spheres of human endeavor. Of special note are the Inter-Religious Federation for World Peace, The International Federation for World Peace and the Women's Federation for World Peace. These are surrounded by a constellation of cultural, educational, relief, and humanitarian projects. Two important elements must be considered in order to develop an accurate grasp of the Unification Church: 1) the teachings which guide the Unification community, namely the *Divine Principle*; and 2) the status of Reverend and Mrs. Moon.

Reverend Moon was born in what is now North Korea, January 6, 1920, during the period of brutal Japanese occupation. The fifth of eight children, Sun Myung Moon came from a family well respected for its great hospitality and who were referred to as "those who could live without law," a Korean phrase indicating people who were capable of guiding themselves by conscience alone. Reverend Moon's religious foundations combined the ancient traditions of Korea with the message of Christian missionaries. According to Reverend Moon, Jesus appeared to him while deep in prayer on a Korean mountainside, on Easter Sunday, 1936. Jesus asked him to complete the responsibility left unfinished since the origin of humankind. From that point the life of Sun Myung Moon changed dramatically. For nine years he researched the Bible, the natural world, and the spiritual world to produce what is known today as the *Divine Principle*.

The *Divine Principle* is divided into three sections—Creation, Fall, and Restoration. It teaches that God's original ideal is expressed in "the three great blessings" found in the Genesis account of human origins. To "be fruitful" is understood as the commission for each person to perfect his or her unique individuality by uniting mind and body and being in full union with God.

These perfected individuals, man and woman, were to "multiply," forming families born of the unconditional love of a husband for his wife, of a wife for her husband. It is taught that the original human couple were thus to become "True Parents." This ever-expanding family should "have dominion," namely establish a perfect ecological relationship with the natural universe. This ideal was not achieved by the first human ancestors, who instead violated God's commandment "not to eat the forbidden fruit," by engaging in physical love without receiving God's blessing to do so. This act of disobedience, in which the Archangel Lucifer participated, created the personage of Satan and bound the first human ancestors with him. Satan participates in human affairs through the perpetuation of impure love and lineage.

Salvation providence reveals God's work to re-create the conditions for 1) the fulfillment of the original three great blessings, and 2) to liberate the descendants of Adam and Eve from their bondage to Satan. This task constitutes the mission of the Messiah, who by the fulfillment of his own responsibility obeys the commandment and fulfills the purpose of creation. Thus Jesus came both as "Adam" and as the Savior to fulfill the three blessings and to liberate all of humankind. The faithlessness of those around Jesus led to his crucifixion, thus preventing him from his opportunity to fulfill the three great blessings. The divine love of Jesus, however, preserved the mission of Savior, allowing Jesus to pro-vide spiritual salvation to those who believe in him and follow his teachings. Jesus promised the "second coming of Christ," knowing that the original will of God, the three blessings, remained unfulfilled despite his own ministry. It is this original mission that Jesus asked Sun Myung Moon to fulfill in 1936.

In the 20th century Sun Myung Moon came as the return of Christ (at the end of World War II, in 1945), but, like Jesus, he was rejected. When this failure occurred, Reverend Moon was forced to establish a religious community that could carry out the mission of Christianity and serve as the Bride of Christ. This community became known as the Unification Church, founded in 1954. In 1960 Reverend Moon married Hak Ja Han Moon, thus fulfilling for the first time in human history the original mission of True Parents. Unification Church members and members of other religions have their marriages "blessed" by Reverend and Mrs. Moon, whereby they inherit the potential to themselves become True Parents.

The mission of the True Parents and Savior is to all people in all religions. The Unification "Church" does not desire to be an enduring religious body. Long before the Unification Church appeared, each world religion was already instructed to await and receive the one who will end evil history and restore an unbroken relationship between God and all humanity. The Unification Church exists to teach the Divine Principle and support the effort of the True Parents freely to give the blessing.

Chapter Seventeen
THE UNITARIAN UNIVERSALIST CHURCH

A History of Diversity and Openness

The Rev. David A. Johnson

Pastor, First Parish in Brookline, Massachusetts

The Unitarian Universalist Association is the modern institutional embodiment of two separate denominations that grew out of movements and faith traditions which extend back to the Christian Reformation era (14–16th centuries C.E.) and well beyond. Universalist convictions are found as early as the church father Origen, who declared that all creation would ultimately be drawn back to its divine source and that nothing and no one would be ultimately and forever excluded.

In its conviction that God is ultimately and absolutely One, Unitarian thought has been a recurring *heresy* within the established church since the 1st century of the Christian era.

The Roumanian-Transylvanian Unitarian Church, now more than four centuries old, stems originally from the sceptical and evangelical rationalist movements within the Roman Catholic Church and the openness engendered in the Reformation era. Its faith and struggle, and that of Socinianism in Poland and the Low Countries, became a fertile seeding ground for the beginnings of British Unitarian thought and structure. American Unitarianism has its own primary roots in the liberal Christian movement within New England's old Puritan establishment; a formal break with that tradition produced the American Unitarian Association in 1825.

Unitarian faith rejected Calvinist double predestination—the belief that original sin fatally flaws all human character—and the doctrine of the full and absolute personhood of each member of the Trinity. Instead, Unitarians affirmed the just and loving character of God, the God-given moral and reasoning capacity of all people, working out one's salvation through both diligence and God's grace, and, above all, one God.

Universalist institutional roots are in the Radical Reformation, intertwined with the histories of several Anabaptist, Separatist, and Pietist movements. The Universalists first organized separately in Britain as an offshoot of the Wesleyan Methodists. What was to become the Universalist Church of America was first gathered in September of 1793, making 1993 its 200th Anniversary. Universalism in this country found its supporters chiefly from Protestants disaffected by the bitter sectarian enthusiasms of much of American Protestantism, whose theologies condemned the great mass of humankind to eternal perdition. Many of those who could not believe that an everlasting fiery pit awaited all who lacked a proper faith and salvation experience joined the Universalists in the heady revival era of the late 18th and early 19th centuries.

Both the Unitarian and Universalist denominations were democratic in church polity and organizational structure. Both rejected absolute and binding statements of faith. Both affirmed freedom of personal belief within the disciplines of democratic community, as well as the freedom of each congregation to shape its own faith and worship, and choose its clergy. Both became clearly unitarian in theology long before the merger of the two associations of churches in 1961. The Unitarian Universalist Association has grown into an international association of churches in the last few years with congregations in several countries.

Because of its openness the Unitarian Universalist movement encompasses persons of liberal Christian, deist, theist, religious humanist, and world religionist persuasions. When the first World

Parliament of Religions gathered in Chicago in September of 1893, Rev. Jenkin Lloyd Jones (a Unitarian) was the secretary and general workhorse of the planning committee. Rev. Augusta Chapin (a Universalist) was the chair of the women's religion committee. Neither denomination was intimidated or feared contamination by the vigorous non-Christian world (as did so many others) there represented. Hundreds of Universalists and Unitarians participated in the Parliament as attendees, participants, and speakers. Again in 1993 at the second Parliament, they were there to share, learn, and inform their own faith.

Our ritual is as diverse as our congregations. While most congregations' worship shows its rootage in mainline Protestantism, it is no surprise to find a tea ceremony, a Jewish high holy days service, a Hindu Festival of Lights, a Muslim prayer, or a Wiccan ritual in a Unitarian Universalist church.

Likewise, no single symbol has universal acceptance among us. For some the cross remains the central symbol, for others a grouping of world religious symbols centers worship, while for some no symbol is acceptable. In recent years the flaming chalice has become the most frequently used symbol. It originates in the movement that spread from the martyrdom of Jan Hus in the 13th century. The flame in the communion cup symbolized the enduring flame of his faith, burning up from the chalice, together forming the shape of a cross. Over time, the flaming chalice has been reshaped in many forms as congregations have used and adapted it; its most common meaning today is the light of knowledge and the search for truth.

Unitarian Universalists remain a small, vigorous, and growing religious body loosely connected to Protestant Christianity. Many members, however, see themselves as separate and different from that tradition (which is why this chapter stands alone).

The UUA is a strong supporter of the International Association for Religious Freedom, an interfaith organization with seventy member groups in more than twenty-five nations, and is a member of a new coalition of Unitarian movements worldwide.

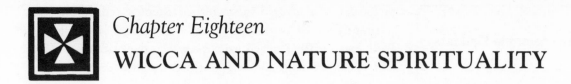

Chapter Eighteen
WICCA AND NATURE SPIRITUALITY

A Portrait of Wicca

H.Ps. Phyllis W. Curott, J.D.

President Emerita, Covenant of the Goddess (COG). COG is one of the largest and oldest Wiccan religious organizations, with members in North America, Europe, and Australia.

Wicca is a vital, contemporary spiritual path reviving the ancient, pre-Christian indigenous religion of Europe. It is a life-affirming Earth religion that is both old and new, "traditional," and vibrantly creative. Wiccans experience the Divine as immanent, as embodied in the Universe, the world in all its aspects, and in humanity, as well as transcendent. Therefore all of life is perceived as sacred and interconnected. Modern Wicca incorporates ancient and modern liturgy, ritual and shamanic practices by which people attune themselves to the natural rhythms of the Earth and the Universe, enabling them to experience communion with the embodied Divine. Wiccans honor nature as a profound spiritual teacher and devote themselves to the contemplation and integration of the spiritual wisdom inherent in the Earth's cycles of seasonal transformation.

Wicca—also known as the Old Religion, Witchcraft, or the Craft—is derived from the old Anglo-Saxon word *wicce*, pronounced "witche," giving rise to the commonly used but frequently misunderstood term *witchcraft*. *Wicce* meant a practitioner of the Old Religion, and reflects the influence of the Old Norse word *vitke*, meaning a priestess, seer, or shaman. The word *pagan* is from the Latin *paganus*, a country dweller. *Heathen*, another related term also misinterpreted as a pejorative, meant one who dwelt on the heath. All were European peoples who, like Native Americans and other indigenous groups, lived close to the Earth and respected their relationship to nature as sacred.

Wicca is nondogmatic. There is no single leader or prophet, nor is there a Wiccan bible or literature of revealed and absolute truth. Rather, Wicca is a dynamic and accessible system of techniques, the mastery of which enables each individual to experience the Divine personally. Most Wiccans consider their practice a priest/esshood involving years of training and passage through life-transforming initiatory rituals. Priestesses and priests are respected as Elders and teachers of these techniques, for it is a basic Wiccan precept that each individual has the capacity and the responsibility to experience the sacred mystery that gives life true meaning.

It is a Wiccan tenet that spiritual insight is achieved through living in harmony with the Earth. Like the spiritual worldview and practices of Native Americans, Taoists, and many indigenous Earth religions, Wiccan spiritual practices are intended to attune humanity to the natural rhythms and cycles of nature. Rituals therefore coincide with the phases of the moon, which are particularly significant for women, and the seasonal changes. Wiccans seek to live in a balanced way with nature and to practice their spirituality not only in sacred rituals but in the way they live each day. Thus the Divine is experienced not only in prayer, meditation, ritual, and shamanic work, but in gardening, preparing a meal, recycling trash, making love, giving birth, and growing old. Divine presence is felt in the air we breathe, the water we drink, the food upon our tables, the creatures and plants with which we share this beautiful planet, and the sacred Earth that nourishes and sustains us.

Our reverence for the Earth expresses our reverence for the Divine, which it embodies, and reflects a deep ecological concern that is more than pragmatic. As an embodiment of the Divine, the Earth is not treated as a utilitarian object, to be exploited,

The Charge of the Goddess

Listen to the words of the Great Mother, she who was of old also called Artemis, Astarte, Athene, Dione, Melusine, Cerridwen, Arianrhod, and many other names:

"Whenever you have need of anything, once in the month, and better it be when the moon is full, then shall you assemble in some secret place and adore my spirit, which is Mother of all creation.

"There shall you assemble, who are fain to learn all mystery, yet have not won the deepest secrets; to you shall I teach things that are yet unknown. And you shall be free from slavery; and as a sign that you are truly free, you shall be naked in your rites, and you shall dance, sing, feast, make music, and love all in my praise. For mine is the ecstasy of the spirit and mine also is joy on earth, for my law is love unto all beings. Keep pure your highest ideal; strive ever towards it; let naught stop you nor turn you aside. For mine is the secret door which opens upon the Land of Youth, and mine is the cup of the wine of life, the Cauldron of Cerridwen, which is the Holy Grail of immortality. I am the gracious Goddess, who gives the gift of joy unto the hearts of humanity. Upon earth I give knowledge of the spirit eternal and beyond death I give peace, and freedom and reunion with those who have gone before. Nor do I demand aught in sacrifice, for behold, I am the Mother of all living and my love is poured out upon the earth."

polluted, and destroyed for man's short-term greed. Rather it is inherently sacred in its value. This fundamental respect for the Earth as sacred has drawn many people to the practice of Wicca and, like other indigenous religions, may be one of its greatest contributions to a world imperiled by ecological crisis.

The Divine is also perceived and experienced anthropomorphically as well, though there is great diversity among Wiccans as to whether they characterize the Divine as exclusively feminine or as a multiplicity or dyad of feminine and masculine forms and metaphors. In contrast to most of the world's religions, Wicca acknowledges the Divine as feminine as well as masculine. The Goddess, who is seen as both transcendent and immanent, is an essential aspect of Wiccan worship. She may be worshipped as the nameless single Goddess, or as any of the many aspects and names by which She has always been known. Personified as the Triple Goddess, the Great Mother, Isis, Gaia, Demeter, Cerridwen, Brigid, Oestara, Innana, Ishtar, Shekinah, Shakti, Kali, Amateratsu, and many others, the Divine feminine is also experienced in the energies of the Universe, the mysteries of the moon, the blessings of the Earth, and the wonders of our own bodies, which like the Earth itself are held to be sacred. This honoring of the Divine in its feminine aspect, as well as the genuine respect for women as spiritual leaders, wise women, and healers, has been a primary reason for the rapid growth in popularity of Wicca among women. According to the Institute for the Study of American Religion (U.C. at Santa Barbara), Goddess spirituality, to which Wicca is a venerable contributor, is the fastest growing religion in America.

Wiccans have one fundamental ethical precept: *An (if) it harm none, do what you will.* This honors the great freedom that each individual has to ascertain truth, to experience the Divine directly, and to determine how to best live her or his own life. With that freedom, however, comes a profound responsibility that none may be harmed by one's choices and actions. As in many religions, individual Wiccans reach different conclusions when applying these fundamental precepts to such issues as vegetarianism, abortion, or participation in war.

Wiccan spiritual practices, often referred to as "magic," are in fact ancient techniques for changing consciousness at will in order to better perceive and participate in Divine reality. A primary purpose of Wiccan techniques is the transformation of the self to fully develop one's gifts and capacities to live a full, joyful, and spiritual life. In this sense, they are also used for practical ends such as healing, divination, purification, blessing, and the raising of energy to achieve positive life goals such as fulfilling work and relationships. All of these techniques, which may include prayer, meditation, ritual, drumming, singing, chanting, dancing, journeying, trance, and others, require and engender wisdom, maturity, patience, passion, and an abiding commitment to the sacred.

The "casting of a spell," frequently misunderstood as a means of having power over people or nature by the use of supernatural forces, is actually a form of ritual and meditation which is very similar to prayer in other religions, except that, instead of beseeching the aid or intervention of an external deity, the indwelling Divine energy is drawn outward into manifestation in the world through harmonious interaction with the Divine presence already present. The idea of controlling and having dominion over nature or others is alien to Wiccan cosmology. Wiccans do not work with supernatural powers nor do they seek to have "power over." The essence of Wiccan spirituality is respect for and attunement with the natural energies of the Earth and the Universe as a means of attuning oneself with the sacred. It is unethical to engage in any form of spiritual work that seeks to control, manipulate, or have power over others. While work may be done on behalf of another, such as healing which is an important and ancient aspect of Wicca, even this is never done without the knowledge and consent of the person who is being assisted.

There are many different traditions or denominations within the Old Religion. Some reflect the particular practices of certain ethnic groups such as Celtic, Norse, Welsh, Greek, Italian, Finno-Ugric, Lithuanian, etc. Some are part of the initiatory traditions made public by such practitioners as Gerald Gardner. Still others practice with the guidance of liturgical works published and taught by contemporary Wiccans. Some practitioners search within themselves for inspiration and direction or work creatively in groups in a mutually agreed-upon group structure. Some traditions are practiced by women only, others by men only, and many include both women and men. Some traditions may date back for hundreds of years or more, and others have been in existence for only a few years.

Whether carrying on the spiritual vocabulary of an ancient lineage or drawing forth the highest creative and spontaneous expression of a single individual, the great strength of Wicca lies in its diversity and vitality—it is a living, growing religious tradition.

(cont. on next page)
The Charge of the Goddess *(cont.)*

Hear the words of the Star Goddess: she in the dust of whose feet are the hosts of heaven, and whose body encircles the universe:

"I am the beauty of the green earth, and the white moon among the stars and the mystery of the waters, and the desire of the hearts of humanity. I call unto thy soul—arise, and come unto me. For I am the soul of nature, who gives life to the universe. From me all things proceed, and unto me all things must return. Before my face, beloved of Gods and humanity, let thine innermost divine self be enfolded in the rapture of the infinite. Let my worship be within the heart that rejoices, for behold, all acts of love and pleasure are my rituals. And therefore, let there be beauty and strength, power and compassion, honor and humility, mirth and reverence, within you. And you who think to seek for me, know your seeking and yearning shall avail you not unless you know the mystery: that if that which you seek you find not within you, you will never find it without. For behold, I have been with you from the beginning, and I am that which is attained at the end of desire."

Composed by Doreen Valiente and Gerals Gardner from inspiration and traditional sources.

A Guide to Nature Spirituality Terms

Selena Fox

Founder and leader of Circle Sanctuary, an internationally linked Nature Spirituality resource center and Shamanic Wiccan church based in Mt. Horeb, Wisconsin

Animism: ancient philosophy that views everything in Nature as having an indwelling spirit/soul, including the plants, rocks, waters, winds, fires, animals, humans, and other life forms. Animism is the foundation of shamanism and has been considered the earliest form of human religion on planet Earth.

Earth-Centered Spirituality: honoring the spiritual interconnectedness of life on planet Earth, often as Mother Earth or Gaia, but sometimes as a gender neutral Earth Spirit. Sometimes called *Earth religion* and *Gaian* (Gaean) religion. Related Eco-Christian form is Creation-Centered Spirituality.

Ecofeminism: feminist environmental philosophy that draws parallels between the oppression of women and the oppression of Nature by patriarchy and which advocates the spiritual and political liberation of both.

Goddess Spirituality: revering Nature and honoring the Great Goddess in one or more of Her many forms. Usually polytheistic and sometimes multicultural in practice. Usually incorporates feminist perspectives.

Heathen: Another name for Pagan. Many contemporary practitioners of Teutonic nature religions prefer this term for themselves and their spirituality.

Nature Religions: religions that include an honoring of the Divine as immanent in Nature. May be premodern, modern, or postmodern in philosophical orientation. Usually polytheistic, animistic, and pantheistic. Include traditional ways of various native peoples of the Americas, Africa, Asia, Australia, Polynesia, Europe, and elsewhere; religions of ancient Pagan cultures, such as Egyptian, Greek, Roman, Minoan, Assyrian, Celtic, Teutonic, and others; and contemporary Paganism.

Nature Spirituality: honoring the spiritual interconnectedness of life not only on planet Earth but throughout the Universe/Cosmos; more encompassing term than Earth-Centered Spirituality because it also includes Celestial religions; used by some as synonymous with contemporary Paganism and by others as also including interfaith blends, such as those that combine Paganism with Eco-Christianity or Eco-Buddhism.

Neo-Pagan: Contemporary Pagan.

Pagan: pertains to a nature religion or a practitioner of an ancient and/or contemporary nature religion; also used to refer to a Nature Spirituality, Earth-Centered Spirituality, and/or Goddess Spirituality group or practitioner.

Pantheism: the Divine as immanent; the Divine is in everything and everything has a Divine aspect.

Panentheism: Pantheism that also includes a transcendent component conceptualized as the Sacred Whole or Divine Unity.

Polytheism: honoring Divinity in two or more forms. Can be belief in/worship of multiple aspects of a particular deity; of the Divine as Goddess and God; or of many Goddesses, Gods, Nature Spirits, and/or other Divine forms. Some, but not all, polytheistic nature religions acknowledge an all-encompassing Divine Unity.

Shaman: an adept who serves as healer and spirit world communicator for her/his tribe or community. Sometimes known as a *Medicine person*. This role is tribal culture/community defined.

Shamanic Practitioner: someone learning and working with shamanistic healing practices for self-development, and in some cases, also for helping others. Sometimes known as a *Medicine worker*. This role is self-defined.

Shamanism: animistic spiritual healing practices usually involving ecstatic trance and spirit world journeys by adepts. Forms of shamanism include *Traditional*, which are rooted in specific indigenous tribal people's cultures, and *Multicultural*, which are contemporary forms that integrate old and new spirit wisdom ways from more than one culture.

Wiccan Spirituality: contemporary paths rooted in one or more nature folk religions of old Europe. Also known as the Old Religion, the Craft, Wicca, Wicce, Ways of the Wise, Neo-Pagan Witchcraft, and Benevolent Witchcraft.

Witch: some Wiccan practitioners use the word "Witch" for themselves in connection with their spirituality to bring back its pre-Inquisition use in Europe as a term of honor and respect, meaning "medicine person/medicine worker," "shaman/ shamanic practitioner," "wise woman/man," "priestess/priest of the Old Religion." Other Wiccans refuse to use the word "Witch" because of later negative definitions of the word which led to its use as a tool of Pagan genocide and religious oppression in Europe and North America for hundreds of years. During the "Burning Times" of the Middle Ages, bigots in power changed its definition, making it a term linked with evil, and used it as a brand to mark and exterminate folk healers, those who refused to convert to state-sanctioned forms of Christianity, political rivals, and others. Contemporary usage of the word "Witch" by non-Wiccans is diverse but in recent years has been changing in academia and elsewhere to reflect the growing public awareness and understanding of Wiccan Spirituality's reclaiming of the word.

Chapter Nineteen
ZOROASTRIANISM

Portrait of an Ancient Monotheistic Religion

Dr. Pallan R. Ichaporia

Chair of the Research and Preservation Committee of the Federation of Zoroastrian Associations of North America

Prayer

"In humble adoration, with hands outstretched, I pray to thee, O Lord, Invisible benevolent Spirit: Vouchsafe to me in this hour of joy, all righteousness of action, all wisdom of the Good Mind, that I may thereby bring joy to the Soul of Creation."

—*Yasna* 28.1 from the *Eathas*

Zoroastrianism is the first revealed monotheistic religion of the world. The date of its founding is lost in antiquity, but general consensus places it between 2000 to 1800 B.C.E. Its founder, Zarathushtra or Zoroaster (as called by the Greeks), flourished on the East Iranian plateau. Zarathushtra saw the God (*Ahura Mazda*—the Wise Lord), felt conscious of His presence, and heard His words, which are recorded in the five Songs or Poems he composed. These are called the *Gathas*. One easily understands Zarathushtra by seeing the Prophet's zeal in the *Gathas* and the visible manifestation of his meeting the God.

Primary Beliefs

Zoroastrians believe in the One Supreme, Omnipotent, Omniscient God, called Ahura Mazda. He is to be understood through his six divine attributes: *Vohu Mana* (Good Mind), *Asha* (Truth, Righteousness), *Spenta Armaity* (Correct Thinking, Piety), *Xsthra Vairya* (Divine Domain), *Haurvatat* (Perfection, Integrity), and *Ameratat* (Immortality). His attributes are also found in each and every human being who must work as a co-worker of God to defeat evil and bring the world to perfection. This can be achieved by good thoughts, good words, and good deeds.

Angels, known as the *Yazatas*, work endlessly to aid humans in bringing the world to perfection. All the natural elements like air, water, and lands are to be kept pure. Their pollutions are to be prevented at all cost. This makes Zoroastrianism the first true ecological religion of the world. After death, the immortal soul of the departed person is judged according to all the good deeds done by him or her in this world; the soul then enjoys the pleasures of paradise or undergoes the tortures of hell.

There is also belief in the appearance of the last savior, called *Sosayant*, and of the final day of judgment with the resurrections of all who have died (these last two are later beliefs).

Main Sources of Religious Knowledge

The primary source is the *Gathas of the Prophet*; this is followed by *Hapatan Haiti*, the seven chapters written by the Prophet's disciples. These scriptures are called *Old Avesta* as their language differs from the later scriptures, called the *Younger Avesta*. Together they are known as the *Avestan*. The *Younger Avesta* consists of the *Yasna* (without the *Gathas*, containing seventy-two chapters), *Vispered*, *Vendidad*, and the *Yasts*. The original *Avestan* scriptures were written in twenty-one books called the *Nasks*, from which only one complete *Nask*—*Vandidad*—has survived the ravages of time. The *Gathas* and the rest of the scriptures survived because they formed part of the long *Yasna* liturgical ceremony, which was passed from generation to generation by oral tradition.

Rituals

The most important ritual which every Zoroastrian has to undergo is the *Navzote* or *Sudraposhi Ceremony*, which is for new initiates (ages seven to fifteen years) entering the religion. Generally the rituals are divided into two classes: 1) those like the *Yasna* ceremony, to be performed in the Zoroastrian Fire-Temples; and 2) those to be performed anywhere outside the Zoroastrian Temples, like *Jashan* (thanksgiving) ceremony.

The word "fire-temple" is a misnomer as the Zoroastrians do not worship the fire. The fire is kept as a symbol of purity, acting as the focal point (like the *Kebla* of the religion of Islam) for prayers.

A Minority Religion

The Zoroastrians are the smallest minority of all religions, having undergone the severest persecutions for centuries in Iran at the hands of its conquerors, after the fall of the last Sassanian Zoroastrian Empire. At one time the number of the community ran into millions (650 C.E.). A small band of the community migrated to India (between the 9th and 10th centuries C.E.) to avoid harassment and persecution; called the Parsees, these now number fewer than 60,000 in India and 2,500 in Pakistan. Still fewer have survived in Iran (10,000), and some have settled in the West, mostly in North America (12,000) and in Europe (7,000); there may be 3,000 in other parts of the world. With such a small total number of the community there are no fixed denominations as such, although the Iranian Zoroastrians and the Parsee have different cultures and mother tongues, which developed due to long separation.

Zoroastrianism in the World Today

Dr. Jehan Bagli

Founding member of the Zoroastrian Association of Quebec, Editor of Gavashni *and first Editor of* FEZANA Journal

Throughout its long history, the Zarathustrian tradition has experienced numerous social environments shaped by various ruling dynasties, in different eras in early Iran. Consequently, from early times the adherents have learned to coexist with people of different beliefs. This has built within the tradition a strong sense of tolerance for other faiths and other religious viewpoints, an attribute that is firmly intertwined with the teachings of the first revealed religion of mankind.

The basic tenets of the faith proclaim respect for creation of nature and of equality for all human beings; these are the fundamental cornerstones of the tradition. With these axioms in focus, Zarathustrians consistently make a concerted effort to learn and comprehend the nature and beliefs of other faiths. The migration of Zarathustrians from Iran to India around 936 C.E. put them within the milieu of the Hindu society. Here they emerged as the most intellectual, honest, and hardworking minority of the world. Despite imbibing the knowledge and customs of other faiths, they have for the past 3,500 years maintained the integrity and identity of their faith with glowing success.

At this time the major challenge for humanity to overcome in the world is a breakdown in true respect and tolerance for other human beings. Much of this is motivated by materialism and greed, but conflicts are frequently perpetrated in the name of religion, under false pretenses. The understanding that all humans emerge from the same creating force has been totally overshadowed by dogmatic and egotistic endeavors, without regard for the needs of others.

The other major issue in our highly technocratic society is the lack of regard for the elements of creation. In the interest of bettering living conditions, the relationship between humanity and the creation has reached an all-time low. The concept of the preservation of the creation, with humans as its stewards and as co-workers with the creator, promoted by various religious traditions, has totally disappeared. Exploitation of our nonrenewable resources, pollution of our waters with chemical wastes, and excessive deforestation are some of the most serious infractions by the human society towards the elements of creation.

There is a great renaissance of spiritual awareness among the Zarathustrian community. Attempts are being made to disseminate the message of the prophet to the youth and to adults to make them aware of these injustices that are perpetrated in the name of religion. The Federation of Zoroastrian Associations of North America (FEZANA) is making all efforts to spread awareness of the Zarathustrian religion through interfaith dialogue with other religious groups and to make our sentiments known.

> *"O Ahura Mazda, and O Spirit of Truth:*
> *Do you grant me and my followers*
> *such strength and ruling power,*
> *that with the help of the Benevolent Mind,*
> *we may bring to the world,*
> *restful joy and happiness,*
> *of which, Thou, O Lord,*
> *art indeed the first Possessor."*
>
> Yasna 29.10,
> from the second chapter of the *Gathas*,
> in "Understanding the *Gathas*, the Hymns
> of Zarathustra" by Dinshan J. Irani

Contributions to Western Thought

Rohinton M. Rivetna

Past President of the Federation of Zoroastrian Associations of North America, and Trustee of the CPWR

Zoroastrian ideas have played a vital role in the development of Western religious thought. Some theological concepts shared by Zoroastrianism with Judaism and Christianity are

- Belief in one supreme and loving God
- Heaven and Hell, resurrection, and final judgment
- Ultimate triumph of good over evil
- A strict moral and ethical code
- The Messiah to come for the final restoration
- The words *satan*, *paradise*, and *amen* are of Zoroastrian origin.

The interchange of Zoroastrian thought with Judeo-Christian ideology first took place when Cyrus the Great defeated the Assyrians and released the Jews from Babylonian captivity. They heralded Cyrus as their messiah, as prophesied two centuries earlier in Isaiah 45:1–3. The Old Testament is replete with references to the Persian emperors Darius, Cyrus, and Xerxes, all of whom were Zoroastrians. . . .

Zoroastrian rituals and prayers are solemnized in the presence of a flame. Scrupulously tended with sandalwood and frankincense, a flame is kept burning in the inner sanctum of every Zoroastrian temple, and often in Zoroastrian homes. Fire is revered as a visible symbol of the inner light that burns within each person. It is a physical representation of the Illumined Mind, Light, and Truth, all highly regarded in the Zoroastrian doctrine. Despite its prehistoric origins, Zoroastrianism has vehemently denounced idolatry in any shape or form.

The *Fravashi* or *Farohar* is the presence of *Ahura Mazda* in every human being. It is the Divinity in Humanity. It is the conscience. The *Fravashi* is immortal and does not die with the person, but lives on forever. The *Fravashi* is ever present to guide and protect the person. It is the duty of a person, in making the choice between good and evil, to seek guidance from his *Fravashi*.

—Excerpts are from "Followers of an Ancient Faith in a Modern World" by Rohinton M. Rivetna, a booklet published by FEZANA.

Part Two

BECOMING A COMMUNITY
OF RELIGIONS

Introduction

Joel Beversluis

While holding on to some key beliefs, practices, and identity, the world's religious and spiritual communities are facing considerable change and challenge. Among them are the growth of "grassroots" and laity-driven spirituality, and exploratory religious quests. Of greater significance are the effects of globalization, technology, and pluralism. While Part Two of this *Sourcebook* is particularly focused on the emergence, especially toward the end of the 20th century, of the interfaith movement, we must also consider the context—both the opportunities and benefits of globalization and technological innovation, and the underside of globalization— increasing economic, social, political, religious, and ecological turmoil. These conditions raise a primary question for many people: How can the religions and quests for richer personal spirituality make positive contributions to resolving the issues and crises of our time?

In reflecting on possible answers, we note that the ideals of the interfaith movement—understanding and mutual respect, religious freedom, and the goal of peace through religiously motivated ethics—are relatively new concepts and are not universally endorsed. It is with justification that some members of most religions are faulted not only for failing to bring peace but also for supporting conflict and oppression. Religions have not generally promoted spiritual or intellectual freedom, and some reactionary elements use religion to generate conflict toward members of other faiths and ethnic communities.

The increasingly common reaction against institutional religions also reflects widespread disappointment that members of the traditions don't live up to their own ideals, lack spiritual vitality, and have little to say to issues of the contemporary world. Unfortunately, this reaction often ignores the wise and progressive elements that may also be found within religious and spiritual traditions and in their contemporary expressions.

What Is Emerging in the Interfaith Movement?

In response to the varied needs of our time, a growing movement is encouraging members of the world's religions and spiritual traditions to be more vital in the "outer" world. Since the 1893 World Parliament of Religions in Chicago and especially

"My dear brothers and sisters:
We are already one, but we imagine that
* we are not.*
What we have to recover is our original
* unity.*
What we have to become is what we
* already are."*

THOMAS MERTON,
speaking to the First Spiritual Summit,
in Calcutta

"A number of philosophers and social sci-
entists have pointed out that the history of
human morals is a story of a developing
sense of community that begins with the
family and tribe and then gradually extends
outward embracing the region, the nation,
the race, all members of a world religion,
and then all humanity. The sense of com-
munity involves an awareness of kinship,
identity, interdependence, participation in a
shared destiny, relationships to a common
good. It gives rise to the moral feelings of
respect and sympathy, leading to a sense of
moral obligation...."

STEVEN C. ROCKEFELLER,
from *Spirit and Nature,* p. 144

during the past thirty years, institutional and popular support of the goals of interfaith dialogue, of religious freedom and harmony, and of peace among and through religions, has grown considerably.

Thus, a viable alternative to rejecting the significant contributions of religions and spiritualities is now emerging. This alternative challenges religionists to delve deeper into their wisdom, to reflect on their own limitations and faults, and to bring their findings and experience to the interfaith table. In this context, the religions are in a better position to offer that wisdom as gifts to the world in dialogical and constructive ways. When this is done, spiritual revitalization within traditions, and healing between religions can—and has—happened.

Interfaith organizations and widely respected leaders are now creating programs that express the wisdom traditionally admired in those sages and masters whose spirituality, though often rooted in a specific tradition, transcended religious myopia. Heroes of this movement are people such as Rumi, St. Francis, Chief Seattle, Vivekananda, Mahatma Gandhi, Albert Schweitzer, Eleanor Roosevelt, Bede Griffiths, Mother Theresa, and the 14th Dalai Lama of Tibet, to name a few.

Another interesting development of this movement is that it now includes not only the official ecclesiastical dialogues between representatives and leaders of religions—including the Pope—and the academic discussions of scholars, but also dialogue with peace and ecology advocates, and with members of new religions and grassroots spiritual movements. There are also increasing opportunities for joint contemplation and multifaith worship at conferences and retreats conducted by distinguished teachers from many traditions.

Yet, despite the fears of conservative Christians, relatively few people or religious communities are trying to define a world theology or promote a single world religion. Rather, the diversity of beliefs and practices is honored even as participants are exploring the unifying elements at the level of ethics and pragmatic action.

Strategies and Tasks

Strategies of the interfaith movement include the dialogue events such as bringing people of faiths together in a safe space, facilitating interpersonal understanding, and raising questions and issues. Complementary tasks include stimulating new conceptual frameworks, encouraging visions of spiritual transformation, clarifying theological and ethical consensus, enrichment, or divergence, and creating collaborative programs of education and service.

To accomplish all of this, the interfaith movement works through a wide range of large and small organizations—in lay, clerical, academic, nongovernmental, and community-based organizations, in ecumenical agencies, and within religious institutions. There is no overarching structure to make it all happen—not one of human devising, anyway—but rather a growing awareness that all of these are ingredients of the changes needed in consciousness and culture. Key characteristics of the movement are determination and hope that the changes are, in fact, taking place.

Concepts for a Community of Religions

An underlying attitude of the interfaith movement is seen in its promotion of the goals and process of respectful and appreciative dialogue for understanding within the diversity of religions and spiritual traditions. Beyond dialogue, however, many in the movement are embracing what Marcus Braybrooke is calling "A New Agenda." This agenda challenges members of all traditions and new movements to reassess their responsibilities regarding the critical issues of the world, and to respond individually and together. Two clear expressions of this are the declaration "Towards a Global Ethic" and "A Call to Our Guiding Institutions," of the Parliament of the World's Religions. But this new agenda is also reaching into civic education, service, and advocacy. Many of the organizations listed in Part Four demonstrate the variety of elements in this new agenda.

The quest for a global ethic and other forms of collaboration are now historically possible because of the emergence of what some of us are naming "the community of religions." This term describes the shift across religious consciousness that encourages partnership and responsibility for the common good. This sense of community also makes possible appreciation for what Brother Wayne Teasdale calls "interspiritual wisdom," which names the growing understanding by the world's contemplative traditions of the common elements and fruits found in practical mysticism and spirituality.

The concept of global spirituality—or "spiritualities"—encompasses many different emphases in different traditions—ranging from eco-justice and stewardship to neo-paganism to advocacy for a sustainable world order, to nonviolence movements, eco-feminism, and the scientific revelations of pioneering biology and quantum physics. In their richest form, global spiritualities include a conscious awareness of the significance of the Earth as part of the larger, sacred community and a deep religious or spiritual commitment by individuals to mitigate the threats by modern civilization to Earth's ecosystems.

"We are rapidly entering the age of interspiritual community. This new axial period will be characterized by the emergence of a profound sense of community among the world's religions and spiritual traditions; it will also draw them into deeper relationships with other areas of human culture, particularly the sciences, arts, economics, politics, and media. The unfolding and expanding reality of this community will slowly dissipate the fears we have collected over the millennia, and it will reveal the precious gift of interspiritual wisdom.

"In this age we will gain access to the treasures hidden in the depths of our own and other traditions of spirituality. These resources have the power to transform our attitudes and behavior toward one another, other species, and the Earth itself. They will lead us into awareness of our larger communion with this sacred reality that is home for us all. The challenge for humankind is to actively participate in this process of transformation, while the task of the religions is to inspire in humanity the will to change and to summon up, within their own ranks, the courage to sustain it."

BROTHER WAYNE TEASDALE

Chapter Twenty
INTERFAITH DIALOGUE
How and Why Do We Speak Together?

Introduction

Joel Beversluis

Interfaith dialogue has evolved out of many factors and experiences. Some of these are the early formal attempts at the World's Parliament of Religions in 1893; the development of the study of world religions; the experiences of the Christian ecumenical movement dating back to the early decades of this century; the challenge of the Holocaust to both Judaism and Christianity; increasing pluralism and globalization; challenges to proselytizing; nuclear weapons and arms proliferation; failures of modern science and worldviews to understand ecological imperatives; ethnic and sectarian conflicts; increased understanding of conflict resolution; and others. Out of these and other factors have come new desire for understanding of the "other," an intensified search for meaning across old boundaries, and the need for respectful conversation between participants who are different or estranged.

There are many kinds of dialogue and many reasons one might pursue it, even within the interfaith movement. Examples of some of these are

1. Intra-religious dialogue between protestant and Catholic Christians, or between Sunni Muslims and Shiite Muslims, for ecumenical harmony.

2. Interreligious dialogue at an official level, for instance, between the Vatican and high-ranking Jewish leaders, as has happened recently.

3. Interfaith dialogue between neighboring clergy or lay persons who express their own faith and practices to others, and who listen and learn from others.

4. The inner dialogue—with the Divine, within one's intellect, or in contemplative practice—of one who encounters meaning in another tradition and wants to integrate it.

5. Scholarly dialogues across diverse traditions, either to understand or to contrast ideas, practices, and worldviews.

6. Thematic dialogues to explore ethical approaches, religious wisdom, and solutions to common problems such as violence or environmental crises.

7. Dialogue of the heart in worship or contemplation together, for fellowship in the presence of the Divine, as the World Congress of Faiths seeks.

8. Dialogue of the hands, seeking collaboration in projects and advocacy.

The most important characteristic of dialogue, and the most difficult in interfaith or inter-ideological arenas, is the willingness to consider the incompleteness of one's own information or truth and to learn from the other.

Although this intention fits well with the uncertainties and needs of the postmodern age, it is not an easy "suspension of belief" for anyone who holds onto truth claims and absolutes. The dialogical intention can also be seen as a part of the "paradigm shift" that is taking place in our cultures, as previous modes of knowing and communicating are inadequate responses to current realities. In recognition of the inclination we all have toward dogmatism and debate, thoughtful guidelines for engaging with others in dialogue have been offered by many theoreticians.

Interfaith dialogue is not new, of course, since interfaith relations have intrigued people throughout history, and even the early Christian St. Paul is said to have engaged in dialogue during his visit to the Areopagus in the 1st century C.E. In the 20th century, we learned from two key figures: David Bohm and Leonard Swidler.

Beginning in the early 1970s, the physicist David Bohm held fruitful dialogues across disciplines with philosophers such as Krishnamurti and other scholars. Bohm explored deep listening—to the "spirit" of the dialogue, to himself, to the others in the group, to the silence, to the impact of listening itself on the individuals and the group. He urged people to suspend their judgments and to make their reasoning explicit so that the conversation itself would be changed in some way and reveal new meaning. Bohm was motivated in part by the need in modern civilization to avoid huge ethical errors by gathering wisdom from dialogues around ideas and issues. He was also intrigued by the process itself, and encouraged heightened awareness of its effects on individuals and groups.

Dr. Leonard Swidler, a systematic theologian, cofounded the *Journal of Ecumenical Studies* in 1964 in the heady ecumenical atmosphere surrounding Vatican II. The journal's first interreligious issue dealt with the problem—for Christians—of Jewish disinterest in Christ and suspicion of Christians, and of Christianity's historical anti-Semitism. This discussion opened the door to consideration of the relations with other religions, especially as the presence of Eastern religions became more noticeable in Western cities and universities. In 1983, Swidler published the "Dialogue Decalogue: Ground Rules for Interreligious, Interideological Dialogue." A recent variation on these ten "commandments," printed in full later in this chapter, were summarized by the Interfaith Dialogue Association of Grand Rapids as

1. Dialogue to learn, to change, and to grow, and act accordingly
2. Dialogue to share and receive from others
3. Dialogue with honesty and sincerity
4. Dialogue comparing ideals with ideals, and practice with practice
5. Dialogue to define yourself and to learn the self-definition of others
6. Dialogue with no hard-and-fast assumptions about someone else's beliefs
7. Dialogue to share with equals
8. Dialogue in trust
9. Dialogue with willingness to look at your beliefs and traditions critically
10. Dialogue seeking to understand the other person's beliefs from within.

The revealing title of a book by Dr. Swidler is *After the Absolute: The Dialogical Future of Religious Reflection*. He also coedited, with John Cobb, Paul Knitter, and Monika Hellwig, *Death or Dialogue? From the Age of Monologue to the Age of Dialogue*, in which Swidler argues that we must leave the age of monologue and accept the age of dialogue if we are to avoid the death that follows from fear, suspicion, misunderstanding, resentment, and hatred.

A New Agenda: What Shall We Do?

But dialogue for its own sake, or even as a means of bringing people of different faiths together, was not a sufficient objective for many participants, especially as contentious social and political issues were also bringing people together in common cause despite their diverse backgrounds. Increasingly, goals such as comparative scholarship, enhancing understanding of the estranged "other," or even finding "fellowship in the presence of the Divine" have become insufficiently compelling reasons for increased participation in the interfaith movement. Instead, the various modes of dialogue have become tools in pursuit of a new agenda that has been emerging over the past half-century. This essay is not the place to trace that evolution, but according to Marcus Braybrooke, the eminent historian of the movement and author of *Pilgrimage of Hope: One Hundred Years of the Interfaith Movement* (Crossroad, 1993) and *Faith and Interfaith in a Global Age* (CoNexus Press, 1998), the commemorations of the Parliament in 1993 were

a milestone in the growth of the interfaith movement. The focus has changed from trying to get people of different religions together to discovering what people of faith can do together for our world. . . . Despite the very practical efforts of some groups, up until 1993 much of the energy in the interfaith movement had to go into persuading people of different faiths to meet. There was first of all ignorance and quite often hostility to overcome. . . . A second task was encouraging people of different faiths to get to know each other, to relax in each other's company, to talk, and perhaps to become friends. As prejudices were dispelled and friendships grew, many people found they had to rethink their attitudes toward the members and theologies of other religions. (pp. 95–96, *Faith and Interfaith in a Global Age*, CoNexus, 1998)

Dr. David Ramage, Chair (Emeritus) of the Council for a Parliament of the World's Religions, noted in a presentation in Grand Rapids in 1994 that it is easier and more productive to get people to work together on common projects, where friendships can form and attitudes re-form, than to bring them to meetings and formal dialogues where defenses and identities are on alert. Both the themes and the organization of the Parliament reflected this insight, and organizers had no difficulty identifying numerous projects and challenges.

The new, emerging agenda has had numerous advocates. Since the 1960s, Martin Luther King, Jr., Rabbi Heschel, Thomas Merton, Thich Nhat Hanh, the Berrigans, and others had been insisting that nonviolent advocacy for peace and justice—and against oppression—can be rooted in one's faith, whether Christian, Jewish, or Buddhist. Dr. Paul Knitter asserts that "the concern for the widespread suffering that grips humanity and threatens the planet can and must be the 'common cause' for all religions." Native Americans, Thomas Berry, and Brian Swimme have taught us how the earth and the universe are integral parts of the sacred community of life. Pope John Paul II noted, at the interfaith 1986 Assisi World Day of Prayer for Peace, that many people long for the religions to be "the moral conscience of humanity." Engaged Buddhists Sulak Sivaraksa and Dr. A. T. Ariyaratne have inspired people of all faiths to seek *sarvodaya*, a new social order which seeks the welfare of all through the interdependent awakening of all. The Dalai Lama has appealed, not only on behalf of Tibet, for compassionate nonviolence and a unifying sense of universal responsibility in all people.

Marcus Braybrooke, who has observed this emerging agenda and also helped shape it through his speaking, writing, and organizing, suggests using Mahatma Gandhi's talisman: "Recall the face of the poorest and weakest man whom you may have seen and ask yourself if the step you contemplate is going to be of any use to him."

The most significant indication of this change in emphasis to the practical and to action was that the primary question of the 1993 Parliament of the World's Religions was not "Shall we meet to talk?" or "Can we pray together?," but "What shall we *do*?" And it was there that the first significant attempt at drafting an interfaith Global Ethic was unveiled. Significantly, it had been shaped through interfaith consultations, and was later discussed in many forums through a process of interfaith dialogue.

Objectives of the 1893 World's Parliament of Religions

NOTE: The 1893 Parliament is widely seen as the beginning of the international interfaith movement. In 1999, as participants in the United Religions Initiative were formulating and sometimes debating the purpose statement for the youngest international interfaith organizations, one of its European organizers, Joseph Boehle, offered a bit of historical perspective by reproducing the ten objectives listed by the organizers of the 1893 Parliament. While some of the language and issues have changed during the past century, many of these late 19th-century objectives express goals similar to those of today's interfaith organizations.

1. To bring together in conference for the first time in history the leading representatives of the great historic religions of the world.

2. To show man, in the most impressive way, what and how many important truths the various religions hold and teach in common.

3. To promote and deepen the spirit of human brotherhood among religious men of diverse faiths, through friendly conference and mutual good understanding, while not seeking to foster the temper of

indifferentism, and not striving to achieve any formal and outward unity.

4. To set forth, by those most competent to speak, what are deemed the important distinctive truths held and taught by each religion and by the various chief branches of Christendom.

5. To indicate the impregnable foundations of Theism and the reasons for man's faith in immortality, and thus unite and strengthen the forces which are adverse to a materialistic philosophy of the universe.

6. To secure from leading scholars (representing the Brahman [Hindu], Buddhist, Confucian, Parsee [Zoroastrian], Mohammedan [Muslim], Jewish, and other faiths, and from representatives of the various churches of Christendom) full and accurate statements of the spiritual and other effects of the religions which they hold, upon the Literature, Art, Commerce, Government, Domestic and Social Life of the peoples among whom these faiths have prevailed.

7. To enquire what light each religion has afforded, or may afford, to the other religions of the world.

8. To set forth, for permanent record to be published to the world, an accurate and authoritative account of the present condition and outlook of religion among the leading nations of the earth.

9. To discover from competent men, what light religion has to throw on the great problems of the present age, especially on important questions connected with Temperance, Labor, Education, Wealth, and Poverty.

10. To bring the nations of the earth into a more friendly fellowship in the hope of securing permanent international peace.

The Interfaith Movement in the 20th Century

The Rev. Dr. Marcus Braybrooke

Author, Trustee of the International Interfaith Centre, World Congress of Faiths, Council for a Parliament of the World's Religions, and the Peace Council

I: Shaping the Present Reality

Hans Küng ends his book *Global Responsibility* with these words:

> No human life together without a world ethic for the nations.
>
> No peace among the nations without peace among the religions.
>
> No peace among the religions without dialogue among the religions.
>
> —*Global Responsibility*, Continuum and SCM Press 1991, p. 138

One hundred years ago, Charles Bonney, who presided at the World's Parliament of Religions in Chicago, ended his closing address like this: "Henceforth the religions of the world will make war, not on each other, but on the giant evils that afflict mankind." Sadly, religions have failed to fulfill that hope. Yet this century, for all its catastrophic wars and acts of genocide, has also seen the growth of a worldwide interfaith movement. Before trying to discern the path ahead, it is worth pausing to see what has been achieved.

The World's Parliament of Religions, Chicago, 1893

The World's Parliament of Religions was held as part of the World Fair or Columbian Exposition which marked the four-hundredth anniversary of Columbus's "discovery" of America. The word "Parliament" was chosen to emphasize that participants of all religions were equal, but, in fact, the body had no executive or legislative authority. It reflected the optimism and self-confidence characteristic of the U.S.A. towards the end of the 19th century.

Most of the participants were Christian from a wide spectrum of denominations. Their presuppositions permeated the gathering. Yet the contribution made by those of other faiths, although their number was small, was very significant.

The World's Parliament of Religions gave much attention to the contribution of religion to peace and social issues. Women were encouraged to play quite a part at the Parliament—more so than at most subsequent interfaith gatherings.

The Study of World Religions

The World's Parliament of Religions gave an impetus to the emerging study of world religions. While such study is an academic discipline in its own right, it has greatly increased awareness of the teachings and practices of world religions at every level. This century has seen an enormous increase in knowledge about world religions. Books, films, and videos are widely available. This study has helped to provide accurate information about the religions of the world. Even so, much ignorance and prejudice still exist.

Initially the study was confined to university departments devoted to the Science of Religions or the Comparative Study of Religions—although such departments were very unevenly spread across the world. Slowly, in some countries, the teaching of world religions has spread to schools, although the situation and law in every country is different. For some time many scholars of the subject stood apart from the interfaith movement partly because they felt that their study should be objective or neutral and partly because they concentrated on the study of the texts and the history of religions. Now, in part because there is more interest in the faith and practice of believers, far more scholars take part in interfaith discussions; their participation has enriched the interfaith movement.

Knowledge may not of itself create sympathy. Opportunities for personal meeting and friendship are important to dispel prejudice and to encourage real understanding. Many interfaith groups attach much importance to providing opportunities for young people to meet. Often they discover that they face similar problems and that in every society many young people are questioning all religions. They may also discover how much people of all faiths can do together to work for a better world.

Organizations for Interfaith Understanding

No continuing organization emerged from the 1893 World's Parliament of Religions. At first slowly and recently more rapidly, interfaith groups have been established in many places. Some are quite small, meeting in a home. Members get to know each other and learn about each other's beliefs and practices. Sometimes members pray together or share in social or peace work. Other interfaith organizations are national bodies and some are international, seeking to coordinate global interfaith concern. By 1993, the established international interfaith organizations were the International Association for Religious Freedom, the World Congress of Faiths, the Temple of Understanding, and the World Conference on Religion and Peace.

Those who take part in interfaith bodies seek for a bond between religious believers, despite the differences of belief and practice between and within the great religions. The interfaith organizations all reject *syncretism*, which implies an artificial mixing of religions, and *indifferentism*, which suggests that it does not matter what you believe. None of these organizations are trying to create one new world religion, although some other groups have that hope.

The interfaith organizations accept that most of their members will be loyal and committed members of a particular faith community. Respect for the integrity of other people's faith commitment and religious practices is essential. A few members of interfaith organizations may have no specific allegiance and describe themselves as seekers. While aware of the distinctiveness of the world religions, members of interfaith organizations hope that some basis of unity exists or may be discovered, although the nature of the relationship of religions to each other is still much debated. For some people the unity rests upon our common humanity; for others there is an essential agreement between religions on moral values; for others there is a mystical unity, by which they mean that religious experience is ultimately the same and that differences are a matter of culture and language; others hope that through dialogue religions will come closer together and grow in their understanding of the Truth; others stress the need of religious people to work together for peace and justice and the relief of human suffering; for some, it is enough that there should be tolerance and respect, without bothering about questions of Truth. All these shades of opinion and many more are reflected within interfaith organizations, which have generally avoided trying to define the relationship of religions. For them, the search for understanding and cooperation is urgent in itself.

In their early years the international interfaith organizations tended to stress what united religious believers. Now, with greater trust and knowledge, equal emphasis is given to appreciating the distinctive contribution each faith—and the various traditions within each faith—make to human awareness of the Divine. Increasingly, those who occupy leadership roles in the various religious communities have begun to take an active part in interfaith organizations, whereas at first the initiative lay with inspired individuals. It has taken a long time to erode the traditional suspicion and competition between religions—and it still persists, especially in the problems created by aggressive missionary work. The main brake on the growth of interfaith understanding has been the conservatism of religious communities. Happily, now, those at the leadership level in many religious traditions recognize the vital importance of interreligious cooperation.

Peace through Religion

While all efforts for interfaith understanding promote a climate of peace, some interfaith organizations, especially the World Conference on Religion and Peace, have concentrated on encouraging religious people to be active in peace work. Attempts to bring together people of different religions to pro-

mote peace date back to the early part of the 20th century. Even so, the first Assembly of the World Conference on Religion and Peace did not meet until 1970. It is hard to assess the impact that religious people can have on political processes, especially as politicians seldom acknowledge those who have influenced them. Modern communications have given added weight to popular opinion.

Religious leaders may play an important role in forming public opinion by insisting on the relevance of spiritual and moral considerations. They have helped to maintain public alarm at the enormous stockpile of nuclear weapons and other means of mass destruction. They have voiced public outrage at the starvation of millions of people due to war, injustice, and unfair patterns of international trade. They have upheld human dignity and protested against torture and racism. They have underpinned efforts to develop internationally agreed standards of human rights and have helped to monitor their application. Interreligious conferences have been among the first to warn of threats to the environment. In local areas of conflict, religious people have often maintained contact across boundaries and divisions. Yet often, too, religious people have used religious loyalties to enflame conflict and have allowed particular interests to outweigh common human and religious moral values. Some extremists stir up religious passions to gain support for their own agendas.

It is even more difficult to evaluate the power of prayer, but certainly remarkable changes have recently taken place in the world scene, especially since the first World Day of Prayer for Peace at Assisi in 1986. Each year some people of all religions join in The Week of Prayer for World Peace. Special days of prayer are held to mark human rights anniversaries and for particular areas of conflict. Many people regularly repeat the Universal Prayer for Peace:

Lead me from death to life, from falsehood to truth.
Lead me from despair to hope, from fear to trust;
Lead me from hate to love, from war to peace.
Let peace fill our heart, our world, our universe.

Religious Institutions Engage in Dialogue

Often those who have pioneered the search for good relations between religions have faced misunderstanding and even hostility in their own faith community. They have been accused of compromising or watering down the distinctive beliefs of their own religion. In fact, however, most pioneers witness that learning about other religions has helped them appreciate their own more deeply. Slowly the value of interfaith dialogue has become more widely recognized. In the Christian world, in 1966, The Second Vatican Council's decree *Nostra Aetate* transformed the Catholic Church's attitude to people of other religions. A Secretariat for non-Christians was established, which is now called The Pontifical Council for Inter-Religious Dialogue. At much the same time, the World Council of Churches established a Unit for Dialogue with People of Living Faiths (now the Office on Inter-Religious Relations), which has arranged various consultations and has encouraged Protestant and Orthodox churches to rethink their theological approach to other religions. Some other religions now have agencies to encourage dialogue; these include the International Jewish Committee on Inter-Religious Consultations and the World Muslim League's office for interreligious affairs.

Clearly, official dialogue has a character of its own. Participants have some representative role. Much of the work is to remove misunderstanding and build up good relations, as well as encouraging practical cooperation on moral issues and social concerns. More speculative discussion about questions of "truth" may be inappropriate. Further, while most organizations fully respect the freedom of all who participate in consultations, the host organization may have its own agenda. This means that official interreligious discussions need to be distinguished from interfaith organizations, where ultimate control rests with a board or executive which is itself interfaith in composition and where funding comes from several religious communities. The growth of discussions between representatives of religious communities is, however, a sign that the importance of harmony between religions is now seen as urgent by the leaders and members of religious communities themselves. This is in part due to the pioneering work of interfaith organizations.

Bilateral Conversations

As in a family, there are times when the whole family wishes to be together and times when two members of the family want to talk by themselves, so there are times when members of just two religions wish to engage in dialogue. A particular example of this is Jewish-Christian dialogue. A major international organization, the International Council of Christians and Jews, was formed in 1975 to foster good relations between the two religions. Other examples are the growing Christian-Muslim dialogue, some Muslim-Jewish dialogue, and considerable Christian-Buddhist dialogue both in North America and in Japan. There are now many study and conference centers in different parts of the world which promote dialogue between members of two or three religions.

The Practical Importance of Interfaith Understanding

The Gulf War, the Salman Rushdie affair, and the conflicts in former Yugoslavia have emphasized the practical importance and urgency of interfaith understanding. No longer can anyone dismiss religion as obsolete or irrelevant to world affairs. But many wonder whether the future belongs to the interfaith movement or whether we are likely to see increasing religious rivalry. Some indeed have an apocalyptic vision of the next century being dominated by renewed conflict between Christendom and the world of Islam. The interfaith movement has serious problems to overcome if it is to achieve its goals.

In all religions there is an increase of extremism, which also alienates others from any religious allegiance. Missionary groups in some religions make exclusive claims that theirs is the only way to truth and salvation. Elsewhere religious differences enflame political and economic divisions and sometimes religion is exploited by the powerful as an instrument of social control. Even India, of whose tolerance Swami Vivekananda boasted at the

World's Parliament of Religions one hundred years ago, has seen the increase of "communalism," or rivalry between different religious and ethnic groups.

In Eastern Europe, the renewed nationalism is often closely linked to religious identity and has been accompanied by anti-Semitism and discrimination against religious minorities. It is easy to deplore intolerance—especially in others. It is harder to understand its causes, which may be psychological or related to a group that is feeling politically, culturally, or economically marginalized. Intolerance may be caused by fear or ignorance or it may be based on exclusive claims to truth.

Even dialogue itself may be misused. As it becomes more popular, it may be "hijacked" for ideological purposes—that is to say, people may have hidden agendas such as wanting to change the views of their dialogue partners or seeking to gain their support for a political cause.

Much to Be Done

Despite all the problems, the interfaith movement has made progress, especially in recent years. Even so, it is still very weak. The initiative was often with "marginal" groups—to whom all credit is due. Gradually liberal members of the major religions began to take part. Now, many religious leaders are committed to this work; even so, the religious communities are still reluctant to fund interfaith work, most of which is semivoluntary. Cooperation between interfaith organizations is still only on an ad hoc basis. Adequate structures for greater coordination and cooperation are required. There is an urgent need, too, for centers of information about worldwide interfaith work. There is also much popular ignorance. The Year of Interreligious Understanding and Cooperation declared by several interfaith organizations in 1993 was intended to increase public awareness of the need for interfaith cooperation and to encourage those involved to assess their progress and to determine priorities for future work.

The educational task is still far from complete. The growth of comparative religious studies has helped to dispel ignorance about the world religions, but ignorance is still widespread. Theologians have helped their communities rethink traditional attitudes to other faiths, yet exclusive attitudes are still common. All religions claim insights into *Truth*. There needs, therefore, to be continuing dialogue so that religions may share their insights and together come to a deeper understanding of Ultimate Reality. This dialogue includes both intellectual discussion and efforts to appreciate each other's patterns of prayer and meditation. Yet in many cases the thinkers are quite remote from religious leaders. Meanwhile, religious rivalries destroy lives. Religious people are reluctant to make clear that their commitment to the search for truth and the defense of human rights is stronger than their group loyalty—costly as this may be.

The interfaith movement is becoming increasingly more practical with a new emphasis on ways of cooperating to face urgent problems and to seek a "global ethic" or consensus on moral values. The discovery of those who attended the first meeting of the World Conference on Religion and Peace in Kyoto, Japan, in 1970, was that "the things which unite us are more important than the things which divide us." The interfaith organizations have shown that people of many religions can agree on the importance of peace and justice and on action to relieve suffering and to save the planet's ecosystem. The events and publicity during 1993, the Year of Interreligious Understanding and Cooperation, provided a chance to make the vital importance of interfaith work far more widely known, not only in combating extremism and communalism but in harnessing the energies of all people of faith and of goodwill to tackle the urgent problems of the world. Only by working together will the dreams of 1893 be realized. Only by standing together will prejudice and discrimination be removed, violence and injustice ended, poverty relieved, and the planet preserved.

II: A New Agenda

Since 1993, there has been rapid growth of interfaith activity throughout the world, with increasing emphasis on its practical importance. The number of local interfaith groups has also increased in several countries. Indeed, I see 1993 as a milestone in the growth of the interfaith movement. The focus has changed from trying to get people of different religions together to discovering what people of faith can do together for our world. Paul Knitter, for example, argues in his recent *One Earth, Many Religions* that "concern for the widespread suffering that grips humanity and threatens the planet can and must be the 'common cause' for all religions." Hans Küng, in his *A Global Ethic for Global Politics and Economics*, seeks to show how moral principles can and should be applied to the affairs of the world. For myself, during the Year of Interreligious Understanding and Cooperation in 1993, I came to see that we were not just talking about cooperation between religious people, but about cooperation within national societies and between nations as essential for our life together.

Despite the very practical efforts of some groups, up until 1993 much of the energy in the interfaith movement had to go into persuading people of different faiths to meet. There was first of all ignorance and quite often hostility to overcome. People of one faith knew little about another faith and what they knew was often erroneous. A second task was encouraging people of different faiths to get to know each other, to relax in each other's company, to talk and perhaps to become friends. As prejudices were dispelled and friendship grew, many people found they had to rethink their attitudes toward the members and theologies of other religions.

Now, however, many people long for the religions to be "the moral conscience of humanity," as Pope John Paul II expressed it to the Assisi World Day of Prayer for Peace. This new agenda reflects the fact that the great problems that threaten human life and the environment concern us all, just because of our common humanity. Since 1993, several international interfaith bodies have focused on practical questions. [These activities are described in more detail in Chapter 21. Ed.]

The question now is, What effect does all this work have? Indeed, the subject of two of the conferences of the International Interfaith Centre at Oxford have been "How effective is interfaith activity in halting and healing conflict?" To have an even greater impact, the interfaith movement must address a number of concerns.

Widening the Circle of Dialogue

1. Traditionalists Are Welcome. The dangers that threaten our world society may be the basis on which traditional members of the faiths may be encouraged to engage more fully in interfaith activity. Yet they are often put off by what they suppose to be the "liberal presuppositions" of the interfaith movement. There are those who reject any meeting with members of another faith tradition. Although these are often labeled "extremists" or "fundamentalists," the cause of their suspicion of and hostility to others may be primarily because of political and economic divisions. Many others who perhaps are best described as "traditionalists" do not wish to give religious legitimacy to another faith tradition. Quite possibly, they have not thought much about the matter, but do recognize that people of different faiths have to live together and therefore need to understand some basic things about each other: for example, what foods should not be served at a civic reception in a religiously plural city?

A pluralist society requires respect for those of other persuasions. Even societies where one religion is dominant may have to take account of significant religious minorities. Teddy Kollek, for example, while mayor of Jerusalem, tried to be sensitive to the religious concerns of Muslim and Christian minorities. Many Islamic states have to make allowance for significant minorities of other faiths.

I doubt if we can reach widespread agreement on the philosophical or theological basis for interfaith work, at least in the immediate future. Perhaps rather than assuming that theological pluralism is the basis for interfaith dialogue, we should acknowledge a pluralism of dialogue. Probably within each religion one can find those to whom the labels "exclusivist," "inclusivist," and "pluralist" can be applied. Perhaps the need is to discover the contribution each group can make to interfaith dialogue.

For instance, the exclusivist stresses commitment, and this is a welcome reminder that interfaith activity should not evade questions of truth. The inclusivist speaks as a member of a particular faith community and can help that tradition reinterpret its theology so that while affirming its central witness it need not deny the witness of others. The pluralist affirms that the richness of the Divine Mystery cannot be contained in one tradition.

I wonder if even as individuals most of us operate within only one model. I recognize that in part I could fit under all the categories. I have a personal commitment as a disciple of Christ; in my theological thinking I seek as a Christian to see God's purpose in the whole religious life of humanity; and as a student of religion and as an interfaith activist, I do not presume that any faith has a privileged position.

2. Listening to Minority Voices. Practical cooperation is not without its difficulties. Is it genuinely interreligious and international or are certain groups recruiting support for their own agenda? Marc Ellis, in his *Unholy Alliance*, reminds us that Palestinians feel that Christian-Jewish dialogue has added to their sufferings, while the Dalits in India feel this about Hindu-Christian dialogue. In some places, women feel they have been excluded from the dialogue.

Does the emphasis on religious consensus allow space for the voices of religious minorities and of those who have no formal religious commitment? A consensus document may be a threat to minorities, especially to those whose religious identity is resented by the mainstream.

3. Listening to Spiritual Movements. We have also to recognize that spiritual wisdom is not the monopoly of religious officials. The Spirit, like the wind, "bloweth where it listeth." I believe that the Chicago Parliament did us all a good turn by opening its doors to all who wanted to come; on the whole, few religions have been in the vanguard of progress. Some groups did withdraw due to the inclusiveness, but that was their choice. It may well be that religious and denominational organizations and hierarchical leadership will become less significant in the next millennium.

4. Listening to Other Disciplines. Equally, we need the wisdom of the experts in many particular disciplines, especially those who are people of faith. Dialogue needs to be multidisciplinary as well as multifaith. Experts in a whole range of disciplines may themselves be committed members of a faith. This was made clear to me when I spoke to the Retired Generals for Peace about the Global Ethic and the role of the military in peacekeeping. Many of those high-ranking officers were committed members of a faith.

If interfaith dialogue is to deal with the vital issues that face human society, it should not be confined to religious specialists or religious leaders. It needs to engage those with expertise in all the relevant disciplines. Particularly, there should be an attempt to involve in this debate those with political and economic power as well as those who control the media. They, however, will perhaps not be interested until there has been far wider public education about the vital importance of interfaith cooperation. Change will begin to happen only as the politically aware public demands that nations act in the interest of the world society and seek to shape that society according to ethical values upheld by the great spiritual traditions as well as by many humanists.

Difficulties to Be Addressed

1. Disagreements within Religions. We are all aware of the disagreements within religions. At one Christian-Jewish dialogue group, it was suggested after our first session that the Jews go into one room to sort out their differences and that the Christians should go into another and solve their disagreements. The differences may be not only theological, but relate to the great social, ecological, and moral issues which we have been suggesting should be the focus of interfaith activity.

Intra-religious dialogue is very important. But in our concern for the environment, the protection of human rights, and the struggle for economic justice, we may well find ourselves in opposition to some members of our own and other faiths. The more socially engaged the interfaith movement becomes, the less it may be a unifying force amongst all believers.

2. Interfaith Organizations Need to Work Together. When people hear of another interfaith organization, the reaction may be "Do we need another interfaith body?" To those on the outside, one interfaith group looks much the same as another, and the motley variety of initials used for the organizations seems designed to confuse.

In fact, there is plenty of work for them all to do. As we have seen, there is a great variety of approaches to interfaith work and each organization has its own particular focus and constituency. Only by working together will the interfaith movement be listened to by the media and by those who control economic and political power.

There have been suggestions that what is needed is a World Council of Faiths, which could perhaps be formed by the merging together of the various international interfaith organizations. It is questionable whether one super organization would be more effective or just more bureaucratic. What seems to me important is a sense of partnership between the organizations and awareness of belonging to a movement that is bigger than any of us. I have hoped that there could be some worldwide coordinating body, rather like the International Council of Christians and Jews, for those engaged in Christian-Jewish dialogue, or the Society for Buddhist-Christian Studies.

The International Interfaith Centre (IIC) at Oxford, which has been set up by the International Association for Religious Freedom, the World Congress of Faiths, and Westminster College, Oxford, has as its purpose to encourage education about interfaith activity and to facilitate cooperation amongst all those engaged in this work. The Centre aims to hold information about interfaith work across the world, to keep those involved in touch with each other, while being a source of information to the media; it also aims to encourage research on questions of concern to many people involved in interfaith work, regardless of their particular organization.

As mentioned above, a particular concern at IIC conferences has been to examine how interfaith

work can be more effective in areas of conflict, such as Sri Lanka, Northern Ireland, former Yugoslavia, and the Middle East. The center is also developing electronic communication capabilities. Nonetheless, hospitality to visitors to the Centre and the many individual contacts and introductions made by the Centre remain at the heart of its work to create a sense of spiritual fellowship amongst all engaged in what has been called a "Pilgrimage of Hope."

Wishful Thinking?

If the interfaith movement is to be effective in helping to rebuild our world on spiritual and moral principles, there is a great deal of work to be done. In many societies, religions are peripheral to the centers of economic and political power. Perhaps the greatest task is to argue that this is a moral and spiritual world.

Is that hope, as Hans Küng asks in his Preface to *A Global Ethic* (Continuum, 1993), a "sheer illusion"? In answer, he points "the eternal skeptic" to the worldwide change of awareness about economics and ecology, about world peace and disarmament, and about the partnership between men and women. Perhaps one special contribution of faith is to inspire hope that change is possible. Such a conviction is based on our inner life. Although I have stressed the needs of the world as our common agenda, the hope and energy to address this will come from the inner life of prayer and meditation. The source of practical action is our spirituality. Inner and outer belong together. The activist will be exhausted without an inner life and the true mystic longs for the world's renewal.

My hopes for interfaith work are graphically expressed in a passage at the end of Choan-Seng Song's *The Compassionate God*. There he described an African's dream of the world:

A giant snake, enormously powerful, was coiling itself around the globe. The globe seemed too weak to withstand the pressure. I could see the first cracks in it. Then I saw a light at the center of the world. Enter into this light, I was told, but I resisted. . . . But the light was irresistible. I went towards it and, as I did so, I saw many others moving towards it, too. And the snake's grip gradually began to loosen.

Choan-Seng Song comments on the dream:

> The world has in fact begun to crack. We seem destined for destruction at our own hands. But behold, miracle of miracles, out of the cracks a light shines. . . . We all need that light, for that light is our only hope—we, the poor and the rich, the oppressed and the oppressors, the theists and the atheists, Christians, Muslims, Jews, Buddhists, and Hindus. We must all get to that light, for it is the light of love and life, the light of hope and the future. The movement of persons toward that light must have constituted a formidable power, for the snake, the demon, begins to loosen its grip on the globe.

—*The Compassionate God*, SCM Press, 1982, pp. 259–60

There is abundant spiritual energy and hope to release our world from the fears and dangers that threaten to crush us, if only we can harness that energy effectively.

—Parts I and II of this essay were previously printed as Chapter 2 and part of Chapter 8 in *Faith and Interfaith in a Global Age*, CoNexus Press and Braybrooke Press, 1998, Grand Rapids and Oxford.

Points of Similarity Found in Dialogue

Father Thomas Keating, O.S.C.O.

Convener of the Snowmass Conference and member of Monastic Interfaith Dialogue

A report on an experience of ongoing interreligious dialogue might be helpful at this point. In 1984 I invited a group of spiritual teachers from a variety of the world religions—Buddhist, Tibetan Buddhist, Hindu, Jewish, Islamic, Native American, Russian Orthodox, Protestant, and Roman Catholic—to gather at St. Benedict's Monastery, Snowmass, Colorado, to meditate together in silence and to share our personal spiritual journeys, especially those elements in our respective traditions that have proved most helpful to us along the way.

We kept no record and published no papers. As our trust and friendship grew, we felt moved to investigate various points that we seemed to agree on. The original points of agreement were worked over during the course of subsequent meetings as we continued to meet, for a week or so each year. Our most recent list consists of the following eight points:

1. The world religions bear witness to the experience of Ultimate Reality to which they give various names: Brahman, Allah, Absolute, God, Great Spirit.

2. Ultimate Reality cannot be limited by any name or concept.

3. Ultimate Reality is the ground of infinite potentiality and actualization.

4. Faith is opening, accepting, and responding to Ultimate Reality. Faith in this sense precedes every belief system.

5. The potential for human wholeness—or in other frames of reference, enlightenment, salvation, transformation, blessedness, *nirvana*—is present in every human person.

6. Ultimate Reality may be experienced not only through religious practices but also through nature, art, human relationships, and service of others.

7. As long as the human condition is experienced as separate from Ultimate Reality, it is subject to ignorance and illusion, weakness and suffering.

8. Disciplined practice is essential to the spiritual life; yet spiritual attainment is not the result of one's own efforts, but the result of the experience of oneness with Ultimate Reality.

At the annual Conference in May 1986, we came up with additional points of agreement of a practical nature:

A. *Some examples of disciplined practice, common to us all:*

1. Practice of compassion

2. Service to others

3. Practicing moral precepts and virtues

4. Training in meditation techniques and regularity of practice

5. Attention to diet and exercise

6. Fasting and abstinence

7. The use of music and chanting and sacred symbols

8. Practice in awareness (recollection, mindfulness) and living in the present moment

9. Pilgrimage

10. Study of scriptural texts and scriptures

And in some traditions:

11. Relationship with a qualified teacher

12. Repetition of sacred words (mantra, *japa*)

13. Observing periods of silence and solitude

14. Movement and dance

15. Formative community

B. *It is essential to extend our formal practice of awareness into all the aspects of our life.*

C. *Humility, gratitude, and a sense of humor are indispensable in the spiritual life.*

D. *Prayer is communion with Ultimate Reality, whether it is regarded as personal, impersonal, or beyond them both.*

We were surprised and delighted to find so many points of similarity and convergence in our respective paths. Like most people of our time, we originally expected that we would find practically nothing in common. In the years that followed we spontaneously and somewhat hesitatingly began to take a closer look at certain points of disagreement until these became our main focus of attention. We found that discussing our points of disagreement increased the bonding of the group even more than discovering our points of agreement. We became more honest in stating frankly what we believed and why, without at the same time making any effort to convince others of our own position. We simply presented our understanding as a gift to the group.

The Deep-Dialogue Decalogue
GROUND RULES FOR PERSONAL AND COMMUNAL DEEP-DIALOGUE

Dr. Leonard Swidler and Global Dialogue Institute

Professor Swidler teaches Catholic Thought and Interreligious Studies in the Religion Department at Temple University, has edited the Journal of Ecumenical Studies *since 1963, and is cofounder and Director of Global Dialogue Institute. He published the first version of "The Dialogue Decalogue" in the* Journal *in 1983. This new version reflects developments based on his and others' experience of the global needs and objectives for dialogue.*

Prologue

Dialogue is a conversation between individual persons—and through them, two or more communities or groups—with differing views; the *primary* purpose of this encounter is for each participant to learn from the other so that s/he can change and grow and thereby the respective groups or communities as well. This very definition of *dialogue* embodies the first Ground Rule of Deep-Dialogue. In the past we encountered those differing with us, for example, labor with management, Catholics with Protestants, either mainly to defeat an opponent, or at best to negotiate with him or her. If we faced each other at all, it usually was in confrontation sometimes more openly polemically, sometimes more subtly so, but nearly always with the ultimate goal of defeating the other, because we were convinced that we alone had the "truth." But *dialogue* is *not* debate, or even negotiation. In *dialogue* each partner listens to the other as openly and sympathetically as s/he can in an attempt to understand the other's position as precisely and, as it were, as much from within, as possible. Such an attitude automatically includes the assumption that at any point we might find the partner's position so persuasive that, if we would act with integrity, we would have to change. Obviously, then, through such *dialogue* and change we will move closer to a deeper, richer understanding of "truth," of the way things really are in the world.

We are here speaking not of superficial *dialogue* or merely "techniques" of *dialogue*, helpful though they may be. Rather, we are speaking of Deep-Dialogue, a way of encountering and understanding oneself and the world at the deepest levels. This opens up possibilities of grasping the fundamental meanings of life, individually and corporately, and its various dimensions, which in turn transforms the way we deal with ourselves, others, and the world. Deep-Dialogue on a broad, communal scale is a whole new way of thinking, of understanding the world. It was understood and practiced in the past by a number of great spiritual geniuses of humankind—Jesus, Gautama, the Sufis, Gandhi—but it never before reached into communal consciousness. Now, applying the insights and experiences of prior giants, it has. In that vital sense it *is* something new under the sun.

The following are some basic Ground Rules of Deep-Dialogue that must be observed if *dialogue* is actually to take place. These are not theoretical rules given from "on high," but ones that have been learned from hard experience. To the extent they are observed, to that degree, dialogue, with all its benefits, will occur.

First Ground Rule: Be Open Within!

Open yourself to your dialogue partner so as to learn, that is, to change and grow in your perception and understanding of reality, and then act accordingly—an intrapersonal move.

We enter into *dialogue* so we can learn, change, and grow, not so we can force change on the other, as one hopes to do in debate—a hope realized in inverse proportion to the frequency and fierceness with which debate is entered into. On the other hand, because in *dialogue* each partner comes with the intention of learning and changing herself, one's partner in fact will also change. Thus the goal of debate, and much more, is accomplished far more effectively by *dialogue*.

Second Ground Rule: Attend!

Be fully present both to yourself and your partner; respond to your partner rather than make your favorite speech.

Since we engage in dialogue so we can learn from our partner, it is imperative that we be fully present, that is, to be conscious of ourselves and of our partner. Otherwise, how can we learn? Likewise, to learn we must focus on our partner, from whom we hope to learn. Again, otherwise, how can we learn? Further, because dialogue is a two-way project, we need to respond to what our partner has said, rather than deliver a pat lecture. Otherwise, we are attending only to ourselves, but not to our partner.

Third Ground Rule: Be Open Between!

Make dialogue a two-sided project—within each community as well as between communities—an intercommunal move.

Because of the "corporate" nature of community or group *dialogue*, and since its primary goal is that each partner learn and change himself, it is also necessary that each participant enter into *dialogue* not only with his partner across the community or group line—labor with management, the Lutheran with the Anglican, for example—but also with his own community, with his fellow workers or fellow Lutherans, to share with them the fruits of the *dialogue*. Only thus can the whole community or group eventually learn and change, moving toward an ever truer, deeper insight into reality.

Fourth Ground Rule: Be Honest and Trusting!

Come to the dialogue with complete honesty and sincerity.

Each participant should attempt to make clear in what direction the major and minor thrusts of her community or group move, what the future shifts might be, and, if necessary, where the participant has difficulties with her own community or group. No false fronts have any place in *dialogue*.

Conversely—*Assume a similar complete honesty and sincerity in your partner.*

Not only will the absence of sincerity prevent *dialogue* from happening, but the absence of the assumption of your partner's sincerity will do so as well. In brief: no trust, no *dialogue*.

Fifth Ground Rule: Cultivate Personal Trust!

Cultivate personal trust by searching first for commonalities, since dialogue can take place only on the basis of mutual trust.

Although group, communal *dialogue* must occur with some kind of "corporate" dimension, that is, the participants must be involved as members of a "community," for instance, as management, as labor, as Buddhists, or . . . it is also fundamentally true that it is only persons who can enter into *dialogue*. But a *dialogue* among persons can be built only on personal trust. Hence it is wise not to tackle the most difficult problems in the beginning, but rather to approach first those issues most likely to provide some common ground, thereby establishing the basis of human trust. Then, gradually, as this personal trust deepens and expands, the more thorny matters can be confronted. Thus, as in learning we move from the known to the unknown, so in *dialogue* we proceed from commonly held matters—which, given our frequent mutual ignorance, will often take us quite some time to discover fully—to discuss matters of likely disagreement.

Sixth Ground Rule: Don't Prejudge; Compare Fairly!

Come to the dialogue with no hard-and-fast assumptions as to where the points of agreement and disagreement are.

Each partner should not only listen to the other with openness and sympathy but also attempt to agree as far as possible, while still maintaining integrity with her own community or tradition; where she absolutely can agree no further without violating her own integrity, precisely there is where agreement ends and disagreement really begins—a point which often turns out to be different from what was falsely assumed ahead of time.

At the same time compare your ideals with your partner's ideals, your practice with your partner's practice.

For example, compare the old Hindu practice of widow-burning with the Christian practice of witch-burning, not with the Christian ideal of loving neighbor as self. In fact, that ideal of the Golden

Rule is found in most religious and ethical traditions, including Confucian, Hindu, Buddhist, Jewish, Christian, Muslim, aboriginal, and secular.

Seventh Ground Rule: Define Yourself in Dialogue!

You and your partner define yourselves in dialogue.

Only the Jew, for example, can define what it means to be a Jew, or a Hispanic what it means to be a Hispanic though the *dialogue* partner can contribute to that self-definition. Because *dialogue* is a dynamic medium, as each participant learns from the other, he will change and hence continually deepen, expand, and modify his self-definition as a Jew or as a Hispanic, being careful to remain in constant *dialogue* with his fellow Jews or fellow Hispanics. Thus it is mandatory that each *dialogue* partner define what it means to be an authentic member of his own community or tradition but in dialogic openness to his partner.

Eighth Ground Rule: Treat Others As Equals!

Treat your partner as an equal, for dialogue can take place only between equals.

Both partners must come to learn from each other. Therefore, if, for example, labor and management do not respect each other, or the Muslim views Hinduism as inferior, or the Hindu views Islam as inferior, there will be no *dialogue*. If authentic *dialogue* is to occur, both labor and management, the Muslim and the Hindu must come mainly to learn from each other. All participants regardless of prior status must enter into a "safe space" of equality if Deep-Dialogue is to be attained. Deep-Dialogue, however, not only requires, but also tends to *produce* an equal empowerment among partners. Deep-Dialogue fosters a "virtuous circle." There can be no such thing as a one-way *dialogue*.

Ninth Ground Rule: Be Healthily Self-Critical!

Be healthily self-critical of yourself and your group or community; only then can you be compassionately critical of your partner.

A lack of self-criticism implies that you and your own group or community already have all the correct answers. Such an attitude makes *dialogue* not only unnecessary, but even impossible, since we enter *dialogue* primarily so we can learn—which is impossible if we have never made a misstep, if we have all the right answers. To be sure, in communal *dialogue* one must stand within a community or tradition with integrity and conviction, but such integrity and conviction must include, not exclude, a healthy self-criticism. Without it there can be no *dialogue* and, indeed, no integrity. Once you have shown yourself to be seriously self-critical, your partner will be open to a compassionate, constructive critique of her position. Thus again, a "virtuous circle" is fostered.

Tenth Ground Rule: Pass Over and Return!

Pass over and experience your partner's community or tradition "from within," and then return to your own, enriched.

A community or tradition is not merely something of the head, but also of the heart, spirit, and "whole being," individual and communal. Hence, in Deep-Dialogue we need to "pass over" into our partner's "interior" world and experience something of its emotional and symbolic impact—then return to our own, enlightened and enriched, bringing something of the Other within us.

Deep-Dialogue among individuals, communities, or groups operates in three areas:

1. The intellectual, where we seek understanding
2. The practical, where we collaborate to help humanity
3. The depth or "spiritual" dimension where we experience something of the partner's emotional and meaning-of-life/spiritual resources "from within."

Deep-Dialogue among individuals, communities, or groups has four phases:

1. In the first phase we unlearn misinformation about each other and begin to know each other as we truly are.

2. In phase two we begin to discern values in our partner's community or tradition and may wish to adapt them into our own. For example, in an American-Japanese business *dialogue*, the American may come to appreciate the value of labor-management cooperation, and the Japanese to appreciate a government "hands-off," antitrust promotion of competition.

3. If we are serious, persistent, and sensitive enough in the *dialogue*, we may at times enter into phase three. Here we together begin to explore new areas of reality and new ways of acting, new insights into meaning—all of which neither of us had previously even been aware. We are brought face to face with this new, until-then-unknown-to-us dimension of reality and possibility of action, insight into meaning, only because of the questions, insights, probings produced in the *dialogue*.

4. If we experience phase three in more than one *dialogue* we will be propelled into phase four, in which we begin along with an increasing appreciation of diversity to perceive in a deep way the oneness of all people and our unity with nature. Thus, it is stamped on the U.S. penny: *E pluribus unum*. This is Deep-Dialogue *par excellence*.

Proposal for a Code of Ethics among Religions in Mexico

Mexican InterFaith Council

NOTE: The Mexican government's Department of the Interior has decided to promote this *Code of Ethics among Religions* as an example to the Mexican people of the harmony that needs to exist in every Mexican community throughout the nation. Created by the Mexican InterFaith Council (CIM), the Department helped the CIM reprint the Code and distributes it in those regions of Mexico where problems of religious intolerance exist as is now the case in the municipality of San Juan Chamula in the state of Chiapas.

Foreword

Religion is a value intrinsically related to mankind's aspirations for some kind of transcendence. Religion is found in the emotional dimension of man as well as his intellectual side: under the banner of religion mankind has constructed cultures and civilizations. Religion has been the foundation for those universal values that support the well-being and happiness not only of individuals but of entire nations.

Nevertheless since man is often contradictory and unsettling in his effect on the world we live in, this is also evident in his religious dimension. Throughout history it has been possible, using religion as an excuse, to discriminate against the dignity of other men, denying their most basic rights and even taking their lives. Examples abound of everything from family disputes to cruel international conflicts beginning and soon becoming inflamed by uncontrollable passions, all in the name of one form of religion or another.

However, we always must be reminded, even in the midst of the most terrible crises of civilized man, and in spite of the contradictions ever present in mankind, that we human beings are marvelously capable of believing and having faith in ourselves and our ability to create and correct our lives and cultures by means of our memory, reason, talent, and willpower.

The sense of the divine and of transcendence which diverse religions share, each from its own point of departure, is the original wellspring which we believers draw on as the foundation and justification for the rights of man and is the ethical imperative that has impelled us to deal here and now with the questions of interfaith relationships.

The religious institutions which are members of the Mexican InterFaith Council offer to the Mexican people this *Code of Ethics* based on our faith both in mankind and in our separate religious convictions because we know that in the final analysis man is born to be content within society, sharing his life including his differences with his fellowman.

In using the word "Code" we do not wish to imply anything either judicial or dogmatic but rather we choose this word used in the spirit of a proposal. Our text attempts to be humbly lucid and boldly critical; it is definitely not our intention to offend the autonomy of any of the diverse religious groups or communities. But the *Code* does constitute a testimony before those groups and before public opinion and we do solicit the adoption of its message by all who read it. Each and every one of the religions possesses an abundant treasure trove of ethical values which when practiced contribute to mankind's happiness and we sincerely believe some of these treasures deserve to be placed in a common setting herein.

We believe it is within each of the religions itself where the possibility exists for a reaction to this *Code* that furthers the creation of a true interreligious and humanitarian fraternity, because our diversity does not condemn us to any permanent contradiction nor does it preclude us from living happily side by side.

The *Code*'s objective, therefore, and the resonance which it may have in Mexico (and worldwide), lies not in attempting to nullify diversity nor in mortgaging the separate identity of each religion. Rather our goal is to unite us in agreement that our diversity is in itself valuable and beautiful as a product of human liberty and to remind each other that our various paths intertwine often and easily in the many shared values and objectives that exist in the human condition, in the air we breath, and on the planet we inhabit together.

Respectfully,
Mexican InterFaith Council

Considering:

1. That the reason for the existence of religions is the belief in an Entity or Supreme Being which has inspired and infused mankind with a dignity from which emanates certain inalienable human rights for every individual.

2. That all religious beliefs have at least the following fundamental ethical principles in common: mercy, compassion, brotherhood, respect, and tolerance, and the search for peace and self-betterment, both for the individual and for society in general.

3. That liberty, justice, and peace have as a basis the intrinsic dignity and equal and inviolable rights of all members of the human family and its different religious communities.

4. That ignorance and contempt among followers of different religions has been a cause throughout human history and still causes today acts of war and other outrages which afflict our lives and stain our collective conscience.

5. That many of the constant outbreaks of violence, personal attacks, and conflicts of war have their origins in religious questions related to the freedom to express different ideas.

6. That oppressive situations including torture, human exploitation, and the imposition of ideologies are the most extreme obstacles to peaceful coexistence among the faithful of the different religions and among society in general.

7. That it has been proclaimed and we hereby reaffirm the highest aspiration of mankind is a world in which all men, liberated from ignorance and all fanaticism, can enjoy freedom of belief, of conscience, and of expression at the same time respecting the rights of all other men.

8. That it is essential to protect the freedom of beliefs by means of a State of Law as well as mutual respect, in order to avoid the danger that persons who profess different religious beliefs might attack each other.

9. That tolerance and respect for the rights of every person both to choose and to freely practice his or her religion are inalienable rights of mankind.

10. That the members from each of the different religions known to mankind do thereby reaffirm their faith in basic human rights, in the dignity and value of every person, and in the equality of men and women.

11. That a general understanding of these rights and freedoms by society is the fundamental prerequisite in order that they be respected in everyday life.

12. That religious groups are resolved to promote human development and progress; and to raise living standards, educational levels, and work toward the well being of human society.

13. That any objective view of our world today shows increasing environmental deterioration.

14. That an intolerably large percentage of mankind today lives in extreme poverty.

15. That a set of fundamental principles is required which will inspire and guide individuals as well as religious institutions and communities so that they promote the respect for the rights and freedoms of each of their members and for those of other religious beliefs.

16. That such principles will produce more dignified and peaceful lives, harmonious relations between persons of differing faiths, and will contribute to the growth of and search for happiness among mankind, and . . .

17. Considering as well the vast acceptance of the Universal Declaration of Human Rights, of the United Nations . . .

THE MEXICAN INTERFFAITH COUNCIL proposes the following CODE OF ETHICS AMONG RELIGIONS:

Art. 1. We recognize as fundamental the rights of man as proclaimed in the Universal Declaration of Human Rights of the United Nations and in the Constitution of the Mexican Republic.

Art. 2. Every human being is born free, equal in dignity and entitled to the same rights in society as his fellowman.

Art. 3. Every human being is entitled to the rights and freedoms mentioned above, without any distinction based on religious beliefs, race, color, sex, country of origin, nationality, tradition, political opinion, or any other conditions.

Art. 4. Every human being is free to follow the religion which in good conscience he desires. At the same time he is entitled to freedom of thought and to change his religion or beliefs without any type of outside pressure.

Art. 5. No person will be attacked, ridiculed, nor defamed because of his form of worship or his beliefs, either individually or as a member of a religious group or institution.

Art. 6. No person will be obligated to belong to any predetermined religious group or institution nor to renounce his or her beliefs.

Art. 7. Whenever any person wishes to separate from a particular religious group or institution, he will not be required to explain the motives for that decision.

Art. 8. Everyone has the right to meet freely to celebrate his or her religious ceremonies, out of mutual respect for peaceful coexistence among diverse expressions of faith.

Art. 9. All persons and religious communities shall abstain from attacking, ridiculing, or otherwise insulting the sacred texts which are considered fundamental scripture by any other religious group or institution.

Art. 10. Religious groups or institutions and particularly their individual members should demonstrate mutual respect for the beliefs and expressions of faith of different religious groups or individuals whenever they make oral or written reference to them.

Art. 11. When any religious institution or group receives requests for admission to its faith, it is responsible for fully and clearly explaining to the applicant all the rights and obligations involved in joining the group.

Art. 12. Whenever religious groups or institutions offer invitations to their meetings, conferences, concerts, or any other type of function, they will clearly identify by name the religious group organizing the event.

Art. 13. Parents or tutors have the inalienable right and freedom to choose the religious education and instruction for their children without any outside compulsion whatsoever.

Art. 14. No one will be excluded from nor discriminated against in public primary or secondary education for reasons of religious belief, politics, race, nationality, social condition, or country of origin of his parents or tutors.

Art. 15. All schools and educational institutes sponsored or managed by religious communities, institutions and particularly by their members will respect the freedom of decision of the parents as regards the religious instruction to be given to their children.

Art. 16. Every person, upon reaching the legal age of maturity as defined by law, has the right to marry freely and without restriction by reason of race, nationality, place of origin, or religious beliefs.

Art. 17. No person, upon marriage, should be forced or obliged to change his or her religious beliefs nor to renounce in any manner his or her rights to participate in decisions concerning the education of the children.

Art. 18. No one will be forced or obliged to break his or her family ties or friendships because of belonging to or separating oneself from a particular religious community or because of expressing any religious belief.

Art. 19. Both the institution of marriage and that of the family are fundamental components of society which ought to be unconditionally protected by the State, the religious communities, and society itself.

Art. 20. No person will be discriminated against, persecuted, deprived of his liberty or property, dispossessed, or exiled because of expressing his or her religious beliefs nor because of his or her membership in a religious institution.

Art. 21. All persons and religious communities whatsoever their religious beliefs, will work together in mutual respect and harmony to promote brotherhood, love and care for creation, well-being, and peace among individuals, religious groups, and institutions and in society in general.

Art. 22. The different religious groups and institutions will establish dialogues among themselves with the goal of mutually increasing their knowledge and understanding and thereby eliminating any prejudices among their members towards other religious beliefs and practices.

Chapter Twenty-one
THE INTERFAITH MOVEMENT
Who Are the Interfaith Organizations and What Do They Do?

Introduction

Joel Beversluis

This chapter provides insights into the diverse character, purposes, and activities of the interfaith movement by highlighting a selection of organizations, as well as terms, strategies, and a speech by Pope John Paul II. In addition to the major international organizations, the alphabetically arranged sampling includes other types of organizations. While it offers insights into the interfaith movement, this list is by no means complete. More lists of organizations and Web-sites are provided in Part Four.

Terminology

Because the terms *interfaith, interreligious, multifaith,* and *ecumenical* are sometimes confused or used interchangeably, here's a useful way of distinguishing among them:

- Groups comprised of members of many faiths whose primary purpose is direct service or advocacy are often called *multifaith* organizations to distinguish them from organizations whose primary goals are interfaith understanding, dialogue, or representation.
- The term *interreligious* is best used in reference to deliberate encounters at a clerical or institutional level and where participants represent a religious community in some official or semiofficial capacity.
- The word *ecumenical* is occasionally used in reference to interfaith and interreligious relationships, as in "the wider ecumenism." However, since this word entered common use during the Christian ecumenical movements of the 20th century, that word is best reserved for interactions among Christian denominations. Equally confusing is the fact that some ecumenical organizations have used the word *interfaith* when referring to "among diverse Christian denominations"; for such uses, the word *ecumenical* is more precise.
- In this book, *interfaith* is reserved for those relationships and deliberate encounters or programs between members of communities based in distinctly different religions, spiritual philosophies, aboriginal communities, or new religious movements. The term *interfaith*, whether used in reference to dialogue, joint services, or collaboration, also suggests encounters at an interpersonal or experiential level, particularly when faith and spirituality are the focus.

However, because these distinctions are not always made consistently, the word *interfaith* is also used in this book and elsewhere to reflect more generic references to the movement as a whole.

Types of Interfaith Organizations and Activities

Interfaith organizations and encounters vary enormously in their programs, relationships, goals, and structures. Following is a brief description of eight general types into which most organizations can be categorized.

a. Metropolitan or regional dialogue and education groups, such as the Interfaith Dialogue Association, based in West Michigan.

b. International organizations and networks, such as the World Conference on Religion and Peace, based in New York, or the InterFaith Network for the United Kingdom.

c. Chapters or affiliates of national or international bodies or networks, such as the U.S. Chapter of the International Association for Religious Freedom, or the Chicago chapter of the National Conference for Community and Justice.

d. Interfaith offices or agencies for single faith or spiritual communities, such as the interfaith offices of the National Council of the Churches of Christ, U.S.A.

e. Projects related to academic pursuits, including campus ministries, dialogue groups, interfaith seminaries, and institutes such as Global Dialogue Institute at Temple University.

f. Media with programming by and about many religious traditions, such as Vision TV, a multifaith cable station based in Toronto.

g. Centers for spirituality, holistic health, adult education, or counseling, such as the Shem Center in the Chicago area.

h. Public and private agencies providing direct services and/or advocacy such as food pantries, health care services, AIDS prevention and treatment programs, and peace and ecology organizations.

Other Organizations

Among these many types of organizations are hundreds of coalitions, associations, institutes, local and regional groups, and Web-sites that are exploring new interreligious relationships and collaborative efforts. (See Part Four.) Some of these are chapters or affiliates of larger organizations, but many others are independent or loosely networked grassroots efforts facilitated by visionary individuals and boards. Very effective interfaith work is done by local organizations not only in North America and Europe, but also, for example, in the former Yugoslavia, Israel/Palestine, Sri Lanka, India, and Brazil. The listings in this *Sourcebook*, however, are primarily in North America, with relatively few listings from other continents.

Some of the many interfaith organizations are supported by religious communities such as the Bahá'í Faith, the National Council of Churches, the Pontifical Council on Interfaith Relations, Buddhist and Hindu associations, and the Unification Church, among others. Some are based in academic institutions, and many others are independent, nonprofit organizations with their own memberships. Many authors, journalists, publishers, educators, scholars, and religious leaders are also promoting the ideals of the interfaith movement. And, increasingly, young adults are participating in existing programs as well as by defining their own agendas for action.

Despite their substantial names, visions, and global representation, the number of people actively involved in these organizations is relatively small, given the enormous memberships among Christian, Muslim, Hindu, and Buddhist communities worldwide. The numbers of interfaith participants and audiences, and the impact of these organizations is difficult to document. Even so, the cumulative effect of the movement's exploration of new concepts and cooperative methods in areas of real need reaches far beyond memberships and mailing lists because most of them are engaged in public activities, education, and media outreach to much wider communities.

As in any movement, there are some problems: some of the large organizations should learn more about collaboration and outreach; most interfaith organizations are not well funded; and there is some competition among them for recognition and for the participation of religious and spiritual leaders in their programs.

While there is some overlap in the agendas and constituencies of the larger international interfaith organizations, leaders among them, such as Dr. Marcus Braybrooke, insist that there is plenty of room for new groups of well-intentioned people to creatively define arenas for their work. And their highly motivated volunteers, staff, and supporters are convinced that they are doing significant work. Most see themselves as planting the seeds of ideas and values that are necessary to harmony and well-being in our increasingly complex and interdependent world.

Many participants in the interfaith movement believe that their efforts are contributing to a subtle but persistent evolution within cultures, in the same way that other significant ideas have spread through mass consciousness because of small groups of pioneering individuals. By helping to define and create a safe space for religious communities and individuals to meet, and by encouraging spiritual, ethical, and personal growth, participants in the interfaith movement are encouraging significant new opportunities for members of diverse religions to relate to each other and to the wider world.

A Sampling of Interfaith Organizations and Programs

Compiled by Joel Beversluis

NOTE: While providing a snapshot of some of the interfaith movement's diverse organizations, this sampling is by no means a complete list, nor does it highlight only the largest programs. Many of these organizations have paid staff and international projects while some others are networks with minimal or volunteer staff and, therefore, minimal programming. The information below comes from many sources, including newsletters, brochures, Web-sites, reports, and meetings. For those interfaith organizations that presented major events in 1999, extended descriptions are found below or by following cross-references to other articles. A directory with many more listings of faith-based and interfaith organizations, including addresses, Internet information, and mission statements for these and numerous other organizations is provided in Part Four. Readers are encouraged to learn more about these worthy and pioneering organizations by contacting them directly.

Association of Interfaith Ministers (AIM)

The Association of Interfaith Ministers was formed in 1986 to support Interfaith Ministers in their professional work. Over the past twelve years, AIM has reached out to clergy of all faiths and denominations who see Interfaith as a growing paradigm for the coming century. As AIM grows, its purpose has expanded beyond networking and support services to include educating the public and working with humanitarian and religious projects.

AIM's goals now include supporting members with services such as Photo-ID Cards for Interfaith Ministers and interfaith clergy entering hospitals, schools, and clinics in order to provide much needed counseling and support services, especially to members of minority religious communities. AIM also provides members with the opportunity to network and share their experiences, challenges, victories, and insight with other Interfaith Ministers.

AIM's quarterly newsletter contains articles about interfaith groups, the ministries of our members, and other individuals who are making contributions to interfaith and world peace, an interfaith calendar, and more. AIM provides a hard-copy directory and an Internet Directory, an online Bulletin Board, an Internet presence, and community services. (See the AIM sidebar, "A Definition of Terms.")

Center for World Thanksgiving

The Center was incorporated in 1964 "to acknowledge thanksgiving to God as a basic human act, and thanksgiving among persons as a common bridge to understanding. Through the exploration of gratitude and praise in world religions and cultures, its mission is to witness, celebrate, and promote the value and spirit of thanksgiving for both sacred and secular cultures throughout the world." Hundreds of international religious leaders have signed the annual Declarations of World Thanksgiving, statements of gratitude published since 1982. The Center's seminars and educational programs have brought academic and spiritual leaders together in Dallas and around the world.

The Center for World Thanksgiving is also working with numerous religious and political leaders to implement the declaration by 185 nations at the United Nations observing the year 2000 as an International Year of Thanksgiving. Among the powerful ideas in this commemoration is the concept that religions can show leadership by thanking one another for their contributions to the common good. The first global event of the International Year of Thanksgiving was a major interfaith conference in March of 1999, sponsored by the Center. The Thanksgiving World Assembly gathered more than one hundred religious and spiritual leaders and scholars from thirty-three countries to consider the healing and uniting spirit of thanksgiving within religions, among religions in dialogue together, and through religions speaking together for the benefit of the world in the new century and new millennium.

Among the many observations and conclusions from the Assembly are these: the spirit of reverence for the gift of life and gratitude to the Divine Source of Life has been a cornerstone of religion and personal happiness since ancient times; the great world religions have seen giving thanks as central, and gratitude has been seen by many as the "parent of all virtues"; the interreligious character of thanksgiving is demonstrated by its importance as a discipline that is taught and practiced in numerous traditions; giving thanks together has special power to unite diverse communities, large and small; thanksgiving implies both receiving and giving, demonstrating our interdependence and fostering forgiveness and healing; thanksgiving is expressed in stewardship—the responsible care of the life and gifts we have been given; and in service—a dependable commitment to the needs and well-being of others.

The delegates at the Assembly also issued a Call to Action, which is available from the Center.

Council for a Parliament of the World's Religions (CPWR)

The CPWR was formed in Chicago in 1988 to plan and celebrate the 100th anniversary of the 1893 Parliament. In 1993, more than seven thousand participants came together to acknowledge both the commonalities and diversities of the world's faith traditions and to explore religious responses to the critical issues that face the human community at the threshold of the 21st century. Since then, CPWR has also developed the Metropolitan Interreligious Initiative in the Chicago area.

CPWR continues to encourage discussion of "Toward a Global Ethic: An Initial Declaration," the groundbreaking document from the 1993 Parliament. In 1997 the International Initiative convened a Preparatory Assembly of Religious and Spiritual Leaders with about one hundred religious and spiritual leaders and observers from several countries to draft "A Call to Our Guiding Institutions" based on the Global Ethic. After a drafting process that included consultants from numerous religions, professions, and countries, these documents were discussed and disseminated at the Cape Town Parliament in December 1999. Additionally, CPWR is encouraging individuals, groups, nations, and religious communities to make strategic "Gifts of Service to the World." (See Chapter 22 for more substantial details on the Parliaments, the "Global Ethic," and the "Call.")

Fellowship of Reconciliation (FOR)

Established during and after World War I in order to promote peacemaking and nonviolence, FOR is composed of men and women who recognize the essential unity of all humanity and have joined together to explore the power of love and truth for resolving human conflict. While it has always been vigorous in its opposition to war, the Fellowship has insisted equally that this effort must be based on a commitment to the achieving of a peaceful world community, with full dignity and freedom for every human being.

As the oldest and largest interfaith peace organization in the United States and the world, FOR began as a movement of protest against war, with its origins in the ethic of love as found in Jesus Christ. FOR seeks the company of those of whatever faith— and no faith—who wish to confront human differences with nonviolent, compassionate, and reconciling love. While many of its members today are Christian, the participation of others is nourished in the Jewish and Muslim communities, with their prophetic emphases on justice and love. The FOR was also deeply affected by Gandhi and the freedom struggle in India, with its roots in the ancient teachings of the Jains and Hinduism. And the powerful pacifist movement in Vietnam brought to FOR still another tradition of nonviolence, that derived from Buddhism.

Members participate in local groups and Religious Peace Fellowships in all major religious denominations, with branches and groups in over forty countries and on every continent. FOR has worked with all the living Nobel Peace Laureates and the United Nations General Assembly, as well as with peacemakers around the world, to proclaim and observe the years 2001–2010 as the "International Decade for a Culture of Peace and Nonviolence for the Children of the World."

Global Dialogue Institute (GDI)

Dr. Leonard Swidler of Temple University and Dr. Hans Küng of Tubingen Ecumenical Institute published the initial challenge for the definition of a global ethic in the *Journal of Ecumenical Studies*, which Dr. Swidler and Arlene Swidler founded in 1963. More recently, Dr. Swidler and others established the Institute for Interreligious and Interideological Dialogue and one of its offshoots, the Global Dialogue Institute.

GDI is dedicated to "the global pursuit of a greater ethical and spiritual awakening in the culture-shaping groups such as business, law, politics, science, religion, education, communications, and the arts, for creative action through *deep-dialogue*." Deep-Dialogue is a "powerful Transformative Technology grounded in classical philosophical and spiritual traditions in a global context. It has been experimentally developed and distilled over many years through a wide range of Inter-World Encounters." For a better understanding of interfaith and interideological dialogue, see Dr. Swidler's "The Deep-Dialogue Decalogue" in Chapter 20.

The InterFaith Network for the UK

Established in 1987 to foster good relations between the religious communities in Britain, at national and local levels, the Network's members now include over eighty organizations. As of 1999, these included nearly thirty representative bodies of faith communities, ten national (and international) interfaith organizations, thirty-five local interfaith groups, and eleven educational and academic bodies. Activities include an information service, publication of interfaith guidelines, resources and directories, networking between faith initiatives, fostering local interfaith cooperation, and arranging meetings and events. The Network believes that "dialogue and cooperation can only prosper if they are rooted in respectful relationships which do not blur or undermine the distinctiveness of different religious traditions" (from *The Local InterFaith Guide*).

The Interfaith Alliance (TIA)

TIA "is a coalition of concerned religious leaders and other citizens who have joined together to articulate and promote the unifying principles of all faiths—compassion, tolerance, and justice. In a world plagued by strife, fear, and hatred, we affirm the values of respect and community against the politics of division. We reject efforts to pit groups of people against each other for personal or political gain. We consider it our moral obligation to promote understanding and participation. We will work to inform and unite citizens, to reinvigorate public discourse, and to hold our leaders accountable for their words and deeds. . . .

"The challenge: Radical right-wing extremists have declared a holy war in America, promoting an agenda based on hate and intolerance. They are preying on Americans' very real concerns about their families and communities in an attempt to impose one narrow set of beliefs on an entire nation. Organizations such as the Christian Coalition, the Oregon Citizen's Alliance, and the Traditional Values Coalition have adopted a broad strategy that is succeeding in state after state. Religious extremism is increasingly being used to attack politicians, pull textbooks out of classrooms, cut back on school breakfast programs, and promote discrimination. This movement has polarized the political debate, choking off discussion with its harsh and unyielding rhetoric. . . ."

The Interfaith Alliance has a three-part strategy: public dialogue, public education, and serving as a national clearinghouse for religious, grassroots, and political citizens looking for ways to respond to the radical right.

The International Association for Religious Freedom (IARF)

Formed in 1900 and inspired by the 1893 Parliament, IARF is the oldest worldwide community of religious organizations. It is interreligious, intercultural, and interracial in composition and vision, encompassing approximately eighty-three member groups in twenty-seven countries, and speaking more than twenty languages. The IARF world community is based on interpersonal sharing to foster openness, understanding, compassion, service, and solidarity.

In cooperation with local IARF groups and members, the Social Service Network has some fifty projects such as emergency relief, cooperative development projects, and women's centers. This scope expands its spiritual horizon, giving IARF a worldwide identity and moral involvement in response to the global issues of our time, especially those surrounding religious freedom.

IARF holds congresses in various parts of the world, every three years; its 29th Congress was held in August 1996, at Won Kwang University in South Korea. Topics included economic justice, religious practice, religion and culture, religious education, and ecological living. Primary attention was given to facilitating increased understanding between Japanese and Korean member groups, to help resolve some of the bitterness remaining from the Japanese occupation of Korea for many years in the mid-20th century.

In 1999 IARF held its 30th World Congress in Vancouver, Canada. Over 650 persons came from around the world "to consider how religious communities might draw from the wellsprings of their traditions the insight and commitment that will be required to overcome the ecological crisis of our time." After five days of discussion, prayer, and dialogue, the closing ceremonies included challenges from the young adults that all, young and old, put their words into action.

The IARF's International Secretariat is in Oxford, UK, and it has regional offices in Amsterdam, India, and the Philippines. The U.S. Chapter is based in Cambridge, Massachusetts, and the Canadian Chapter is in Vancouver. IARF also holds Consultative Status as a nongovernmental organization at the United Nations, where it advocates for religious freedom and contributes its expertise to international conferences.

International Council of Christians and Jews (ICCJ) and NCCJ

Formed in 1975, the ICCJ is the international umbrella organization of twenty-three national Jewish-Christian dialogue organizations. Envisaged to deal with relations between Christians and Jews, its activities also serve as a model for wider interfaith relations and networking. Its North American member recently changed its name from National Conference of Christians and Jews to National Conference for Community and Justice (NCCJ) to indicate its wider conversation and programming across multi-religious and multiethnic lines.

International Interfaith Centre (IIC)

IIC is a joint project of International Association for Religious Freedom and World Congress of Faiths in cooperation with Westminster College. The idea for the Centre emerged out of the cooperation among interfaith groups for the Year of Interreligious Understanding and Cooperation (1993). The Centre's goals include providing a place for study and research, the development of educational materials, a lecture series, consultations and conferences, hospitality, networking among interfaith organizations, and office space. Some conferences have focused on how interfaith work can be more effective in areas of conflict such as Sri Lanka, Northern Ireland, former Yugoslavia, and the Middle East.

Rev. Marcus Braybrooke, a key Trustee of the IIC, notes that the purpose of the Centre is "to serve cooperation on many shared programs—the real work—of providing healing and hope to a divided world. . . . The Centre also encourages the practice of meditation and prayer, which should be at the heart of all our work, so we meet once a month for meditation together." Friends of the IIC provide the staff and trustees with program and financial support, communications, and networking with other organizations and contacts to "heal divisions, foster understanding, and build cooperation between religions."

Inter-Religious Federation for World Peace (IRFWP)

IRFWP brings together believers and scholars from many religious traditions of the world to work for world peace and understanding. IRFWP's program of congresses, conferences, consultations, research, service projects, youth programs, and publications promote peace personally, socially, regionally, and globally. IRFWP has chapters in twenty-six nations. Founded and funded by the Reverend Sun Myung Moon and the Unification Church, IRFWP has a prestigious interreligious Board of Presidents and Presiding Council.

Peace among the religious traditions of humankind as well as the utilization of religious wisdom and ethics are seen as essential to the development of both interpersonal and universal peace. Recent projects include the discussion and development of more substantial cooperation and mutually supportive relationships among the world's statesmen and religious leaders. A new sister organization, the Inter-religious and International Federation for World Peace, will work with religious leaders and with the United Nations to facilitate such collaboration. Other interfaith projects have focused on topics such as "The Family and the Interfaith Ideal," "Forgiveness: Faith in Practice," and, through the Religious Youth Service in South Africa, on the role of youth in creating a culture of peace.

Mexican InterFaith Council (Consejo Interreligioso de Mexico—CIM)

Reminding us that Mexico is also part of North America, Jonathan Rose writes that "beginning in 1992, the initial faith groups in the CIM were the Anglican, Catholic, Lutheran, Mormon, and Presby-

terian churches and the Buddhist, Hindu, Jewish, and Sufi-Islamic communities with a presence in Mexico. Subsequently the Greek Orthodox Church and the Sikh community have also joined the CIM, whose Board of Directors includes a leading figure from each member faith."

CIM's three objectives are to promote interfaith acceptance throughout Mexican society; to encourage greater understanding of each faith's tradition among the others; and to work together on projects reflecting universal values that unite humankind regardless of one's religion, faith, or spiritual practice. In November 1998 CIM published its "Proposal for a Code of Ethics among Religions" (printed in Chapter 20). Currently underway is a project called "Love and Care for Creation," an environmental initiative to involve faith communities in practical local activities dealing with the ethical problem of the ecological disaster in Mexico and the world.

In an exciting endorsement of CIM's work and value to Mexican society, the government's Department of the Interior is promoting the "Code of Ethics" as an example to the Mexican people of the harmony that needs to exist in every Mexican community throughout the nation. The Mexican Department of the Interior helped the CIM to reprint the *Code* and will distribute it in those regions of Mexico where problems of religious intolerance exist, as is now the case in the municipality of San Juan Chamula in the state of Chiapas.

Monastic Inter-religious Dialogue (MID)

Originally called the North American Board for East-West Dialogue, MID was established in 1978 by the Benedictine Confederation to assume a leading role in dialogue between Christianity, especially Catholicism, and the great religions of the East. Since the documents of Vatican II clearly encouraged appreciation for, and interaction with, other religious traditions, MID aims to foster the contribution of Christian monastics and other religious persons engaged in the dialogue between contemplative traditions.

MID publishes a bulletin, assists in networking, participates in conferences, and promotes dialogical sessions such as the Buddhist-Christian dialogue on Spiritual Practices held at the Abbey of Gethsemane during the summer of 1996 with contemplative leaders from around the world.

The National Religious Partnership for the Environment (NRPE)

In July 1993, four major faith groups—the U.S. Catholic Conference, the National Council of Churches of Christ, the Consultation of the Environment and Jewish Life, and the Evangelical Environment Network—initiated a three-year, $5 million mobilization representing environmental integrity and justice. Now representing religious communities numbering over 100 million people, the Partnership began at a Summit on the Environment in 1992, sponsored by the Joint Appeal in Religion and Science. Its origins, however, date back to the Open Letter to the Religious Community issued in January 1990 by thirty-four internationally prominent scientists. Each of the four traditions has published its own Resource Kits for congregational uses, which may be gotten directly from the affiliated partners.

North American Interfaith Network (NAIN)

NAIN is a nonprofit association for communication between, and mutual strengthening of, interfaith organizations, agencies, and programs along with offices of religious or denominational institutions pertaining to interfaith relations in the United States and Canada. The Network seeks to affirm humanity's diverse and historic spiritual resources and bring these to bear on contemporary global, national, regional, and local issues. While it has minimal program or staff of its own, the Network sees its role as facilitating the networking possibilities of these organizations by providing information. It seeks to provide a coalition model for cooperative interaction based on serving the needs and promoting the aspirations of all member organizations. Membership benefits include a newsletter, invitation to the annual conferences, support of the growing interfaith movement, and links to other affiliates.

The Peace Council

Formed since the 1993 Parliament, the Peace Council had its inaugural meeting at Windsor Castle in November 1995. Since then the Council has offered spiritual leadership and support for peace and nonviolence in several conflicts, including Chiapas, Mexico, where Bishop Samuel Ruiz has been leading efforts in conflict resolution.

Councilors include H.H. the 14th Dalai Lama of Tibet, Bishop Samuel Ruiz Garcia, Dr. Oscar Arias Sanchez, Dr. Dalil Boubakeur, Dr. Elise Boulding, Swami Chidananda Saraswati, Maha Ghosananda, Sister Joan Chittister, Dr. Chung Hyun Kyung, Rev. Thomas Keating, Imam W. Deen Mohammed, Dr. L. M. Singhvi, Rabbi Levi Weiman-Kelman, [former] Archbishop Desmond Tutu, Ven. Samdhong Rinpoche, and Chatsumarn Kabilsingh.

The Councilors responded vigorously to the plea of Maha Ghosananda, supreme leader of Cambodian Buddhism and leader of the Cambodian Peace Marches, that the Council join the International Campaign to Ban Land Mines. The Peace Council arranged interfaith prayer services with local interfaith councils at the Conventions on Landmines in Mozambique and Oslo, Norway, and produced a booklet, "Prayers for a World with No Land Mines," in French and English.

The Pluralism Project at Harvard University

Dr. Diana Eck has directed this multiyear research project, funded by the Lilly and Ford Foundations, into the current state of religious diversity and relationships in North America. The extensive results, much of it researched by her students and academic affiliates, include essays, photos, and databases about the thousands of temples, mosques, *gurdwaras*, and other minority religious centers in North America. Another of the project's subject areas is the interfaith movement itself. This research has been published as a multimedia CD-ROM titled "On Common Ground: World Religions in America," by Columbia University Press. The project's Web-site includes a survey and listing of North American interfaith organizations compiled by Joel Beversluis

(www.fas.harvard.edu/~pluralism/affiliates/
beversluis/interfaith_survey.html).

Society for Buddhist-Christian Studies

This Society, which was founded in Hawaii in 1980, brings together both scholars, religious leaders, and practitioners of Buddhism and/or Christianity in a holistic and interdisciplinary approach to dialogue. It is the most dynamic of the academic interfaith organizations because, as Dr. Sallie King, president of the Society, notes, "We are human beings first, and as humans we have intellectual, spiritual, activist, caring, and cultural dimensions. Ideally, dialogue will address us in all of these dimensions."

The fifth International Buddhist-Christian Conference was held at DePaul University during the summer of 1996. Participants included H.H. the 14th Dalai Lama of Tibet, Samdech Preah Maha Ghosananda, Supreme Buddhist leader of Cambodia, and Engaged Buddhism leaders Dr. Ariyaratne of Sri Lanka and Sulak Sivaraksa of Burma, as well as other internationally respected leaders and scholars.

In a historic milestone in Buddhist-Christian dialogue, fifty Buddhist and Christian monastics and over one hundred observers met immediately before this conference at the Abbey of Gethsemani to discuss key elements of the spiritual life. The Sixth Conference will be held in August 2000, at Pacific Lutheran University, with the theme, "Buddhism, Christianity, and Global Healing." The Society, along with the University of Hawaii Press, also publishes a journal titled *Buddhist-Christian Studies*.

Temple of Understanding (ToU)

Formed in 1960, ToU has held a series of Summit Conferences in several parts of the world with many politicians, scientists, UN delegates, and religious leaders. The purpose of this global interfaith organization is the promotion of interfaith dialogue and education to achieve understanding and harmony among the people of the world's religions and beyond. The Temple of Understanding maintains a strong commitment to the integrity of each religion or faith tradition and believes that each can better

remain true to itself by honoring the truths inherent in all traditions. ToU is very active in New York, especially, where it has assisted in the development of the North American Interfaith Network, the Association of Religious NGOs and the Values Caucus at the UN, numerous interfaith services for UN delegates, educational programs, and the Interfaith Center of New York.

United Communities of Spirit

The United Communities of Spirit network project "has begun to realize its potential as a framework for a comprehensive global network, intended to mediate the relationship between the various religious and spiritual traditions of this planet. The network, created and maintained by Bruce Schuman, presents a series of Web pages that include interfaith dialogue "chat rooms," an occasional newsletter, useful links, plus parts of the 1995 edition of *A SourceBook for Earth's Community of Religions*, and *World Scripture: A Comparative Anthology of Sacred Texts*. In addition, Bruce is developing sophisticated polling and database technology to "identify, correlate, and gather together the 'common factors' in the beliefs" of members. Bruce is also codirector, with Gloria Weber, of the groundbreaking Web-site, *Interfaith Voices for Peace and Justice*, which lists mission statements and contact information for over 900 organizations in an interactive database. (See Part Four for a large portion of the IFV database.)

United Religions Initiative (URI)

The URI began during the planning for the 1995 commemoration of the United Nations Charter in San Francisco's Grace Episcopal Cathedral. Since then, Bishop William Swing and many others have promoted the vision, which has recurred several times over the past half-century, of an organization where members of religions would meet on a daily basis "for the sake of peace and healing between religions, peoples, and nations, and to bring the wisdom of religious traditions to bear on economic, environmental, and social crises . . . " ("URI 2000: Declaration of Vision and Purpose"). Since then, this vision has grown and changed in many ways, based on a series of consultations and conferences. Three URI Charter-development conferences have been held in San Francisco, and others in Oxford, New York, Washington, Buenos Aires, and Pittsburg; related activities have been held in other cities as part of an extensive organizational development process.

Rev. Paul Chaffee, Secretary of the URI Board, reports that the energy for this exploration comes from "a very person-centered approach and the development of trust and commitment. The organization is also very spiritually grounded; the 1997 conference in Stanford was marked by frequent time for prayer and meditation."

URI's most extensive public project as of January 2000 has been coordination of 72 Hours, An Interfaith Peace-Building Project. More than 160 events in over forty countries engaged over a million people during the period from December 31, 1999, to January 2, 2000. A similar project supported by the Initiative's Charter signing activities in June of 2000. That Global Summit and Signing Celebration was centered in Pittsburgh, with complementary local ceremonies throughout the world. These activities were organized by founding URI Affiliates and Cooperation Circles, whose supporters acclaim the following pledge:

> We, people of diverse religions, spiritual expressions and indigenous traditions throughout the world, hereby establish the United Religions Initiative to promote enduring daily interfaith cooperation, to end religiously motivated violence, and to create cultures of peace, justice, and healing for the Earth and all living beings.

Vision TV

Based in Toronto, this unique coalition of seventy-five faith and ministry partners provide multifaith cable television broadcasts to Canada's very diverse cultures. No single faith group "owns" Vision TV since all partners pay for broadcast time and for the costs of producing their programs. All of the partners subscribe to its Code of Ethics, which includes pro-

hibitions against slandering other faith communities, proselytizing from other faiths, and on-air fundraising. Vision TV celebrated its tenth anniversary in 1998.

World Conference on Religion and Peace

The World Conference on Religion and Peace (WCRP) was formed as a consolidation of movements in Japan, the United States, and India to promote interreligious encounter and cooperation throughout the world. Members have formed three regional committees—in Asia, Africa, and Europe—and twenty-three national committees.

The Kyoto Declaration of the First World Assembly in 1970 noted that their gathering represented "an historic attempt to bring together men and women of all major religions to discuss the urgent issue of peace. We meet at a crucial time. At this very moment we are faced by cruel and inhuman wars and by racial, social, and economic violence." Since 1970, conditions have not improved much, and more issues, including environmental catastrophes, have been added to the list of crises.

On the local, national, regional, and global levels, WCRP convenes periodic meetings and assemblies, gathering religious leaders and representatives for the purpose of exploring urgent issues, sharing experiences in working for peace with justice, and making commitments. These have included common actions and statements to promote peace and harmony among religious bodies, nations, and ethnic groups, as well as between human beings and the natural environment. Topics include conflict resolution, peace education, human rights, children and youth, assistance to refugees, economic and social development, and environmental protection.

WCRP held its Sixth World Assembly in Riva del Garde, Italy, in November 1994, attended by about one thousand people from sixty-three countries. In an opening address, Pope John Paul II stressed that "religion and peace go together," and added that "to wage war in the name of religion is a blatant contradiction" (from *Faith and Interfaith in a Global Age* by Marcus Braybrooke, CoNexus Press, 1998).

In November of 1999, WCRP held its Seventh World Assembly in Amman, Jordan. The session was attended by more than one thousand religious, civil, and political leaders from more than sixty countries.

At a preliminary session, a unique gathering of 120 women of the world's many religious traditions convened for a three-day session aimed at the creation of the world's first international network of religious women's associations. In welcoming remarks, His Majesty King Abdullah II of Jordan noted that "now more than ever...it is imperative to build bridges to link religious and academic leadership in tandem with political leadership in order to create appropriate forums for debate where the various problems besetting the world can be addressed." (Contact WCRP for a copy of the Proceedings document, which presents many of the speeches, reports, and the Amman Declaration.)

World Congress of Faiths (WCF)

At the heart of the World Congress of Faiths has been a mystical vision which sees that beyond our particularities there is, in the presence of the Divine, something that unites all people. Founded in the 1930s in Oxford, England, WCF offers conferences, interfaith events such as tours to Tibet and the Middle East, and the annual Younghusband Lecture, given in 1998 by the Archbishop of Canterbury.

The WCF has also encouraged initiatives to bring interfaith groups as well as religious leaders together in partnership. For example, WCF is one of the founding members of the International Interfaith Centre in Oxford. In the mid-1980s, WCF was instrumental in bringing many international interfaith organizations together for the Ammerdown Conference, which began discussions of commemorating 1993 as the centennial of the 1893 World's Parliament of Religions. Because interfaith meeting is seen as a form of spiritual pilgrimage, WCF also sponsors meetings and retreats that bring people together for dialogue, study, prayer, and worship.

WCF's journal, *World Faiths Encounter,* is an important resource for dealing with new questions and issues that arise from living in religiously plural-istic societies. In recent decades, WCF has pioneered interfaith services and prayers "as a witness to a common God-given humanity and as an expression of the yearning for peace, justice, human rights, the relief of poverty, and the protection of the planet" (*All in Good Faith,* by Marcus Braybrooke, from WCF and CoNexus Press). WCF also publishes or encourages publication of books by its members and staff; for instance, in 1997, WCF published *All in Good Faith: A Resource Book for Multifaith Prayer,* which includes articles by members of many faiths on approaches to multifaith services. The book also includes a selection of services and an anthology of prayers and short readings.

World Council of Churches; Team on Interreligious Relations

As a fellowship of 337 churches in more than 120 countries, from virtually all Christian traditions, the WCC promotes worldwide Christian unity. It does so through its programs of sharing, support, and advocacy, through its studies and publications, through its assemblies and conferences with a rich diversity of Christians.

The Team on Interreligious Relations promotes contact between Christians and neighbors of other faiths primarily through multilateral and bilateral dialogue with partners of other faiths. The dialogue aims at building trust, meeting common challenges, and addressing conflictive and divisive issues. An important aspect of the team's work is to interpret trends in the religious, intellectual, and political life of various faith communities and to consider the future of religion, interreligious relations, secularization, and religious plurality, and their significance for Christian identity and witness.

The WCC has organized a number of Hindu-Christian, Christian-Muslim, Buddhist-Christian, and Jewish-Christian dialogues; their progress as well as articles highlighting local efforts are published in the biannual *Current Dialogue.* The WCC has also published study guides and other publications.

As an example of its recent work, the WCC held a Christian-Muslim consultation on "Religious

Freedom, Community Rights, and Individual Rights: A Christian-Muslim Perspective," in October of 1999. Thirty-five international participants gathered to address these issues and to begin to build a common understanding of such concepts as proselytism, mission, tolerance, respect, citizenship, and freedom.

World Faiths Development Dialogue (WFDD)

This organization grew out of interfaith conversations in 1998 between leaders and scholars from the world's religious communities along with the development community, including the World Bank and other donor agencies. The subjects of the conversations are poverty and development. Co-chairs of the WFFD (1998–2000) are Dr. George Carey, the Archbishop of Canterbury; and Mr. James D. Wolfensohn, President of the World Bank.

The WFDD brochure notes that the organization is focusing on four main areas of work (which do not exclude others): hunger and food security; post-conflict reconstruction; culture as an element of development; and the delivery of social services. In a booklet titled *Poverty & Development* (available free from WFDD), a great deal of thinking is synthesized into an outline that reveals both the multidimensional nature of poverty and the meaning of true development, from the standpoint of the religions. Common ground is uncovered, but above all, the faith communities recommend that development should be grounded on moral values and focused on people rather than on economic processes.

A Grassroots Model
THE GRAND RAPIDS INTERFAITH DIALOGUE ASSOCIATION

Dr. Lillian Sigal

Professor of Humanities; organizer of Interfaith Dialogue Association, Grand Rapids, and board member of Global Dialogue Institute

NOTE: For those thinking about initiating interfaith dialogue meetings or a local organization, here is a model with practical organizing suggestions and goals, based on the experience of people in western Michigan.

Introduction

The Interfaith Dialogue Association in Grand Rapids began as the brainchild of two women—Rev. Marchiene Rienstra, a Christian, and myself, a Jew. Marchiene and my late husband, Rabbi Phillip Sigal (a New Testament scholar), met at Calvin College, where they frequently dialogued about Judaism and Christianity. Phillip dreamt of establishing a Jewish-Christian ecumenical center. After he died, Marchiene and I determined to make his dream a reality; however, we decided to broaden its scope to include all the world religions. The seed for the Interfaith Dialogue Association (IDA) was planted in 1988; it flowered as a chartered, nonprofit organization in 1990. In 1999, it is still needing consistent nurturance, but betokening greater growth and outreach to fulfill its mission.

Based on my experience as past president of IDA, I offer below suggestions for organizing, dialoguing, and developing programs for an association such as ours.

Forming a Dialogue Organization

We began the process of establishing IDA by first brainstorming with a cross-section of leaders from the religious and academic community—both lay and clergy—to determine whether our community needed such an organization. These people strongly endorsed our concept, and many of them became members of our Board of Directors, providing us with ideas, contacts, and resources to fulfill our objectives.

Subsequently, we met with a core group to create bylaws and appoint an executive committee consisting of two copresidents, a secretary, and a treasurer. We established membership dues (with option of reduced rate or no fee, depending upon financial status), a quarterly newsletter, and a brochure stating our goals and activities.

Practical Ideas for Dialogue Groups

If possible, have two groups meeting monthly on different nights to accommodate different people's schedules. Ideally, discussion thrives in a group of nine to twelve people. However, realistically, the mailing list should be fifteen to eighteen, because of absenteeism. Other ideas:

- Encourage members to put the dates of the monthly meetings on their calendars and to be committed to them.
- Strive to make the group as religiously and ideologically diverse and balanced as possible, and include humanists.
- Meet in members' homes to enhance development of personal relationships, opportunities to see and experience the cultural milieu of different members—their food, art, ritual objects, etc.
- Begin with a prayer or ritual led by a member of a different religion each time, who explains its meaning.
- Discuss various festivals at seasons when they are observed.
- Generate ideas from members for a text to read in advance of each meeting. This should be done at the beginning of the year. Huston Smith's *The World Religions* was an excellent choice one year.
- Begin the first meeting with a discussion of Leonard Swidler's "The Deep-Dialogue Decalogue" [in Chapter 20] to establish guidelines for meaningful and sensitive dialogue.
- Appoint a group coordinator who sends reminders of meetings.
- Appoint a group leader for each session to keep the discussion focused, to encourage full participation, to avoid monopolization of the discussion by a few members, and to faithfully follow the guidelines of the Deep-Dialogue Decalogue.
- Make one person responsible for summarizing or providing historical background for the reading material.
- Occasionally, invite an outside speaker, especially on a subject in which no group member has any expertise.
- Use the comparative method, i.e., when a theme is discussed in one religion, elicit responses from members of the other religions on that theme.
- Allow time for announcements of events, religious festivals, or news of interfaith activities in the community.
- Occasionally, share a potluck to provide opportunities for personal friendships to develop.
- Ask members for feedback on how things are going.

Major Programs

- Have an annual membership meeting with a program and a social hour to bring together the dialoguers and people on your mailing list who support you, but do not attend dialogue groups. Open these programs to the public to help advertise the organization and gain new members. The best source of members, nevertheless, is the members themselves—their friends and acquaintances.
- Offer an annual conference with an outstanding leader who has contributed to interfaith dialogue. So far, our guests have included Dr. Leonard Swidler, director of the Global Dialogue Institute at Temple University, and Dr. Huston Smith; our third conference featured Muslim feminist Riffat Hassan, chair of Religious Studies at the University of Louisville, Kentucky. These conferences included an interfaith panel of respondents to the keynoter and conference themes, and offered small discussion groups of those attending the conference, facilitated by members of our organization.

Our fourth annual conference followed a more academic model, offering more than thirty papers and presentations with respondents. The keynote address was given by Dr. David Ramage, Jr., chair of the Council for a Parliament of the World's Religions (Emeritus).

Some funding for these conferences has been provided by three local colleges who served as cosponsors in support of our educational objectives.

Goals

1. To eliminate prejudice that creates tension between members of different religious traditions and ideologies.

2. To advance understanding of religions and ideologies by study, dialogue, and sharing of religious experiences.

3. To foster appreciation for the richness of diverse ideologies and religions.

4. To identify commonalities and differences among religions and ideologies to enhance personal growth and transformation.

5. To promote friendship and trust among people of diverse ideologies and religions.

Conclusion

I have discovered that interfaith dialogue that is serious and not superficial involves challenges and risks, but also opportunities for personal growth and spiritual enrichment. Bahá'ís compare humanity to a rose garden. A garden where all the roses are white or red would be boring—the beauty of the garden resides in its variety of colors. Grassroots interfaith activity enables us to join the growing momentum—evidenced in the Parliaments of the World's Religions—for global bonding to displace the hostility that religious differences have unfortunately created. Indeed, as Hans Kung has noted, "There will be peace on earth when there is peace among the world religions."

A Definition of Terms

Association of Interfaith Ministers (AIM)

How Do We Define Interfaith?

AIM currently recognizes three different aspects or definitions of interfaith. The first and most widely used definition refers to dialogue and cooperation between leaders and/or members of different religions for the purpose of better understanding each other and working together on joint projects.

The second definition of interfaith refers to the union of two or more faiths, beliefs, or practices in the context of a specific situation, such as the marriage of a Catholic and a Jew and the raising of their children.

The third definition of interfaith refers to the search for the mythic, poetic basis of all religions and to the need to get in touch with that basis through whatever means are appropriate for that person's life journey. Also included within this definition is the search to create new religious forms that speak to an individual's particular lifestyle or personal orientation.

What Is the Difference between Interfaith Ministers and Interfaith Clergy?

"Interfaith Ministers" are ordained graduates of the newer interfaith seminaries. Interfaith seminaries give the student a broad, multifaith, theological education that includes any or all of the following activities: training and practical experience in spiritual counseling, ministering to those with special needs, and performing ceremonies such as weddings and funerals, in addition to emphasis on inner, contemplative development. Because of their broad training, Interfaith Ministers have an understanding of the different faiths represented plus a basic orientation that accepts interfaith as a growing phenomenon. This enables them to act as an effective bridge in any situation that involves interfaith needs and concerns. In their own personal spiritual lives, Interfaith Ministers may be members of any faith.

"Interfaith clergy" is a generic term that describes clergy members and religious leaders trained in any one specific faith, who are working with interfaith issues and are open to interfaith concerns. Because they possess an in-depth understanding of their own religion, they are able to provide a foundation for individuals of that faith who are striving to reach across religious boundaries.

AIM honors both Interfaith Ministers and interfaith clergy as visionaries whose service and direction is much needed at this time in history.

Collaboration among the Diverse Religions

Pope John Paul II

NOTE: This speech was given by the Pope at the conclusion of the Interreligious Assembly of several hundred invited guests from twenty religions, hosted by the Vatican and the Pontifical Interreligious Council in October 1999. In it, he repeats his vision of "a new civilization of love, founded on the universal values of peace, solidarity, justice, and liberty." He also takes a clear stand against any attempt to use religion in support of violence. These are important statements coming from one of our world's most venerated religious leaders. John Paul II has increased the Catholic Church's participation in dialogue and has increasingly seen the need for interreligious understanding. At the same time, his remarks must be evaluated in light of his trip to India, shortly before he made this speech. While there, the Pope's call for increasing evangelism by Christians greatly offended many Hindus. The Christian mandate to preach the gospel remains an offense to members of other traditions. Which is more important and effective in the building of "a new civilization of love," conversion or dialogue?

Distinguished Religious Representatives, Dear Friends,

1. In the peace which the world cannot give, I greet all of you gathered here in Saint Peter's Square at the conclusion of the Interreligious Assembly which has been taking place during the last few days. Throughout the years of my Pontificate, and especially on my pastoral visits to different parts of the world, I have had the great joy of meeting countless other Christians and members of other religions. Today this joy is renewed here, close to the tomb of the Apostle Peter, whose ministry in the Church it is my task to continue. I rejoice in meeting you all, and give thanks to Almighty God who inspires our desire for mutual understanding and friendship.

I am conscious of the fact that many esteemed religious leaders have traveled long distances to be present at this concluding ceremony of the Interreligious Assembly. I am grateful to all who have worked to foster the spirit which makes this Assembly possible. We have just listened to the Message which is the fruit of your deliberations.

2. I have always believed that religious leaders have a vital role to play in nurturing that hope of justice and peace, without which there will be no future worthy of humanity. As the world marks the close of one millennium and the opening of another, it is right that we take time to look back, in order to take stock of the present situation and move forward together in hope towards the future.

As we survey the situation of humanity, is it too much to speak of a crisis of civilization? We see great technological advances, but these are not always accompanied by great spiritual and moral progress. We see as well a growing gap between the rich and poor—at the level of individuals and of nations. Many people make great sacrifices to show solidarity with those suffering want or hunger or disease, but there is still lacking the collective will to overcome scandalous inequalities and to create new structures which will enable all peoples to have a just share in the world's resources.

Then there are the many conflicts continually breaking out around the world—wars between nations, armed struggles within nations, conflicts that linger like festering wounds and cry out for a healing that seems never to come. Inevitably it is the weakest who suffer most in these conflicts, especially when they are uprooted from their homes and forced to flee.

3. Surely this is not the way humanity is supposed to live. Is it not therefore right to say that there is indeed a crisis of civilization which can be countered only by a new civilization of love, founded on the universal values of peace, solidarity, justice, and liberty (cf. *Tertio Millennio Adveniente*, 52)?

There are some who claim that religion is part of the problem, blocking humanity's way to true peace and prosperity. As religious people, it is our duty to demonstrate that this is not the case. Any use of religion to support violence is an abuse of religion. Religion is not and must not become a pretext for conflict, particularly when religious, cultural, and ethnic identity coincide. Religion and peace go together: to wage war in the name of religion is a blatant contradiction. Religious leaders must clearly show that they are pledged to promote peace precisely because of their religious belief.

The task before us therefore is to promote a culture of dialogue. Individually and together, we must show how religious belief inspires peace, encourages solidarity, promotes justice, and upholds liberty.

But teaching itself is never enough, however indispensable it may be. It must be translated into action. My revered predecessor Pope Paul VI noted that in our time people pay more attention to witnesses than to teachers, that they listen to teachers if they are at the same time witnesses (cf. *Evangelii Nuntiandi*, 41). It suffices to think of the unforgettable witness of people like Mahatma Gandhi or Mother Teresa of Calcutta, to mention but two figures who have had such an impact on the world.

4. Moreover, the strength of witness lies in the fact that it is shared. It is a sign of hope that in many parts of the world interreligious associations have been established to promote joint reflection and action. In some places, religious leaders have been instrumental in mediating between warring parties. Elsewhere common cause is made to protect the unborn, to uphold the rights of women and children, and to defend the innocent. I am convinced that the increased interest in dialogue between religions is one of the signs of hope present in the last part of this century (cf. *Tertio Millennio Adveniente*, 46). Yet there is a need to go further. Greater mutual esteem and growing trust must lead to still more effective and coordinated common action on behalf of the human family.

Our hope rises not merely from the capacities of the human heart and mind, but has a divine dimension which it is right to recognize. Those of us who are Christians believe that this hope is a gift of the Holy Spirit, who calls us to widen our horizons, to look beyond our own personal needs and the needs of our particular communities, to the unity of the whole human family. The teaching and example of Jesus Christ have given Christians a clear sense of the universal brotherhood of all people. Awareness that the Spirit of God works where he wills (cf. John 3:8) stops us from making hasty and dangerous judgments, because it evokes appreciation of what lies hidden in the hearts of others. This opens the way to reconciliation, harmony, and peace. From this spiritual awareness spring compassion and generosity, humility and modesty, courage and perseverance. These are qualities that humanity needs more than ever as it moves into the new millennium.

5. As we gather here today, as people from many nations representing many of the religions of the world, how can we fail to recall the meeting in Assisi thirteen years ago for the World Day of Prayer for Peace? Since that time, the "spirit of Assisi" has been kept alive through various initiatives in different parts of the world. Yesterday, those of you taking part in the Interreligious Assembly journeyed to Assisi on the anniversary of that memorable gathering in 1986. You went to claim once more the spirit of that meeting and to draw fresh inspiration from the figure of *il Poverello di Dio*, the humble and joyful Saint Francis of Assisi. Let me repeat here what I said at the end of that day of fasting and prayer:

"The very fact that we have come to Assisi from various parts of the world is in itself a sign of this common path which humanity is called to tread. Either we learn to walk together in peace and harmony, or we drift apart and ruin ourselves and others. We hope that this pilgrimage to Assisi has taught us anew to be aware of the common origin and common destiny of humanity. Let us see in it an anticipation of what God would like the developing history of humanity to be: a fraternal journey in which we accompany one another toward the transcendent goal which he sets for us."

Our gathering here today in Saint Peter's Square is another step on that journey. In all the many languages of prayer, let us ask the Spirit of God to enlighten us, guide us, and give us strength so that, as men and women who take their inspiration from their religious beliefs, we may work together to build the future of humanity in harmony, justice, peace, and love.

Young Adult and Youth Organizations

Joel Beversluis

Not surprisingly, several major interfaith organizations have encouraged programs for youth and young adults. This is not merely an outreach or patronizing effort; in some cases the energy comes from young adults themselves, requesting or creating new organizations. While each organization has its own unique program structure and goals, the participants have much more than youthfulness in common.

Bishop William Swing begins the Epilogue to his book, *The Coming United Religions*, with these words about the responses of youth to interfaith ideals:

> The United Religions Initiative is a voice. A young voice. It belongs to coming generations that I can only vaguely imagine. It is the youth that have resonated with the Initiative right from the beginning, and in the end it will be theirs.

> The United Religions Initiative started with a Youth Conference in June 1995. . . . During the Conference adults met early in the mornings and late at night debating whether or not a United Religions organization was worthy of pursuit. While the adults argued, the youth lived it. Two hundred young people from forty-six different religions spontaneously walked to an open field, held hands, and prayed. They lived out something that adults could not work out.

In June 1997, I spoke to 1,200 high school students (Rotary International Scholars) at the University of Wisconsin. My speech was merely an introduction to the United Religions Initiative. Even so, on nine occasions the youth began to applaud and twice there were standing ovations. I was blown away. The youth heard

something in the United Religions vision that resonated with their secret and highest hopes.

> . . . When I travel the world, I am looking for a degree of restlessness, a sense of urgency to get on with the task of religious peacemaking. Among adults I see a deep satisfaction with the state of religion and interreligious life as it now exists. Among young people I sense a readiness for building community among faiths.

> —from *The Coming United Religions*, by William E. Swing, CoNexus Press, 1998

Ebrahim Patel is one of those young people. A recent college graduate who taught urban minority high school dropouts in Chicago and, at the time of this writing, is a Rhodes Scholar at Oxford, Eboo has also participated in and helped lead Next Generation activities for the Parliament of the World's Religions. In addition, he is Coordinator of the new **Interfaith Youth Corps**, which in some ways is modeled on the Peace Corps. In an essay responding to the Parliament's "Call to Our Guiding Institutions," Eboo writes:

> Young people are the arms and legs of the institutions with which "The Call" seeks creative engagement. We are organizers in the labor movement, teachers in the schools, social workers in the community development corporations, program deliverers in NGOs, artists in the neighborhoods, beat reporters at the newspapers, aides in government and international institutions. We implement at the grassroots level the details of the declarations. Our lives are about action and our spirituality needs to support our work.

> My first experience of the power of interfaith was with a group of young people at the 1998 **United Religions Initiative** Global Summit. On one level, we couldn't have been more different— coming from as far apart as Malaysia, Ghana, and the United States and calling ourselves practitioners of at least a half dozen spiritual paths. But, through a week of dance, discussion, and

prayer, we discovered profound similarities and developed deep connections with one another. The theoretical encounters that had previously only taken place in my head were now happening with real people. A Hindu woman quoted from Swami Vivekananda and called herself a *karma-yogi*, someone who seeks God through the path of action. A young Jew pointed out the commonalities between the Hindu tradition of service and the call for Jews to engage in *tikkun olan*, "repair of the world." Christians saw parallels between these and the Sermon on the Mount.

Hearing other people's stories brought clarity to my own Ismaili Muslim identity. "Relationship," as Krishnamurti has said, "is the mirror in which we see ourselves as we really are...." The Global Summit lasted for only a week, but it was a time that changed us all. Even with our diverse backgrounds, we found that we were all concerned with common issues—identity, pluralism, and peace. We were convinced that there were other young people out there who, like us, were inspired by faith to improve both their own lives and the world around them by action, reflection, and encounter.

We discussed this vision with leaders of three major interfaith organizations—the Council for a Parliament of the World's Religions, the Interfaith Center of New York, and the United Religions Initiative. They agreed to sponsor a small youth conference where we would have the space to hammer our ideas into a concrete project. In June 1999, sixteen young people from Japan, Uganda, South Africa, and the United States came together to discuss the following question: What experiences do today's young people need to become tomorrow's global, compassionate leaders?

. . . We were convinced that we were entering a new world, and that this world needs new kinds of heroes—spiritual citizens. The rite of passage for these heroes must include experiences of service, intercultural encounter, and interfaith reflection.

The initial design for the Interfaith Youth Corps is the result of our three days together. It is an opportunity for young people to do sustained service at a host site that welcomes their contribution. Each young person will be exploring his or her faith tradition through service and encounter. A Muslim might be inspired by *zakat*, a Native American by 7th Generation Thinking. Through living and working together, they will watch one another becoming better Jews, Muslims, Jains, and Zoroastrians. The Interfaith Youth Corps volunteers will form a powerful community of faith, service, dialogue, and reflection. Buddhists will recognize this as *sangha*, Muslims as *usrah*, and Jews might refer to the group as *haimish*—a warm gathering of homies.

As more and more young people become involved in interfaith, it is increasingly apparent that our contribution will be in the realm of direct action. Our faith encourages and respects diversity, and compels us to build bridges of understanding through cooperative service. My generation recognizes the truth of Marcus Braybrooke's observation that "Inner and outer belong together. The activist will be exhausted without an inner life and the true mystic longs for the world's renewal."

—from "A Call to an Interfaith Youth Corps" by Ebrahim Patel

The **Next Generation** project of the Council for a Parliament of the World's Religions is dedicated to mobilizing the power, energy, and enthusiasm of the world's young leadership. It has focused particularly on the 1993 and 1999 Parliaments, but the preparation and follow-up for each have been substantial, engaging young people in planning and programs in South Africa as well as in the Chicago area, and including support for the Interfaith Youth Corps.

In contrast with the young and self-organizing

Interfaith Youth Corps, the **Religious Youth Service (RYS)** was founded in 1985 by Rev. Sun Myung Moon through the International Religious Foundation. RYS has been providing service-learning opportunities since its inaugural project in the Philippines, when 120 young adults from all faiths and thirty-six nations gathered to work, discuss, listen, and engage in a unique project. In fifteen years, RYS held nearly seventy service projects in over twenty-five nations, working with existing charitable organizations, schools, and agencies that are providing models of cooperation crossing religious and national barriers.

RYS is a peace project designed to eradicate the root causes of conflict. It allows its participants to directly experience the problems of society while encouraging them to look towards their religious values as the source of solutions for these problems. RYS is designed to demonstrate that religion is essentially about true love and service, and to contribute to world peace through interreligious dialogue and action.

A different model of youth activities, utilizing weekend workshops and evening events, takes place in Metropolitan Washington, D.C., where the **Interfaith Conference (ICMW)** has developed a fascinating high school program. For example, "Why I love to be a . . . (Muslim, Jew, Sikh, Christian, etc.)" brought seventy high school students from nine faiths together "to internalize and appreciate their own faith traditions and the faith traditions of other youth for the sake of establishing a cohesive spirit of unity."

During a workshop in the spring of 1999, young people explored the core values of each tradition in detail and created the following pledge: "We pledge to act from our core values, to promote harmony among all religious traditions, and to be Champions of the Millennium—working to create a better world." The follow-up fall program gathered "more than 170 high school youth and adults [who] shared in an incredible evening about how to apply core values of our faiths to the challenges of the Millennium" (from the ICMW newsletter).

During the 30th World Congress of the **International Association for Religious Freedom** in Vancouver in the summer of 1999, the IARF Young Adult Program met in its own sessions as well as with the larger and older group. Approximately eighty young adults, ages eighteen to thirty-five, gathered from around the world to present their faith and cultural traditions, to articulate their concerns, and to formulate strategic action plans on a broad range of issues. They learned firsthand about the challenges facing the people of the First Nations, and visited the world-renowned Museum of Anthropology. In the closing ceremony, many participants made action pledges as manifestations of their support for the IARF's work and mission. The young adult program also met three years ago in Iksan City, South Korea, and will meet again at the World Congress in 2002. In addition, IARF sponsors young adult activities among some of its regional chapters throughout the world.

The **North American Interfaith Network (NAIN)** invites young adults from its nearly sixty member organizations to participate in its annual conference, NAINConnect. Although the Young Adult program does not continue formally throughout the year, participants do make friends and establish connections. Interfaith organizations that constitute NAIN's membership are encouraged to develop their own young adult programs and to sponsor young adult participation in the annual Network events. Scholarships help defer registration and lodging costs for those who attend. Since networking, fellowship, and resource sharing are among NAIN's goals, the conference provides young adults with invaluable opportunities to meet and learn from their peers in other organizations as well as from the "old-timers" at the conference workshops.

Yet another model is offered by the new **International Religious Youth Organizations' Seminar (IRYOS)**, which offers the great promise of providing a two-year academic program and Certificate in interfaith dialogue and multireligious cooperation. Developed through the joint efforts of the World Conference on Religion and Peace (WCRP) and Connecticut College, the IRYOS program will have up to one hundred students meeting for annual two-week seminars and bimonthly online courses, with guidance from the participant's own religious community. The initiating committee includes WCRP's Young Leadership Section and Peace Education Standing Committee, as well as the College's Office of Religious and Spiritual Life and Department of Religious Studies. Advisors are selected from among other youth sections of international interfaith organizations.

In India, the **National Youth Project (NYP)** is a response to the enormous diversity there of languages, cultures, and religions, and to the overwhelming needs in that country. Inspired by Gandhi and Vinoba Bhave, the NYP has conducted camps throughout India since 1970 to inspire youth and give them experience in choosing a life of service, self-help, self-discipline, harmony with others' religions and languages, and the dignity of manual work. The camps normally serve 200 youth for a week, but a camp in November 1999 had 2,546 young men and women and an earlier camp had 23,500 youths for ten days.

(Readers may contact the young adult programs through their sponsoring organizations, which are listed in Part Four.)

Chapter Twenty-two
THE PARLIAMENTS AND THE QUEST FOR A GLOBAL ETHIC

Introduction

Joel Beversluis

Surveying the 1993 and 1999 Parliaments of the World's Religions, can we find any lasting significance in them? Or will they seem to fade and leave imprecise markings on the course of religions and history, as seemed to happen following the 1893 event? Then, the dominant North American religious communities mostly ignored the World's Parliament of Religions despite its now apparent impact on the study of world religions and on the interfaith movement.

On the other hand, the impact of the 1893 event was much more widely remembered in India and Japan than in North America because that Parliament highlighted the beginning of the missionary journeys from Eastern religions to the West and greatly enhanced Western fascination with those traditions. Will there be comparable, long-lasting effects from the two 20th century Parliaments, and is there any way they can be considered watershed events?

It seems to this observer that the lasting significance of the Parliaments resides in the vision that the religions of the world—through their spiritual and ethical values, their institutions, and their potential influence on personal behavior—can and must play a positive role in the increasingly challenging matrix of our planetary life. The Parliaments were both symbolic of this vision and a major step towards its fulfillment. Religious leaders and members from all traditions, members of numerous planning and host committees, and trustees and staff from the Parliaments all broadcast one aspect or another of this inspiring message: Despite the problems caused by religions, in the face of increasing secularization, and contradicting the assumptions of scientism and reductionistic technique, the people of

the Parliaments affirmed that the holistic nature of religious and spiritual experience, in its noblest forms, guarantees religion's ongoing relevance to life, peace, and well-being.

Conspiracy or CoNexus?

Some fearful observers, particularly those who picketed the event in 1993 from the sidewalk outside Chicago's Palmer House Hotel and on the sidewalks in Cape Town, were concerned that the Parliament's underlying significance was its pursuit of a convergence of beliefs into one world religion, which for many is an apocalyptic scenario. Others tied the Parliament to the spectre of one world religion and a one-world government, via the United Nations or a United Religions Organization. And some were simply declaring their beliefs: one sign in Cape Town argued that the only "global ethic" is the Qur'an, while another quoted the Bible as the only Word of God.

These protests were generally ignoring the organizers' intentions and the evidence. Both the intentions and the actions of most participants indicated a healthy respect for the uniquenesses and diversity of religions; indeed, most participants would not have been there if their religious identities or sacred texts were being threatened in any way. Participation and responsibilities were highly diffuse and democratic. The eight hundred or more programs in each Parliament were defined by those who volunteered to make presentations, and audiences voted with their feet.

Although some religions and individuals, including some of the contributors to this *SourceBook*, do affirm the convergence of religions or believe in a common spiritual destiny, the presentation of these concepts was neither a goal of the Parliaments nor an overarching voice there. Organizers took pains to avoid the appearance of that agenda, and the interfaith movement in general is clearly leaning towards the goal of understanding and appreciation of diversity. Likewise, while issues of global policies and responsibilities were quite apparent, many people also affirmed the greater effectiveness of local and regional efforts for the resolution of those problems.

My perception of the two contemporary Parliaments is not of a conspiracy or convergence leading to either structural or doctrinal unity. Rather, I see a gathering of members of religious and spiritual traditions into an historic *nexus*. A nexus is a focal point or convergence of a sometimes overwhelming assortment of factors. In this case they include religious and spiritual worldviews, the seemingly increasing critical global and local issues, unprecedented amounts of information, the search for wisdom and appropriate responses, and experiences of disaster as well as success and grace. An important quality of a nexus is that the future—beyond the nexus—is open to numerous possibilities that are determined by the choices people make as they encounter the many factors and proceed through the focal point. As I see it, the Parliaments' participants recognized that the time had come to acknowledge the broad scope of this nexus and to help the world move through it, cooperatively.

Our task was to acknowledge the critical issues and the sometimes harsh realities of a pluralistic world, but we also chose to look beyond the differences so that we could focus on the changes in attitude that are necessary if we are to meet our common challenges and aspirations. In short, Parliament participants arranged to meet "within the nexus" and to begin responding together in whatever ways were appropriate to us as individuals, out of our personal commitments to our religiously based ethics.

Lessons on Unity and Diversity

A closer look at the two Parliaments suggests their significance to the wider community of religions and to the understanding of a new role for religious and spiritual communities in the 21st century. One major lesson is that the Parliaments are eloquent witnesses to assertions of religious identity and diversity, and to the ideal of unity amidst diversity.

In 1993, the Palmer House and the streets of Chicago were filled with the costumes, languages and accents, ritual smells and sounds, and the goodwill of more than 7,500 participants (some estimates claim up to 10,000 due to shared registrations) from fifty-six countries and most of the world's organized religions. During an intense eight days, participants encountered the richness of the religious and cultural experience of those whom we met in the lobbies, elevators, bathrooms, and meeting halls. Although an impressive 43 percent of the participants lived outside of the United States, by no means did all the diversity leave town after the final sessions. Members of the world's religions and cultures have moved permanently and in large numbers into Chicago, across North America, into Cape Town, and increasingly into most major cities throughout the world.

South Africa's Cape Town, site of the 1999 Parliament attended by people from some ninety countries, is now enmeshed in the difficult work of building a new "rainbow nation," as Desmond Tutu calls it, out of the ashes of apartheid. Diversity of all kinds is increasing rather than decreasing in Cape Town as immigrants from elsewhere in Africa are streaming in, bringing more languages, cultures, religions, and problems. The diversity of Cape Town, like that of Chicago, provided a symbolic and stimulating setting for the diversity of the Parliament.

At the same time, Cape Town was also chosen for the 1999 Parliament because interreligious cooperation was an established method and reality during South Africa's struggle for freedom. Following the elections and the birth of new social freedom and democracy for the black and "coloured" majorities, religious leaders who had participated in the resistance to apartheid were invited to participate in shaping the new constitution, in the Truth and Reconciliation hearings, and in addressing crises such as HIV-AIDS, poverty, and education.

Likewise, throughout the world, new interfaith centers and revitalized chapters of international organizations are increasing their presence and activities as diverse cultures and religions encounter each other and as frictions also increase. New publications—

about the world's religions, about interfaith and interideological dialogue, for use in religious education and in education about religions within public school systems—are supporting these grassroots efforts to encourage understanding of religious identity and diversity.

The lesson is that we don't need to look or travel very far to see the increasing need for new modes of interreligious understanding and cooperation. There can be benefits to all when we discover and appreciate the diversity in our midst.

Disasters, Wisdom, and New Alliances

Environmental disasters that are already taking place, as well as more serious prognoses of ecological crises and identity-based conflicts are, ironically, drawing many well-meaning members of religious and spiritual communities into new alliances. The lesson from the Parliaments' focus on the critical issues is the growing consensus that these crises are, essentially, matters of the human heart and will, and furthermore, that religious and spiritual traditions have much to offer in motivations and techniques for personal changes of heart. Since we all will face these ecological challenges, either cooperatively or competitively, we are invited to learn from the ecological experiences of traditions other than our own. For instance, an understanding of indigenous peoples' sustainable relationships with the earth can help inform our own responses to these issues and re-sensitize us to the wisdom within our own traditions.

Parliament participants acknowledged the ugly realities of religiously sanctioned violence, but we also noted the religiously based ideals that can ameliorate it. The Parliaments also presented the needs of suffering and dispossessed brothers and sisters, and asserted that we share responsibility for meeting those needs with others of goodwill, beyond the parameters of our own traditions and institutions.

The "Global Ethic" and "A Call to Our Guiding Institutions"

The declaration "Towards a Global Ethic" defines the context and principles for a minimum global ethic. Derived from core values found in all the major religious and spiritual traditions, this effort of the 1993 Parliament was unprecedented in its scope and intent. Its primary value and lesson lies in the explicitly interreligious consensus on ethical principles and responsibilities—necessary ingredients in the development of any community. Having this consensus in written form provides us with a tool for increased understanding and self-criticism. Furthermore, because the "Ethic" is grounded in humanity's common wisdom and experience rather than in any specific scriptures or claims of transcendence, it is also useful to nonreligious persons.

Many people are searching for ways to facilitate the changes that seem necessary if humans are to sustain the ecological and cultural systems on which we and our heirs depend. To make the Global Ethic more specific and applicable, a new document, titled "A Call to Our Guiding Institutions," was created during the several years preceding the 1999 Parliament and became a focal point of discussion at that meeting's Assembly. The objective of these statements is to provide a useful and authoritative catalyst for reflection, creative engagement, and appropriate change. (See related articles and the documents in this chapter.)

Experiences of the Heart

The Parliaments were as much experiences of the heart as of the head, and many participants were deeply moved by their programs, atmosphere, and interpersonal encounters. For these, the Parliaments offered an alternative to the insular approach common to many religious and spiritual traditions. It would be a mistake, however, to think that the Parliaments affected only the registrants. Cape Town's citizens, from politicians to taxi drivers, claimed benefits for that city, and that it would never be the same. Colleagues and friends of registrants and many others wished they could have attended and want to know more about the Parliaments. There's a romance to it that intrigues people.

Most participants at the Parliaments are, I believe, part of a much larger movement that can be described as a global spiritual awakening. One characteristic of this movement among practicing members of diverse religious traditions is the rediscovery of the genius at the heart of their own traditions. It is also noteworthy that for many people, the awakening includes revitalized faith in diverse forms of divine intervention, despite the contrary effects of secularization and scientific education. Worldwide, there is a growing sense that a "divine orchestration," emanating from divine love and compassion, is assisting us in responding to our crises.

Opening the Gates

Another element in this movement is the individual's desire to clarify ethical, religious, and spiritual commonalities and differences. While some people believe that the doctrinal differences between religions should be resolved and perhaps erased, many others believe that religious identities and distinctions will be preserved even while our hearts and hands reach across such boundaries. In either case, this clarification of ethics and spiritual meaning meets very personal existential needs of searching individuals. The answers provide a place for people to stand, from which they can identify purpose and generate hope, even in hard times. Significantly, the clarification of ethical commonalities also serves the very pragmatic desire to galvanize the spiritual and institutional resources of the world's religions into responsible and compassionate action.

These shifting attitudes indicate that the resurgence of fundamentalisms is not the only contemporary religious feature to watch. Both movements are responding to pluralism in our cultures, to turmoil, and to portents of crisis. Each of these movements is naming its perception of the dangers, and each develops its best defensive maneuvers. One movement feels the need to guard the gates, to focus on the truth and well-being of those within, and to open the gates only when its disciples are bringing that truth to those outside, or bringing outsiders within. The other movement identifies common threats and common aspirations on both sides of the walls; with its "open-gate policy," it finds friends on the outside

as well. Its best strategy calls for a unified response, which it does with an openness to mysteries, to the experiences of other persons, and to their perceptions of the Other—the Divine Mystery. The lesson is that the "opening of the gates" in this movement allows participation in a wider community of religions and enables collaborative responses on behalf of the larger community of the earth.

Although one may or may not appreciate the vision of a community of religions, we cannot ignore that there was also a great range of goals and participation at the Parliaments. As in any village or religion affected by human nature and diversity, the community was not always harmonious. Some members did not carry their share; some never came to the interfaith table, or withdrew; some were not respectful of others or were too self-centered; and some were angry; some expressed their pain, exposing others to discomfort. Yet, many needs were met, new connections were joined, new voices were heard, and numerous members of the community were enriched. The following observations demonstrate some of this range in more detail.

- The frequent uses of God-language during plenary sessions was problematic for some, particularly Buddhists.
- At the same time, the absence of references to God, Allah, or Deity in the declaration "Towards a Global Ethic" and in the "Call" was problematic for others, particularly Muslims and Christians.
- Some major speakers assumed universalistic beliefs among participants, without acknowledging those who disagree. Those with exclusivist commitments were offended.
- Some minority religions and new religious movements got extensive recognition and media attention, to the dismay of those in the large historic religions.
- Members of some religions felt they could not associate with others with whom they had major differences of culture, politics, or doctrine.
- Religious and ethnic traditions that were not present or substantially represented in 1893, including African Americans, Native Americans, Baháʼís,

Sikhs, and Zoroastrians, to name a few, made important contributions to these Parliaments.

- At the same time, some of these also revealed their great pain and, in the process, raised real-world tensions.

- Hindus and Buddhists had a very substantial presence commensurate with the significance they attach to the 1893 Parliament. Muslims, almost completely absent in 1893, were present at these Parliaments in substantial numbers.

- Though still a minority at plenary session podiums, women were much more present within the organization, making presentations, and among the registrants.

- Western Christian participants did not dominate the Parliaments as in 1893, and they were not out to "Christianize" the world. Perhaps because of the agreement by cosponsors and presenters to refrain from proselytizing, conservative white evangelical Christians were notably underrepresented.

- On the other hand, many Chicago-area African-American churches and young people participated with enthusiasm in the 1993 Parliament, and many Black African Christians did as well in Cape Town.

The lesson is that, despite the tensions and range of participation, the vast majority at the Parliaments were able to show a remarkable degree of harmony, respect, and appreciation for others.

Growth in the Movement

The number of interreligious encounters has increased geometrically during the past fifty years, and they have been sponsoring a wide variety of interfaith programs. Though it was a major event, the 1993 Parliament was only one of many activities that took place in that year, which had been designated as the Year of Interreligious Understanding and Cooperation by a coalition of international, interfaith organizations. For instance, four international interfaith organizations held their own substantial centennial commemoration in Bangalore, India, and numerous other local, regional and inter-national meetings were held then and have been held since the Parliament—including one in Delhi, India, which attracted more than one hundred thousand participants to some events.

In 1999, there were several other significant conferences—by the World Conference on Religion and Peace, the International Association for Religious Freedom, the Vatican's Pontifical Interreligious Institute, and others. (These are described in Chapter 21.) The continuing growth of this movement is both necessary and inevitable. A renewal of religious concern and engagement is afoot across the planet, with potential for both good and ill. It is becoming apparent that even statecraft, international economic policies, and remedial development plans will have limited success unless they collaborate in strategic ways with the values and influence of members of the world's religions. The lesson and challenge to the community of religions are to use the interfaith movement and the dialogue process to help form relationships and to influence structures that will evoke the best that religions can offer.

Studying the Parliaments and Religious Change

As significant examples of a new form of what might be called "ceremonies of pluralism," the Parliaments of the World's Religions are manifestations of change in the world's religions. Those who reflect on the larger context of meetings like the Parliament will benefit from insights into the dynamism of living religions. This phenomenon has implications for the ever-changing, current history of religions, religious education, interfaith dialogue, the study of ethics, and religious freedom and human rights, to name a few areas of study. Like governments, businesses, and international agencies, religions are being reshaped and are redefining themselves. Those who wish to learn more about religions can study this phenomenon as an indicator of change, particularly in these areas:

1. Participants from some conservative traditions are moving beyond sectarianism and exclusivity toward tolerance, inclusivity, and congenial interaction; among more liberal traditions, the Parliament

signifies movement toward a pluralism that celebrates a diversity of religious and cultural forms in new approaches to spirituality.

2. The competing truth claims of the religious participants are acknowledged in such forums as the Parliament, but do not receive priority treatment within the more pragmatic framework of these events. The atmosphere of the Parliaments transcends that diversity through an appeal to common concerns, the search for wisdom and ethics—ancient and new—in response to the needs of our time, and cooperative action. Many religious and spiritual leaders are trying to reshape their communities with these new agendas.

3. The Parliaments are publicly reaffirming the significance of religion in human experience, proposing that engagement with present and future global realities are vital concerns of the religions. Religious leaders and activists are experimenting with new forms of response to issues and realities.

4. The Parliaments prompt self-criticism and self-understanding by asking institutions and individuals to face tough questions: What aspects of my tradition may cause or perpetuate the critical issues? and Are our beliefs, practices, and institutional structures helping or hindering the goal of meeting the needs of humanity and the earth?

5. The process is identifying ethical propositions drawn not only from the wisdom and experience of religious heritages but guided as well by the insights of physics, earth sciences, and the social sciences. Some changes are springing from the force of religious ideals placed within the cauldron—or nexus—of new realities.

6. Strategies and "technologies" of transformation—old and new—are helping to resolve the paradox between religious ideals and the day-to-day operational beliefs of people, many of which block solutions and continue to threaten the community.

The Vision and Legacy of the Parliaments

The vision of the Parliaments is not about building an institution. It is about individuals and organizations joining a movement to help engage religions

and spiritual communities with the challenges and opportunities of the future. The legacy of the Parliaments will be significant to the extent that

1. They challenge the widespread assumption that religions or spiritualities have nothing to do with the pragmatic concerns of modernity

2. Those in the community of religions are inclined to live in harmony, with unity-in-diversity

3. They contribute to an equitable and sustainable life for all in the community of the earth.

The Quest for a Global Ethic

Joel Beversluis

In the first half of the 20th century, interfaith organizations such as the World Congress of Faiths, the International Association for Religious Freedom, and the National Conference of Christians and Jews focused on fellowship, understanding, and mutual tolerance among religions, especially in the context of anti-Semitism.

The "new agenda" of the interfaith movement, as Marcus Braybrooke terms it, in *Faith and Interfaith in a Global Age*, began its slow emergence during the last half-century alongside the growing understanding that the global village needed to find some consensus on behavior, for justice, and to ensure peaceful coexistence among diverse peoples. In the 1960s, especially, interfaith organizations, religious ethicists, and advocates addressed specific issues such as civil and human rights, religious freedom, wars, militarism and nuclear weapons, economic and social justice, and then, the overarching concern for the planet's ecological well-being. With increasing cross-fertilization across disciplines and movements, they held conferences, issued declarations, formed nongovernmental organizations, and lobbied governments and at the UN. This process is illustrated in *Stepping Stones to a Global Ethic* (SCM, 1992), edited by Marcus Braybrooke, which presents a selection of declarations as well as the story of the unfolding

An Ancient Precept

NOTE: Known by some as "The Golden Rule," this ancient principle is described in "Towards a Global Ethic" as one that has "persisted in many religious and ethical traditions of humankind for thousands of years . . . [and should, therefore] be the irrevocable, unconditional norm for all areas of life, for families and communities, for races, nations, and religions."

Bahá'í

"Blessed is he who preferreth his brother before himself."

BAHÁ'U'LLÁH,
Tablets of Bahá'u'lláh, 71

Buddhism

"Hurt not others in ways that you yourself would find hurtful."

UDANA-VARGA,
5:18

Christianity

"All things whatsoever ye would that men should do to you, do ye even so to them."

JESUS,
in Matthew 7:12

Confucianism

"Do not unto others what you would not have them do unto you."

Analects 15:23

Hinduism

"This is the sum of duty: do naught unto others which would cause you pain if done to you."

Mahabharata 5:1517

vision, beginning with the Universal Declaration of Human Rights in 1948.

Yet these efforts were rarely presented as an integral ethical system with widespread support. Rather, the issues were too often seen as unconnected, and they sometimes even competed ideologically and for public support. Furthermore, many people were suspicious of religions and of religiously declared ethics in a pluralistic and scientific age. During the '80s, however, this situation began to evolve toward a new resolution as single-issue advocates began to understand the systemic nature and interconnectedness of both the problems and the solutions. Disillusionment that big government policy alone could change matters substantially revitalized consideration of the role of religions, personal responsibility, spirituality, and a consistent global ethic.

The publication in 1991 of Hans Küng's ringing call, in *Global Responsibility* (first published in 1990 as *Projekt Weltethos*), for a new world ethos moved the conversation further along. Küng and Leonard Swidler then published, in the *Journal of Ecumenical Studies*, a proposal for the development of a "Universal Declaration of a Global Ethos." This document, which included signatures of some twenty-five renowned scholars of religion, broadened the perception that a global ethic could and should be formulated. The Council for a Parliament of the World's Religions (CPWR) then caught the vision and, in 1992, invited Küng to coordinate the drafting of a "Declaration of a Global Ethic" which would serve as a focal point of the 1993 Parliament.

The challenge of formulating a global ethic is not insignificant. Can the world's religious and spiritual communities agree on a written Ethic that defines crucial minimum standards for human attitudes, values, and behavior toward fellow humans and toward the natural world? To find the answer, Küng consulted with more than one hundred scholars and leaders, and prepared a draft by the fall of 1992. The CPWR, wanting a short document, themselves drafted an introductory statement, contextualizing and summarizing Küng's more detailed principles.

The document itself affirms the answer: "a fundamental consensus already exists" among the teachings of the religions describing the minimum ethic for establishing a sustainable, peaceful, and just world order. For example, "there is a principle found in many religious and ethical traditions of humankind for thousands of years: What you do not wish done to yourself, do not do to others. Or, in positive terms: What you wish done to yourself, do to others!" (See sidebar, "An Ancient Precept.")

The declaration defines itself as "a fundamental consensus on binding values, irrevocable standards, and personal attitudes." A large majority of the Assembly of Religious and Spiritual Leaders at the Parliament did reach consensus on, and sign, this document, but they first renamed it "Towards a Global Ethic: An Initial Declaration" to indicate that it is yet another stepping-stone in an ongoing quest.

Some have rightly wondered, "What use is a Declaration of a Global Ethic?" Several books by Hans Küng and Marcus Braybrooke, as well as essays by others explain potential applications for the education and transformation of individuals and institutions. These publications also address the process of drafting, and a number of useful critiques and suggestions for improvement.

While this document will probably not be revised, the CPWR used it as the basis for the development of a more specific ethical "Call to Our Guiding Institutions"—Religion, Government, Commerce and Agriculture, Education, Arts and Media, Civil Society, Intergovernmental Organizations, and Science and Medicine—which were issued at the 1999 Parliament in Cape Town, South Africa. The CPWR's vision for the "Calls" is to identify and publicize the ideals that call us as individuals and as members of guiding institutions to our highest good, similar to the beacon held up by the Universal Declaration of Human Rights.

Beyond the Parliament, other interfaith organizations, including the World Congress of Faiths, the Global Ethic Foundation, the International Interfaith Centre, and others such as the Brahma Kumaris have also committed resources to exploring and promoting a global ethic. Besides Küng and Braybrooke, Dr. Leonard Swidler and the Global Dialogue Institute, ethicists, and religionists from many traditions are also working with the ideas and implications of a global ethic. Additionally, a new project, based in Germany and Japan, is being developed to create a "Universal Declaration of Human Responsibilities" to parallel the 1948 Declaration of Human Rights. All of these are intent on calling our cultures to grapple with a set of significant moral standards that are affirmed by the teachings and wisdom found in the world's religions and spiritual traditions.

It is important to note that others, usually individual philosophers, have attempted to define a universal ethical system or perennial philosophy. What remains unique about this effort—especially "A Call to Our Guiding Institutions"—is the intention to use a dialogical method of research among numerous religious and spiritual leaders to incorporate scholarship, contemporary experience, and personal insight.

It is likewise significant that since the early '90s, the conversa-

---

An Ancient Precept (cont.)

Islam

"No one of you is a believer until he desires for his brother that which he desires for himself."

SUNNAH

Jainism

"In happiness and suffering, in joy and grief, we should regard all creatures as we regard our own self."
LORD MAHAVIRA,
24th Tirthankara

Judaism

"What is hateful to you, do not to your fellowman. That is the law: all the rest is commentary."

Talmud, Shabbat 31a

Native American

"Respect for all life is the foundation."
The Great Law of Peace

Sikhism

"Don't create enmity with anyone as God is within everyone."

Guru Arjan Devji 259,
Guru Granth Sahib

Zoroastrianism

"That nature only is good when it shall not do unto another whatever is not good for its own self."

Dadistan-i-Dinik, 94:5

(Compiled by Temple of Understanding)

tion about an interfaith global ethic, like the Parliament itself, represents a momentous shift in interreligious and interspiritual relationships. The focus includes but has also moved beyond dialogue about beliefs, practices, and experience. This conversation appreciates and utilizes the wisdom found in diversity, but also transcends it. The quest for a global ethic seeks to define a minimum standard of universal criteria by which we may live and act together, and it perceives both the dialogue and the criteria as signs of a much-needed transformation of consciousness. This activity invites participants to address our common life together at those depths where the inner life of the individual commits to an ethical response to our global community and some of its most significant and critical issues.

Towards a Global Ethic
An Initial Declaration

Council for a Parliament of the World's Religions

NOTE: This interfaith declaration is the result of a two-year consultation among approximately two hundred scholars and theologians from many of the world's communities of faith. On September 2–4, 1993, the document was discussed by an assembly of religious and spiritual leaders meeting as part of the 1993 Parliament of the World's Religions in Chicago. Respected leaders from all the world's major faiths signed the declaration, agreeing that it represents an initial effort—a point of beginning for a world sorely in need of ethical consensus. The Council for a Parliament of the World's Religions and those who have endorsed this text offer it to the world as an initial statement of the rules for living on which the world's religions can agree.

The Declaration of a Global Ethic

The world is in agony. The agony is so pervasive and urgent that we are compelled to name its manifestations so that the depth of this pain may be made clear.

Peace eludes us...the planet is being destroyed... neighbors live in fear... women and men are estranged from each other... children die!

This is abhorrent!

We condemn the abuses of Earth's ecosystems.

We condemn the poverty that stifles life's potential; the hunger that weakens the human body; the economic disparities that threaten so many families with ruin.

We condemn the social disarray of the nations; the disregard for justice which pushes citizens to the margin; the anarchy overtaking our communities; and the insane death of children from violence. In particular we condemn aggression and hatred in the name of religion.

But this agony need not be.

It need not be because the basis for an ethic already exists. This ethic offers the possibility of a better individual and global order, and leads individuals away from despair and societies away from chaos.

We are women and men who have embraced the precepts and practices of the world's religions:

We affirm that a common set of core values is found in the teachings of the religions, and that these form the basis of a global ethic.

We affirm that this truth is already known, but yet to be lived in heart and action.

We affirm that there is an irrevocable, unconditional norm for all areas of life, for families and communities, for races, nations, and religions. There already exist ancient guidelines for human behavior which are found in the teachings of the religions of the world and which are the condition for a sustainable world order.

We Declare:

We are interdependent. Each of us depends on the well-being of the whole, and so we have respect for the community of living beings, for people, animals, and plants, and for the preservation of Earth, the air, water, and soil.

We take individual responsibility for all we do. All our decisions, actions, and failures to act have consequences.

We must treat others as we wish others to treat us. We make a commitment to respect life and dignity, individuality and diversity, so that every person is treated humanely, without exception. We must have patience and acceptance. We must be able to forgive, learning from the past but never allowing ourselves to be enslaved by memories of hate. Opening our hearts to one another, we must sink our narrow differences for the cause of the world community, practicing a culture of solidarity and relatedness.

We consider humankind our family. We must strive to be kind and generous. We must not live for ourselves alone, but should also serve others, never forgetting the children, the aged, the poor, the suffering, the disabled, the refugees, and the lonely. No person should ever be considered or treated as a second-class citizen, or be exploited in any way whatsoever. There should be equal partnership between men and women. We must not commit any kind of sexual immorality. We must put behind us all forms of domination or abuse.

We commit ourselves to a culture of nonviolence, respect, justice, and peace. We shall not oppress, injure, torture, or kill other human beings, forsaking violence as a means of settling differences.

We must strive for a just social and economic order, in which everyone has an equal chance to reach full potential as a human being. We must speak and act truthfully and with compassion, dealing fairly with all, and avoiding prejudice and hatred. We must not steal. We must move beyond the dominance of greed for power, prestige, money, and consumption to make a just and peaceful world.

Earth cannot be changed for the better unless the consciousness of individuals is changed first. We pledge to increase our awareness by disciplining our minds, by meditation, by prayer, or by positive thinking. Without risk and a readiness to sacrifice there can be no fundamental change in our situation. Therefore we commit ourselves to this global ethic, to understanding one another, and to socially beneficial, peace-fostering, and nature-friendly ways of life.

We invite all people, whether religious or not, to do the same.

THE PRINCIPLES OF A GLOBAL ETHIC

Our world is experiencing a fundamental crisis: a crisis in global economy, global ecology, and global politics. The lack of a grand vision, the tangle of unresolved problems, political paralysis, mediocre political leadership with little insight or foresight, and in general too little sense for the commonweal are seen everywhere: too many old answers to new challenges.

Hundreds of millions of human beings on our planet increasingly suffer from unemployment, poverty, hunger, and the destruction of their families. Hope for a lasting peace among nations slips away from us. There are tensions between the sexes and generations. Children die, kill, and are killed. More and more countries are shaken by corruption in politics and business. It is increasingly difficult to live together peacefully in our cities because of social, racial, and ethnic conflicts, the abuse of drugs, organized crime, and even anarchy. Even neighbors often live in fear of one another. Our planet continues to be ruthlessly plundered. A collapse of the ecosystem threatens us.

Time and again we see leaders and members of religions incite aggression, fanaticism, hate, and xenophobia—even inspire and legitimize violent and bloody conflicts. Religion often is misused for purely power-political goals, including war. We are filled with disgust.

We condemn these blights and declare that they need not be. An ethic already exists within the religious teachings of the world that can counter the global distress. Of course this ethic provides no direct solution for all the immense problems of the world, but it does supply the moral foundation for a better individual and global order: a vision which can lead women and men away from despair, and society away from chaos.

We are persons who have committed ourselves to the precepts and practices of the world's religions. We confirm that there is already a consensus among the religions which can be the basis for a global ethic—a minimal *fundamental consensus* concerning binding *values*, irrevocable *standards*, and fundamental *moral attitudes*.

I. No new global order without a new global ethic!

We women and men of various religions and regions of Earth therefore address all people, religious and nonreligious. We wish to express the following convictions which we hold in common:

- We all have a responsibility for a better global order.
- Our involvement for the sake of human rights, freedom, justice, peace, and the preservation of Earth is absolutely necessary.
- Our different religious and cultural traditions must not prevent our common involvement in opposing all forms of inhumanity and working for greater humaneness.
- The principles expressed in this global ethic can be affirmed by all persons with ethical convictions, whether religiously grounded or not.
- As religious and spiritual persons we base our lives on an Ultimate Reality, and draw spiritual power and hope therefrom, in trust, in prayer or meditation, in word or silence. We have a special responsibility for the welfare of all humanity and care for the planet Earth. We do not consider ourselves better than other women and men, but we trust that the ancient wisdom of our religions can point the way for the future.

After two world wars and the end of the cold war, the collapse of fascism and Nazism, the shaking to the foundations of communism and colonialism, humanity has entered a new phase of its history. Today we possess sufficient economic, cultural, and spiritual resources to introduce a better global order. But old and new ethnic, national, social, economic, and religious tensions threaten the peaceful building of a better world. We have experienced greater technological progress than ever before, yet we see that worldwide poverty, hunger, death of children, unemployment, misery, and the destruction of nature have not diminished but rather have increased. Many peoples are threatened with economic ruin, social disarray, political marginalization, ecological catastrophe, and national collapse.

In such a dramatic global situation humanity needs a vision of peoples living peacefully together, of ethnic and ethical groupings and of religions sharing responsibility for the care of Earth. A vision rests on hopes, goals, ideals, standards. But all over the world these have slipped from our hands. Yet we are convinced that, despite their frequent abuses and failures, it is the communities of faith who bear a responsibility to demonstrate that such hopes, ideals, and standards can be guarded, grounded, and lived. This is especially true in the modern state. Guarantees of freedom of conscience and religion are necessary but they do not substitute for binding values, convictions, and norms which are valid for all humans regardless of their social origin, sex, skin color, language, or religion.

We are convinced of the fundamental unity of the human family on Earth. We recall the 1948 Universal Declaration of Human Rights of the United Nations. What it formally proclaimed on the level of rights we wish to confirm and deepen here from the perspective of an ethic: the full realization of the intrinsic dignity of the human person, the inalienable freedom and equality in principle of all humans, and the necessary solidarity and interdependence of all humans with each other.

On the basis of personal experiences and the burdensome history of our planet we have learned:

- That a better global order cannot be created or enforced by laws, prescriptions, and conventions alone
- That the realization of peace, justice, and the protection of Earth depends on the insight and readiness of men and women to act justly
- That action in favor of rights and freedoms presumes a consciousness of responsibility and duty, and that therefore both the minds and hearts of women and men must be addressed
- That rights without morality cannot long endure, and that *there will be no better global order without a global ethic*.

By a global ethic we do not mean a global ideology or a single unified religion beyond all existing religions, and certainly not the domination of one religion over all others. By a global ethic we mean a fundamental consensus on binding values, irrevocable standards, and personal attitudes. Without such a fundamental consensus on an ethic, sooner or later every community will be threatened by chaos or dictatorship, and individuals will despair.

II. A *fundamental demand: every human being must be treated humanely.*

We all are fallible, imperfect men and women with limitations and defects. We know the reality of evil. Precisely because of this, we feel compelled for the sake of global welfare to express what the fundamental elements of a global ethic should be—for individuals as well as for communities and organizations, for states as well as for the religions themselves. We trust that our often millennia-old religious and ethical traditions provide an ethic which is convincing and practicable for all women and men of goodwill, religious and nonreligious.

At the same time we know that our various religious and ethical traditions often offer very different bases for what is helpful and what is unhelpful for men and women, what is right and what is wrong, what is good and what is evil. We do not wish to gloss over or ignore the serious differences among the individual religions. However, they should not hinder us from proclaiming publicly those things which we already hold in common and which we jointly affirm, each on the basis of our own religious or ethical grounds.

We know that religions cannot solve the environmental, economic, political, and social problems of Earth. However they can provide what obviously cannot be attained by economic plans, political programs, or legal regulations alone: a change in the inner orientation, the whole mentality, the "hearts" of people, and a conversion from a false path to a new orientation for life. Humankind urgently needs social and ecological reforms, but it needs spiritual renewal just as urgently. As religious or spiritual persons we commit ourselves to this task. The spiritual powers of the religions can offer a fundamental sense of trust, a ground of meaning, ultimate standards,

and a spiritual home. Of course religions are credible only when they eliminate those conflicts which spring from the religions themselves, dismantling mutual arrogance, mistrust, prejudice, and even hostile images, and thus demonstrating respect for the traditions, holy places, feasts, and rituals of people who believe differently.

Now as before, women and men are treated inhumanely all over the world. They are robbed of their opportunities and their freedom; their human rights are trampled underfoot; their dignity is disregarded. But might does not make right! In the face of all inhumanity our religious and ethical convictions demand that *every human being must be treated humanely!*

This means that every human being without distinction of age, sex, race, skin color, physical or mental ability, language, religion, political view, or national or social origin possesses an inalienable and untouchable dignity, and everyone, the individual as well as the state, is therefore obliged to honor this dignity and protect it. Humans must always be the subjects of rights, must be ends, never mere means, never objects of commercialization and industrialization in economics, politics and media, in research institutes, and industrial corporations. No one stands "above good and evil"—no human being, no social class, no influential interest group, no cartel, no police apparatus, no army, and no state. On the contrary: possessed of reason and conscience, every human is obliged to behave in a genuinely human fashion, to do good and avoid evil!

It is the intention of this global ethic to clarify what this means. In it we wish to recall irrevocable, unconditional ethical norms. These should not be bonds and chains, but helps and supports for people to find and realize once again their lives' direction, values, orientations, and meaning.

There is a principle which is found and has persisted in many religious and ethical traditions of humankind for thousands of years: *What you do not wish done to yourself, do not do to others.* Or in positive terms: *What you wish done to yourself, do to others!* This should be the irrevocable, unconditional norm for all areas of life, for families and communities, for races, nations, and religions.

Every form of egoism should be rejected: all selfishness, whether individual or collective, whether in
the form of class thinking, racism, nationalism, or
sexism. We condemn these because they prevent
humans from being authentically human. Self-
determination and self-realization are thoroughly
legitimate so long as they are not separated from
human self-responsibility and global responsibility,
that is, from responsibility for fellow humans and for
the planet Earth.

This principle implies very concrete standards to
which we humans should hold firm. From it arise
four broad, ancient guidelines for human behavior
which are found in most of the religions of the world.

III. Irrevocable directives.

1. COMMITMENT TO A CULTURE OF NONVIOLENCE AND
RESPECT FOR LIFE

Numberless women and men of all regions and
religions strive to lead lives not determined by egoism but by commitment to their fellow humans and
to the world around them. Nevertheless, all over the
world we find endless hatred, envy, jealousy, and violence, not only between individuals but also between
social and ethnic groups, between classes, races,
nations, and religions. The use of violence, drug traf-
ficking and organized crime, often equipped with
new technical possibilities, has reached global proportions. Many places still are ruled by terror "from
above"; dictators oppress their own people, and institutional violence is widespread. Even in some countries where laws exist to protect individual freedoms,
prisoners are tortured, men and women are muti-
lated, hostages are killed.

a. In the great ancient religious and ethical traditions of humankind we find the directive: *You shall
not kill!* Or in positive terms: *Have respect for life!* Let
us reflect anew on the consequences of this ancient
directive: All people have a right to life, safety, and
the free development of personality insofar as they
do not injure the rights of others. No one has the
right physically or psychically to torture, injure,
much less kill, any other human being. And no

people, no state, no race, no religion has the right to
hate, to discriminate against, to "cleanse," to exile,
much less to liquidate a "foreign" minority which is
different in behavior or holds different beliefs.

b. Of course, wherever there are humans there will
be conflicts. Such conflicts, however, should be
resolved without violence within a framework of justice. This is true for states as well as for individuals.
Persons who hold political power must work within
the framework of a just order and commit themselves
to the most nonviolent, peaceful solutions possible.
And they should work for this within an international
order of peace which itself has need of protection and
defense against perpetrators of violence. Armament is
a mistaken path; disarmament is the commandment
of the times. Let no one be deceived: There is no survival for humanity without global peace!

c. Young people must learn at home and in school
that violence may not be a means of settling differences with others. Only thus can a culture of nonviolence be created.

d. A human person is infinitely precious and must
be unconditionally protected. But likewise the lives
of animals and plants which inhabit this planet with
us deserve protection, preservation, and care.
Limitless exploitation of the natural foundations of
life, ruthless destruction of the biosphere, and militarization of the cosmos are all outrages. As human
beings we have a special responsibility—especially
with a view to future generations—for Earth and the
cosmos, for the air, water, and soil. We are all intertwined together in this cosmos and we are all
dependent on each other. Each one of us depends on
the welfare of all. Therefore the dominance of
humanity over nature and the cosmos must not be
encouraged. Instead we must cultivate living in harmony with nature and the cosmos.

e. To be authentically human in the spirit of our
great religious and ethical traditions means that in
public as well as in private life we must be concerned
for others and ready to help. We must never be ruthless and brutal. Every people, every race, every religion must show tolerance and respect—indeed high
appreciation—for every other. Minorities need pro-

tection and support, whether they be racial, ethnic, or religious.

2. Commitment to a culture of solidarity and a just economic order

Numberless men and women of all regions and religions strive to live their lives in solidarity with one another and to work for authentic fulfillment of their vocations. Nevertheless, all over the world we find endless hunger, deficiency, and need. Not only individuals, but especially unjust institutions and structures are responsible for these tragedies. Millions of people are without work; millions are exploited by poor wages, forced to the edges of society, with their possibilities for the future destroyed. In many lands the gap between the poor and the rich, between the powerful and the powerless is immense. We live in a world in which totalitarian state socialism as well as unbridled capitalism have hollowed out and destroyed many ethical and spiritual values. A materialistic mentality breeds greed for unlimited profit and a grasping for endless plunder. These demands claim more and more of the community's resources without obliging the individual to contribute more. The cancerous social evil of corruption thrives in the developing countries and in the developed countries alike.

a. In the great ancient religious and ethical traditions of humankind we find the directive: *You shall not steal!* Or in positive terms: *Deal honestly and fairly!* Let us reflect anew on the consequences of this ancient directive: No one has the right to rob or dispossess in any way whatsoever any other person or the commonweal. Further, no one has the right to use her or his possessions without concern for the needs of society and Earth.

b. Where extreme poverty reigns, helplessness and despair spread, and theft occurs again and again for the sake of survival. Where power and wealth are accumulated ruthlessly, feelings of envy, resentment, and deadly hatred and rebellion inevitably well up in the disadvantaged and marginalized. This leads to a vicious circle of violence and counterviolence. Let no one be deceived: There is no global peace with-

out global justice!

c. Young people must learn at home and in school that property, limited though it may be, carries with it an obligation, and that its uses should at the same time serve the common good. Only thus can a just economic order be built up.

d. If the plight of the poorest billions of humans on this planet, particularly women and children, is to be improved, the world economy must be structured more justly. Individual good deeds and assistance projects, indispensable though they be, are insufficient. The participation of all states and the authority of international organizations are needed to build just economic institutions.

A solution that can be supported by all sides must be sought for the debt crisis and the poverty of the dissolving second world, and even more the third world. Of course conflicts of interest are unavoidable. In the developed countries, a distinction must be made between necessary and limitless consumption, between socially beneficial and nonbeneficial uses of property, between justified and unjustified uses of natural resources, and between a profit-only and a socially beneficial and ecologically oriented market economy. Even the developing nations must search their national consciences.

Wherever those ruling threaten to repress those ruled, wherever institutions threaten persons, and wherever might oppresses right, we are obligated to resist—whenever possible nonviolently.

e. To be authentically human in the spirit of our great religious and ethical traditions means the following:

- We must utilize economic and political power for service to humanity instead of misusing it in ruthless battles for domination. We must develop a spirit of compassion with those who suffer, with special care for the children, the aged, the poor, the disabled, the refugees, and the lonely.

- We must cultivate mutual respect and consideration, so as to reach a reasonable balance of interests, instead of thinking only of unlimited power and unavoidable competitive struggles.

- We must value a sense of moderation and modesty

instead of an unquenchable greed for money, prestige, and consumption. In greed humans lose their "souls," their freedom, their composure, their inner peace, and thus that which makes them human.

3. COMMITMENT TO A CULTURE OF TOLERANCE AND A LIFE OF TRUTHFULNESS

Numberless women and men of all regions and religions strive to lead lives of honesty and truthfulness. Nevertheless, all over the world we find endless lies and deceit, swindling and hypocrisy, ideology and demagoguery:

- Politicians and business people who use lies as a means to success
- Mass media which spread ideological propaganda instead of accurate reporting, misinformation instead of information, cynical commercial interest instead of loyalty to the truth
- Scientists and researchers who give themselves over to morally questionable ideological or political programs or to economic interest groups, or who justify research which violates fundamental ethical values
- Representatives of religions who dismiss other religions as of little value and who preach fanaticism and intolerance instead of respect and understanding.

a. In the great ancient religious and ethical traditions of humankind we find the directive: *You shall not lie!* Or in positive terms: *Speak and act truthfully!* Let us reflect anew on the consequences of this ancient directive: No woman or man, no institution, no state or church or religious community has the right to speak lies to other humans.

b. This is especially true

- For those who work in the mass media, to whom we entrust the freedom to report for the sake of truth and to whom we thus grant the office of guardian—they do not stand above morality but have the obligation to respect human dignity, human rights, and fundamental values; they are duty-bound to objectivity, fairness, and the preservation of human dignity; they have no right to intrude into individuals' private spheres, to manipulate public opinion, or to distort reality.
- For artists, writers, and scientists, to whom we entrust artistic and academic freedom; they are not exempt from general ethical standards and must serve the truth.
- For the leaders of countries, politicians, and political parties, to whom we entrust our own freedoms—when they lie in the faces of their people, when they manipulate the truth, or when they are guilty of venality or ruthlessness in domestic or foreign affairs, they forsake their credibility and deserve to lose their offices and their voters; conversely, public opinion should support those politicians who dare to speak the truth to the people at all times.
- Finally, for representatives of religion—when they stir up prejudice, hatred, and enmity towards those of different belief, or even incite or legitimize religious wars, they deserve the condemnation of humankind and the loss of their adherents. Let no one be deceived: There is no global justice without truthfulness and humaneness!

c. Young people must learn at home and in school to think, speak, and act truthfully. They have a right to information and education to be able to make the decisions that will form their lives. Without an ethical formation they will hardly be able to distinguish the important from the unimportant. In the daily flood of information, ethical standards will help them discern when opinions are portrayed as facts, interests veiled, tendencies exaggerated, and facts twisted.

d. To be authentically human in the spirit of our great religious and ethical traditions means the following:

- We must not confuse freedom with arbitrariness or pluralism with indifference to truth.
- We must cultivate truthfulness in all our relationships instead of dishonesty, dissembling, and opportunism.
- We must constantly seek truth and incorruptible sincerity instead of spreading ideological or partisan half-truths.

- We must courageously serve the truth and we must remain constant and trustworthy, instead of yielding to opportunistic accommodation to life.

4. COMMITMENT TO A CULTURE OF EQUAL RIGHTS AND PARTNERSHIP BETWEEN MEN AND WOMEN

Numberless men and women of all regions and religions strive to live their lives in a spirit of partnership and responsible action in the areas of love, sexuality, and family. Nevertheless, all over the world there are condemnable forms of patriarchy, domination of one sex over the other, exploitation of women, sexual misuse of children, and forced prostitution. Too frequently, social inequities force women and even children into prostitution as a means of survival, particularly in less developed countries.

a. In the great ancient religious and ethical traditions of humankind we find the directive: *You shall not commit sexual immorality!* Or in positive terms: *Respect and love one another!* Let us reflect anew on the consequences of this ancient directive: No one has the right to degrade others to mere sex objects, to lead them into or hold them in sexual dependency.

b. We condemn sexual exploitation and sexual discrimination as one of the worst forms of human degradation. We have the duty to resist wherever the domination of one sex over the other is preached— even in the name of religious conviction—wherever sexual exploitation is tolerated, wherever prostitution is fostered or children are misused. Let no one be deceived: There is no authentic humaneness without a living together in partnership!

c. Young people must learn at home and in school that sexuality is not a negative, destructive, or exploitative force, but creative and affirmative. Sexuality as a life-affirming shaper of community can only be effective when partners accept the responsibilities of caring for one another's happiness.

d. The relationship between women and men should be characterized not by patronizing behavior or exploitation, but by love, partnership, and trustworthiness. Human fulfillment is not identical with sexual pleasure. Sexuality should express and rein-

force a loving relationship lived by equal partners.

Some religious traditions know the ideal of a voluntary renunciation of the full use of sexuality. Voluntary renunciation also can be an expression of identity and meaningful fulfillment.

e. The social institution of marriage, despite all its cultural and religious variety, is characterized by love, loyalty, and permanence. It aims at and should guarantee security and mutual support to husband, wife, and child. It should secure the rights of all family members.

All lands and cultures should develop economic and social relationships which will enable marriage and family life worthy of human beings, especially for older people. Children have a right of access to education. Parents should not exploit children, nor children parents. Their relationships should reflect mutual respect, appreciation, and concern.

f. To be authentically human in the spirit of our great religious and ethical traditions means the following:

- We need mutual respect, partnership, and understanding, instead of patriarchal domination and degradation, which are expressions of violence and engender counterviolence.
- We need mutual concern, tolerance, readiness for reconciliation, and love, instead of any form of possessive lust or sexual misuse.

Only what has already been experienced in personal and familial relationships can be practiced on the level of nations and religions.

IV. *A transformation of consciousness!*

Historical experience demonstrates the following: Earth cannot be changed for the better unless we achieve a transformation in the consciousness of individuals and in public life. The possibilities for transformation have already been glimpsed in areas such as war and peace, economy, and ecology, where in recent decades fundamental changes have taken place. This transformation must also be achieved in the area of ethics and values!

Every individual has intrinsic dignity and inalienable rights, and each also has an inescapable responsibility for what she or he does and does not do. All our decisions and deeds, even our omissions and failures, have consequences.

Keeping this sense of responsibility alive, deepening it and passing it on to future generations, is the special task of religions.

We are realistic about what we have achieved in this consensus, and so we urge that the following be observed:

1. A universal consensus on many disputed ethical questions (from bio- and sexual ethics through mass media and scientific ethics to economic and political ethics) will be difficult to attain. Nevertheless, even for many controversial questions, suitable solutions should be attainable in the spirit of the fundamental principles we have jointly developed here.

2. In many areas of life a new consciousness of ethical responsibility has already arisen. Therefore we would be pleased if as many professions as possible, such as those of physicians, scientists, business people, journalists, and politicians, would develop up-to-date codes of ethics which would provide specific guidelines for the vexing questions of these particular professions.

3. Above all, we urge the various communities of faith to formulate their very specific ethics: what does each faith tradition have to say, for example, about the meaning of life and death, the enduring of suffering and the forgiveness of guilt, about selfless sacrifice and the necessity of renunciation, about compassion and joy? These will deepen, and make more specific, the already discernible global ethic.

In conclusion, we appeal to all the inhabitants of this planet. Earth cannot be changed for the better unless the consciousness of individuals is changed. We pledge to work for such transformation in individual and collective consciousness, for the awakening of our spiritual powers through reflection, meditation, prayer, or positive thinking, for a conversion of the heart. Together we can move mountains! Without a willingness to take risks and a readiness to sacrifice there can be no fundamental

change in our situation! Therefore we commit ourselves to a common global ethic, to better mutual understanding, as well as to socially beneficial, peace-fostering, and Earth-friendly ways of life.

We invite all men and women, whether religious or not, to do the same.

The 1999 Parliament

Joel Beversluis with CPWR Press Releases

More than seven thousand people from some ninety countries participated in the 1999 Parliament of the World's Religions in Cape Town. The South African Codirector of the Parliament, Afrika Msimang, called it a "banquet for the soul," and indeed it was a feast. The program book contained over 850 programs and presentations, so participants were nearly overwhelmed by the choices we had to make among conflicting opportunities. But we were also nourished by the array of stimulating offerings: key-note addresses by Nelson Mandela, the Dalai Lama, and others, plenary sessions, symposia, major presentations, workshops and panel discussions, films and theatre, music and dance, single- and multifaith meditations and worship, a large art gallery, exhibit halls, and much more.

The primary organizer of this unique interreligious extravaganza was the Council for a Parliament of the World's Religions (CPWR), based in Chicago. Working with CPWR was a strong staff in Cape Town, which provided services and support for six major venues, logistics, outreach, registration, program, fundraising, transportation, security, and hundreds of volunteers. In both cities, participation and planning was clearly interreligious and highly motivated.

Parliament programs illuminated many themes: 1) Religious and Spiritual Traditions and Practices; 2)

Interreligious Organizations and Dialogue; 3) the Critical Issues and Significant Ideas of Our Time; 4) Religious Performance, Art, and Film; and 5) South African Religious, Interreligious, and Political History. In addition, the Next Generation program provided opportunities for more than 120 young adults to develop their own agendas and interpersonal connections as well as to participate in the larger program. The young people held their own symposia on urban youth, intergenerational bonds, and sustainable initiatives.

Building on the declaration "Towards a Global Ethic" from the 1993 Parliament, organizers developed a new document titled "A Call to Our Guiding Institutions." The "Call," which went through a lengthy process of consultations and revisions over several years, invites creative engagement and ethical reflection within the institutional systems of the world. The "Call" counts religion as an important force for social and moral guidance, but also invites cooperation from the other institutional systems that have significant cultural influence: governments; agriculture, labor, industry and commerce; education; arts and communication media; science and medicine; intergovernmental institutions; and voluntary associations of civil society.

The 1999 Parliament also highlighted "Gifts of Service to the World," projects illustrating effective ways to work for a more just, peaceful, and sustainable world. More than three hundred such gifts were collected in a book distributed to participants and many were featured in presentations and plenary sessions. The CPWR will not only monitor the development of these gifts and projects but is also inviting new gift proposals.

The Parliament Assembly

Over a three-day period, religious and spiritual leaders in the Parliament Assembly worked with members of other spheres of influence to design hundreds of model projects illustrating how religious and spiritual traditions, working in collaboration with other fields of influence, can affect the major global issues. Using the key Parliament document, "A Call to Our Guiding Institutions" as its touchstone, the nearly 400 participants generated some 240 commitments to new and existing projects of service. Participants identified issues such as poverty, ecological damage, governmental and media abuses, and deprivation of human rights, which the guiding institutions could address through the process of ethical reflection and creative engagement.

These Assembly designs and commitments were essentially the first steps toward new and ongoing projects. The slogan expressed by the Next Generation, "Activate the Call, Live the Call," challenged older participants to take their commitments seriously. According to Jim Kenney, International Interreligious Director for CPWR, "The idea is to stimulate concrete action both by the Assembly and the participants. Although CPWR cannot provide funding, it can identify potential allies, resources, and recipients for whatever action is proposed." The project commitments "are entered in our database, classified by issue and by guiding institution," and will be shared with the Assembly to confirm the information and to determine what assistance CPWR and others might provide.

(A full listing of Parliament events can be found in the Program book, available from CPWR. "A Call to Our Guiding Institutions" and "Towards a Global Ethic" are also available from CPWR, as is the book *Gifts of Service to the World*. Reports on the Parliament and additional information on the projects designed at the Assembly are also available on the CPWR Web-site: http://www.cpwr.org.

A Call to Our Guiding Institutions

Council for a Parliament of the World's Religions
Presented on the Occasion of the 1999 Parliament of
the World's Religions

December 1 through 8, 1999, Cape Town, South Africa

FROM THE GLOBAL ETHIC TO A CALL TO OUR GUIDING INSTITUTIONS

Introduction

"Earth cannot be changed for the better unless
the consciousness of individuals is changed
first.... [And] without risk and a readiness to
sacrifice there can be no fundamental change in
our situation. Therefore we commit ourselves to
this global ethic, to understanding one another,
and to socially beneficial, peace-fostering, and
nature-friendly ways of life. We invite all people,
whether religious or not, to do the same."

—"Towards a Global Ethic: An Initial Declaration,"
1993 Parliament of the World's Religions, Chicago

We find ourselves at a moment when people
everywhere are coming to recognize that the
world is a global village. The perils and promises of
this new reality bring to mind several ancient understandings: that human beings are interdependent
and responsible for the care of the Earth; that we are
each worthy of a meaningful life and obliged to help
the human community toward a life of peace and
dignity; that the choices shaping a just, peaceful, and
sustainable future are choices we must make
together.

Unique to this moment is the possibility of a new
level of creative engagement between the institutions of religion and spirituality and the other powerful institutions that influence the character and
course of human society.

What is needed now is a persuasive invitation to
our guiding institutions to build new, reliable, and
more imaginative partnerships toward the shaping of
a better world. In the face of unprecedented challenges to the well-being of the Earth and its people,
a clear, calm call to such creative engagement may
be the harbinger of a new day. As we find new ways
to cooperate with one another, an unprecedented
process of transformation can unfold, and new hope
can emerge.

At the threshold of a new century and a new mil-
lennium, therefore, and on the occasion of the 1999
Parliament of the World's Religions in Cape Town,
South Africa, the Council for a Parliament of the
World's Religions (CPWR) extends such an invita-
tion: "A Call to Our Guiding Institutions."

Continuing the Parliament Tradition

The 1999 Parliament of the World's Religions and
this document continue a tradition born in Chicago
in 1893. At the first Parliament of Religions, several
hundred leaders, scholars, theologians, and other
representatives of the world's religions came together
to ponder the place of faith and spirituality in the
modern world. As the deliberate formal encounter of
many religions, East and West, this unprecedented
gathering marked the beginning of modern interreligious dialogue.

This tradition was reborn in 1993 as more than
seven thousand people from a wide spectrum of the
world's religious and spiritual communities gathered
again in Chicago. Throughout the 1993 Parliament,
participants were challenged to think critically and
holistically about the role of religious and spiritual
communities in the pursuit of creative solutions to
the world's most pressing problems. They explored
issues of religious and spiritual identity, engaged in
thoughtful dialogue with persons of other traditions
and cultures, and searched for effective ways of
bringing the attention, energy, and influence of religion and spirituality to bear on the critical issues
confronting the planetary community.

In order to provide a context for these reflections, the 1993 Parliament offered a thoughtful and provocative statement of fundamental ethical principles shared by the world's religious and spiritual traditions. That statement took form in a groundbreaking document, "Towards a Global Ethic: An Initial Declaration," which was signed by nearly two hundred religious and spiritual leaders from around the world. It set forth four fundamental commitments that remain powerfully relevant in the face of the issues that the 1993 Parliament addressed—nonviolence and respect for life, solidarity and a just economic order, tolerance and a life of truthfulness, and equal rights and partnership between men and women.

The Next Step

The Council for a Parliament of the World's Religions urges continuing reflection on the commitments at the heart of the Global Ethic and renewed efforts to apply them. Essential to such efforts is the acknowledgment that we live in a world in which powerful institutions exercise a significant and inescapable influence on our collective future. Woven through the core documents and practices of these institutions are values, perspectives, and assumptions that can be examined in the light of the principles of the Global Ethic. In inviting them to examine their roles for a new century, the Call will make it clear that the principles and commitments of the Global Ethic relate directly and immediately to their functioning. It will also propose a process of creative engagement that will involve not only the religions of the world but all other guiding institutions as well.

The Council's hope is that the Call will also provide encouragement and direction for those wishing to offer gifts of service to the world. Such gifts express a fundamental spiritual inclination toward good will, generosity, hospitality, compassion, righteousness, and justice. Indeed, the existence of goodness in the world has often been directly related to the spirit in which such gifts are given. Though ambitious endeavors and noble projects have made

undeniable contributions, the world needs and continues to thirst for such individual and collective gifts of service—now, more than ever.

The Nature of the Call

"A Call to Our Guiding Institutions" is not a prescriptive or admonitory document. It is instead an appeal for active, ongoing dialogue about the creation of a just, peaceful, and sustainable future on behalf of the entire Earth community. For this reason, the Call consists of specific, particular invitations rather than sweeping declarations or hectoring injunctions.

Furthermore, the authority of the Call will come only in small measure from its endorsement by religious and spiritual leaders. Its strength flows primarily from its expression of beliefs and convictions already deeply held—and held in common—by the world's religious and spiritual communities, and from the collaborations each part of the Call may inspire.

In the pages that follow, key excerpts from the document "Towards a Global Ethic: An Initial Declaration" appear in the margins of the various sections. These serve as reminders that the Global Ethic sets the stage for the Call and informs its core. All are invited to reflect on this document and to respond in ways that will move our world toward a just, peaceful, and sustainable future.

Rationale
Visions of the World

Visions of the world-as-it-might-be have always found expression through the world's religious and spiritual traditions. These traditions embody human aspirations: for meaning and purpose in life; for respect and mutuality between diverse peoples, cultures, and religions; for justice and peace; for the alleviation of suffering; and for harmony with the Earth. In the practice of these traditions, their respective communities have gained a glimpse and a taste of the world as it might be.

In the long historical struggle to realize their respective visions, however, the world's religious and spiritual communities have sometimes adopted divisive, unjust, inhumane, and Earth-denying attitudes and practices. Sadly, this phenomenon has been most clearly manifested in interreligious relations. All too often, these relations have been marred by intolerance, oppression, and even violence, dramatically undermining efforts to build a better world.

Yet, today there is a broad and deep movement toward openness, goodwill, and warmhearted and loving engagement among religious and spiritual communities around the world. Sustained encounters between people of different religious, spiritual, and cultural traditions have created heightened momentum toward actualizing our many visions of a better world, as well as stronger possibilities for establishing ethical common ground. New awareness of shared ethical principles opens the way into a new era of creative engagement—where we find and implement new modes of outreach, cooperation, and constructive common action, not only among the world's religions but among all of the world's guiding institutions.

Towards a Global Ethic

While the world's religious and spiritual traditions differ profoundly with respect to various beliefs and practices, they nevertheless hold in common certain ethical principles. One formulation of this ethical common ground is found in the document, "Towards a Global Ethic: An Initial Declaration," issued on the occasion of the 1993 Parliament of the World's Religions.

The document identifies four universal directives that offer a basis for a "global ethic":

- Do not kill.
- Do not steal.
- Do not lie.
- Do not commit sexual immorality.

These directives are further described and emphasized in the following affirmations:

- Have respect for life.
- Deal honestly and fairly.
- Speak and act truthfully.
- Respect and love one another.

"Towards a Global Ethic" then proposes that these affirmations lead to four vital commitments (listed here with excerpts from the text):

COMMITMENT TO A CULTURE OF NONVIOLENCE AND RESPECT FOR LIFE

"All people have a right to life, safety, and the free development of personality insofar as they do not injure the rights of others. No one has the right physically or psychically to torture, injure, much less kill any other human being. And no people, no state, no race, no religion has the right to hate, to discriminate against, to 'cleanse,' to exile, much less to liquidate a 'foreign' minority which is different in behavior or holds different beliefs...

"As human beings we have a special responsibility—especially with a view to future generations—for Earth and the cosmos, for the air, water, and soil. We are all intertwined together in this cosmos and we are all dependent on each other. Each one of us depends on the welfare of all. Therefore the dominance of humanity over nature...must not be encouraged. Instead we must cultivate living in harmony with nature and the cosmos."

COMMITMENT TO A CULTURE OF SOLIDARITY AND A JUST ECONOMIC ORDER

"No one has the right to rob or dispossess in any way whatsoever any other person or the commonweal.... No one has the right to use her or his possessions without concern for the needs of society and Earth....

"We must utilize economic and political power for service to humanity instead of misusing it in ruthless battles for domination. We must develop a spirit of compassion with those who suffer, with special care for the children, the aged, the poor, the disabled, the refugees, and the lonely."

COMMITMENT TO A CULTURE OF TOLERANCE AND A LIFE OF TRUTHFULNESS

"No woman or man, no institution, no state or church or religious community has the right to speak lies to other humans...

"We must cultivate truthfulness in all our relationships instead of dishonesty, dissembling, and opportunism. . . . We must courageously serve the truth and we must remain constant and trustworthy, instead of yielding to opportunistic accommodation to life."

COMMITMENT TO A CULTURE OF EQUAL RIGHTS AND PARTNERSHIP BETWEEN MEN AND WOMEN

"No one has the right to degrade others to mere sex objects, to lead them into or hold them in sexual dependency. . . .

"The relationship between women and men should be characterized not by patronizing behavior or exploitation, but by love, partnership, and trustworthiness."

These commitments have profound implications for the inner life of individuals and the shared life of the human community.

First, they "can provide what obviously cannot be attained by economic plans, political programs, or legal regulations alone: A change in the inner orientation, the whole mentality, the 'hearts' of people, and a conversion from a false path to a new orientation for life."

Second, they suggest the outlines of "a vision of peoples living peacefully together, of ethnic and ethical groupings and of religions sharing responsibility for the care of the Earth," a vision made possible by the discovery and embrace of common ethical principles (quotations from "Towards a Global Ethic").

Addressing the Critical Issues

Reflecting on the shared ethical principles expressed in the Global Ethic sets the critical issues of our time in stark relief: disintegrating community, unrelenting demand on the Earth's limited resources, aggravated injustice, growing divisions between rich and poor, spiritual indirection. At the same time, if we address these agonies from the perspective of shared moral commitments, we can find hope. That endeavor can be described in the following ways:

BUILDING COMMUNITY IN DIVERSITY

Diversity is a hallmark of our contemporary experience. Today every metropolitan center is home to a striking variety of cultures, ethnic and national groups, and religions. Never before has the encounter between people from different paths and perspectives been so widespread, touching individuals and communities everywhere, enriching the tapestry of our lives together, and recasting the dynamics of our world. When such encounters take place in an atmosphere of respect and mutuality, then new understanding and cooperation can emerge. More evident at present, however, are the tensions, hostilities, and even violence that arise from misunderstanding, fear, and hatred of those who are different. The urgent task is to embrace human diversity in such a way that we no longer erect barriers out of differences but, by understanding and appreciating them, build bridges to harmonious, vibrant community.

COMMITMENT TO SUSTAINABILITY

The issue of sustainability addresses the relationship of basic human needs to the continued viability of the Earth. Today the human family numbers nearly six billion. If our present rate of population growth and resource consumption continues, we are likely to approach and then exceed the limits of the Earth's ability to support us. Economic analysis suggests that to meet even the basic needs of so many would require a huge increase in agriculture and industry, prompting thoughtful persons to ask whether the Earth can possibly sustain such demands. For example: levels of atmospheric carbon dioxide have risen dramatically; one-half of all land has already been transformed for human use; and one-half of all accessible fresh water has been claimed to meet current human needs. As a result, one of every eight plant varieties and ever-greater numbers of animal species are at risk of extinction, a prospect that further imperils the planet and its human community. The challenge is to find sustainable ways to peacefully meet the needs of all people while preserving the integrity of the whole community of life on Earth.

STRIVING FOR JUSTICE

Currently, four-fifths of the world's people live on one dollar (U.S.), five rand (South Africa), or fifty rupees (India) per day or less. Wrenching poverty, exacerbated by systemic injustice and inequitable distribution of resources, gives rise to disease, crime, violence, and hopelessness. Current trends toward globalization and modern models of "development," which are rarely community oriented, have often increased hardship and privation for millions of people. Injustice of this kind and scope poisons the familial, social, and spiritual life of us all. It is imperative, from both an idealistic and a pragmatic point of view, that the sufferings of a majority of the human community be alleviated through urgent economic, political, and social reform.

SOLIDARITY AND SERVICE

The division of the world into rich and poor, north and south, empowered and disenfranchised, privileged and exploited, is growing. These divisions feed, and then feed upon, a pervasive alienation. If we are unaware of our fundamental connection to one another, we will not choose to work for justice and therefore will find no peace. The remedy is to identify compassionately with others—with their joys and sorrows, their sufferings and struggles, and their essential human needs. Such solidarity is the root of justice and the wellspring of service. In rediscovering our shared humanness and in serving one another, we emerge from estrangement into community.

SEEKING SPIRITUAL GROUNDING

Without spiritual grounding, visions of a far better world cannot be realized. In an age of profound spiritual yearning, the religious and spiritual traditions of the world offer wisdom

- To move beyond our narrow self-interest, and to build community in the spirit of hospitality
- To recognize the interdependence of all life and

the systems that support it, and to choose sustainable ways of living
- To see that the needs of others make a claim on our lives and to strive for justice and peace
- To remember our place in the human family and to find compassion that must be expressed in service
- To deepen spiritual awareness as the wellspring of personal transformation and to embrace the whole human community.

Creative Engagement

When reflecting on the future of the human community, one must consider the world's most powerful institutions—institutions, whose policies, for better and for worse, influence every aspect of life on the planet. Clearly, the critical issues facing the world today present an acute ethical challenge to these institutions. What is urgently needed is a new opening to creative engagement among the guiding institutions—an active, attentive, and inventive collaboration, rooted in shared moral principles and expressed in mutually sustained programs on behalf of the peoples of the 21st century.

A Final Note

"A Call to Our Guiding Institutions" is offered with the understanding that those who helped to craft this document and those who choose to endorse and implement it are themselves—like all human beings—influenced by the very institutions addressed here. And because all of us, as social beings, participate in one or more of these institutions, each of us therefore shares responsibility for their endeavors and effects.

This document reflects the collective wisdom of the many thoughtful persons from within each of the guiding institutions who have participated in its drafting—leaders, scholars, workers, teachers, executives, activists, and others. We are deeply indebted to the hundreds of women and men from around the world, young and old, of diverse religious, cultural, and professional backgrounds, who have participated over the past three years in the shaping of this Call.

A CALL TO OUR GUIDING INSTITUTIONS

- Religion and Spirituality
- Government
- Agriculture, Labor, Industry, and Commerce
- Education
- Arts and Communications Media
- Science and Medicine
- International Intergovernmental Institutions
- Organizations of Civil Society

Guided by a vision of the world as it might be, with deep concern for the well-being of the Earth, its people, and all life, the Council for a Parliament of the World's Religions respectfully calls upon the world's guiding institutions to reassess and redefine their roles in order to assure a just, peaceful, and sustainable future. We invite these institutions to join with each other in a process of creative engagement to address the critical issues that face the world. We seek common cause with those who strive for justice, peace, and sustainability. We seek to join with those whose lives embody the process of creative engagement. We do this with the knowledge that the future of the whole community of life on Earth depends on the realization of a collaborative, coherent, and moral vision of a better world.

Preamble

As human beings

. . . we are all interdependent and must relate to each other respectfully and peacefully;

. . . we are all—children, women, men—worthy of a meaningful life, and must treat all others with fairness, kindness, encouragement, and love;

. . . we are all responsible for the care of the Earth on which we depend and the well-being of the communities in which we live;

. . . we know that our individual and collective futures will be reshaped by the extent to which we link our societies in partnerships that reach across the continents and across racial, ethnic, cultural, sexual, social, political, economic, and religious lines.

As religious and spiritual persons

. . . we center our lives in an Ultimate Reality, which our traditions call by various names (the Absolute, Allah, Brahman, Dharmakaya, God, Great Spirit, the One, Waheguru), drawing hope and strength therefrom, in trust and vision, in word and silence, in service and solidarity;

. . . we seek to foster creative engagement among the guiding institutions that so profoundly influence life on Earth, in order that they may find imaginative new ways to address the critical issues that confront us all.

As members of the Earth community

. . . we affirm the keystone principle of the document "Towards a Global Ethic: An Initial Declaration":

Every human being must be treated humanely!

We further affirm the four commitments ensuing from this principle:

- Commitment to a Culture of Nonviolence and Respect for Life
- Commitment to a Culture of Solidarity and a Just Economic Order
- Commitment to a Culture of Tolerance and a Life of Truthfulness
- Commitment to a Culture of Equal Rights and Partnership between Men and Women.

Together, on the occasion of the 1999 Parliament of the World's Religions in Cape Town, we extend this Call to these guiding institutions whose decisions and actions will mean so much to the future of the entire community of the Earth, urging each to reassess and redefine its role for a new century toward the realization of a just, peaceful, and sustainable future.

THE CALL TO RELIGION AND SPIRITUALITY

"We know that religions cannot solve the environmental, economic, political, and social problems of Earth. However, they can provide what obviously cannot be attained by economic plans, political programs, or legal regulations alone: A change in the inner orientation, the whole mentality, the 'hearts' of people, and a conversion from a false path to a new orientation for life.

"...Humankind urgently needs social and ecological reforms, but it needs spiritual renewal just as urgently. As religious or spiritual persons we commit ourselves to this task. The spiritual powers of the religions can offer a fundamental sense of trust, a ground of meaning, ultimate standards, and a spiritual home."

—"Towards a Global Ethic: An Initial Declaration"

A. *We envision a world in which*
...the diverse religions, spiritual paths, and cultures are recognized and respected;
...religious and spiritual communities exist in harmony;
...the pursuit of justice and peace is nurtured by religion and spirituality and by dialogue between religious and spiritual communities;
...religious and spiritual teachings on wisdom, love, and compassion are prized;
...service is seen as an essential, uplifting religious or spiritual act;
...the Earth and all life are revered and cherished.

B. Religion helps human beings find meaning in life and history. It offers paths to enlightenment and salvation and encouragement to follow such paths. Among the noblest functions of religion is the promulgation of systems of beliefs, practices, and ethics that honor the humanity and dignity of each person and foster the vitality and moral well-being of the society.

When individuals and communities struggle with ethical questions, religion and spirituality provide necessary and trustworthy values, norms, motivations, and ideals, all grounded in an ultimate reality. At the same time, ethical challenges demand that religious and spiritual people bring their most cherished principles to bear in the real world. How should we treat the stranger in our midst? What claim do the needs of others make on our lives and energies? How should we respond to the threats of an enemy? It is in answering such questions that religious and spiritual communities live their convictions.

Today, we face these enduring questions and age-old problems in the context of new global realities. Greed, injustice, hatred, and violence are everywhere exacerbated by a burgeoning human population and unprecedented ecological pressures. It is vital that we develop a global perspective in order to meet adequately our ethical responsibilities as human beings.

With such a perspective, our religious and spiritual communities can best serve by extending to each of us the hospitality that our traditions teach. In solidarity with those in need, we can act with compassion, generosity, and courage to build a just and joyous life for all. In so doing, however, we must realize that religious and spiritual individuals and communities cannot act alone but must engage with people from all walks of life, who possess expertise and experience of every sort. Only in such a collaborative spirit can we find the basis for real service and genuine hope.

C. We call on the institutions of religion and spirituality to develop practical ways to engage creatively with other guiding institutions in pursuit of a just, peaceful, and sustainable world.

In this spirit, we invite all individuals, communities, groups, and organizations engaged with the institutions of religion and spirituality to reassess their roles for the next century.

Each is invited
1. To deepen respect and mutual welcome between religious and spiritual communities—in that spirit of hospitality which is to be found in each of their respective traditions
2. To strengthen the search for those shared ethical and spiritual values and principles that can enable religious and spiritual communities to engage creatively with one other and with the world
3. To encourage religious and spiritual individuals and communities to speak out for the welfare of all human beings in the name of their own values and in solidarity with others
4. To provide leadership to assure that the Earth is respected, revered, and protected
5. To find practical means to bring those elements

of their teachings that address justice, peace, and care for future generations to wider and more immediate effect through engagement with the other guiding institutions

6. To work closely with the institutions of government to bring religious teachings and values to bear in the struggle against corruption, dishonesty, and bribery at all levels

7. To safeguard against the use of religious and spiritual belief and practice as briefs for intolerance, tools for political manipulation, or warrants for conflict, terror, and violence

8. To urge their adherents to work together—within and across traditions—to respond directly to the critical issues facing the world: intolerance; racism; violence; social, political, and economic injustice; systematic deprivation and exploitation of children and women; and ecological degradation

9. To promote service—in solidarity and in partnership with the poor and vulnerable—to the entire human family and to the Earth as an affirmation of their teachings on personal spiritual growth, social justice, and life lived in ever-deepening relationship to Ultimate Reality.

THE CALL TO GOVERNMENT

"On the basis of personal experience and the burdensome history of our planet we have learned:

. . . that a better global order cannot be created or enforced by laws, prescriptions, and conventions alone;

. . . that the realization of peace, justice, and the protection of Earth depends on the insight and readiness of men and women to act justly;

. . . that action in favor of rights and freedom presumes a consciousness of responsibility and duty, and that therefore both the minds and hearts of women and men must be addressed;

. . . that rights without morality cannot long endure and that there will be no better global order without a global ethic."

—"Towards a Global Ethic: An Initial Declaration"

A. *We envision a world in which*

. . . *universal human rights and responsibilities, grounded in fundamental ethical and moral principles, are upheld;*

. . . *the structures of power are accountable to and serve the needs of all generations;*

. . . *our leaders are worthy of public trust;*

. . . *peace within and among nations is the rule and not the exception;*

. . . *the great decisions in human affairs are made with a thoughtful care for the future of the planetary community.*

B. Among the noblest functions of government is securing for its citizens their individual and collective well-being. This end can only be achieved through the honoring and safeguarding of human dignity and the constructive mediation between individual freedoms and collective action. When government succeeds in this purpose, it assures the social, political, and ecological integrity of the community.

Mere laws, prescriptions, and conventions alone cannot achieve a better social order. Freedom, justice, and peace rest on a common, enduring regard for the equal and inalienable rights of all people. What is required is that we as citizens live by a shared ethic that clarifies our mutual concerns and common values while transcending narrowly defined boundaries and interests.

Nowhere is the need for such a shared ethic more apparent than in international relations. Today, our world is a field of competing nations. For the world to become a true community, we must work toward a profound affirmation of global interdependence, moving beyond the present model of tenuously balanced power among nation-states toward a model of robust cooperation within the human family.

The art of governing—at local, regional, national, and international levels—can be understood in terms of the skillful application of ethical mandates and moral convictions to political realities. How can governments move beyond national concerns toward global responsibility? What steps can be taken toward the responsible use of power and the nurture of a global culture of justice, peace, and sustainability? What is the responsibility of the citizenry in fostering ethical government in a global context? To meet these responsibilities effectively will demand of both those who govern and of the governed an unshakable commitment to the cultivation of a high moral will and a truly global perspective.

C. We call on the institution of government to develop practical ways to engage creatively with other guiding institutions in pursuit of a just, peaceful, and sustainable world. In this spirit, we invite all individuals, communities, groups, and organizations engaged with the institution of government to reassess their roles for the next century.

Each is invited

1. To recognize and realize universal human rights—with all their civic, political, economic, social, and cultural implications, and with particular regard to women, children, the aged, and the poor

2. To encourage and create initiatives and alliances to foster a culture of justice and peace at local, national, regional, and international levels

3. To work most urgently and effectively to encourage and implement sustainable ways of living in a rich yet fragile world

4. To seek the advice and cooperation of religious and spiritual leaders and communities in an effort to bring their teachings and values to bear in the struggle to end bribery, dishonesty, and corruption at all levels of government

5. To enter into close dialogue and counsel with religious and spiritual communities concerning the peaceful resolution of conflicts and the criteria (if any) for a "just war"

6. To mitigate the factors that lead to violent conflict and war: government (and government-authorized) sales of arms; proliferation of weapons of mass destruction; and policies that underwrite economic exploitation, social or political injustice, or the destruction of communities and habitats

7. To denounce, counter, and deter genocide, as well as persecution, oppression, and terrorism of any sort, whether directed at members of a religious or spiritual community, of an ethnic or national group, of a culture, generation, or gender

8. To broaden the role of the military to include such peacemaking functions as meeting the challenges of natural disasters, famine, and epidemic; building or repairing vital infrastructure; or conducting ecological surveys

9. To take up their responsibility in the international effort to remedy the indebtedness of the poorest nations and establish more transparent, holistic, and culturally sensitive measures for assessing economic development

10. To move toward a model of "communities of communities," from the village level through the international, with an ethos of service to the common good.

THE CALL TO AGRICULTURE, LABOR, INDUSTRY, AND COMMERCE

"There is no global peace without global justice!

"... In the developed countries, a distinction must be made between necessary and limitless consumption, between socially beneficial and nonbeneficial uses of property, between justified and unjustified uses of natural resources, and between a profit-only and a socially beneficial and ecologically oriented market economy.

"... We must utilize economic and political power for service to humanity instead of misusing it in ruthless battles for domination. We must develop a spirit of compassion for those who suffer, with special care for children, the aged, the poor, the disabled, the refugees, and the lonely.

"... We must value a sense of moderation and modesty instead of an unquenchable greed for money, prestige, and consumption. In greed, humans lose their 'souls,' their freedom, their composure, their inner peace, and thus, that which makes them human."

—"Towards a Global Ethic: An Initial Declaration"

A. *We envision a world in which*

. . . *our productive activities are creative and vital and give meaning to our lives;*

. . . *high moral standards and trustworthiness guide all interactions in the marketplace and the workplace;*

. . . *economic, social, and physical well-being is not the exception but the normal human condition;*

. . . *agricultural policies, labor relations, industrial development, and commercial exchange are just, harmonious, and culturally enriching;*

. . . *agriculture, industry, business, and investment are conducted with constant thoughtful regard for the vitality and fragility of the Earth and all life;*

. . . *the essential needs of all are met in a manner that can be sustained well into the future.*

B. Among the noblest functions of agriculture, labor, industry, and commerce are the creative development and production of goods, services, and information to meet the basic physical and social needs of each human community—in a sustainable, renewable, and nondisruptive manner.

What we human beings desire, however, often eclipses material interests. What we work toward is often other than material prosperity. People everywhere feel the need to make something of themselves and their world that goes well beyond calculations of solvency. This perspective on human happiness and fulfillment is a considerable complement to current theories of the dominance of the market economy.

Consequently, economic power should be wielded in the service of economic justice and the commonweal. Wealth should be used equitably. State economic plans, corporate financial investments, agricultural techniques, and industrial processes should always do justice to human dignity and the community of life on Earth.

In the modern world, instances of the exploitation of human beings, the Earth itself, and all life are more numerous than ever. The reality of globalization, the profound interconnectedness of the world economy, and the inherent fragility of the Earth's ecosystem heighten the need for new strategies. At the same time, an extraordinary prospect has opened up: a worldwide awareness of the sensitive roles of agriculture, labor, industry, and commerce in relation to the pursuit of a more equitable and humane world.

C. We call on the institutions of agriculture, labor, industry, and commerce to develop practical ways to engage creatively with other guiding institutions in pursuit of a just, peaceful, and sustainable world.

In this spirit, we invite all individuals, communities, groups, and organizations engaged with the institutions of agriculture, labor, industry, and commerce to reassess their roles for the next century.

Each is invited

1. To develop and extend common statements of ethical standards and practices for production, exchange, investment, lending, and employment that could be accepted, implemented, and monitored around the world

2. To expand long-term goals to include not only the increase of wealth, but also the alleviation of poverty and the advancement of the social, cultural, spiritual, and ecological well-being of communities

3. To afford all peoples and nations the opportunity to participate equally in a global market, operating on trade agreements that safeguard and promote community-based economics and regional trade

4. To act immediately and comprehensively to ensure that fair compensation and humane working conditions are the norm, and the scourges of forced child labor, prison labor, sweatshops, and virtual slavery are put to an end

5. To bring their collective experience, knowledge, and skills at persuasion and innovation into partnerships with organizations of civil society dedicated to the rights of working men and women, intercultural and interreligious understanding, social justice, ecology, and community-based economics

6. To pay careful attention to corollary effects of patterns of agriculture, manufacture, investment, marketing, and distribution in light of their impact on local communities and ecological systems worldwide

7. To become at once exemplars and advocates of sustainability, carefully weighing short-term economic benefits against the continued viability of the Earth's ecosystem and the constant basic needs of the whole human community

8. To create joint structures with other guiding institutions to address more immediately and effectively the principal problems of our time, including severe ecological degradation, the deep indebtedness of poorer countries, massive unemployment, the widely unrewarded labors of women, and generations of poverty and malnutrition.

THE CALL TO EDUCATION

"Every human being without distinction of age, sex, race, skin color, physical or mental ability, language, religion, political view, or national or social origin possesses an inalienable and untouchable dignity, and everyone, the individual as well as the state, is therefore obliged to honor this dignity and protect it.

" . . . Young people must learn at home and in school that violence may not be a means of settling differences with others. Only thus can a culture of nonviolence be created.

" . . . Young people must learn at home and in school that property, limited though it may be, carries with it an obligation, and that its uses should at the same time serve the common good. Only thus can a just economic order be built up.

" . . . Young people must learn at home and in school to think, speak, and act truthfully. They have a right to information and education to be able to make the decisions that will form their lives. Without an ethical formation they will hardly be able to distinguish the important from the unimportant. In the daily flood of information, ethical standards will help them discern when opinions are portrayed as facts, interests veiled, tendencies exaggerated, and facts twisted."

—"Towards a Global Ethic: An Initial Declaration"

A. *We envision a world in which*

. . . learning, as a singularly enlivening human pursuit, is available to all;

. . . intergenerational learning is cherished;

. . . ethical, moral, and spiritual questions are an integral part of academic and civil discourse;

. . . the world's ethnic groups, cultures, and religious and spiritual communities are taught lifelong about each other in such a way that each becomes appreciative of the other;

. . . every human being has the opportunity to grow in personal and intellectual responsibility and committed service to the entire community of life;

. . . understanding and reverence for the vital yet fragile Earth provides the groundwork and incentive for sustainable living.

B. Among the noblest functions of education is the discovery of imaginative, enduring ways to translate and then to question humanity's knowledge, traditions, travails, and insights. Through this process of discovery and reflection, education equips the members of each successive generation to lead honorable, grateful, and engaged lives, which enrich their respective communities.

The principles of a global ethic make it clear that education should be a basic and universal human right. Girls and boys around the world should have full access to learning. Educators must seek out and adapt astute methods and well-researched materials to advance literacy in their regions, thus laying foundations for the equity and well-being of all societies. Young learners should be protected from child labor and other kinds of exploitation harmful to their development. Moreover, lifelong learning should be a cultural opportunity and a personal challenge for people of all ages.

Particular attention must be paid to learning about values, since an understanding of how values are adopted and shared is crucial to a peaceful and harmonious life. As no institution can do this work alone, it is important that families, schools, neighborhoods, local religious and spiritual communities, and each of the guiding institutions collaborate in this effort. Public education must never be used to further the exclusive aims of interest groups, ideologies, political parties, or religions. Education is one of the most precious gifts a society can give for the enrichment of the society itself. We are obliged to make wise and equitable investments to develop excellent teachers and to build a basic infrastructure capable of carrying out essential educational tasks.

C. We call on the institution of education to develop practical ways to engage creatively with other guiding institutions in pursuit of a just, peaceful, and sustainable world. In this spirit, we invite all individuals, communities, groups, and organizations engaged with the institution of education to reassess their roles for the next century.

Each is invited

1. To renew their commitment to universal education and to develop and extend common statements of ethical standards and practices that can be accepted, implemented, and monitored around the world

2. To work together with other guiding institutions to provide and strengthen the economic and material base for the development of educational systems worldwide

3. To address the needs of the world's poorest and least educated, with full-fledged universal literacy as a primary goal

4. To explore the most substantial and expedient ways to expand and enrich the education of girls and women worldwide

5. To make the best use of new media and new technologies to broaden intercultural access and exchange, while at the same time honoring local knowledge and traditional ways of knowing

6. To ensure that broadened intercultural access and exchange have a positive impact in areas of vital concern, with particular emphasis on sanitation, literacy, parenting, and enrichment of the lives of the neglected and dispossessed

7. To integrate learning about different cultures, religions, and spiritual practices into the standard educational process

8. To promote and teach respect for other ways of life, nonviolence, and peacemaking, at every stage of learning

9. To promote ecological literacy and the study of sustainability as essential to education at all levels

10. To acknowledge that moral and spiritual questions are as critical to academic as to civil discourse by including considerations of values, personal responsibility, moral integrity, and community service throughout higher education.

THE CALL TO THE ARTS AND COMMUNICATIONS MEDIA

"In the great ancient religious and ethical traditions of humankind we find the directive: You shall not lie! Or in positive terms: Speak and act truthfully! Let us reflect anew on the consequences of this ancient directive: No woman or man, no institution, no state or church or religious community has the right to speak lies to other humans.

"This is especially true

• For those who work in the mass media, to whom we entrust the freedom to report for the sake of truth and to whom we thus grant the office of guardian. They do not stand above morality but have the obligation to respect human dignity, human rights, and fundamental values. They are duty-bound to objectivity, fairness, and the preservation of human dignity. They have no right to intrude into individuals' private spheres, to manipulate public opinion, or to distort reality

• For artists, writers, and scientists, to whom we entrust artistic and academic freedom. They are not exempt from general ethical standards and must serve the truth...."

—"Towards a Global Ethic: An Initial Declaration"

A. *We envision a world in which*

...the stories and images that matter most are those that enrich understanding, deepen responsibility, and nurture personal growth amid development;

...the networks of communication and modes of

artistic expression that link diverse peoples, regions, and ways of life are characterized by integrity and mutuality;

. . . the arts and communications media play an active, thoughtful role in enabling a much wider discussion and more profound analysis of the most critical issues and decisions facing the human community;

. . . the sacred stories, symbols, and wisdom of the world's religious and spiritual traditions are broadly disseminated and cherished.

B. Among the noblest functions of the arts and of communications media is the weaving of a sense of community that comes from shared access to the central stories of a culture and the signal events of an era. As a transformative force, the arts and communications media have a special role: to inspire, warn, inform, challenge, set in perspective, and dramatize both our deeds and our dilemmas. In so doing, they energize, broaden, embolden, and deepen public discourse.

The freedom of the arts and of communications media to inform the public and critique society or government is essential to a just social order. This freedom must be exercised with care for the fabric of each society and the whole cloth of humanity. On the part of the arts, freedom demands a sensitivity to cultural and historical context. On the part of communications media, it also demands accurate and truthful reporting. Privacy and intimacy must be honored. Art or journalism that degrades or injures individuals or communities must be avoided. Any calls to hate or to violence must be rejected.

Today, movies, television, the music industry, the news media, and the Internet have unprecedented significance as sources of information and influence on cultural life and social change. What is our role as consumers and patrons in shaping the character of art and media? How can we best employ the technologies of the near future for education and enrichment and not merely for entertainment? How can we better recognize, understand, and be nurtured by the presence of artistic genius?

C. We call on the institutions of the arts and communications media to develop practical ways to engage creatively with other guiding institutions in pursuit of a just, peaceful, and sustainable world.

In this spirit, we invite all individuals, communities, groups, and organizations engaged with the institutions of the arts and communications media to reassess their roles for the next century.

Each is invited

1. To develop and disseminate common statements of ethical standards and practices—where possible, across cultures and disciplines—addressing such issues as the universal professional code for news media, socially responsible journalism, and commitments to cross-cultural understanding

2. To design coherent, widely acceptable approaches to such issues bearing on the news media as rights of privacy, rules of investigational conduct, remedies for misreporting or misquotation, and retractions for the mistaking or perpetuating of rumor as fact

3. To safeguard the means and open up the methods of global communication so that they serve all segments of society equitably

4. To counter the often dehumanizing sameness of globalized mass culture by supporting local and regional traditions and cultures

5. To promote models for the arts and communications media that give voice to all peoples, cultures, and conditions, ensuring their active involvement in deliberations on issues that face the world

6. To establish and enliven liaisons with religious, interreligious, and intercultural groups, in order to increase journalistic coverage and artistic representation of society's religious, spiritual, interreligious, and intercultural dimensions

7. To eliminate religious, ethnic, and cultural caricatures and stereotypes that devalue the experience of human beings and demean their essential dignity

8. To invest effectively in artistic and journalistic projects that address in long-range terms the most critical problems facing the human community and the Earth

9. To further art and aesthetic appreciation by offering all children art education, to include inter-

nationally and nationally acclaimed art—both contemporary and historical—as well as the traditional art and crafts of each region.

THE CALL TO SCIENCE AND MEDICINE

"Humans must always be the subjects of rights, must be ends, never mere means, never objects of commercialization and industrialization in economics, politics and media, in research institutes, and industrial corporations.

"...A human person is infinitely precious and must be unconditionally protected. But likewise the lives of animals and plants that inhabit this planet with us deserve protection, preservation, and care. Limitless exploitation of the natural foundations of life, ruthless destruction of the biosphere, and militarization of the cosmos are all outrages. As human beings we have a special responsibility—especially with a view to future generations—for Earth and the cosmos, for the air, water, and soil.

"...A universal consensus on many disputed ethical questions (from bio- and sexual ethics through mass media and scientific ethics to economic and political ethics) will be difficult to attain. Nevertheless, even for many controversial questions, suitable solutions should be attainable in the spirit of the fundamental principles we have jointly developed here."

—"Towards a Global Ethic: An Initial Declaration"

A. *We envision a world in which*
...we wisely explore the mysteries of life;
...our various systems of knowing enhance one another;
...access to knowledge and to the healing arts is not a privilege but a right;
...our methods of seeking the truths of existence and well-being draw us together (rather than separate us);
...humanity is enhanced by technology, in a manner consistent with our responsibility to the rest of the Earth community.

B. To enlarge our understanding of the physical world and of ourselves is among the noblest functions of science and medicine. From these material and human realities we draw many of our metaphors, operating principles, and therapeutic practices. Science and medicine provide essential tools in our efforts to nurture the life and growth of individuals and communities.

As disciplines engaged in observation, experiment, analysis, and discovery, science and medicine also have a social dimension. Researchers and teachers, physicians and engineers, physicists, chemists, and biologists should be committed to benefiting human life and reducing suffering. In fact, civilization has found ways to make most scientific and medical discoveries and technologies beneficial and productive. Some of these, however, have been employed in dangerous, destructive, life-threatening ways. Therefore, we must always consider the consequences of scientific research, medical programs, and technological development in the context of the well-being of the human community and of the Earth's systems of life.

The influence and power of science, medicine, and technology are now so enormous that scientists, physicians, and engineers bear an unprecedented responsibility for the future. Not only their knowledge and technical skills but also their conscientiousness and prudence are critical to what we make of ourselves and our world in the next decades.

Over the course of history, science and religion have often been seen as contradictory or even as mutually exclusive. Increasing openness, however, has recently produced a new level of dialogue between the two. This development could not be more fortuitous: in the final analysis, the wisdom of religion, the knowledge of science, and the art of medicine are indispensable to each other and to a sustainable future.

C. We call on the institutions of science and medicine to develop practical ways to engage creatively with other guiding institutions in pursuit of a just, peaceful, and sustainable world.

In this spirit, we invite all individuals, communities, groups, and organizations engaged with the institutions of science and medicine to reassess their roles for the next century.

Each is invited

1. To enter into dialogue with competent persons from the world's religious and spiritual traditions with regard to the ethical and moral dimensions of research programs and the long-range consequences of scientific, medical, and technological innovation

2. To reflect sincerely on the limitations and moral boundaries of science and medicine in continual dialogue and exchange with other guiding institutions

3. To develop and disseminate common statements of ethical standards and practices for science, medicine, and technology—across cultures and disciplines

4. To resist efforts at control, redirection, or even domination of scientific and medical enterprises by narrowly defined interests, whether economic, political, military, or religious

5. To keep in mind, for new programs of research, application, and outreach, those children, women, and displaced peoples around the world who have little access to advanced systems, tools, and modalities of healing

6. To honor and learn from traditional modes of healing in concert with modern technological perspectives on the human body

7. To take always into account, at each step in the design of experimental protocols, public health programs, laboratories, research centers, clinics, and hospitals, the constellation of values, cultural norms, and spiritual concerns of local communities

8. To find ways to focus the creative energies of science and medicine more intentionally, systematically, and intensively on the most pressing issues of human survival, such as food, health, demographic change, and ecological sustainability

9. To enter into dialogue with religious and spiritual communities about the evolving scientific understanding of the origins and complex dynamics of the universe.

THE CALL TO INTERNATIONAL INTERGOVERNMENTAL ORGANIZATIONS

"No new global order without a global ethic!

"... We all have a responsibility for a better global order. Our involvement for the sake of human rights, freedom, justice, peace, and the preservation of the Earth is absolutely necessary.

"... We must utilize economic and political power for service to humanity instead of misusing it in ruthless battles for domination.

"... Today we possess sufficient economic, cultural, and spiritual resources to introduce a better global order. But old and new ethnic, national, social, economic, and religious tensions threaten the peaceful building of a better world.

"... In such a dramatic global situation humanity needs a vision of peoples living peacefully together, of ethnic and ethical groupings and of religions sharing responsibility for the care of the Earth.

"We are convinced of the fundamental unity of the human family on Earth. We recall the 1948 Universal Declaration of Human Rights of the United Nations. What is formally proclaimed on the level of rights we wish to confirm and deepen here from the perspective of an ethic: the full realization of the intrinsic dignity of the human person, the inalienable freedom and equality in principle of all humans, and the necessary solidarity and interdependence of all humans with each other."

—"Towards a Global Ethic: An Initial Declaration"

A. *We envision a world in which*

... all peoples of the Earth have an equal voice and an equal claim to be heard;

... each person has an undeniable claim to universal human rights, complemented by a personal moral responsibility based on care for others;

... each person has a right to the fulfillment of basic human needs, balanced by a personal ethical obligation to share;

. . . national and regional concerns for equality, security, prosperity, and sustainability are informed by a truly global perspective;

. . . any resort to arms to resolve a dispute is understood as a moral failure to engage in heartfelt dialogue;

. . . the regional and the global do not subsume but supplement and sustain the local;

. . . people from across the planet, from all walks of life, come to see themselves as world citizens.

B. Among the noblest functions of international intergovernmental organizations is the fostering of communication and cooperation, among nations and peoples, toward greater global harmony, security, and peace. With this in mind, these organizations invoke and act on principles of international law while appealing on ethical and political grounds for a broadly held vision of a better world.

The 20th century has been punctuated by two world wars and plagued by regional and world conflicts. These conflicts have been fueled by ethnic, racial, and religious antagonisms, as well as by economic imbalances and insecurities. In this century, we also have seen pervasive abuse of human rights, alarming ecological and environmental degradation, and the steady increase of economic and social inequities. Yet we have also witnessed a series of strongly worded international affirmations—beginning with the Universal Declaration of Human Rights in 1948—that served as the basis for countless economic, social, and political movements and reforms. Furthermore, a heightened environmental awareness and ecological consciousness has prompted a new willingness and new ways to address significant problems related to sustainability. Now, at century's end, the reality that the world has in so many ways become a global village impels our search for new models of international relations.

These two contrasting dimensions of the 20th century have given rise to an array of international intergovernmental organizations. These include the United Nations, the European Union, the Pacific Community, the Association of Southeast Asian Nations, the Organization of African Unity, the Organization of American States, the International Court of Justice, the World Bank, the International Monetary Fund, the World Trade Organization, the International Labor Organization, the World Health Organization, and many others.

If these international organizations are to wield their enormous influence for the public good, they must pursue economic and social justice, support efforts at self-determination and self-sufficiency, and move the world further along toward the equitable sharing of resources. Each organization must also acknowledge, honor, and act to promote a sense of the world as a single, albeit admirably diverse, community that attends patiently and comprehensively to human needs within a larger, delicately balanced environment.

A singular question emerges: How can citizens of the world ensure that all international intergovernmental organizations are grounded in the same shared ethical principles—fairness, equity, compassion, and concern for the abiding welfare of every succeeding generation?

C. We call on international intergovernmental organizations to develop practical ways to engage creatively with other guiding institutions in pursuit of a just, peaceful, and sustainable world.

In this spirit, we invite all individuals, communities, groups, and organizations engaged with international intergovernmental organizations to reassess their roles for the next century.

Each is invited

1. To operate with transparency in exchanges with peoples and cultures around the world, and in such a way that the fullest participation of civil society is guaranteed

2. To work together with the other guiding institutions to reduce and soon to eliminate the crushing debt of the poorest nations

3. To monitor transnational economic concerns, enterprises, and projects so that forced labor, forced relocation, and enforced isolation are relics of the past

4. To find effective ways to screen agricultural and technological innovations introduced on behalf of

peoples whose local sustainability may thereby be jeopardized

5. To help establish more equitable and comprehensive international policies with regard to asylum, sanctuary, and emigration/immigration

6. To work together with the other guiding institutions to reduce and soon to eliminate the financial, technical, social, legal, and political barriers to swift, secure, and easily accessible regional, continental, and global communication

7. To influence international policy and to mobilize the personnel and funds to assure that every human being has, for the foreseeable future, sufficient food, fresh water, clean air, adequate shelter, and medical care

8. To safeguard the integrity and uniqueness of the world's diverse cultures, particularly of those peoples most vulnerable in the face of the globalization of the world economy

9. To assure that resources are available for emergency relief for famine, epidemic, natural disaster, industrial pollution, and other catastrophes; and that such relief campaigns are conducted on a fair, impartial, and apolitical basis, and in a manner that preserves the dignity of the recipient

10. To protect the natural resources of the Earth from depredation, pollution, waste, and exhaustion.

THE CALL TO ORGANIZATIONS OF CIVIL SOCIETY

"In conclusion, we appeal to all the inhabitants of this planet. Earth cannot be changed for the better unless the consciousness of individuals is changed. We pledge to work for such transformation in individual and collective consciousness, for the awakening of our spiritual powers through reflection, meditation, prayer, or positive thinking, for a conversion of the heart. Together we can move mountains! Without a willingness to take risks and a readiness to sacrifice there can be no fundamental change in our situation! Therefore we commit ourselves to a common global ethic, to better mutual understanding, as well as to socially beneficial, peace-fostering, and Earth-friendly ways of life.

"We invite all men and women, whether religious or not, to do the same."
—"Towards a Global Ethic: An Initial Declaration"

A. *We envision a world in which*
. . . freedom of association is assured and encouraged;
. . . open discourse is cherished and cooperative common action is nurtured;
. . . "public life" is understood as broader and more fundamental than government, which exists by the will of the people and for the sake of the society;
. . . societies are constituted and reconstituted through a multitude of voluntary associations that give voice to all;
. . . conversation about values and visions is a highly regarded and well-protected element of public life;
. . . the generations and genders speak and listen to each other with mutual respect, at home and abroad;
. . . every society understands how to listen and to learn as alternative perspectives and courses of action are presented, discussed, and debated, and implemented.

B. Civil society has come to mean the network of voluntary, nongovernmental associations—clubs, youth groups, sports and service groups, professional organizations, trade unions, cultural alliances, independent political parties, philanthropic funds, advocacy centers, community coalitions—that provide the fertile soil in which an expansive, responsible citizenship takes root and flourishes. Among the noblest functions of civil society is mediation between the power of the state and the rights, needs, and responsibilities of individuals and groups.

The astonishing growth in numbers, projects, and influence of organizations of civil society is one of the most important phenomena of our time. Organizations of civil society are involved in all areas of human concern, providing essential social services, humanitarian relief, and innovative programs for social, economic, and political reform. Moreover, because governments do not easily or naturally extend rights to their citizens, civil society often takes on a prophetic role as the body politic struggles to identify and secure basic rights and meet unfulfilled needs. Such organizations act regionally and globally as monitors—and sometimes as guarantors—of the freedoms, rights, and the very survival of individual citizens. In time, the civil social process can come both to exemplify and to sustain the ethical character and public life of a society.

As individual citizens facing larger societal dynamics and world events, we may often feel that our voices are not heard and our actions are viewed as inconsequential. Yet movements bringing transformation most often have arisen from the grassroots, because it is at this most vital level that rights, needs, and responsibilities are brought into sharpest relief. Because its lifeblood is voluntary association, civil society is an expression of the grassroots. Choosing to associate with others in common cause amplifies our voices and strengthens our actions. Speaking and acting in concert with others, we make a difference in the world.

In itself, civil society is never complete or perfect. It is grounded in the reality that communities—whether rural or urban—are not simply spaces occupied by numbers of discrete people but hubs where history, habits, and harbingers converge. Thus, the chief task of civil society is to broaden the scope of citizen participation, to mediate between the community and the state, and to deepen the pluralistic exchange of ideas. Organizations of civil society have a special responsibility to cultivate and demonstrate moral leadership if they are to contribute to the elevation of public discourse and collective action on behalf of a better world.

C. We call on the organizations of civil society to develop practical ways to engage creatively with other guiding institutions in pursuit of a just, peaceful, and sustainable world.

In this spirit, we invite all individuals, communities, groups, and organizations engaged with the organizations of civil society to reassess their roles for the next century.

Each is invited

1. To operate on principles of transparency, democracy, accountability, and cooperation

2. To exemplify and cultivate moral leadership through thoughtful, consistent service and advocacy

3. To commit to service to a larger social good, rather than to the self-interest of a particular group

4. To establish firm, friendly, supportive alliances among themselves, toward eventual collaboration in support of larger constituencies and causes

5. To work together with other guiding institutions to assure the poor, the illiterate, and the inarticulate a strong, cogent voice in the public forum

6. To broaden access to participation in civil society, with particular outreach to women, to youth, to indigenous peoples, and to the physically or mentally challenged

7. To clear the public forum of all assumptions that disagreement is equivalent to treason, so that opinion and action are neither compelled nor withheld out of fear

8. To listen to critics and consult with opponents, and to attend patiently to internal controversy, promoting the active, positive agency of each individual and group

9. To make dialogue possible and promising where it seems most unlikely, especially among groups that consider themselves long-standing rivals for power, prestige, or pride of place

10. To help establish new templates of interaction and participation as they expand their partnerships with national governments and international agencies, so that cooperative, inclusive, and nonadversarial approaches to decision making become the norm at every level of society.

ENDORSEMENT

As persons reflecting the broad diversity of the Earth's religious, spiritual, cultural, ethnic, and racial communities, we the undersigned join with the Council for a Parliament of the World's Religions in issuing this "Call to Our Guiding Institutions."

We embrace the spirit of this document.
We applaud its invitation to creative engagement.
We commit ourselves to the realization of its aims.
We seek to serve as role models and examples within the institutions with which we are engaged.
We urge all thoughtful and concerned persons to join with us.

Visions of Challenge, Harmony, and Transformation

REFLECTIONS ON THE PARLIAMENT OF THE WORLD'S RELIGIONS

Brother Wayne Teasdale and Joel Beversluis

Known historically for its hospitality and energized by its potential for change, Cape Town enthusiastically embraced the Parliament during those eight days in early December 1999. Its program and participants captured the attention, imagination, and hearts of Africans of all colors, especially those from Cape Town. There are many reasons, of course, beyond the presence of numerous tourists from around the world in a relatively small city: the visitors' spiritual orientation and messages of hope; their economic and cultural impact; their understanding of the demands and opportunities of pluralism; and their clear message of appreciation for the dramatic changes and challenges in South Africa.

The Parliament's diversity of cultures, races, and traditions was breathtaking, with members and leaders from some two hundred religious communities as well as from numerous educational, interfaith, and advocacy organizations. From around the world, they joined an already vibrant and historic community of religions at the southern tip of Africa, nestled into ancient mountains where two great oceans meet.

Hidden among the Parliament's impressive attendance figures—more than seven thousand badges were issued—is the unfortunate fact that because of the costs of travel, registration, and lodging, relatively few Africans registered for its programs. As a result, the voices of indigenous Africans, including those who've been "dispossessed," were not often heard. On the other hand, many Africans from all classes and religions volunteered with great generosity. Even so, the largest contingent of registrants was from North America, with its surplus of disposable wealth.

The Parliament opened on December 1st with an AIDS awareness commemoration. Because AIDS is a huge problem in South Africa—20 percent of the population is infected with HIV, and many more are directly affected—the Parliament wanted to draw attention to this critical matter by identifying with South Africa's suffering. Speakers lamented the extent of the problem, both the personal devastation it brings and the high cost and inaccessibility of drugs such as AZT. Portions of the AIDS quilt, including new panels memorializing some who've died recently in South Africa, were displayed for all to see. At the conclusion of this event in Company Gardens, which is also the site of the South African Parliament, thousands marched in procession through the city streets.

Along the way, marchers were greeted by the voices and placards of evangelical Christians and fundamentalist Muslims who had found rare common cause in their opposition to the event. Other placards wondered what we would do about global hot spots such as East Timor, or accused the Parliament of "conspiracy" or of a godless motivation. Some marchers ignored the placards or felt a bit indignant, but many others greeted our challengers with smiles and blessings, acknowledging that those on the sidewalks were also, in their way, part of the diversity of the Parliament of the World's Religions. A few days later, four of the protesting Muslims approached Parliament leaders to apologize after they discovered the positive nature of what was happening in Cape Town.

We marched to District Six, which has been a desolate yet sacred place for South Africans of color in their struggle to overcome the apartheid regime. The empty fields there were once a thriving intercultural neighborhood of businesses, schools, churches, and homes, where people of all races and religions had lived in relative harmony. The neighborhood had been destroyed—plowed under—in one of the tragic apartheid actions of the '60s and '70s. Most of its occupants had been sent to the townships outside the city in a crass legislative attempt to create more space for whites in Cape

Town. Even the streets had been torn up, but the land had never been reoccupied.

At the end of the procession, Parliament marchers gathered with former residents in an open field in District Six for a ceremony of prayers, dance, and music in the subtropical sunshine. There, the Parliament celebrated its opening on the African continent and invoked "a new day dawning."

A Sampling of Program Highlights

Among the Parliament's more than eight hundred programs—too many to detail here—were several symposia that lasted two or more days. One of the most fascinating of these was the Science and Religion Symposium entitled *At Home in the Universe*, a meeting demonstrating the growing congeniality between scientists and sages. Some of the other symposia of interest considered interfaith action in a global context; religious responses to the Earth Charter; ethics, values, and spirituality in the workplace; and new initiatives in micro-credit and sustainable development.

Nine plenary sessions accented themes such as sharing sacred space, human rights, celebrating life, creative engagement, meeting essential needs, and the Next Generation's nurturing and transformative vision of community among youth and young adults. Dance and musical events were spectacular; the noteworthy stars were the very athletic and disciplined Taiko drummers from Japan and the young Zulu dancers; both groups appeared at various points during the Parliament's eight exhaustingly rich days. In addition, several choirs from Black African congregations provided energetic music, including the new and inspirational national anthem.

Among the highlights of the Cape Town gathering was the appearance of Nelson Mandela at an evening plenary session. The former president's humility, warmth, and graciousness complemented his speech, which was substantive and brilliant. In it, he drew attention to the role of the religions—and interreligious cooperation—in South Africa's struggle against racism and the apartheid system. Mandela also remarked how the religions—Christians, Hindus,

Muslims, and Jews—had supported education for blacks, and were the only means whereby most blacks and "coloreds" could achieve an education, since the best schools were reserved for the white minority. It was the religious leaders who regularly visited the prisoners and "gave us the hope that one day we would return." "Religion," he said, "was one of the motivating forces of everything we did and will have a crucial role in inspiring humanity to meet the enormous challenges we face," not only in material development, but "the redefinition of values."

His words were meaningful in an age when it is common to criticize and even reject organized religion; they were particularly welcome at the Parliament, where religions are respected and challenged to respond to issues such as racism and economic oppression. At the same time, we were humbled by the knowledge that religion, particularly some branches of protestant Christianity, had helped create and support the oppressive apartheid system.

One of the most meaningful services relating to South Africa's heritage was held early on a Sunday morning, on Robben Island. Approximately four hundred people ferried out to this historically painful site, which was used first as a "colony" to isolate lepers and later as a harsh prison for those who resisted apartheid. Nelson Mandela was one of many who spent long years in the prison, working under the hot sun in the glare of the limestone quarries. The island prison has now been converted into a museum and monument to the history of South Africa, to those who resisted oppression, and to the African renaissance.

At a moving service of commemoration, Mr. Ahmed Kathrada, who'd been an inmate there for eighteen years and is now curator of Robben Island, spoke about how the prisoners had welcomed and attended whatever religious services were provided from all faiths, and why the new government believes religious communities must continue to play a guiding role in South Africa. Religious and indigenous spiritual leaders then blessed a Peace Pole as a symbol of the victory over oppression and as a reminder of the power of prayer for peace. Inscribed in four South African languages, the Peace Pole bears the message, "May Peace Prevail on Earth!"

The Dalai Lama's presence and participation at the Parliament represented another high point for registrants as well as a significant attraction for the general public. When he was asked, during a news conference, about the value of the Parliament, he responded by pointing out that it was definitely a positive force, but that it needed to walk the path of action, not simply words. Later, in his address at the final plenary, he reiterated his plea for concrete action motivated by compassion.

His Holiness also spent two wonderful hours with twenty-five young adults of the Next Generation program who had been invited to interact with him and participate in the Parliament Assembly. Many of these had also written essays reflecting on the Parliament document, "A Call to Our Guiding Institutions." During their conversations, the Dalai Lama was his usual playful but wise self, and he and the young people clearly enjoyed themselves.

The Assembly itself considered ways to implement the "Call" and disseminate it far and wide, and ideas for programs in service to the planet. To do their work, participants sat at tables of eight to ten people, alternating between working alone and group discussions. The conversations were useful, often profound, and provided a lot of ideas for the participants and for CPWR as it considers how to proceed with the document. Because it is a substantive challenge to the leaders of the political, economic, educational, media, religious, scientific, and other segments of culture that influence our lives in the world, the "Call to Our Guiding Institutions" is regarded by many as an innovative, imaginative, and bold step by this third Parliament.

In retrospect, the concept of the Assembly as a separate, by-invitation-only gathering may be an obsolete carryover from an older paradigm where religious and spiritual elites have a special function and privilege. Because of the significance of the "Call," it would have been more fulfilling, and certainly less discriminatory, to invite all Parliament registrants into the process of reflection, design, and

commitment. This step would also have demonstrated creative engagement with much more of the extraordinary talent that had assembled in Cape Town.

The Parliament was major news in South Africa, and received substantial media attention in Asia and Europe. However, with the exception of *The New York Times* and a few other papers, North American media displayed its usual myopia regarding things spiritual despite efforts of the CPWR to generate news coverage. Unfortunately, the Parliament had to compete with excitement over the World Trade Organization and its opponents in the streets of Seattle.

Ironically, both the Parliament and the protesters in Seattle had significant common cause: challenging the world to make a shift from exploitive personal and corporate interests to sustainable development and economics, environmental protection, and peace with justice. In fact, some who attended the 1993 Parliament chose to go to Seattle in 1999 to help organize and participate in the overwhelmingly nonviolent aspects of that protest. The media, however, focused instead on the scattered violence and the militant police response to it as well as to the nonviolent protests. What media reported on about Cape Town was the unrelated bombing that occurred just before the Parliament met, plus some political conflict over AIDS funding and whether South Africa's president would meet with the Dalai Lama. Interestingly, one of the guiding institutions that the "Call" addresses is the media itself, challenging it to reflect on what it finds newsworthy and to pay attention to the numerous efforts at cultural transformation.

For those who do appreciate good news, some powerful symbolism broke out around the perimeter of Parliament events. For example, when His Holiness the Dalai Lama spoke at a luncheon for the Assembly, hosted by Nomaindia Mfeketo the black female mayor of Cape Town, the group spontaneously broke into refrains of "We Shall Overcome," thus linking the Tibetan struggle with the victorious campaigns of South Africa and the Civil Rights movement in the United States. The same song had broken out spontaneously—and with healing effects—in 1993, when disputants over Indian policy in Kashmir disrupted a plenary session. A further link joined the successful struggle of India for her independence with South African and American struggles: Ela Gandhi, the granddaughter of Mahatma Gandhi, a member of the South African Parliament from Durban, and a vigorous supporter of the Parliament's agendas, presented Nelson Mandela with the Gandhi-King Award for Nonviolence.

Other meaningful symbolism was evident on the last evening, immediately following the closing plenary session, when a small group went to the top of Table Mountain for a final interfaith ceremony. Overlooking Cape Town, the ocean, Robben Island, District Six, and dramatic cloud formations on the plateau, participants from a dozen religious communities took turns praying, chanting, and singing in our own ways and tongues. This experience was wonderfully moving in the wind and sunset, as the clouds rolled down to the sea, reminding us of how Spirit moves across earth and water.

Among us was a young Japanese Buddhist monk who had been fasting for the week of the Parliament, sitting on the sidewalk across from the main venue. While we'd been busy with events, he had spent each day, from early morning till evening, chanting, drumming, and praying for the Parliament's success and safety. After our service, he told us with great excitement that he'd gone off alone to a place where he could stand on one edge of a gorge while the cloud waves tumbled down over the facing cliff, just fifty feet away. While he was standing there in the setting sun, a bright rainbow had appeared in the fog, in the shape of an arch. His shadow then appeared as a silhouette in the white of the fog, surrounded by the rainbow. It was, in Buddhist terms, very auspicious! He was greatly blessed, as he had blessed us with his week of prayer and fasting.

This Parliament was memorable, like the previous two (1893 and 1993) in Chicago. Wonderful meetings and synchronicities, networking, giving, and creativity took place among people with common ideals, inspired by uncommon Spirit. Heroic acts of sacrifice and commitment by organizers, volunteers, and presenters prove the significance attached to these Parliaments by their tens of thousands of participants. The agendas and organizing principles of the Parliaments have emerged as a world force that draws leaders, educators, advocates, organizers, and inquirers—nearly all of whom are committed members of the world's religious and spiritual communities. Of most significance is the discovery, once again, that numerous energetic, well-intentioned, and capable people are doing good work in the world!

The next Parliament is planned for 2004, at a site to be selected following a careful evaluation process. It will be even more significant if it can help religious and spiritual communities to incarnate its message into guidance and practices to help transform human consciousness on this planet. For, ultimately, it is not simply ethics but transformation itself that the Global Ethic invites and that the *global problematique* and the "Call" require of us and our guiding institutions.

Suggestions to Strengthen and Broaden the Parliament

Dr. Allan Mott Keislar

A third-generation missionary in India and Pakistan, Dr. Keislar also received direct spiritual instruction from His Divine Grace A.C. Bhaktivedanta Swami Prabhupada and Hazrat Baba Farid Ganj Shakkar. He now teaches South Asian Religion and Interfaith Dialogue at the Graduate Theological Union, Berkeley, California.

In 1989, Dr. Paulos Mar Gregorios spoke these pointed words at the inaugural ceremonies for celebrating the Centennial of the 1893 World's Parliament of Religions:

> Let me say something now which I hope can be understood: so long as Western civilization or Western Christianity dominates the World Parliament or Concourse, it will not work. . . .

Western civilization has been a largely one-way mission, in which both the civilization and the church claimed to know the truth and refused to listen to aspects of truth in the experience of the rest of humanity. And, therefore, I want to say this from the heart: I love my Western brothers and sisters; I love my Western *Christian* brothers and sisters also. But where they dominate, an impasse prevails which does not allow the other cultures of the world to function. They are help-lessly dominant. Men or women, they cannot do anything but dominate. And, therefore, the most important thing for a Global Concourse of Religions is for the Western civilization and Western Christianity to be humble and courte-ous enough to take a backseat. . . . Then we might be able to use your God-given capacity [for organization] in our common work, not as a leader, but in a more modest way.

In a similar vein, Joel Beversluis wrote in 1998 to the Internet forum of *Interfaith Voices for Peace and Justice:*

Members of different faith traditions can and must work together with common ethics and goals, despite differences of commitments and despite political and social diversity. The inter-faith movement must accommodate differences as great as conflicting faith commitments, Truth claims, exclusivity, and lifestyle values. This phi-losophy must be explained to members of the reli-gions and even to members of interfaith organizations, some of whom believe that "funda-mentalists" should give up their claims. . . . If the interfaith movement is merely an expression of liberal religion and progressive political and social agendas, it will not only alienate many oth-ers of other persuasions, it will in fact contribute to the same kinds interreligious conflicts it claims to want to "heal."

How did the 1999 Parliament of the World's Religions live up to these insightful appeals? The Parliament was held where the Indian Ocean meets the Atlantic, where East meets West, in South Africa—a country long identified with a most unpro-gressive Christian tradition. Great strides were made in broadening the representation of non-Western and more conservative religious groups, and espe-cially encouraging was the significant participation of South Africans of a wide range of ethnicities and religious persuasions.

To further strengthen the foundation of the Parliament's work, what can we do to insure that Parliaments in the future are still less dominated by 1) a restrictive Western approach, and 2) "expres-sions of liberal religion and progressive political and social agendas"?

1. An Underlying Western Presupposition of the Parliament

If we compare the Parliament with interfaith pro-grams more directed by non-Westernized persons, there is a striking difference. The latter are rarely "conferences," but are spiritual gatherings where Spirit is expected to often directly guide the pro-ceedings. No doubt the Parliament gave ample opportunity—to give just a few examples—to Indians, both native American and South Asian, to Muslims, and to indigenous Africans, to offer prayers and blessings. These traditions, however, had little opportunity to share what I consider a much greater strength of theirs. We did not see Native American medicine men or women, non-Westernized yogis or Sufi mystics, or African shamans deciding the direc-tion of the conference proceedings. In a traditional gathering, they would have done this, according to their mystic visions of the supernatural world. But this very idea, due largely to our bad experience with false "spiritualists," may appear irrational, if not abhorrent, to us. Can the Westernized leadership of the Parliament "be humble and courteous enough to take a backseat," quoting Paulos Mar Gregorios, at least until we learn how to better perceive the direct inspiration of God in our hearts. Can the leadership allow those who are far better trained in such spiri-tuality to direct future Parliaments, using our special

Western capacity for organization "not as a leader, but in a more modest way"?

One of the most telling, if not shocking, revelations of the dominance of organization over Spirit in the 1999 Parliament was how the audience often applauded after prayers or Scripture readings were offered, almost as if they had been organized for entertainment. I don't want to make too much of this point, for there was plenty of sincere appreciation in the applause, but it certainly revealed some of the problems involved in attempting to organize Spirit this rigidly.

There is a valid fear, in organizing such huge interreligious gatherings, that something may easily go awry if the happenings are not well controlled. Nevertheless, I would suggest that the organizers of the Parliament, and of other major interfaith gatherings, should try to depart as much as possible from the Western conference model. We have much to learn, for example, from both American and Eastern Indians. The recent great intertribal powwows, incredible manifestations of the resurgent Spirit in Native America, or the *Kumbha melas* in India, by far the largest regular religious gatherings on the planet, are instructive examples of more spiritual, multireligious "parliaments." I have attended two of these events, and observed others by video. Although organization sometimes seems pitifully lacking, the spiritual atmosphere, generated by the dominant presence of genuine spiritual masters, is far more palpable than in more highly-organized conferences. I suggest that, to become even more of a true "Parliament of the World's Religions," we need to review the conference-like procedures, and perhaps even the very goals and purposes of the Parliament, humbly accepting the direction of less Westernized (rather than simply non-Western) spiritual guides.

2. The Social Agenda of the Parliament

Most clearly revealed by the document, "A Call to Our Guiding Institutions," the entire thrust of the 1999 Parliament, especially of the quite deliberately organized Parliament Assembly, was the effort to "make the world a better place to live." This is at least

partly because the organizers of the Parliament correctly understand that social action is an area where different religions can more easily cooperate with each other. Yet such almost exclusive emphasis on this primary concern of many liberal traditions (again more the Western ones) can easily, in Joel Beversluis's words, "alienate many others of other persuasions." Indeed, despite considerable pressure to endorse the "Call," at least one spiritual leader in the Parliament Assembly refused to sign it for precisely this reason.

Jesus Christ said, as many spiritual masters have, "Seek ye first the Kingdom of Heaven and all these things shall be added unto thee." If we take this seriously, we will understand that no program of social action can succeed without giving primary attention to the spiritual dimension. "A Call to Our Guiding Institutions," in my opinion, fails to acknowledge this, and for this reason (among others) will fail to accomplish its purpose. Nevertheless, I hope that future Parliaments will correct this lopsided emphasis, and will have great success in introducing programs to effectively implement the demands of a Global Ethic.

To suggest a few examples of how to bring the "Call" into better harmony with the most important, the spiritual aspect of religion, I wrote the following response to "A Call to Our Guiding Institutions." The organizers of the Parliament kindly allowed me to distribute it to the members of the Parliament Assembly.

Broadening the Base of Support for the "Call"

We thank the organizers of the Parliament of the World's Religions for gathering together so many important leaders of religious and spiritual traditions, along with leaders of other guiding institutions, youth, and other committed individuals, to discuss the vital document, "A Call to Our Guiding Institutions."

The "Call" is an outstanding example of what concerned individuals of various faiths can do when we reflect on the ethical guidelines of our religious and spiritual communities. However, most religious persons of a more conservative bent, and even many "middle-of-the-roaders," have rejected the "Call" as too watered-down. Such critics accuse the

Parliament of the World's Religions of catering too much to the preferences of humanistic or nonspiritual thinkers.

To try to broaden the base of support for the "Call" (and for the work of the Parliament more generally), the following suggestions are humbly offered:

- All religious traditions (except humanistic ones, which may not even be properly called "religious") stress the importance of understanding that this world is temporary. Our bodies are temporary, our families, societies, and nations are temporary, and our planet is temporary. According to most traditions, even the material universe itself is temporary. This realm is not all-in-all. Therefore, let the "Call" emphasize or at least acknowledge the universal and fundamental religious truth that human life is meant to reach beyond this temporary world.

- The "Call" is concerned with "our individual and collective futures," but does not mention our future after death. Almost every religious tradition not only has a concept of a future life (or lives), but enjoins its followers to prepare for that afterlife. Indeed, in most religious traditions the preparation for life after death is considered far more important than trying to make this world a better place to live (and some go so far as to reject as illusory the attempt to improve this fleeting existence). Instead of being solely concerned with our future on this planet, let the "Call" address the almost universally accepted religious truth that there are more lasting worlds that we will enter after death.

- In virtually every religious tradition, Scripture, or revelation is accepted as a most important source of knowledge. Therefore, let the "Call" mention the validity of revelation, or at least the inspired realization of saints, and let it appeal to the leaders of our guiding institutions to mold their own lives and guide their citizens according to the teachings of their Scriptures and the examples of their saints.

- The "Call" evinces a "deep concern for the well-being of the Earth, its people, and all life," and affirms a "commitment to a culture of nonviolence and respect for life." Almost all religious traditions extend this concept of *ahimsa* (nonviolence) to include protection of nonhuman life, or at least they restrict violence against animals within religiously prescribed limits. Therefore let the "Call" appeal to our guiding institutions to discourage cruelty to animals, including the inhuman practices associated with slaughterhouses that ignore the more humane, Scripturally sanctioned procedures of sacrifice (kosher, hilal, etc.).

Many other suggestions could be made for broadening the base of support for the "Call" and the declaration "Towards a Global Ethic," and for strengthening the work of the Parliament and the interfaith movement more generally. Nevertheless, it must be noted that the 1999 Parliament in Cape Town made notable progress toward incorporating the offerings of non-Westerners and conservatives, and we may hope that the organizers of future Parliaments will redouble this effort.

Chapter Twenty-three
FACING RELIGIOUS INTOLERANCE, VIOLENCE, AND OTHER EVILS

Introduction

Joel Beversluis

At the end of October 1999, Pope John Paul II invited representatives of twenty of the world's religions to the Vatican to address common problems of the world's people. Among the problems loomed the cancer of extremism and violence in the name of religion, which this council addressed with a forceful denunciation. The two hundred clergy and lay people appealed to world leaders to "refuse to allow religion to be used to incite hatred and violence." "Any use of religion to support violence is an abuse of religion," John Paul noted.

Sitting next to him at the closing ceremony was the Dalai Lama of Tibet; also present were numerous Buddhists, Africans, American Indians, Jewish leaders, Muslims, and many others. This council and its appeal were certainly necessary, and this theme was reiterated at several other interfaith conferences and religious councils in 1999 as well as in previous years. "Peace among religions" is also a centerpiece theme of the United Religions Initiative, and was a focal point for the numerous "72 Hours for Peace" events it encouraged throughout the world.

Even so, readers may well be distraught over continuing religious intolerance, warfare, and other forms of violence in many countries, including in North America. For most, violence and intolerance fly in the face of the religious and spiritual ideals we profess. Yet they take many forms.

A few of the various forms are intolerant activities by members of a religious majority against a minority; violence by a religious minority seeking freedom or justice; state intolerance of one or more religious communities through legislative, judicial, or extrajudicial means; intolerance or violence fanned by perceptions of religious superiority and exclusivity; media caricatures and demonizing of others; segregation and social fear of the unknown other; and so on.

Interreligious Political Conflict

As this book goes to press, the international news offers plenty of evidence of religious conflict. Political and media responses also sometimes caricaturize or betray those who are being violated. Dr. Mustafa Ceric, Supreme Head of the Islamic Community in Bosnia-Herzegovina, clearly felt abandoned by both the international and the religious communities in a 1993 letter to the Parliament. Inaction by national and international bodies also betrays our standards of good and evil and our proclamations regarding human rights.

The United Nations' goal of peacekeeping is being sorely tested by violence with religious aspects in places like Kosovo, East Timor, Northern Ireland, the Middle East, Cambodia, Rwanda, and Sudan, to name a few. Yet that goal must be reinforced; casualties and failures notwithstanding, the United Nations must preserve its peacekeeping function as an expression of international will. Member nations of the UN are bound to uphold international agreements that include statements about human rights, including religious freedom and the elimination of religious intolerance or discrimination.

Wars like the ones in Kosovo and East Timor have numerous subtle and interrelated causes and factors other than religion, including tribal or racial, economic, and political. Like most other human interactions, conflicts are wholistic in that they engage many interconnected aspects of individuals and societies. It is therefore not accurate to suggest, as some do, that in this modern era the religions are a primary source of conflict, that they are the main source of division and war. Religious differences are often, however, part of group identity, one that is easily labeled. For example, in the conflict over Kashmir, the media repeatedly identified the Pakistani soldiers as Muslims, while the Indian soldiers were not labeled religiously.

Even so, religions do often contribute greatly to conflicts by *sanctifying* causes and political decisions. Thus violent thoughts and actions are not only justified in the name of religion, but are often made "holy" by religious and spiritual leaders.

The Nonviolent Response

Is there room midst this unholy alliance between religions and violence for a religious response that serves a culture of peace? Despite the contributions of religions to conflict, the most persistent voice for nonviolence also comes from the religions and those who practice their precepts. Jainism is one of the oldest sources of nonviolence through its insistence on *ahimsa*. Many other traditions, including Christianity, emphasize forgiveness and have peacemaking and pacifist inclinations that some Christians consider to be divine mandates.

Citizens at Work

National and international diplomacy, whether successful or not, should not blind us to other possibilities of nonviolent action that originate in popular and religious movements. Growing numbers of citizens from many countries and religions are discovering the simple truth that diplomacy for peace and intervention for human rights are the right and responsibility of the people, and not the domain only of nation-states. More and more committed citizens are engaged in conflict resolution, ecological preservation, disaster relief, and solidarity movements. These activities operate independently of the nation-states and sometimes even stand in opposition to their policies, as with the Witness for Peace program of intervention and public disclosure in Central America. Nongovernmental organizations and citizens' movements are also developing creative strategies for conflict resolution, the pursuit of justice, and approaches to sustainable development in the face of consumerism and the perceived ultimacy of the marketplace.

The motivations for these autonomous actions are often spiritual as well as ethical, and their members are often based in religious organizations, embodying religious responses to humanitarian, political, and ecological crises, especially those evils caused by human choices. These groups are, in fact, modeling strategies for the development of a culture of peace.

Media and the Religions

The media do not pay much attention to these citizens' activities. Instead of seeing them as pioneering attempts to implement the highest values of religious and political will, media often ignore them as fringe protests, out of touch with mainstream thought. In fact, however, mainstream thought is changing, in part because of the success of these efforts as well as because military methods are always expensive and often fail. Now, international agencies, governments, and military departments are exploring and utilizing conflict resolution techniques and peace teams to defuse tensions.

Organized religions must also learn, now, how to support and participate in these nonviolent and idealistic challenges to the destructive impulses of humans that have such power within our societies.

Prophetic Nonviolence

True nonviolent responses are not passive, and do not shy away from analyzing and speaking the truth in the face of the abuses of power, as Gandhi demonstrated. This is, in fact, a prophetic task, consistent with that of the prophets of ancient Judaism, Christianity, and Islam. Those who work for peace without taking sides, whether through medical services or quiet diplomacy, who risk their lives in solidarity with those who are suffering, and who are making injustice visible, are expressing the power of nonviolence. Movements emphasizing "engagement" are growing as well among Buddhists, Muslims, Hindus, and others.

Those who do this work often have religious commitments that compel them to their chosen form of service, and are expressions of the increasing power of institutions of civil society. They are, at the same time, embodying some fundamental truths of the religions of the world. They require the support of religious communities, the media, the governing structures, as well as the other "guiding" institutions.

The Interreligious Assembly at the Vatican

NOTE: Approximately two hundred participants from twenty of the world's religions were invited to Vatican City by the Pontifical Council for Interreligious Dialogue from October 24–29, 1999. At the conclusion of this Assembly for the Great Jubilee of the Year 2000, Pope John Paul II spoke to the guests. Some of his comments follow:

There are some who claim that religion is part of the problem, blocking humanity's way to true peace and prosperity. As religious people, it is our duty to demonstrate that this is not the case. Any use of religion to support violence is an abuse of religion. Religion is not and must not become a pretext for conflict, particularly when religious, cultural, and ethnic identity coincide. Religion and peace go together: To wage war in the name of religion is a blatant contradiction. Religious leaders must clearly show that they are pledged to promote peace precisely because of their religious belief. The task before us therefore is to promote a culture of dialogue. Individually and together, we must show how religious belief inspires peace, encourages solidarity, promotes justice, and upholds liberty.

The following statement was issued by participants in the Interreligious Assembly:

On the eve of the third millennium, we the representatives of different religious traditions who have gathered in the Vatican City from many corners of the globe wish to share the fruits of our experiences during these days, the convictions that we have matured and the hope with which we face the future of our world.

We are conscious of the urgent need

• To confront together responsibly and courageously the problems of our modern world (i.e., materialism, consumerism, globalization, breakdown of family and community, etc.)

• To work together to affirm human dignity as the source of human rights and their corresponding duties, in the struggle for justice and peace for all

• To create a new spiritual consciousness for all humanity so that the principles of tolerance and respect for freedom of conscience may prevail.

We are convinced that our religious traditions have the necessary resources to overcome the fragmentations which we observe in the world and to foster peaceful coexistence between peoples.

We are aware that many tragic conflicts around the world are the result of convenient but often unjust association of religions with nationalistic, political, economic, or other interests.

We are aware that if we do not fulfill our common obligations to live out our religious traditions, then we shall be held liable for the consequences and we shall be judged severely.

We know that the problems in the world are so great that we cannot solve them alone. Therefore there is an urgent need for interreligious collaboration.

We are all aware that interreligious collaboration does not imply giving up one's own religious identity but is rather a journey of discovery.

We learn to respect one another as members of the one human race.

We learn to appreciate both our differences and the common values that bind us to one another.

Therefore, we are able to work together to strive to prevent conflict and to overcome the crises existing in different parts of the world.

Collaboration among the different religions must be based on the rejection of fanaticism and extremism, which lead to violence.

We are all aware of the importance of education

as a means for promoting mutual understanding, cooperation and respect. It implies

- Supporting the family as a fundamental building block of society
- Shaping the conscience of the younger generation
- Underlining common fundamental moral and spiritual values
- Cultivating a spiritual life (e.g., through prayer, meditation, and mindfulness according to the practice of each religious tradition)
- Using all means, including the mass media, to impart objective information about each other's religious tradition
- making sure that history and religious textbooks give an objective presentation of religious traditions acceptable to their followers.

Everyone is called to engage in this interreligious and intercultural dialogue. This leads us to address a number of appeals:

We appeal to religious leaders to promote the spirit of dialogue within their respective communities and to be ready to engage in dialogue themselves with civil society at all levels.

We appeal to all the leaders of the world whatever their field of influence

- To refuse to allow religion to be used to incite hatred and violence
- To refuse to allow religion to be used to justify discrimination
- To respect the role of religion in society at national and international levels
- To eradicate poverty and strive for social and economic justice.

In the spirit of Jubilee, we appeal to each one of us gathered here today

- To seek forgiveness for past wrongs
- To promote reconciliation where the painful experiences of the past have brought divisiveness and hatred
- To commit ourselves to overcoming the gulf between rich and poor
- To work for a world of true and lasting peace.

It is with joy and a spirit of thanksgiving, some of us would say thanksgiving especially to God, that

those gathered here for the Interreligious Assembly offer to their brothers and sisters this message of hope.

Temples Firebombed in Sacramento
A SABBATH REQUEST

Alan Canton

NOTE: This eloquent statement speaks about the effects of religious violence here in North America, as well as meaningful responses to it by others in the community of religions. It was first sent as a letter by e-mail to users of software that the author and his company provide for small publishers. It has been forwarded to other mailing lists—literally around the world. The response? Hundreds of notes of condolence and more than $180,000 in donations within two months, approximately 60 percent of it from Christians. For Alan and other Jews in Sacramento, this response was overwhelming and unprecedented.

I'm sure that most of you have heard about how three synagogues in my home of Sacramento, California, were firebombed early Friday morning and perhaps you have heard about the pains of despair that so many Jews around the country are feeling. And, of course, these feelings run even stronger among those of us who are members of one of the temples.

I have been a member of Congregation B'nai Israel for the past seventeen years. This is our 150th anniversary. We are the oldest congregation west of the Mississippi. All day yesterday members of our temple (as Jewish congregations go, we're on the large side with nine hundred families) phoned each other seeking news about how bad it really was, since we were not allowed anywhere near the site.

Was this the beginning of another reign of terror for us? Was this another *Kristalnacht*?

We talked about how this could happen in America? What have we done? Why do they (still) hate us so much? Aren't we good members of the community? We volunteer for local services and donate funds to good civic causes. All we ask is to be allowed to worship the way we wish and to be allowed to keep our culture alive in our own homes and temples. We don't seek converts. It is not a religion of "we're better than you are," or "God loves us more than you." All we ask is that we be allowed to live in peace, brotherhood, and safety within the dominant Christian community. We don't want to bother or threaten the dominant community. Just allow us to "to be." Is that so hard?

And on one night, in my hometown, they firebombed three of our temples. Not in New York or Los Angeles, but here. They must live here. Who would come in from out of town to our small city and our small Jewish congregation? It must be local people, and if so, why? We don't bother anyone.

We heard via our phone tree as well as the local media that our weekly Friday Sabbath service would be held in the 2,000-seat Community Theatre. I was not going to go at first. I'm not religious and don't often go to Friday night services. However I thought that someone should be there to "stand up" to the terrorists who would attempt to rend and destroy us. Even though it was announced that everyone (Jew/non-Jew) was invited (this is normal for Reform congregations) I figured that there would only be 150 or 250 people there, enough to fill up a few rows in the huge theatre, which has two balconies.

When I arrived I was totally surprised. Eighteen hundred people were there, from all over our community—Jews, Catholics, Buddhists, Hare Krishnas, and members from every sect of the Protestant community. There were members from black churches, gay churches, Asian churches, as well as atheists, agnostics, and followers of so-called "new age" spiritual leaders. There were ministers, bishops, city council members, the police chief, the FBI, ATF, and representatives from the state legislature and governor's office. Never have I seen such an outpouring of grief and concern from the community...for Jews.

One of the most touching groups was the Methodists. It seems they were having a large convention here in Sacramento. When they heard about the bombings, many decided they wanted to pray with us. And so there were hundreds of them, all wearing their convention badges. They circulated through the waiting crowd explaining who they were and why they were there. What a wonderfully kind thing to do.

A Reform Jewish Friday night service is not what you might expect. It is not solemn and "dignified." It is the Celebration of the Sabbath where workday thoughts are put aside and the hearts of the parents turn toward the children and the hearts of the children turn to the parents. We sing, clap hands, say prayers, listen to the Rabbi and Cantor (who leads the music), banter with each other, and, of course, hear a sermon, often filled with humor. It is a happy service...and usually short.

But who could be happy? Our house of worship had been torched. Our entire library of five thousand books was gone. Yet our Rabbi told us that we must persevere and that to not celebrate the Sabbath would be exactly what the terrorists would hope to achieve. And so we went on with our service.

There were a number of speakers from our congregation and from the community. All were inspirational and devoid of the kind of sorrow, sadness, grief, or anger that you might expect. Our previous Rabbi, now retired, who served us for twenty-two years, flew in from Phoenix and reminded us that "we are the JEWISH people and that we have always survived and we will survive this as well." And we were putting on a brave front. We laughed, we sang, we applauded, we said the ancient prayers. We held up the best we could. Then something happened that I will never forget.

Seated on the stage, known as a *bema* (bee-mah) in Hebrew, were a number of our Temple's officers, as well as some of the dignitaries from the city. There was also one very attractive woman whom no one seemed to recognize. I heard the "buzz" of "who is that woman and why is she there." Toward the middle of the service our Rabbi said he wanted to introduce us to a Rev. Faith Whitmore and she got up and went to the podium. She was either the local or regional head of the United Methodist Church, which was having their convention. And she spoke briefly about how appalled she and her brethren were about these incidents.

We've heard it before. From the Pope on down, all through the years it's been "Gee, sorry for the Holocaust but there's nothing I could have done about it."

She reached into her suit coat and took out a piece of paper. "I want you to know that this afternoon we took a special offering of our members to help you rebuild your temple and we want you to have this check for $6,000." For two seconds there was absolute dead quiet. We were astounded. Did we hear this correctly? Christians are going to do this? On the third second the hall shook with a thunderous applause. I've never heard applause like that before. And it went on for two minutes. And then people broke into tears. Me too. It was like all of the emotion of the day and evening poured out in those few minutes.

Those in my parent's generation were dumbfounded. Who ever heard of Gentiles caring about Jews? The idea of a Gentile coming up to a Jew and saying, "I want you to know how sorry I am," was beyond the ability of many of our members to cope. And I have to admit that I too, old curmudgeon that I am, felt so much emotional gratitude for these lovely people, who were not even part of our community or city.

As Rev. Whitmore gave the check to the Rabbi and hugged him, it was one of the most emotional moments I've ever been witness to. In my entire lifetime I've never known an organized Christian denomination to officially do anything "nice" for a Jewish congregation. Our congregation, some 1,100 of us stood with tears in our eyes. Christians who for centuries sent the Cossacks to pillage our towns, who put us through their Inquisitions, who burned us at the stake as heretics, who expelled us from their countries, who locked us away in tiny *shtetls* (shtet-ell: a poor Jewish town like in *Fiddler on the Roof*), who eagerly turned us into the Nazi SS, and who ran the trains, who produced the poison gas, or just "knew" about the greatest human tragedy of this century . . . were doing something good for a Jew.

Nothing in my life prepared me for that. It's one thing to say, "I'm sorry, it's too bad," but it is quite

another to put $6,000 behind it and not even be from the community! When this is all behind me, I'm going to find out who is the head Methodist deacon, pope, minister, or whatever he/she is called, get the address, and write a warm thank-you letter . . . as will every member of our congregation.

The evening closed with a final hymn and we all went home feeling a bit better.

It didn't really hit me until I drove down to the temple and saw the charred remains of the library wing. The place was swarming with ATF, FBI, and other agents, collecting materials for the investigations. One ATF agent said that this is being classified as an "act of domestic terrorism" and has been given the highest priority.

We lost our entire 5,000-volume library. I saw it. It was soot. Not even a page remained. Nothing. It was a wonderful library of Jewish-oriented books and films. It was a treasure of our congregation and it was used by hundreds of our members, especially the young people. In our community, mothers took their children to the Temple library as much as they took their children to the public library. It was part of "what we do." Our books and videos were one of the ways we socialized our young people into our culture. And it works. We don't have a very high incidence of crime, substance abuse, or academic problems with our young people. We expect a lot from them and we make sure they have the tools and opportunities not to disappoint us.

As publishers, you of all people should know what the loss of a library means to we who are known as "the people of the book." When you see the destruction of something that was yours, something you helped build, and something you were proud of, it hits you. The depression is awesome. It is just awesome.

Why here? Why us? Why me? I'm sure there are answers, but I don't have them at the moment. The only answer I do have is that we must pick ourselves up as a congregation and community (there were two other temples also heavily damaged) and move on. They can't beat us. We are the Jewish people. We were here five thousand years ago, and we will be here five thousand years from today.

As our Torah teaches us: "And this too shall pass." And as the final benediction to every one of our services reads: "May the Lord bless you, and keep you, and give you peace."

Lutherans and Judaism—
A New Possibility

Dr. Stephen A. Schmidt

Professor of Pastoral Studies, Loyola University, Chicago

NOTE: Among the steps needed to transcend religious discrimination and intolerance is theological and cultural recognition of the errors of the past. This article presents one recent attempt to rectify those errors and the tragedies they helped create.

The Evangelical Lutheran Church in America (ELCA) has taken a dramatic step to heal centuries of distrust between Lutherans and Jewish Americans. That healing process happened because Lutherans are taking both their Scripture studies and their Gospel seriously. They are attending to matters of political history, and their new awareness of past experiences of anti-Semitism. They now are able to acknowledge that such bigotry was a denial of the Gospel and to face many other issues of social justice and compassion.

Last April 18, The Church Council of the ELCA adopted a sensitive statement on Lutheran-Jewish relations (to follow). What this "Declaration" announces is a beginning of new relationships between the two religious traditions. It begins with a straightforward confession of past social sins by the worldwide community of Lutherans. It particularizes the terrible actions of Lutheran Christians in relationship to the Nazi Holocaust. It names the sin and the sinner. It explicitly acknowledges Luther's "anti-Judaic diatribes and violent recommendations in his later writings against the Jews." It makes public con-

fession and it asks for reconciliation with the (American) Jewish Community. All this in mutual words of prayer for the "continued blessing of the Blessed One," Yahweh/God for both communities.

On November 13, Chicago Lutherans with representatives from the larger American church met at Grace Lutheran Church in River Forest, Illinois, for evening prayer of public confession and repentance. After this service of repentance and confession, the assembly walked to West Suburban Temple Har Zion for words of healing and reconciliation. A public presentation of the "Declaration" was given to the Jewish community, and a first step toward a modest future of dialogue and new possibilities for trust and healing has begun.

This action could not have transpired if Lutherans were not serious about their theological traditions. This was an event more about confession and absolution than about face-saving or guilt. It was possible, I think, because for this time in this small but important event Lutherans are taking the Gospel seriously, and acting out of their own sin and the clear understanding of the need for repentance and absolution. It is an event that took history seriously, in this case the history of a religious tradition. And it was an event that cared about acts that denied God's justice in a particular time and place, in a very political setting.

So Lutherans did what they will continue to do if they take the core of the Gospel seriously. They will cease attempting justification by action or by some kind of public gesture. They can confess and they can begin renewal because they know they are judged and loved by a God who calls them to justice and love in return. They kept covenant. They theologized out of historical reality. They prayed and ritualized the event around word and sacrament and they turned a page to a new horizon for Jewish-Lutheran dialogue. They participated in a little process of creating public documents that in some small measure contributes to the public *paideia*. A small step, faithfully taken. And I am glad.

DECLARATION OF THE EVANGELICAL LUTHERAN CHURCH IN AMERICA TO THE JEWISH COMMUNITY

In the long history of Christianity there exists no more tragic development than the treatment accorded the Jewish people on the part of Christian believers. Very few Christian communities of faith were able to escape the contagion of anti-Judaism and its modern successor, anti-Semitism. Lutherans belonging to the Lutheran World Federation and the Evangelical Lutheran Church in America feel a special burden in this regard because of certain elements in the legacy of the reformer Martin Luther and the catastrophes, including the Holocaust of the 20th century, suffered by Jews in places where the Lutheran churches were strongly represented.

The Lutheran communion of faith is linked by name and heritage to the memory of Martin Luther, teacher and reformer. Honoring his name in our own, we recall his bold stand for truth, his earthy and sublime words of wisdom, and above all his witness to God's saving Word. Luther proclaimed a gospel for people as we really are, bidding us to trust a grace sufficient to reach our deepest shames and address the most tragic truths.

In the spirit of that truth-telling, we who bear his name and heritage must with pain acknowledge also Luther's anti-Judaic diatribes and the violent recommendations of his later writings against the Jews. As did many of Luther's own companions in the 16th century, we reject this violent invective, and yet more do we express our deep and abiding sorrow over its tragic effects on subsequent generations. In concert with the Lutheran World Federation, we particularly deplore the appropriation of Luther's words by modern anti-Semites for the teaching of hatred toward Judaism or toward the Jewish people in our day.

Grieving the complicity of our own tradition within this history of hatred, moreover, we express our urgent desire to live out our faith in Jesus Christ with love and respect for the Jewish people. We recognize in anti-Semitism a contradiction and an affront to the Gospel, a violation of our hope and calling, and we pledge this church to oppose the deadly

working of such bigotry, both within our own circles and in the society around us. Finally, we pray for the continued blessing of the Blessed One upon the increasing cooperation and understanding between Lutheran Christians and the Jewish community.

Universal Declaration on Nonviolence

THE INCOMPATIBILITY OF RELIGION AND WAR

NOTE: This document is an attempt to set forth a vision of nonviolence within the context of an emerging global civilization in which all forms of violence, especially war, are totally unacceptable as means to settle disputes between and among nations, groups, and persons. This new vision of civilization is global in scope, universal in culture, and based on love and compassion, the highest moral/spiritual principles of the various historical religions. Its universal nature acknowledges the essential fact of modern life: the interdependence of nations, economies, cultures, and religious traditions.

As members of religious groups throughout the world, we are increasingly aware of our responsibility to promote peace in our age and in the ages to come. Nevertheless, we recognize that in the history of the human family, people of various religions, acting officially in the name of their respective traditions, have either initiated or collaborated in organized and systematic violence or war. These actions have at times been directed against other religious traditions, groups, and nations, as well as within particular religious traditions. This pattern of behavior is totally inappropriate for spiritual persons and communities. Therefore, as members of world religions, we declare before the human family, that

> Religion can no longer be an accomplice to war, to terrorism, or to any other forms of violence, organized or spontaneous, against any member of the human family.

Because this family is one, global, and interrelated, our actions must be consistent with this identity. We recognize the right and duty of governments to defend the security of their people and to relieve those afflicted by exploitation and persecution. Nevertheless, we declare that religion must not permit itself to be used by any state, group, or organization for the purpose of supporting aggression for nationalistic gain. We have an obligation to promote a new vision of society, one in which war has no place in resolving disputes between and among states, organizations, and religions.

In making this declaration, we the signatories commit ourselves to this new vision. We call upon all the members of our respective traditions to embrace this vision. We urge our members and all peoples to use every moral means to dissuade their governments from promoting war or terrorism. We strongly encourage the United Nations organization to employ all available resources toward the development of peaceful methods of resolving conflicts among nations.

Our declaration is meant to promote such a new global society, one in which nonviolence is preeminent as a value in all human relations. We offer this vision of peace, mindful of the words of Pope Paul VI to the United Nations in October 1965: "No more war: war never again!"

Signatories: *Thomas Keating, Johanna Becker, Wayne Teasdale, Dom Bede Griffiths, Raimundo Panikkar, Katherine Howard, Pascaline Coff, Theophane Boyd, Ruth Fox, Timothy Kelley, and other members of the North American Board for East-West Dialogue;* and *His Holiness the Dalai Lama*

—Promulgated and signed on April 2, 1991, at Santa Fe, New Mexico, U.S.A.

Eliminating Intolerance and Discrimination Based on Religion or Belief

Introduction

One of the basic purposes of the United Nations, as set forth in its Charter, is the promotion and encouragement of respect for human rights and fundamental freedoms for all without distinction as to race, sex, language, or religion.

Freedom of belief is one of the rights proclaimed in the Universal Declaration of Human Rights, adopted by the General Assembly in 1948, and in the International Covenant on Civil and Political Rights, adopted in 1966.

The Preamble to the Universal Declaration of Human Rights states that "the advent of a world in which human beings shall enjoy freedom of speech and belief and freedom from fear and want has been proclaimed as the highest aspiration of the common people."

Article 2 declares that "everyone is entitled to all the rights and freedoms set forth in this Declaration, without distinction of any kind, such as race, color, sex, language, religion, political or other opinion, national or social origin, property, birth, or other status."

Article 18 of the Universal Declaration of Human Rights states that "everyone has the right to freedom of thought, conscience, and religion; this right includes freedom to change his religion or belief, and freedom, either alone or in community with others and in public or private, to manifest his religion or belief in teaching, practice, worship, and observance."

This right was transformed into a legal obligation for ratifying States in article 18 of the International Covenant on Civil and Political Rights, which states that

"1. Everyone shall have the right to freedom of

thought, conscience and religion. This right shall include freedom to have or to adopt a religion or belief of his choice, and freedom, either individually or in community with others and in public or private, to manifest his religion or belief in worship, observance, practice, and teaching.

"2. No one shall be subject to coercion which would impair his freedom to have or to adopt a religion or belief of his choice.

"3. Freedom to manifest one's religion or beliefs may be subject only to such limitations as are prescribed by law and are necessary to protect public safety, order, health, or morals or the fundamental rights and freedoms of others.

"4. The States party to the present Covenant undertake to have respect for the liberty of parents and, when applicable, legal guardians to ensure the religious and moral education of their children in conformity with their own convictions."

Preparation of a draft Declaration on the elimination of all forms of intolerance and of discrimination based on religion and belief originated in 1962, when the idea of a United Nations instrument on this issue was first approved by the General Assembly. Two distinct documents were then envisaged: a declaration and an international convention.

In 1972 the General Assembly decided to accord priority to the completion of the Declaration before resuming consideration of the draft International Convention. At the Assembly's request, the question of a draft Declaration was considered by the Commission on Human Rights at each of its annual sessions from 1974 to 1981.

In March 1981, the Commission adopted the text of a draft Declaration, which was submitted, through the Economic and Social Council, to the General Assembly at its regular session later that year.

On 25 November 1981, the General Assembly proclaimed the Declaration on the Elimination of All Forms of Intolerance and of Discrimination Based on Religion and Belief, stating that it considered it essential "to promote understanding, tolerance, and respect in matters relating to freedom of religion and belief" and that it was resolved "to adopt

all necessary measures for the speedy elimination of such intolerance in all its forms and manifestations and to prevent and combat discrimination on the grounds of religion or belief."

DECLARATION ON THE ELIMINATION OF ALL FORMS OF INTOLERANCE AND OF DISCRIMINATION BASED ON RELIGION OR BELIEF

Adopted by the General Assembly of the United Nations on 25 November 1981 (Resolution 36155)

The General Assembly,

Considering that one of the basic principles of the Charter of the United Nations is that of the dignity and equality inherent in all human beings, and that all Member States have pledged themselves to take joint and separate action in cooperation with the Organization to promote and encourage universal respect for and observance of human rights and fundamental freedoms for all, without distinction as to race, sex, language, or religion,

Considering that the Universal Declaration of Human Rights and the International Covenants on Human Rights proclaim the principles of nondiscrimination and equality before the law and the right to freedom of thought, conscience, religion, and belief,

Considering that the disregard and infringement of human rights and fundamental freedoms, in particular of the right to freedom of thought, conscience, religion, or whatever belief, have brought, directly or indirectly, wars and great suffering to mankind, especially where they serve as a means of foreign interference in the internal affairs of other States and amount to kindling hatred between peoples and nations,

Considering that religion or belief, for anyone who professes either, is one of the fundamental elements in his conception of life and that freedom of religion or belief should be fully respected and guaranteed,

Considering that it is essential to promote understanding, tolerance, and respect in matters relating to freedom of religion and belief and to ensure that the use of religion or belief for ends inconsistent with the Charter, other relevant instruments of the United Nations and the purposes and principles of the present Declaration is inadmissible,

Convinced that freedom of religion and belief should also contribute to the attainment of the goals of world peace, social justice and friendship among peoples and to the elimination of ideologies or practices of colonialism and racial discrimination,

Noting with satisfaction the adoption of several, and the coming into force of some, conventions, under the ægis of the United Nations and of the specialized agencies, for the elimination of various forms of discrimination,

Concerned by manifestations of intolerance and by the existence of discrimination in matters of religion or belief still in evidence in some areas of the world,

Resolved to adopt all necessary measures for the speedy elimination of such intolerance in all its forms and manifestations and to prevent and combat discrimination on the grounds of religion or belief,

Proclaims this Declaration on the Elimination of All Forms of Intolerance and of Discrimination Based on Religion or Belief:

Article 1

1. Everyone shall have the right to freedom of thought, conscience, and religion. This right shall include freedom to have a religion or whatever belief of his choice, and freedom, either individually or in community with others and in public or private, to manifest his religion or belief in worship, observance, practice, and teaching.

2. No one shall be subject to coercion which would impair his freedom to have a religion or belief of his choice.

3. Freedom to manifest one's religion or beliefs may be subject only to such limitations as are prescribed by law and are necessary to protect public safety, order, health, or morals or the fundamental rights and freedoms of others.

Article 2

1. No one shall be subject to discrimination by any State, institution, group of persons, or person on the grounds of religion or other beliefs.

2. For the purposes of the present Declaration, the expression "intolerance and discrimination based on religion or belief" means any distinction, exclusion, restriction, or preference based on religion or belief and having as its purpose or as its effect nullification or impairment of the recognition, enjoyment, or exercise of human rights and fundamental freedoms on an equal basis.

Article 3

Discrimination between human beings on the grounds of religion or belief constitutes an affront to human dignity and a disavowal of the principles of the Charter of the United Nations, and shall be condemned as a violation of the human rights and fundamental freedoms proclaimed in the Universal Declaration of Human Rights and enunciated in detail in the International Covenants on Human Rights, and as an obstacle to friendly and peaceful relations between nations.

Article 4

1. All States shall take effective measures to prevent and eliminate discrimination on the grounds of religion or belief in the recognition, exercise, and enjoyment of human rights and fundamental freedoms in all fields of civil, economic, political, social, and cultural life.

2. All States shall make all efforts to enact or rescind legislation where necessary to prohibit any such discrimination, and to take all appropriate measures to combat intolerance on the grounds of religion or other beliefs in this matter.

Article 5

1. The parents or, as the case may be, the legal guardians of the child have the right to organize the life within the family in accordance with their religion or belief and bearing in mind the moral education in which they believe the child should be brought up.

2. Every child shall enjoy the right to have access to education in the matter of religion or belief in accordance with the wishes of his parents or, as the case may be, legal guardians, and shall not be compelled to receive teaching on religion or belief against the wishes of his parents or legal guardians, the best interests of the child being the guiding principle.

3. The child shall be protected from any form of discrimination on the grounds of religion or belief. He shall be brought up in a spirit of understanding, tolerance, friendship among peoples, peace and universal brotherhood, respect for freedom of religion or belief of others, and in full consciousness that his energy and talents should be devoted to the service of his fellowmen.

4. In the case of a child who is not under the care either of his parents or of legal guardians, due account shall be taken of their expressed wishes or of any other proof of their wishes in the matter of religion or belief, the best interests of the child being the guiding principle.

5. Practices of a religion or beliefs in which a child is brought up must not be injurious to his physical or mental health or to his full development, taking into account article 1, paragraph 3, of the present Declaration.

Article 6

In accordance with article 1 of the present Declaration, and subject to the provisions of article 1, paragraph 3, the right to freedom of thought, conscience, religion, or belief shall include, *inter alia*, the following freedoms:

a. To worship or assemble in connection with a religion or belief, and to establish and maintain places for these purposes;

b. To establish and maintain appropriate charitable or humanitarian institutions;

c. To make, acquire, and use to an adequate extent the necessary articles and materials related to the rites or customs of a religion or belief;

d. To write, issue, and disseminate relevant publications in these areas;

e. To teach a religion or belief in places suitable for these purposes;

f. To solicit and receive voluntary financial and other contributions from individuals and institutions;

g. To train, appoint, elect, or designate by succession appropriate leaders called for by the requirements and standards of any religion or belief;

h. To observe days of rest and to celebrate holidays and ceremonies in accordance with the precepts of one's religion or belief;

i. To establish and maintain communications with individuals and communities in matters of religion and belief at the national and international levels.

Article 7

The rights and freedoms set forth in the present Declaration shall be accorded in national legislation in such a manner that everyone shall be able to avail himself of such rights and freedoms in practice.

Article 8

Nothing in the present Declaration shall be construed as restricting or derogating from any right defined in the Universal Declaration of Human Rights and the International Covenants on Human Rights.

—United Nations Department of Public Information, Document DPI/714-84-33131

How May I Help?

NONVIOLENT SOCIAL CHANGE IN THE GANDHIAN TRADITION

Dr. Guy de Mallac

NOTE: Dr. de Mallac is a founder of the Ways of Peace and Service and the United Peace Network, professor emeritus at the University of California, Irvine, in the School of Humanities, and editor of *The Wisdom of Humankind* by Leo Tolstoy. This comprehensive outline of practical steps for implementing social change also outlines nonviolent ways of resisting intolerance, violence, and other evils.

As we know from previous essays, the people of this planet face major global issues. One temptation for any individual is to be overwhelmed by their magnitude, so overwhelmed that one does nothing...which is very much against authentic spiritual endeavor, and very much against the Gandhian spirit as well.

The correct view is that every step, however minor, matters—every step that I take, trying to be of service, to be of help. Every such step contributes to fulfilling the purpose of my life. Albert Schweitzer wrote that "the purpose of life is to serve and to show compassion and the will to help others." A key statement on the Volunteer Commitment Card of the Alabama Christian Movement for Human Rights in 1960 translates that attitude or principle into a suggested practice: "Seek to perform regular service for others and for the world."

Let us now see what nonviolence can contribute toward finding concrete ways in which one can help.

Nonviolence—Another Name for Loving, Dynamic Outreach

Following in the footsteps of his mentor Leo Tolstoy, Mahatma Gandhi felt there are two global forces at work in the world: 1) the Law of Love, and 2) the Law of Violence or Aggression. He felt Love is stronger and can prevail, given our best efforts.

For those who feel that the word "love" has been unduly cheapened, we might substitute synonyms for it: "nonviolence" (although, like the Sanskrit word *ahimsa*, nonviolence is a negative definition, conveying: not hurting, or the failure to do violence). Or, with Carl Rogers we might talk of "unconditional positive regard." Again, we might say, "loving, dynamic outreach."

Whatever term we use, we must realize the existence in ourselves and others of a positive force based on warmth, understanding, love, cooperation. Attuned to that force within ourselves, we reach out and turn on that force in others. This force, which reaches out to meet the other, promotes sharing and cooperation, and thus resolves conflicts. Generally speaking, love has been defined as having the following four characteristic attitudes toward the loved one(s): care, responsibility, respect, and knowledge (Erich Fromm, *The Art of Loving*).

In usual practice, we tend to love in a restricted way within a set of circles: most strongly, our spouse and/or close family; then other relatives, and friends; and finally perhaps members of affinity groups or associations, and fellow country-people. To universalize love, we should reach out to all within these concentric circles as sincerely and efficiently as possible.

There are several stages in dynamic outreach: first, develop acquaintance with the member or members of the "other" group, with those who are first seen as "different" from me; then, cultivate greater awareness of those "others" as worthy of respect, as unique, as close to me; demonstrate greater sensitivity, respect and acceptance; and, finally, work toward joint goals together.

If we fail to reach out in that way, but rather insist on viewing the others as radically or forever "different" from us, then the crystallized feeling of difference or estrangement leads to such ills as racism, ethnocentrism, or triumphalism; these can give rise to enmity and, in time, generate conflict and war.

Concrete suggestions for implementing nonviolence:

1. Practice the Law of Love: Love all humans as brothers and sisters, with respect, promoting universal acceptance and familyhood. Challenge all

discriminations and prejudices. Promote the dignity of human beings regardless of age, sex, race, or creed. Practice strategic nonviolence as part of an active struggle: denounce injustice.

2. Alongside reasonable concern for self, work and serve for the welfare of all. Practice the Golden Rule. "I can never be what I ought to be until you are what you ought to be" (Martin Luther King, Jr.).

3. Practice thoughtful attentiveness and creative listening to the other's side. In dealing with an opponent, search actively for common/mutual interests; on the basis of these interests, build projects to encourage the development of increasing mutual trust.

4. Respect other societies, cultures, races, and the heritage of each. Conduct intercultural, interreligious, interethnic, interclass, and intergender exchange and interaction. Support human freedom and dignity at home by endorsing civil liberties; not granting such liberties is also a form of violence. Persistently denounce and oppose injustice.

5. Work for reduction in military budgets. Actively pursue alternatives to military intervention. Support human freedom and dignity by ending foreign military intervention; interfering in another country's internal affairs is a form of violence.

6. Instead of supporting narrow, parochial approaches, develop broader horizons—pluralize and globalize issues.

7. Foster togetherness, unity, harmony. When two or more individuals come together to achieve that aim, the Godhead is with them.

Nonviolent Economics

Awareness of the need for nonviolent economics comes with an awareness of what Mahatma Gandhi called "the wide gulf separating the few rich from the hungry millions." If a few decades ago he was warning us that this gap was significant, how much more concerned should we not be today, knowing that this gap has been widening markedly? Gandhi saw a direct, causal relationship between a) the extreme of considerable wealth and idleness and b) the extreme of considerable poverty and crushing labor.

We need a fuller awareness of what poverty really means: its lack of access to work and basic amenities; the biological damage it causes; the heavy restrictions and waste of human potential that it brings about. We can each develop a fuller awareness of the meaning of the absolute poverty that is the lot of close to 1 billion human beings. We need to become better acquainted with the mechanisms that stop many rich individuals from even perceiving the gap between rich and poor.

Concrete suggestions for implementing nonviolent economics:

1. Our caring for others should lead us to insist on nothing short of full economic justice—leaving behind traditional "charity" and handouts.

2. Gandhi and Tolstoy urge us all to do some necessary manual work, to commune with all those who are condemned to especially alienating and harsh forms of manual work.

3. Practice frugality and a simple lifestyle. Over the last two decades more than a dozen stimulating books have discussed intentional simplicity as part of strategies to achieve fairer distribution of available resources.

4. Give all a chance to work. Especially, give the right to work to the weak, the poor, and the disenfranchised so that they might achieve greater autonomy and self-sufficiency.

5. Learn to share, to give, to practice generosity on a daily basis. Share resources, including land. In third world countries there is a crying need for land reform to make land available to the landless, who often are landless as a result of documented injustice. Establish a fairer and saner balance of resources, and view ourselves merely as stewards or trustees, to whom resources have been entrusted for a broader purpose, transcending the individual.

6. Implement appropriate or intermediate technology as defined in E. F. Schumacher's landmark book, *Small Is Beautiful.*

7. To whatever extent is feasible, practice local or regional self-sufficiency; support local agriculture and manufacture; practice economic and political decentralization.

8. Nurture the environment: practice right ecology.

9. Stop designing and manufacturing weapons. Achieve economic conversion of military jobs to *jobs with peace!*

10. Support cooperative approaches to work and economic problems. Gandhi's plea was to avoid and denounce the practices of exploitive capitalism.

Nonviolent Communication

To combat violent communication (which often is synonymous with oppression) and the lack of communication, foster the more complete and effective nonviolent, cooperative communication.

Concrete suggestions for implementing nonviolent communication:

1. Let our attitude toward the person we are communicating with be one of Love (care + respect + responsibility + knowledge) as opposed to an attitude of domination.

2. Let our attitudes toward the other party be ones of flexibility: tolerance, humility, and openness to other viewpoints—as opposed to arrogance.

3. Let us practice trust in the other: regard for the other, patience toward the other, and assuming the other's goodwill—as opposed to scorn for the other and disbelief in the other's potential and goodwill.

4. Let me have a reasonably open and questioning attitude toward my ideas and positions, and be prepared to view them in a new light on occasion—as opposed to a closed and dogmatic mentality.

5. Let us be prepared to engage in a two-way process of sharing information, facts, ideas, opinions as opposed to a close-minded attitude.

6. In the process of dialoguing, let us systematically listen to the other party or parties and be prepared to express differences as well as commonalities. Let us consider signing up for workshops in listening skills and undergoing training in that area. (Mostly, we are very poor listeners.)

7. Let us engage in authentic dialogue which, according to the definition of that term, implies a two-way flow.

8. Practice cooperation as part of the process of communication and dialogue. This supposes a willingness to view issues and problems in a more general perspective, and to pluralize or globalize the issues.

9. Practice consultation, which is the process whereby we seek information, opinions, advice, or guidance from others.

10. If the above approaches have not been attempted or have not worked and we are in a situation of exacerbated conflict, practice the various skills and approaches relevant to conflict-solving/conflict-resolution: negotiation, mediation, arbitration, and reconciliation.

War is the ultimate breakdown in communication, and is the ultimate evil, which the process of communication seeks to avoid.

Nonviolent Government/Politics (Including International Politics)

Reasonable participation in the governmental process is a basis of the Gandhian doctrine of nonviolence; civic awareness and involvement in activities are viewed as important as a prayer or religious duty or act.

We must train ourselves to examine the institutions we have created. If a governing body or road repair service does not achieve what our best judgment and our moral selves want it to achieve, we must reconsider why we as citizens created such a service.

Gandhi has warned us that "the State represents violence in a concentrated and organized form." We must therefore always be on the lookout for the violence which the State and its agencies are perpetrating, claiming it is done in our name. It is a mistake to assume that the judiciary or the military or the government stands for justice or peace; our duty as citizens is to make sure they come closer to that ideal.

Concrete suggestions for implementing nonviolent government:

1. Participate by making sure that through representation of our opinions, through our votes and actions, government agencies achieve their original

purpose—the administration of a required service in accordance with our aims and values.

2. Decentralize: go back to human scale.

3. Interrelate through adequate communication with other groups within a nation or among nations or continents.

4. Build a society that provides for basic human needs (such as adequate housing, health, education, jobs in humane working conditions, and a safe environment). Change social structures which exploit the poor.

5. Democratize: respect the rights and opinions of all groups, and especially of minorities.

6. Ensure that the laws are just. If a given law is not just, convey our wish to have it repealed; as needed, get involved in actions to achieve that end.

7. Democratize the international world order. Democratize relations among nations.

8. Pluralize issues: view them in the light of the concerns of all parties involved; in a domestic context, this means all the groups involved; in the international context, all the nation-states involved.

Nonviolent Education

Concrete suggestions for implementing nonviolent education:

1. Develop education for peace and nonviolence, education in nonviolent communication, in mutual understanding and cooperation. This should be the basis for curriculum and the framework within which all educational subjects fit.

2. Have the students/learners learn from work and learn from life. Encourage full and responsible (not just token) involvement in various crafts and in various other forms of work (such as agriculture). All should do some necessary manual work.

3. Work on self-improvement, on achieving knowledge and mastery of self, on educating the individual character and on development of truthfulness and fearlessness. This naturally leads to spiritual training.

4. Self-sufficiency is to be developed on the basis of students' ability to learn from life, and to cope with a variety of manual tasks. Self-sufficiency is the

ability to adapt to tomorrow's knowledge and context, after aspects of today's knowledge become obsolete. Educate for tomorrow's context.

5. Develop the crucial dimension of outreach. Learn to intuit or discover the needs of others, to meet such needs, and to do committed volunteer service for the welfare of all.

The Seville Statement on Violence

NOTE: A scientific statement that says that peace is possible because war is not a biological necessity, this document was written by an international team of specialists in 1986 for the United Nations–sponsored International Year of Peace. Based on scientific evidence and endorsed by scientific and professional organizations around the world, the statement was adopted by UNESCO in 1989.

Believing that it is our responsibility to address from our particular disciplines the most dangerous and destructive activities of our species, violence and war; recognizing that science is a human cultural product that cannot be definitive or all encompassing; and gratefully acknowledging the support of the authorities of Seville and representatives of the Spanish UNESCO, we, the undersigned scholars from around the world and from relevant sciences, have met and arrived at the following statement on violence. In it we challenge a number of alleged biological findings that have been used, even by some in our disciplines, to justify violence and war. Because the alleged findings have contributed to an atmosphere of pessimism in our time, we submit that the open, considered rejection of these misstatements can contribute significantly to the International Year of Peace.

Misuse of scientific theories and data to justify violence and war is not new but has been made since the advent of modern science. For example, the theory of evolution has been used to justify not only war, but also genocide, colonialism, and the suppression of the weak.

We state our position in the form of five propositions. We are aware that there are many other issues about violence and war that could be fruitfully addressed from the standpoint of our disciplines, but we restrict ourselves here to what we consider a most important first step.

1. It is scientifically incorrect to say that we have inherited a tendency to make war from our animal ancestors. Although fighting occurs widely throughout animal species, only a few cases of destructive intra-species fighting between organized groups have ever been recorded among naturally living species, and none of these involve the use of tools designed to be weapons. Normal predatory feeding upon other species cannot be equated with intra-species violence. Warfare is a particularly human phenomenon and does not occur in other animals.

The fact that warfare has changed so radically over time indicates that it is a product of culture. Its biological connection is primarily through language that makes possible the coordination of groups, the transmission of technology, and the use of tools. War is biologically possible, but it is not inevitable, as evidenced by its variation in occurrence and nature over time and space. There are cultures which have not engaged in war for centuries, and there are cultures which have engaged in war frequently at some times and not at others.

2. It is scientifically incorrect to say that war or any other violent behavior is genetically programmed into our human nature. While genes are involved at all levels of nervous system function, they provide a developmental potential that can be actualized only in conjunction with the ecological and social environment. While individuals vary in their predispositions to be affected by their experience, it is the interaction between their genetic endowment and conditions of nurturance that determines their personalities. Except for rare pathologies, the genes do not produce individuals necessarily predisposed to violence. Neither do they determine the opposite. While genes are co-involved in establishing our behavioral capacities, they do not by themselves specify the outcome.

3. It is scientifically incorrect to say that in the course of human evolution there has been a selection for aggressive behavior more than for other kinds of behavior. In all well-studied species, status within the group is achieved by the ability to cooperate and to fulfill social functions relevant to the structure of that group. Dominance involves social bondings and affiliations; it is not simply a matter of the possession and use of superior physical power, although it does involve aggressive behaviors. Where genetic selection for aggressive behavior has been artificially instituted in animals, it has rapidly succeeded in producing hyperaggressive individuals. This indicates that aggression was not maximally selected under natural conditions. When such experientially created hyperaggressive animals are present in a social group, they either disrupt its social structure or are driven out. Violence is neither in our evolutionary legacy nor in our genes.

4. It is scientifically incorrect to say that humans have a violent brain. While we do have the neural apparatus to act violently, it is not automatically activated by internal or external stimuli. Like higher primates and unlike other animals, our higher neural processes filter such stimuli before they can be acted upon. How we act is shaped by how we have been conditioned and socialized. There is nothing in our neural physiology that compels us to react violently.

5. It is scientifically incorrect to say that war is caused by instinct or any single motivation. The emergence of modern warfare has been a journey from the primacy of emotional and motivational factors, sometimes called *instincts*, to the primacy of cognitive factors. Modern war involves institutional use of personal characteristics such as obedience, suggestibility, and idealism, social skills such as language, and rational considerations such as cost calculation, planning, and information processing. The technology of modern war has exaggerated traits associated with violence both in the training of actual combatants and in the preparation of support for a war in the general population. As a result of this exaggeration, such traits are often mistaken to be the causes rather than the consequences of the process.

We conclude that biology does not condemn humanity to war, and that humanity can be freed from the bondage of biological pessimism and empowered with confidence to take the transformative tasks needed in this International Year of Peace and in the years to come. Although these tasks are mainly institutional and collective, they also rest upon the consciousness of individual participants for whom pessimism and optimism are crucial factors. Just as wars begin in the minds of humans, peace also begins in our minds. The same species who invented war is capable of inventing peace. The responsibility lies with each of us.

May the Light Dawn

Dr. Paulos Mar Gregorios

H.G. Metropolitan Dr. Paulos Mar Gregorios (deceased) was Bishop of the Syrian Orthodox (Christian) Church in India, and a President of Inter-Religious Federation for World Peace. He also was a participant and leader in numerous interreligious gatherings and dialogues. Mar Gregorios presented this address at the Opening Plenary of the 1993 IRFWP Congress in New Delhi, India, in February 1993, shortly after the militant Hindu Kar Sevaks had destroyed the Muslim mosque at Ayodhya. Dr. Gregorios identifies elements of evil not only in religious violence but also in the scientism, secularism, and corporate fascism that define the purpose and character of our urban-technological civilization.

Today, as I welcome you to this first global celebration of the Centenary Year of the Chicago Parliament of World Religions and to this New Delhi Congress of the Inter-Religious Federation of World Peace on Global Harmony through Inter-Religious Action, I do so with sadness in my heart. My land to this day moans with pain at what took place in Ayodhya on December 6th last year, and in the whole country in the aftermath.

This land of the *Vedas* and the *Upanishads*, the *Gita* and the *Guru Granth Saheb*, of Gautama Buddha and Ashoka Priyadarshin, of Jaina Mahavira and Kabir, of Ramakrishna Paramanhansa and Swami Vivekananda, of Nizamuddin and Sri Aurobindo, of Rabindranath Tagore and Maulana Abu'al Kalam Azad, of Sri Ramana and Mahatma Gandhi, of Sadhu Sundar Singh and Sirdi Sai Baba; this land of *Dharma* and *Ahimsa*; this unique land where people of many religions have for two-and-a-half millennia lived together in peace and harmony; this land of the rishis and sages, weeps today because religion has been hijacked by some politicians and prostituted by a few religious leaders.

Political parties abuse and pervert religion as a mere means to get votes, even at the expense of hurting the feelings of other communities or of destroying the places of worship of other religions! Neither these political leaders nor these religious dignitaries show any compassionate concern about what happens to people or the nation in the process.

Pity on Religious Fanatics

Swami Vivekananda, in an address to the Shakespeare Club in Pasadena, California (January 27, 1900), said that in India, even if you want to set up a gang of robbers, the leader will have to preach some sort of religion. The Swami used his statement to show that in India, in all things, religion has to be uppermost. But what he said in his address to the concluding session of the Parliament of World Religions in Chicago in 1893, exactly a hundred years ago, is more significant and memorable:

> If the Parliament of Religions has shown anything to the world it is this: It has proved to the world that holiness, purity, and charity are not the exclusive possessions of any church in the world, and that every system has produced men and women of the most exalted character. In the face of this evidence, if anybody dreams of the exclusive survival of his own religion and the destruction of others, I pity him from the bottom of my heart.

Well, sisters and brothers in the Spirit, who have come to us from all regions and religions of the world, Swami Vivekananda meant by that pity for the fanatic Christian missionaries whom he had encountered. Now there are people of my country also who think along the lines Swami Vivekananda condemned, who deserve to be pitied from the bottom of your hearts. But give us a little more than your pity. Give us also your generous understanding and kind compassion.

This nation and our great neighbor, Pakistan, both bear the trauma of being born in the midst of violence and hatred in 1947; we were drawn, even through all that murder and bloodshed, by two different pious hopes: India's "Tryst with Destiny," understood as a secular liberal democratic paradise where Hindu and Muslim, Christian and Sikh, Buddhist and Jaina, Jew and Parsi, Adivasi and people of no specific religious faith could all live and work together in peace with mutual respect, where justice would rule, where no one religion would dominate, and where the poor and the downtrodden would flourish in dignity and freedom; and Pakistan's fond dream of a perfect Islamic society where all would be equal and free from what they see as the arrogant and godless culture of the West, to live by the noble *shariyah*, worshipping Allah, in a nation where the lofty ideals of the Qur'an would become a social-historical reality.

Now both dreams have gone sour. Please forgive us for behaving irrationally. We are not in our best elements. We are a bit confused. That goes for all of us, Christians and Sikhs, Hindus and Muslims. Even our intellectuals are not at their best. Bear with us. We will come around to our senses, we promise you
. . . .

The question today is, Shall religion still look to the technological civilization as its patron and censor, as it did a hundred years ago? Shall it meekly accept the insignificant corner in the margin allotted to it by a secular and earthbound culture dominated by the dazzle of modern science/technology, which was beating its drums of triumph at the Columbian Exposition a hundred years ago? Shall we continue to pin our hopes on a secular culture that has not been able to provide us with interreligious and inter-

ethnic harmony within a nation, not to speak of global harmony? Or shall all religions go back to their own sources in conversation with other religious traditions, to seek renewal and gain a new self-understanding, so that we can develop again the spiritual depth and the cultural creativity necessary for functioning as humanity's true guides and advocates?

The human race first needs to be rescued from the adolescent hubris of an unreflective secularism and scientism on the one hand, and from the meaning-distorting and soul-destroying urban-technological civilization developed by the White West and their allies on the other hand. That is only part of the mammoth task facing humanity.

The secularism we want to be rescued from is the one that glibly assumes that the world open to our senses is the chief part of reality; that meaning can be found without reference to anything transcending that world; that religion is a matter of private individual choice (free enterprise religion, I suppose), to be banished from the public sphere, in such a way that the main human activities like economic activity, politics, education, and health care can be undertaken without any transcendent reference.

The scientism from which we seek liberation is the one that assumes that modern empirical science is the chief way to get hold of reality, and that scientific knowledge is the higher kind of human knowledge. Our purpose in this civilization shaped by scientism-technologism seems to be to make reality too our colony, so that we can have a domineering, imperialist, exploiting grip on reality through our technology. We want to make reality our slave and our hoard.

[This attitude] looks like the same imperialist-fascist greed that drives rioting mobs to loot and arson, rape and plunder in Ayodhya or Bombay. The only difference between the industrial-urban-technological civilization and the rioting mobs seems to be one of style and scale and sophistication. Corporate and brutal violence exercised by the many over the few (the essence of fascism), monumental, heartless injustice with no concern for the victim, and plunder and looting, with or without sophistication, seem to be common to both.

Different versions of the same are taking place everywhere—in former Yugoslavia, in Somalia, in the Middle East, and elsewhere. Adherents of religions are fully involved in the arson and plunder, in the torture and persecution, in the corporate violence of groups and governments that perpetrate injustice with impunity. . . .

The Future of Interfaith Dialogue

If we can see the present darkness and gloom that shroud the globe as a challenge along these lines, this Congress of leaders of many religions can bring hope, to us in India, and to depressed people anywhere else. But I am slightly anxious. I do not see such signs of creativity among the religious leadership, even among the world's best-known religious leaders.

Therefore I am coming to a strange conclusion. The kind of interreligious dialogue we have been promoting is getting to be more and more pointless, beyond, of course, its rich symbolic value. I am beginning to envisage a somewhat different kind of interreligious dialogue. My friends who are leaders of religions may or may not like what I have to propose. It cannot be carried out without their full cooperation.

Very simply put, my proposal is this: Let us give the lay men, women, and youth in our various religions their full role in interreligious dialogue and cooperation. I welcome what is being attempted here. But let us go beyond. I want the best talent in our religions, especially women who form more than half our membership, to be drawn in: the literary writers, the artists, the philosophers, the poets, the painters, the musicians, the professionals like doctors, lawyers, and teachers, housewives and businessmen, political and social activists. Not in separate groupings, but coming together to reflect on the issues facing humanity. I would like to keep the religious leadership as well as the political activists as important minorities, but would not want either group to set the agenda or set up the program. Something more sane and healthy, therefore more

hopeful, than what has been hitherto achieved may emerge.

With those words may I welcome you all most heartily once again. Let us make this Centenary Year a time of soul-searching and pioneering. Let Ayodhya and its aftermath never happen again, anywhere.

The Threat of Nuclear Weapons

NOTE: The statement is introduced by Jonathan Granoff, Cochair, American Bar Association Committee on Arms Control, Board Member of Global Security Institute, NGO Committee on Disarmament (Vice President), Bawa Muhaiyaddeen Fellowship, UN Representative to State of the World Forum.

At the beginning of the 21st century, 30,000 nuclear warheads stand ready and able to end life on planet Earth. Over five thousand remain at high alert, on hair-trigger status. Just the triggering devices on these thermonuclear weapons are equivalent to the destructive force that devastated Hiroshima.

During the genocide of World War II, 6 million people were transported to the furnaces. We now have thousands of "portable furnaces," each one with destructive capacities that dwarf the horrors of the Holocaust.

There are five declared nuclear weapons states—United States, the United Kingdom, Russia, China, and France—and three nuclear-capable states—India, Pakistan, and Israel. The five declared states have obligated themselves, under the Nuclear Nonproliferation Treaty, to negotiate nuclear abolition. Yet, as we enter the 21st century we continue to see a failure of political will and action to eliminate this unacceptable risk.

The religious communities had an enormous impact in ending apartheid in South Africa. They have had an enormous impact in raising awareness about our responsibilities regarding the environment. It is time that religions exercise their moral persuasion to end nuclear apartheid and prevent the greatest environmental catastrophe—ending all life. This moral evil is inherent in the ongoing pursuit of security by utilizing the threat of total annihilation.

The following Moral Call is an initiative that will continue in process until the clarion call for a rational security system resonates from our mosques, churches, synagogues, and temples. The State of the World Forum, the Global Security Institute, and numerous interfaith organizations such as the Temple of Understanding and the Interfaith Center of New York are pleading for wider and stronger engagement by religious communities, for we are in a race against time. We ask all to join this initiative as a matter of spiritually awakened conscience.

A MORAL CALL TO ELIMINATE THE THREAT OF NUCLEAR WEAPONS

A Statement by Religious Leaders and People of Faith

Our common humanity brings us together to eliminate a threat to us all. Our diversity will strengthen our efforts. As people of faith, we accept our responsibility to provide moral and ethical clarity and leadership for the common good of all life on the Earth.

The threat posed to humanity and all other forms of life by the sheer destructiveness of nuclear weapons presents an unacceptable risk for this and future generations. This unacceptable risk presents a moral imperative for the elimination of nuclear weapons.

We cannot hold life sacred and at the same time seek security by placing its entirety at risk.

Security concerns and spiritual concerns often seem at odds with each other. Here, that is not the case. The imperatives of global security and the demands of spirituality have converged to bring us to the necessity of outlawing and eliminating nuclear weapons worldwide.[1]

It is immoral for states to place all life at risk in their own perceived self-interest. The creation is a gift and an immeasurable and beautiful mystery; the

state is a human construction. We join together in humility to serve and protect the majesty of the mystery of life.

The belief held by the nuclear weapons states that the alleged security benefits of nuclear weapons should be reserved for them and denied to all others violates the most basic principles of fairness. The solution is simple: States should treat other states as they wish to be treated.

Nuclear weapons are more hazardous than any problem they seek to solve. Their possession and threatened use by any nation provide an impetus for their proliferation by others.

Effective leadership in opposing the growing threat of nuclear proliferation will be credible only if nuclear powers demonstrate a commitment to the universal outlawing of these weapons. Continued reliance on nuclear deterrence puts at risk our moral integrity.

The proposition that nuclear weapons can be retained in perpetuity and never be used—accidentally or by decision—defies credibility.

The unprecedented and immeasurable destructive potential of nuclear weapons threatens the genetic pool. The production and possession of nuclear weapons are an unacceptable threat to the health of the environment.

The threat and use of nuclear weapons is incompatible with civilized norms, standards of morality, and humanitarian law which prohibit the use of inhumane weapons and those with indiscriminate effects. The trillions of dollars spent in this irrational pursuit of a false security constitutes a theft from those who are hungry and a waste of the gift of intelligence.

We say that a peace based on terror, a peace based on threats of inflicting annihilation and genocide upon whole populations, is a peace that is morally corrupting.

We refuse to accept living under an unworthy peace which might make us the Earth's last generation.

The responsibility for banning nuclear weapons does not lie solely with governments of nuclear weapons states and their citizens. It is a responsibility shared by every sovereign state and each precious and sacred individual.

Generals and admirals from many nations have addressed this still-urgent matter of nuclear weapons from a military perspective and advocate that nuclear weapons be taken off hair-trigger alert; that swift and deep reductions in nuclear arsenals be made; and that these steps be taken within the framework of an unequivocal commitment to the achievement of their universal, verifiable, enforceable prohibition and elimination. We agree.[2]

We pledge to work together in our homes, communities, temples, mosques, and churches, transcending differences of religion, race, and nationality, to rid the world of this universal threat.

As people of faith and moral conviction, we believe it is our duty to address this global evil, for no person is removed from its effect. The magnitude of this threat requires that we learn to live in greater cooperation and harmony or we shall all perish together. It is time to move the world from the irrational love of power to the wise power of love. We call upon our faith communities and all concerned citizens to mobilize, to pray, and to act in support of this noble cause.

For these and other reasons of conscience and wisdom we pledge to

1. Include the moral imperative of the abolition of nuclear weapons in our studies and teachings and to encourage our families, friends, congregations, and institutions to do likewise

2. Make efforts to persuade the governments of the nuclear weapons states to pledge never to use nuclear weapons first, remove all nuclear weapons from hair-trigger alert status, dramatically reduce nuclear arsenals, and commence multilateral negotiations on their global elimination.

We personally pledge to express our common humanity by standing up to and challenging the arrogance of power and apathy of bureaucracies behind which nuclear weapons policies hide, and to affirm our faith that human affairs can be governed with cooperation, courage, faith, and wisdom.

NOTES

1 We note the historic International Court of Justice opinion of July 8, 1996, in which the Court unanimously held that "there exists an obligation to pursue in good faith and bring to a conclusion negotiations leading to nuclear disarmament in all its aspects under strict and effective international control." This is consistent with moving the world from the law of power to the power of law.

2 The Nuclear Weapons Elimination Initiative, through the State of the World Forum, gathered signatures on two other abolition statements of international significance. The first, on December 5, 1996, included sixty-three retired generals and admirals from seventeen countries. Among these military leaders were U.S. Generals Lee Butler, former Commander-in-Chief of the Strategic Air Command, and Andrew Goodpaster, former Supreme Allied Commander in Europe; General Charles Horner, Commander of Allied Forces in the recent Gulf War; and Russian General Alexander Lebed. The second, on February 2, 1998, included over 130 prominent civilian leaders. Among these were fifty-two past or present presidents and prime ministers from forty-nine countries. Among them are Jimmy Carter, Mikhail Gorbachev, and Nelson Mandela.

The State of the World Forum has gathered an extraordinary community representing over one hundred nations and nearly four thousand exceptional individuals, ranging from leaders of states to poets, from scientists to youth. Its goal is to help create a more compassionate, environmentally sustainable, just and nonviolent world. The Forum has spawned several gifts to humanity, including the Global Security Institute, which is specifically dedicated to the abolition of nuclear weapons and is coordinating the promotion of the above statement. For more information, call (415) 256-5305 or e-mail info@gsinstitute.org.

Chapter Twenty-four
SPIRITUALITY AND COMMUNITY

Introduction

Joel Beversluis

This chapter explores approaches to spirituality as it can be understood in this new pluralistic and global age. These articles were selected because, for this editor, they contribute to the vision of "community" among religious and spiritual communities. They also relate spirituality and community to the larger community of the Earth and, in Thomas Berry's article, to the cosmos itself as the primary, sacred community. The articles help to identify essential conditions for a new understanding of spirituality through our unity-in-diversity and our interconnectedness.

The first article, by Dr. Peter Laurence, introduces the term "spirituality" as it is coming to be understood, especially in North America. The article also clarifies distinctions between the terms "religion" and "spirituality," and introduces the terms "exclusivism," "inclusivism," and "pluralism." Based on the author's extensive experience in several interfaith organizations, he suggests that many participants in the interfaith movement are operating within a "pluralistic" approach to religious truth claims.

Other articles—notably, Wayne Teasdale's on a universal understanding of spirituality and mysticism—make a similar proposal. While this perspective is intriguing, readers should also consider this—that the interfaith movement and discussions of spirituality must not presume universalism or a pluralistic spirituality among its participants. Unfortunately, some participants in some interfaith venues do make that presumption, thereby excluding those with a strong "exclusivistic" approach to truth from the interfaith table. On some occasions, unfortunately, the inclination to embrace pluralism even takes the form of intolerance of those who "cling to truth claims" and argue for them. The interfaith movement, especially those participants in liberal traditions, should strenuously guard against this religious vice.

The concept of "community" among religions does not require consensus on beliefs, truth claims, or experiences of spirituality. While the search for commonalities in these areas can provide fascinating theological and interpersonal dialogue, this book's claim is that the community of religions must not only tolerate but can even appreciate and benefit from diversity. Among other benefits, religious and cultural diversity provides a process of checks and balances on our own limited knowledge and experience. A clear example of this is the industrial world's need to learn about establishing a sustainable relationship with the Earth from indigenous cultures.

So, conflicting truth claims must not be an impediment to the overarching civil and cooperative character of the community's participants. As many articles in this book point out, we have a great deal in common anyway, and an underlying interconnectedness at many levels—physical, environmental, ethical, genetic, atomic, cosmic—and some ambiguous but common relationship with Ultimate Reality. This community of communities does not require us to seek religious or spiritual uniformity, but to welcome, with sincere hospitality, the community's members, wisdom, and experience into a greater and richer whole.

Exploring Spirituality

Dr. Peter Laurence

Director of the EDUCATION as Transformation Project at Wellesley College and Chair of the Board of the North American Interfaith Network

Emerging from Interfaith Activity

In 1893, representatives of many of the world's religions were brought together at the World's Parliament of Religions, a gathering held during the World Columbian Exposition in Chicago. This event marked the beginning of a century of interfaith activity, carefully documented by Marcus Braybrooke in his book, *Pilgrimage of Hope*.[1] Attitudes toward the existence of a plurality of religions have varied over the intervening time. One classic scheme that has been developed to describe these attitudes uses the terms "exclusivism," "inclusivism," and "pluralism." As recently articulated by Diana Eck, director of the Pluralism Project at Harvard University, an *exclusivist* feels that "our own community, our tradition, our understanding of reality, our encounter with God is the one and only truth, excluding all others." An *inclusivist* would say that "there are, indeed, many communities, traditions, and truths, but our own way of seeing things is the culmination of the others, superior to the others, or at least wide enough to include the others under our universal canopy and in our own terms." The *pluralist* might express it this way: "Truth is not the exclusive or inclusive possession of any one tradition or community. Therefore the diversity of communities, traditions, understandings of the truth, and visions of God is not an obstacle for us to overcome, but an opportunity for our energetic engagement and dialogue with one another. It does not mean giving up our commitments; rather, it means opening up those commitments to the give-and-take of mutual discovery, understanding, and indeed, transformation."[2]

The pluralistic view has become the most supportive environment for interfaith activity, generating the formation of a growing number of interfaith organizations at local, national, and international levels. Religious representation for such organizations has traditionally been accessed in several ways: through official designation by participating religious institutions, by inviting members of faith traditions who have distinguished themselves as individuals, and sometimes by including anyone who identifies with a tradition and is willing to participate. The organizational model in which religious representatives make joint decisions, issue proclamations, or carry out collaborative projects is predicated on the assumption that these individuals somehow do represent a religious tradition.

The Question of Religious Identity

Within any given tradition, however, there is usually a wide disparity of beliefs among its adherents. The divisions within religions are often more deeply felt than the differences between them. A number of long-standing religious institutions have recently been shrinking in size and influence. Many people are either abandoning those institutions or are reserving the right to disagree with official doctrines and policies. Where representatives are chosen, their ability to adequately represent the diversity within their tradition is always a concern. In addition, there is a large and growing population whose sense of personal identity is not linked to any traditional religion. This raises the question of whether religious identity and representation continue to be the most important qualities to utilize in the search for ways to overcome the historic tensions among religions. In the process of addressing this question, we are discovering that there is, instead, a common bond that unites people without requiring that they abandon their religious roots, or that they identify with a particular tradition at all. The term that has been emerging to describe this common bond is "spirituality."

The Problem of Language

Recently, writers in a variety of publications have turned their attention to exploring the concept of spirituality, particularly as it stands in contrast with "religion." An article in *America* by Michael Downey, Flannery Professor of Theology at Gonzaga University, begins with this statement: "Spirituality is no longer tied to the notion that only priests and religious are called to the fullness of the spiritual life....Today a great variety of persons and groups discern the presence of the Spirit in a diversity of living situations. This has called for new ways of understanding spirituality."[3] One of those new ways is the attempt to define spirituality so that it transcends the limitations of what we have traditionally called "religion." There seems to be a widespread hunger for something that moves beyond structures that have characteristically divided us.

For example, an article in the *Journal of Holistic Nursing* by Joni Walton of St. Luke's Hospital in Kansas City described this perspective as follows: "Religion may or may not play a role in individual spirituality and is quite distinctive from spirituality....Religion is described as a framework for beliefs, values, traditions, doctrine, conduct, and rituals.... Whereas spirituality is a much more encompassing term...a spiritual individual may or may not be religious....Spiritual relationships are defined as relationships to self, others, a higher power, or the environment that brings forth a sense of inner strength, peace, harmonious interconnectedness, and meaning to life."[4]

On a somewhat more technical note, Andrés Niño writes in the *International Journal of Psychotherapy* that "there are many individuals who either do not have identified traditional religious sources for the construction of meaning or cannot integrate them in their experience at the service of a coherent self. The religious factor has been diffused through an unprecedented diversity. Even amongst groups previously considered homogeneous within their own faith, substantial numbers of people have modified their attitudes to adopt unorthodox forms of religiosity or have abandoned them altogether. Yet, very often one finds that individuals in this predicament consider themselves to be cultivating a spiritual life."[5]

Spirituality is transcendent, unlimited by the distinctions that separate people. In an article in *Ebony*

Man, Stephen C. Rasor, who teaches at the Interdenominational Theological Center in Atlanta, is quoted as saying that "[spirituality] is something that all persons have, regardless of finances or background. I don't think age, income level, gender, or race separates us."[6]

William Raspberry, a popular columnist, found spirituality to be the common ingredient in successful neighborhood social programs. Quoting the founder and president of the National Center for Neighborhood Enterprise in Washington, he writes, "For twenty years, says Robert L. Woodson, Sr., he had been observing the phenomenon but not really seeing it. 'People, including me, would check out the successful social programs—I'm talking about the neighborhood-based healers who manage to turn people around—and we would report on such things as size, funding, facilities, or technique. Only recently has it crystallized for me that the one thing virtually all these successful programs had in common was a leader with a strong sense of spirituality....The thing I'm talking about may or may not be specifically religious,' Woodson says. 'It can happen with people who don't even go to church. But it's spiritual, and the people who are touched by it know it.'"[7]

What Is Spirituality?

Throughout these articles on the subject of spirituality there is a common theme that emerges. It is the concept of connectedness. *U.S. Catholic* describes it this way: "Curiously, there's a remarkable consistency in readers' definitions of the word spirituality, according to the responses to a *U.S. Catholic* reader survey. Normally one would suppose that in describing such an ineffable, intensely personal experience such as spirituality, the answers would be as varied as the hues in Joseph's multicolored coat. But no. Young and old, religious and lay, women and men define spirituality as consistently as if they were reciting the Baltimore Catechism. Rare is the definition that fails to mention relationship or connectedness....Spirituality 'is an awareness of my connection to God, earth, and others,' writes Karen Fitzpatrick of

Burnsville, Minnesota. Many acknowledge that spirituality is not some otherworldly, escapist pursuit but rather, in the words of one reader, an intermingling of all that is divine with 'the delicious humanness' of our humble earthly existence. 'Too often we separate our spiritual life from what we call our regular life. It should be our life—what completes us as human beings,' suggests Judi Gualtiere of Amarillo, Texas."[8]

In a forthcoming book, Robert Forman, Associate Professor of Religion at Hunter College and Director of the Forge Institute, describes the outcomes of a series of interviews conducted nationally to arrive at a better understanding of spirituality. In compiling the results, Forman noticed several patterns in the way people use the term. The first had to do with "inner" rather than "outer" experiences, drawing on meditation and other techniques for access to the inner world. A second pattern might be identified by the terms "whole, or holistic," seeing ourselves and the rest of the universe as part of a single spiritual reality. A third pattern was associated with impressions of connectedness and being in relationship with everything in that spiritual reality. Finally, spirituality was identified as being nonrational and nonlinear—emphasizing the subjective rather than the objective. As Forman summarizes his conclusions, "...spirituality seems to point to the intuitive, nonrational meditative side of ourselves, the side that strives for inner and outer connection and a sense of wholeness."

As reported in *Holistic Education: Principles, Perspectives and Practices*, edited by Carol Flake, a statement adopted by eighty international holistic educators affirms that "spiritual experience and development manifest as a deep connection to self and others, a sense of meaning and purpose in daily life, an experience of the wholeness and interdependence of life, a respite from the frenetic activity, pressure, and overstimulation of contemporary life, the fullness of creative experience, and a profound respect for the numinous mystery of life." Specifically addressing their concern about education, they state that "one of the functions of education is to help individuals become aware of the connectedness of all

life. Fundamental to this awareness of wholeness and connectedness is the ethic expressed in all of the world's great traditions: 'What I do to others I do to myself.'"[9]

Another prominent educator, Parker Palmer, in his book *The Courage to Teach*, advises that "if we want to develop and deepen the capacity for connectedness at the heart of good teaching, we must understand—and resist—the perverse but powerful draw of the 'disconnected' life." As educators in all parts of the world look for ways to help their students prepare for life and work in a diverse world, spirituality becomes a natural vehicle for overcoming the inherent fragmentation between individuals, groups and institutions. Toward this end, the EDUCATION as *Transformation* Project at Wellesley College was formed in 1996 and has initiated an international dialogue with two goals: 1) to explore the impact of religious diversity on higher education and the potential of religious pluralism as a strategy to address the desire of educational institutions to prepare their students for a religiously diverse world; and 2) to consider the role of spirituality at colleges and universities, and particularly its relationship to teaching and learning pedagogy, the cultivation of values, moral and ethical development, and the fostering of global learning communities and responsible global citizens.

Interest in spirituality is beginning to take shape in the world of organizational development. Diana Whitney, writing in *World Business Academy Perspectives*, tells us that "spirituality has entered organizational discourse through the back door and is now sitting in the drawing room awaiting a proper welcome....The modern focus on objectivity and the separation of science and spirituality, taken to fullness, leaves people separate from one another, separate from nature, and separate from the divine.... Organizations are still suffering under the modern fiction of fragmentation, functionalism, and division of labor." Diana's vision of spirituality includes a description of "Spirit as Sacred," which she explains, "acknowledges the connection of all life and all energy such that actions of the part affect the whole.... A s modern communication and transportation enable us to experience the world as one being, we see the reality of our connectedness. As we see the effect of local actions on global existence, we wonder if perhaps we have been connected all along and just didn't know it.... With this sense of wholeness and connectedness comes a deep reverence for relationships. Spirit as Sacred places relationships at the center of social organization."[10]

Even the popular literature follows the same pattern. *Self* magazine recently conducted its own survey on spirituality and recorded the following ways its readers distilled the spiritual life: "connection to a reality that is more than self and comforts me and guides us"; "belief in a higher power"; "a connection to all living things and to the Earth and universe." The magazine further reports that, "no matter how you define it, though, hunger for the spiritual life is nearly universal: 93 percent of you believe that having a spiritual life is important."[11]

The Need for a Spiritual Renaissance

An article in the *Utne Reader* by Jon Spayde entitled "The New Renaissance" identifies a new breed of visionaries who "view recorded history and the growth of societies as phases of a much longer and more profound process of evolution....For them, human society in the 20th century has reached a crisis point at which our species could descend into ecocidal disaster or—if we make the right choices— bring off a sort of second Renaissance on the global scale....Most of all, the new Renaissance would spark the widespread proliferation of new modes of thinking and feeling into the far reaches of global society: true partnership between the sexes; the conviction that racial and ethnic identities are complex and valuable human options, not fixed fates; and the ever-growing sense that our daily struggles serve something greater than ourselves: a universal Higher Power toward which all religions point."[12]

Brother Wayne Teasdale calls this spiritual renaissance "The Interspiritual Age," and attributes its emergence to the maturing of the world's religions. Writing in the *Journal of Ecumenical Studies*, he pro-

poses that "global spirituality or interspiritual wisdom has become possible because of a tangible sense of community among the religions and the real necessity for the religions to collaborate on the serious challenges to the world, notably the ecological crisis. Only spirituality can move us from within to change and become more responsible for the Earth and one another....Spirituality is a resource for building a universal and enlightened civilization."[13]

Indian-born Raimundo Panikkar gives us the following poetic vision of the transcendent harmony of faiths: "The rivers of the earth do not actually meet each other, not even in the oceans, nor do they need to meet in order to be truly life-giving rivers. But they do meet: they meet in the skies—that is, in heaven. The rivers do not meet, not even as water. They meet in the form of clouds, once they have suffered a transformation into vapour, which eventually will pour down again into the valleys of mortals to feed the rivers of the earth. Religions do not coalesce, certainly not as organised religions. They meet once transformed into vapour, once metamorphosized into Spirit, which is then poured down in innumerable tongues."[14]

Exploring Spirituality

Spirituality is a connectedness that transcends our various religious traditions, which have historically placed boundaries on community. Because everything is connected we care for each other, for the Earth, and for all its forms of life. This is the primary relationship. Our programs in peacemaking, ecology, and caregiving all flow from this basic understanding. By placing a priority on spirituality, we have an opportunity to explore a new dimension of relationship, moving with the spirit that seems to be emerging in every aspect of human activity.

NOTES

1   Braybrooke, Marcus. *Pilgrimage of Hope: One Hundred Years of Global Interfaith Dialogue*. New York: Crossroad, 1992.

2   Eck, Diana L. *Encountering God: A Spiritual Journey from Bozeman to Banaras*. Boston: Beacon Press, 1993.

3 Downey, Michael. "Books on Spirituality." *America*, November 2, 1996.

4 Joni Walton. "Spiritual Relationships." *Journal of Holistic Nursing*, September 1996.

5 Niño, Andrés G. "Assessment of Spiritual Quests in Clinical Practice." *International Journal of Psychotherapy*, November 1997.

6 Collier, Aldore. "Exploring Your Spirituality." *Ebony Man*, September 1997.

7 Raspberry, William. "Spirituality, the Secret Ingredient in Many Successes." *Chicago Tribune*, December 21, 1992.

8 Hendrickson, Mary Lynn. *"U.S. Catholic* Takes a Spirituality Check." *U.S. Catholic*, October 1997.

9 Global Alliance for Transforming Education. "Education 2000: A Holistic Perspective." In *Holistic Education: Principles, Perspectives and Practices.* Edited by Carol L. Flake. Brandon, Vermont: Holistic Education Press, 1993.

10 Whitney, Diana K. "Spirituality as an Organizing Principle." *World Business Academy Perspectives*, Vol. 9, No. 4, 1995.

11 Grant, Priscilla. "How Spiritual Are You?" *Self*, December 1997.

12 Spayde, Jon. "The New Renaissance." *Utne Reader*, January–February 1998.

13 Teasdale, Wayne. "The Interspiritual Age: Practical Mysticism for the Third Millennium." *Journal of Ecumenical Studies*, Winter 1997.

14 Panikkar, Raimundo. *The Unknown Christ of Hinduism: Towards an Ecumenical Christophany.* Maryknoll, New York: Orbis Books, 1981.

Toward a Global Spirituality

Dr. Patricia M. Mische

NOTE: This statement by Dr. Patricia Mische is excerpted from an essay titled "Toward a Global Spirituality," and was first published in 1982 by Global Education Associates, which she cofounded with her husband, Gerald Mische. The excerpt suggests the wholistic approach Dr. Mische takes in thinking about spirituality, yet a major focus of her work has been defining the conditions for a just, peaceful, and sustainable world order. For Pat Mische and many others, spirituality is meaningless unless it has very real connections to the state of the Earth and its people, especially those in marginal or oppressive conditions.

Authentic spirituality is awakening awareness and conscious attunement to the sacred source of life. At the deepest part of every and all being is the sacred. Spirituality is the process of ordering our life in intimate communion with this sacred center and source. Spirituality is not static. It is not a finished state we ever finally achieve and then hold onto. It is a process. It is a sacred journey.

. . . In a certain sense we each make this journey alone. No one else can make it for us. But in another sense we make this journey together, in communion with others. The whole planet with all its life-forms and billions of people—indeed the whole cosmos— is on a collective journey. This is true in a physical sense as we hurtle through space. This is also true in a spiritual sense. There is a sacred source at our collective center from which all our separate journeys originate and in which we all find life and direction.

There is a flow between this collective Earth journey and our personal journeys. They cannot be separated. . . .

True spirituality—the authentic religious journey—can never be an escape from life's problems. God, the sacred center at the source of all authentic spiritual journeys, must be met in the midst of life, not in escape from life. Today we live in a global age—an age of planetary exploration and communications and new global interdependencies. Our spiritual journey—our search for life in God—must be worked out now in a global context, in the midst of global crises and global community. Our spirituality must be a global spirituality. . . .

The skin of deeply spiritual persons is not a dividing membrane that separates them from the world, but a connecting membrane, a permeable membrane, through which events of the world and events of their inner life flow into one another.

Global Spiritualities

Joel Beversluis

As we explore the concept of global spirituality, consider this—that there is no single global spirituality but rather a multitude of spiritualities, and they may be more or less global depending on the choices and experience of the individual person. So, although some use the term "global spirituality" in a generic sense, its many possible emphases may well be tied to particular insights carried by one or more of the world's religions and spiritual philosophies, as well as to ideologies of a political or economic nature.

Even so, the spirituality of any one individual need not have explicit reference to the larger world or to other traditions or cultures. For instance, pure expressions of compassion, simplicity, and service by a committed member of one faith, acting quite locally, may also express a mature and "global" spirituality to the extent that it reflects universal and intrinsic factors common to many contemplative and spiritual traditions.

Especially in this age, however, many of us are eclectic by nature, wanting to learn from others, to consider answers and perspectives beyond those offered in our root tradition. For this writer, the *global* aspect of spirituality suggests, among other things, a relationship between the earth and human culture as an integral system, for good or ill; a vision of humanity as a single, interconnected community; the discovery of an ethical system that serves the whole; an acknowledgement of numerous sources of inspiration and revelation; and trust in Divine mystery, power, and love for all humanity and all creation and cosmos.

To be more specific, the following examples illustrate the enrichment that can be drawn from the community of religions and the accumulated experience of our species, whether religious or not:

- The analyses of eco-justice are clearly supported by the prophetic traditions found in Judaism, Christianity, and Islam. Its focus on justice sees connections between governments, economic systems, consumption patterns, and ecological systems with the inner worlds and attachments of individual people.

- The new interest in the earth religions, expressed through Wiccan, Neo-pagan, Native American, and Christian Creation Spirituality, shares a perception of the Earth as sacred and of ultimate value in the religious life.

- Global spirituality is enriched by eco-feminism and has benefited from its analysis of patriarchal attitudes and domination—whether of women, the poor, or the earth. Like the earth religions, its mode of spirituality encourages partnership, caring, stewardship and appreciation for feminine aspects of the Divine.

- Jain and Buddhist commitments to nonviolence and respect for all life are a standing challenge to some Jewish and Christian attitudes toward the earth, and can thus enrich what is sometimes a very myopic spirituality.

- Bahá'ís, theosophic traditions, and new religious movements bring a vision of planetary community and systems guided by spiritual laws for a pluralistic civilization.

- Sikhs and Vedantists remind us to respect all religions and spiritual philosophies as paths seeking the Divine, and they teach us much about service and devotion.

- Christianity and Buddhism bring strong notes of

compassion, service, and the sense of responsibility to the common good.

- Islam brings a long tradition of philosophy and science enriched by a clear sense of the One, and it is a living example of the acceptable diversity of the *ummah* (community); Muslims also demonstrate a sense of discipline in prayer and worship.

- Judaism and many other religions bring appreciation for story, celebration, and family and community ritual.

- Awareness of the community of religions and its search for a global ethic contributes its inclusiveness and respect for diversity. This awareness also analyzes the worldviews that guide or fail us, and it is clear about its objective of establishing peace and sustainable relations between humans and the earth.

- The common elements of interspiritual wisdom found in contemplative and mystical traditions set a high standard for spiritual practice and discipline.

- Humanistic culture makes contributions to global spirituality in its understanding of human dignity, social behavior, the scientific method, and the psychological factors that shape our lives and world.

- Global spirituality even benefits from the revelation of science, the mysteries of quantum physics, and technological developments; the sciences also help us understand and monitor a systems approach to ecology and culture.

- Finally, global spirituality can build upon the deep human instincts for both survival and interconnectedness, and thereby include a commitment to mitigate the threats by modern civilization to Earth's ecosystems.

The fabric of global spirituality is not being sewn as new cloth or as a new religion, but rather, to adapt a metaphor by Pat Mische, consists of a permeable membrane, a "skin" woven and worn and patched together by each of us. Through it, events of the world and events of our inner lives flow into one another. In promoting the exploration of these concepts, participants in the interfaith movement are some of the many who are seeking an emerging, "integral" culture.

It would be misleading, however, to conclude that many or most people are in consensus regarding the meaning and practice of "spirituality," of the concepts of global spirituality and interspiritual wisdom, or even the idea of the community of religions. This is, in part, because of the particularities each participant brings to his or her portion of the interfaith fabric.

Even so—and perhaps even as a benefit of this diversity—the interfaith movement has a unique opportunity to assist as a midwife to the emerging culture and its community of religions, because it is forging new connections across old borders and among very large and particular religious constituencies. It is through these new connections, as well as by way of the time-tested patterns, that the Divine can be seen doing its transforming work.

Sacred Community at the Dawn of the Second Axial Age

Brother Wayne Teasdale

A Christian sannyasi (monk) in the lineage of Father Bede Griffiths; author, most recently, of The Mystic Heart; lecturer and retreat master; and trustee of the Council for a Parliament of the World's Religions

We are rapidly entering an axial time, a new age which may well be decisive for humanity and the Earth. It will be an age unlike any other in the issues it will resolve, in the direction it assumes, in the consciousness that guides it, and in the truly global civilization it will fashion. Nationalism and fanaticism will diminish before the human family's discovery of a more universal identity. Humankind will come of age, and will outgrow these forms of association as doubtful luxuries no longer desirable or affordable.

Curiously, it is the religions that are playing a central role in leading the world into this new age. Mahatma Gandhi first observed so prophetically that there would never be peace on Earth unless there was first peace among the religions. Hans Kung has reiterated this truth in our time. A subtle shift is occurring in how the religions relate to one another. Often antagonists in the past, their rivalry produced tens of thousands of wars throughout recorded history. Suspicion, competition, and conflict have characterized their relationship, in part because their cultures developed in isolation, only occasionally influencing one another. Now, a new paradigm of relationship is emerging as the barriers dividing the world's religions collapse. Faced with the same critical issues threatening all of us—the ecological crisis, escalating violence, economic instability, hunger, poverty, disease, the population explosion, racism—the religions have found a new mode for cooperation, and through collaboration, the possibility of genuine community among the traditions.

Living in community was always a potential among religions because of the deeper reality out of which we have all come, but the dark forces of fear, insecurity, and ignorance led us into patterns of competition and bloody conflict. When we see this tragic history in the light of our profound and primordial unity, then these conflicts resemble the petty squabbles of children on a playground where cruelty and mean-spiritedness take over.

The cultural transformations occurring are global in scope, comprehensive in extent—affecting everything—and radical in their depth. A new awareness of our interconnectedness but also of our fragility and the fragility of the Earth is changing how we look at the planet and one another. The media are an important tool in breaking down the exclusivistic attitudes that each society, culture, and religion has followed. It was television that brought us the breathtaking image of the Earth from *Apollo*. In that precious image of the planet—like some ethereal jewel—a new consciousness was born, the fruit of an enlightening revelation that compelled us to confront our essential interdependence and our inescapable fragility. It is this realiza-

tion that is the basis of the new age we are now entering.

This approaching period, which is singularly important to the survival and well-being of our planet and its species, has the character of an *axial* event. Thus far in human history only one other Axial Age has been identified. This term was popularized by the German philosopher Karl Jaspers to designate the time frame from 1000 B.C.E. up to and including the time of Christ. That millennium is called the Axial Age because it was the golden age of so many spiritual geniuses whose insights became the foundations of all the great ancient civilizations, and which are enduring even into our century. These figures include the Jain saint Mahavira, Gautama the Buddha, Zoroaster, Socrates and Plato in Greece, Lao-Tzu and Confucius in China, Elijah, Isaiah, and Jeremiah in Israel, and numerous sages in India who inspired the *Vedas* and *Upanishads*. These extraordinary beings provided the axis of our cultures up until the present, and their influence will continue till the end of time because of the perennial nature of their wisdom.

Now, the radical changes taking place around the globe are propelling us quickly into what can be called the Second Axial Age. Like the first period, the second will provide the foundation for culture, but this culture will be universal in scope. The coming age will not, however, dispense with the spiritual, psychological, and moral wisdom of the First Axial Age; rather, it will build on the experience, wisdom, and insight of the great sages of that first period of humankind's awakening.

The latter half of the 20th century has witnessed at least three revolutionary religious/cultural events: the Second Vatican Council (1962–1965), the arrival of Tibetan Buddhism and the Dalai Lama on the world stage, and the Parliament of the World's Religions in 1993.

The first two events will impact life and culture for centuries and both have implications for the new axial period; indeed, they are part of it. The third event, the Parliament of the World's Religions, is so radically significant as to be a catalyst into the next age. This is where a shift in relationships among the great world religions and smaller ones became explicit.

What happened at the 1993 Parliament of the World's Religions was singular and miraculous. Some 8,700 people representing 125 religions, along with a large number of groups standing for various causes, came from around the world. They participated in the grandest display of diversity and creativity ever recorded, even more diverse than the Rio Earth Summit of June 1991. The Parliament was a transcendent moment in history animated by a spirit of genuine openness, mutual listening, and respect. Aside from a few minor exceptions greatly exaggerated by the media, it was as if there had never been any religious wars and other struggles.

During those momentous days at the end of summer 1993, a revelation was given to humanity. For the brief period of eight days, a new awareness became evident among the participants, those with and without a religious tradition or spirituality. This extraordinary awareness revealed some of the attributes we will need for our planet to survive and flourish. These skills include dialogue, sustainable economic and social life, conflict resolution, a Global Ethic, a Universal Spirituality, a willingness to share, mutual openness, trust, respect, and the capacity for profound listening to others, to ourselves, and to the planet itself.

Sacred Community

These attributes also encompass the values and practices we need in order to actualize the deeper, more inclusive type of community that was glimpsed during the 1993 Parliament. That experience gave us a vision of sacred community that includes all religions, nations, groups, organizations, species, the Earth with the entire cosmos. If we want this dream to be, then we must exercise these skills. We must always be willing to dialogue or communicate in an authentic manner; no one should be excluded! Our economic and social life has to be in harmony with the natural world; sustainability with the Earth and with one another demands genuine justice: for the

planet itself (eco-justice), for other species, and for members of our own species. How we utilize resources affects justice and peace. There can be no actual peace unless there is true justice that is both ecological, that is, towards the Earth, and social, or within our communities. More and more this will be the case, so it is imperative that we embrace the practice of sharing our resources. Sharing will create the conditions for justice and will contribute to sustainable economics.

The ecological crisis has emerged as the most pressing of the critical issues and the chief moral concern of the coming age. The Earth has become the matrix of interfaith dialogue just as it is the medium in and through which we live. For far too long we have abused the natural world unaware of what we were doing. Now we neglect it to our own peril. We need a whole new vision of human life as part of and in harmonious interaction with the natural world and the cosmos.

Thomas Berry reminds us that the Second Axial Age is also the Ecozoic Age, the shift away from an exclusively anthropocentric culture to a geocentric and cosmocentric one. Such a momentous and radical alteration of culture, and the evolution of a global society or civilization that is friend to the Earth, requires the active participation of the religions. For just as there can be no world peace unless there is first peace between and among the religions, there can be no new vision of life, culture, and the human family's relationship to nature unless all the religious traditions support it and realize its critical necessity.

Because there already exists an emerging sense of community of the faith traditions within the larger identity of the Earth Community, spiritual interdependence is a growing insight, and with this realization is the further creative possibility of inter-spiritual wisdom. These truths were explicit developments in the consciousness of the Parliament event, and are now integral to its process of self-awareness and vision. The notes of interfaith community, spiritual interdependence, and interspiritual wisdom are equally axial in significance. They represent good news for the planet as a whole in all its glorious variety.

Elements of a Universal Spirituality

The declaration "Towards a Global Ethic," prepared for the Parliament and signed by most of the 250 members of the Assembly of Religious and Spiritual Leaders, is the first explicit expression of a consensus on ethics among the religions. The declaration contains general norms of behavior and responsibility that are universally acceptable and applicable. It is one thing, however, to recognize and outline these norms, but quite another to implement them around the world.

"A Call to Our Guiding Institutions," the document from the 1999 Parliament, helps inspire humankind and offers practical applications of the Global Ethic to those institutions with such power to shape culture. But something more is needed to give humankind the capacity to live this more mature expression of moral life, as the Global Ethic itself suggests in its last paragraphs appealing for the transformation of consciousness. What is needed is a universal spirituality that enables humankind to actualize its potential for the inner, transformative experience, to achieve the fruition of the human adventure in contemplative consciousness.

A universal spirituality does not mean a "super-spirituality." The aim of describing a global spiritual life is not the reduction of the rich variety of humanity's inner life to one common form or generic type. That would be neither possible nor desirable. There are literally thousands of forms of spirituality; indeed it can be said that each person has his or her own kind of spirituality.

Yet we can describe common elements; just as there is a consensus on ethics among religions, there can also be consensus on the essential elements of a universal spirituality. Likewise, just as the goal of a Global Ethic and the "Call" is to identify common standards of practice for the transformation of consciousness, so all authentic spirituality is itself transformative. True spirituality, in its social dimension, is a deep and personal appropriation of the moral life,

and makes each of us better than we were before.

There is a spiritual interdependence among the various religions in the same way as there is a metaphysical interconnectedness to all reality. Each religious tradition and each form of spirituality develops in relation to actual life. Spirituality is a personal response and commitment to reality in its deepest sense. It is the source of self-knowledge that sees our human condition with all its woundedness, but which also offers us the possibility of real growth toward becoming an integrated person, one who is alive, holy, and wise. It gives us a sensitivity to life in all its variety.

Spirituality is an inner stand in relation to the Divine or Ultimate Reality that calls us to higher realization. Spirituality embodies our profoundest and purest desire, our passionate yearning for the Divine itself. It is a longing for union and communion with God, with Ultimate Reality. Characterized by this passionate commitment to the Ultimate, all spirituality takes the form of embracing the spiritual journey, the road to inner transformation and growth. Each kind of spirituality awakens us to reality as it is and to our own condition. Spirituality itself, as the deepest dimension of life and being, is common to all religions.

In identifying the essential elements of a universal spirituality—those elements that will be part of any viable tradition—eight are clearly discernable:

1. An actualized moral capacity and commitment. The capacity to live morally or ethically is the indispensable foundation of the spiritual life in any tradition. One who is on the spiritual journey is always a morally committed individual. A universal spirituality would easily adopt the code of the Global Ethic, and spirituality would provide the inner motivation for implementing its norms in one's life, or in the life of a community.

2. Deep nonviolence and reverence for all life. A deeply rooted attitude of nonviolence is also an important aspect of spirituality. As one becomes more awake within, one also becomes gentle and sensitive without—that is, in relations with others. Not just nonviolence, but *deep nonviolence* must be emphasized because of the growing problem of violence all over the world. Deep nonviolence means a nonharming that is the fruit of wisdom and compassion; it is really a form of love, and it is also a way to spread peace: by living nonviolently! If we truly wish to teach peace, we must live nonviolently!

3. A sense of interdependence and spiritual solidarity. Every person who follows the call of the inner life knows there is a deep bond of human and spiritual solidarity that unites us all. It emanates from the unity of reality itself, and because of this oneness, there is also a spiritual oneness, the basis of our interdependence. That means actually that reality has degrees of subtlety and unity—subtlety-in-unity. Spirituality has a high degree of unity that can be seen as solidarity on the human level. Practically speaking it implies a responsibility to assist and guide any seeker on the spiritual journey who asks for our aid. Thus, a spiritual solidarity exists in life, and we receive what we need, while the journey provides what is required for us.

At the same time, we have a spiritual solidarity with the other species and with the Earth in a special way. It manifests in the possibility of harmony and communion with them both. This harmony and communion is not as rare as we might imagine; it is common to many very advanced in holiness who also have a highly evolved sensitivity towards the created order. Examples include St. Francis of Assisi, the nature mystics and poets, and certain monastics, as well as some unusual lay persons.

4. Spiritual practice. All genuine spirituality has a spiritual practice, the heart of spirituality that brings about the process of inner change. Without it, spirituality is not authentic nor viable. Spiritual practice may consist of some form of mature prayer, meditation, or interiority, a discipline of contemplation, spiritual reading, reflection, study, work, or a simple resting in the Divine. Spiritual practice often involves all or most of these activities. It also may involve liturgy or some kind of ritual. The only rule is that spiritual practice must be transformative. It must initiate, follow through, and sustain fundamental, indeed radical change in the aspirant. Spiritual practice, with the aid of grace, initiates a fourfold transformation: of consciousness, of will, of character, and of action.

5. Mature self-knowledge. The fourfold transformation that grows out of a rich spiritual practice has self-knowledge as its core. One's consciousness grows by addition of greater knowledge and awareness. Perception of reality becomes more profound and all-embracing. This includes an awareness of the three primary worlds: the material, the psychological, and the spiritual dimensions of all reality, life, and being. The person becomes proficient in spiritual wisdom as his or her consciousness becomes more and more subtle. The individual acquires a progressively deeper understanding of hidden motives and unconscious emotional programs originating from infancy. Eventually these give way to spiritual maturity. The person's will, like the mind, is transformed; it no longer seeks selfish ends, and becomes more other-centered. It seeks the permanent in the midst of what is passing away, and pursues harmony with the divine will and with the totality of life. Similarly, the human character knows a far-reaching transformation whereby the person becomes more and more grounded in virtue, grace, and holiness. Saintliness of character emerges as the person submits to love and is shaped by this into a loving, wise, compassionate being. One's behavior is altered as selfish patterns give way to altruistic actions governed by love, kindness, compassion, mercy, and wisdom.

6. Simplicity of life. The sixth element of a universal spirituality is simplicity of life or lifestyle. Its power and truth are eloquently expressed in the admonition: "Live simply so that others may simply live!" Simplicity in style of life, in the use of the Earth's goods, has for millennia in every tradition been a requirement and a sign of the genuine nature of one's spiritual witness. In monasticism and other forms of religious life the vow of poverty is meant basically to emphasize the need for simplicity in living. Simplicity also has a direct bearing on the cultivation of detachment, and detachment facilitates growth in our spiritual lives, especially in holiness and our attachment to the Eternal—that is, to God.

"Live simply so others may simply live" refers, of course, to the poor in its original social context, but it also has a direct bearing on the Earth. Our self-indulgent consumer society has caused and continues to cause a serious deficit to the planet itself. Simplification of life means above all using only what we need of resources and nothing beyond. This principle of spirituality thus translates into a benefit for the Earth and all its inhabitants, and indicates the eminently practical nature of spirituality itself. As Gandhi recognized, we don't need much to live and be happy; he often remarked that the Earth has sufficient resources for humankind's needs, but not for its greeds.

7. Compassionate and selfless service. The seventh principle or guideline in a universal spirituality is selfless service. The transformation of the person living an intense inner life, especially the radical change in character and will, leads spontaneously to the development of a sensitivity to the needs of others. One's relationship with others is grounded on compassion, kindness, love, and the possibility of service or compassionate action. One becomes capable of thinking and acting beyond self-interest, able to discern among the needs of others what is required, based upon justice and charity. This pattern of behavior is found in every valid expression of the spiritual life and is one of the infallible signs of its genuineness. These enduring fruits of enlightened awareness unfold in the spiritual journey.

8. A witness to justice. A final element of a universal spirituality is the freedom to exercise prophetic action calling for change; it may mean taking a courageous stand for others in matters relating to justice, peacemaking, economic policy, refugees, hunger, poverty, women, the elderly, children, the unemployed, the homeless, AIDS and other diseases, and the whole critical issue of the environment. Prophetic action requires spiritual leadership and the courage to take a stand that may have political implications and consequences.

The issue of Tibet, for instance, is one that cries out for an effective voice. For nearly five decades now the Tibetan people have endured immense suf-fering, oppressed by the Chinese who have carried out physical and cultural genocide against them, inflicting on them unspeakable forms of torture and numerous other indignities. The world has stood by in utter silence. The United Nations has ignored the whole question, and the religious leaders of the world, with the notable exception of Buddhists, have been equally reticent. Can they not sense the extreme anguish and pain of the Tibetan people? Genuine spirituality demands prophetic speech and action in such cases.

Another example is the plight of indigenous peoples. We have not dealt adequately with their complaints nor have we been sensitive to their intense pain over the centuries, a suffering for which we bear a certain historical responsibility. Healing must take place between native peoples and the Europeans who have oppressed and nearly destroyed indigenous tribes in the Western Hemisphere and Australia. For instance, the indigenous population in Guatemala is nearly 75 percent of the total, yet they are still treated as a minority in their own country; their rights are systematically denied them by the 25 percent of European descent who rule Guatemala. Authentic spirituality demands a prophetic response.

In this age of spiritual interdependence, when we have finally discovered the profoundly rich bonds of sacred community that unite us, our global spiritual tradition must possess the ability to speak out when the occasion requires it. Such moral leadership is yet another fruit of a genuine spiritual life, and in our age it is much more. It is an essential demand and function of a global culture.

Forging a New Vision

The great religions, indeed all the religions and all organizations concerned in any way with human responsibility, must work together in forging such a vision. Collectively, the spiritual heritage of humankind is deposited among the traditions. This heritage belongs to each one of us and is accessible to all in differing degrees. The religions possess enormous psychological, moral, educational, and spiritual resources. These may now be marshaled in the

Olympian task of creating and expressing the new vision; it can and will happen eventually. The Global Ethic and a tentative, emerging knowledge of universal spirituality are but two examples of what can be achieved by drawing on these vast inner resources, the treasures of humanity's religious consciousness.

The members and leaders of all religious and spiritual communities in the community of religions have a sacred responsibility to create the conditions for formulating, spreading, and implementing the new vision. They have been groping forward now for more than a century, since the first Parliament of 1893. Participants in recent Parliaments and those in other international interfaith organizations—the World Conference on Religion and Peace, the International Association for Religious Freedom, the Temple of Understanding, the Fellowship of Reconciliation, the World Congress of Faiths, the International Interfaith Centre, the United Religious Initiative, and many other groups—have the duty to help create a platform for the religions.

This new global community of religions will only be achieved if the world's religions and other organizations and groups accept together their universal responsibility for the planet. Together, however, we can inaugurate the vehicle that will inspire a new global culture and civilization, one that will be a mature expression of humankind's collective wisdom: a civilization, a society, and a spirituality with a heart!

The Cosmology of Religions and the Sacred Story of the Universe

Dr. Thomas Berry

Eco-theologian, anthropologist, philosopher, Catholic monk, and scholar of Teilhard de Chardin. Father Thomas Berry's many important books and his vision challenge the religions and cultures to consider a new story of the universe and of our place in it.

The universe is the primary sacred community; all human religions are participants in the religious aspect of the universe itself. With this recognition, we are moving from the theology and anthropology of religions to the cosmology of religions. In the past fifty years in America there has been intense interest in the sociology and psychology of religions, and even more interest in the history of religions, yet these all fall within the general designation of the anthropology of religions.

Because none of these have been able to deal effectively with the evolutionary story of the universe or with the ecological crisis, we are led on to the cosmological dimension of the religious issue both from our efforts at understanding and from our concerns for survival.

What is new about this sense of the universe's religious mode of being is that the universe itself is now experienced as an irreversible time-developmental process, not simply as an abiding season-renewing universe. Not so much cosmos as cosmo-genesis.

Our recent knowledge of the universe comes primarily through the empirical, observational sciences rather than from intuitive processes. We are listening to the Earth tell its story through the signals that it sends to us from outer space, through the light that comes to us from the stars, through the geological formations of the Earth and through a vast number of other evidences of itself that the universe manifests to us.

In its every aspect the human is a participatory reality. We are members of the great universe community. We participate in its life. We are nourished, instructed, and healed by this community. In and through this community we enter into communion with that numinous mystery on which all things depend for their existence and activity. If this is true for the universe entire, it is also true in our relations with the Earth.

From its own evidences we now know the story of the universe as an emergent process in its fourfold sequential story: the galactic, the Earth, the life, and the human story. These constitute for us the primordial sacred story of the universe.

The original flaring forth of the universe carried the present within its fantastic energies as the present expresses those original energies in their articulated form. This includes all those spiritual developments that have occurred in the course of the centuries. In its sequence of transformations, the universe carries within itself the comprehensive meaning of the phenomenal world. In recent secular times this meaning was perceived only in its physical expression. Now we perceive that the universe is a spiritual as well as a physical reality from the beginning.

This sacred dimension is especially evident in those stupendous moments of transformation through which the universe has passed in these 15 billion years of its existence. These transformations include moments of great spiritual as well as physical significance—the privileged moments in the Great Story. The numinous mystery of the universe now reveals itself in a developmental mode of expression, a mode never before available to human consciousness through observational processes.

Yet all this means little to our modern Western theologians who have shown little concern for the natural world as the primary bearer of religious consciousness. This is one of the basic reasons why both the physical and spiritual survival of the planet have become imperiled.

Presently we in the West think of ourselves as passing into another historical period or undergoing another cultural modification. If we think that the changes taking place in our times are simply another in the series of historical changes, we are missing the real order of magnitude of the events taking place. We are at the end of an entire biological era in Earth history! We are now in a religious-civilizational period. In virtue of our new knowledge we are changing our most basic relations to the world about us. These changes are of a unique order of magnitude.

Our new acquaintance with the universe as irreversible developmental process is the most significant religious, spiritual, and scientific event since the beginning of the more complex civilizations some five thousand years ago. But we are bringing about the greatest devastation the earth has ever experienced in the 4 $1/2$ billion years of its formation. Norman Myers, a specialist in the biosystems of the planet, estimates that we are causing an extinction spasm that is liable to result in the greatest setback to the abundance and variety of life on earth since the first flickerings of life some 4 billion years ago.

We are changing the chemistry of the planet, disturbing the biosystems, altering the geological structure and functioning of the planet—all of which took billions of years of development. In this process of closing down the life systems of the planet we are devastating a sacred world, making the earth a wasteland, not realizing that as we lose the more gorgeous species, we thereby lose modes of divine presence, the very basis of our religious experience.

Because we are unable to enter effectively into the new mystique of the emergent universe available to us through our new modes of understanding, we are unable to prevent the disintegration of the life systems of the planet taking place through the misuse of that same scientific vision. Western religion and theology have not yet addressed these issues or established their identity in this context. Nor have other religious traditions done so. The main religious traditions have simply restated their beliefs and their spiritual disciplines. This new experience of the religious being of the universe and of the planet earth is not yet perceived on any widespread scale within academic, theological, or religious circles.

We cannot resolve the difficulties we face in this new situation by setting aside the scientific venture. Nor can we assume an attitude of indifference toward this new context of earthly existence because it is too powerful in its effects. We must find a new way of interpreting the process itself, because, properly interpreted, the scientific venture might even become one of the most significant spiritual disciplines of these times. This task is particularly urgent just now because this new mode of understanding has such powerful consequences on the very structure of the planet Earth. We must learn to respond to its deepest spiritual content or we will be forced to submit to the devastation that lies before us.

The assertions of our traditions cannot by themselves bring these forces under control. We are involved in the future of the planet in its geological and biological survival and functioning as well as in the future of our human and spiritual well-being. We will bring about the physical and spiritual well-being of the entire planet or there will be neither physical nor spiritual well-being for any of our earthly forms of being.

The traditional religions have not dealt effectively with these issues or with our modern cosmological experience because they were not designed for such a universe. Traditional religions have been shaped within a predominantly spatial mode of consciousness. The biblical religions, although they have a historical developmental perspective in dealing with the human spiritual process, perceive the universe itself from a spatial mode of consciousness. Biblical religions only marginally provide for the progress of the divine kingdom within an established universe that participates in the historical process. They seem to have as much difficulty as any other tradition in dealing with the developmental character of the universe.

Although antagonism toward the idea of an evolutionary universe has significantly diminished, our limitations in speaking the language of this new cosmology are everywhere evident. Much has been done in process theology in terms of our conceptions of the divine and the relations of the divine to the phenomenal world, but little has been done in the empirical study of the cosmos itself as religious expression.

To envisage the universe in its religious dimension requires that we speak of the religious aspect of the original flaming forth of the universe, the religious role of the elements, the religious functioning of the earth and all its components. Since our religious capacities emerge from this cosmological process, the universe itself may be considered the primary bearer of religious experience.

Thinking about the emergent universe in this way provides a context for the future development of religious traditions. Indeed all the various peoples of the world, insofar as they are being educated in a modern context, are coming to identify themselves in time and space in terms of the universe as described by our modern sciences, even though none of us have learned the more profound spiritual and religious meaning indicated by this new sense of the universe.

This story of the universe is at once scientific, mythic, and mystical. Most elaborate in its scientific statement, it is nevertheless among the simplest of creation stories and, significantly, the story that the universe tells about itself. We are finally overcoming our isolation from the universe and beginning to listen to it in some depth. In this we have an additional context for the religious understanding of every tradition. Through listening to the universe we also gain additional depth of spiritual understanding that was not available through our traditional insights. Just as we can no longer live simply within the physical universe of Newton so we can no longer live spiritually within the limits of our earlier traditions.

The first great contribution this new perspective on the universe makes to religious consciousness is the sense of participating in the creation process itself. We bear within us the impress of every transformation through which the universe and the planet earth have passed. The elements out of which we are composed were shaped in the supernova implosions. We passed through the period of stardust dispersion resulting from this implosion-explosion of the first generation of stars. We were integral with the attractive forces that brought those particles together in the original shaping of the earth. Especially in the rounded form of the planet we felt the gathering of the components of the earthly community and we experienced the self-organizing spontaneities within the megamolecules out of which came the earliest manifestations of the life process and the transition to cellular and organic living forms. These same forces that brought forth the genetic codings of all the various species were guiding the movement of life on toward its latest expression in human consciousness.

This sacred journey of the universe is also the personal journey of each individual. We cannot but marvel at this amazing sequence of transformations.

Our reflexive consciousness, which allows us to appreciate and to celebrate this story, is the supreme achievement of our present period of history. The universe is the larger self of each person since the entire sequence of events that has transpired since the beginning of the universe has been required to establish each of us in the precise structure of our own being and in the larger community context in which we function.

Earlier periods and traditions have also experienced their intimacy with the universe, especially in those moments of cosmic renewal that took place periodically, particularly in the springtime of each year. Through these grand rituals powerful energies flowed into the world. Yet it was the *renewal* of the world or the sustaining of an abiding universe, not the irreversible and nonrepeatable *original* emergence of the world that was taking place. Only such an irreversible self-organizing world such as that in which we live could provide this special mode of participation in the emergent creation itself. This irreversible sequence of transformations is taking shape through our own activities as well as through the activities of the multitude of component members of the universe community.

It is not a straight line sequence, however; the component elements of the universe move in pulsations, in successions of integration-disintegration, in spiral or circular patterns, especially on earth in its seasonal expressions. On Earth, in particular, the basic tendencies of the universe seem to explode in an overwhelming display of geological, biological, and human modes of expression, from the tiniest particles of matter and their movement to the vast movements of the seas and continents, with the clash and rifting of tectonic plates, the immense hydrological cycles, the spinning of the Earth on its own axis, its circling of the Sun, and the bursting forth of the millionfold variety of living forms.

Throughout this disorderly, even chaotic process, we witness an enormous creativity. The quintessence of this great journey of the universe is the balance between equilibrium and disequilibrium. Although so much of the disequilibrium falls in its reaching toward a new and greater integration, the only way to consistent creativity is through the breakdown of existing unities. That disturbed periods of history are the creative periods can be seen in the Dark Ages of Europe as well as in the period of breakdown in imperial order in China at the end of the Han Dynasty around the year 200 C.E.

So too religiously, the grand creativity is found in the stressful moments. It was in a period of spiritual confusion that Buddha appeared to establish a new spiritual discipline. Prophets appeared in the disastrous moments of Israel. Christianity established itself in the social and religious restlessness of the late Roman Empire. Now we find ourselves in the greatest period of disturbance that the Earth has ever known, a period when the continued existence of both the human and the natural worlds are severely threatened. The identity of our human fate with the destiny of the planet itself was never more clear.

In terms of liturgy, a new sequence of celebrations is needed based on those stupendous moments when the great cosmological transformations took place. These moments of cosmic transformation must be considered as sacred moments even more than the great moments of seasonal renewal. Only by a proper celebration of these moments can our own human spiritual development take place in an integral manner. Indeed these were the decisive moments in the shaping of human consciousness as well as in the shaping of our physical being.

First among these cosmic celebrations might be that of the emergent moment of the universe itself as a spiritual as well as a physical event. This was the beginning of religion just as it was the beginning of the world. The human mind and all its spiritual capacities began with this first shaping of what was to become the universe as we know it. A supremely sacred moment, it carries within it the high destinies of the universe in its intellectual and spiritual capacities as well as in its physical shaping and living expression.

Also of special import is the rate of emergence of the universe and the curvature of space, whereby all things hold together. The rate of emergence in those first instants had to be precise to the hundred-billionth of a second. Otherwise the universe would have exploded or collapsed. The rate of emergence was such that the consequent curvature of the universe was sufficiently closed to hold the universe together within its gravitational bondings and yet open enough so that the creative process could continue through these billions of years, providing the guidance and the energies we need as we move through the dangers of the present into a more creative and perhaps more secure future.

This bonding of the universe, whereby every reality attracts and is attracted to every other being in the universe, was the condition for the rise of human affection. It was the beginning and most comprehensive expression of the divine bonding that pervades the universe and enables its creative processes to continue.

It might be appropriate then if this beginning moment of the universe were the context for religious celebration, perhaps even for a special liturgy; it should be available, in a diversity of expressions, to all the peoples of the planet as we begin to sense our identity in terms of the evolutionary story of the universe rather than in purely physical terms or in mythic modes of expression. Although it seems difficult, at first, to appreciate that these are supreme spiritual moments, these and other transformative moments did help establish both the spiritual and the physical contours of the further development of the entire world.

Among these supreme moments we might list the supernova explosions that took place as the first generation of stars collapsed into themselves in some trillions of degrees of heat; this process generated the heavier elements out of the original hydrogen and helium atoms, and then exploded into the stardust with which our own solar system and planet shaped themselves. New levels of subjectivity came into being, new modalities of bonding, new possibilities for those inner spontaneities whereby the universe carries out its self-organization. Along with all this came a magnificent array of differentiated elements and intricate associations. The Earth, in all of

its spiritual as well as its physical aspects, became a possibility.

To ritualize this moment would provide a depth of appreciation for ourselves and for the entire creative process. Such depth is needed because the entire earthly process has become trivialized, leaving us with no established way of entering into the spiritual dimension of the story that the universe is telling us about itself.

The human is precisely that being in whom this total process reflects on and celebrates itself and its numinous origins in a special mode of conscious self-awareness. At our highest moments we fulfill this role through the association of our liturgies with the supreme liturgy of the universe itself. Since the earliest times of which we have information, the human community has been aware that the universe itself is the primary liturgy. Human personality and community have always sought to insert themselves into space and time through this integration with the great movement of the heavens and the cycles of the seasons, which were seen as celebratory events with profound numinous significance. What is needed now is integration with a new sequence of liturgies related to the irreversible transformation sequence whereby the world as we know it has come into being.

We could continue through the entire range of events whereby the universe took shape, inquiring about the religious meaning and celebrating a great many of the mysteries of the Earth. The invention of photosynthesis is especially important in this context. Then the coming of the trees, later the coming of the flowers, 100 million years ago; and finally the birth of the human species.

Only such a selective sequence of religious celebrations could enable the cosmology of religions to come into being. If the sacred history of the biblical world is recounted with such reverence, how much more so the recounting of the sacred history of the universe and of the entire planet Earth.

We find this difficult because we are not accustomed to thinking of ourselves as integral with, or subject to, the universe, to the planet Earth, or to the community of living beings, especially not in our religious or spiritual lives. There we tend to identify the sacred precisely as that which is atemporal and unchanging even though it is experienced within the temporal and the changing. We think of ourselves as the primary referent and the universe as participatory in our own achievements. Only the present threats to the viability of the human as a species and to the life systems of the Earth are finally causing us to reconsider our situation.

This leads us to a final question in our consideration of the various religious traditions, the question of the religious role of the human as species. History is being made now in every aspect of the human endeavor, not within or between nations, or ethnic groups, or cultures, but between humans as a species and the larger Earth community. We have been too concerned with ourselves as nations, ethnic groups, cultures, religions. We are presently in need of a species and interspecies orientation in law, economics, politics, education, medicine, religion, and whatever else concerns the human.

If until recently we could be unconcerned with the species level of human activities, this is no longer the situation. We now need a species economy that will relate the human as species to the community of species on the planet, and that will ultimately be an integral Earth economy. Already the awareness is beginning to dawn that the human is overwhelming the entire productivity of the Earth with its excessive demands, using up some 40 percent of the entire productivity of the Earth. This leaves an inadequate resource base for the larger community of life. The cycle of renewal is overburdened, to such an extent that even the renewable life systems are being extinguished.

We could say the same thing for medicine; the issue of species health has come into view and beyond that the health of the planet. Since human health on a toxic planet is a contradiction, the primary objective of the medical profession must be to foster the integral health of the earth itself. Only then can human health be adequately attended to.

We can in a corresponding manner outline the need for a species, interspecies, and even planetary legal system as the only viable system that can be functionally effective in the present situation. As in economics and medicine, the planet itself constitutes the normative reference. There already exists a comprehensive participatory governance of the planet. Every member of the Earth community rules and is ruled by the other members of the community in such a remarkable manner that the community as a whole and its individual members have prospered over the centuries and millennia. The proper role for the human is to articulate its own governance within this planetary governance.

What remains is the concept of a religion of the human as species in the larger Earth and universe communities. This concept implies a prior sense of the religious dimension of the natural world within the cosmos. Just as we can see the Earth in economic, biological, and legal modes of being, so might we think of the earth as having a religious mode of being. Although this concept is yet to be articulated effectively in the context of our present understanding of the great story of the universe, the ideas seem to be explicit in many of the scriptures of the world.

In general, however, we have thought of the Earth as joining in the religious expression of the human rather than the human joining in the religious expression of the Earth. This has caused difficulties in most spheres of human activity. We have consistently thought of the human as primary and the earth as derivative; in the future, and in a cosmology of religions, we must understand that the Earth is primary and the human is derivative. Only when the cosmos is acknowledged as the matrix of all value will we be able to solve the ecological crisis and arrive at a more comprehensive view of who we are in the community of the Earth.

—Previously published in *Pluralism and Oppression: Theology in a World Perspective*, Annual Volume #34, published by College Theology Society, pp. 99–113

A Universal Understanding of Spirituality and Mysticism

Brother Wayne Teasdale

Brother Wayne Teasdale, Ph.D., is a Christian lay monk and contemplative, retreat leader, author of The Mystic Heart, *professor and trustee of the Council for a Parliament of the World's Religions.*

Introduction

If a culture of peace is to develop and grow deep roots in history, the religions themselves must regard one another differently than has been the case in the past; they must understand one another in a new light. Such a new approach is indispensable, since the religions have often been agents of a culture of war and violence.

Many scholars have believed that the contribution the religions can make to an emerging culture is to seek out what is common, or universal in all the religions. However, discovering a universal ground upon which the various religions could relate is problematic when it is attempted at the level of belief or ideology, or in the doctrinal sphere. At that level agreement is nearly impossible, for we are overwhelmed by the sheer diversity of views.

I am convinced that it is not at this level of religion that common ground will be discovered and nourished, but in the area of spirituality. Spirituality is not quite the same thing as religion, but every religion has different forms of spirituality, and all forms of spirituality are intrinsically relatable.

Religion and Spirituality

Religion is essentially derivative from primary spiritual experience; it is an institutionalization of this experience, a way of handing on a revelation. It represents the social, communal dimension in the historical process of preserving and cultivating the original impulse in a mystical, revelational moment. Religion is way of holding on to this moment by building a system of theological reflection and doc-

trine around it, of rites and tradition. Religion provides, indeed maintains the tradition through which one may ascend or descend into ultimate levels of mystical awareness, the domain of what has come to be called spirituality. The call of the biblical prophets, of Moses, the experience of intimacy with the Divine Reality, with the Father, that Jesus speaks about, the Buddha's enlightenment, the Prophet Muhammad's encounter with Allah through the mediation of the Archangel Gabriel, and his reception of Allah's revelation, the process of mystical illumination and union of the *rishis*, the forest sages of Indian antiquity—all these figures and their unique mystical consciousness generated the great world religions of Judaism, Christianity, Islam, Buddhism, and Hinduism. Religion is born from mystical consciousness.

Spirituality is primary, primordial, numinous, or religious experience, and the emphasis is decidedly on experience, not on doctrine or belief. Frithjof Schuon makes a useful distinction between the esoteric and exoteric to distinguish between spirituality (or mysticism) and religion, the realm of ideological doctrine or belief. The former allows for a certain degree of common ground, while the latter involves us in endless problems trying to find common ground.[1] Mysticism and numinous experience are part of the esoteric dimension, and they demonstrate that the real religion of humankind is not religion itself, but this ultimate kind of consciousness. Spirituality is thus the real religion in the larger sense.

The mystical dimension of consciousness puts the human in touch with the ultimate realms of reality, the frontiers of experience. It is the Divine and the human on the way to union; the person, or soul is surrounded on every side by the Divine. Mysticism is a vast domain. It involves the human in the elevation to awareness of God, where the normal parameters of life are set aside; it has its own laws, its own parameters, and these are infinite. Mystical experience and consciousness is of the infinite reality that is beyond time in the Eternal. All mystical consciousness happens in eternity, not in time. It is the human taken out of finitude and temporality and placed in the unlimited and endless/beginningless realms of the Divine itself. It is imperative to realize that mysticism is not belief, opinion, conjecture, but actual experience, and so, in that sense, is empirical, even scientific. There are, however, options in understanding mystical consciousness, and that is where a certain diversity is introduced.

Pluralism in the Subject and "Object" of Mystical Experience

The subject—the knower, the person who is conscious and having experience—can be approached through diverse conceptions of identity. Plato viewed the essentially real in the human as the soul, which was conceived by him as a "prisoner" of the body. In this position he was similar to the Hindu understanding in which the *atman*, the self, is eternal, but goes from body to body, that is, from life to life, and discards bodies as we would old clothing. Aristotle interpreted the soul as the form of the body, the principle of life and structure, and Thomas Aquinas in the Christian view followed him in this avenue of formulation. The Buddhist conception of no-self—no soul, no intrinsically real identity that is individual and permanent in this world—denies all these other approaches. So, there are numerous understandings, and the gap among them seems to grow wider.

There is a way, however, to span this gap between the Buddhist denial of a self, or soul, and the other traditions of self-identity as a permanent, substantial actuality. If we shift to a model of human identity that puts the emphasis on consciousness itself as the abiding reality regardless of whether we are here in this world or in eternity, then it is possible to bridge the ontological chasm between Buddhism and those views that hold to the existence of soul, or self as a permanent identity.

Consciousness is in fact the "place" of all experience, of perception, of thought, memory, feeling, and all sorts of sensations. There is no *outside* to consciousness, for we only know, or can know, the inside of it. We are phenomenologically[2] bound, by our experience itself, to our own consciousness. We are not able, as it were, to get out of our skins, and see what's there precisely because there is nothing beyond, or outside consciousness. There is only reality and world, self and others, where consciousness is present. Divine Consciousness would then be the ultimate knowing holding everything in being. Consciousness is a community of knowing-subjects, a community of spirit; there is thus a continuity existing between and among all knowers. In this approach, this paradigm of identity, I see consciousness as a medium we inhabit, not a property we own, or have. There is no private ownership of the self in this ontological realm. Consciousness itself is the nature of the self, the soul, or our personal identity, and we have this in common with all other knowers, including God.

I am convinced that this model of identity provides common ground for all the traditions to meet. All traditions depend on consciousness to have and express their various approaches. Consciousness is central to them all.

Of course there are also diverse interpretations of the "object" of mystical experience and of the mystical process[3] itself. Basically, for our purposes here, we can identify these options as two: theism, and nontheism, or again, between the Buddhist notion, and the rest of humanity's experience, which is of the Divine Reality. These two positions seem like polar opposites, but in reality they may be two sides of the same coin, because the Ultimate Mystery is greater than these two views, and can easily accommodate them. We can conceive of them apart, as has been done for centuries, but the more enlightened view would see them as together forming a larger understanding of the Absolute.

Traditionally there have been two categories of ultimate mystical consciousness: God, or theism, and Nirvana, or nontheism. I don't think it is accurate to call Buddhism atheistic, because it does in fact have an approach to the Absolute. Theism usually entails personalism, although not always, as in *Advaita Vedanta*. Personalism requires its fulfillment in an intimate relational mode, or union with God, while nontheism entails transpersonalism, or impersonalism.

Transpersonalism is ordered to realization of the Absolute, like Nirvana and *shunyata*, rather than union, because Buddhism doesn't speak of a personal God. I believe that the Divine can be approached through both personalism and transpersonalism, and that union and realization are both necessary. Let us take a closer look at three possible options on the mystical path: the Hindu, Buddhist, and Christian.

Varieties of Mystical Consciousness

The Hindu tradition is referred to by Hindus themselves as the *Sanatana Dharma*, the Eternal Religion, because it belongs to a revelation of the Eternal by the Eternal, or the Divine itself. The ultimate experience, in this rich understanding, is what is called *advaita*, or nonduality, that is, that absolute awareness is characterized by saying it is "not two," and "not one" either; it is somewhere in between. That which is not two or one is the relationship between the person, soul, individual *atman*, and the Supreme, the *Atman, Brahman*, or God. This is mystical perception, not mere conception.[4] To say the relationship is not two and not one, is to suggest, I think, that it is inwardly dynamic, that within unity there are distinctions.

This unitive experience in *advaitic* awareness, or this experiential awareness that is *advaita*, or nonduality, can be further characterized as *saccidananda*.[5] *Saccidananda* is first a term that unites three attributes: *sat*, or being, the pure act of existence itself, said only of the Brahman, the Godhead; *cit*, or pure consciousness, again, a property of the Absolute, and *ananda*, or pure bliss, joy, the third attribute of the Brahman. *Saccidananda* is, thus, the pure, infinite bliss or joy of being total awareness, of being the fullness of unlimited existence. This is absolute consciousness, or the awareness of the Absolute, the Godhead, the Brahman itself. What should be immediately clear is that *saccidananda* is not primarily a theology of the Absolute, but the inner experience of its own awareness, in which the mystic-sage participates, or shares.

Buddhist mysticism is oriented to the awakening to Nirvana, an absolute condition of freedom from all cultural/social conditioning in which all desire has been extinguished; free from craving and selfish projects for personal happiness, the person is then in a position to understand the nature of reality as *karuna*, or compassion. *Karuna* arises from the recognition of our essential interdependence with all beings, our co-arising with everything else. The suffering, anxiety, existential angst, the lack of satisfaction we feel from the impermanent, allows us to feel compassion and empathy for all sentient beings, all creatures that feel, including plants. We are able to arrive at compassion because we have understood *shunyata*, that everything is *empty* of inherent existence. What that means is that nothing exists in isolation from everything else. There is no intrinsic existence to any being as a separate entity; each has its being only in relation to the totality. In the ultimate, transcendental sense, *shunyata* is the Whole beyond the diversity of arising beings in the cosmic multiplicity that we now experience.

Nirvana, more positively, is the unconditioned, ultimate nature of our reality; its definitive attributes are absence of coming into being, of passing out of being, of subsisting, and changing. It is wholly immutable, ungraspable, beyond comprehension and description, the permanent realm of total bliss and safety. Nirvana unites in itself *samsara*, this realm of becoming and the eternal realm of changeless, transcendent being; we are part of that reality. The experience of Nirvana brings with it the awareness that we are in identity with it, and so, we will always be.

To know Nirvana in a mystical sense is also enlightenment, or what in the Zen tradition is called *satori*, or *kensho*, the breakthrough to a nonrational, nonconceptual, intuitive manner of experiencing reality, which is nondual and ineffable. One feels no distance, no separation from anyone or anything else.

The quintessence of Buddhist esotericism is the Tibetan mystical state, or original condition called *Dzogchen*, the "original," or "great perfection" of the mind. It is named "great" because it is regarded as the ultimate level of attainment, and it is called "perfection" because it is the end of all effort; nothing more is needed once one attains to this profound awareness.[6] It is an *advaitic* level of awareness that is essentially beyond time and corruption; it is the original and primordial nature of the mind. It is not something to achieve beyond ourselves, but our actual nature, requiring only that we awaken to it, leaving behind our ignorance of who we really are. Meditation is a sure way to come to a breakthrough to this awareness, as it is also in arriving at a knowledge of the Brahman, or the *Atman* in the Hindu tradition.

Christian mysticism aims at the final goal of a permanent, or stable union with God. In this goal it is similar to Judaic and Sufi mysticism as well. This union is an experience of intimacy with the Divine. Contemplation is a mystical process, the inner life of interior relationship with the Divine Lover; it is intensely personal, relational, but there is also a direct, existential knowledge of God that arises out of this love. The soul or person who is granted this grace is elevated into the Divine Reality; the human is transformed in God, and on every side is saturated by Love, transfigured by the radiance of glory that emanates from the Divine Light itself. Christian mysticism, and all mysticism, is experiential; it is direct awareness and experience of the Ultimate Reality. In this sense, it is highly empirical; it is not based on a belief, opinion, or speculation, but on an absolutely certain and objective reality.[7] When this state of union becomes stabilized in a permanent relationship of love, the mystical marriage exists. John of the Cross provides an eloquent description of this mystical condition:

> This spiritual marriage is incomparably greater than the spiritual espousal, for it is a total transformation in the Beloved in which each surrenders the entire possession of self to the other with a certain consummation of the union of love. The soul thereby becomes divine, becomes God through participation, insofar as is possible in this life. And thus I think that this state never occurs without the soul's being confirmed in grace, for the faith of both is confirmed when God's faith in

the soul is here confirmed. It is accordingly the highest state attainable in this life.[8]

It is my firm conviction that the various forms of mystical consciousness are internally related; they exist in the unity of the one Ultimate Reality in Divine Consciousness itself. The essential difference of types, divided between theism and nontheism, between a personal Divine Absolute, God, who is also the Creator, and the transcendent Consciousness of the Buddha, represents two sides of the same Absolute. I believe up the road of history we will find that this is the case.

NOTES

1 Frithjof Schuon. *The Transcendent Unity of Religions*. Wheaton, Ill.: Quest Books, 1993, rev., pp. xii–xxvii and 7–60.

2 Phenomenology is an epistemological method that emphasizes how reality, perception, thought appear to the conscious knower. It is concerned primarily with how things appear to the mind.

3 It is important to distinguish between mystical experience(s) and the mystical process, for although mystical experiences are common they are not entirely beneficial unless they lead to a commitment to live a spiritual life. When that happens, one embarks on the spiritual journey, or the mystical process. Then all spiritual experiences impact one's inner life, and do their work.

4 It is necessary to remember that we lack a proper language to talk about mystical consciousness, and especially in its unitive modes. This lack has led to so many misunderstandings of statements made by mystics in all of the traditions, particularly in the Hindu, Buddhist, Christian, Sufi, and Jewish schools of mysticism.

5 For a good treatment of *advaita* and *saccidananda*, see Abhishiktananda, *Saccidananda: A Christian Approach to Advaitic Experience* (Delhi: ISPCK, 1974), or Richard King, *Early Advaita Vedanta and Buddhism: The Mahayana Context of the Gaudapadiya-karika* (Albany, N.Y.: SUNY, 1995).

6 For further exploration of *Dzogchen*, see Tulku Thondup Rinpoche, *Buddha Mind: An Anthology of Longchen Rabjam's Writings on Dzogpa Chenpo (Dzogchen)*, ed. Harold Talbott (Ithaca, N.Y.: Snow

Lion, 1989), and Chokyi Nyima Rinpoche, *Indisputable Truth: The Four Seals That Mark the Teachings of the Awakened Ones*, ed. Erik Pema Kunsang and Kerry Moran (Hong Kong: Rangjung Yeshe Publications, 1996).

[7] In the Christian tradition alone, there are some forty thousand volumes on mystical subjects, covering every aspect of the spiritual journey. For love, or bridal mysticism, see St. Teresa of Avila, *The Interior Castle, in The Collected Works of St. Teresa*, vol. two, trans. Otilio Rodriguez, O.C.D. and Kieran Kavanaugh, O.C.D. (Washington: ICS Publications, 1980), and St. John of the Cross, *The Collected Works of St. John of the Cross*, trans. Kieran Kavanaugh, O.C.D. and Otilio Rodriguez, O.C.D. (Washington: ICS Publications, 1973).

[8] Ibid., *The Spiritual Canticle*, 22, 3, *Collected Works*, p. 497.

The World House

NOTE: As the Reverend Dr. Martin Luther King, Jr., once said, we live in a "world house." During the Persian Gulf War in 1991, the interfaith community of metropolitan Chicago recognized that, regardless of perspective, one day the war would end and that everyone had to live peacefully with their neighbors. The interfaith community recognized that it was in a unique position to offer guidance to the community at large on how to live together when hostilities had ceased. The following texts were first published in a pamphlet by the National Conference on Community and Justice (formerly the National Conference of Christians and Jews) in cooperation with representatives from twelve religious traditions in metropolitan Chicago. The intention was to help people think in terms of those values they wished to live by once the war was over. Here are the thoughts and prayers of these religious communities—each presented in their own way and in their own words.

American Indian

The sacred hoop of any nation is but one of many that together make the great circle of creation. In the center grows a mighty flowering tree of life sheltering all the children of one mother and one father. All life is holy.

People native to this land have long lived by the wisdom of the circle, aware that we are part of the Earth and it is part of us. To harm this Earth, precious to God—to upset the balance of the circle—is to heap contempt on its Creator. Therefore, with all our heart and mind, we must restore the balance of the Earth for our grandchildren to the seventh generation.

> —compiled by Native American Indians of Chicago at Anawim Center, from the wisdom of Black Elk, Chief Seattle, and many other American Indian spiritual leaders

Bahá'í

The primary question to be resolved is how the present world, with its entrenched pattern of conflict, can change to a world in which harmony and cooperation will prevail.

World order can be founded only on an unshakable consciousness of the oneness of mankind, a spiritual truth that all the human sciences confirm.

Acceptance of the oneness of mankind is the first fundamental prerequisite for reorganization and administration of the world as one country, the home of humankind. Universal acceptance of this spiritual principle is essential to any successful attempt to establish world peace. It should therefore be universally proclaimed, taught in schools, and constantly asserted in every nation as preparation for the organic change in the structure of society which it implies.

> —"The Promise of World Peace," a statement by the Universal House of Justice to the Peoples of the World, October 1985, submitted by Spiritual Assembly of Bahá'ís of Chicago

Judaism

In Jewish tradition, there are many deeply held values that govern a nation's conduct in war, so that the subsequent peace may be based on dignity and justice. We are told:

"Rejoice not when your enemy falls and be not glad in your heart when (he) stumbles."

                                                    PIRKE AVOT

Who is the greatest hero? The one who changes an enemy into a friend.

AVOT D' RABBI NATAN

How great is peace? Even in time of war, peace must be sought.

SIFRE DEUTERONOMY

When besieging a city to capture it, one may not surround it on all four sides . . . (so that) anyone who wishes to flee may escape.

MISHNEH TORAH

Peace without truth is false.

MENDEL OF KOTZK

—from the Chicago Board of Rabbis

Anglican Christianity

O God, you made us in your own image and redeemed us through Jesus your Son: Look with compassion on the whole human family; take away the arrogance and hatred which infect our hearts; break down the walls that separate us; unite us in bonds of love; and work through our struggle and confusion to accomplish your purposes on earth; that, in your good time, all nations and races may serve you in harmony around your heavenly throne; through Jesus Christ our Lord. Amen.

—Episcopal Diocese of Chicago

Zoroastrianism

In this worldly abode of ours,

May communication drive away miscommunication.

May peace drive away anarchy.

May generosity drive away selfishness.

May benevolence drive away hostility.

May compassionate words prevail over false protestations.

May truth prevail over falsehood.

—From the *Dahm Afringan* prayer, submitted by Federation of Zoroastrian Associations of North America

Catholic Christianity

"But I say to you that listen, Love your enemies." (Luke 6:27) Because Jesus' command to love our neighbor is universal, we hold that the life of each person on this globe is sacred.

Communion with God, sharing God's life, involves a mutual bonding with all on this globe. Jesus taught us to love God and one another and that the concept of neighbor is without limit. We know that we are called to be members of a new covenant of love. We have to move from our devotion to independence, through an understanding of interdependence, to a commitment to human solidarity. That challenge must find its realization in the kind of community we build among us. Love implies concern for all—especially the poor—and a continued search for those social and economic structures that permit everyone to share in a community that is a part of a redeemed creation (cf. Rom 8:31–33).

—"Economic Justice for All" (#326 and #365), National Conference of Bishops, November 18, 1986, submitted by Catholic Archdiocese of Chicago

Buddhism

We are what we think.
All that we are arises with our thoughts.
With our thoughts we make the world . . .

"Look how he abused me and beat me,
How he threw me down and robbed me."
Live with such thoughts and you live in hate.

"Look how he abused me and beat me,
How he threw me down and robbed me."
Abandon such thoughts, and live in love.

In this world, hate never yet dispelled hate.
This is the law,
Ancient and inexhaustible.

—The *Dhammapada*, submitted by Buddhist Council of the Midwest

Islam

Is he who knoweth that what is revealed unto thee from thy Lord is the truth like him who is blind? But only men of understanding heed;

Such as keep the pact of Allah, and break not the covenant;

Such as unite that which Allah hath commanded should be joined (taking care of their mutual duties), and fear their Lord, and dread a woeful reckoning;

Such as persevere in seeking their Lord's countenance and are regular in prayer and spend of that which We bestow upon them secretly and openly, and overcome evil with good. Theirs will be the sequel of the (heavenly) Home,

Gardens of Eden which they enter, along with all who do right of their fathers and their helpmates and their seed. The angels enter unto them from every gate,

(Saying): Peace be unto you because ye persevered. Ah, passing sweet will be the sequel of the (heavenly) Home.

And those who break the covenant of Allah after ratifying it, and sever that which Allah hath commanded should be joined, and make mischief in the earth: theirs is the curse and theirs the ill abode.

Allah enlargeth livelihood for whom He will, straiteneth (it for whom He will); and they rejoice in the life of the world, whereas the life of the world is but brief comfort as compared with the Hereafter.

—The Qur'an 13:19–26, submitted by the Muslim Community Centers of Chicago

Hinduism

O Lord, lead us from the unreal to the Real,
Lead us from darkness to Light,
And lead us from death to Immortality.

May all be free from dangers,
May all realize what is good,

May all be actuated by noble thoughts,
May all rejoice everywhere.

May all be happy,
May all be free from disease,
May all realize what is good,
May none be subject to misery.

May the wicked become virtuous,
May the virtuous attain tranquility,
May the tranquil be free from bonds,
May the freed make others free.

May good betide all people,
May the sovereign righteously rule the earth,
May all beings ever attain what is good,
May the worlds be prosperous and happy.

May the clouds pour rain in time,
May the earth be blessed with crops,
May all countries be freed from calamity,
May holy men live without fear.

May the Lord, the destroyer of sins,
The presiding Deity of all sacred works,
be satisfied.
For, He being pleased, the whole universe becomes pleased,
He being satisfied, the whole universe feels satisfied.

—Swami Yatiswsarananda, *Universal Prayers*, submitted by Vivekananda Vedanta Society

Orthodox Christianity

Lord our God it is truly just and right to the majesty of Your holiness to praise You and to offer to You our spiritual worship.

We entreat You Lord to,

Remember us and grant us profound and lasting peace. Speak to our hearts good things concerning all people, so that through the faithful conduct of our lives we may live together peacefully and serenely. As Your children, may we come to understand that we are all brothers and sisters to one another, created in Your Image and Likeness.

We call upon You, the God of Peace, to enlighten us to treat all people with the very same dignity, freedom, and respect which You will for all humans to enjoy; for You have revealed to us that dignity is the essence of life itself and from it alone do we obtain the right to call ourselves Your children.

Remember us, O Lord, and all Your people. Pour out Your rich mercy upon us. Be all things to all, You, who know each person. Receive us all into Your kingdom. Declare us to be sons and daughters of the light and of the day. Grant us Your peace and love, Lord our God, for You have given all things to us. Amen.

—submitted by the Greek Orthodox Diocese of Chicago

Protestant Christianity

O Thou whose love embraces every child of the world, forgive our easy labels and simple answers. As Thou hast created every living organism in complexity and beauty, give us grace to see each other as people with many needs and hopes and dreams. In some way touch us with the spirit of Jesus, whose love embraced everyone and whose sympathy knew no bounds.

In times of stress and disappointment, through every dark valley and every moment of limited vision, be Thou our stay. And when we come through those moments, stop us, O God, that we may remember on whose grace we have depended, and we may give Thee the thanks and praise.

This prayer and all prayers we are able to make because Thou hast first put the spark of divinity within us. Amen.

—submitted by Church Federation of Greater Chicago

Sikhism

Says Nanak:
There are many dogmas, there are many systems,
There are many spiritual revelations,
Many bonds fetter the self (mind):
But Release is attained through God's Grace;
Truth is above all these,
But even higher is life lived in Truth.
All God's creatures are noble,
None are base.
One Potter has fashioned all the pots,
One Light pervades all Creation.
Truth is revealed through Grace.
And no one can resist Grace.

—*Siri Rag, Ashtpadiyan,* p. 62

Adds Tegh Bahadur:
Oh saints (seekers of Truth), real peace is achieved through God,
The virtue of studying the scriptures lies in contemplating the Name.

—*Gauri,* p. 220

We all pray for peace in the world, through peace of mind.

—Copyright © NCCJ, used with permission

Part Three

CHOOSING OUR FUTURE

Introduction: Making the Connections

Joel Beversluis

As we move into the new century (in the Gregorian calendar), many of us are increasingly conscious of relentless change and mind-boggling crises. We seem to be at a point in time where circumstances created by numerous historical and cultural factors are converging into a nexus, a focal point where the energies are intense and swirling around us. Although it is difficult to find our way through this unprecedented convergence of factors, we are learning that crises contain not only danger, but also opportunities—a better word is imperatives—for transforming the systems in which we live. What the future holds for us and future generations will be determined in great part by how well we as a species use these opportunities to think and act in new ways.

We cannot easily escape the awareness that this mix of crises has the potential to cause enormous trauma and social conflict. Indeed, emergencies and disasters are already commonplace; the threats and warning signals that transcend national borders are so well known, in fact, that we are numbed to them and to our seeming powerlessness to respond adequately: poverty, hunger, disease, ethnic and regional wars, violence in our cities and among our youth, unsustainable ecological and population patterns, ozone depletion and, though it has receded from our consciousness, the possibility of nuclear war.

Many speakers and writers, including some in this book, claim that we live in a time of profound crisis and that the heart of the crisis is a moral or spiritual dilemma. Numerous conditions ranging from crimes of hate to the unethical dumping of toxic by-products reveal that the human species and the world we inhabit are threatened most by humanity's own inner decay. Though we placed our trust in science and technology, it is increasingly clear that these tools cannot save us. We are realizing that, despite our material "progress," the human species is threatened, along with many others, by our moral ambiguity and inertia.

These threats and conditions are the "critical issues," sometimes called "the global problematique," that must be addressed with greater engagement by the world's religious and spiritual communities.

Seeking a Culture of Peace

Within most human hearts lies a strong desire for peace: we want harmony with our neighbors and we long for beautiful and healthy natural surroundings. Nevertheless, we willingly forfeit these when fear, greed, or even lofty goals seem more compelling. Our hearts also call out for justice for ourselves and, in principle, for others. Yet, for some, the pursuit of personal or group "justice"—in the form of revenge or self-interest—is another one of those compelling reasons to compromise the ideals of peace. Likewise, the crises mentioned above also have increasing power to disrupt the peacefulness of our daily lives, health, and security.

Aren't there more durable and persistent meanings of "peace" that can offer us the power to transcend those forces that disturb our peacefulness? Where shall we look for the true meaning of peace that can help us face the future with wisdom and effective action?

In Part Three of this *Sourcebook*, we propose a closer look at the wisdom of the world's religions, spiritual traditions, and venerable philosophies as it pertains to creating a culture of peace—in many of its meanings. Their diverse insights on peace and other subjects are derived from the many sources, including the experiences of life—physical and spiritual—that have tested the insights and found them meaningful.

We also propose a closer look at the pioneering ideas and commitments of those individuals and organizations who are advocating transformation and who are themselves participants in transformative responses to the critical issues. They bring proposals based in philosophy and the social and physical sciences, and they bring real-world tests of their visionary hypotheses.

The primary challenge and opportunity of this age is to identify the values, conditions, tasks, and agents of peace—so that we can know what it is we seek and when we are finding it. When this pilgrimage bears fruit, the insights give us a place to stand and a vision of the future we want. The true meaning of peace provides a spiritual compass and a set of moral imperatives that can guide us through the nexus of our times.

Connecting Religions, Ecology, Human Rights, and Peace

Beyond the *deadly* connections among the critical issues—between avarice and hunger, consumerism and ecological degradation, tribalism and suffering, the marketplace and exploitation—are there also life-enhancing connections to help us define the tasks before us?

Along with the crises described above, transformative ideas and visions are also gathering in the global nexus in response to the increased need for them. Operating something like a funnel that consolidates the elements, the nexus is also creating new "chemical reactions," breaking up old allegiances and revealing new connections. Among them is the evolving understanding of the idea of interconnectedness itself.

Thirty years ago ecology and environment were generally understood in terms of the interactions of the natural world and our impact on it. Now the terms are increasingly linked with the entire material and conceptual system in which we function, including economics, governance, sustainable development, human rights, peace, and justice. This holistically understood system now also encompasses shifting worldviews, the new insights of physics and life sciences, creation stories of the religions, personal spirituality, and studies of the future. New myths and cosmological stories are arising as science and religions find unexpected bonds within the nexus.

The idea that ecology, human rights, institutional leadership, and spirituality are vitally connected is a liberating and empowering worldview. The policies and methods of leadership at all levels have never had more influence on the global future than they do now. At the same time, each individual's responsibility for the whole must ensure that there is appropriate participation at all levels. This personal quality of universal responsibility, though innate, must be acknowledged and activated by religions, spiritual traditions, and worldviews to generate compassion and personal commitment.

The future, on the far side of the nexus, is, for the most part, unpredictable. Many things may happen there. Their shape will come through the convergence of very real crises with equally real opportunities for personal and global change.

Beyond the Borders of Self-Interest

It seems only common sense that in order for our species and Earth's ecosystems to survive gracefully, we humans must change our ways. But, we may well ask, is there any hope? Is it possible for the species to change so substantially? Can an emerging global consciousness buttressed by wisdom from the world's religious and spiritual traditions, as well as by the best contemporary knowledge, save us from ourselves? And, within the context of this book, can an energetic community of religions empower their adherents to cooperate in changing our ways and reversing the threats?

Growing numbers of people worldwide do have these hopes and have committed themselves to assisting in the process of doing the right thing for future generations. Many people of all countries are busy acting locally, working to recreate the world as it should be. The universal persistence of the "ideal" is itself a hope-engendering factor in the nexus; envisioning it is the first step in the process of creativity. As Goethe wrote, and many traditions affirm, the next step is to act boldly and with pure intention, for then the powers of the universe act with us.

Many necessary changes are possible simply because the opportunities and needs are found everywhere and call out to everyone to respond in very local and personal ways. Each person who acts for the well-being of others engages in a journey of personal growth, envisioning a future and acting locally in his or her own way. The teacher who recycles and the investor who chooses socially responsible funds are acting within a global context. Each student with a pen pal across the planet, each man who plants a fruit tree, and each child who cares for a pet is acting beyond the borders of self-interest. So it is that, through the little actions and the multiplier effect, momentous changes will evolve.

In this process of change, we can gain needed sustenance from the knowledge that we are not alone. Understanding the deadly connections and the scope of crises can be intimidating, but becoming familiar with helpful ideas and joining other motivated people is also highly energizing. The best energy in any transformative process is that which flows through us when we reflect on it, respond to it from our hearts and through our bodies, and then pass it on to others.

St. Francis sang, "Lord, make me an instrument of thy peace!" With the same prayer we may become instruments of peace, pioneers working the connections that link members of the world's religions and spiritual traditions into a community of peace, as fully responsible citizens of the larger community of the Earth.

Chapter Twenty-five
CREATING A CULTURE OF PEACE

Introduction

Joel Beversluis

The growing efforts among religious, philosophical, political, and activist communities to understand and implement the conditions for peace have led to a series of conferences, consultations, and declarations during the past decade. While these efforts themselves do not necessarily bring change, they reflect the development of ideas at the cusp of our culture and are promoted in a "trickle-out" method of dissemination to other institutions and individuals. Quite often the meetings and declarations are the result of substantial interdisciplinary, interreligious, and intercultural consultations that, by their nature, bring much more insight and substance to the table than any single group, movement, or discipline can, by itself, consider. This chapter brings together the results of several such consultations and documents.

The Contribution by Religions to the Culture of Peace

Since its first conference in 1993 on this subject, the United Nations Educational, Scientific, and Cultural Organization (UNESCO) has taken new interest in the role of religions, churches, and spiritual traditions in promoting a culture of peace. The Programme for an April 1993 conference on this topic sponsored by UNESCO noted the roles that religions may play in conflictive situations:

Looking at international problems, it is easy to find religious components in existing wars and conflicts. Religions are often used to legitimate the ideological, economic, or political interests which are the most immediate cause of conflicts. But religions can be of great help in the creation of a culture of peace that would make it possible to prevent conflicts, defuse violence and build structures that are fairer and freer....

Religions can remind us of fundamental aspects of human dignity, of openness to others, of the real priorities in individual lives and the lives of all peoples. Religions can encourage us on the paths of generosity and cooperation. Religion is a great source for insight and ethical courage.

The following excerpt is from a statement distributed by UNESCO in preparation for a meeting held in Barcelona from 12 to 18 December 1994. Following the statement is a Declaration signed by the delegates to the meeting who, while acting in their individual capacities, are also influential religious or cultural leaders. UNESCO presented the Declaration to the United Nations General Assembly and promoted it as part of UNESCO's program for 1995, the International Year of Tolerance.

... One of the priorities UNESCO has set itself for the coming years is to promote reflection on the cultural changes that make it possible to imagine and encourage new concepts and actions for peace. War seems more meaningless every day. In the past, wars and violence were considered natural and inevitable. Today, we know that more rational and human alternatives for resolving conflicts are available to us. But we do not yet have the ideas, beliefs, symbols, and methods we need to orient culture as whole towards peace. In many respects, finance and industry are designed by war, science is committed to developing weapons, and the media provide coverage of war and fail to explain the paths of peace. The whole of culture needs to be reoriented and a new consensus reached on the possibility of peace, the foundations of peace, and the responsibility of peace. UNESCO wants to provide the setting, the drive, and the consensus for reflections on the culture of peace. It is therefore once more inviting personalities from the religious world and from the world of culture to contribute to defining the culture of peace and above all to defining themselves publicly as builders for peace.

Declaration on the Role of Religion in the Promotion of a Culture of Peace

UNESCO

We, participants in the meeting, "The Contribution by Religions to the Culture of Peace," organized by UNESCO and the Centre UNESCO de Catalunya, which took place in Barcelona from 12 to 18 December 1994,

Deeply concerned with the present situation of the world, such as increasing armed conflicts and violence, poverty, social injustice, and structures of oppression;

Recognizing that religion is important in human life;

DECLARE:
Our World
1. We live in a world in which isolation is no longer possible. We live in a time of unprecedented mobility of peoples and intermingling of cultures. We are all interdependent and share an inescapable responsibility for the well-being of the entire world.

2. We face a crisis which could bring about the suicide of the human species or bring us a new awakening and a new hope. We believe that peace is possible. We know that religion is not the sole remedy for all the ills of humanity, but it has an indispensable role to play in this most critical time.

3. We are aware of the world's cultural and religious diversity. Each culture represents a universe in itself and yet it is not closed. Cultures give religions their language, and religions offer ultimate meaning to each culture. Unless we recognize pluralism and respect diversity, no peace is possible. We strive for the harmony which is at the very core of peace.

4. We understand that culture is a way of seeing the world and living in it. It also means the cultivation of those values and forms of life which reflect the worldviews of each culture. Therefore neither the meaning of peace nor of religion can be reduced to a single and rigid concept, just as the range of human experience cannot be conveyed by a single language.

5. For some cultures, religion is a way of life, permeating every human activity. For others it represents the highest aspirations of human existence. In still others, religions are institutions that claim to carry a message of salvation.

6. Religions have contributed to the peace of the world, but they have also led to division, hatred, and war. Religious people have too often betrayed the high ideals they themselves have preached. We feel obliged to call for sincere acts of repentance and mutual forgiveness, both personally and collectively, to one another, to humanity in general, and to Earth and all living beings.

Peace
7. Peace implies that love, compassion, human dignity, and justice are fully preserved.

8. Peace entails that we understand that we are all interdependent and related to one another. We are all individually and collectively responsible for the common good, including the well-being of future generations.

9. Peace demands that we respect Earth and all forms of life, especially human life. Our ethical awareness requires setting limits to technology. We should direct our efforts towards eliminating consumerism and improving the quality of life.

10. Peace is a journey—a never-ending process.

Commitment
11. We must be at peace with ourselves; we strive to achieve inner peace through personal reflection and spiritual growth, and to cultivate a spirituality which manifests itself in action.

12. We commit ourselves to support and strengthen the home and family as the nursery of peace.

In Homes and Families, Communities, Nations, and the World

13. We commit ourselves to resolve or transform conflicts without using violence, and to prevent them through education and the pursuit of justice.

14. We commit ourselves to work towards a reduction in the scandalous economic differences between human groups and other forms of violence and threats to peace, such as waste of resources, extreme poverty, racism, all types of terrorism, lack of caring, corruption, and crime.

15. We commit ourselves to overcome all forms of discrimination, colonialism, exploitation, and domination and to promote institutions based on shared responsibility and participation. Human rights, including religious freedom and the rights of minorities, must be respected.

16. We commit ourselves to assure a truly humane education for all. We emphasize education for peace, freedom, and human rights, and religious education to promote openness and tolerance.

17. We commit ourselves to a civil society that respects environmental and social justice. This process begins locally and continues to national and transnational levels.

18. We commit ourselves to work towards a world without weapons and to dismantle the industry of war.

Religious Responsibility

19. Our communities of faith have a responsibility to encourage conduct imbued with wisdom, compassion, sharing, charity, solidarity, and love; inspiring one and all to choose the path of freedom and responsibility. Religions must be a source of helpful energy.

20. We will remain mindful that our religions must not identify themselves with political, economic, or social powers, so as to remain free to work for justice and peace. We will not forget that confessional political regimes may do serious harm to religious values as well as to society. We should distinguish fanaticism from religious zeal.

21. We will favor peace by countering the tendencies of individuals and communities to assume or even to teach that they are inherently superior to others. We recognize and praise the nonviolent peacemakers. We disown killing in the name of religion.

22. We will promote dialogue and harmony between and within religions, recognizing and respecting the search for truth and wisdom that is outside our religion. We will establish dialogue with all, striving for a sincere fellowship on our earthly pilgrimage.

Appeal

23. Grounded in our faith, we will build a culture of peace based on nonviolence, tolerance, dialogue, mutual understanding, and justice. We call upon the institutions of our civil society, the United Nations system, governments, governmental and nongovernmental organizations, corporations, and the mass media, to strengthen their commitments to peace and to listen to the cries of the victims and the dispossessed. We call upon the different religious and cultural traditions to join hands together in this effort, and to cooperate with us in spreading the message of peace.

Religion and World Order

Dr. Patricia M. Mische

Patricia Mische is cofounder of Global Education Associates, Professor at Antioch College, and author of numerous works, including Toward a Human World Order *(with Gerald Mische) and "Toward a Global Spirituality." This essay is from the Introduction to "Religion and World Order: Proceedings of the Symposium on Religion and Global Governance," which was held February 4, 1994, in Washington, D.C.*

It is now commonplace to speak of a new world order. But there is not yet a shared vision of what that new world order should be. We live in a transformative moment, but how deep will that transformation go? The task of shaping a new world order has yet to be undertaken. It beckons to us on the road ahead as a challenge and opportunity to create the not yet but possible future.

Thus, the question now before us is not *whether* there will be a new world order, but *what kind* of world order? Based on what values? With what underlying vision and spirit? Guided by what kind of ethical principles and policies? By what systems and structures? Who will shape this new world order? For whose benefit? Will the 21st century see a repeat of the violence, ethnic cleansings, apartheids, genocides, and ecocides of the 20th? Or will we who live on the cusp between two centuries use the openness of this historical moment to develop a more humane, just, peaceful, and ecologically sustainable world order? Can we shape a world order that benefits not only some of us, but all of us; not only those of us living now, but also those yet to come who will inherit the world we create?

These are some of the questions addressed in Project Global 2000 (PG2000), a partnership of four UN agencies and thirteen nongovernmental organizations that are collaborating to expand public discourse and action for more humane and ecologically sustainable global systems. People from different walks of life who want to participate in this process can do so through the Project's six program councils: Business, Communications, Education, Health, Youth, and Religion....

The Need

The 50th anniversary of the United Nations in 1995 provides a special framework and point of reference for exploring the kind of world structures needed for the next century. When the United Nations Charter was drafted and signed in 1945, the world faced a particular set of problems and challenges. Now, fifty years later, there is a new nexus of military, economic, environmental, population, human rights, and health problems that were not anticipated at that time. These problems can only be dealt with through new levels of global cooperation and strengthened global systems.

Existing international institutions were shaped in the shadows of World War II and the Cold War that followed. While the war was still on, Allied powers began planning for a new world order and institutions that would focus on two main concerns: 1) the prevention of future wars, and 2) the reconstruction of war-devastated economies and international monetary relationships. The United Nations was designed to address the first; the World Bank and International Monetary Fund the second.

Those involved in drafting the UN Charter were not aware of work on an atomic bomb. Even when the final document was signed in June 1945, those who signed it were not among the few select military, scientific, and political leaders who knew of the secret work under way on a new weapon. They did not anticipate Hiroshima and Nagasaki. Nor could they foresee the nuclear arms race and threat of nuclear proliferation that followed. Nor did they anticipate the Cold War and how it would obstruct the UN's effectiveness.

Instead of the new world order based on collective security that had been envisaged, what emerged instead was a bipolar world order—one driven by the arms race and economic and ideological conflict between the military powers aligned on either side of the Cold War divide. This division dominated and obstructed the UN Security Council and some other UN agencies. It dominated international relations. The major powers viewed all their international relations through this screen. An entire generation of national and international policy makers was trained to think and act within this framework. They, and the institutions they created and maintained, are now ill prepared to lead their nations or the world toward solutions to the new economic and environmental threats that have emerged.

Also, in 1945 much of the world was still colonized. Great numbers of the world's peoples were under foreign domination and not represented or consulted in the San Francisco negotiations that shaped the UN Charter. Only fifty-one nation-states participated in determining the principles and structures that would frame the new international organization. In the

The Causes of Peace Failure

It is now widely recognized that the present plight of civilization is, in the last analysis, due to our spiritual anarchy and our spiritual impotence. The power, which new and in the last resort destructive ideologies exert over the minds of millions of men today, has forced us to face in a new way the problem of the basic presuppositions of all common living. It is now clear that no durable international settlement can possibly be arrived at unless the nations accept certain common convictions and common standards as the basis of their own life and of their relations with each other.

All schemes for a future international order depend for their realization on this presupposition of a willingness to live together in harmony, which itself depends upon some underlying unity of spirit. It is the absence of any such basis which has brought civilization to the brink of catastrophe.

As it becomes increasingly evident that the crisis of Western civilization is in the last resort a spiritual crisis which is due to the absence of great common and compelling convictions, and that none of the ideologies which are at present in control can pretend to bring about a true integration, men everywhere are searching for a new universalism. It is rightly believed that international society has become so interdependent that it will only be able to live in a harmonious and orderly fashion if some fundamental common convictions concerning man and society are held by all nations, however different they may remain in all other respects....

—*The Causes of Peace Failure, 1919–1939*, the report of the International Consultative Group of Geneva, which met in 1940 sponsored by the Carnegie Endowment for International Peace

decades that followed, self-determination and democratization movements spread worldwide. More than one hundred new nation-states came into existence, seeking equal representation and decision-making power in the international community.

Environmental concerns were also not on many people's minds in 1945. None of the drafters of the UN Charter or the subsequent Declaration and Covenants on Human Rights foresaw threats to the Earth's air, water, soil, rain forests, and plant and animal species on the scale we do today. They never imagined that human activities would one day threaten global climate change and a growing hole in the Earth's protective ozone layer, or that the transboundary shipment or dispersal of toxic and radioactive wastes would become a bone of international contention. Nor did they consider the need to protect the rights of future generations to a healthy environment. Today all these issues are before the world community, but without adequate global structures to respond effectively.

Furthermore, when the Charter was drafted, the underlying assumption was that states were the only legitimate international actors. "We the peoples" were the first words in the UN Charter, but, in fact, "the peoples" were not given a real role or voice. The centrality and ultimate authority of the nation-state was enshrined in the new Charter and other international agreements that followed. Thus, in the new community of nations there was not only a failure of democratization between the member states (some states were more equal than others), there was also a failure of democratization or representation from below—i.e., a failure to recognize the source of sovereignty or authority in peoples.

At the same time, because states were so determined to hold on to absolute national sovereignty, they failed to delegate sufficient sovereignty or authority at the global level to make the new global institutions really effective in protecting peace and security and human rights. Consequently the UN was left relatively powerless to prevent or effectively deal with acts of aggression and mass violations of human rights.

In the last few years, this state-centric system has been increasingly challenged from both above and below. From below, people's movements and non-governmental organizations, often acting in solidarity across state borders, are pushing for a greater voice and role in shaping the global policies and structures that affect their lives. There is a growing global civic literacy and sense of global citizenship. This new global literacy is generating demands for democratization of global institutions; demands to let "we the peoples" have a greater role in global governance. At the same time there is growing recognition—including among some heads of states—that, in an interdependent world, national sovereignty is largely an illusion.

Global environmental and economic threats pay little attention to national borders or sovereign banners. If there is to be an adequate response to these trans-boundary threats, some sovereignty must be delegated to global-level institutions to make them more effective. The question is not one of totally abandoning the principle of state sovereignty. Rather, it is one of determining how much sovereignty to invest at local, national, and global levels of governance, and for which purposes. There is a need for effective systems at all the appropriate levels where decisions have to be taken—local, national, and global.

Our generation lives in a rare moment of history, a transformative moment. The end of the Cold War, the emergence of global communications systems, the continuing pressure for democratization at all levels—from local and national to global structures—are all signs of a historic window of opportunity. This is a very open and malleable period in history. Old systems are breaking down and new ones are in process of being created.

But this malleability will not last forever. There is a very narrow margin of time to make a difference in the shape of these new systems and structures. For better or worse, new systems and structures will be developed. Once institutionalized they will be very difficult to change. Decisions are being made now that will shape the norms, policies, and systems that

govern the world far into the 21st century.

The Important Role of Religious Networks

Societies, cultures, and human institutions are shaped not only by political and economic forces, but also by religious and spiritual forces. Throughout history spiritual visionaries and religious leaders have had a powerful influence on the shaping and maintaining of worldviews and culture. The teachings of Lao Tzu, Confucius, Buddha, Abraham, Moses, Jesus, Paul, Mohammed, and Bahá'u'lláh, for example, have had a far more profound and lasting effect on thought patterns and lives than have political revolutionaries.

The great world religions include members from different races, nationalities, and ethnic backgrounds. Their loyalties and identities often transcend national boundaries. They are global communities in microcosm, with shared values, beliefs, and social agendas.

Of course, this does not mean that religion always plays a positive role in human interactions. The very features that contribute to a sense of belonging for some may contribute to a sense of exclusion for others. Religious differences have often turned into divisiveness, self-righteousness, and fanaticism, contributing to conflict, hostilities, and sometimes brutality, atrocities, and war. Organized religion has also sometimes been a tool of the state, used to manipulate people's loyalties toward blind obedience and unquestioning allegiance to state power. Or it has sometimes made itself indistinguishable from the state, wielding political power for its own gains. And one does not need to be a Marxist to know that religion has sometimes been an opiate that numbed people into acceptance of hunger, poverty, and injustice and thus impotent to effect change.

But the very fact that organized religion can and has sometimes been such a powerful force in war and human destructiveness also suggests that it can play a powerful role in building and sustaining systems of global peace, human rights, social justice, and ecological balance. Just as there is ample evidence of human destructiveness perpetrated in the name of religion, so is there evidence of the creative force that religion and spirituality have sometimes been in inspiring creative solutions or energizing new directions in history. In his explorations of the rise and fall of great civilizations, the historian Arnold Toynbee found that spirituality and religion played a significant role in bridging the time/space between the fall of one civilization and the rise of another. The creative minorities that helped build new civilizations from the ashes of the old were often operating from a strong spiritual impulse. In contrast, civilizations that lost their spiritual core were not long sustained.

If we accept Toynbee's conclusions about the importance of spirituality and religion in the rise and fall of civilizations, then we are led to certain conclusions about the importance of spirituality in the development of any truly new world order or *global* civilization in our time. Inner spiritual growth and transformation may be as, or even more, important than external political changes in global systems. Put another way, inner, spiritual growth, and the development of more democratic, effective, and humane global systems may be inseparable parts of a holistic world order. They develop in conformity to one another and are mutually reinforcing. The nurturing of a deeper, global consciousness, and the harnessing of spiritual and moral energies for a more just and humane world order, are vital aspects of its healthy development.

The more destructive behavior of some members of organized religions needs to be distinguished from the "authentic" spiritual or religious impulse. The Latin word *religare*, from which the word for religion in many Western languages is derived, means "harmony," or "to unify, bind together, make whole." In Eastern languages the words for religion have the same or similar meanings. In Sanskrit, for example, one of the original meanings for *dharma* (eternal religion) is to bind together the whole universe.

Despite some major variations between different religions and religious experience in different historical periods and societies (e.g., belief in gods or a God is not common to all religions), there are some important similarities or commonly shared aspects of religious experience. Spirituality and religion usually include a sense of the numinous or transcendent. They have evolved from a sense that reality is greater than self or the sum total of measurable physical, economic, political, or other phenomena. Religion and spirituality have been defined as our unitive experience—i.e., the experience of "the holy" or "whole," or of the "ultimate," "sacred," and "unknowable." It has also been defined as the human effort to discover some order (cosmos) in disorder (chaos).

Some have described religion as a means by which societies interpret life and develop and reinforce codes of morality and conduct in keeping with those interpretations and the requirements of community life. It has also been described as those beliefs and practices by means of which a group designates and seeks to deal with its deepest problems of meaning, suffering, and injustice.

In these understandings of authentic religion and spirituality, then, world order is not something peripheral or outside the realm of religion, but rather at its deepest core of interest, experience, and concern.

In addition to the meanings, spiritual experience, and moral/ethical considerations religion brings to questions of world order, there is also the power of its networks and institutions. The major world religions have worldwide networks of organizations, educational and medical institutions, alumni, research institutes, local communities, and social- and civic-action projects. They can and often do operate across national boundaries with greater ease than many government officials, unbound by the constraints that often tie the hands of governmental actors. They can be major actors in the development of a more peaceful, equitable, and ecologically sustainable world order. They can contribute important scholarship and professional expertise to help resolve some of the grave issues that confront humanity. Their members, programs, and institutions put them in touch with leaders and shapers of public policy. They can be important partners and cocreators in the development of a more humane and just world order.

There is a growing interest by UN agencies and secular NGOs to collaborate with religious institutions and networks to develop a relevant framework of values and leadership for global systemic change. These secular bodies recognize the valuable contributions that religious networks can play in building a viable future. For example, for some years the UN Environment Programme (UNEP) has sponsored the Environmental Sabbath (or Environmental Holy Days) with the cooperation of world religions and spiritual traditions. UNEP also welcomed the cooperation and support of religious NGOs in the process leading to the Earth Summit and in efforts to develop global environmental ethics. UNESCO has sponsored conferences on the Contributions of Religions to the Development of Cultures of Peace. UNICEF and the World Conference on Religion and Peace (WCRP) collaborated in promoting the Convention on the Rights of the Child. Since 1971, the WCRP has been convening regional and global conferences of religious leaders to cooperate in building world peace, and it recently undertook an initiative in collaboration with UN officials to explore ethical guidelines for humanitarian intervention. The Global Forum of Parliamentary and Spiritual Leaders sponsors conferences bringing together governmental and religious leaders to address global issues. And UNICEF and UNESCO are working with Global Education Associates and Project Global 2000 to link religious networks....

The Religion and World Order Program provides a process and context for religious and spiritual communities to reflect on what and how, from their tradition and experience, they can contribute to the values and systemic challenges we face today . . . to conceptualize and work together for the fundamental elements of a cooperative world order and a global vision that affirms the oneness of the human community and the sacredness of all life.

Seeking the True Meaning of Peace

Introduction

Joel Beversluis

From June 25 to 30, 1989, an unusual conference met in Costa Rica to explore the meaning and implications of the concept of peace. Present at the conference were a large number of persons concerned with various aspects of this highly pertinent topic. Participants gained new appreciation for the very real connections between such factors as population pressures, ecological crises, development and resource use, religious teachings and spirituality, and international political activity.

Noteworthy among the participants were two Nobel Peace laureates, Oscar Arias, former president of Costa Rica, and His Holiness Tenzin Gyatso, the 14th Dalai Lama of Tibet. In addition, other distinguished guests and more than five hundred persons of various creeds, professional training, political orientation, and nationalities—including representatives of indigenous populations—came together to study, reflect, visualize new content for the idea of *peace*, and take action that would have impact throughout the planet.

The Declaration and Its Uses

In preparation for the conference, a commission of representatives from the Foreign Ministry of the Government of Costa Rica and the University for Peace held an international consultation to draft the "Declaration of Human Responsibilities for Peace and Sustainable Development." This document is a sophisticated attempt to identify universally acceptable principles, based upon diverse philosophical and religious wisdom as well as recognizing the requirements of the ecological systems of the earth. The Declaration was enthusiastically considered and adopted by the participants in the conference, and has been distributed by the government of Costa Rica, by the University for Peace, and by conference attendees as an instrument for reflection and commitment.

Since the conference, the Declaration was presented in October 1989 to the General Assembly of the United Nations and was formally adopted through a presidential decree of the government of Costa Rica as an instrument for reflection and commitment. As a statement of universal principles, the document has many applications in forums ranging from religious and ethical studies to economics and political science.

By linking the pursuit of peace with the concepts of sustainability, personal responsibility, and interdependence, the Declaration's insights provide a holistic perspective and have important implications for the development of personal and planetary resources. The values it promotes have implications for economic aid programs, as well as for international policies and cooperation. Its greatest value, however, is its focus on the universal responsibility of each individual, so it is through personal reflection and commitment that the Declaration has its most significant impact.

Declaration of Human Responsibilities for Peace and Sustainable Development

Preamble

Considering that both the report of the World Commission on Environment and Development[1] and the United Nations Environmental Perspective to the Year 2000 and Beyond[2] have recognized the imminent danger threatening the existence of the Earth as a result of war and environmental destruction;

Recognizing that the world has been evolving from a group of separate communities towards interdependence and the beginnings of a world community, a process reflecting global concerns, common goals, and shared ideals;

Recalling that, according to the Universal Declaration of Human Rights, recognition of the inherent dignity and of the equal and inalienable human rights of all members of the human family is the foundation of freedom, justice, and peace in the world;

Considering the aspirations of all the members of the human family to realize their potential to the maximum through the cultural, social, political, and economic development of individuals and of communities, recognized in the Declaration on the Right to Development[3] as an inalienable human right;

Recognizing the necessity of ensuring the full and equal participation of women and men in the decision-making processes relating to the promotion of peace and development;

Bearing in mind that the international community has proclaimed that people have a sacred right to peace[4] and has recommended that national and international organizations should promote peace;[5]

Observing that the international community has recognized the fundamental right of human beings to live in an environment of a quality that permits a life of dignity and well-being;[6]

Bearing in mind the challenge posed by the growing imbalances in the dynamic relationship between population, resources, and the environment;

Considering that the General Assembly has established that all human rights and fundamental freedoms are indivisible and interdependent;[7]

Aware that the attainment of those rights has been recognized as being the responsibility of individuals as well as of state;[8]

Concerned because the efforts of human society thus far have not been sufficient to achieve the full recognition of those rights;

Considering that the United Nations has emphasized that wars begin in the minds and through the actions of human beings[9] and that the threats to continuing development and the conservation of the environment arise from diverse but interrelated forms of human behavior;[10]

Bearing in mind that the General Assembly has determined that, in order to ensure the survival of natural systems and an adequate level of living for all, human activity should be reoriented towards the goals of sustainable development;[11]

Considering that the present generation, having reached a crossroads where new challenges and decisions must be faced, bears the immediate responsibility for its own development and for the survival of future generations, so that they may consciously constitute a single world, just, peaceful, and based on cooperation with nature;

Convinced, therefore, that there is an urgent need for a greater awareness of the unity of life and of the special character of each of the expressions of life, and for a more profound human sense of responsibility and a reorientation of human thoughts, feelings, and actions;

Considering that this Declaration can contribute to the achievement of this reorientation and can inspire many practical applications at the level of the individual, the family, and the community as well as at the national and international levels;

In accordance with all the foregoing considerations, the Government of Costa Rica offers the present Declaration of Human Responsibilities for Peace and Sustainable Development as an instrument for reflection and action.

NOTES

[1] Accepted by General Assembly resolution 42/187 of 11 December 1987.

[2] Adopted by General Assembly resolution 42/186 of 11 December 1987.

[3] General Assembly resolution 41/128 of December 1986.

[4] Declaration on the Right of Peoples to Peace, General Assembly resolution 39/11 of 12 November 1984.

[5] Declaration on the Preparation of Societies for Life in Peace, General Assembly resolution 33/73 of 15 December 1978.

[6] Report of the United Nations Conference on the Human Environment (the Stockholm Declaration), 16 June 1972.

[7] General Assembly resolution 37/199 of 18 December 1982.

[8] See World Charter for Nature: General Assembly resolution 37/7 of 28 October 1982, and resolution 38/124 of 16 December 1983.

[9] Declaration on the Preparation of Societies for Life in Peace: General Assembly resolution 33/73 of 15 December 1978; Constitution of the United Nations Educational, Scientific, and Cultural Organization, preamble, paragraph 1.

[10] General Assembly resolutions 37/7 of 28 October 1982; 42/186 of 11 December 1987 and 42/187 of 11 December 1987.

[11] General Assembly resolutions 42/186 of 11 December 1987 and 42/187 of 11 December 1987.

We Declare

Chapter I. Unity of the World

Article 1. Everything which exists is part of an interdependent universe. All living creatures depend on each other for their existence, well-being, and development.

Article 2. All human beings are an inseparable part of nature, on which culture and human civilization have been built.

Article 3. Life on Earth is abundant and diverse. It is sustained by the unhindered functioning of natural systems that ensure the provision of energy, air, water, and nutrients for all living creatures. Every manifestation of life on Earth is unique and essential and must therefore be respected and protected without regard to its apparent value to human beings.

Chapter II. Unity of the Human Family

Article 4. All human beings are an inseparable part of the human family and depend on each other for their existence, well-being, and development. Every human being is a unique expression and manifestation of life and has a separate contribution to make to life on Earth. Each human being has fundamental and inalienable rights and freedoms, without distinction of race, color, sex, language, religion, political or other opinion, national or social origin, economic status, or any other social situation.

Article 5. All human beings have the same basic needs and the same fundamental aspirations to be satisfied. All individuals have the right to development, the purpose of which is to promote attainment of the full potential of each person.

Chapter III. The Alternatives Facing Mankind and Universal Responsibility

Article 6. Responsibility is an inherent aspect of any relation in which human beings are involved. This capacity to act responsibly in a conscious, independent, unique, and personal manner is an inalienable creative quality of every human being. There is no limit to its scope or depth other than that established by each person for himself. The more activities human beings take on and become involved in, the more they will grow and derive strength.

Article 7. Of all living creatures, human beings have the unique capacity to decide consciously whether they are protecting or harming the quality and conditions of life on Earth. In reflecting on the fact that they belong to the natural world and occupy a special position as participants in the evolution of natural processes, people can develop, on the basis of selflessness, compassion, and love, a sense of universal responsibility towards the world as an integral whole, towards the protection of nature and the promotion of the highest potential for change, with a view to creating those conditions which will enable them to achieve the highest level of spiritual and material well-being.

Article 8. At this critical time in history, the alternatives facing mankind are crucial. In directing their actions towards the attainment of progress in society, human beings have frequently forgotten the inherent role they play in the natural world and the indivisible human family, and their basic needs for a healthy life. Excessive consumption, abuse of the environment, and aggression between peoples have brought the natural processes of the Earth to a critical stage which threatens their survival. By reflecting on these issues, individuals will be capable of discerning their responsibility and thus reorienting their conduct towards peace and sustainable development.

Chapter IV. Reorientation towards Peace and Sustainable Development

Article 9. Given that all forms of life are unique and essential, that all human beings have the right to development and that both peace and violence are the product of the human mind, it is from the human mind that a sense of responsibility to act and think in a peaceful manner will develop. Through peace-oriented awareness, individuals will understand the nature of those conditions which are necessary for their well-being and development.

Article 10. Being mindful of their sense of responsibility towards the human family and the environment in which they live and to the need to think and act in a peaceful manner, human beings have the obligation to act in a way that is consistent with the observance of and respect for inherent human rights and to ensure that their consumption of resources is in keeping with the satisfaction of the basic needs of all.

Article 11. When members of the human family recognize that they are responsible to themselves and to present and future generations for the conservation of the planet, as protectors of the natural world and promoters of its continued development, they will be obliged to act in a rational manner in order to ensure sustainable life.

Article 12. Human beings have a continuing responsibility when setting up, taking part in, or representing social units, associations, and institutions, whether private or public. In addition, all such entities have a responsibility to promote peace and sustainability, and to put into practice the educational goals that are conducive to that end. These goals include the fostering of awareness of the interdependence of human beings among themselves and with nature and the universal responsibility of individuals to solve the problems they have engendered through their attitudes and actions in a manner that is consistent with the protection of human rights and fundamental freedoms.

*Let us be faithful to the privilege
of our responsibility.*

Toward a Universal Civilization with a "Heart"

Brother Wayne Teasdale

Christian monk and sannyasi in the lineage of Father Bede Griffiths, author of books and numerous essays on mysticism, Christian Vedanta, and other topics

There is a longing that stirs deep within all of us, innate to the human family, found in every nation, culture, every religious tradition, in the ancient myths, in poetry, song, and historical experience. It is the inspiration behind them all—the desire for the paradisal state of life, the beatitude of the perfect society. Whether it is conceived as a garden of heavenly delights, a pure utopian state, or a more realistic process that brings transformation of society gradually over many years through a deliberate approach, the desire itself is real; it's in touch with something ultimate, something that is as mysterious as it is inviting.

In this essay I am suggesting that a universal society of a higher order than is presently the case is not only possible, but perhaps inevitable! I will try to show how the culture of peace is related to the emergence of a new civilization, what the foundation of this global society is, and what its characteristic elements are, especially the roles of nonviolence and spirituality.

Remembrances of Paradise

All the myths about the original state of the human condition speak of it in terms that convey a kind of intimacy with the Divine, with Ultimate Reality and mystery. This is clear not only in the Bible, but is also true of the Hindu tradition, especially in the *Bhakti* school, but also, more generally, in every other school of Hindu mysticism. It is equally true of Greek mythology as it is of the experience of indigenous societies of Africa, Australia, and the Americas. It is true, in its way, of Buddhist, Jewish, and Islamic or Sufi mysticism, as it is of Taoism, Confucianism, Shintoism, and Shamanism. In all these forms there is present the faint memory of *beatitude* as a real experience of intimacy with the Source of Being.

As the ancient cultures became more stable and were informed by the spirit of their original revelation experiences, they evolved societies that were deeply peaceful and in a state of inner harmony. This pacific quality is evident in the great pre-Vedic Harappa culture of the Indus Valley. This culture is probably the prototype[1] of the one that arose from the Aryan-Dravidian union. We still do not know the age of the Harappa-Mohenjo-Daro civilization, but the discovery of two seals with the image of a deity seated in the meditation *asana*[2] (posture) suggests a high degree of spiritual awareness coming from the practice of meditation and an attitude of contemplative interiority. It may be that the Harappans were the progenitors of the *rishic* seers of Indian antiquity, and perhaps were the recipients of a primordial revelation from which they learned the cosmic and social harmony that is enshrined in the Vedic notion of *rta*.[3]

Similar to the notion of *rta*, on a social and political level in Chinese history and civilization, is the Confucian ideal of *Ta-t'ung*, the "Great Society," or "Great Commonwealth."[4] It can also be translated as the Great Unity in Common, or simply as the "Great Harmony." I prefer the latter two expressions. China knew centuries of civil peace when her empire was socially and politically cohesive, centuries in which crime and corruption were nearly nonexistent, when relationships within the family, the state, and the society were harmonious. These periods of China's golden ages, for example, the Tang dynasty (A.D. 618–906), were the consequence of the *Ta-t'ung*, when it prevailed.

We also marvel at the example of tolerance and enlightened government of the Buddhist emperor Ashoka, of the Maurya Empire in India, who reigned from 268–233 B.C. His example is often cited as constituting a brilliant star in the constellation of ancient rulers.

In the West, we have the seemingly perfect blueprints of Plato's *Republic* and Thomas More's *Utopia*—seemingly perfect because both of these attempts, though originating in spiritual wisdom, still are somewhat abstract, untried, and so, theoretical, even though they portray societies where genuine justice exists. But it was St. Augustine who, in his monumental *City of God*, his philosophy of history, describes the perfect Christian society, whose foundation is peace, as "the tranquillity of order."[5] He elaborates this order in its highest sense: "The peace of the celestial city (the City of God, Heaven) is the perfectly ordered and harmonious enjoyment of God, and of one another in God."[6] The harmonious order of human society derives from its heavenly archetype, and the basis of the latter realm is this mystical relationship with the divine Source, which is also the end for each of us.

There is also the extremely ancient Tibetan legend of Shambhala, a mystical kingdom hidden away somewhere in or beyond the Himalayas, where a perfect utopia exists. Many of Tibetan Buddhism's secret or esoteric writings are attributed to Shambhala, including the texts associated with the Kalacakra initiation. The Dalai Lama is said to have once remarked: "If so many Kalacakra texts are supposed to have come from Shambhala, how could the country be just a fantasy?"[7]

Whether or not these legends refer to real places, however, they are found in most cultures, and we must garner their spirit, their deep spiritual truth, and apply it to our own attempts at building a new civilization. For all of these myths and treatises are inspired by an intuition that we are meant for something better.

The Parliament vis-à-vis a Universal Society

All memories of paradise and the attempts to create it in this world again point to the possibility and, indeed, the urgency of moving toward this "something better," this new civilization. I believe that we have a unique opportunity today to introduce the possibility of such a new global order as the child of enlightened values and wisdom. The introduction of a new universal civilization, as well as its dissemination, require the permanent collaboration of the world's religions. For just as there can be "no peace on Earth unless there is peace among the religions," as Hans Kung has rightly observed, no advance to an enlightened global order is possible unless these same religions decide to work together. That much seems obvious. How to achieve this kind of sustained cooperation is less obvious.[8]

The logic of our global life and situation with all its complexity and all the international problems we face as a planet, the fact of interdependence on all levels, and our precious and rich pluralism have brought us to this intense moment of focus in history. We are compelled and challenged to leap beyond, transcend, even outgrow our old limits, and become a *new humanity*. This new humanity receives its direction and inspiration from the discovery of our common, larger identity in what Thomas Berry, the eloquent ecological thinker, calls the *Earth Community*.[9] The term suggests a natural commonwealth of species united in the one planetary world, *living* in genuine harmony with one another and with the Earth itself.

I see great potential for the Parliament of the World's Religions to become a significant instrument and catalyst for a new civilization by focusing world attention upon the need and the potential for it. In many ways, the Parliament of 1893, in historical terms, was a prophetic act because—just by happening—it pointed to the need for the religions to have a forum in which they can discover, through trial and error, their common voice and acceptance of a *universal responsibility*[10] for the Earth.

The Parliament in our time represents an historical promise, a unique opportunity to forge ahead towards a deeper sense of our identity as the *Community of Religions* within the Earth Community itself. From this profound realization—that religions constitute a larger reality of community than any one tradition standing alone—we can begin to place the stones in the edifice of the new, enlightened civilization. The Council for a Parliament of the World's Religions and other interfaith organizations, along with the individual religious traditions, the nation-states, the United Nations, and nongovernmental and international organizations, could become essential partners for the actualization of a culture of peace on a global scale. We have a historic responsibility to cast light on this unique and unprecedented opportunity. Thus the prophetic direction of the first Parliament can be realized in our time.

Nonviolence and the Culture of Peace

I am convinced that we must become aware of the culture of peace that is slowly developing within the larger context of the new global civilization. It is unquestionably fundamental to it, one of its enduring pillars. More basic still, and essential to the growth and deep-rootedness of the culture of peace and the new civilization, is the value and attitude of nonviolence. As Mahatma Gandhi, Martin Luther King, and the Dalai Lama well understood, one of the most effective tools in educating for peace is teaching nonviolence.

To set the stage for the introduction of nonviolence as a serious option on a global scale, particularly as we enter into the next century, "The Seville Statement on Violence"[11] (in Chapter 23) presents the highly significant conclusions of an international group of scientists and researchers. Endorsed by UNESCO, "The Seville Statement" offers great and solid hope to the world by underscoring the *good news* that violence is not innate to the human species, that it is a learned behavior, and that, consequently, it can and must be left behind as humans, in effect, unlearn it.

All of us know that we must come to grips with the escalating problem of violence, both in society and in ourselves. It is especially critical that we confront it as it emanates from communities of faith in conflict. Everything would seem to depend on getting violence under control; one way to do this—a way which serves the culture of peace and brings us nearer to the universal civilization—is to make a solid commitment to nonviolence among religions, nations, groups, and persons. In committing ourselves to nonviolence in our individual intentions and actions, and, collectively, through the Parliament and our religious institutions, our international organizations, and our governments, we are making a quantum leap forward.

In his books, Teilhard de Chardin spoke eloquently of the eventual emergence into a higher, planetary consciousness. I believe that we have arrived at the very threshold of this exciting process. We require only the radical, childlike courage and wisdom to walk through that door! In passing through this threshold we assume the responsibility of what is essentially a new commandment for us; that commandment is nonviolence.

Nonviolence is the active living out of peace and the very essence of a culture of peace. It is infinitely more effectual to *be* a concrete example of peace than merely to talk about it. Nonviolence means a sensitivity towards all life, a respect and reverence for it, without exception. Nonviolence—*ahimsa*—is rich and all-embracing as a virtue, an attitude, a habit, and a value. It is at once an active commitment to nonharming in any form, whether physical, emotional, intellectual, social, economic, political, and spiritual. It is also the disposition of gentleness, of humility, of selflessness, and yet includes moral clarity, firmness, patience, perseverance, and openness. Nonviolence is all of these and more. In its ultimate depth of reality, nonviolence is love! Thus it is necessarily not only the basis of a culture of peace—the way to teach peace in the deepest sense—but also the basis of the new universal society, the civilization of love.

With these goals, the North American Board for East-West Dialogue (now called Monastic Interreligious Dialogue) developed and signed the "Universal Declaration on Nonviolence" [12] (reprinted in Chapter 23) with the Dalai Lama. Its primary intention is to be a first step towards a new civilization where violence has no place, and nonviolence, as a value and a practice, is preeminent.

The Shape of the New Civilization

In this space I can offer only the barest of outlines of the future global society: It will require a new metaphysics, cosmology, theology, ethics, and, of course, a new way to conduct economics and politics. On the social level, in the relationship of the various religious traditions to one another, and in the interest of peace among the traditions, this planetary society will be established firmly on the insight that the community of religions is the primary religious organization of humankind.

Spirituality is the soul of this civilization, and what will animate it. For it is spirituality that unites us all on the deepest level, and each one of us has some kind of personal spirituality. As a universal tradition of wisdom and an individual process of inner development, as the unfolding and flowering in relationship to Ultimate Reality and as the fruits of this inner process reflected in one's life, spirituality is the foundation of the new civilization's culture and vitality. The universal spirituality of humankind emphasizes the mystical awareness of unity as the essence of enlightenment, whether conceived or experientially understood as *Advaita*, Nirvana, *Dzogchen*, *Satori*, *Fana*, or the Unitive Life. This intense and ultimate awareness of unity is the ground of genuine solidarity in the evolving universal tradition of wisdom.

The moral[13] foundations of the new civilization include the values of love, compassion, nonviolence, empathy, respect for pluralism, justice, courage, respect for human rights, and for the rights of all species, and solidarity. The new civilization also relies upon personal commitment to universal responsibility, especially as this embraces the total Earth Community, its environmental needs and values, the guarding of justice, and making peace.

The social, political, material, and economic foundations[14] of a new culture lie in the balance between the individual's rights and those of the Earth Community. The common well-being is the basis of personal well-being, but personal well-being guides the interpretation of communal welfare. Society exists for the person—for his or her protection and development, but equally, the person has a responsibility to the Earth Community always to consider the larger welfare of the whole, and always to live in harmony with it.[15]

A Universal Order of *Sannyasa*

Finally, I'd like to offer one last vision: the creation of a universal order of *sannyasa*, an order of mystics or contemplatives coming from all the great world religions that possess a mystical life and teaching. This would not be a new form of elitism, for it would be open to all who have the desire and the potential for spiritual development within and, perhaps, beyond their traditions and to those who are open to integrating insights and experiences from other traditions.

In the Sanskrit of the Hindu tradition, *sannyasa* means renunciation: of desire, wealth, power, sex, and oneself. The purpose of this great renunciation that the renunciate, monk, or nun makes is to be free to go in quest of the Absolute. In an essential way, the *sannyasi* stands beyond all formal religion while still being loyal to and rooted in his or her own tradition. In this usage, "beyond" religion means that the *sannyasi* knows interiorly that Ultimate Reality cannot be circumscribed by theological formulations. In the inner awareness he or she transcends the limits of understanding. So, in this essential way, the *sannyasi* is "beyond."

Since the 17th century there has been a Christian form of *sannyasa*, and it has been growing steadily in India during the course of this century. This proposal suggests the extension of *sannyasa* to the other traditions as a spiritually uniting medium, though not a formally synthetic act of integration. Its primary purpose would be to promote peace among the members of the community of religions, not confusion or syncretism. A universal order of *sannyasa* could, thus, be profoundly beneficial to interreligious dialogue, encounter, and reconciliation.

A Civilization with Heart

Solutions to humankind's problems must originate in and flow from the heart, from an inner change of attitude and direction. Although the intellect will make its contribution, our problem is not one of understanding. We all grasp the crisis of our planet in its many facets. Our problem, rather, is one of will: the capacity to change before it's too late for our beloved Earth. Together, the religions have the immense challenge of *inspiring* this will to change in the human family. Building the culture of peace is a major step toward a new civilizational reality that is truly global in scope, universal in culture, and informed by our ultimate values. The culture of peace is the ambience of this new global society, this civilization with a heart.

We are all collaborators in the construction of this civilization. In this great labor, the emergence of a permanent forum for the world's religions is an absolute necessity and an urgent responsibility to which, I believe, the Spirit calls us in our time of monumental transition. In view of this necessity and responsibility, the existing interfaith organizations should work together with the religions and other organizations, disciplines, and institutions, to see to it that some such entity becomes a permanent reality. We must seize the initiative to make it happen.

Let us realize the historic opportunity we are being offered; the emerging forum of the world's religions will provide a place for all of us who wish to serve the Earth Community. The question comes to this: can we model in ourselves, for the sake of the world, that quality of dynamic change so indispensable to our planet? Much depends on the answer we give to this question.

NOTES

1 See Mircea Eliade, *Yoga: Immortality and Freedom*, Bollingen Series, Princeton Univ. Press, 1969, pp. 353–358.

2 Ibid., pp. 355–356.

3 For a profound and comprehensive study of *rta*, see Jeanine Miller, *The Vision of Cosmic Order in the Vedas*, Routledge & Kegan Paul, London, 1985.

4 Dun J. Li, *The Essence of Chinese Civilization*, Von Nostrand, New York, 1967, p. 109. See also K'ang Yu-wei (1858–1927), a modern Confucian thinker, especially his *Ta-t'ung shu* (*Book of Great Unity*), Peking, 1956.

5 S. Augustinus, *De Civitate Dei*, bk. 19, ch. 13.

6 Ibid.

7 Edwin Bernbaum, *The Way to Shambhala: A Search for the Mythical Kingdom beyond the Himalayas*, Tarcher, Los Angeles, 1989, p. 27.

8 Hans Küng, "No Peace in the World without Peace among Religions," *World Faiths Insight*, New Series 21, Feb. 1989, p. 14.

9 Thomas Berry, *The Dream of the Earth*, Sierra Club Books, San Francisco, 1988 cf. ch. 2, "The Earth Community," pp. 6–12.

10 The term *universal responsibility* is the Dalai Lama's. He has been and is popularizing it. See, for instance, his *Global Community and the Need for Universal Responsibility*, Wisdom Pub., Boston, 1992.

11 Reproduced in Chapter 23 of this book, "The Seville Statement on Violence" was written in 1986 by an international group of scientists for the UN, and was adopted by UNESCO in 1989. See *The Seville Statement on Violence: Preparing the Ground for Peace*, ed. David Adams, UNESCO, Paris, 1991.

12 All documentation relating to the "Universal Declaration on Nonviolence" is with Sister Katherine Howard, OSB, Committee for the Universal Declaration, St. Benedict's Convent, St. Joseph, MN 56374–0277.

13 Some beginnings have been made here by the UN and various interfaith organizations, i.e., The International Association for Religious Freedom, Temple of Understanding, Anuvrat Global Organization, World Conference on Religion and Peace, Monastic Interreligious Dialogue, etc. These groups and others have all generated documents or statements of principles. See Marcus Braybrooke's *Stepping Stones to a Global Ethic*, SCM Press, London, 1992.

14 Two important books here are E. F. Schumacher's *Small Is Beautiful: Economics As If People Mattered*, Harper & Row, New York, 1973, and the less known, but significant work by Gerald and Patricia Mische, *Toward a Human World Order*, Paulist Press, 1977.

15 Mention should also be made of the role of the media, especially journalism, which must exercise a greater sense of responsibility, always keeping in mind the common good of the entire Earth Community. It cannot be a tool of special interests, nor operate in isolation from the guiding values of a universal society. The media has to become more accountable to the community through a process of self-regulation, that is, imposed on it by its own standards of enlightened journalism.

New Roles for Religious Nongovernmental Organizations

Joel Beversluis

The past few decades have seen a considerable increase in the number and effectiveness of nongovernmental organizations affiliated with the United Nations. Although the common image of the United Nations depicts the Security Council, the General Assembly, and a few high-profile events and crises, much more goes on behind the scenes in numerous agencies, in the creation of many important treaties, declarations, conferences, and in programs of action such as education, health, commerce, development, and relief. It is in these diverse activities that NGOs have greatly increased their value and influence at the UN.

Background

The Benchmark Survey of NGOs notes that, as they were originally conceived in the UN Charter discussions, NGOs were to be recognized only by the Economic and Social Council of the UN as important participants in considering issues before that Council. (ECOSOC still serves the function at the UN of granting "consultative status" to those who apply for it and are qualified.) In subsequent years, when large numbers of NGOs began arriving at conferences with their own agendas, and making their presence felt through counter-conferences, demonstrations, and parallel events, other UN agencies and venues began to open up to their contributions.

During the '70s, special arrangements allowed some experts and individuals from leading NGOs to participate in specialized conferences and staff planning meetings. Some NGOs began providing important services such as background data, in-house news services, and even the monitoring of Member States and reporting back to intergovernmental agencies regarding compliance on matters such as human

rights conventions. NGO expertise is valued by agencies such as the World Heath Organization; the Bergen conference on sustainable development employed the consensus of governments, business, labor, youth, and environmental organizations. In 1993, for the first time in its eighteen-year history, the United Nations Non-Governmental Liaizon Service (NGLS) received explicit recognition from the UN General Assembly as well as a financial contribution from the UN's regular budget. This move makes NGLS a jointly financed activity of the UN system and reflects the UN's increased commitment to NGO participation in its work.

Roles and Importance of the NGOs

Dr. Keith Suter has identified a number of important roles of NGOs (in *Global Change*, Albatross Books, 1992, Australia):

1. NGOs investigate and identify problem areas, as an early warning system that brings data to public attention.

2. NGOs generate ideas and then advocate and promote them widely, as an important educational medium.

3. NGOs lobby governments to change their own policies and to influence the policies of other governments.

4. NGOs provide services and model behaviors unrestrained by the self-interested boundaries of national sovereignty.

5. NGOs provide citizens with opportunities for service, self-help, and the expression of personal commitments on a global scale.

6. NGOs represent people or issues which otherwise have no voice or power at national or international levels.

7. NGOs offer new methods of addressing and settling international issues.

"We the People ..."

Women's NGOs and caucuses are especially credited for helping to shape the new roles and influence of all NGOs. Their effective work since the mid-1970s on the International Women's Conferences (in '75, '80, '85, and '95), the Decade for Women, the Earth Summit, and at the Cairo Conference on Population and Development, as well as at numerous smaller conferences and preparatory meetings, has helped to bring a whole new power base into the United Nations.

This democratic power is expressed in the service of dedicated advocates based in nongovernmental organizations, representing not governments or profit-oriented groups but "we the people," whose loyalties are quite often transnational and altruistic. There are now well over ten thousand NGOs worldwide who represent concerns that cross national boundaries; some of these are affiliated with the UN.

While some of these NGOs are sponsored by business, professional, or political associations, others represent educational, disaster relief, or development organizations; still others are focused on critical global issues—human rights, environment, population, disarmament, hunger, children-at-risk, medical and health care, peace, justice, or social concerns. Within this mix, religiously based and motivated NGOs have always been present; since the founding of the UN, they have brought their own combinations of altruism, values, worldviews, and perspectives; they may also bring highly politicized or ideological agendas.

Religiously Based NGOs

In the mid-1990s, several historic circumstances and developments provided religious NGOs with new opportunities within the United Nations. They may now take advantage of the end of the Cold War and the collapse of the most powerful antireligious state. Religious NGOs also are seeing new needs arising among global issues and are identifying new ways that religious and spiritual traditions may respond to these issues out of their traditional wisdom and values. In addition, the environmental, population, and social summits, and the new emphases on interreligious cooperation and global ethics, are providing religions and their NGOs with a new image in the international community.

There are numerous religiously based NGOs func-

tioning within the UN community (some of these are annotated in the Directory at the end of this *Sourcebook*). They also come together in several interfaith forums. The Temple of Understanding, the World Conference on Religion and Peace, and the International Association for Religious Freedom have provided excellent interfaith leadership at the UN. NGOs such as the Brahma Kumaris, the Bahá'ís, the National Council of Churches, the Won Buddhist Association and many others have also contributed their energies and resources to many projects. Collaborative forums for religious and like-minded NGOs include the Association of Religious NGOs, the NGO Committee on Freedom of Religion or Belief, and the Values Caucus, which formed around the desire to have an impact at the UN Summit on Social Development and beyond.

Religions and spiritual traditions have many new opportunities to be active in the international arena. They may act individually, but they also are discovering the value of interreligious cooperation in the NGO processes at the UN as well as locally and regionally. The transnational and transethnic memberships of religions and spiritual traditions, their ethical base, and their potential for providing much-needed leadership to their congregations offers them an unprecedented and historic role in good governance and in the creation of cultures of peace.

Prayers, Scriptures, and Reflections on Peace

A Native American Prayer

Let us know peace.
For as long as the moon shall rise,
For as long as the rivers shall flow,
For as long as the sun will shine,
For as long as the grass shall grow,
Let us know peace.

A CHEYENNE INDIAN

A Jewish Teaching

In that hour when the Egyptians died in the Red Sea,
the ministers wished to sing the song of praise before the
Holy One, but he rebuked them saying:

> *"My handiwork is drowning in the sea;*
> *would you utter a song before me in honor*
> *of that?"*

—from the Sanhedrin

A Buddhist Reflection

Now under the loving kindness and care of the Buddha, each
believer of religion in the world transcends the differences of
religion, race and nationality, discards small differences and
unites in oneness to discuss sincerely how to annihilate strife
from the earth, how to reconstruct a world without arms,
and how to build welfare and peace of mankind, so that
never-ending light and happiness can be obtained for the
world of the future.

May the Lord Buddha give His loving-kindness and blessing
to us for the realization of our prayers.

—from Buddhist Prayers in Religion for
Peace, 1973, WCRP

A Hindu Prayer

May the winds, the oceans, the herbs, the nights and days,
the mother earth, the father heaven, all vegetation, the sun,
be all sweet to us.

Let us follow the path of goodness for all times, like the sun
and the moon moving eternally in the sky.
Let us be charitable to one another.
Let us not kill or be violent with one another.
Let us know and appreciate the points of view of others.

And let us unite.

May the God who is friendly, benevolent, all-encompassing,
measurer of everything, the sovereign, the lord of speech, may
He shower His blessings on us. . . .

Oh Lord, remove my indiscretion and arrogance; control my
mind. Put an end to the snare of endless desires. Broaden the
sphere of compassion and help me to cross the ocean of existence.

—excerpted from Hindu Prayers
in Religion for Peace, 1973, WCRP

A Christian Promise

In the tender compassion of our God,
the dawn from heaven will break upon us,
to shine on those who live in darkness,
under the shadow of death,
and to guide our feet into the way of peace.

—from "Song of Zechariah," Luke 1:78–79

A Taoist Teaching

I have three precious things that I hold fast and prize.

The first is gentleness; the second is frugality; the third is
humility, which keeps me from putting myself before others.

Be gentle, and you can be bold; be frugal, and you can be
liberal; avoid putting yourself before others, and you can
become a leader of men.

Gentleness brings victory to him who attacks, and safety to
him who defends.

Those whom Heaven would save, it fences round with
gentleness.

The greatest conquerors are those who overcome their
enemies without strife.

LAO TSU

A Bahá'í Teaching

When love is realized and the ideal spiritual bonds unite the hearts of men, the whole human race will be uplifted, the world will continually grow more spiritual and radiant, and the happiness and tranquillity of mankind be immeasurably increased.

Warfare and strife will be uprooted, disagreement and dissension pass away, and Universal Peace unite the nations and peoples of the world.

All mankind will dwell together as one family, blend as the waves of one sea, shine as stars of one firmament, and appear as fruits of the same tree.

This is the happiness and felicity of humankind.
This is the illumination of man, the glory eternal and life everlasting; this is the divine bestowal.
      'ABDU'L-BAHÁ

A Jain (Universal) Prayer for Peace

Lead me from Death to Life,
from Falsehood to Truth.

Lead me from Despair to Hope,
From Fear to Trust.

Lead me from Hate to Love,
From War to Peace.

Let Peace fill our Heart, our World, Our Universe.
      SATISH KUMAR

A Sikh Prayer

May the kingdom of justice prevail!
May the believers be united in love!
May the hearts of the believers be humble,
high their wisdom,
and may they be guided in their wisdom by the Lord.

O Khalsa, say "Wahiguru, Glory be to God!" . . .
Entrust unto the Lord what thou wishest to be accomplished.
The Lord will bring all matters to fulfillment:
Know this as truth evidenced by Himself.
      —excerpted from Sikh Prayers
            in *Religion for Peace*, 1973, WCRP

A Shinto Prayer

O Most High, help to bring thy Light into the darkened conditions of the world!

Be gracious to us thy humble servants and bless us with illumination as to that which is Divinely relevant to the fulfillment of thy will!

O Most High, inspire thy servants throughout the world to further efforts towards leading back thy children who are led astray to the right way, and to live and act on the faith of what has been taught by the great founders of the religions!

Bless all spiritual leaders with thy power and enable them to give help, joy, comfort and reassurance to those suffering, to whom they minister!
      —from Shinto Prayers in *Religions for Peace*, 1973, WCRP

Islamic Prayer

Oh God, You are Peace.
From You comes Peace,
To You Returns Peace.
Revive us with a salutation of Peace,
and lead us to your abode of Peace.
      —a saying from *The Prophet*,
            used in daily prayer by Muslims

A Zoroastrian Prayer

With bended knees, with hands outstretched, do I yearn for the effective expression of the holy spirit working within me:
            For this love and understanding, truth and justice;
            for wisdom to know the apparent from the real
            that I might alleviate the sufferings of men on earth. . . .

God is love, understanding, wisdom and virtue.
Let us love one another, let us practice mercy and forgiveness, let us have peace, born of fellow-feeling. . . .

Let my joy be of altruistic living, of doing good to others. Happiness is unto him from who happiness proceeds to any other human being.

RESPONSE:

We will practice what we profess.
      —excerpted from the Avesta Prayer
            in *Religion for Peace*, 1973, WCRP

Chapter Twenty-six
RELIGIONS, ECOLOGY, AND SPIRITUALITY

NOTE: The environmental issues of the late 20th and early 21st century have played an increasingly significant role in the interfaith and religious communities. Many of the "critical issues" discussed at the Parliaments in the '90s and other interfaith conferences, beginning in the early '80s, focused on responses of religious and spiritual communities to the ecological questions of our time. The articles and documents in this chapter, along with prayers and reflections drawn from religious communities, demonstrate the conviction that environmental issues are not only of scientific and economic impact but are equally of religious and spiritual concern.

Signed by numerous scientists, the following "Letter" was facilitated and disseminated in 1989–1990 by the Joint Appeal in Religion & Science. Out of these efforts grew the coalition now known as the National Religious Partnership on the Environment, or NRPE, a coalition of four major faith groups serving more than 100 million Americans. Member groups of NRPE include the U.S. Catholic Conference, the National Council of Churches of Christ, the Evangelical Environmental Network, and the Coalition on the Environment and Jewish Life. NRPE's mission is to offer a distinctively religious response linking issues of environmental protection and social justice.

Preserving and Cherishing the Earth—A Joint Appeal in Religion and Science

AN OPEN LETTER TO THE RELIGIOUS COMMUNITY FROM THE SCIENTIFIC COMMUNITY

The Earth is the birthplace of our species and, as far as we know, our only home. When our numbers were small and our technology feeble, we were powerless to influence the environment of our world. But today, suddenly, almost without anyone's noticing, our numbers have become immense and our technology has achieved vast, even awesome, powers. Intentionally or inadvertently, we are now able to make devastating changes in the global environment—an environment to which we and all other beings with which we share the Earth are meticulously and exquisitely adapted.

We are now threatened by self-inflicted, swiftly moving environmental alterations about whose long-term biological and ecological consequences we are still painfully ignorant: depletion of the protective ozone layer; a global warming unprecedented in the last 150 millennia; the obliteration of an acre of forest every second; the rapid-fire extinction of species; and the prospect of a global nuclear war which would put at risk most of the population of the Earth. There may well be other such dangers of which we are still unaware. Individually and cumulatively, they represent a trap being set for the human species, a trap we are setting for ourselves. However principled and lofty (or naive and shortsighted) the justifications may have been for the activities that brought forth these dangers, separately and taken together they now imperil our species and many others. We are close to committing—many would argue we are already committing—what in religious language is sometimes called "Crimes against Creation."

By their very nature these assaults on the environment were not caused by any one political group or any one generation. Intrinsically, they are transnational, transgenerational and transideological. So are all conceivable solutions. To escape these traps requires a perspective that embraces the peoples of the planet and all the generations yet to come.

Problems of such magnitude, and solutions demanding so broad a perspective, must be recognized from the outset as having a religious as well as a scientific dimension. Mindful of our common responsibility, we scientists—many of us long engaged in combatting the environmental crisis—urgently appeal to the world religious community to commit, in word and deed, and as boldly as is required, to preserving the environment of the Earth.

Some of the short-term mitigations of these dangers—such as greater energy efficiency, rapid banning of chloro-fluorocarbons, or modest reductions in nuclear arsenals—are comparatively easy and at some level are already underway. But other, more far-reaching, long-term, and effective approaches will encounter widespread inertia, denial, and resistance. In this category are conversion from fossil fuels to a nonpolluting energy economy, a continuing swift reversal of the nuclear arms race and a voluntary halt to world population growth—without which many other approaches to preserve the environment will be nullified.

As with issues of peace, human rights, and social justice, religious institutions can be a strong force here, too, in encouraging national and international initiatives in both the private and public sectors, and in the diverse worlds of commerce, education, culture, and mass communications.

The environmental crisis requires radical changes not only in public policy, but also in individual behavior. The historical record makes clear that religious teaching, example, and leadership are able to influence personal conduct and commitment powerfully.

As scientists, many of us have had profound experiences of awe and reverence before the universe. We understand that what is regarded as sacred is more likely to be treated with care and respect. Our planetary home should be so regarded. Efforts to safeguard and cherish the environment need to be infused with a vision of the sacred. At the same time, a much wider and deeper understanding of science and technology is needed. If we do not understand the problem, it is unlikely we will be able to fix it. Thus, there is a vital role for both religion and science.

We know that the well-being of our planetary environment is already a source of profound concern in your councils and congregations. We hope this appeal will encourage a spirit of common cause and joint action to help preserve the Earth.

Spiritual Dimensions of the Environmental Crisis

Dr. Daniel Gomez-Ibanez

Executive Director, The Peace Council and formerly of the Council for a Parliament of the World's Religions, Dr. Gomez-Ibanez first presented this essay at an interfaith meeting in 1990. The insights offered here have informed his work at the Parliament, with the declaration Towards a Global Ethic, *and with the Peace Council.*

In the spirit of interreligious understanding, I wish to begin this discussion of the critical issue of environment, and its relationship to spiritual matters, with a Sanskrit invocation from the *Vedas*. I ask those of you who are not Hindus to understand that any invocation must arise from one tradition or another, and to reflect on the relevance of these words for your own tradition or to reflect on their meaning for the earth and for those of us who would restore it to health. This is a chant for peace from the *Yajur Veda*.

Om
Dyauh Shantir Antariksham Shantih
Prithivii Shantir Aapah Shantir
Oshadayah Shantih Vanaspatayah Shantir
Vishvedevaah Shantir Brahma Shantis
Sarvam Shanti Shantireva Shanti
Saa Maa Shantiredhi

Yajur Veda 36, 17

May there be peace in the heavens,
peace in the skies and peace on earth.
May the waters be peaceful.
May the grasses and herbs bring peace to all creatures,
and may the plants be at peace also.
May the beneficent beings bring us peace,
and may the way of all creation bring peace throughout the world.
May all things be peaceful,
and may that peace itself bring further peace.
May we also bring peace to all.

The attention given to the environment has varied enormously over the last few decades. In 1990, however, over 100 million people observed Earth Day and in some way gave thanks for the earth, which sustains us all. One hundred million people are about 2 percent of humankind—more than enough to start a revolution! Since then, newspapers and television networks of all political shades have been featuring the plight of the earth, and this ten-year period is widely held to be the decade of the environment.

We have made some progress since 1970. The rate of growth of the earth's population has begun to slow down, although the numbers of people added each year—nearly 90 million this year—are unprecedented and still rising. The United Nations predicts that the total world population will stabilize around the end of the 21st century at somewhere between 8 and 13 billion persons.[1] The margin of error is about the same as the present population of the world: 5 billion persons. It is in the developing countries that population growth will be greatest and where increasing demand for energy and material goods will put enormous strains on the earth's resources of air, water, and soil. Twenty years ago, leaders in those nations often voiced the cynical attitude that the environmental concerns of the industrialized nations were yet another ploy to keep the developing regions in a state of subjugation. But today that attitude is giving way to the realization that environmental problems are indeed a threat to every country and perhaps especially threatening to the welfare of developing regions.

In wealthy countries, people now nearly unanimously say they support environmental causes. In the United States, 80 percent of those questioned in a June 1989 New York Times/CBS News poll agreed that protecting the environment is so important "that requirements and standards cannot be too high and continuing environmental improvements must be made regardless of cost." Forty-three percent had agreed with the statement in September 1981.[2] Laws protecting the environment have been passed in most developed countries, and in Germany the Green Party has significantly changed the political landscape, if not yet the physical landscape. Even the normally conservative and complacent business community is awakening to environmental issues. Articles about the environment appear frequently in periodicals such as Business Week, Fortune, Forbes, The Economist, and the Wall Street Journal.

Despite these encouraging signs, by most measures we have failed during the last twenty years to improve the health of the planet on which we all depend. The rate of extinction of species has quickened, not slowed. At least two or three species are lost irretrievably each day. Not only are we strangling the creation's genetic diversity, but entire ecosystems are being ravaged. Deforestation and erosion are destroying the once pristine Himalayas. Deserts are spreading in Africa south of the Sahara. We are losing twenty hectares of tropical forest each minute—an area the size of Ohio every year. The rate is increasing. Eighty percent of all Amazonian deforestation has occurred in the last ten years.[3]

In industrialized regions, forests, lakes, and fields suffer increasingly from acid precipitation. There have been ominous decreases in crop and forest yields recently. Production, consumption, and dissipation of toxic chemicals have increased since 1970. We have a landfill crisis, an ocean dumping crisis, and an air quality crisis. The energy efficiency of Western economies increased during the last two decades, but after a brief slowdown around 1980, overall energy use continued to climb. Carbon emissions from fossil fuels increased worldwide by about 40 percent between 1970 and 1990.[4] The increase in atmospheric carbon dioxide may be causing significant global warming. We may not know enough about the earth's climate to know exactly what we are doing to it, but many scientists are deeply concerned. In my opinion, the uncertainty itself is cause for concern, and restraint is the prudent response.

And finally, as if these and other assaults on life were not enough, global spending on weapons and military activities has nearly doubled (in constant dollars) in twenty years. Each year we spend about 1 trillion dollars on arms which, if ever they were used, would lay waste to the entire biosphere.[5] We should be spending the money instead on healing the earth; and if we are to survive, we soon will need to do so.

These threats to creation are not just numerous or widespread, they encompass the whole ecosphere, and this emergence of the universal scale of our influence is what distinguishes our activities from those of previous generations. The natural resources we are consuming are no longer simply local, such as deposits of minerals, or tracts of forest, prairie, or marsh. They now include the global reserves of air, water, soil, and genetic material on which we all depend.

Furthermore, our environmental problems are intertwined with and in a real sense indistinguishable from the other great afflictions of the world: the divisions which wound the human community, such as racism, sexual discrimination, or xenophobic nationalism; the grotesque coexistence of affluence and poverty; the prevalence of all kinds of violence, oppression, and exploitation; and the alienation of individuals: these ills, like our environmental problems, all have common origins in the vision which increasingly has guided human affairs during the last two centuries.

In most of our daily affairs, in our prognoses for the human condition and in prescriptions for making the world a better place to live in, we accept or assume this vision. It is the vision in which material progress produces increasing happiness and well-being.

For millennia people have had faith in progress, or at least believed that progress was the birthright of humankind, but it is only relatively recently that we have come to associate progress almost exclusively with increases in *material* prosperity. When the great teachers of the world—Christ, Buddha, Mohammed, Krishna, Confucius, LaoTzu, and others—point the way to joy and fulfillment, they are not talking about money and material goods, but today these have become the nearly universal talismans of goodness and wealth. In the Sermon on the Mount, Christ puts the issue clearly, but few have listened. "... Where your treasure is, there will your heart be also."[6]

Many individuals understand that spiritual growth brings greater freedom and more lasting happiness than material growth, but as a society we are reluctant to admit that premise in our collective, corporate, or political debates on the purposes of society or the future of the world.

A result of this vision of a purely material prosperity is that we usually use material, that is economic, criteria to allocate worldly resources. The familiar concepts of economics—calculations of costs and benefits, rent, the laws of supply and demand, rights of property (ownership), the concept of a free market—are defended in the delusion that an economy somehow operates independently of cultural or spiritual biases. On the contrary, the economy is an especially clear reflection of our spiritual or metaphysical priorities. One brief example will make this point.

Before the British colonized Nigeria, the land in that part of West Africa was not a commodity. Land was an attribute of the community or kinship group that inhabited it, but it was not property. It could not be owned (in the European sense), much less bought or sold. Land was associated with the group perhaps similarly to the way we associate last names with families. Boundaries were correspondingly fluid. In fact the idea that something so essential as land might be an object of trade was beyond the experience of many non-Western peoples.

Not understanding how the landscape mirrored West African attitudes, the British simply saw this state of affairs as primitive and as a hindrance to economic progress. So they surveyed the land, determined ownership on the basis of occupation, set up a system of *cadastral* records, and issued titles to parcels of land. Suddenly it became possible to own land, to buy and sell it, to use it as collateral, and to enforce rights of property against others. Thinking they had done the Nigerians a great service, the British proceeded to purchase the land for farms and plantations and to develop the colonial economy. The Nigerians reacted with bewilderment. They were dispossessed before they could understand what was happening to them. One can only imagine the social and cultural upheaval which this bit of European "progress" caused. Of course the British assumed that the money they paid Nigerians for the land was appropriate compensation. The whole process was sustained and enforced by the British legal system—another "gift" to the colonies.[7]

European settlers produced a similar effect in North America, though without resorting to the niceties of surveys and titles. Here is the response of Chief Seattle, speaking in 1855: "How can you buy or sell the sky, the warmth of the land? The idea is strange to us. If we do not own the freshness of the air and the sparkle of the water, how can you buy them?"[8]

I give this example simply to make the point that attitudes we take for granted have enormously important consequences for the way we treat the earth and the way we treat each other. Reducing the earth's resources and creatures to the status of commodities has made it difficult to discuss or even to recognize their transcendent values. How does one put a "value" on diversity, or beauty, or life itself, which can somehow be compared with the "values" of the conventional transactions of the marketplace, such as building a road or a factory, or sales of automobiles, television sets, or tuna fish.

Conventional economists assume that markets are indeed able to put a price on sunsets, for example, because people willing to pay for an unobscured view will do so, forcing the factory owner to build elsewhere. But not everyone who wants to see the sunset can afford to buy the view. Further, many potential "customers" have no access to the market, hence no say in determining the sunset's "value," for the simple reason that they have not been born yet. They are the future generations for whom we ought to be holding this beautiful earth in trust. Their welfare, or the beauty they inherit, depends on our willingness to defer our own gratification for the sake of theirs. (Sadly, the marketplace simply mirrors our intentions: in fact many of us heavily discount the future. The proof is our willingness to pay very high rates of interest to be able to satisfy our desires immediately.) A few economists, like Nicholas Georgescu-Roegen, Kenneth Boulding, Herman Daly, and E. F.

Schumacher have worked to construct an economics grounded in environmental realities and designed for a sustainable future, but they are as yet a small voice in the wilderness.[9]

Society's powerful, materialistic vision of progress seems to leave little room for the gentler, more loving vision that also finds a home in us. This is the vision of the heart and spirit we all share: the vision in which progress means caring for creation, for each other, for the earth and the environment we live in; building a peaceful community and world; and living harmoniously together, with fairness and justice. With such a vision we are moved by love.

But the modern, materialistic vision of progress depends on self-interest as the motivation for transactions, rather than love. So it can only be maintained by coercion—usually tacit, sometimes explicit. Coercion is violence to the spirit as well as to creation. Listen to the words of Wendell Berry, written twenty years ago:

> Do we really hate the world? Are we really contemptuous of it? Have we really ignored its nature and its needs and the problems of its health? The evidence against us is everywhere. It is in our wanton and thoughtless misuse of the land and the other natural resources, in our wholesale pollution of the water and air, in strip mining, in our massive use and misuse of residual poisons in agriculture and elsewhere, in our willingness to destroy whole landscapes in the course of what we call "construction" and "progress," in the earth-destroying and population-destroying weapons we use in our wars, in the planet-destroying weapons now ready for use in the arsenals of the most powerful and violent nations of the world. It is in our hatred of races and nations. It is in our willingness to honor profit above everything except victory. It is in our willingness to spend more on war than on everything else. It is in our unappeasable restlessness, our nomadism, our anxiousness to get to another place or to "the top" or "somewhere" or to heaven or to the moon.

Our hatred of the world is most insidiously and dangerously present in the constantly widening discrepancy between our power and our needs, our means and our ends. This is because of machinery and what we call efficiency. In order to build a road we destroy several thousand acres of farmland forever, all in perfect optimism, without regret, believing that we have gained much and lost nothing. In order to build a dam, which like all human things will be temporary, we destroy a virgin stream forever, believing that we have conquered nature and added significantly to our stature. In order to burn cheap coal we destroy a mountain forever, believing, in the way of lovers of progress, that what is of immediate advantage to us must be a permanent benefit to the universe. Fighting in Vietnam in the interest, as we say and would have ourselves believe, of the Vietnamese people, we have destroyed their villages, their croplands, their forests, herded the people into concentration camps, and in every way diminished the possibility of life in that country; and the civilian casualties are vastly greater than the military. In order to protect ourselves against Russia or China, or whoever our enemy will be in ten years, we have prepared weapons the use of which will, we know, involve our own destruction and the destruction of the world as well. Great power has always been blinding to those who wield it.[10]

A great danger in this materialistic and mechanistic view of the universe is that even when we see the problems it has wrought, we often assume that the solutions are to be found only in the same material realm, perhaps because we forget to consider any other possibility. For example, in the many stories on the environment which have appeared in the business press recently, the most frequently cited reasons for our environmental ills are ignorance, inefficiency, misapplied technology, population growth, institutional inertia, and lack of political will. All these reasons are true, but they are symptoms, not the root causes, of our failure to create a friendly and sustainable world.

Similarly, most proposals for cleaning up the environment focus on technical fixes. We want more miles-per-gallon, aerosols, and refrigerants that don't destroy the ozone, more efficient homes and factories, and nontoxic pesticides. All these things will help. We have used science and technology to get us into this predicament and I think we will use science and technology to get us out.

But the greatest help and the only lasting solution to the violence we do to the world and to each other will arise from an ethic based on compassion and love rather than self-interest. Aldo Leopold's vision of a land-ethic is one expression of this truth:

In short, a land ethic changes the role of *Homo sapiens* from conqueror of the land community to plain member and citizen of it. It implies respect for his fellow-members, and also respect for the community as such.[11]

But the hour is late. The signs of our heedlessness, selfishness, and fear are all about us. This beautiful earth, mother to us all, groans beneath the blows. The trends are worrisome rather than reassuring. For the first time in many generations our children are no longer confident of being able to live in a better world. Have we reached the end of hope?

I think not. We only reach the end of hope when we abandon our claim to being whole human beings. If we believe that the future will be simply a projection of past trends, then we yield it and ourselves helplessly to the notion that our destiny has already been determined by the destructive processes we have set in motion.[12]

We cannot assume that only one possible future lies before us without being guilty of idolatry, because to do so would amount to worshipping our present technological civilization, submitting to the thralldom of the machine rather than accepting our responsibility to control it. We would be guilty of forgetting the importance of human consciousness, of divine purposes and transcendent visions which might call us to a different destiny. There are many instances when the path of history has taken an unforeseeable turn because of the passions and convictions of dreamers, heroes, and saints. We stand at such a place today and the earth calls us to recognize and create a new way forward.

Against the strength, even the apparent omnipotence, of the machine, we need to call forth a power that is greater still, the power of compassion and love. In place of self-interest let us cultivate selflessness. We must be willing to restore the primacy of the heart, and to make every intention and action an expression of kindness and love.

In all the world's religions we find the ethic of loving kindness, compassion, and relatedness. In some, this earth and all upon it are sacred because they are created by God: "The earth is the Lord's and the fullness thereof, the world and those who dwell therein..."; or because creation is a reflection of God's glory: "The heavens are telling the glory of God; and the firmament proclaims his handiwork." "O Lord, how manifold are thy works! In wisdom hast thou made them all; the Earth is full of thy creatures."[13]

All creation is part of the divine, only differentiated by our power to respond. From the Hindu *Isha Upanishad*:

The Spirit moves, and it moves not. It is far, and it is near. It is within all, and it is outside all. Who sees all beings in his own Self, and his own Self in all beings, cannot hate. To the seer, all things have truly become the Self. What delusion, what sorrow, can there be for the one who sees this unity?

The words of Black Elk, a holy man of the Oglala Sioux:

My friend, I am going to tell you the story of my life, as you wish; and if it were only the story of my life I think I would not tell it; for what is one man that he should make much of his winters, even when they bend him like a heavy snow? So many other men have lived and shall live that story, to be grass upon the hills.

It is the story of all life that is holy and is good to tell, and of us two-leggeds sharing it with the four-leggeds and the wings of the air and all green things; for these are children of one mother and their father is one Spirit.

And from the great vision he had when he was a boy:

...I was seeing in a sacred manner the shapes of all things in the spirit, and the shape of all shapes as they must live together like one being. And I saw that the sacred hoop of my people was one of many hoops that made one circle, wide as daylight and as starlight, and in the center grew one mighty flowering tree to shelter all the children of one mother and one father. And I saw that it was holy.[14]

Listen again to the voice of Chief Seattle:

Every part of this earth is sacred to my people. Every shining pine needle, every sandy shore, every mist in the dark woods, every clearing and humming insect is holy in the memory and experience of my people.... We are part of the earth and it is part of us. The perfumed flowers are our sisters; the deer, the horse, the great eagle, these are our brothers. The rocky crests, the juices of the meadows, the body heat of the pony, and man—all belong to the same family. . . . What is man without the beasts? If all the beasts were gone, men would die from a great loneliness of spirit. For whatever happens to the beasts, soon happens to man. All things are connected.[15]

Here is a metaphor from Saint Paul: "God has arranged the body so that...each part may be equally concerned for all the others. If one part is hurt, all parts are hurt with it."[16]

Ecologists know that everything is connected to everything else. That is one of Barry Commoner's "four laws of ecology." Other scientists also are moving towards an explanation of the universe as infinitely related. The new science of chaos and the mathematics of fractal geometry draw attention to this essential unity.[17]

Let me borrow a lesson from the teachings of a Buddhist monk, Thich Nhat Hanh:

If you are a poet, you will see clearly that there is a cloud floating in this sheet of paper. Without a cloud, there will be no rain; without rain, the trees cannot grow; and without trees, we cannot make paper. The cloud is essential for the paper to exist. If the cloud is not here, the sheet of paper cannot be here either. So we can say that the cloud and the paper *inter-are*. "Inter-being" is a word that is not in the dictionary yet, but if we combine the prefix "inter-" with the verb "to be," we have a new verb, *inter-be*. Without a cloud, we cannot have paper, so we can say that the cloud and the sheet of paper inter-are.

If we look into this sheet of paper even more deeply, we can see the sunshine in it. If the sunshine is not there, the forest cannot grow. In fact, nothing can grow. Even we cannot grow without sunshine. And so, we know that the sunshine is also in this sheet of paper. The paper and the sunshine *inter-are*. And if we continue to look, we can see the logger who cut the tree and brought it to the mill to be transformed into paper. And we see the wheat. We know that the logger cannot exist without his daily bread, and therefore the wheat that became his bread is also in this sheet of paper. And the logger's father and mother are in it too. When we look in this way, we see that without all of these things, this sheet of paper cannot exist.

Looking even more deeply, we can see we are in it too. This is not difficult to see, because when we look at a sheet of paper, the sheet of paper is part of our perception. Your mind is in here and mine is also. So we can say that everything is in here with this sheet of paper. You cannot point out one thing that is not here—time, space, the earth, the rain, the minerals in the soil, the sunshine, the cloud, the river, the heat. Everything coexists with this sheet of paper. That is why I think the word "inter-be" should be in the dic-

tionary. "To be" is to *inter-be*. You cannot just *be* by yourself, alone. You have to *inter-be* with every other thing. This sheet of paper is, because everything else is.[18]

This lesson on interdependence is at the heart of understanding. (In fact it is part of a commentary on the *Sutra* of the Heart of Wisdom.) Once you begin to see the world in this way, you are forever changed. At first you may think that seeing yourself as one with all that is might put an intolerably heavy burden on you. If everything is everything else, then everyone is responsible for everyone else too; and everyone's suffering is also our own. But this *is* the truth that sets you free, because now you know who you are and what you can do. From this heart of wisdom come compassion and loving-kindness to all.

The violence we wreak on the earth is a kind of hatred done in ignorance, and it comes back to haunt us in many ways. We poison the soil, water, and air, and they in turn poison us. We build terrifying arsenals, and live in fear.

But when we live fully aware of the creation and the web of life in which we humans are but a strand, we will begin to do unto the earth as we would have done unto us. It is ignorance that drives us apart from creation.

When we accept the earth as our home and mother, and all the inhabitants as our kin, then we will be able to find the peace that now eludes us. Black Elk's prayer was "Grandfather, Great Spirit, give me the strength to walk the soft earth, a relative to all that is!"[19]

Our new awareness brings both joy and suffering, because the newfound kinship demands new responsibility. When we accept the responsibility of seeing, we learn how to love. Let me turn to Thich Nhat Hanh again:

At the beginning of each meal, I recommend that you look at your plate and silently recite, "My plate is empty now, but I know that it is going to be filled with delicious food in just a moment." While waiting to be served or to serve yourself, I suggest you breathe three times and look at it even more deeply, "At this very moment many, many people around the world are also holding a plate, but their plate is going to be empty for a long time." Forty thousand children die each day because of the lack of food. Counting children alone. We can be very happy to have such wonderful food, but we also suffer because we are capable of seeing. But when we see in this way, it makes us sane, because the way in front of us is clear—the way to live so that we can make peace with ourselves and with the world. When we see the good and the bad, the wondrous and the deep suffering, we have to live in a way that we can make peace between ourselves and the world.[20]

Seeing more clearly and the transcendence of self are the most fundamental teachings of all religions. Truly to restore the earth we must first restore ourselves. The inner and outer worlds are inseparable. They must be in harmony. Here is the prayer of a Sufi (Muslim) mystic, Ansari of Herat:

Watch vigilantly the state of thine own mind.
Love of God begins in harmlessness.

Know that the Prophet built an external kaaba of clay and water,
And an inner kaaba in life and heart.

The outer kaaba was built by Abraham, the holy;
The inner is sanctified by the glory of God himself.

On the path of God
Two places of worship mark the stages,
The material temple
And the temple of the heart.
Make your best endeavor
To worship at the temple of the heart.[21]

A heedless person cannot bring caring to the world. A fearful person cannot see clearly; a selfish person does not embrace the wholeness of all creation and an angry person does not bring peace to the world. We must ourselves be whole and healthy if we would heal the earth. Its peace begins with ours, at home, in our daily lives, in our peaceful hearts.

The healing of creation will not be accomplished by the judicious application of technology alone, but by a commitment that must be as intense as any religious faith. Our personal commitment to spiritual growth will lead us to ecologically responsible behavior, because it will make clear the interrelatedness of all beings.

In fact caring for creation is a commitment for which the religions of the world provide the essential teachings. Faced with unprecedented global environmental and social crises, the challenge to us all is to recover the meaning of those teachings for today, to renew our kinship with all creation, to restore the primacy of spiritual values and of communal and personal spiritual growth, and to rediscover the simple truths: that there is no separateness and therefore there can be no selfishness, and that compassion for all is the heart of understanding.

NOTES

This essay is adapted from a lecture given on July 21, 1990, at the conference on "Spiritual Values in the Global Village," at Vivekananda Monastery, Ganges, Michigan.

[1] United Nations Department of International Economic and Social Affairs, *World Demographic Estimates and Projections* (New York, 1988), cited in *The Economist*, January 20, 1990.

[2] *The Economist*, September 2, 1989. A poll in April 1990 by the *Wall Street Journal/NBC News* indicated that 86 percent of respondents want to protect the environment even if it means they will have to pay higher prices (*Wall Street Journal*, April 20, 1990).

[3] Lester Brown, et al, *State of the World*, 1990 (New York: Norton, 1990).

[4] Ibid.

[5] Lester Brown, et al, *State of the World*, 1989 (New York: Norton, 1989).

[6] Matthew 6:21.

[7] See Paul Bohannan, "The Impact of Money on an African Subsistence Economy," *Journal of Economic History*, XIX (1959), 491–503; and Paul Bohannan, "Africa's Land," *The Centennial Review*, IV (1960), 439–449.

[8] *Chief Seattle's Testimony* (London: Pax Christi & Friends of the Earth, 1976).

9 Nicholas Georgescu-Roegen, *The Entropy Law and the Economic Process* (Cambridge: Heard University Press, 1971); E. F. Schumacher, *Small Is Beautiful* (New York: Harper, 1973); Herman Daly, ed., *Toward a Steady-State Economy* (San Francisco: Freeman, 1973); Herman Daly, *Steady-State Economics* (San Francisco: Freeman, 1977); and Herman Daly and John Cobb, Jr., *For the Common Good* (Boston: Beacon Press, 1989).

10 Wendell Berry, "A Secular Pilgrimage," in *A Continuous Harmony* (New York: Harcourt Brace Jovanovich, 1975) pp. 10–11.

11 Aldo Leopold, "The Land Ethic" in *A Sand County Almanac* (New York: Ballantine, 1970), p.40.

12 See Lewis Mumford, "Prospect," in W. L. Thomas, ed., *Man's Role in Changing the Face of the Earth* (Chicago: University of Chicago Press, 1956) pp. 1141–1152.

13 From Psalms 24, 19, and 104.

14 John G. Neihardt, *Black Elk Speaks* (New York: Pocket Books, 1972), pp. 1, 36.

15 *Chief Seattle's Testimony.*

16 1 Corinthians, 12:24–26. Christianity has been criticized for emphasizing separation between humans and creation and for teaching that creation is subservient and intended for humankind's use and enjoyment. See Lynn White, Jr., "The Historical Roots of Our Ecologic Crisis," *Science*, v. 155 (1967), pp. 1203–1207. The first two chapters of Genesis appear to support these views, although there are also thoughtful contrary interpretations. The true picture is more complex. Attitudes towards the environment are rooted in the secular culture as well as in religion, and neither the West nor Christianity has any monopoly on environmental damage or disrespect.

The Christian mystical tradition reveals the sense of relatedness and responsibility for creation. From a sermon by Meister Eckhart:

> Though we talk about human beings, we are speaking at the same time of all creatures, for Christ himself said to his disciples: "Go forth and preach the gospel to all creatures." God poured his being in equal measure to all creatures, to each as much as it can receive. This is a good lesson for us that we should love all creatures equally with everything that we have received from God.... So God loves all creatures equally and fills them with his being. And we should lovingly meet all creatures in the same way.

(Matthew Fox, *Breakthrough: Meister Eckhart's Creation Spirituality* in New Translation [New York: Doubleday, Image Books, 1980], p. 92.)

Many Christians are deeply sensitive to the tensions between Christian doctrine and a creation in urgent need of healing. See, for examples: Gerald Barney, "The Future of the Creation: The Central Challenge for Theologians," *Word & World*, v. 4 (1984), pp. 422–429; William E. Gibson, *Keeping and Healing the Creation* (Louisville, Ky.: Presbyterian Church [USA], Eco-Justice Task Force, 1989); Thomas Beny, *The Dream of the Earth* (San Francisco: Sierra Club, 1988); Matthew Fox, *Original Blessing* (Santa Fe, N.M.: Bear, 1983).

17 Barry Commoner, *The Closing Circle* (New York: Knopf, 1971); see also Benoit B. Mandelbrot, *The Fractal Geometry of Nature* (New York: Freeman, 1983); James Gleick, *Chaos* (New York: Viking, 1987).

18 Thich Nhat Hanh, *The Heart of Understanding* (Berkeley, Calif.: Parallax Press, 1988), pp. 3–4. This is a commentary on the *Maha Prajnaparamita Hridaya Sutra*.

19 Neihardt, p. 5.

20 Nhat Hanh, p. 54.

21 Abdullah al-Ansari al-Harawi (d. 1088). This translation is by Sardar Sir Jogendra Singh, quoted in Eknath Easwaran, *God Makes the Rivers to Flow* (Petaluma, Calif.: Nilgiri Press, 1982), p.55.

The Gaia Hypothesis

Joel Beversluis

Most of us sense that the Earth is more than a sphere of rock with a thin layer of air, ocean, and life covering the surface. We feel that we belong here, as if this planet were indeed our home. Long ago, the Greeks, thinking this way, gave to the Earth the name of Gaia.

JAMES LOVELOCK,
The Ages of Gaia

A New Scientific Paradigm and a New Mythology

Despite Greek, pagan, and other indigenous approaches to Earth, for many hundreds of years the intellectual crest of Western civilization has believed and acted on a clear distinction between "dead" earthly matter and the very precious and improbable forms of life. Furthermore, this scientific belief system—a major paradigm of past and present western civilization with clear ties to Judeo-Christian beliefs—has placed humanity at the pinnacle of Earthly life, and perceived all else, alive or not, as arranged for the convenience of humans. This worldview, as many Christians and Jews have pointed out, overlooks some of the wisdom from the biblical tradition, and certainly overlooks other religious traditions; nevertheless, this anthropomorphic view of creation, especially the view that the Earth has no intrinsic value apart from human utility, undergirds our religion, science, industry, and ethical systems.

What is remarkable now, in the midst of technological marvels utilizing those assumptions, is that this view is now undergoing a major set of challenges, both scientific and philosophical. It now seems likely that the perspectives of the "dead Earth," and mechanistic evolutionary theories about the selection and survival of the fittest, are inadequate science. It also seems that the assumptions that generated these beliefs and methods have led us to the disasters that we are now courting, including widespread extinction of countless species of life.

Earth As a Self-Regulating Organism

Many people are reevaluating both the science and some of the underlying assumptions of Western civilization. They include indigenous friends of the Earth and neo-pagans, but also biochemists, atmospheric scientists and climatologists, geologists, geophysicists, eco-philosophers, and activists, as well as advocates of spiritual and mystic traditions. The Gaia Hypothesis, presented to a once-skeptical but now somewhat-interested community of scientists by Dr. James Lovelock, is one focal point of that reevaluation.

Lovelock is a brilliant and highly respected inter-disciplinary scientist with advanced degrees and professorships in medicine, cybernetics, chemistry, marine biology, and atmospheric analysis. In his research he uses state-of-the-art equipment (some of which he invented) to analyze atmospheric, geological, and biochemical conditions. His hypothesis—that Earth functions as though it is a self-regulating organism—is currently undergoing considerable scrutiny by a large and growing body of scientists forced into interdisciplinary studies by his work and its implications.

According to Dr. Michael Cohen, an environmental educator and founder of the National Audubon Society Expedition Institute, and author of *How Nature Works*, the Gaia Hypothesis Symposium sponsored by the National Audubon Society had to turn away more than one hundred prospective speakers. Held at the University of Massachusetts in 1985, the excited synthesis and research of respected scientists, philosophers, and others were recorded in conference proceedings that exceeded 1,300 pages. This major conference explored the startling question: Is the Earth a living organism?

The hypothesis suggests that over a long period, the Earth self-regulates its temperature, atmospheric gas ratios, salinity, chemistry, and geology, utilizing sunlight which it ingests as energy and converts as needed; in short, it functions like a cell. Lovelock doesn't say it *is* one, but that the Earth *behaves* like a living organism. Furthermore,

> All the entities [of the Earth] interact as a whole, like organelles in a cell. Only when [the scientist] separates them or observes them individually for a short time, do they assume different properties including life and death. Long term, in congress, the entities appear to sense and communicate, thereby sustaining the optimum environment for their cell's life (Cohen, *How Nature Works*, p. 78).

Biologist and author Lewis Thomas, in *The Lives of a Cell*, suggests that the atmosphere is the Earth cell's membrane wall as it regulates precise amounts of energy capture, storage, and release.

Life means holding out against equilibrium—banking against entropy by using membranes. The Earth has its own membrane, the atmosphere, to filter the sun. In Lovelock's words,

> The biota—the sum of all living things, including plants, animals, and microorganisms—not only profoundly affects the Earth's environment, but acts to maintain and enhance life on the planet (*Gaia: A New Look at Life*).

Despite Entropy

Some evidence suggests that the systems of Earth are preserved by life-enhancing direction in response to circumstances, despite the apparent laws of chemistry and of entropy. Examples include the following: Earth's many atmospheric gases do not settle into a lifeless equilibrium; oxygen levels remain a constant, life-enhancing 21 percent by means of the photosynthesis of countless organisms; planetary temperatures tend to remain constant, maintained not only by clouds and carbon dioxide, but by the actions of micro-organisms in the oceans in an extensive interdependent network of geology, biology, and chemistry; the massive excess of poisonous carbon now stored (buried) in the Earth in the form of oil and coal, as well as other signs of the control of dis-equilibrium suggest that unidentified regulating mechanisms are at work on a global scale, with the apparent purpose of the maintenance of life.

From Hypothesis to Mythology

There is much more to the hypothesis and its debate than I comprehend or can present in this introduction. I'm not able to confirm or critique its science, though that also has its critics. I can appreciate the hypothesis, however, as part of a new metaphor for Earth, as contributing to the story of a new relationship with it. The bottom line here is, What difference does it make to us or to Earth's survival?

At the simplest level, as we learn more about the processes of regulation and adaptation, we may be heartened somewhat by the possibility that we could get unexpected help from Earth as it self-regulates the biosphere. On the other hand, we are also learning how complex the interconnections are, and how serious is the damage that we are doing to those regulating mechanisms. Perhaps we will learn how to work *with* the Earth in processes it once performed autonomously. Certainly, we can better learn to anticipate new causes of damage.

We are learning that Gaia may be resilient, but we also see that we are changing nature, permanently. Increasingly, acts of nature are not "acts of God," but of humanity or, we might say, *inhumanity*. Nature is no longer an independent and autonomous force, and it's no longer true that "everybody talks about the weather, but nobody does anything about it." We are, in fact, doing much about it; for instance, recent storms that have ripped into the Caribbean and southeastern U.S. coasts, and across Asian islands and continents, are increasing in intensity as a direct result of the oceans' warming. As the band of warm water in which such storms incubate widens and deepens, the size of the storms increases, and the power of the wind increases geometrically. It is most likely not coincidence but rather human intervention which has brought us in the last fifteen years many of the most destructive tropical storms ever recorded.

Stewards or Pirates?

In response to the Gaia paradigm, we may learn to see Earth-life as inherently valuable; we are coming to see ourselves as part of a whole system, not above it or separate from it. We can, if we accept that place in it, reestablish our role as stewards of the Earth rather than as abusive, short-term tenants, owners, or profiteers.

Another impact of Lovelock's hypothesis and subsequent responses to it is that the mechanistic sciences are forced to reevaluate their methodologies of specialization and reductionism. It is becoming apparent that holistic, interdisciplinary approaches are crucial to an accurate understanding of the larger picture. Much current science and technology is revealed as inadequate when it appears that a deeper system and apparent "purpose" drive the interconnected forces of evolution, geology, and atmospheric balances.

At the level of popular culture and religion, the hypothesis will encourage appreciation for the relationship of indigenous peoples to Earth. Within Christianity, the Gaia hypothesis can revitalize the appreciation of what it has called "Natural Revelation," reinforcing its wisdom that Earth and life are created blessings and are themselves revelation from God, and that, at our best, we are gardeners or stewards of Earth. Within the wider culture, the Gaian mythology and derivative Earth stories may play a role in the conversion of secular cultures to new appreciation for various forms of creation spirituality.

One unexpected consequence of the theory is the assessment—or *hope*, in the face of despair— that the Earth's restorative abilities are to some extent counteracting the damage we do. As Stephen Scharper notes in "The Gaia Hypothesis," the Gaia theory offers an inspiring vision of interrelatedness, but "it may also diminish the human by neglecting our ability to build the world—or to destroy it."

Nature, Gaia, or God?

Some purely scientific proponents of the hypothesis resist referring to any source of power or purpose outside of Earth itself, claiming that, since Earth and life-forms are the only knowable objects of our science, they also represent the proper limits of reflection. Those who are agnostic, atheist, or who insist on separating their science from metaphysics, are uncomfortable with speculative thinking about God or spiritual powers. It may well be that their science suffers rather than gains from those self-imposed blinders.

Religious people of numerous traditions have always maintained that Earth-life and visible creation have origins and direction from outside of this system. From the perspective of logic, it is equally reasonable for humans to believe in transcendent sources of life and purpose as it is to believe that all the intelligent direction, interaction, and apparent

self-regulation within Nature have evolved autonomously on Earth, out of primordial chaos. While the "scientific" approach claims to believe only in what it can prove, it too requires a substantial leap of faith when it claims that what it can't prove doesn't exist.

The Gaia hypothesis, along with other personal and species-wide inclinations, may help nudge science and our modern cultures back to the concept that a directive energy is functioning within Earth's systems. The witness of many religious traditions, of course, declares it—there is One (with many names and descriptions) who created and sustains Earth-life and the mediating forces that act as beneficent caretakers of the systems of this biosphere.

The Locus of Consciousness

One chapter of the Gaia mythology describes humans as the locus of Earth-life's upward drive to intelligent and moral consciousness. This scenario places contemporary humans in a period of testing, a window of opportunity where we can choose to match our technological powers with corresponding inner development. That choice may be our only alternative to destroying much of life and ourselves.

This *story* can empower us through helping us envision that the species *Homo sapiens* is now challenged by—take your pick—Earth-life, the crises, the Creator, and/or laws of the cosmos, to join as co-creators in this work of the renewal and care of the Earth. As in mythologies and religions, our response to the challenge can be a spiritual journey, a vision quest in which we discover our values, our calling, and the meaning of our lives within the greater meaning of the cosmos.

REFERENCES

The Ages of Gaia: A Biography of Our Living Earth, James Lovelock. New York: Bantam Books. Originally published by W.W. Norton, 1988.

Gaia: A Way of Knowing. Political Implications of the New Biology, William Irwin Thompson. Great Barrington, Mass.: Inner Traditions/Lindisfarne Press, 1987.

"The Gaia Hypothesis: Implications for a Christian

Political Theology of the Environment," Stephen B. Scharper. *Cross Currents*, Summer 1994, pp. 207–221.

How Nature Works: Regenerating Kinship with Planet Earth, Michael Cohen, Stillpoint International, Inc., P.O. Box 640, Walpole, N.H., 1988.

Microcosmos: Four Billion Years of Evolution from our Microbial Ancestors, Lynn Margulis and Dorion Sagan, N.Y.: Summit Books, 1986.

The Universe Story: From the Primordial Flaring Forth to the Ecozoic Era; A Celebration of the Unfolding of the Cosmos, Thomas Berry and Brian Swimme. San Francisco: HarperCollins, 1992.

Prayers, Scriptures, and Reflections in Celebration of the Earth

Introduction

Established in 1987 by the United Nations Environment Programme (UNEP) and its advisory board and planning committee, and originally named Environmental Sabbath/Earth Rest Day, UNEP's new outreach program is titled "Celebration of the Earth." Through publications and publicity, the "Celebration" project provides a way to meld spiritual values with environmental sciences and humanitarian concerns. Many churches, temples, synagogues, mosques, and other institutions have committed to remembering the needs and value of the Earth through worship and liturgy, education and personal engagement, drawing on UNEP's resource base to develop programs of their own.

The United Nations Environment Programme is the international organization given authority to monitor and control the global environment, responding to the problems that transcend national boundaries. It is a world leader in dissemination of global environmental information. Within the United Nations, UNEP oversees the environmental work being done by all other agencies to ensure that an ecological perspective is incorporated in develop-

ment projects supported by the UN.

UNEP played a major role in the Montreal Protocol on ozone depletion; the Rio Earth Summit (UNCED). More recent developments include the Global Environmental Monitoring System offering early warning alerts on immediate and potential dangers; INFOTERRA, a global computer network; and the annual *State of the Environment* reports.

The primary publication produced for use by religious communities is *Only One Earth*, a substantial resource guide containing scientific environmental data, action guides, and declarations from religious bodies in response to contemporary environmental deterioration. This booklet, first published in 1990, also includes selected scriptures, prayers, and reflections from many of the world's religious traditions which suggest the historic wisdom of the traditions regarding the Earth and how members of the religions may respond to contemporary environmental issues. A new, enhanced edition has been prepared by the Interfaith Partnership on the Environment for publication in the year 2000. Most of the prayers, scriptures, and reflections below were originally published (with permission) in the 1990 edition of *Only One Earth*.

Bahá'í Reflections

With respect to environment…

We cannot segregate the human heart from the environment outside us and say that once one of these is reformed everything will be improved. Man is organic with the world. His inner life molds the environment and is itself also deeply affected by it. The one acts upon the other and every abiding change in the life of man is the result of these mutual reactions.

Nature is God's will and is its expression in and through the contingent world. It is a dispensation of Providence ordained by the Ordainer, the All-Wise. The earth is but one country, and mankind its citizens.

Look not upon the creatures of God except with the eye of kindliness and of mercy, for Our loving providence hath pervaded all created things, and Our grace encompassed the earth and the heavens.

. . . It is not only their fellow human beings that the

beloved of God must treat with mercy and compassion, rather must they show forth the utmost loving- kindness to every living creature.... The feelings are one and the same, whether ye inflict pain on man or on beast.

Blessed is the spot, the house, and the place, and the city, and the heart, and the mountain, and the refuge, and the cave, and the valley, and the land, and the sea, and the island, and the meadow where mention of God hath been made, and His praise glorified.
— from Bahá'í Sacred Writings

Buddhist Prayers
The Rain Cloud

It is like a great cloud rising above the world,
Covering all things everywhere—
A gracious cloud full of moisture; lightning-flames flash and
    dazzle,
Voice of thunder vibrates afar, bringing joy and ease to all.
The sun's rays are veiled, and the earth is cooled;
The cloud lowers and spreads as if it might be caught and
    gathered;
Its rain everywhere equally descends on all sides,
Streaming and pouring unstinted, permeating the land.
On mountains, by rivers, in valleys,
In hidden recesses, there grow the plants, trees, and herbs;
Trees, both great and small, the shoots of the ripening grain,
Grapevine and sugarcane.
Fertilized are these by the rain and abundantly enriched;
The dry ground is soaked; herbs and trees flourish together.
From the one water which issued from that cloud,
Plants, trees, thickets, forests, according to need receive
    moisture.
All the various trees—lofty, medium, low, all according to
    its sizes—
Grow and develop roots, stalks, branches, leaves,
Blossoms and fruits in their brilliant colors;
Wherever the one rain reaches, all become fresh and glossy.
According as their bodies, forms, and natures are great and
    small,
So the enriching rain, though it is one and the same,
Yet makes each of them flourish.

In like manner also the Buddha appears here in the world
Like unto a great cloud universally covering all things;
And having appeared in the world, for the sake of living,
He discriminates and proclaims the truth in regard to all laws.
The Great Holy World—honored One among the gods and

humans,
And among all living beings proclaims abroad this word:
"I am the Tathagata, the Most Honored among humans;
I appear in the world like this great cloud,
To pour enrichment on all parched living beings,
To free them from their misery to attain the joy of peace,
Joy of the present world and joy of Nirvana...
Everywhere impartially, without distinction of persons...
Ever to all beings I preach the Law equally; ...
Equally I rain the Law—rain untiringly."
— from the Lotus Sutra, the "Thus-Gone"

Loving Kindness

May every creature abound in well-being and peace.
May every living being, weak or strong, the long and the
    small,
The short and the medium-sized, the mean and the great—
May every living being, seen or unseen, those dwelling far
    off,
Those near by, those already born, those waiting to be
    born—
May all attain inward peace.

Let no one deceive another. Let no one despise another in
    any situation.
Let no one, from antipathy or hatred, wish evil to anyone at
    all.
Just as a mother, with her own life, protects her only son
    from hurt,
So within yourself foster a limitless concern for every living
    creature.
Display a heart of boundless love for all the world
In all its height and depth and broad extent—
Love unrestrained, without hate or enmity.
Then as you stand or walk, sit or lie, until overcome by
    drowsiness,
Devote your mind entirely to this, it is known as living here
    the life divine.

Christian Prayers and Scriptures
A Call to Prayer

The earth is at the same time mother.
She is mother of all that is natural, mother of all that is
    human.
She is the mother of all, for contained in her are the seeds of
    all.

The earth of humankind contains all moistness,
all verdancy, all germinating power.
It is in so many ways fruitful.
All creation comes from it.
Yet it forms not only the basic raw material for mankind,
but also the substance of the incarnation of
  God's son.

HILDEGARD OF BINGEN

A Reflection on Our Present Plight

The high, the low, all of creation, God gives to humankind
  to use.
If this privilege is misused, God's Justice permits creation to
  punish humanity.

HILDEGARD OF BINGEN

A Prayer of Gratitude

Most High, all powerful, good Lord, to you all praise, glory,
and honor and all blessing; to you alone, Most High, they
belong and no man is worthy of naming you.

Praised be you, my Lord, with all your creatures, especially
My Lord Brother Sun, who brings day, and by whom you
enlighten us; he is beautiful, he shines with great splendor;
of you, Most High, he is the symbol.

Praised be you, my Lord, for Sister Moon and the Stars: in
the heavens you formed them, clear, precious and beautiful.
Praised be you, my Lord, for Brother Wind and for the air
and for the clouds, for the azure calm and for all climes by
which you give life to your creatures.

Praised be you, my Lord, for Sister Water, who is very
useful and humble, precious and chaste.

Praised be you, my Lord, for Brother Fire, by whom you
enlighten the night: he is beautiful and joyous, indomitable
and strong.

Praised be you; my Lord, for Sister our Mother the Earth
who nourishes us and bears us, and produces all kinds of
fruits, with the speckled flowers and the herbs.

FRANCIS OF ASSISI,
Canticle of the Sun

The Mystery of Mankind

When I look at the heavens,
the work of thy fingers,
the moon and stars which thou has established—
what is mankind that thou art mindful of them, and the
  children of mankind that thou dost care for them?

Yet thou hast made them little less than God,
and dost crown them with glory and honor.
Thou hast given them dominion over the works of thy
  hands;
thou has put all things under their feet.

PSALM 8:3–6

In the Day of the Lord
The wolf shall dwell with the lamb,
and the leopard shall lie down with the kid,
and the calf and the lion and the fatling together,
and a little child shall lead them.

The cow and the bear shall feed;
their young shall lie down together;
and the lion shall eat straw like the ox.
The sucking child shall play over the hold of the asp,
and the weaned child shall put his hand on the adder's den.

They shall not hurt or destroy in all my holy mountain; for
  the earth shall be full of the knowledge of the Lord as the
  waters cover the sea.

ISAIAH 11:6–9

A Voice from the Earth

Enoch looked upon the earth; and he heard a voice from the
bowels thereof, saying,
"Woe, woe is me, the mother of men;
I am pained, I am weary, because of the wickedness of my
children.
When shall I rest and be cleansed from the filthiness which is
gone forth out of me?
When will my Creator sanctify me, that I may rest,
and righteousness for a season abide upon my face?"

And when Enoch heard the Earth mourn, he wept, and
cried unto the Lord, saying,
"O Lord, wilt thou not have compassion upon the Earth?"
Pearl of Great Price,
MOSES 7:48–49,
from the scriptures of the
Church of Jesus Christ
of the Latter-day Saints

Hindu Prayers
The Waters of Life

Waters, you are the ones who bring us the life force. Help
us to find nourishment so that we may look upon great joy.
Let us share in the most delicious sap that you have, as if
you were loving mothers.

Let us go straight to the house of the one for whom your
waters give us life and give us birth. For our well-being let
the goddesses be an aid to us, the water be for us to drink.
Let them cause well-being and health to flow over us.

Mistresses of all the things that are chosen, ruler over all
peoples, the waters are the ones I beg for a cure. Soma has
told me that within the waters are all cures and Agni who is
salutary to all.

Waters, yield your cure as an armor for my body, so that I
may see the sun for a long time. Waters, carry far away all
of this that has gone bad in me either what I have done in
malicious deceit or whatever lie I have sworn to.
I have sought the waters today; we have joined with their
sap.
O Agni full of moisture, come and flood me with splendor.

Prayer for Blessing

May the axe be far away from you; May the fire be far
away from you; May there be rain without storm; Lord of
Trees, may you be blessed; Lord of Trees, may I be blessed.

Prayer for Peace

Supreme Lord, Let there be peace in the sky and in the
atmosphere, peace in the plant world and in the forests; Let
the cosmic powers be peaceful; let Brahma be peaceful; Let
there be undiluted and fulfilling peace everywhere.
Atharva Veda

The Waters, Who Are Goddesses

They who have the ocean as their eldest flow out of the sea,
purifying themselves, never resting.

Indra, the bull with the thunderbolt, opened a way for them;
let the waters, who are goddesses, help me here and now.

The waters of the sky or those that flow, those that are dug
out or those that arise by themselves, those pure and clear
waters that seek the ocean as their goal—let the waters, who
are goddesses, help me here and now.

Those in whose midst King Varuna moves, looking down
upon the truth and falsehood of people, those pure and clear
waters that drip honey—let the waters, who are goddesses,
help me here and now.

Those among whom King Varuna, and Soma, and all the
gods drink in ecstasy the exhilarating nourishment, those into
whom Agni Of-all-men entered—let the waters, who are
goddesses, help me here and now.
Rig Veda

Jewish Prayers and Reflections

And God saw everything that He had made, and found it very good. And He said: "This is a beautiful world that I have given you. Take good care of it; do not ruin it."

How wonderful, O Lord, are the works of Your hands!
The heavens declare Your glory,
the arch of sky displays Your handiwork.
The heavens declare the glory of God.

In Your love You have given us the power to behold the beauty of Your world, robed all its splendor. The sun and the stars, the valleys and hills, the rivers and lakes all disclose Your presence.

The Earth reveals God's eternal presence. The roaring breakers of the sea tell of Your awesome might; the beasts of the field and the birds of the air bespeak Your wondrous will. Life comes forth by God's creative will.

In Your goodness You have made us able to hear the music of the world. The raging of the winds, the whisperings of trees in the wood, and the precious voices of loved ones reveal to us that You are in our midst. A divine voice sings through all creation.

Gates of Prayer, p. 652

It is said: Before the world was created, the Holy One kept creating worlds and destroying them. Finally He created this one, and was satisfied. He said to Adam: "This is the last world I shall make. I place it in your hands: hold it in trust."

Gates of Prayer, p. 655

Let the sea roar, and all its creatures;
the world, and its inhabitants.
Let the rivers burst into applause,
let the mountains join in acclaim with joy.
The Lord is coming to sustain the Earth.
He will sustain the Earth with kindness,
its people with graciousness.

PSALM 98

Let the heaven rejoice, let the Earth be glad. Let the sea and all it contains roar in praise.

PSALM 96

Environmental Responsibility

The Earth is Adonai's and the fullness thereof.

PSALM 24:1

God acquired possession of the world and apportioned it to humankind but God always remains the Master of the world.

ROSH HASHANAH 31a

All that [we] see — the heaven, the Earth, and all that fills it—all these things are the external garments of God.
SHNEUR ZALMAN OF LIADI, TANYA, Chapter 42

In the hour when the Holy One created the first human being, God took the person before all the trees of the garden of Eden, and said to the person:

"See my works, how fine and excellent they are! Now all that I have created, for you have I created. Think upon this, and do not corrupt and desolate my world; for if you corrupt it, there is no one to set it right after you."
ECCLESIASTES RABBAH 7:28

The Land Is for Our Use

And God said: "Behold, I have given you every herb-yielding seed, which is upon the Earth, and every tree in which is the fruit of a tree-yielding seed—to you shall it be for food."

GENESIS 1:29

God blessed them; and God said to them: "Be fruitful and multiply, and replenish the Earth, and subdue it; and have dominion over the fish of the sea, and over the fowl of the air, and over every living thing that moves on the Earth."

GENESIS 1:28

Reforestation—Reclaiming the Land

One day he, Honi the circle-drawer, was journeying on the road and he saw a man planting a carob tree; he asked him, "How long does it take [for this tree] to bear fruit?" The man replied, "Seventy years." He then further asked him, "Are you certain that you will live another seventy years?" The man replied, "I found [ready grown] carob trees in the world; as my ancestors planted these for me, so I too plant these for my children."

TAANIT 23a, RABBI YOCHANAN BEN ZAKAI

Environmental Land Usage

Six years shall you sow your field, and six years shall you prune your vineyard, and gather in the produce thereof. But the seventh year shall be a Sabbath of solemn rest, Sabbath unto the Lord, you shall neither sow your field, nor prune your vineyard."

LEVITICUS 25:3–4

The Holy One blessed be God said to the children of Israel: "Sow for six years and leave the land at rest for the seventh year, so that you may know the land is Mine!"

SANHEDRIN 39a

Muslim Reflections and Prayer

Under Islam, everything is created by Allah (God) and therefore everything is sacred, useful and has its place in the general scheme of things and in the interest of man.

The protection of God's creation is therefore the duty of the Muslim and God will reward all who protect his creation.

God has created the skies, the Earth, the sun, and the moon, the rivers and the mountains. God has created the animals and vegetables, the birds, the fish, and all that exists between the Earth and sky! The totality of the environment is God's creation and man's responsibility to protect.

The Holy Qur'an declares, "We have created everything from water." Hence the importance of water resources for human life. The survival of human life also depends upon agriculture and animal husbandry. Hence the Muslim obligation to be kind to animals and grateful for the availability of the rivers and the rain. Indeed, there are special prayers for rain in which Muslims express appreciation for God's bounty and beg Him to continue it by providing the faithful with rain.

The relationship of the Muslim to God is a direct and simple one. A Muslim calls upon his Creator for everything! When he is sick, he prays for God to provide him with health. If he is poor and hungry, he begs God for food and support, and so on. Hence, the permanent link between man and the environment through God and prayers to the Creator.

Islam is a religion which started in the deserts of Arabia with a universal message. Its concern for the environment is a universal concern, cutting across national, religious, and geographical barriers. Its major commandments are directed, not to the Muslims, but to the human race. Hence its call upon "people" (not the Arabs nor the Muslims) to conserve the natural resources which are God's gift to mankind.

There are many verses from the Holy Qur'an and Hadith (statements by the Prophet) urging people to be kind to the land, to the rivers, to the air and not to abuse the fertile valleys. Kindness to "those who cannot speak" (animals) is urged by the Prophet again and again.

In his letter of recommendation, the First Muslim Khalifa, Abu-Baker, ordered his troops, "Do not cut down a tree, do not abuse a river, do not harm animals, and be always kind and humane to God's creation, even to your enemies."

Muslim commitment to the sanctity of life is most pronounced during the Hajj to Mecca, where the pilgrims are not permitted even to kill an insect.

Under Islam, the individual is responsible for the "good" and for the "bad." "En Ahsantutn, Ahsantum le-Anfosekum wa en Asaatumfa-lahaa." (If you do good things, you do that for yourselves, and if you do wrong things, that is for you, too!) Hence, the responsibility for the protection of the environment is an individual responsibility in the first place and a "collective" obligation of the society secondarily.

Following is a Muslim prayer for rain, called "Prayer for *Istesquaa*."

O God! The Creator of everything!
You have said that water is the source of all life!
When we have needs, You are the Giver.
When we are sick, You give us health.
When we have no food, You provide us with Your bounty.
And so God, presently, we have no rain. We need water.
    Our water resources are dry; we need You to help us with
    rain—rain for our fields, our orchards and our animals.
We need water for ablution and general cleanliness to
    prepare for worshiping You, O Lord.
Our confidence, O Lord, is in You and Your unlimited
    mercy and compassion.
Please, Merciful God, provide us with rain.
        —provided by Dr. Mohammed Mehdi, Secretary
        General, National Council on Islamic Affairs

Native American Prayers and Reflections

A Call to Prayer

O Great Spirit, Whose breath gives life to the world
    and whose voice is heard in the soft breeze,
We need your strength and wisdom—
    May we walk in beauty.
May our eyes ever behold the red and purple sunset;
Make us wise so that we may understand what you have
    taught us.
Help us learn the lessons you have hidden in every leaf and
    rock;
Make us always ready to come to you with clean hands and
    straight eyes,
So when life fades, as the fading sunset, our spirits may
    come to you without shame.

A Prayer of Awareness

Now, Talking God, with your feet I walk,
I walk with your limbs.
I carry forth your body,
For me your mind thinks,
Your voice speaks for me.
Beauty is before me,
Above and below me hovers the beautiful—
I am surrounded by it,
I am immersed in it.
In my youth I am aware of it,
And in old age I shall walk quietly
The beautiful trail.

The Rights of the Natural World

There is a hue and cry for human rights—human rights,
    they said, for all people. And the indigenous people said:
What of the rights of the natural world?
Where is the seat for the buffalo or the eagle?
Who is representing them here in this forum?
Who is speaking for the waters of the earth?
Who is speaking for the trees and the forests?
Who is speaking for the fish—for the whales—for the
    beavers—for our children?
We said: Given this opportunity to speak in this
    international forum, then it is our duty to say that we
    must stand for these people, and the natural world and
    its rights; and also for the generations to come.
                    CHIEF OREN LYONS
of the Onondaga Nation and the Iroquois Confederacy, in
his account of speaking to the United Nations in Geneva

Sikh Reflections

Guru Nanak, the founder of Sikhism, very aptly said:

Air is the vital force, water the progenitor
The vast earth the mother of all.
Day and night are nurses, fondling all creation in
    their lap.

Nature is not only the source of life, beauty, and power, but it is also an inspiration of strength in formulation of our character. Man is composed of five elements. According to the Sikh Scripture, *Guru Granth Sahib*, these five elements of nature teach us valuable lessons:

Earth teaches us:	patience, love
Air:	mobility, liberty
Fire:	warmth, courage
Sky:	equality, broadmindedness
Water:	purity, cleanliness

We have to imbibe these fine traits of nature in our personality for fuller, happier, and nobler lives.

For the sake of posterity, those countless generations of unborn children to come, let us save this Earth. Let us not misuse our privileges.

Please don't let the song of birds die. Don't let the

water babies perish.

Don't let magnificent animals become extinct. Above all, don't let human beings die of starvation and man-made disasters.

Live and let live.

Taoist Reflections

Trees and animals, humans and insects, flowers and birds: these are active images of the subtle energies that flow from the stars throughout the universe. Meeting and combining with each other and the elements of the Earth, they give rise to all living things.

The superior person understands this, and understands that one's own energies play a part in it. Understanding these things, the superior one respects the Earth as mother, the heavens as father, and all living things as brothers and sisters.

Those who want to know the truth of the universe should practice...reverence for all life. This manifests as unconditional love and respect for oneself and all other beings.

LAO TZU

Universal Prayers

NOTE: These new prayers from *Only One Earth* are deliberately given "secular" language, making them useful either as they are for those who so choose, or modified for a particular congregation's use in a celebration of care and appreciation for Creation. (Where a *Reader* is noted, he or she repeats the italicized phrases between responses from the congregation.)

A Call to Prayer

We who have lost our sense and our senses—our touch, our smell, our vision of who we are; we who frantically force and press all things, without rest for body or spirit, hurting our Earth and injuring ourselves: we call a halt.

We want to rest. We need to rest and allow Earth to rest. We need to reflect and to rediscover the mystery that lives in us, that is the ground of every unique expression of life, the source of the fascination that calls all things to communion.

We declare a time of rest, a space of quiet: for simply being and letting be; for recovering the great, forgotten truths; for learning how to live again.

A Prayer of Awareness

Today we know of the energy that moves all things: the oneness of existence, the diversity and uniqueness of every moment of creation, every shape and form, the attraction, the allurement, the fascination that all things have for one another.

Humbled by our knowledge, chastened by surprising revelations, with awe and reverence we come before the mystery of life.

A Prayer of Sorrow

Reader: *We have forgotten who we are.*

We have forgotten who we are.
We have alienated ourselves from the unfolding of the cosmos.
We have become estranged from the movements of the earth.
We have turned our backs on the cycles of life.

Reader: *We have forgotten who we are.*

We have sought only our own security.
We have exploited simply for our own ends.
We have distorted our knowledge.
We have abused our power.

Reader: *We have forgotten who we are.*

Now the land is barren, and the waters are poisoned,
And the air is polluted.

Reader: *We have forgotten who we are.*

Now the forests are dying,
And the creatures are disappearing,
And the humans are despairing.

Reader: *We have forgotten who we are.*

We ask forgiveness.

We ask for the gift of remembering.
We ask for the strength to change.

Reader: *We have forgotten who we are.*

[Silence]

A Prayer of Healing

Reader: *We join with the Earth and with each other.*

To bring new life to the land,
To restore the waters,
To refresh the air.

Reader: *We join with the Earth and with each other.*

To renew the forests,
To care for the plants,
To protect the creatures.

Reader: *We join with the Earth and with each other.*

To celebrate the seas,
To rejoice the sunlight,
To sing the song of the stars.

Reader: *We join with the Earth and with each other.*

To recall our destiny.
To renew our spirits.
To reinvigorate our bodies.

Reader. *We join with the Earth and with each other.*

To create the human community,
To promote justice and peace.
To remember our children.

Leader: *We join together as many and diverse expressions of one loving mystery: for the healing of the earth and the renewal of all life.*

[Meditation]

Prayer of Gratitude

Reader: *We rejoice in all life.*

We live in all things.
All things live in us.

Reader: *We rejoice in all life.*

We live by the sun.
We move with the stars.

Reader: *We rejoice in all life.*

We eat from the Earth.

We drink from the rain.
We breathe from the air.

Reader: *We rejoice in all life.*

We share with the creatures.
We have strength through their gifts.

Reader: *We rejoice in all life.*

We depend on the forests.
We have knowledge through their secrets.

Reader: *We rejoice in all life.*

We have the privilege of seeing and understanding.
We have the responsibility of caring.
We have the joy of celebrating.

Leader: *We are full of the grace of creation.*

We are graceful.
We are grateful.
We rejoice in all life.

The Earth Charter

Introduction

For over a decade diverse groups throughout the world, including many with religious and spiritual commitments, have endeavored to create an Earth Charter. Hundreds of organizations and thousands of individuals have been involved in the process. Representatives from government and non-governmental organizations worked to secure adoption of an Earth Charter during the Rio Earth Summit in 1992, but that time was not right.

In 1994, a new Earth Charter Campaign was launched by the Earth Council and Green Cross International. Objectives of the Campaign include

- To promote a worldwide dialogue on shared values and global ethics
- To draft an Earth Charter that sets forth a succinct and inspiring vision of fundamental ethical prin-

ciples for sustainable development

- To circulate the Earth Charter throughout the world as a people's treaty, promoting awareness, commitment, and implementation of Earth Charter values
- To seek endorsement of the Earth Charter by the United Nations General Assembly by the year 2002.

On the text of the document.In March 1997, the Earth Charter Commission issued Benchmark Draft I of the Earth Charter and called for ongoing international consultations on its text. During 1997 and 1998, thirty-five national Earth Charter committees were formed, and numerous conferences considered its principles and wording. Recommendations from all regions of the world were forwarded to the Earth Council and the Drafting Committee. Guided by these, in April 1999 the Earth Charter Commission issued Benchmark Draft II. The consultation and refinement process continued throughout 1999 in order to provide individuals and groups with a further opportunity to make their contributions.

Throughout its drafting, religious and spiritual leaders and scholars have been closely engaged in Earth Charter consultations and revisions. Indeed, the energetic chair of the drafting commission, Dr. Steven Rockefeller, is professor of religion at Middlebury College.

The sixteen main principles of the Earth Charter and their fifty-five supporting principles are closely interrelated. Together they provide a conception of interdependence, responsibility, and an urgent call to build a global partnership for sustainable development. These principles are drawn from international law, science, philosophy, religion, recent UN summit meetings, and the extensive international conversation on global ethics and on the Charter. The Commission issued this final version of the Earth Charter in March of 2000.

Preamble

We stand at a critical moment in Earth's history, a time when humanity must choose its future. As the world becomes increasingly interdependent and fragile, the future at once holds great peril and great promise. To move forward we must recognize that in the midst of a magnificent diversity of cultures and life forms we are one human family and one Earth community with a common destiny. We must join together to bring forth a sustainable global society founded on respect for nature, universal human rights, economic justice, and a culture of peace. Toward this end, it is imperative that we, the peoples of Earth, declare our responsibility to one another, to the greater community of life, and to future generations.

Earth, Our Home

Humanity is part of a vast evolving universe. Earth, our home, is alive with a unique community of life. The forces of nature make existence a demanding and uncertain adventure, but Earth has provided the conditions essential to life's evolution. The resilience of the community of life and the well-being of humanity depend upon preserving a healthy biosphere with all its ecological systems, a rich variety of plants and animals, fertile soils, pure waters, and clean air. The global environment with its finite resources is a common concern of all peoples. The protection of Earth's vitality, diversity, and beauty is a sacred trust.

The Global Situation

The dominant patterns of production and consumption are causing environmental devastation, the depletion of resources, and a massive extinction of species. Communities are being undermined. The benefits of development are not shared equitably and the gap between rich and poor is widening. Injustice, poverty, ignorance, and violent conflict are widespread and the cause of great suffering. An unprecedented rise in human population has overburdened ecological and social systems. The foundations of global security are threatened. These trends are perilous—but not inevitable.

The Challenges Ahead

The choice is ours: form a global partnership to

care for Earth and one another or risk the destruction of ourselves and the diversity of life. Fundamental changes are needed in our values, institutions, and ways of living. We must realize that when basic needs have been met, human development is primarily about being more, not having more. We have the knowledge and technology to provide for all and to reduce our impacts on the environment. The emergence of a global civil society is creating new opportunities to build a democratic and humane world. Our environmental, economic, political, social, and spiritual challenges are interconnected, and together we can forge inclusive solutions.

Universal Responsibility

To realize these aspirations, we must decide to live with a sense of universal responsibility, identifying ourselves with the whole Earth community as well as our local communities. We are at once citizens of different nations and of one world in which the local and global are linked. Everyone shares responsibility for the present and future well-being of the human family and the larger living world. The spirit of human solidarity and kinship with all life is strengthened when we live with reverence for the mystery of being, gratitude for the gift of life, and humility regarding the human place in nature.

We urgently need a shared vision of basic values to provide an ethical foundation for the emerging world community. Therefore, together in hope we affirm the following interdependent principles for a sustainable way of life as a common standard by which the conduct of all individuals, organizations, businesses, governments, and transnational institutions is to be guided and assessed.

Principles

I. RESPECT AND CARE FOR THE COMMUNITY OF LIFE

1. Respect Earth and life in all its diversity.
a. Recognize that all beings are interdependent and every form of life has value regardless of its worth to human beings.
b. Affirm faith in the inherent dignity of all human beings and in the intellectual, artistic, ethical, and spiritual potential of humanity.

2. Care for the community of life with understanding, compassion, and love.
a. Accept that with the right to own, manage, and use natural resources comes the duty to prevent environmental harm and to protect the rights of people.
b. Affirm that with increased freedom, knowledge, and power comes increased responsibility to promote the common good.

3. Build democratic societies that are just, participatory, sustainable, and peaceful.
a. Ensure that communities at all levels guarantee human rights and fundamental freedoms and provide everyone an opportunity to realize his or her full potential.
b. Promote social and economic justice, enabling all to achieve a secure and meaningful livelihood that is ecologically responsible.

4. Secure Earth's bounty and beauty for present and future generations.
a. Recognize that the freedom of action of each generation is qualified by the needs of future generations.
b. Transmit to future generations the values, traditions, and institutions that support the long-term flourishing of Earth's human and ecological communities.

In order to fulfill these four broad commitments, it is necessary to:

II. ECOLOGICAL INTEGRITY

5. Protect and restore the integrity of Earth's eco-

logical systems, with special concern for biological diversity and the natural processes that sustain life.

a. Adopt at all levels sustainable development plans and regulations that make environmental conservation and rehabilitation integral to all development initiatives.

b. Establish and safeguard viable nature and biosphere reserves, including wild lands and marine areas, to protect Earth's life support systems, maintain biodiversity, and preserve our natural heritage.

c. Promote the recovery of endangered species and ecosystems.

d. Control and eradicate nonnative or genetically modified organisms harmful to native species and the environment, and prevent introduction of such harmful organisms.

e. Manage the use of renewable resources such as water, soil, forest products, and marine life in ways that do not exceed rates of regeneration and that protect the health of ecosystems.

f. Manage the extraction and use of nonrenewable resources such as minerals and fossil fuels in ways that minimize depletion and cause no serious environmental damage.

6. Prevent harm as the best method of environmental protection and, when knowledge is limited, apply a precautionary approach.

a. Take action to avoid the possibility of serious or irreversible environmental harm even when scientific knowledge is incomplete or inconclusive.

b. Place the burden of proof on those who argue that a proposed activity will not cause significant harm, and make the responsible parties liable for environmental harm.

c. Ensure that decision making addresses the cumulative, long-term, indirect, long distance, and global consequences of human activities.

d. Prevent pollution of any part of the environment and allow no build-up of radioactive, toxic, or other hazardous substances.

e. Avoid military activities damaging to the environment.

7. Adopt patterns of production, consumption,

and reproduction that safeguard Earth's regenerative capacities, human rights, and community well-being.

a. Reduce, reuse, and recycle the materials used in production and consumption systems, and ensure that residual waste can be assimilated by ecological systems.

b. Act with restraint and efficiency when using energy, and rely increasingly on renewable energy sources such as solar and wind.

c. Promote the development, adoption, and equitable transfer of environmentally sound technologies.

d. Internalize the full environmental and social costs of goods and services in the selling price, and enable consumers to identify products that meet the highest social and environmental standards.

e. Ensure universal access to health care that fosters reproductive health and responsible reproduction.

f. Adopt lifestyles that emphasize the quality of life and material sufficiency in a finite world.

8. Advance the study of ecological sustainability and promote the open exchange and wide application of the knowledge acquired.

a. Support international scientific and technical cooperation on sustainability, with special attention to the needs of developing nations.

b. Recognize and preserve the traditional knowledge and spiritual wisdom in all cultures that contribute to environmental protection and human well-being.

c. Ensure that information of vital importance to human health and environmental protection, including genetic information, remains available in the public domain.

III. SOCIAL AND ECONOMIC JUSTICE

9. Eradicate poverty as an ethical, social, and environmental imperative.

a. Guarantee the right to potable water, clean air, food security, uncontaminated soil, shelter, and safe sanitation, allocating the national and international resources required.

b. Empower every human being with the education and resources to secure a sustainable livelihood, and provide social security and safety nets for those who are unable to support themselves.

c. Recognize the ignored, protect the vulnerable, serve those who suffer, and enable them to develop their capacities and to pursue their aspirations.

10. Ensure that economic activities and institutions at all levels promote human development in an equitable and sustainable manner.

a. Promote the equitable distribution of wealth within nations and among nations.

b. Enhance the intellectual, financial, technical, and social resources of developing nations, and relieve them of onerous international debt.

c. Ensure that all trade supports sustainable resource use, environmental protection, and progressive labor standards.

d. Require multinational corporations and international financial organizations to act transparently in the public good, and hold them accountable for the consequences of their activities.

11. Affirm gender equality and equity as prerequisites to sustainable development and ensure universal access to education, health care, and economic opportunity.

a. Secure the human rights of women and girls and end all violence against them.

b. Promote the active participation of women in all aspects of economic, political, civil, social, and cultural life as full and equal partners, decision makers, leaders, and beneficiaries.

c. Strengthen families and ensure the safety and loving nurture of all family members.

12. Uphold the right of all, without discrimination, to a natural and social environment supportive of human dignity, bodily health, and spiritual well-being, with special attention to the rights of indigenous peoples and minorities.

a. Eliminate discrimination in all its forms, such as

that based on race, color, sex, sexual orientation, religion, language, and national, ethnic, or social origin.

b. Affirm the right of indigenous peoples to their spirituality, knowledge, lands, and resources and to their related practice of sustainable livelihoods.

c. Honor and support the young people of our communities, enabling them to fulfill their essential role in creating sustainable societies.

d. Protect and restore outstanding places of cultural and spiritual significance.

IV. DEMOCRACY, NONVIOLENCE, AND PEACE

13. Strengthen democratic institutions at all levels, and provide transparency and accountability in governance, inclusive participation in decision making, and access to justice.

a. Uphold the right of everyone to receive clear and timely information on environmental matters and all development plans and activities which are likely to affect them or in which they have an interest.

b. Support local, regional and global civil society, and promote the meaningful participation of all interested individuals and organizations in decision making.

c. Protect the rights to freedom of opinion, expression, peaceful assembly, association, and dissent.

d. Institute effective and efficient access to administrative and independent judicial procedures, including remedies and redress for environmental harm and the threat of such harm.

e. Eliminate corruption in all public and private institutions.

f. Strengthen local communities, enabling them to care for their environments, and assign environmental responsibilities to the levels of government where they can be carried out most effectively.

14. Integrate into formal education and life-long learning the knowledge, values, and skills needed for a sustainable way of life.

a. Provide all, especially children and youth, with

educational opportunities that empower them to contribute actively to sustainable development.

b. Promote the contribution of the arts and humanities as well as the sciences in sustainability education.

c. Enhance the role of the mass media in raising awareness of ecological and social challenges.

d. Recognize the importance of moral and spiritual education for sustainable living.

15. Treat all living beings with respect and consideration.

a. Prevent cruelty to animals kept in human societies and protect them from suffering.

b. Protect wild animals from methods of hunting, trapping, and fishing that cause extreme, prolonged, or avoidable suffering.

c. Avoid or eliminate to the full extent possible the taking or destruction of nontargeted species.

16. Promote a culture of tolerance, nonviolence, and peace.

a. Encourage and support mutual understanding, solidarity, and cooperation among all peoples and within and among nations.

b. Implement comprehensive strategies to prevent violent conflict and use collaborative problem solving to manage and resolve environmental conflicts and other disputes.

c. Demilitarize national security systems to the level of a nonprovocative defense posture, and convert military resources to peaceful purposes, including ecological restoration.

d. Eliminate nuclear, biological, and toxic weapons and other weapons of mass destruction.

e. Ensure that the use of orbital and outer space supports environmental protection and peace.

f. Recognize that peace is the wholeness created by right relationships with oneself, other persons, other cultures, other life, Earth, and the larger whole of which all are a part.

The Way Forward

As never before in history, common destiny beckons us to seek a new beginning. Such renewal is the promise of these Earth Charter principles. To fulfill this promise, we must commit ourselves to adopt and promote the values and objectives of the Charter.

This requires a change of mind and heart. It requires a new sense of global interdependence and universal responsibility. We must imaginatively develop and apply the vision of a sustainable way of life locally, nationally, regionally, and globally. Our cultural diversity is a precious heritage and different cultures will find their own distinctive ways to realize the vision. We must deepen and expand the global dialogue that generated the Earth Charter, for we have much to learn from the ongoing collaborative search for truth and wisdom.

Life often involves tensions between important values. This can mean difficult choices. However, we must find ways to harmonize diversity with unity, the exercise of freedom with the common good, short-term objectives with long-term goals. Every individual, family, organization, and community has a vital role to play. The arts, sciences, religions, educational institutions, media, businesses, nongovernmental organizations, and governments are all called to offer creative leadership. The partnership of government, civil society, and business is essential for effective governance.

In order to build a sustainable global community, the nations of the world must renew their commitment to the United Nations, fulfill their obligations under existing international agreements, and support the implementation of Earth Charter principles with an international legally binding instrument on environment and development.

Let ours be a time remembered for the awakening of a new reverence for life, the firm resolve to achieve sustainability, the quickening of the struggle for justice and peace, and the joyful celebration of life.

(For more information, explore the Earth Charter Web site: http://www.earthcharter.org.)

The Declaration of the Sacred Earth Gathering

NOTE: The Declaration below was created for and supported by the many indigenous, religious, political, and NGO leaders who participated in the Sacred Earth Gathering for two days preceding the Earth Summit (UNCED) in 1992. They had come to Rio from throughout the world to be a witness for spiritual perspectives on ecological issues and decision making midst the highly politicized atmosphere of this United Nations summit conference. The presence and contribution of the indigenous leaders at the Summit was strongly supported by Maurice Strong, Secretary-General of the United Nations Conference on Environment and Development, who noted in his opening remarks, June 3, 1992, that

> We are reminded by the Declaration of the Sacred Earth Gathering, which met here last weekend, that the changes in behavior and direction called for here must be rooted in our deepest spiritual, moral, and ethical values. We must reinstate in our lives the ethic of love and respect for the Earth, which traditional peoples have retained as central to their value systems. This must be accompanied by a revitalization of the values common to all of our principal religious and philosophical traditions. Caring, sharing, cooperation with and love of each other must no longer be seen as pious ideals, divorced from reality, but rather as the indispensable basis for the new realities on which our survival and well-being must be premised.

The Gathering was cosponsored by the Manitou Foundation in cooperation with the Organization for Industrial, Spiritual and Cultural Advancement, a Japanese-based NGO. The Gathering was followed by the Wisdom Keepers Convocation, which met from June 1–14 at a secluded location near Rio. A sacred fire, drumbeat, and prayers from many indigenous and religious traditions continued twenty-four hours a day for the duration of the Summit, seeking to bring enlightenment to its meetings and decisions.

The planet earth is in peril as never before. With arrogance and presumption, humankind has disobeyed the laws of the Creator which are manifest in the divine natural order.

The crisis is global. It transcends all national, religious, cultural, social, political, and economic boundaries. The ecological crisis is a symptom of the spiritual crisis of the human being, arising from ignorance [greed, lack of caring, and human weakness]*. The responsibility of each human being today is to choose between the forces of darkness and the force of light. We must therefore transform our attitudes and values, and adopt a renewed respect for the superior law of Divine Nature.**

Nature does not depend on human beings and their technology. It is human beings who depend on nature for survival. Individuals and governments need to evolve "Earth Ethics" with a deeply spiritual orientation or the earth will be cleansed [of all destructive forces].

We believe that the universe is sacred because all is one. We believe in the sanctity and the integrity of all life and life-forms. We affirm the principles of peace and nonviolence in governing human behavior towards one another and all life.

We view ecological disruption as violent intervention into the web of life. Genetic engineering threatens the very fabric of life. We urge governments, scientists, and industry to refrain from rushing blindly into genetic manipulation.

We call upon all political leaders to keep a spiritual perspective when making decisions. All leaders must recognize the consequences of their actions for the coming generations.

We call upon our educators to motivate the people towards harmony with nature and peaceful coexistence with all living beings. Our youth and children must be prepared to assume their responsibilities as citizens of tomorrow's world.

We call upon our brothers and sisters around the world to recognize and curtail the impulses of greed, consumerism, and disregard of natural laws. Our survival depends on developing the virtues of simple living and sufficiency, love and compassion with wisdom.

We stress the importance of respecting all spiritual and cultural traditions. We stand for preservation of the habitats and lifestyle of indigenous people and urge restraint from disrupting their communion with nature.

The World Community must act speedily with vision and resolution to preserve the earth, nature, and humanity from disaster. The time to act is now. Now or never.

*Brackets indicate that consensus was not reached on this wording.

***Alternative reading*: "the superior law of the Divine manifest in nature and the created order."

An Evangelical Christian Declaration on the Care of Creation

NOTE: One significant indication of the growing environmental concern among Christians is the work of the Evangelical Environmental Network. Initiated by Evangelicals for Social Action (ESA) and World Vision, EEN is a part of the National Religious Partnership on the Environment, an interfaith environmental movement with four partners: Roman Catholic, mainline Protestant, Jewish, and evangelical Protestant. The following is adapted from an EEN press release.

After a year of preparation, leaders representative of a wide cross-section of evangelical constituencies recently issued [early 1994] the first substantial evangelical call for environmental stewardship. Within a few months, the resulting document, *An Evangelical Declaration on the Care of Creation*, had been endorsed by over two hundred evangelical leaders and organizations.

The Declaration's intent is to call evangelical Christians to greater ecological faithfulness. The document addresses the environmental "degradation" that the church has silently been complicit in, and calls Christians to both theological reflection and practical repentance. Noting that many have become convinced that environmental healing is outside the realm of the Church, the Declaration decries the tendency of Christians to let environmental activism become the realm of only the nonbeliever. While carefully distancing itself from the pantheistic notions of the New Age, and reaffirming the notion of a fallen creation and humanity's creatureliness, the document makes clear the biblical responsibility of every Christian to care for God's Earth. Indeed, the document affirms that the impact of the redemptive work of Christ extends to the whole of the Earth, and the reconciliation Christ offers the Christian reaches to all relationships.

The presence of the Kingdom of God is marked not only by renewed fellowship with God, but also by renewed harmony and justice between people, and by renewed harmony and justice between people and the rest of the created world.

The authors of *An Evangelical Declaration on the Care of Creation* include a distinguished group of evangelical leaders. The EEN will continue its effort to provide a biblical basis for evangelical churches to use in responding to environmental issues and challenges. EEN has distributed many thousands of environmental awareness kits to evangelical congregations across the country. These kits contain resources to help churches both provide biblical environmental education and concrete approaches to action in their communities.

As well, the EEN will continue to work closely with other evangelical environmental groups, including the Christian Society of the Green Cross. The Society also publishes a magazine titled *Green Cross*.

(Copies of the *Declaration* itself can be obtained from EEN, 10 East Lancaster Avenue, Wynnewood PA 19096–3495.)

The Jain Declaration on Nature

There is nothing so small and subtle as the atom nor any element so vast as space. Similarly, there is no quality of soul more subtle than nonviolence and no virtue of spirit greater than reverence for life.

One who neglects or disregards the existence of earth, air, fire, water, and vegetation disregards his own existence which is entwined with them.

MAHAVIRA, 500 C.E.

The Jain tradition that enthroned the philosophy of ecological harmony and nonviolence as its lodestar flourished for centuries side-by-side with other schools of thought in ancient India. It formed a vital part of the mainstream of ancient Indian life, contributing greatly to its philosophical, artistic, and political heritage. During certain periods of Indian history, many ruling elites as well as large sections of the population were Jains, followers of the *Jinas* (Spiritual Victors).

The ecological philosophy of Jainism, which flows from its spiritual quest, has always been central to its ethics, aesthetics, art, literature, economics, and politics. It is represented in all its glory by the twenty-four *Jinas* or *Tirthankaras* (Path-finders) of this era whose example and teachings have been its living legacy through the millennia.

Although the 10 million Jains estimated to live in modern India constitute a tiny fraction of its population, the message and motifs of the Jain perspective, its reverence for life in all its forms, and its commitment to the progress of human civilization and to the preservation of the natural environment continue to have a profound and pervasive influence on Indian life and outlook.

In the 20th century, the most vibrant and illustrious example of Jain influence was that of Mahatma Gandhi, acclaimed as the Father of the Nation. Gandhi's friend, Shrimad Rajchandra, was a Jain. The two great men corresponded until Rajchandra's death, on issues of faith and ethics. The central Jain teaching of *ahimsa* (nonviolence) was the guiding principle of Gandhi's civil disobedience in the cause of freedom and social equality. His ecological philosophy found apt expression in his observation that the greatest work of humanity could not match the smallest wonder of nature....

The ancient Jain scriptural aphorism *Parasparopagraho jivanam* (all life is bound together by mutual support and interdependence) is refreshingly contemporary in its premise and perspective. It defines the scope of modern ecology while extending it further to a more spacious "home." It means that all aspects of nature belong together and are bound in a physical as well as a metaphysical relationship. Life is viewed as a gift of togetherness, accommodation, and assistance in a universe teeming with interdependent constituents.

—excerpted by the Editor from *The Jain Declaration on Nature* by Dr. L. M. Singhvi

On the Urgency of a Jewish Response to the Environmental Crisis

Issued by the Consultation on the Environment and Jewish Life—March 10, 1992

We, American Jews of every denomination, from diverse organizations and differing political perspectives, are united in deep concern that the quality of human life and the earth we inhabit are in danger, afflicted by rapidly increasing ecological threats. Among the most pressing of these threats are depletion of the ozone layer, global warming, massive deforestation, the extinction of species and loss of biodiversity, poisonous deposits of toxic chemical and nuclear wastes, and exponential population growth. We here affirm our responsibility to address this planetary crisis in our personal and communal lives.

For Jews, the environmental crisis is a religious challenge. As heirs to a tradition of stewardship that goes back to Genesis and that teaches us to be partners in the ongoing work of Creation, we cannot accept the escalating destruction of our environment and its effect on human health and livelihood. Where we are despoiling our air, land, and water, it is our sacred duty as Jews to acknowledge our God-given responsibility and take action to alleviate environmental degradation and the pain and suffering that it causes. We must reaffirm and bequeath the tradition we have inherited which calls upon us to safeguard humanity's home.

We have convened this unprecedented consultation in Washington, D.C., to inaugurate a unified Jewish response to the environmental crisis. We pledge to carry to our homes, communities, congregations, organizations, and workplaces the urgent message that air, land, water, and living creatures are endangered. We will draw our people's attention to the timeless texts that speak to us of God's gifts and expectations. This Consultation represents a major step toward

- Mobilizing our community toward energy efficiency, the reduction and recycling of wastes, and other practices which promote environmental sustainability
- Initiating environmental education programs in settings where Jews gather to learn, particularly among young people
- Pressing for appropriate environmental legislation at every level of government and in international forums
- Convening business and labor leaders to explore specific opportunities for exercising environmental leadership
- Working closely in these endeavors with scientists, educators, representatives of environmental groups, Israelis, and leaders from other religious communities.

Our agenda is already overflowing. Israel's safety, the resettlement of Soviet Jewry, anti-Semitism, the welfare of our people in many nations, the continuing problems of poverty, unemployment, hunger, health care, and education, as well as assimilation and intermarriage—all these and more have engaged us and engage us still.

But the ecological crisis hovers over all Jewish concerns, for the threat is global, advancing, and ultimately jeopardizes ecological balance and the quality of life. It is imperative, then, that environmental issues also become an immediate, ongoing, and pressing concern for our community.

Cairo Declaration on Population and Development

An Interreligious Statement

NOTE: The Inter-Religious Federation for World Peace (IRFWP), which drafted this statement, is an international and interreligious peace organization incorporated in New York State. Its contacts from the world's major religious traditions include seven thousand religious leaders and scholars of religion. The Introduction below appeared in the *IRFWP Newsletter*, Vol. II, No. 2, along with the Declaration, which was first issued in a press release on September 9, 1994, in Cairo.

Introduction

Delegates from 189 nations gathered in Cairo, Egypt, from September 5 to 14, 1994, for the United Nations–sponsored International Conference on Population and Development. This, perhaps more than any previous UN conference, brought to the fore a fascinating interplay of forces, both spiritual and secular, that currently inform the evolution of human affairs. The high-profile figures who emerged in this setting as those through whom these powers manifest and interact included Pope John Paul II, U.S. Vice President Albert Gore, Conference Chairwoman Nafis Sadik, Prime Ministers Brundtland of Norway and Bhutto of Pakistan, and the Sheikh Al-Azhar. These leaders communicated such diverse perspectives on the issues as Catholic, Muslim, Secular Feminist, and Secular Rationalist.

As the conference approached, leaders of the Inter-Religious Federation for World Peace (IRFWP) felt that the debate on the all-important issues of population and development had degenerated on at least two important levels:

1. By having only Catholics and Muslims identified as representing religious and spiritual concerns, the potential benefits which could come from a broad spectrum of religions were lost.

2. The decision on the part of the religious spokespeople to focus debate on concrete issues such as abortion and contraception forfeited a golden

opportunity to present on the world stage a more comprehensive expression of religious and spiritual concerns regarding the all-important considerations of family life and human development.

For these and other reasons, IRFWP Presidents and Presiding Council Members drafted the following statement. The IRFWP sought to present a position representing a broader constituency of the world's religions, and offer a more broadly defined set of religious and spiritual concerns.

The Cairo Declaration on Population and Development

The United Nations Conference on Population and Development, held in Cairo from September 5–14, 1994, has highlighted the pressing problem of the earth's finite capacity to support the growing human population. This issue should receive paramount attention from all, parallel to the equally urgent issue of a sustainable life environment on our planet.

We note that the Conference has been controversial. At least four nations—Iraq, Lebanon, Saudi Arabia, and Sudan—with large Muslim populations, have chosen to boycott the Conference. The Vatican has used strong words to protest elements of the Conference working documents. In the Roman Catholic constituency many have expressed dissent from the official Vatican position. Thus in dealing with birth and death, sexuality, marriage and family, and human development, the Conference obviously has touched upon issues directly affecting the religious consciousness of humanity.

It is in this context that Presidents and Members of the Presiding Council of the Inter-Religious Federation for World Peace wish to make the following modest observations for the prayerful consideration of all concerned.

1. Religion—a central issue

Given the importance of religion for peoples throughout the world, no serious effort to engage crucial global problems should discount the core values and wisdom represented in the world's religious traditions. The course of the deliberations of this Conference has demonstrated how unwise it is to ignore the religious perspective and to presume that a purely secular analysis and secular solutions could adequately or effectively handle this perplexing problem which involves such momentous issues as human reproduction and the regulation and planning of the family. Reason demands that religious organizations should be fully involved in discussing these problems and finding solutions.

2. Sciences as well as religions have their limits

We recognize the enormous contribution made by science and technology in promoting general health, in increasing life expectancy, in reducing infant mortality, in eliminating epidemics, and in facilitating general health care. But as regards the problems of population stabilization and human development, even when all significant and relevant findings and discoveries of the physical and social sciences have been fully taken into account, the sciences cannot offer the necessary ethical elements of social policy; what ought and needs to be done is a moral judgment, which science by definition is not designed to provide. Scientific data can clarify aspects of the human situation and point to possible options in an ethical issue; but the final decision on what to do depends on the moral conscience, which is largely shaped by the religious heritage of humanity.

Religions also have their limits, and sometimes represent vested interests. But the same is true of the physical and social sciences. They too are prone to misuse and manipulation by vested interests willing to finance scientific research; military establishments and large corporations can be cited as examples.

While religions are often accused of dogmatism, it should be noted that advocates of secular causes are not entirely free from this characteristic.

Ideological dogmatism in the pursuit of moral positions, passionately held, may belie claims of scientific objectivity. Religions and sciences need to cooperate in facilitating debate and public discussion of issues pertaining to human development and population stabilization.

3. Religion and education

Despite the quickening pace of the process of global secularization, religions still play a leading role in shaping the moral consciousness of humanity. Eighty percent of the world's people still profess one religion or another. If programs for promoting human development and stabilizing population growth are to succeed at all, the religions of the world must take a major part of the responsibility for educating and inspiring the people.

The role of governments and secular programs for sexual education and family planning should not be minimized; but neither should that role be overvalued or absolutized. A purely secular approach can have only limited effect. There are few societies which do not link sexuality, marriage, and childbirth with religion. Throughout the world marriages are performed in religious contexts precisely in order to place sexuality and childbirth in a sacred context. Societies where these biological and social practices are divorced from authentic religious norms and rites suffer grave consequences manifested in the proliferation of promiscuous behavior, the denigration of women, epidemics of sexually transmitted diseases, rising divorce, and grossly defective forms of child rearing. In technologically advanced societies, social scientific strategies for arresting such problems have been largely unsuccessful. Social policies, however well intentioned, which encourage the violation of important religious values may be counterproductive.

What needs to be reoriented is the religious and moral attitudes of people. The religions of the world have an enormous infrastructure for education. If in addition, the vast number of conscientious religious teachers in the world can be mobilized and projected by the public media, with free and frank discussion of issues relating to human development and population stabilization, the effect can be quite phenomenal.

4. Interreligious cooperation

All religions need to learn from each other in this regard and to coordinate their efforts. If, for example, Muslims and Roman Catholics have special convictions in matters of human reproduction, such convictions can be discussed in interreligious gatherings; only then will their validity or questionability come clearly to light. The presence of interreligious strife plays a large part in the advocacy of a-religious, and sometimes even anti-religious secularism. Yet in this century the world's religions have made great strides toward concord, through dialogue and discussion.

A consensus among major religious leaders can have a high positive value. The religions owe it to humanity to come together in dialogue and cooperation on this crucial issue.

5. Religion and women

The women of the world should have a major role in the debate on human development and population stabilization. No programs in this area can be conceived properly, or effectively implemented, without benefit of the unique insights and universal talents of women. In actual fact women now play a major, but often unrecognized, role in maintaining religious traditions, in the practice of religion, and in education both in the family and in society.

Many religions have tended to marginalize women from their teaching, decision-taking, and implementing structures. All religions need to reexamine their position and practice in relation to discrimination against women, and to marginalization, denigration, oppression, and abuse of women. When women are oppressed the entire social world is oppressed, the youth are impoverished, and prosperity flees. Thus all religions have responsibility to provide for women to play a leading role in decision-making and implementation of programs.

6. Abortion, family, and promiscuity

The debate on the ethics of abortion of the human fetus is far from concluded. Although there is much disagreement as to whether a fetus is a person entitled to rights, few deny that an abortion is the termination of human life at some very early stage of development. While there may indeed be cases where abortion may be morally legitimate, at the very least when a mother's life is endangered, it should never be viewed simply as a morally neutral medical procedure. No strategy for solving population growth should rely on or encourage abortion as a solution. Any society that is cavalier about abortion will tend toward discounting the value of human life.

Religions of the world have a special responsibility to deepen our understanding of the moral implications of abortion, for this is an issue which calls for deeper, more informed, more enlightened attention.

Conclusion

We applaud the open and straightforward debate on these issues, which the Cairo Conference has freshly stimulated. The United Nations cannot on its own decide which religious views to promote, or which particular religious leaders to invite or boycott. Religions have to come forward to help the United Nations in this regard, and to discuss these questions in an ambience of harmony, cooperation, and mutual openness. Consensus may be difficult to achieve immediately; but a consensus eliminating inconvenient positions can hardly be worthwhile, in the long run.

Our Children, Their Earth

NOTE: The Environmental Sabbath/Earth Rest Day, established in 1987 by the United Nations Environment Programme (UNEP), focused its Spring 1991 publication on children and the environment, and produced the resource guide *Our Children Their Earth.* The following scriptures and reflections have been drawn from that publication to help us remember that it is not only our children but all future generations that will live with our decisions and impact on the Earth, for good or ill.

Bahá'í

O God! Educate these children. These children are the plants of Thine orchard, the flowers of Thy meadow, the roses of Thy garden. Let Thy rain fall upon them; let the Sun of Reality shine upon them with Thy love. Let Thy breeze refresh them in order that they may be trained, grow and develop, and

appear in the utmost beauty. Thou art the Giver. Thou art the Compassionate.

'ABDU'L-BAHÁ, *Bahá'í Prayers*, p. 35

Train your children from their earliest days to be infinitely tender and loving to animals. If an animal be sick, let the children try to heal it; if it be hungry, let them feed it; if thirsty, let them quench its thirst; if weary, let them see that it rests.

From the writings of 'ABDU'L-BAHÁ,
No. 130, p. 158

Buddhist

It's time for elders to listen to the child's voice. You see, in the child's mind there is no demarcation of different nations, no demarcation of different social systems of ideology. Children know in their minds that all children are the same, all human beings are the same. So, from that viewpoint, their minds are more unbiased. When people get older, though, they start to say, "our nation," "our religion," "our system." Once that demarcation occurs, then people don't bother much about what happens to others. It's easier to introduce social responsibility into a child's mind.

His Holiness the 14th Dalai Lama,
TENZIN GYATSO, in *My Tibet*,
written with Galen Rowell

Christian

One generation passeth away,
and another generation cometh:
but the earth abideth forever.

ECCLESIASTES 1:4

They brought young children to Christ, that he should touch them: and his disciples rebuked those that brought them. But when Jesus saw it, he was much displeased, and said unto them, "Allow the little children to come unto me, and forbid them not: for of such is the kingdom of God. Verily I say unto you, whosoever shall not receive the kingdom of God as a little child, he shall not enter therein."

And he took them in his arms, put his hands upon them, and blessed them.

MARK 10:13–16

Hindu

The Hindu mind is singularly dominated by one paramount conception: the divinity of life. Regarding the creation of the universe, Hindu tradition, based on the experience of illumined mystics, asserts with deep conviction that God is the supreme creator of every thing and every being.... [We] Hindus give God a favored place in our homes as mother, friend, child, even husband or sweetheart. God, being the most beloved object of life, must find a place in our family life. He must be dear and near to us. This ideal of the sweet God, lovable God, playmate God, child God has been admirably illustrated in Hinduism in the personality of Sri Krishna. So, every child can be looked upon by anyone as a baby God, and spiritual life can be quickened in this manner.

SWAMI TATHAGATANANDA,
Vedanta Society, New York

Let us declare our determination to halt the present slide towards destruction, to rediscover the ancient tradition of reverence for all life and, even at this hour, to reverse the suicidal course upon which we have embarked. Let us recall the ancient Hindu dictum: "The earth is my mother, and we are all her children."

DR. KARAN SINGH,
at the World Wide Fund for Nature
gathering of religious leaders, Assisi, Italy

Jewish

Just as you found trees which others had planted when you entered the land, so you should plant for your children. No one should say, "I am old. How many more years will I live? Why should I be troubled for the sake of others?" Just as he found trees, he should add more by planting even if he is old.

MIDRASH TANCHUMA, Kedoshim 8

A person's life is sustained by trees. Plant them for the sake of your children.

From SEDER TU BISHEYAT, the Festival of Trees,
Central Conference of American Rabbis

Muslim

The Prophet [Mohammed] was very concerned about wasting and polluting water. Even when we were very young, our mothers taught us that whoever soils the river, on the day of judgment that person is going to be given the responsibility of cleaning the river. So we were really learning about preserving the purity of water from childhood.

SHEIKH AHMAD KUFTARO,
Grand Mufti of Syria, in *Shared Vision*, 1990

Native American

We are taught to plant our feet carefully on Mother Earth because the faces of all future generations are looking up from it.

OREN LYONS,
Chief Joagquisho of the Haudenosaunee
(Iroquois) Confederation

Teach your children what we have taught our children, that the earth is our mother. Whatever befalls the earth, befalls the children of the earth. If we spit upon the ground, we spit upon ourselves. This we know. The earth does not belong to us; we belong to the earth. One thing we know, which the white man may one day discover, our God is the same God. You may think now that you own Him as you wish to own our land, but you cannot. He is the God of all people, and His compassion is equal for all. This earth is precious to God, and to harm the earth is to heap contempt on its Creator.... So love it as we have loved it. Care for it as we have cared for it. And with all your mind, with all your heart, preserve it for your children, and love it...as God loves us all.

CHIEF SEATTLE,
of the Squamish, circa 1855

Sikh

For the sake of posterity, those countless generations of unborn children to come, let us save this Earth. Let us not misuse our privileges. Please don't let the song of birds die. Don't let the water babies perish. Don't let magnificent animals become extinct. Above all, don't let human beings die of starvation and man-made disasters.

—from the World Wide Fund for Nature gathering of religious leaders at Assisi, Italy

A Declaration of Independence— from Overconsumption

Vicki Robin

President of the New Road Map Foundation, author, and a frequent speaker on fiscal and resource frugality

We are all consumers. Every human takes sustenance from and returns waste to the environment. But overconsumption means taking more than we can productively use—or more than the environment can sustainably provide. Overconsumption has become our way of life in the United States. We put our faith in "more," but it's never enough; we report being no happier now than we were in 1957, when cars were fewer, houses smaller and microwaves, VCRs, and personal computers did not even exist. Worse yet, our lifestyle, which threatens our social fabric and the very web of life on which we depend, has become the envy of much of the world.

As Robert Muller, retired Assistant Secretary-General of the United Nations, says, "The single most important contribution any of us can make to the planet is a return to frugality."

Overconsumption Is a Mounting Catastrophe

Quantity as well as type of consumption defines the individual's impact on the environment. With population rising and expectations for more, better, and different stuff increasing, humanity is taxing the earth's life-sustaining systems, its "carrying capacity." Each overconsumer is responsible; we must face this catastrophe in the making.

Overconsumption is a catastrophe for ourselves:

- *Declining quality of life.* Our habit of overconsumption enslaves many of us to longer hours at tedious or morally questionable jobs. We say we value relationships over possessions, yet our behavior says the opposite. As we spend less time with our families and communities, we end up with more crime, violence, and teen suicides.

Overconsumption is a catastrophe for our countries:

- *Economic weakness.* Our habit of overconsumption has led the U.S.A. into debt, bankruptcy, and the lowest savings rate in the industrialized world. We don't have money to invest in infrastructure, in education, in the future.

- *Personal excess encourages institutional abuses.* The more-is-better mentality allows us to tolerate wars over oil, and corporate practices that are wasteful, polluting, and unethical. We can't say "no" to Nintendos for our children or new gadgets for ourselves, so how can we expect our government to say "no" to deficit spending or CEOs to say "no" to exorbitant salaries?

Overconsumption is a catastrophe for humanity:

- *Modeling an unattainable and unsustainable lifestyle to the global community.* The earth cannot support everyone in the manner to which Americans have become accustomed. We must find a way to limit our excess and maintain or increase our quality of life while providing the world's people with our best knowledge and technologies so that they too can enjoy sustainable livelihoods and lifestyles.

Overconsumption is a catastrophe for the earth:

- *Environmental destruction.* Overconsumption accelerates species extinction, water and air pollution, global warming, and accumulation of toxic waste and garbage.

- *Resource depletion.* Overconsumption means we're using renewable resources faster than nature can restore them! Twenty percent of the groundwater we use each year is not restored. One million acres of cropland are lost to erosion annually. Ninety percent of our northwestern old-growth forests is gone.

We Can Change! Strategies for Ending Overconsumption

Break the silence

We must begin to talk about our consumption and challenge the conspiracy of silence. We can't solve a problem we won't acknowledge. Challenge yourself. Challenge others. Risk being uncomfortable. Risk offending others. Ask:

- Should we be able to buy whatever we can afford, no matter what the effect on others or the earth?
- Should we allow credit cards to lure us into excessive debt?
- When is personal consumption a matter of public concern?
- Who or what will set limits for us, if we won't do it ourselves?
- Does overconsumption really make us happy?

At the 1992 Earth Summit the United States refused to talk about consumption, saying that a country such as ours could not tell its citizens what kind of lifestyles and consumption patterns to have. By the 1994 Cairo Population Conference, the United States at least acknowledged the need to reduce our consumption. The door is opening. Speak out. And keep speaking.

Reframe the game

Saving money—"creating a nest egg," "saving for a rainy day," "recession-proofing your life," ensuring a decent retirement income independent of shaky pensions or social security—benefits you, the economy, and the planet. By getting out of debt, saving money, and building financial security, you consume less. By living life at a slower pace, you consume less.

Frugality isn't deprivation. Deprivation is pouring your time and talent into your job while ignoring your health and your loved ones. Poverty is wanting more than you have. Wealth is having more than you want. So make overconsumption sound dull-witted and frugality smart. (It's easy, because it's true.)

Debunk the myths

Myth: *"Standard of living equals quality of life."* Once we have enough for survival and comforts, quality of life suffers when we continue to focus on quantity of stuff. Studies show that good relationships, meaningful work, and restorative leisure are core components of quality of life.

Myth: *Overconsumption is natural.* No, it isn't! It began in this century as a deliberate strategy on the part of business, media, and government to educate people to want what they don't need in order to increase markets for American products. Overconsumption is selling your life and mortgaging your future so the economy can grow. Now that's unnatural.

Myth: *The U.S. (or any) economy is dependent upon overconsumption.* Respected economic observers like Lester Thurow of M.I.T., Charles Schultze of the Brookings Institute, and Alfred E. Kahn of Cornell all assert that economic health in the '90s depends on consuming less and saving more.

Myth: *Government programs, revolutionary business practices, or new technologies will take care of it.* Green taxes! Renewable energy! Fuel-efficient cars! Clean industry! Better living through chemistry! All are valuable—but, even all together, they are not sufficient. Creating a sustainable future requires a new way of thinking. We must reexamine our desires, transform our perceptions and develop a new ethic. Only then can the larger systems with which we operate be transformed.

Myth: *One person can't make a difference.* There is no "they." There is only us, a society of individuals making personal and collective choices. Legislators, CEOs, and consumers are all people who can change their minds and thus change the world, no matter what they did yesterday. Lowering consumption happens one transaction at a time.

Educate about overconsumption

Every conversation is an opportunity. Share your ideas and success stories with friends, neighbors, and colleagues; write about them in your letters. Discuss and debate. Put together a study circle. Talk to the media. Show the link between overconsumption and environmental and social issues. Begin to notice all the ways that others can benefit from what you have learned.

Live a sustainable lifestyle yourself

Each of us has the mandate to consume in moderation. Ask yourself now and every day, "How much is enough?"

A call to action

The shift away from excess and back to balance is on. "Voluntary Simplicity" is one of the top ten trends in the '90s, according to the Trends Research Institute in Rhinebeck, New York. Books on getting out of debt, saving money, and working less are hot. Churches are exploring stewardship, not dominion. Foundations are funding projects to explore the issue of consumption and activate solutions. People are taking back their lives.

The can-do American character has faced challenges before. When science showed us the dangers of being couch potatoes, of smoking, of too much fat, we responded with lifestyle changes. The mandate to reduce consumption can energize our country in a similar fashion, this time in a fiscal fitness campaign.

Let's transform the American way of life and pave the way to a sustainable future.

NOTE
Tools for Personal Change

Beyond the what and why of overconsumption, people need the "how to." Based on twenty-five years of experience in living and educating about lowconsumption, high-fulfillment lifestyles, Joe Dominguez and Vicki Robin wrote the best-selling book *Your Money or Your Life*. Among the other resources available from The New Road Map Foundation is the popular booklet, *All-Consuming Passion: Waking Up from the American Dream*.

Chapter Twenty-seven
HUMAN RIGHTS AND RESPONSIBILITIES

The articles and documents in this chapter demonstrate the central role of religious freedom and human rights, especially for minorities, in the relationship between individuals and the communities in which they live. Dr. Robert Traer indicates how two differing theories about rights can lead to substantial differences of practice and how one interreligious organization attempts to work with those who adopt both theories.

The articles about indigenous cultures and dispossessed peoples show how they, in particular, have been victims of human rights abuses by more powerful cultures. Of particular need is the emphasis on the rights of half the human race—women, as they are facing abuses and new perceptions of their place in religions and in the world. Emerging alongside the emphasis on rights is a complementary focus on human responsibilities, a movement that has been shaped, in part at least, by Hans Küng's work on the Global Ethic. This Declaration is also inspired by the realization of many world and religious leaders that an overemphasis on rights leads to a loss of understanding of the responsibilities that individuals have to the larger community.

Faith in Human Rights

OUR CHALLENGE IN THE NEW CENTURY

Dr. Robert Traer

Dr. Traer served as General Secretary of the International Association for Religious Freedom (IARF) until June of 2000. IARF is an interreligious organization based in Oxford, England, with NGO affiliation at the United Nations. Dr. Traer has advanced degrees in both law and religious studies.

We are challenged both by the events of our time and by our faith commitments to support human rights. Brutal warfare, starvation, ethnic cleansing, and religious intolerance make the struggle for human rights more necessary than ever. At the same time greater cooperation among people of different faith traditions and the support within their communities for human rights make the struggle for human rights more encouraging. Human rights are violated everywhere, but everywhere men and women of faith assert that every person has the right to human dignity.

I say "men and women of faith" are asserting human rights, because human rights are not simply a matter of law but of faith. The Universal Declaration of Human Rights, which was passed without dissenting vote by the General Assembly of the United Nations in 1948 and is the foundation of international human rights law, affirms that

> the peoples of the United Nations have in the (UN) Charter reaffirmed their *faith in fundamental human rights*, in the dignity and worth of the human person and in the equal rights of men and women and have determined to promote

social progress and better standards of life in larger freedom. (Emphasis added.)

Human rights cannot simply be derived from legal precedents of the past, nor from empirical evidence or logic, but require a "leap of faith."

Human Rights in the 20th Century

Prior to World War II, international law was the law of nations, and thus the rights of a human person were the rights granted by his or her government. This understanding of rights was supported by modern legal theory, which holds that laws are simply the decisions of governments and that there is no other "higher law." Faith in this theory and system of law was shattered by the acts of Nazi Germany, for the Nazis legislated the extermination of the Jews. These Nazi laws were clearly wrong, but how were they to be condemned by a system of international law which allowed for no standards by which to judge the authority of a state?

The Nuremberg trials assessed a higher standard, and the United Nations codified this as international human rights law. Since 1948 these laws have grown to include numerous covenants (or treaties) and international mechanisms such as the UN Human Rights Commission and Subcommission. At the same time the number of nations in the UN has expanded rapidly, due to the liberation of peoples in Africa and Asia from colonial rule. The UN has become more prominent, if not less controversial, and assertions of human rights have continued to capture international attention.

In the last fifty years human rights have expanded conceptually as well. The Universal Declaration of Human Rights was dominated by notions of civil and political rights, which are most familiar to Westerners. But economic and social rights concerning employment, food, shelter, education, and health care were also affirmed. More recently, accompanying the growing strength of formerly colonized peoples in the UN, cultural and peoples' rights have been asserted. We see here a shift in emphasis from the individual to the group, from protection of the dignity of the individual from state intervention, to providing for communities the elements of life deemed necessary for human dignity through state intervention.

Agreement on the nature and scope of human rights is a matter of debate, of course, not only among political leaders and international lawyers, but also among religious leaders from a variety of cultures and traditions. As conflict between religious communities seems to be increasing in many parts of the world, support for human rights among religious leaders may prove ever more important.

Religious Support for Human Rights

When we reflect on the historical development of human rights, we see immediately that for most of human history religious leaders resisted what we today describe as human rights. Traditionally, religious leaders have been primarily concerned with enforcing their authority and with the welfare of their community, rather than with the rights of its members, especially if recognizing these rights meant permitting dissent. Thus, religious people who now support human rights should in good conscience confess that their traditions and teachings have generally been used to deny many of these rights.

Yet, religious leaders were among the first to assert that the UN must promulgate a Declaration of Human Rights, and Christian and Jewish leaders actively lobbied the UN Commission that drafted it. The World Council of Churches provided leadership among Protestant Christian groups, and, after Vatican II, members of the Roman Catholic Church have been in the forefront of the human rights struggle in Asia, Africa, and Latin America. Jewish participants in the human rights movement are far more numerous than their small numbers in the world would lead one to expect. And more recently prominent Muslims have asserted that the Islamic tradition supports fundamental human rights.

Within the theistic traditions human rights are understood as God-given. Men and women created in the image of God are seen as having rights, because of the freedom of God. The nature of these rights is discerned from the scriptures of the particular tradition. As the word "right" rarely appears in these scriptures, notions of human rights tend to be derived from teachings about duty.

The idea that rights are part of relationships is something that all religious traditions share, although the emphasis on individual rights may vary considerably. From the religious point of view a person has a right in relation to others, in the context of relationships and mutual obligations. These duties and rights are part of the fabric of community. Communities are constituted by religious teachings, common discipline, and (from the point of view of theistic traditions) by God. Rights are thus a fundamental part of the nature of communities.

This is different from the view which dominated the drafting of the Universal Declaration of Human Rights, and the development of human rights law in the first part of the second half of the 20th century. From this other point of view, which dominates modern Western political thought, rights are inherent in the individual, who joins together with other individuals to form communities. Thus rights are brought into society by individuals, who in theory form a "social contract" with one another in order to live together. In this perspective the community is a voluntary association, which the individual can leave or join, as he or she chooses.

These two different understandings of the nature of human rights can lead to disagreements. For example, the more individualistic perspective dominates the formulation of religious freedom in the Universal Declaration of Human Rights and the Covenant on Civil and Political Rights. In the words of the Universal Declaration, it is "freedom of thought, conscience, and religion" which is protected and this includes the freedom to change one's religion or belief as well as the freedom to join with others in teaching, practicing, worshipping, and observing the religious disciplines of one's tradition. Thus freedom of religion is primarily an individual right, although it may be asserted by a group of individuals.

This understanding of the right to religious freedom reflects the Western notion of religion, as a voluntary activity of individuals who join together to practice what their individual consciences tell them is right. Because this is largely a modern Western notion of religion, it is not surprising that more traditional religious communities are less than enthusiastic about this emphasis on the rights of the individual believer. In their view, if rights are given by God to the community of the faithful, then individual rights are secondary, not primary. The rights of the entire community take precedence.

For example, many Muslims are loath to support the right of an individual to convert from Islam to another religion. They believe that God has constituted the Islamic community to rule in his stead. To convert from Islam is thus to reject God and those who are charged to rule for God. It is inconceivable, for many Muslims, that one can have a right to turn away from God, to err, and to go astray.

This position is not unique to Islam. Prior to the 18th century it was the view of most religious communities, at least among the theistic traditions. It was the position of the Roman Catholic Church until the latter part of this century, and it is affirmed in slightly different ways by many Christian groups today. What is neglected in such a position, of course, is the idea that God wants obedience to be freely given. Muslims who support the right of conversion quote from the Qur'an: "Let there be no compulsion in religion." Such a text, however, envisions the religious community more as a voluntary association of believers, rather than as a community constituted by God which must be protected from deviation by its leadership. And this view of religious community is strongly opposed by the leaders of many religious traditions.

It is not helpful to characterize a position which stresses community interests over individual interests as counter to human rights, for those who assert such a position believe they are affirming the community's right to religious freedom. The claim of the Unitarian Church in Romania may put this perspective in a more sympathetic light for many of us. The Unitarians in Romania, who are part of the Hungarian minority community, claim the right to operate confessional secondary schools in their own language, for their own people, but to have these schools supported by the state. The Romanian government asserts the right to integrate Romanian students (who are neither Hungarian nor Unitarian) into state-supported schools, claiming that the right to religious freedom is protected by freedom of worship and religious education in the churches, and that the government has no obligation to support confessional schools for minority students so that they may study their religion with one another in their own language.

The International Association for Religious Freedom (IARF) has supported the Unitarians in its struggle with the Romanian state, as it is clear that integrating Romanian students into the confessional schools, which have for centuries nurtured the minority Hungarian Unitarian community, is part of the government's plan to destroy the minority Hungarian community by assimilating it into Romanian society. Denying places for the public education of young people in the Hungarian Unitarian tradition would make it much more difficult for that minority community to pass on its religious traditions and identity to its young people.

Yet, the issue is not a clear-cut one, and thus assertions of the right of religious freedom may genuinely be made by those who stress community rights as well as those who recognize only individual rights. What is needed here is communication between the two, respect for their differences, and protection within the society for minority views whatever the law may decide about the balance between the two positions.

Notwithstanding these differences, it must be stressed that support for human rights among leaders of different religious traditions is substantial. Given the history of conflict between religious communities, both in different religious traditions and within the same tradition, we might well conclude that this agreement is astonishing. Certainly it is unprecedented, as is the *faith* in human rights as expressed in the Universal Declaration of Human Rights and as affirmed by men and women of faith all around the world.

Human Rights Enforcement

The religious communities have played and can now play a significant role in the enforcement of human rights law. This is particularly the case because of the unique nature of international law in our time. Unlike the laws of a state, international human rights law has no coercive authority to back it up. The United Nations does not have enforcement powers, except as granted by its member nations, and then only for very limited purposes.

For many, this fact suggests that human rights law is merely a legal fiction, a romantic idea, until a world government with enforcement powers is created. Others argue, however, that the enforcement of international human rights law is an experiment in nonviolent community building. Nonviolent methods for enforcing human rights laws include exposing human rights violations to public scrutiny and shame, economic and political sanctions, and forms of cooperation among community groups including religious organizations.

Religious ideals and discipline may help keep the human rights struggle nonviolent, may encourage political leaders to live up to the higher aspirations of their religious and cultural traditions, and may help build trust between minority and majority communities in a society. We see examples of this in the movement led by Gandhi in India, in the role of Christians and Jewish leaders during the civil rights movement in the United States during the 1960s, in the leadership of Christians and Muslims in fighting apartheid in South Africa, and in the martyrdom of religious leaders in the struggle for human rights all around the world.

Thus support in religious traditions not only provides a foundation for human rights, which may otherwise appear to be merely the consensus of a particular culture or a particular time, but also translates the imperatives of human rights into the moral and spiritual language of different religious and cultural traditions, allowing more people to claim these rights as their own heritage.

Our Challenge Now

What then is our challenge now? Often human rights issues seem beyond our control, involving governments and political forces that are hard to influence. Yet, the human rights struggle is compelling, because it affirms the fundamental human dignity of each person. This is a radical assertion and deserves our active support. It is a leap of faith to claim that each person, regardless of his or her intelligence, morality, or circumstances, is a human being who deserves to be treated with respect. There is little in the history of civilization to support this claim and much to deny it. It is simply wonderful that this claim even has a hearing today.

In the IARF we support the claim to human dignity both as a legal claim under international law and as a religious claim, which has found support within many of the world's religious traditions. As an association of religious and humanist groups, the IARF does not hold to one theory of the nature of human rights, but urges members within all the religious traditions to find their own way of understanding and supporting human dignity. It acknowledges that different conclusions may be drawn within different religious communities, and that these different conclusions deserve to be taken seriously and discussed in good faith.

This is why the IARF supports interfaith activities that bring together people of different religious traditions. It seeks to discover areas of agreement and cooperation among members of diverse religious communities. Conceptual differences may not necessarily inhibit cooperation among different religious communities in support of human rights. In fact, it is the experience of the IARF that members of all the major religious traditions are able to join together in support of many fundamental human rights.

Because of its heritage as an association of minority groups who have suffered ostracism and been oppressed, the IARF focuses on the human right of religious freedom. Moreover, as its constituency of religious and humanist groups includes a diversity of traditions, the IARF has developed a particular methodology emphasizing support for constructive community leadership. Specifically, the IARF assists religious communities, rather than taking up individual cases in the way that Amnesty International does. It seeks to help local religious leaders create the social conditions necessary for the enforcement of laws protecting religious freedom. Wherever there are cases of individual violations of religious freedom, there are religious communities that are oppressed. But in these same communities, there are religious leaders struggling to create viable alternatives to being victimized. The IARF supports the initiatives of these local leaders.

Thus, the IARF supports efforts to develop respect among the different religious and ethnic communities and the enforcement of international law in the society. It sponsors interfaith activities to develop the social understanding and consensus necessary for the protection of religious freedom. It promotes and publicizes constructive programs in divided societies, programs which bring together people of different faith and ethnic traditions.

For example, at the IARF Congress in Bangalore, India, in August 1993, Muslims, Hindus, Christians, Buddhists, members of indigenous traditions, and others talked and ate and prayed together. Muslims who had not previously been involved in interfaith dialogue invited more than two hundred visitors to their College in order to share their views and to listen to those who might disagree with them (and some did, rather vociferously). Visitors went to a village of Muslims and Hindus, where the IARF has supported efforts to improve agriculture and education and to care for orphans.

As an association of religious and humanist groups, the IARF is founded on the belief that people of different faith traditions and philosophies can become friends, can share in eating and celebrating, can act in solidarity with minority religious communities which are being persecuted, and can help religious people of different traditions understand each other and cooperate together. The work of the IARF puts this belief to the test.

In the end, this all comes down to what you and I do in our own communities. All life is local. There is no global or international life, although today there is a global or international dimension to all local life. We are all affected by what is happening all over the world. But we live our lives in the world of our friends and neighbors and communities and voluntary associations and societies.

Our religious traditions are real for us in our fellowships and churches and synagogues and mosques and temples and, for some, in our interfaith activities as well. But it is here, among people we know and others we hope to know, that the human rights struggle goes on and will either be won or lost. The IARF is thus nothing other than the local activities of people like you and me, people who care enough about the whole world to care about their part of it, people who care enough about human dignity to care about the persons in their own communities, people who care enough about those yet to be born to care about what kind of neighborhood and community they will inherit.

The IARF methodology is basic to every religious tradition. It involves reaching out in friendship, getting to know others who are different, sharing by listening as well as talking, respecting differences and building on agreements, supporting constructive leadership, being compassionate, and standing by our friends when they are in trouble. Support for religious freedom is as simple, and as challenging, as that.

Universal Declaration of Human Rights

Adopted by the United Nations General Assembly, December 10, 1948.

NOTE: This Declaration, now more than fifty years old, remains highly relevant. It continues to be the standard for numerous international declarations and conventions on topics ranging from the rights of children and women, to religious freedom, and political, social, and economic development. The United Nations Conference on Human Rights, held in Vienna from June 14–25, 1993, drew more

than 2,000 representatives of 171 Member States along with more than 3,000 representatives of 813 NGOs, and many others. The conference was marked by an unusually high level of passion and clash over the universality of the principles and over the mesh of human rights, democracy, national sovereignty, and development. In addition, other issues such as torture, sexual slavery of women, and mistreatment of indigenous peoples vied for attention. Many NGO groups were frustrated by missed opportunities and by a lack of new initiatives for promoting and protecting human rights. Pierre Sane of Amnesty International summed up this critique: "There has been no reprieve for the victims, as governments [merely] fine-tuned their official declarations. . . . No radically new principles have been articulated. . . to move. . . from a 'common standard of achievement' to 'an obligation under international law.'" Among the challenges that remain are

1. Identifying the political, economic, and cultural world views that cause human rights violations
2. Challenging those systems that allow human rights abuses to continue even where, in principle, they are found objectionable
3. Moving to effective enforcement through international law.

The Universal Declaration of Human Rights

Whereas recognition of the inherent dignity and of the equal and inalienable rights of all members of the human family is the foundation of freedom, justice, and peace in the world,

Whereas disregard and contempt for human rights have resulted in barbarous acts which have outraged the conscience of mankind, and the advent of a world in which human beings shall enjoy freedom of speech and belief and freedom from fear and want has been proclaimed as the highest aspiration of the common people,

Whereas it is essential, if man is not to be compelled to have recourse, as a last resort, to rebellion against tyranny and oppression, that human rights should be protected by the rule of law,

Whereas it is essential to promote the development of friendly relations between nations,

Whereas the peoples of the United Nations have in the Charter reaffirmed their faith in fundamental human rights, in the dignity and worth of the human person and in the equal rights of men and women and have determined to promote social progress and better standards of life in larger freedom,

Whereas Member States have pledged themselves to achieve, in cooperation with the United Nations, the promotion of universal respect for and observance of human rights and fundamental freedoms,

Whereas a common understanding of these rights and freedoms is of the greatest importance for the full realization of this pledge,

Now, therefore, the General Assembly proclaims this Universal Declaration of Human Rights as a common standard of achievement for all peoples and all nations, to the end that every individual and every organ of society, keeping this Declaration constantly in mind, shall strive by teaching and education to promote respect for these rights and freedoms and by progressive measures, national and international, to secure their universal and effective recognition and observance, both among the peoples of Member States themselves and among the peoples of territories under their jurisdiction.

Article 1. All human beings are born free and equal in dignity and rights. They are endowed with reason and conscience and should act towards one another in a spirit of brotherhood.

Article 2. Everyone is entitled to all the rights and freedoms set forth in this Declaration, without distinction of any kind, such as race, colour, sex, language, religion, political or other opinion, national or social origin, property, birth, or other status.

Furthermore, no distinction shall be made on the basis of the political, jurisdictional, or international status of the country or territory to which a person belongs, whether it be independent, trust, nonselfgoverning, or under any other limitation of sovereignty.

Article 3. Everyone has the right to life, liberty, and security of person.

Article 4. No one shall be held in slavery or servitude; slavery and the slave trade shall be prohibited in all forms.

Article 5. No one shall be subjected to torture or to cruel, inhuman, or degrading treatment or punishment.

Article 6. Everyone has the right to recognition everywhere as a person before the law.

Article 7. All are equal before the law and are entitled without any discrimination to equal protection of the law. All are entitled to equal protection against any discrimination in violation of this Declaration and against any incitement to such discrimination.

Article 8. Everyone has the right to an effective remedy by the competent national tribunals for acts violating the fundamental rights granted him by the constitution or by law.

Article 9. No one shall be subjected to arbitrary arrest, detention, or exile.

Article 10. Everyone is entitled in full equality to a fair and public hearing by an independent and impartial tribunal, in the determination of his rights and obligations and of any criminal charge against him.

Article 11. 1) Everyone charged with a penal offense has the right to be presumed innocent until proved guilty according to law in a public trial at which he has had all the guarantees necessary for his defence.

2) No one shall be held guilty of any penal offense on account of any act or omission which did not constitute a penal offense, under national or international law, at the time when it was committed. Nor shall a heavier penalty be imposed than was applicable at the time the penal offense was committed.

Article 12. No one shall be subjected to arbitrary interference with his privacy, family, home, or correspondence, nor to attacks upon his honour and reputation. Everyone has the right to the protection of the law against such interference or attacks.

Article 13. 1) Everyone has the right to freedom of movement and residence within the borders of each State.

2) Everyone has the right to leave any country,

including his own, and to return to his country.

Article 14. 1) Everyone has the right to seek and to enjoy in other countries asylum from persecution.

2) This right may not be invoked in the case of prosecutions genuinely arising from nonpolitical crimes or from acts contrary to the purposes and principles of the United Nations.

Article 15. 1) Everyone has the right to a nationality.

2) No one shall be arbitrarily deprived of his nationality nor denied the right to change his nationality.

Article 16. 1) Men and women of full age, without any limitation due to race, nationality, or religion, have the right to marry and to found a family. They are entitled to equal rights as to marriage, during marriage, and at its dissolution.

2) Marriage shall be entered into only with the free and full consent of the intending spouses.

3) The family is the natural and fundamental group unit of society and is entitled to protection by society and the State.

Article 17. 1) Everyone has the right to own property alone as well as in association with others.

2) No one shall be arbitrarily deprived of his property.

Article 18. Everyone has the right to freedom of thought, conscience, and religion; this right includes freedom to change his religion or belief, and freedom, either alone or in community with others and in public or private, to manifest his religion or belief in teaching, practice, worship, and observance.

Article 19. Everyone has the right to freedom of opinion and expression; this right includes freedom to hold opinions without interference and to seek, receive, and impart information and ideas through any media and regardless of frontiers.

Article 20. 1) Everyone has the right to freedom of peaceful assembly and association.

2) No one may be compelled to belong to an association.

Article 21. 1) Everyone has the right to take part in the government of his country, directly or through freely chosen representatives.

2) Everyone has the right of equal access to public service in his country.

3) The will of the people shall be the basis of the authority of government; this will shall be expressed in periodic and genuine elections which shall be by universal and equal suffrage and shall be held by secret vote or by equivalent free voting procedures.

Article 22. Everyone, as a member of society, has the right to social security and is entitled to realization, through national effort and international cooperation and in accordance with the organization and resources of each State, of the economic, social, and cultural rights indispensable for his dignity and the free development of his personality.

Article 23. 1) Everyone has the right to work, to free choice of employment, to just and favourable conditions of work and to protection against unemployment.

2) Everyone, without any discrimination, has the right to equal pay for equal work.

3) Everyone has the right to just and favourable remuneration ensuring for himself and his family an existence worthy of human dignity, and supplemented, if necessary, by other means of social protection.

4) Everyone has the right to form and to join trade unions for the protection of his interests.

Article 24. Everyone has the right to rest and leisure, including reasonable limitation of working hours and periodic holidays with pay.

Article 25. 1) Everyone has the right to a standard of living adequate for the health and well-being of himself and of his family, including food, clothing, housing and medical care, and necessary social services, and the right to security in the event of unemployment, sickness, disability, widowhood, old age, or other lack of livelihood in circumstances beyond his control.

2) Motherhood and childhood are entitled to special care and assistance. All children, whether born in or out of wedlock, shall enjoy the same social protection,

Article 26. 1) Everyone has the right to education. Education shall be free, at least in the elementary and fundamental stages. Elementary education shall be compulsory. Technical and professional education shall be made generally available and higher education shall be equally accessible to all on the basis of merit.

2) Education shall be directed to the full development of the human personality and to the strengthening of respect for human rights and fundamental freedoms. It shall promote understanding, tolerance and friendship among all nations, racial or religious groups, and shall further the activities of the United Nations for the maintenance of peace.

3) Parents have a prior right to choose the kind of education that shall be given to their children.

Article 27. 1) Everyone has the right to freely participate in the cultural life of the community, to enjoy the arts, and to share in scientific advancement and its benefits.

2) Everyone has the right to the protection of the moral and material interests resulting from any scientific, literary, or artistic production of which he is the author.

Article 28. Everyone is entitled to a social and international order in which the rights and freedoms set forth in this Declaration can be fully realized.

Article 29. 1) Everyone has duties to the community in which alone the free and full development of his personality is possible.

2) In the exercise of his rights and freedoms, everyone shall be subject only to such limitations as are determined by law solely for the purpose of securing due recognition and respect for the rights and freedoms of others and of meeting the just requirements of morality, public order, and the general welfare in a democratic society.

3) These rights and freedoms may in no case be exercised contrary to the purposes and principles of the United Nations.

Article 30. Nothing in this Declaration may he interpreted as implying for any State, group, or person any right to engage in any activity or to perform any act aimed at the destruction of any of the rights and freedoms set forth herein.

The NGO Committee on Freedom of Religion and Belief

The Non-Governmental Committee on Freedom of Religion and Belief is composed of representatives of many organizations working within the UN community. The Committee was formed in 1990–91 to seek to strengthen the effectiveness of the United Nations in the prevention of religious intolerance and discrimination and in the advancement of religious freedom. While working to enhance the effectiveness of existing UN human rights mechanisms, the Committee also continues consultations and encourages the drafting and passage of a UN convention on freedom of religion and belief.

The United Nations has long been concerned with promoting greater religious freedom, beginning with the adoption of Article 18 of the Universal Declaration of Human Rights in 1948. Its most recent achievement was the adoption in 1981 of the "Declaration on the Elimination of All Forms of Intolerance and/or Discrimination Based on Religion or Belief." Among the official UN offices concerned with religious freedom is a Human Rights Committee which monitors the Covenant on Civil and Political Rights and a Special Rapporteur on Religious Intolerance who works out of the office of the Commission on Human Rights in Geneva.

Another effort of the NGO Committee is a World Report on Freedom of Thought, Conscience, Religion, or Belief, which are situation reports on more than sixty countries. The NGO Committee and the Committee of Religious NGOs also organize the annual Day for Freedom of Religion or Belief at the UN.

This committee provides a very good example of an interfaith affiliation that is working for the common good, including for those with no organized voice in international forums. Its members come from more than thirty religiously diverse NGOs, including Anglicans, Bahá'ís, Franciscans, the Humanist and Ethical Union, the International Association for Religious Freedom, Mahavir Jains, the Women of Reform Judaism, Lutherans, Pax Christi, Presbyterians, Seventh-Day Adventists and the World Conference on Religion and Peace, among many others.

—Compiled by the Editor from documents provided by the Committee

The Enduring Revolution

Charles W. Colson

NOTE: These excerpts present the opening sentences of the Templeton Address delivered by Charles Colson as he received the Templeton Prize for Progress in Religion. The Address was delivered at the University of Chicago, September 2, 1993, during the Parliament of the World's Religions. A "born-again" evangelical Christian (following the Watergate cover-up and his conviction on related charges), Colson spoke forcefully about the need and right to maintain and witness to one's own truth while, at the same time, sharing aspirations and common ground in common tasks with others from different faith traditions. The Templeton Prize was awarded for Colson's dedicated work of creating and organizing Prison Fellowship, which uses Christianity to help prisoners break from the cycle of crime; the Fellowship also advocates humanitarian treatment of prisoners, supports victims' rights and reform of sentencing laws. At that time, Prison Fellowship and its international affiliate had staff of over 280 who coordinated efforts of nearly 50,000 volunteers in 800 state and federal prisons and in more than 50 nations.

I speak as one transformed by Jesus Christ, the living God. He is the Way, the Truth, and the Life. He has lived in me for twenty years. His presence is the sole explanation for whatever is praiseworthy in my work, the only reason for my receiving this award.

That is more than a statement about myself. It is a claim to truth. It is a claim that may contradict your own. Yet on this, at least, we must agree: the right to do what I've just done—to state my faith without fear—is the first human right. Religious liberty is the essence of human dignity. We cannot build our temples on the ruins of individual conscience. For faith does not come through the weight of power, but through the hope of glory.

It is a sad fact that religious oppression is often practiced by religious groups. Sad—and inexcusable. A believer may risk prison for his own religious beliefs, but he may never build prisons for those of other beliefs.

It is our obligation—all of us here—to bring back

a renewed passion for religious liberty to every nation from which we came. It is our duty to create a cultural environment where conscience can flourish. I say this for the sake of every believer imprisoned for boldness or silenced by fear. I say this for the sake of every society that has yet to learn the benefits of vital and voluntary religious faith. . . .

The Conversion Dilemma

Joel Beversluis

One substantial source of conflict between religions is the problem of missions—witnessing to one's own faith commitments and efforts to convert others to those beliefs. While the missions of evangelical and Pentecostal Christians seem to be on the front edge of the problem in places such as the former Soviet Union and in India, in fact, missions take many forms and missionaries go both ways. This dilemma fits Robert Traer's analysis of the conflict between communal religious identity and authority, and individual rights of belief and free speech.

Vivekananda, the Indian sage who took the 1893 Parliament of Religions by storm, engaged in what is sometimes referred to as the first Eastern missionary voyages to Western Christendom. By force only of his eloquence and charisma, Vivekananda laid the groundwork for Vedanta centers in North America and Europe. Many others came after him, and are still coming to the West. When the gurus and swamis came to North America in the middle of the 20th century, and when the Hari Krishna sect appealed not only for funds but for the souls of American students, and when the Buddhist Dalai Lama makes the dilemma even more complex with his very appealing but nontheistic call for compassion and universal responsibility, many Christians here are offended—or confused or fearful—just as some Hindus are by Christian missionaries in India.

In the fall of 1999, during the Hindu festival of lights known as *Diwali*, both the Pope and the Southern Baptist Convention offended Hindus by encouraging Christian evangelism of Hindus. Southern Baptists were urged to pray for Hindus' deliverance from "the power of Satan," and published statements claiming that Hindus have no concept of sin or personal responsibility, and "worship gods which are not God." While Christians felt they were expressing their faith, love, and gospel mandate to convert the "lost" peoples to Christ, Hindus and others reacted to the language of evangelism with dismay, interpreting it as religious intolerance and hate language. Compounding the issue, when various enticements implicated in conversions, as in India where food, education, and health care are often parts of the Christian witness to the love of God, the conflict is exacerbated by suspicions of manipulation and new kinds of imperialism.

Taking a longer view of the dilemma, one that may be found among participants in the interfaith movement, cross-fertilization from religious witnessing and dialogue can serve the common good and enrich each community. One term for this enrichment is "mutual irradiation." Two examples demonstrate this interpretation, as well what is, for some, the offense of it:

1. The respect and self-respect given by Christian missionaries to the lowest castes and the poorest women, who are typically victims of the illegal but still functioning caste system in India, offers a model of human dignity that substantial segments of the Hindu community are not providing. The witness can stimulate self-analysis and appropriate change. Or, as sometimes happens, it can cause offense if the analysis and change are met with suspicion or denial.

2. Unfulfilling forms of Christian and Jewish spirituality have, for many people, been renewed and enriched by Hindu commitments to nonviolence, devotion to the presence of the Divine, and meditative practices. This exposure can deepen the faith and practice of Christians and Jews. Or, it can be interpreted as syncretism or worse by concerned parents and community leaders.

There's no simple answer to the dilemma, but

here are some key questions:

1. Does the concept of religious freedom guarantee the freedom to seek conversion of individuals despite the will of the majority community or family interests when the spiritual identity and destiny of its members seems to be challenged or changing?

2. Is it intolerant and disrespectful of another's religious beliefs to witness by offering both physical and spiritual comfort to those in need? Perhaps the disrespect comes with attitudes or style; are some styles—some words—offensive?

3. Can the interfaith movement allow for the witnessing of eager evangelicals, pious Muslims, or enlightened Hindus, or should the interfaith arena attempt to guarantee "no proselytizing"?

4. What models of witnessing, service, or dialogue offer solutions to this dilemma?

Voices of the Dispossessed

David Nelson

Music producer and member of the Vedanta Society of Southern California, David Nelson wrote the essay which follows as part of his privately published Notes and Reflections on the Parliament of the World's Religions, *1993.*

NOTE: Choosing our future wisely requires insight into the problems of the past and present. Humanity's mistakes and human rights abuses are clearly evident in their impact on those who have been forcibly separated from their cultures and lands. Whatever the causes—ranging from colonialism and ecological disasters to wars and cultural/religious conflict—the 1993 Parliament of the World's Religions recognized these matters as among the most significant issues of our time and made substantial commitments to addressing it. Because the news media grabbed onto some of the conflict expressed when these issues were aired at the Parliament, giving the whole event an inaccurate aura, this article provides a factual corrective; more importantly, the article introduces important dimensions of the issue, including the dignity and persistence of those whose voices speak for all of the dispossessed among us. Even as fugitives or disempowered minorities, these peoples carry with them insight, tradition, and culture. Those of us in dominant cultures can learn much about ourselves—our hospitality to strangers

and the ways our choices, governments, and businesses participate in disenfranchising people in other countries. These are lessons the community of religions needs to learn and teach if we claim compassion as our ideal and are guided by a global ethic.

The Monday morning plenary of the Parliament turned out to be a dramatic high point. It was one of the few events deemed newsworthy by the press, though for all the wrong reasons.

The plenary "Voices of the Dispossessed" belonged to 18.9 million international refugees [the number has increased dramatically since 1993], to an equal number who are displaced within their own national borders, and to countless others who suffer dispossession in subtler forms of discrimination and human rights abuses. The organizers felt that these issues, plaguing every continent, had to be faced early in the Parliament. They planned this plenary session around experiences of loss but also to identify affirmations of the spirit that have given the victimized around the world the strength to survive.

The opening prayer by Charles Nolley of the National Assembly of Bahá'ís preceded a filmed presentation by Luis Valenzuela of Brazil and Lourdes Sylvia of Cuba. The film portrayed how today, 500 million people go hungry. Many have a short life expectancy. To 1.5 billion of the world's citizens no medical care is available. Unemployment, poverty, and the lack of water and life's other basic necessities are rife. One out of every 135 people on Earth has been uprooted by persecution, and most of these are women and children. Dispossession is not the natural human condition but the product of processes that create extreme wealth and extreme poverty. Dispossession destroys the sense of human community, it destroys sacred places, and it creates the human degradation of homelessness.

Policies of border control leave the causes of flight unanswered, and thus far humanitarian efforts have proven inadequate. They can also serve as a smokescreen, creating the illusion that we are doing something. Dropping parcels of food from 10,000 feet does not stop genocide. Finally, the film asserted that all life is sacred, and any act against life is an act against God.

Personal stories and testimonies formed the substance of this plenary session, which diverged considerably from the printed schedule owing not just to changes beforehand but to unforeseen events.

From the main entrance of the conjoined State and Grand Ballrooms, Haitians made their way in procession toward the stage, singing and dancing. Watching them pass close by, I thought, these people have borne such suffering, yet with what dignity and humanity they come here to share something of their lives. Bishop Willie Romelus from the Diocese of Jeremie spoke with an interpreter.

Before the fall of the Duvalier dictatorship he had been a voice for the voiceless, and after the ouster of President Aristide he became the only one of Haiti's twelve Roman Catholic bishops to denounce the campaign of terror.

I come to say that Haitian people are tired of injustices. Together let us find a way to peace. In Haiti there is no freedom of speech, thought, or movement. Haitians chose a leader but were dispossessed of that choice. Supporters of the exiled president are still beaten and jailed, even for possessing a photo of him, although there is now an agreement for his return. There is also spiritual dispossession. One is not free to worship as one chooses, and there are no safe refuges. Beaten people are hunted down even in hospitals.

Ladjamaya, a Baha'i actress and dramatist from Colorado, speaks to and from the heart on issues of peace and racial harmony. She asked,

Is there strength enough in democracy? Virtue enough in our civilization? Strength enough in religion to bring justice to the Americas? Our civilization has produced magnificent results, but American civilization lacks two things: simple justice and a humanity that lets us all look at each other as brothers.

Those words were not her own but came from a speech made in 1875, when racism ruled the South.

One hundred eighteen years later, those words reflect the hypocrisy and injustice of present-day America. From the beginning the United States embraced a contradictory set of values. Alongside the highest principles there was slavery, and it took a Civil War to abolish that. Still, its evil consequences linger on in the nation's continuing neglect of the ravages of racism. Racism is the most pressing issue confronting America today; it affects the hearts of black and white Americans, and both races must strive for unity. We need close association and fellowship.

Ghulam Nabi Fai of Kashmir started his address with the statistics that Kashmir is larger in population than 114 sovereign nations and larger in land area than 87. His implication was that Kashmir should be independent. "When we lose our homeland, we lose more than real estate. We lose tradition, memories, family. We cannot recreate a homeland in a refugee camp. Occupying forces destroy beliefs, sacred books, and sacred sites." With the partition of India and Pakistan in 1947, Kashmir was forcibly occupied by the Indian government, 1.5 million refugees were created, families were divided, and a culture was destroyed. Ghulam Nabi Fai was now speaking in exile, cut off from his family....

At this point disturbances erupted. There was shouting all around, and I couldn't understand much. For the most part I wrote furiously in my notebook, but toward the front a Hindu in *gerua* was standing and shouting, and waving his right arm accusingly. "Point of order, Mr. Chairman!" he said. Calls came from the audience to remove the speaker. Some were protesting what they felt to be a politicization of the Parliament. But in India is it possible to disentangle the volatile mix of religion and politics?

The moderator took charge, reaffirming the Parliament's commitment to giving a voice to the dispossessed, and enthusiastic applause concurred. Before long, order returned, and Thomas M. Johnson from Liberia began a litany of the political events in Monrovia that led to his persecution. He had been arrested, beaten, and tortured as a rebel in the civil war. He was imprisoned with more than two hundred others in a small room without hygienic facilities. The daily meal was rice and oil, served in the small sort of bowl used in latex tapping, and the rice was half stones. The prisoners slept on a concrete floor. On 25 July the warring factions signed a peace treaty, which a newly formed interim government, in an about-face, decided to reject. Relief trucks with food were turned back, and three hundred people starved to death. Once the most stable nation on the African continent, Liberia today lies in ruins, while its religions, Christian and non-Christian, work for peace.

"Bismillahi rakhman i rahim," intoned the black speaker, thus identifying himself as a Muslim. Resplendent in an ivory-colored silk robe and a gold crown that conjured up visions of the patriarchs of antiquity, Sheikh Ahmed Tijani Ben Omar of Ghana chanted in Arabic, then in English, and launched into a high-minded exhortation. His impassioned manner reminded me of an African-American gospel preacher, and there was power in his utterances.

> Suspicions of each other are great sins. Throw away negative attitudes. You call yourselves Christian, Jew, Hindu, Muslim, but God says, "I made you all from a single man and woman, and I made you to look different, with different languages. I made you tall, short, fat, clumsy, pale, dark..." All look beautiful to the creator! Who am I to find fault with you if God is pleased with your deeds? This Parliament should be a truthful Parliament. It is not a crime to be a Christian, a Jew, a Hindu, or a Buddhist. If you trust in God, treat all believers equally. I am a Muslim. I believe in Moses [so] I am a Jew. I believe in Jesus Christ [so] I am a Christian. I believe in the prophet Muhammad; I am a Muslim.

My heart swelled with respect for this man, and I thought what a lesson this was. A follower of Islam had laid aside his own tale of dispossession and exhorted us as brothers and sisters to seek that which is best within us all. I reflected and regretted that fundamentalism has poisoned some of the faithful, and by extension our perception of the Islamic world. And fundamentalism, that scourge of our time, is a virus to which no religion is immune.

Father Thomas Kocherry related the experiences of fishermen in southern India. In the global market where all members fight for a share of the profits, anything without monetary value is rejected. Since India is becoming a part of that market, traditional ways of life are under threat. In cooperation with the West, the Indian government has put Western technology in direct competition with traditional fishing methods, and if that were not harmful enough, mechanization is also depleting the stocks of fish. Other forms of development are causing deforestation and water pollution and together with the construction of dams are further diminishing the fishermen's livelihood. With the arrival of more and more American companies the situation spirals ever downward. In India's coastal states a growing resistance movement has begun to win concessions from the government even as new threats appear. Japanese machines are replacing the women netmakers. Opposition to a nuclear power plant led to arrests. Now there is an emerging alliance throughout India of various dispossessed groups against the development measures of the government.

Norbu Samphell had come to Chicago the previous January with ninety-two Tibetans. He recalled in vivid detail his family's difficult escape over the snowy mountains and his thirty-year stay in India, a nation of wonderful kindnesses, like no other in the world. Tibet, he urged, needs to gain independence.

The session's moderator interrupted to say that God's greatest gift is the power of speech. That same speech can unleash terrible forces and threaten our unity. This impromptu message came at the request of a consultation group, including the Parliament's trustees, which had met downstairs immediately following the controversy. There, Sikh, Jain, Hindu, Muslim, Buddhist, Zoroastrian, and Christian leaders expressed their wish to see the purpose of the Parliament reaffirmed. At one time each of them had suffered at the hands of another, but they came together here in harmony to encourage all by moderate speech to find ways to unity. Applause signaled the audience's approval.

Molefe Tsele from Soweto represents one of 5 million black families whose land was stolen by the white government. The experience of relocation, misery, and death energized him in the struggle against apartheid, and he participated in the 1976 uprising. Three times he was imprisoned and tortured, but, he noted, that is nothing compared to the pain and suffering of millions today.

The accounts of human misery had become all too familiar by now, and Hayelom Ayele added an almost predictable picture of cruelty in his native Ethiopia. Two million have fled the country, and 1.5 million are dead of famine or were killed by the communist junta.

When Gurmit Singh Aulakh from Punjab came to the podium wearing the characteristic Sikh turban, this one bright orange, I feared that discord might flare up again. He began with a simple statement of facts. The 1947 Partition had separated the Sikhs from the birthplace of their Guru Nanak. They had tried to make the best of their diminished Punjabi homeland, but they were only 2 percent of the population and were discriminated against. A brief history brought us up to the storming and desecration by Indian military forces of the Golden Temple at Amritsar, the holiest shrine. Thirty other temples were also attacked. Twenty thousand Sikhs were tortured or killed, and their scriptures were burned. Later thousands were killed with government compliance, he said, in anti-Sikh pogroms. (He failed to mention that in retaliation Sikhs assassinated the prime minister, Indira Gandhi.) The cycle of violence continues. The death toll has reached 100,000 while 70,000 more languish in prisons without charges or trial. He began to speak about rape and torture, and that is when protest erupted again.

The same Hindu whom I described earlier was on his feet again, shouting with upraised arm. This time one of the security guards tried to calm him down. Shouting was erupting all over the room, and this time it was worse than before. As tension mounted, the lights came on to full brightness, and the waiting speakers were ushered off the platform. Protesters leapt to their feet. One was an Indian woman just

three seats to my right. People around tried to quiet her but to no avail. From just behind and all around, Sikhs chanted, "Let him speak! Let him speak!" Daniel Gomez-Ibanez joined the lone Gurmit Singh Aulakh, who remained at the podium, and other Parliament organizers came to the stage. They seemed mired in indecision. Confusion reigned throughout the room.

I noticed the television cameras on the balconies and to the left and the right of the platform and wondered if this would make the news. When the presenter left the platform, dismay rang out from the audience, and Sikh voices called, "Let him speak! This is not fair! This is a democracy! These are human rights!" Daniel announced that the session would proceed.

Then, amid the welter of voices, I detected the strains of "We Shall Overcome," first quietly then swelling in numbers and volume. Hands joined everywhere, and we stood up and sang, clasped hands held high in solidarity. It was hard to sing through all the tears, but sing I did, and before long the atmosphere in the room was transformed.

Much time had been lost, and the last presentations had to be postponed. We did not hear from Sharifa Sharif of Afghanistan, David Hernandez of the Chicago homeless, Juanita Baltzibal and the sacred dancers who had come with her from Guatemala. Nor did we hear from Waldemar Boff, of Petropolis, São Paulo, Brazil, who was to summarize the "voices" and formulate their questions and challenge to the Parliament.

Instead, Jennie Joe, a Navajo, spoke on behalf of all the indigenous peoples of the Americas who have suffered dispossession and genocide for five-hundred years. White men justified the taking of land from those people whom they deemed "without religion." She remembered in her youth greeting the rising sun with cornmeal and praying for all humankind. "That is spirituality. Our religion does not believe in divine retribution." She spoke of the healing ceremonies being the most misunderstood aspect of her religion, because they are the most visible. Bad thoughts can bring illness; everything is interrelated. She recalled how Indian youths were forced into boarding schools and taught that their beliefs were heathen and valueless, how they were taught to be ashamed of their backgrounds, their families, and those closest to them. Native Americans have had to fight hard to regain their religion. They have had to go through the white man's courts. And Native Americans were excluded from the first Parliament in 1893. "[Now] it is encouraging," she concluded, "that you recognize that we *do* have a religion."

Onstage, led by four Native Americans resplendent in feathers, a circle formed of speakers and dancers from every continent. The drumming enticed more and more people to take part, and the dancers came down from the stage and merged with that larger humanity. Around the ballroom, people also joined hands and danced in a line that stretched up the aisles and circled the room's periphery. With everyone placed in it and sharing the dance, the circle was a symbol of reconciliation on behalf of humanity.

Burdened with notebook and *chaddar*, I felt constrained from joining the line. Instead I joined friends from the Vedanta Society of New York, who stood nearby. We shared our thoughts on what had been an extraordinary morning. When the drumming stopped, the moderator asked us all to embrace the next person. "Well, fellow Vedantist!" I laughed, hugging one. Another, spotting a blue-turbaned Sikh not far away, ran to embrace him. I think we all left that room better for having been there.

The Sweetgrass Hills

Native American Rights Fund

NOTE: This description provides an example of the dispossession which is a common experience of indigenous peoples throughout the world. It was adapted by the editor from an informational letter about the destruction of sacred lands and the work of the Native American Rights Fund.

"Every society needs sacred places. A society that cannot remember its past and honor it is in peril of losing its soul."

VINE DELORIA,
Standing Rock Sioux,
Native American author and legal scholar.

In the far north of Montana lie the Sweetgrass Hills. It is a magnificent land of mountainous buttes and rocky ridges, separated by sweeping open grasslands. It is also a sacred place. For 12,000 years, Blackfeet, Chippewa-Cree, Salish, Kootenai, and other Indian tribes have journeyed to the Sweetgrass Hills to perform religious ceremonies that bind them to each other, to the earth, and to past generations.

In the mid-1990s, the U.S. Bureau of Land Management planned to give a foreign mining company the go-ahead to rape these sacred hills in search of gold.

Plundering temples and destroying sacred relics is an age-old way to debase a conquered people. Spanish conquistadors leveled the temples of the Aztecs. Hitler's Nazis burned and defaced Jewish synagogues all across Europe. And for over two hundred years, the U.S. government has torn down, dug up, bulldozed, dammed, logged, mined, and paved over Native American sacred worship sites.

But they still aren't done with us. More than sixty Native American sacred sites in addition to the Sweetgrass Hills are threatened with total destruction or massive desecration.

You must understand what this means to Native

Women Struggle for Survival

"There are, however, many [women] who have difficulty in tuning in to these thoughts and spiritual problems, because the daily struggle for life and survival, against death in all its varied forms, demands all the energy they can get....

"Among them, and even right in their vanguard, are women like Domitilla de Chungara from the tin mines of Bolivia. She organized a hunger strike in the midst of starvation, in order to obtain better living conditions. Or Rigoberta Menchu from Guatemala who has experienced how her people are being destroyed, and rises up against it. Among them are also the women of the Plaza de Mayo in Argentina, who each Thursday for years now have been marching up and down in silent protest in front of the government palace in Buenos Aires, in order to obtain information about their disappeared children. And the Philippino nuns who are demonstrating their concern for the young prostitutes, and exposing the scandal of the human slave trade. Or the Babushkas in Russia who are keeping the church alive.

"The women in the peace movements and the anti-apartheid movements everywhere: they get to grips with these issues through practical action, for, whatever the question about God-father or mother-goddess may be, the surest way of finding an answer lies in looking at the faces of the women, men, and children who have been entrusted to us, and in whom God, as woman, man, or child, meets us and waits for our response."

from *We Will Not Hang Our Harps on the Willows*,
by Barbel Von Wartenberg-Potter,
World Council of Churches

American religions, where the land and the religion cannot be separated. For Native Americans, the sacred site is the wellspring of religious beliefs. The land is our "church," and it cannot be rebuilt down the road.

The tribes that worship at the Sweetgrass Hills come to this land because the center of their spirituality lies here and nowhere else. If the Bureau of Land Management succeeds in selling the land out from under them, the wellspring of their religion will be gone—forever.

We must secure for Native Americans the fundamental right that every other American takes for granted—the right to freely practice our religions—by passing the Native American Free Exercise of Religion Act (NAFERA).

We do not worship creation: we worship the Great Spirit in the creation he has made. We pray to the pail of water in the sweat lodge but that represents all the waters everywhere, the Great Lakes, the Mississippi River, the Missouri, all the waters in the world. The pail of water represents all of that. We pray through the water to the Great Spirit.

Finally—Choosing Our Future As Women

Rev. Marchiene Vroon Rienstra

Author, minister (Reformed Church of America), interfaith leader at Mother's Trust, Mother's Place, and counselor

For the first time in recorded human history, women who are adherents of the world's religions are claiming the right and power, in a whole new way, to choose their faith and their future for themselves. This empowerment has two contexts—within their separate religious communities and in the emerging globalization of the women's movement.

No longer can it be said that this movement is primarily a white, middle-class, Euro-American women's movement. It has become a worldwide phenomenon, transcending national, cultural, racial, and economic boundaries. It defies definition and dismissal as simply feminist. In fact, the movement is in such ferment, charged with such energy, so fast-growing, and filled with such variety, that it is itself only beginning to come to a kind of self-understanding and clarity about its goals.

Fortunately, at this point in history, certain common ground is emerging in this women's movement in the context of the community of the world's religions. One piece of that common ground is the ever-clearer understanding of the ways in which all of the major religions of the world have been, to a greater or lesser degree, patriarchal, and therefore limiting of women's gifts and roles in the religious community and society as a whole. As women scholars representing the major religions of the world have had increasing opportunity to meet in global religious forums, they have compared notes and found that in spite of their many differences, there are certain striking similarities in their experience and observation. The Preface to *The Spiral Path* sums it up in eloquent words:

> Women have been given steps to spirituality by the same patriarchal groups that have given them their place in society, in politics, in the arts, in the workplace. Her spirituality was developed for her alongside her subjugation and invalidation. Masculine values have been taught as the norm in spirituality. . . . Women have so internalized these concepts that they themselves guided young women in those same male norms.... The resultant pain of women throughout the ages, the loss of the gifts in spiritual literature and service that they might have given humankind, can only be mourned. But after our mourning, we must begin again the process of discovery. There is much to discover. (p. ix)

As women have discovered the specific ways in which their experience and views have not been taken into account in the scriptures, theology, worship, and customs of their various religious traditions, they have begun to review those traditions with a view to recovering what is life-giving in them for women. Gifted women like Islamic scholar Riffat Hassan, Buddhist scholar Rita Gross, Hindu scholar Lina Gupta, Jewish scholar Judith Plaskow, and Christian scholar Phyllis Tribble have found neglected elements in their respective traditions which can be recovered and reinterpreted to establish claims for a just and equal treatment of women in the world's religions. Even more, their studies are helping to lay the foundation for transforming the world's religions into traditions that are respectful of and hospitable to the special wisdom and gifts women can contribute to the future of religious life around the globe.

An important element of such studies is the asking of hard questions which serve to arouse the kind of creative dissonance out of which real learning arises. These questions are often painful for both women and men, and they can shake the very foundations of the faiths to which they are addressed, for they go the the root of the religious systems which express these faiths.

Ursula King, editor of *Women in the World's Religions*, summarizes these dissonance-creating questions:

> Looking at the past, one can ask: what do the sacred scriptures, the theological and spiritual writings of the religions of the world, teach about women? How far do the different religions draw on feminine symbols in speaking about ultimate reality, about the nature and experience of the spirit? To what extent do women take part in ritual and religious practices, choose to follow the religious life, or hold positions of authority in particular religions? Most important, what is the religious experience of women? Why has it been so little reflected in the official theological literature whereas it has contributed so much to the wealth of mystical and spiritual writings in different religions? Perhaps the central question today is how far women are still hindered or, alternatively, encouraged in giving full expression to their religious experience. Contemporary feminists often sharply criticize traditional religions

and explore the meaning of religion for women in a new way. Although this challenge has barely been met by the official religious leaders of the world, in each tradition women and men are beginning to reflect on its meaning. (p. vii)

Along with such questions come discoveries that are the result of the consciousness raised by such questions. In the past, this sort of consciousness was rare among the adherents of the world's religions. But in our age, for the first time, believers of various faiths are beginning to realize that sexual differentiation has been taken for granted without being critically reflected upon by both men and women in positions of authority in past human history. The critical reflection now necessary highlights gender differences in religious experience and expression, but also seeks eventually to embrace them in a new, more meaningful unity. This new unity requires religious symbol-systems, action, and organization which fully reflect the experience and wisdom of both women and men in equal measure.

For example, Friday M. Mbon has this to say about the role of women in African traditional religions.

> While educated African women in the towns and cities today can sing, "What men can do, women can also do," in the areas of political, educational, and scientific achievements, the uneducated women in African villages could sing the same slogan in areas of African traditional religious life. Yet if they dare sing such a slogan, the menfolk may mistake it as a song of equality between them and the women and therefore a threat to their supposed divinely sanctioned superiority over the womenfolk. (p. 10, *Women in the World's Religions*)

Anne Bancroft has this to say about women in Buddhism.

> It is interesting to speculate on the extent of fear which women seemed then and still seem to engender in men. They are regarded as not only

personal but universal obstacles, preventing the spiritual progress of humankind and even filling the Buddha with fear that they would bring about the fall of the Sangha. Denise Carmody takes the view that early conservative Buddhism linked desire and productive becoming with *samsara*, the realm of change and endless redistribution of the life-force. Since *samsara* was the enemy and the trap, so too was femaleness. Thus, women took on symbolic force as epitomizing karmic bonds. (p. 86, *Women in the World's Religions*)

Lina Gupta critiques the Hindu tradition, and brilliantly reshapes the understanding of the goddess Kali in Hinduism to envision a new order of mutuality and equality between women and men.

> Scripturally, both the husband and the wife are considered to be reflections of the divine nature. Therefore, any hierarchical order negates the very premise on which it appears to be based. Manu used the symbols of duality found in the principles of Siva and Sakti to support a hierarchical and patriarchal system in which women's understanding and experience of their own power have been severely restrained. In doing so, he violated the very spirit of those symbols. The more the patriarchal mind recognized the force of the creative power present in the divine female, the more it created an environment for the feminine to be restricted and restrained.... The patriarchal reading neglects the source of both subject and object, the One unmanifested Brahman who is neither a subject nor an object, male nor female. Both subject and object in reality are the same. Union transcends sexual differences and the individual ego. Kali illustrates this.... As we listen to the various stories of the goddess Kali we see them take shape into a definite pattern of experience.... By reviewing these stories over and over again, understanding them in their most liberating sense, and reappropriating from them those elements which are most powerful as resources for the liberation of both

men and women—taken as authentic and genuinely spiritual those aspects that promote our overall welfare—we can eliminate the unessential details and the patriarchal distortions and finally identify the sources and patterns of our oppressed past and present. It is this pattern that finally reveals the way we are now, and what we could possibly become. It shows the ways in which the images and the stories of Kali can be liberating and empowering to all through exposing an essence that goes beyond male and female, beauty and ugliness, life and death, and all forms of alienation and separation. (pp. 35–37, passim, *After Patriarchy*)

Lina Gupta's words reveal the essential method and approach being taken by women scholars and leaders in all of the world's great religions. The women writers mentioned above, and others too numerous to mention, are challenging traditional religious teachings and practices. A veritable torrent of books and papers are carrying this flood tide of new questions and ideas into the minds and hearts of men and women the world over. At heart, they challenge the dualistic thought patterns about men and women which were the matrix of and became enshrined in the great historical religions, whether one looks at their scriptures, teachings, worship, rites, or institutions. Not only do they probe just how far women's experience has been taken into account in the world's religious traditions; they also ask how far traditional religious teachings can still speak to women and men today whose consciousness has been changed, and who find the old patriarchal assumptions incredible.

So far, as many women scholars and leaders are noting, the loss of the plausibility of much traditional religious doctrine and worship has escaped the attention of many male religious authorities, who are inexcusably ignorant of the wider issues being raised by the women's movement, and often do not wish to take its critique of religion seriously. This situation contains within it the serious possibility of crisis for the world's religions as the women's movement grows in power

and credibility, winning men as well as women to a point of view which poses a profound challenge to the religious status quo all over the world.

The societal changes brought about by the ongoing processes of Westernization and globalization simply make the challenge all the greater as more and more women the world over exercise leadership in more and more fields previously closed to them. "Nothing is as powerful as an idea whose time has come," goes an old saying. Indeed. And the power of the idea that women may and must choose their future also in terms of how they will participate in the world's religious communities is one that is growing daily. News magazines and religious periodicals carry constant accounts of the changes taking place as more and more women and men refuse to believe that women must take an inferior place. Women are in the forefront now of the ecological, peace, and interfaith movements which value the interconnection of all people and things, and seek a global order which makes the survival and flourishing of this fragile planet a priority. The very violence of certain reactions to all of this by fundamentalist wings of various religious communities only serves to reinforce the power of this turn in the tide of human history. The world community of religions really has no choice but to accept the challenge of this historic movement in which women are choosing their own future in terms of their faith commitments.

The world's religions contain within them a rich deposit of hard-won wisdom which is universal and life-giving for men and women the world over. Though it is buried under patriarchal layers of interpretation and custom, it is crucially important to preserve this treasure trove of wisdom. If women and men in increasing numbers desert their faith traditions because they cannot find in them the spiritual resources they need for a flourishing spirituality that equally honors the gifts and wisdom of women and men, then those faith traditions will gradually weaken and perhaps even fade away, be it ever so slowly. That would be a great loss to the human race, which is in desperate need of the accumulated wisdom of the world's religions. If there is to be a future worth choosing for any of us, a recovery of religious wisdom and a transformation of the religious traditions in which wisdom is embedded—making them equally hospitable to women and men—are urgent necessities. For too long, the human race and the world's religions have flown with only one wing fully outspread. When women's wings are added to men's, what a glorious flight of the Spirit there will be!

REFERENCES (*Books quoted in this article and useful for further study*):

After Patriarchy, edited by Paul M. Cooey, William R. Eakin, and J.B. McDaniel (Faith Meets Faith: An Orbis Series in Interreligious Dialogue) published by Orbis Books, Maryknoll, N.Y., 1991.

Women in the World's Religions, edited by Ursula King (God: The Contemporary Discussion Series) published by Paragon House, N.Y., 1987.

The Spiral Path, edited by Theresa King O'Brien (Essays and Interviews on Women's Spirituality) published by YES International Publishers, St. Paul, Minn., 1988.

The World's Religions for the World's Children

NOTE: Prior to the World Summit for Children, held at the United Nations in September 1990, a Conference on the World's Religions for the World's Children was held in Princeton, New Jersey. Organized by the United Nations Children's Fund (UNICEF) and by the World Conference on Religion and Peace, it was attended by 150 people from forty countries drawn from twelve major religions. The participants agreed that there is still time to reclaim the future for our children and succeeding generations. And they said that "despite differences in our traditions, our practices, our beliefs, and despite our inadequacies" they would work together to influence their nation's political leaders and their own religious communities so that children's basic needs will be given priority. To this end they issued the following declaration and an action plan with specific goals.

Conscious of the plight of vast numbers of children throughout the world, we representatives of twelve religions from forty countries participating in the World's Religions for the World's Children conference, meeting in Princeton, New Jersey, U.S.A., July 25–27, 1990, speak with common voice. We commend the United Nations for its efforts in creating and adopting the Convention on the Rights of the Child. We urge its ratification and adherence in practice by all governments. We commend those government leaders who have recognized the urgency and priority of addressing the needs and rights of children. Cognizant of the efforts of earlier generations represented by the 1924 League of Nations Geneva Declaration on the Rights of the Child, and the United Nations 1959 Declaration on the Rights of the Child, we are aware of the difficulty of moving from the statement of rights to their realization. Our common voice resounds despite differences in our traditions, our practices, our beliefs, and despite our inadequacies. Our religious traditions summon us to regard the child as more than a legal entity. The sacredness of life compels us to be a voice of conscience. We speak hereby to heads of state and government, to the United Nations, to our religious communities and to all, throughout the world, who have held a child in love, with joy for its life, with tears for its pain.

Recognizing the Rights of the Child

The Convention on the Rights of the Child, which acknowledges the rights of the world's children to survival, protection, and development, is rooted in the Universal Declaration of Human Rights which recognizes the inherent dignity and the equal and inalienable rights of all members of the human family. We recognize that, lamentably, such rights are not universally respected or legally guaranteed, nor are they always accepted as moral obligations.

As religious men and women, however, we dare to assert that the state of childhood, with its attendant vulnerability, dependence, and potential, founds a principle that the human community must give children's basic needs priority over competing claims—and a "first call"—upon the human and material resources of our societies. Such a principle needs to be both recognized and accepted as a guide for relevant actions in human communities.

Society's Responsibility to Children

The survival, protection, and development of children is the responsibility of the whole world community. However, for countless girls and boys there is no survival, no protection, no chance for development. Societies are morally bound to address the obscene conditions which result in the death of 14 million children during every year, two-thirds from preventable causes, and the other conditions of abject poverty that result in wasted bodies, stunted physical development, or permanent handicaps. Existing health care knowledge and technology, promptly and persistently applied, have the potential to make dramatic improvements in child survival and health with relatively moderate financial costs. Such possibilities underscore our obligations. To fail to make such efforts for the well-being of children is morally unconscionable.

Societies are also bound to rectify the gross injustices and violations which children suffer, such as child abuse, sexual and labor exploitation, homelessness, victimization due to war, and the tragic consequences of family disintegration, cultural genocide, social deprivations stemming from intolerance based upon race, sex, age, or religion, to name but a few. Addressing these issues will require fundamental structural change.

Societies are obliged to confront the broad constellation of human forces and failures which affect children. The social and international order necessary for the full realization of children's rights does not exist. Our interdependent political and economic systems can be restructured and refined to provide children their basic needs. The world has the resources to provide the basic needs of children. Wars, in which children are increasingly the victims and even the targets of violence, need not be the inevitable expression of human conflict. Our readiness to resolve conflict through violent means can be changed. Development cannot succeed under the illusion that our resources are inexhaustible or uni-

formly self-renewing. While our air, water, and soil are polluted, we still have the chance to reverse the most devastating trends of environmental degradation. What will we bequeath to our children? The dangerous forces that impact upon children jeopardize the full realization of freedom, justice, and peace.

The grim realities we confront demand our outrage because they exist; they demand our repentance because they have been silently tolerated or even justified; they demand our response because all can be addressed, some of them quite readily.

Responsibilities of Governments and International Organizations

We religious women and men gathered in Princeton urge governments and relevant international organizations to fulfill their responsibilities to children through at least the following:

- To sign, ratify, fully implement, and monitor compliance with the Convention on the Rights of the Child.
- To undertake those actions which would have a dramatic impact upon child survival at very low cost.
- To take vigorous and immediate action to rectify the myriad obscene injustices which children suffer, such as abuse from exploitation.
- To take the steps necessary, in each country, to achieve the goals for children and development in the 1990s, as defined by the international community.
- To utilize peaceful means of conflict resolution in order to protect children from the ravages of war.
- To create new, or adjust existing, political and economic structures that can provide access to and distribution—or all—of both the natural resources and the products of human labor, including information, so that the claims of justice may be met.
- To undertake the bold steps known to be necessary and to develop new steps to protect and reclaim the environment as the heritage for our children and succeeding generations' development.
- To allocate adequate funds to undergird the global programs addressing health, education, and devel-

opment.

- To ensure full participation of NGOs in the implementation of appropriate actions.
- To provide basic education for all children.
- To reduce the burden of debt that robs a nation's children of their rightful heritage.
- To support the family, help keep it intact, and provide the resources and services for the adequate care and protection of its children.
- To provide resources and develop programs for the survival, health, and education of women, the bearers and primary caregivers of children.
- To ensure the participation of women in the entire range of social governance and decision making.
- To take steps to ensure that children actually receive a first call on society's resources.

Religious and Spiritual Responsibilities

Our consciences as religious men and women, including those of us bearing governmental and other forms of social responsibility, will not allow us to evade the responsibilities of our religious traditions. We therefore call upon religious women and men and institutions:

- To order our own priorities so as to reaffirm our central claims about the sacredness of life.
- To examine any of our own traditional practices that may violate the deeper spirit of our faiths and indeed the sacredness of human life.
- To provide resources for families, from single parent to extended in size, so that they can fulfill their roles in spiritual formation and education.
- To protect and support parents in their rights and responsibilities as the primary religious educators.
- To undertake actions to promote the well-being, education, and leadership roles of female children and their right to equal treatment with male children
- To engage in services of nurture, mercy, education, and advocacy, and to exemplify before the world the possibilities for compassion and care
- To cooperate with all agencies of society, including other religious bodies, that have as their purpose the well-being of the children in our societies.
- To advocate the ratification and implementation of the Convention on the Rights of the Child in our respective countries and communities.
- To work for the protection of the unborn in accord with the teachings of our respective religious traditions.
- To establish independent systems to monitor the state of children's rights.
- To coordinate with other religions in the removal of religious and other forms of prejudice and conflict in all contexts.
- To reorder our communities' resources in accord with the principle of the right of children to a first call on those resources.

Political will is necessary to create the social and international climate in which survival, protection, and development can be achieved. We call on governments and the international community to manifest that will.

Spiritual will is necessary to establish a shared ethos in which children can flourish in freedom, justice, and peace. We call on all spiritual and religious peoples and institutions to manifest that will.

The Convention on the Rights of the Child

Children are especially vulnerable to rights violations. Each day nearly 35,000 children die from lack of food, shelter, or primary health care. About 30 million children live in the world's streets, and another 20 million have been displaced, physically disabled, or otherwise traumatized by armed conflict.

The United Nations Convention on the Rights of the Child is an international treaty establishing an international legal framework for the civil, social, economic, and political rights of children. Unanimously adopted by the UN General Assembly on November 20, 1989, as of February 1993, 129 countries have ratified the Convention so far. Drafted over a ten-year period by the forty-three nations that are members of the United Nations Human Rights Commission, the Convention is the most comprehensive international expression of children's rights. By gathering them into a single legal instrument, the Convention represents an unprecedented international consensus.

The Convention commits all ratifying nations to recognize that children have special needs and encourages all governments to establish standards for their survival, protection, and development. *Survival* means the right to food, shelter, and essential health care. *Protection* includes sheltering children from abuse and from involvement in war, and gives them the right to a name and nationality. *Development* guarantees the right to a basic education and provides special care for handicapped children.

The preamble recalls the basic principles of the United Nations Charter and specific provisions of relevant human rights treaties such as the Universal Declaration of Human Rights. It reaffirms the fact that children, because of their vulnerability, need special care and protection, and it places special emphasis on the primary caring responsibility of the family and extended family.

The Convention also reaffirms the need for legal and other protection of the child before and after birth, the importance of respect for the cultural values of the child's community, and the vital role of international cooperation in securing children's rights. It also includes provisions never before recognized in an international treaty, requiring countries to

- Do everything possible to ensure child survival
- Pursue full implementation of the child's right to the highest level of health possible by working to provide primary health care, to educate mothers and families about breast-feeding and family planning, and to abolish harmful practices such as the preferential treatment of male children
- Work toward achieving universal primary education, and take measures to reduce dropout rates and encourage regular school attendance.

The World Summit for Children

Nearly one year later, in September 1990, a unique summit meeting was held at the United Nations in an extraordinary effort to address the problems of the world's children. With seventy-two heads of state and government, the World Summit for Children was the biggest gathering of national leaders in the history of humankind up to that time. It also was the first time that leaders from around the globe had met for a single, common purpose—to give children priority on governmental agendas in the 1990s.

The World Summit's goals were to

- Draw attention to major problems affecting children—debt, war, and other hostilities, environmental deterioration, drugs, and AIDS
- Give children first call on society's resources
- Accelerate implementation and monitoring of the Convention on the Rights of the Child
- Encourage people and their governments to "do the doable"—mass, low-cost, available means of action.

—Excerpted and adapted by the Editor from *Our Children Their Earth*, p. 21, from the UNICEF *Backgrounder*, and from the Convention on the Rights of the Child.

A Universal Declaration of Human Responsibilities

The InterAction Council

NOTE: The first public draft of a declaration emphasizing responsibilities was presented in 1997. Due to the process of discussion and refinement, a final draft has not yet been prepared; and, while its language suggests adoption by the United Nations, it had not yet been formally considered there as of November 1999. The early draft of the document was substantially influenced by religious leaders as well as other scholars, including Dr. Hans Küng, who had drafted the Global Ethic. Other contributions and amendments came from numerous retired world leaders who constitute the InterAction Council, as well as from consultations with representatives of the United Nations, media organizations, and current government officials.

Because it is undergoing refinement, the document is not printed here.

Introductory Comment by the InterAction Council

It is time to talk about human responsibilities. Globalization of the world economy is matched by global problems, and global problems demand global solutions on the basis of ideas, values, and norms respected by all cultures and societies. Recognition of the equal and inalienable rights of all the people requires a foundation of freedom, justice, and peace—but this also demands that rights and responsibilities be given equal importance to establish an ethical base so that all men and women can live peacefully together and fulfill their potential. A better social order both nationally and internationally cannot be achieved by laws, prescriptions, and conventions alone, but needs a global ethic. Human aspirations for progress can only be realized by agreed values and standards applying to all people and institutions at all times.

The year 1998 was the 50th anniversary of the Universal Declaration of Human Rights adopted by the United Nations. The anniversary was an opportune time to consider adoption of a Universal Declaration of Human Responsibilities, which would complement the Human Rights Declaration and strengthen it and help lead to a better world.

The Declaration of Human Responsibilities seeks to bring freedom and responsibility into balance and to promote a move from the freedom of indifference to the freedom of involvement. If one person or government seeks to maximize freedom but does it at the expense of others, a larger number of people will suffer. If human beings maximize their freedom by plundering the natural resources of the earth, then future generations will suffer.

The initiative to draft a Universal Declaration of Human Responsibilities is not only a way of balancing freedom with responsibility, but also a means of reconciling ideologies, beliefs, and political views that were deemed antagonistic in the past. The proposed declaration points out that the exclusive insistence on rights can lead to endless dispute and conflict, that religious groups in pressing for their own freedom have a duty to respect the freedom of others. The basic premise should be to aim at the greatest amount of freedom possible, but also to develop the fullest sense of responsibility that will allow that freedom itself to grow.

The InterAction Council has been working to draft a set of human ethical standards since 1987. But its work builds on the wisdom of religious leaders and sages down the ages who have warned that freedom without acceptance of responsibility can destroy the freedom itself, whereas when rights and responsibilities are balanced, then freedom is enhanced and a better world can be created. The InterAction Council commends the draft Declaration to the United Nations and to all others for examination and support.

Chapter Twenty-eight
WHAT SHALL WE DO NEXT?

Introduction

MOVING THROUGH THE NEXUS

Joel Beversluis

Because this book is intended to promote appropriate responses and action, the selections in Chapter 28 offer a few strategies and inspirational pieces for those who will take the next steps. Preceding chapters have offered numerous ideas and resources for our knowledge and use—the perceptions, wisdom, and beliefs of the world's religions and spiritual traditions, insights into a global ethic, visions of a community of religions, the experience of indigenous voices, and the needs of future generations. Part Four, which follows, presents the hopeful programs of nearly seven hundred organizations. Taken together, these begin to reveal the awesome and glistening web that connects us—hence my use of the word *nexus*.

This *Sourcebook* has also affirmed a basic interconnectedness between the challenges we face and our own values and practices. Yet, when we map the connections from situations of crisis back into our homes and communities, this knowledge can cause us pain and frustration. We tend to assume that *our* society is basically generous and principled, that *our* values and *our* tribal and religious or spiritual identifications are righteous. The evidence, however, suggests that there is a chasm between our personal beliefs and the impact of our collective actions on the larger world.

Some of the questions that are once again challenging our cultural assumptions include: Who is my neighbor? What are my personal responsibilities to the future? How will our species survive? The answers to these old questions have new, planetary implications. The human desire for community, once expressed in tribal and religious allegiances, now encounters the global village. It is no simple matter for us to become a community of religions or to pledge allegiance to the community of the Earth.

Other assumptions are also under assault. We can no longer pretend

- That our community is or should be composed of people who believe, worship, and live as we do
- That the creating and consuming of products and luxuries is *progress*
- That our desire for *the good life* justifies the exploitation of resources or people, or that it grants us the right to protect our short-term interests, even at the expense of long-term values
- That if change is needed, *other* people, religions, corporations, and governments must change first.

We are learning how our lifestyles have been built on the intersections of global business, national military power, consumer demand, and inadequate values. These intersections connect us to the world's problems and bring those issues into our homes and into our religious and secular communities.

Truth or Consequences

How do we respond to views of reality that diverge from the world we thought we knew? They seem to make unreasonable demands on us. It's certainly tempting to rewarm the American Dream, to retreat to comfort and entertainment, to beat the dangers back out of sight and mind, and to place our hopes in technology. However, old ways of thinking and technological fixes can't save us from ourselves. We need new models, new ways of perceiving the meaning of life.

Although it can be painful, we can begin to cut loose from dying assumptions, from inappropriate attachments, and from being overwhelmed by it all. We can begin to live in ways that demonstrate that we do respect each other and honor the Earth. To do that, however, we must learn from traditions of meaning and spirituality far wiser than the toxic worldviews that drive modern culture. As a culture we must find an alternative to the pursuit of industrial and commercial luxury—what Thomas Berry calls our cultural pathology—because too much of humanity is enticed to imitate us and because such a life is neither sustainable nor ethical.

This liberation won't come cheap. We'll have to make commitments to specific values and concrete tasks. We'll need to nurture hope, act boldly, and watch for signs of grace. As we deal with failure—our own and that of others—and are tempted by apathy, we must trust in our commitments and in gradual but persistent transformations.

New Approaches

Along with the challenges, helpful concepts are also swirling in the nexus that surrounds us, offering new approaches to the expression of our spiritual impulses. Transformative perceptions can illuminate our paths through the nexus of crises and opportunities. We can also derive hope from seeing that many others are already on this journey and that they, too, are attempting an appropriate analysis and response. For example:

- Those who've worked on single-focus issues such as the peace or environmental movements are learning that most problems and solutions are tied to other issues.
- Increasingly, religious and spiritual leaders are making the connections between ecology, justice, peace, and spirituality.
- Hungry people and those who advocate for them are discovering that corporate profits and national policies also cause starvation.
- Human rights issues are getting higher profile in political and economic arenas, and are balanced by calls for human responsibilities.
- Freedom-loving people are experiencing the power of nonviolent resolution of problems and resistance to injustice; most of those who choose nonviolence are motivated by spiritually informed ideals.

Truth and Reverence Will Carry Us Through

When we have seen the connections and want to begin to move through the nexus, we can do as Gandhi proposed: invite the truth-force to work in us. It requires a process of action and reflection, steps that move us toward personal and collective truths—if we don't resist or shortchange it. As we engage in this process, we must test all the spirits, including the "emerging global consciousness," to distinguish the highest spiritual values from fashion, personalities, and deception. The following insights may be used as a perceptual matrix to guide such an inquiry:

- All the world's human affairs—politics, culture, commerce, and religious life— are rooted in and interconnected with the ecology, or systems, of Earth.
- Our choices and actions reflect ethical and spiritual values; we're always voting with our time or energy or money, even when we're apathetic or following cultural patterns.
- Our personal spirituality is revealed in our relationships with other life, the Earth, the cosmos, and the creative One.
- There is no separate, neutral, or higher ground where our religions and spiritual communities may stand; they either help or hinder solutions and processes of transformation.

And, in conclusion,

- Reverence and gratitude for the beauty, interconnectedness, and mysteries of life provide the strongest foundation for new ways of living.

These qualities, combined with our responsiveness to the *global problematique* and inspired by our religious commitments, point us toward what we seek: the true substance of peace within the community of religious and spiritual communities of the Earth.

A Response to Those Who Despair about the State of the World

Dr. Willis W. Harman

Director (deceased) of the Institute of Noetic Sciences, Sausalito, California, and Professor (emeritus) of Engineering–Social Systems at Stanford University

Anyone who is sanguine about the global future probably doesn't understand. The problems of a progressively degraded environment, ravaged resources, uncontrolled man-made climate change, chronic hunger and poverty, persistent ethnic and religious conflicts, ever-increasing militarization of societies, and systemic mal-distribution of wealth and opportunity seem sufficiently overwhelming, and the political responses so pathetic, that despair seems a reasonable response.

It is important to remind ourselves of the creative response which can be found at the core of the esoteric understanding in any one of the world's religious traditions. But first we need to make explicit a number of principles.

Six Principles for Creative Action

1. Each of us can discover within ourselves a deep sense of purpose; the deepest yearning of each of us is to make sense of our lives, to know that our lives have meaning. The ultimate learning is that we are spiritual beings in a spiritual universe, that ultimate cause is not to be found in the physical world but in spirit, and that meaning comes through contributing creatively to the whole.

2. The present world order is not sustainable in the long term. The world has become unmanageable; fundamental change is required, at the level of the most basic underlying assumptions. We are all reluctant to realize this fact. But like the first step of the twelve-step programs for addiction, we can make no advance without this recognition.

3. Part of our collective confusion comes from the fact that the scientific worldview, which is at the heart of the modern world order and is taught throughout the modern world from kindergarten to university, explicitly denies the validity of the discovery described in the first principle.

4. We intuitively know what are the characteristics of a sustainable and glorious society. We know what is required at a family and community level, and we only have to extend that to the whole world. This sounds simplistic; the goal is simple—it's just getting there that is not.

5. Each of us can discover our particular role. There is a place in the system where we uniquely fit, a place where our unique gifts and the demands of the situation fit together perfectly. We may find that place partly through following intuition; partly through trying things and seeing what "wants to happen"; partly by watching for "meaningful coincidences."

6. Each of us can say "yes" to that role. There is a new pattern of understanding and valuing which is emerging from the various social movements and deliberations of recent decades. That "new paradigm"—which draws on the perennial wisdom of the world's spiritual traditions—affirms that all things are parts of a single, ultimately spiritual whole, and that each of us, as a part of that whole, has access to an "inner knowing" which can guide us to ultimately meaningful action.

Elements of a Personal Program

How can one play one's part in all this? The following three elements comprise an effective personal program:

1. Personal transformation (inner work). Many guides to inner transformation are available; ultimately one has to work with what feels intuitively right. Intention is the key requirement for discovering within oneself the inner wisdom and deep sense of purpose that will lead to making an effective contribution. The right way will appear. It may be within an established religious tradition, or it may not—or it may be for a time one and later on the other. It will probably involve a meditative discipline, prayer, or

yoga. It may or may not be with a personal spiritual teacher.

2. Local action (outer work). Whole-system transformation involves the transformation of all parts of the system; we can contribute anywhere. Wherever we are in the system is a good place to start—our families, our jobs, our communities. All creative action is with a small group, locally—although the effects may ripple out worldwide. Taking action is essential: it provides "grounding" through which we receive feedback. Action leads to experience, and "all experience is feedback." The guidance of deep intuition as it develops in our inner work, together with feedback from our outer work, will direct us toward discovering our particular role—the place in this whole-system evolution where we uniquely fit.

3. Global re-perception (inner work). Modern society, like all societies that have ever existed, rests on some set of basic assumptions about who we are, what kind of universe we are in, and how we relate to one another and to the whole. The present world order is not long-term sustainable because its worldview is not accurate. But we have complicity in that order because we "buy into" the underlying belief system. It is not comfortable to discover that the experienced reality we come to through deep inner work is not that of the materialistic scientific worldview. The re-perception of a sustainable worldview reveals neither the manipulative rationality that passes for knowledge nor the prevailing ethic of acquisitive materialism, and it does not lead to the conventional belief system of economic rationality. Yet it is necessary to come to this realization if we are to clear the path to our own intuitive wisdom and make a meaningful contribution to the whole. There is no resolution of our global dilemmas short of changing these collective beliefs, beginning with ourselves.

Towards the Dialogue of Love

Robert L. Fastiggi

The story is told of a young Capuchin friar who had consulted the great French Islamicist Louis Massignon about how to overcome his negative feelings towards Islam. The scholar provided the friar with two thoughts to ponder. The first was from Augustine, "*Amor dat novos oculos*," ("Love gives new eyes"); the second was from John of the Cross: "Where there is no love put love, and you will find love Himself." These two thoughts helped to transform the young friar into an Islamic scholar capable of finding in a religion he once feared "the reflection of the infinite goodness of God" (see Giulio Basetti-Sani, *The Koran in the Light of Christ*, p. 18).

This story serves as an example of the central role of love in authentic interreligious dialogue. The new eyes given by love enable us to see people of other religions as brothers and sisters engaged in a common search for wisdom and truth. Without love there is the danger of demonizing those of other faiths—of seeing them as competitors and enemies rather than as fellow human beings who share a common humanity and common human questions. In reflecting on the meaning of the 1993 Parliament of the World's Religions, one question continuously comes to my mind: "Is it possible for people of many religions, of many races, and of many languages to truly love one another?" It is a deceptively simple question—for in the answer lies the destiny of our planet.

The amazing truth is that love is possible in spite of the differences of belief and practice that exist among the religions. These differences are real and will not go away. We should not attempt to ignore them and pretend that all religions are homogeneous, for they are not. However, the people who practice these religions do share a common language of love and compassion. For in every continent people have learned the language of love—whether from the arms of a mother or the gentle wisdom of a grandfather or the companionship of a friend. It should come as no surprise to learn of the beautiful words for love and compassion that emerge from the different traditions—from the *karuna* of the Bodhissatva to the *hesed* of YHWH; from the *agape* taught by Jesus to *Allah Ar-Rahman, Ar-Rahim* there is a common recognition that compassion, mercy, and loving-kindness are the qualities we most wish to imitate as humans reaching towards transcendence.

As we enter this new century, we must look for ways of growing in love. One way is that of collaborative work. When people of different religions work on common projects for better health care and family life, for cleaner air and safer cities, for more just laws and structures of peace, then the common humanity of fellow workers is perceived and loved. Another way is through study of a different religion—not a study that simply looks for patterns and archetypes—but a study that seeks to penetrate the heart of each tradition with empathy and a true desire to understand (insofar as is possible) how the world is seen from within the vision of that tradition. And, finally, we learn to love, as John of the Cross tells us, by putting love where there is no love, be being loving even when others are not loving, by seeking to understand even when others do not understand.

The dialogue of love is the first step needed for what has been envisioned as "the civilization of love." The shadows of war and fratricidal killing still hang like gloomy clouds over the sky of a world that is taking its first steps in learning to love. However, if love is the starting point for the survival of our planet, then all will be in vain if the various religions that preach love, compassion, and mercy fail in the exercise of these virtues. If religious people cannot learn to love each other, what are we to expect from nonreligious people?

"*Amor dat novos oculos.*" Love gives new eyes. Let us love so we may have new eyes—eyes that see into the hearts of our brothers and sisters with love, and eyes that can see in the future a civilization of love.

Hope

"St. Augustine says that Hope has two lovely daughters, Anger and Courage. . . . In the famous Pauline statement, of faith, hope, and love, love is the greatest (1 Cor. 13), but Augustine praises Hope for she tells us that God will work God's will. . . . Anger so that what cannot be will not be, and Courage so that what must be will be."

DOROTHY SOLLE

"*. . . for in the tender compassion of our God,*
the dawn from heaven will break upon us,
to shine upon those who live in darkness,
under the shadow of death,
and to guide our feet into the way of peace."

— from the "Song of Zechariah";
LUKE 1:78, 79

"Hope without risk is not hope,
which is believing in risky loving,
trusting others in the dark,
the blind leap,
letting God take over."

DOM HELDER CAMARA,
The Desert Is Fertile, p. 10

A Dual Awakening Process

Dr. Ahangamage T. Ariyaratne

The word *sarvodaya* was coined by Mahatma Gandhi to describe a new social order, which he envisioned as being very different from the capitalist and communist systems prevalent at that time.

Make Love Your Aim

If I speak in the tongues of men and of
*   angels, but have not love,*
I am a noisy gong or a clanging cymbal.
And if I have prophetic powers, and
*   understand all mysteries*
and all knowledge, and if I have all faith so
*   as to remove mountains,*
but have not love,
I am nothing. . . .

Love is patient and kind;
love is not jealous or boastful;
it is not arrogant or rude.
Love does not insist on its own way;
it is not irritable or resentful;
it does not rejoice at wrong,
but rejoices in the right.

Love bears all things,
believes all things,
hopes all things,
endures all things.

Love never ends. . . .
So faith, hope, and love abide, these three;
but the greatest of these is love.
Make love your aim.

PAUL, THE APOSTLE,
in 1 Corinthians 13

Literally it means "the welfare of all." With my Buddhist outlook, when I came across the word *sarvodaya* I interpreted it as "the awakening of all." . . . I cannot awaken myself unless I help awaken others. Others cannot awaken unless I do. So it is an interconnected and interdependent dual process of awakening oneself and society that we have chosen in the *Sarvodaya* [organization, of which he is Director]. . . . Lord Buddha's admonition to us was [to serve] ". . . by helping those who suffer physically to overcome physical suffering, those who are in fear to overcome fear, those who suffer mentally to overcome mental suffering, be of service to all living beings."

This is *sarvodaya* in the most profound sense. Transcending all man-made barriers of caste, race, religion, nationality, and other ways of separating human beings, *sarvodaya* serves all. *Sarvodaya* works to remove the causes of human physical suffering, anxiety, and fear. Working for interreligious and interracial harmony, eradicating poverty and empowering the poor, promoting peace by religious education and spiritual development programs, engaging in every kind of peacemaking process, taking nonviolent action against human rights violations and other forms of injustice, are all part of the *Sarvodaya* portfolio of activities.

—excerpted from Dr. Ariyaratne's acceptance speech for the Ninth Niwano Peace Prize

The Family of Abraham

Dom Helder Camara

Archbishop of Recife, Brazil, author, advocate for peace, justice, and the human rights of the poor

Jews, Muslims, and Christians know the story of the father of believers. . . . Did Abraham receive great gifts? He gave a faithful return, the best he could. He served. . . . If you feel in you the desire to use the qualities you have, if you think selfishness is narrow and choking, if you hunger for truth, justice, and love, you can and should go with us. . . .

The Violence of the Truth

In underdeveloped countries the Abrahamic minorities must try to find out what is involved in a subhuman situation. "Subhuman" is an explosive word. Take it in detail.

Find out about housing. Do the places where some people live deserve to be called houses?...Look at the water, drains, electricity, the floor, the roof.

Investigate clothing, food, health, work, transport, leisure. You should ask the right questions. With work, for example, does it pay a living wage sufficient to support a family? Is employment guaranteed or are there frequent redundancies (layoffs)? Are trade unions encouraged, tolerated, interfered with, forbidden? What are the apprenticeship conditions? the sanitary conditions? holidays? retirement provisions? Are the laws on social conditions kept? Are human beings treated with respect?

This sort of inquiry could of course arouse suspicion, and that could have unpleasant consequences. But it is necessary to find out what the real situation is in conditions of internal colonialism. What other way is there of becoming convinced and convincing others of the huge gap between those who suffer from an almost feudal situation in which the masses have no voice and no hope? Such information would not aim at inciting anger and rebellion but at providing a solid argument for the necessity to change the structures....

Its aim is to supply liberating moral pressure. For many, this in itself is dangerous and subversive. But one day it will be understood that this violence of the peaceful is greatly preferable to the explosion of armed violence....Choosing the way of moral pressure is not choosing the easy way out. We are replacing the force of arms by moral force, the violence of the truth. We must believe that love can strengthen the courage of these Abrahamic minorities who want justice but who refuse to answer violence with violence....

—excerpted from *The Desert Is Fertile*

Decide to Network

Use every letter you write,
Every conversation you have,
Every meeting you attend,
To express your fundamental beliefs and
    dreams.
Affirm to others the vision of the world
    you want.
Network through thought.
Network through action.
Network through love.
Network through spirit.
You are the center of a network.
You are a free, immensely powerful
    source of life and goodness.
Affirm it.
Spread it.
Radiate it.
Think day and night about it.
And you will see a miracle happen:
    the greatness of your own life.
In a world of big powers, media, and
    monopolies,
But of five billion individuals,
Networking is a new freedom.
The new democracy.
A new form of happiness.

ROBERT MULLER

The Practice of Meditation

K.G. von Durckheim

The aim of practice [meditation] is not to develop an attitude that allows the man to acquire a state of harmony and peace wherein nothing can ever trouble him. On the contrary, practice should teach him to let himself be assaulted, perturbed, moved, insulted, broken, and battered. That is to say, it should enable him to dare to let go his futile hankering after harmony, surcease from pain, and a comfortable life, in order that he may discover in doing battle with the forces that oppose him, that which awaits him beyond the world of opposites. The first necessity is that we should

Action and Prayer

Righteous action among the people saves prayer from becoming an escape into self-satisfied piety.

Prayer saves righteous action among the people from self-righteousness.

Righteous action saves prayer from the hypocrisy among the pious which the children of this world will never fail to spot.

Prayer saves righteous action from the fanatical ideologizing through which those who are committed to change become bad representatives of their own commitment.

Righteous action saves prayer from pessimism. Prayer saves righteous action from resignation.

Action keeps prayer in the realm of reality; prayer keeps action within the realm of truth.

EBERHARD BETHGE
Am gegebenen Ort

have the courage to face life, and to encounter all that is most perilous in the world. When this is possible, meditation itself becomes the means by which we accept and welcome the demons that arise from the unconscious (a practice very different from the practice of concentration on some object as a protection). Only if we venture repeatedly through zones of annihilation can our contact with Divine Being, which is beyond annihilation, become firm and stable. The more a man learns wholeheartedly to confront the world that threatens him with isolation, the more are the depths of the ground of Being revealed, and the possibilities of new life and Becoming opened.

—from *The Way of Transformation*

Who Will Tell Us What to Do?

Thich Nhat Hanh

The [Vietnamese] boat people said that every time their small boats were caught in storms, they knew their lives were in danger. But if one person on the boat could keep calm and not panic, that was a great help for everyone. People would listen to him or her and keep serene, and there was a chance for the boat to survive the danger. Our Earth is like a small boat. Compared with the rest of the cosmos, it is a small boat indeed, and it is in danger of sinking. We need such a person to inspire us with calm confidence, to tell us what to do. Who is that person?

> The Mahayana Buddhist *sutras* tell us that you are that person. If you are yourself, if you are your best, then you are that person. Only with such a person—calm, lucid, aware—will our situation improve.

> I wish you good luck. Please be yourself. Please be that person.

—from "Please Call Me by My True Names,"
in *The Path of Compassion*, ed. by Fred Eppsteiner

Concerning Acts of Initiative and Creation

Until one is committed,
there is hesitancy,
the chance to draw back,
always ineffectiveness.

Concerning acts of initiative (and creation)
there is one elementary truth
the ignorance of which kills countless ideas
and splendid plans:
    that the moment one definitely commits oneself,
    then Providence moves too.

All sorts of things occur to help one
that would never otherwise have occurred.

A whole stream of events issues from the decision,
raising in one's favor all manner
of unforeseen incidents and meetings
and material assistance
which no one could have dreamed
would come one's way.

Whatever you can do,
or dream you can, begin it.
Boldness has genius, power, and magic in it.
Begin it now.

                GOETHE

A Critical Point in History

Man has reached a critical point in history, where he must turn to God to avoid the consequences of his own faulty thinking. We must pray, not a few of us, but all of us. We must pray simply, fervently, sincerely, and with increasing power as our faith grows. We must condition the world's leaders by asking God's Spirit to descend upon their hearts and minds. We must condition ourselves, each and every one, by asking God's help in living so that peace may be possible.

We must pray in church, at home, on the train, while driving, on the job—and keep at it. Each of us is important now. The ability of every individual to seek divine help is a necessary link in the golden chain of harmony and peace.

Prayer is a dynamic manifestation of love by the concerned, reaching out for God's help for man. You can help change the world by your prayers and your prayerful action.

                DAG HAMMARSKJOLD,
                former UN Secretary-General,
                at the dedication of the
                United Nations Prayer Room

Prayer for the Sacred Community

O Blessed Source,
eternal Lord of creation,
sustainer of all worlds,
you embrace the whole cosmos within yourself,
for everything exists in you.

Let your winds come
and breathe your everlasting Spirit in us.
Let us inhale your divine Spirit and be inspired.
Enlighten us in your truth.
Pour your grace into our hearts.
Wipe away our sin and all negativity.

Transform us into your Love,
and let us radiate that Love to all others.
Inflame us with your unending life.
Dissolve our limited way of being.
Elevate us into your divine Life.
Give us your capacity to share that Life with everyone.
Shape us in your wisdom.

Grant us your joy and laughter.
Let us become that divine wisdom, sensitivity,
laughter and joy for all beings.

Let us realize fully that we are members
of that Sacred Community
with all humankind, with other species,
with nature and the entire cosmos.
Grant us a heart that can embrace them all in you.

Let us be in communion with you forever
in the bliss of that Love:
the Love that sustains all
and transforms all into your Divine Radiance.

                    BROTHER WAYNE TEASDALE

Part Four

SELECTED RESOURCES FOR THE COMMUNITY OF RELIGIONS

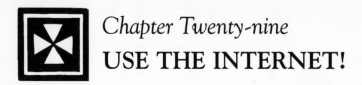

Chapter Twenty-nine
USE THE INTERNET!

An Online Congress of World Religions?

Interfaith Networking and Internet Communications

Bruce Schuman

NOTE: Developer of Internet projects supporting the emergence of interfaith community, including United Communities of Spirit (UCS) and Interfaith Voices for Peace and Justice (IFV), the author argues that an ongoing "electronic congress of world religions" is feasible and ought to be developed. The IFV Web site and the interactive capacity in the UCS site are examples of electronic venues for such a congress. (Mail to: bruce@origin.org or see UCS or IFV site listings.)

In a global context of dissolving barriers and intensified communications, the process of intercultural encounter is transforming the understanding of religion. The Buddhist meets the Baptist in the supermarket in Cleveland, and both are shaped by the exchange. Influenced by every culture and by every academic and scientific discipline, new religious ideas are emerging that portend the globalization of religion, in much the way the global economy is being redefined. The ancient traditions are vitalized and reaffirmed in this process, and new movements appear that are influenced by hundreds of sources. The result is a burst of creativity in religion that points towards a vibrant and enlightened future.

Among the most powerful influences contributing to this process is the connectivity of the Internet. With 100 million or more persons linked in a vast and complex global network, interaction among members of diverse cultures has never been easier. Thousands of instantly available religious Web sites offer their perspective to the seeker through the net. Innumerable reference works, scriptural texts, scholarly articles and theological commentaries are available online. And there are any number of discussion forums and mailing lists where the seeker can join others in extended conversation on any aspect of religion.

Inexpensive, operating continuously, truly global, inherently democratic, decentralized, and nonhierarchical, the Internet reaches everywhere that people can afford computers, and is drawing them all into a vast network of conversations. From Africa, Asia, Australia, from all over North and South America, from Europe and Russia—individual humans are placing their insights into the dialogue and finding themselves influenced by other participants. Lovers of the Divine and the sacred are coming together from all corners of the world in a process of cross-fertilization that is broadening the popular understanding of religion. Against this backdrop, the Internet offers an opportunity for the emergence of a profoundly empowered interfaith movement. Diverse voices can easily come together into a common context, expressing their opinions, working on common projects, seeking a common agenda, or defending particular positions. An ongoing congress of world religions could readily be organized, basing its interactions not on the brief and costly conferences of the past, but instead building on what these conferences have accomplished in an electronic format.

This interaction could be organized in any number of ways. Do we wish to seek consensus on critical issues? Well-defined procedures can now pursue this course. Do we wish to develop a collaborative agenda and a universal statement of policy? We can use established tools for developing cooperative documents. Do we wish to poll our participants, or take a vote? We can create sophisticated voting and polling procedures. Do we wish to expand the conversation to others, such as those in "the guiding institutions" ? We can now reach out to them via the Web.

The challenge for the interfaith community is a simple one: do we *want* to do these things? Do we care enough about building the global interfaith movement to give our resources to this new style of organizing? Do we want to take deliberate steps to bring together official representatives of religious traditions through this medium, drawing them into an ongoing creative conversation that addresses the spiritual challenges facing the world?

If our answer to these questions is "yes," we are standing at the edge of a new universe of interfaith cooperation and development. We can build a powerful and influential system that resolves the challenges involved in bringing people together. This system can provide the means whereby our common values and inspirations can be articulated in a clear and public way and, furthermore, communicated to the entire online world.

Internet Sites for Comparative Religious Studies and World Religions

Compiled by James T. Cloud

Editor, The Sacred Books Library (CD-ROM) and Director of the Multifaith Institute

General and Academic Sites

ACADEMIC INFO:
http://www.academicinfo.net/religindex.html
An annotated directory of Internet resources, including links, for the academic study of religion.

AMERICAN ACADEMY OF RELIGION:
http://www.aarweb.org
The major learned society and professional association for scholars whose object of study is religion.

CENTER FOR THE STUDY OF WORLD RELIGIONS, HARVARD UNIVERSITY:
http://www.hds.harvard.edu/cswr/index.html

A research institute with the goal to understand the meaning of religion, with sympathetic insight into religious communities, and to analyze with scholarly integrity the role of religion in global perspective.

CENTER FOR THEOLOGY AND NATURAL SCIENCES:
http://www.ctns.org
Focuses primarily on the relation between contemporary physics, cosmology, technology, environmental studies, evolutionary and molecular biology, and Christian theology and ethics.

CONEXUS PRESS:
http://www.conexuspress.com
Offers substantial information about selected books (including this *Sourcebook*), calendars, CD-ROM, links, and other resources for interreligious understanding, wisdom, and cooperation.

MULTIFAITH INSTITUTE:
http://www.multifaith.net
Information, products, and services, including research and database resources for interfaith organizations and the public.

MYSTICISM IN WORLD RELIGIONS:
http://www.digiserve.com/mystic
An excellent and extensive site which explores the mystical traditions of six religions by comparing and contrasting quotations drawn from their respective literatures.

RELIGIOUS MOVEMENTS PAGE:
http://cti.itc.virginia.edu/~jkh8x/soc257/welcome/welcome.htm
This academic site provides information on more than 200 religious groups.

WORLD INTERFAITH EDUCATION ASSOCIATION (WIFEA):
http://www.connect.ab.ca/~lfahlman/wifea.htm
Formerly the World Interfaith Colleges Association, WIFEA is part of a global network of societies working together for interfaith education.

WORLD NETWORK OF RELIGIOUS FUTURISTS:
http://www.wnrf.org
A professional association of scholars and activists

from around the world who study the future of their religious tradition in view of world civilization.

Sites by Religion

African

AFRICAN TRADITIONAL RELIGION:

http://isizoh.net/afrel/index.html

An excellent site providing text, links, maps, and topical information.

ORISHANET/SANTERIA:

http://www.seanet.com/~efunmoyiwa/ocha net.html

This personal site offers information, products, and services related to practicing Santeria.

Bahá'í Faith

BAHÁ'Í COMPUTER & COMMUNICATION ASSOCIATION:

http://www.bcca.org

A valuable resource for exploring the global Bahá'í community with information and links to other resources.

THE BAHÁ'Í WORLD:

http://www.bahai.org

This official site of the Bahá'í Faith is posted in five languages and includes selections of the sacred writings.

Buddhism

DHARMANET INTERNATIONAL:

http://www.dharmanet.org

News, calendar of retreats, biographies of teachers, and a guide to the Buddhist marketplace, much more.

ZEN MOUNTAIN MONASTERY:

http://www.zen-mtn.org

A residential retreat center in the Catskills of New York, providing resources and support for Zen Buddhist practice.

Christianity

CHRISTIANITY ONLINE:

http://www.christianity.net

Advice, goods, and services for the Protestant community, provided by *Christianity Today* magazine.

ECUMENICAL PATRIARCH OF CONSTANTINOPLE:

http://www.patriarchate.org

Official site for Orthodox news linked with the resources of the Greek Archdiocese of America.

THE VATICAN, HOLY SEE:

http://www.vatican.va

Official site of the Roman Catholic Church.

WORLD COUNCIL OF CHURCHES:

http://www.wcc-coe.org

A global association of Christian churches, available in five languages. Includes listings of member churches, Christian world communions, and ecumenical councils.

Confucianism

CHINESE PHILOSOPHY PAGE:

http://www-personal.monash.edu.au/~sab/index.html

Bibliography and links to Confucian and other philosophies.

Hinduism

HINDU UNIVERSE:

http://www.hindu.org

Online resources for all aspects of Hindu tradition: art, customs, languages, scriptures, and temples.

SIVANANDA YOGA:

http://www.sivananda.org

Official Site of the International Sivananda Yoga Vedanta Centers.

Islam

AL-ISLAM, BY THE AHLUL BAYT DIGITAL ISLAMIC LIBRARY PROJECT:
http://al-islam.org

Offers introductory and advanced study of Islam through resources of many kinds.

ISLAMIC SOCIETY OF NORTH AMERICA:
http://www.isna.net

An educational and social service association.

INTERNATIONAL ASSOCIATION OF SUFISM:
http://www.ias.org

Articles, publications, and services about the Islamic mystical tradition.

Jainism

JAIN PRINCIPLES, TRADITION, AND PRACTICES:
http://www.cs.colostate.edu/~malaiya/jainhlinks.html

Some essential information and a huge list of links to Jain sites arranged by topic.

JAINWORLD:
http://www.jainworld.com

A high-quality and well-illustrated site with many resources for exploring this religion of nonviolence.

Judaism

AMERICAN JEWISH COMMITTEE:
http://www.ajc.org

The AJC works to protect Jewish welfare globally, to preserve and nurture Jewish life in the U.S. The site provides information about Israel, Jewish life, and international issues.

JEWISH INTERNET CONSORTIUM:
http://www.shamash.org

This site offers access to a variety of Judaic resources including the Tanach.

JUDAISM 101:
http://www.jewfaq.org

An online encyclopedia of Judaism—an excellent introductory resource on all aspects of Jewish beliefs and customs.

Native American

NATIONAL MUSEUM OF THE AMERICAN INDIAN:
http://www.si.edu/nmai

The Smithsonian Institute site provides information about the museum, its collections, programs, educational resources, and links to other sites.

NATIVE AMERICAN TRIBES:
http://www.rr.gmcs.k12.nm.us/domagala.namericans.htm

Here you will finds links to sites by or about specific tribes.

Shinto

INTERNATIONAL SHINTO FOUNDATION:
http://shinto.org/menu-e.html

The ISF promotes understanding of Shinto, "the *kami* way" through publications, symposia, and academic efforts.

SHINTO:
http://www.jinja.or.jp/english/s-0.html

Introduction to Shinto, with English text on a Japanese site.

Sikhism

SIKHISM:
http://www.sikhs.org

Impressively illustrated site tells about the origin and development of this religion, with scriptures online.

SIKH MEDIA ACTION AND RESOURCE TASK FORCE:
http://www.sikhmedia.org/resources/mansukhani

Introduction to Sikhism for beginners, other resources.

Taoism

CENTER OF TRADITIONAL TAOIST STUDIES:
http://www.tao.org/

A virtual temple of Tao, providing information about Taoist philosophy, religion, and martial arts.

TAOIST RESTORATION SOCIETY:

http://www.taorestore.org/index2.html

Calendar, interviews, library, Q&A, and much more about ancient Chinese religion.

Unitarian-Universalist

UNITARIAN UNIVERSALIST ASSOCIATION:

http://www.uua.org

This official site provides essential information about this liberal faith including finding a community near you.

Zoroastrianism

AVESTA—ZOROASTRIAN ARCHIVES:

http://www.avesta.org

Scriptures and answers to questions about one of the oldest and most influential religions.

FEDERATION OF ZOROASTRIAN ASSOCIATIONS OF NORTH AMERICA:

http://www.fezana.org

This group publishes a directory of Zoroastrian communities as well as online resources.

Interfaith Internet Links
A Selection of Web Sites and Online Indices

Compiled by Susan Sarfaty

ALLFAITHS PRESS:

http://allfaithspress.com

Interreligious information, news, polls.

AREOPAGUS ONLINE:

http://www.areopagus.com

A living encounter with today's religious world with an index of news, articles, and discussion.

CENTER FOR GLOBAL ETHICS:

http://astro.temple.edu/~dialogue/geth.htm

Coordinates the work of thinkers, scholars, and activists who are working to define, implement,

and promote policies of responsible global citizenship.

CONEXUS PRESS:

http://www.conexuspress.com

Offers books (including this *Sourcebook*), calendars, CD-ROM, and other resources for interreligious understanding, wisdom, and cooperation.

COUNCIL FOR A PARLIAMENT OF WORLD RELIGIONS:

http://www.cpwr.org

The mission of CPWR is to foster interreligious dialogue and cooperation in metropolitan Chicago and around the world.

EXPLORING RELIGIONS:

http://august.uwyo.edu/ReligioNet/er

Exploring Buddhism, Christianity, Hinduism, Islam, and Judaism.

GAIAMIND:

http://www.gaiamind.org

Explores the idea that we, humanity, are the Earth becoming aware of itself. Also affirms the Great Spirit of Oneness found at the heart of all the world's great spiritual traditions.

GLOBAL DIALOGUE INSTITUTE:

http://astro.temple.edu/~dialogue

Promotes dialogue in the broadest sense among individuals and groups of different religions and cultures, focusing especially on scholars, professionals, and institutional and business leaders.

INNER EXPLORATIONS:

http://www.innerexplorations.com

Where Christian mysticism, theology, and metaphysics meet Eastern forms of meditation, Jungian psychology, and a new sense of the Earth.

INTEGRALSPIRIT:

http://www.integralspirit.com

Online community and book source for integral culture and spirituality.

INTERFAITH VOICES FOR PEACE & JUSTICE:
http://interfaithvoices.org/ifv.cfm
Directory of faith-based and interfaith activist organizations.

INTERNATIONAL INTERFAITH CENTRE:
http://www.interfaith-center.org/oxford
Aims to support the work of organizations and individuals to further peaceful relations, respect, and understanding between people with different faith beliefs.

JEWISH-CHRISTIAN RELATIONS:
http://jcrelations.com/
Concerning issues in the ongoing and expanding Jewish-Christian dialogue, with history, bibliography, and links to organizations world-wide.

MOVEMENT FOR BELOVED COMMUNITY:
http://home.earthlink.net/~rflyer/index.html
Our dream is the creation of a global network of individuals, villages, neighborhoods, and communities who share a vision of a beloved community—and want to realize it.

MULTIFAITH PRAYERS:
http://www.silcom.com/~origin/sbcr/sbcr453
Reflections from many traditions.

NORTH AMERICAN INTERFAITH NETWORK:
http://www.nain.org
Provides communication and mutual strengthening of interfaith organizations and agencies, and the interfaith relations programs and offices of religious and denominational groups.

ONTARIO CONSULTANTS ON RELIGIOUS TOLERANCE:
http://www.religioustolerance.org
Major multifaith site has three main purposes: 1) to disseminate accurate religious information, 2) to expose religious fraud, hatred, and misinformation, and 3) to disseminate information on "hot" religious topics.

THE PLURALISM PROJECT:
http://www.fas.harvard.edu/~pluralsm/html/links.html
Developed at Harvard University to study and document the growing religious diversity of the United States, with a special view to its new immigrant religious communities.

RELIGION DEPOT:
http://www.edepot.com/religion.html
A listing of religions from the perspective of the point of origin and the source of influence (what religion it adapted from, and the religions that it spawned).

RELIGIONS IN RENEWAL:
http://www.usao.edu/~facshaferi/relren/relren4.htm
Dedicated to efforts by people all over the globe to renew their religions or ideologies in such a way that they will be open to ongoing transformation while remaining solidly rooted in what is essential in their past.

SPIRITWEB:
http://www.spiritweb.org
Spiritual consciousness on World Wide Web: Largest spiritual Web site of its kind; a major hub for connecting to global network of spirit-conscious truth-seekers.

UNITED COMMUNITIES OF SPIRIT:
http://origin.org/ucs.cfm
A global interfaith network, linking people of diverse faiths and beliefs who want to work with others to build a better world.

UNITED RELIGIONS INITIATIVE:
http://www.united-religions.org
A global initiative to bring diverse religions to a common table so they might work together for the good of all life and the healing of the world.

VIRTUAL RELIGION INDEX:
http://religion.rutgers.edu/vri/index.html
Rutgers University tool for students with little time. It analyzes and highlights important content of religion-related Web sites to speed research.

WORLD CONFERENCE ON RELIGION AND PEACE:
http://www.wcrp.org
The largest interfaith peace organization, its programs, chapters, links, and reports.

WORLD CONGRESS OF FAITHS:
http://www.interfaith-center.org/oxford/wcf
A pioneering fellowship dedicated to bringing people of different faiths together.

WORLD NETWORK OF RELIGIOUS FUTURISTS:
http://www.wnrf.org/index.html
Professional association dedicated to understanding and advancing the future of religion.

WORLD SCRIPTURE:
http://origin.org/ws.cfm
A comparative anthology of sacred texts.

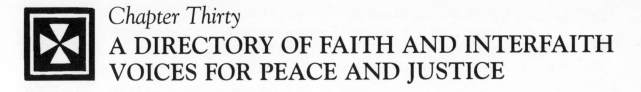

Chapter Thirty
A DIRECTORY OF FAITH AND INTERFAITH VOICES FOR PEACE AND JUSTICE

Gloria Weber and Bruce Schuman

Gloria Weber, a clergy member of the Lutheran Church-ELCA, has also been a teacher and state legislator. She is Founder and Editor of Interfaith Voices for Peace and Justice. Bruce Schuman is Webmaster for Interfaith Voices for Peace and Justice and Founder of the United Communities of Spirit Web project.

NOTE: One significant way of responding to the question asked by the 1993 Parliament, "What shall we do?" is to participate with others in cooperative action that serves the common good. This Directory is the first comprehensive listing of faith and interfaith groups who use religious ethics to organize and inspire action for peace and justice. Because the terms "peace" and "justice" have many connotations and preconditions, the list is very inclusive. Peace is not just the absence of war. Justice is not simply the absence of crime. Their preconditions include, for example, basic human rights, economic opportunity, family cohesiveness, religious freedom, spiritual training, a sustainable ecology, and tolerance among religious and ethnic groups.

Introduction

Why would people of faith want to work for peace? Why would they seek the same justice for others that each wants for him or herself?

Sacred scriptures of all of the world's major religions have a similar, ancient precept, known by some as "The Golden Rule." (Eleven versions are listed in Chapter 22.) This common ethic of goodness, love, trust, and peace is at the core of the teachings of the major faiths. Each perceives the divine as the source of unity and peace. Each faith directs its members to do for others what they'd like done for themselves.

Do all people of faith have a common goal?

People of faith are, by the very essence of their beliefs, allies in the struggle to achieve peace on earth and justice for all—the same justice that each wants for him or herself.

Why are people of faith vital to the quest for peace and justice?

The major problem of the new century is how to live in constructive peace in the face of forces that thrust humans into destructive conflict. In an age of dissolving cultural and geographic boundaries, the ethical foundations of society are weakened. In response, people of all religious and spiritual communities must increasingly teach and act on their common behavioral ethic. The foundation for this new global society must be rooted in moral and ethical actions that support the conditions for peace and justice. In this task, religion is not a "museum piece"; religious faith motivates, enlivens, encourages, and directs millions of people around the globe to rebuild that foundation.

How can this Directory be empowering?

No one seeking peace and justice, no person, group, denomination, or religious community, need ever feel isolated again. With this common goal, thousands of groups and millions of people are allies. Knowing this and engaging with one's co-workers—their motivations, missions, methods, and objectives—enlivens and empowers each person and organization. Cooperative action escalates impact!

How can it be used?

The Directory is a tool for communicating, networking, sharing, planning, and effecting cooperative action! It lists nearly seven hundred faith-based and interfaith groups and coalitions in alphabetical order, giving location, phone, fax, e-mail or Web site, focus, and a mission statement for each. Use of the Directory is enhanced by nineteen shorter lists that index all organizations according to the particular focus of each group's work. This index makes it easy for readers to locate organizations in the

Directory according to interests and tasks.

How are the groups categorized?

The nineteen focus areas in the Directory and in its Index are

- Advocacy
- Communication
- Ecumenical & Interfaith Cooperation
- Training & Resources
- General Peace & Justice
- Children, Youth & Family
- Criminal Justice System
- Discrimination
- Ecology & Environment
- Economic Concerns
- Global Peace & Security
- Health Issues
- Human Rights
- Indigenous or Displaced Persons
- Peace and Nonviolence
- Religious & Civil Liberty
- Renewal of a Faith Group
- Societies, Seminaries & Funds
- Women

Each of these focus areas helps create the conditions for peace and justice in our world.

What's in the Web version?

An online version of this Directory offers additional flexibility and potential. It contains all the information in this printed version, plus it includes new groups, which are added regularly. The Web version contains links to each organization's e-mail and Web site (where there is one), has a search capacity, the ability to poll, to distribute electronic newsletters, and to exchange policy statements. It also allows member groups to make needed changes to their entries online. An unlisted group may join the listing by applying to the IFV office.

This Directory may be shared with others. Reproduction of large sections in print or online requires written permission and appropriate credit. We welcome your contributions and comments at Interfaith Voices for Peace and Justice, P.O. Box 270214, St. Louis, MO 63127.
Tel. 314/892-1192 or Fax 314/892-1255.
E-mail: ifvoices@aol.com
*Web:*http://www.interfaithvoices.org

Directory of Faith and Interfaith Voices for Peace and Justice

20/20 Vision

1828 Jefferson PL NW, Washington, DC 20036 USA; (202) 833-2020; Fax (202) 833-5307; http://www.2020vision.org

Focus: Advocacy; Ecology & Environment; Peace & Nonviolence
Mission: To enable concerned individuals to take 20 minutes a month to protect the environment and promote peace, 20/20 sends a monthly action postcard with information needed to write or call policy makers facing crucial decisions.

50 Years Is Enough: US Network for Global Economic Justice

1247 E St SE, Washington, DC 20003 USA; (202) 463-2265; Fax (202) 544-9359; http://www.50years.org

Focus: Advocacy; Economic Concerns
Mission: A coalition of 205 US secular and faith-based organizations dedicated to the profound transformation of the World Bank and International Monetary Fund. Through education and action, the Network is committed to making international financial institutions democratic and accountable to those who have to live with the effects of their policies.

AAAS Dialogue on Science, Ethics & Religion

1200 New York Ave NW, Washington, DC 20005 USA; (202) 326-6600; Fax (202) 289-4950; http://www.aaas.org/SPP/DSER/default.htm

Focus: Societies, Seminaries & Funds
Mission: The Dialogue promotes knowledge about developments in science and technology, provides opportunities for dialogue on matters of mutual concern between scientists, ethicists, and religious scholars and leaders, and facilitates collaboration on projects that explore the ethical and religious implications of scientific and technological developments.

ABC/USA Association of Welcoming & Affirming Baptists

PO Box 2596, Attleboro Falls, MA 02763-0894 USA; (508) 226-1945; Fax (508) 226-1945; http://users.aol.com/wabaptists

Focus: Discrimination; Renewal of Faith Group
Mission: To create and support a community of churches and individuals committed to the inclusion of gay, lesbian, bisexual, and transgendered persons in the full life and mission of American Baptist churches.

American Baptist Church—USA National Ministries

PO Box 851, Valley Forge, PA 19482 USA; http://www.abc-usa.org/natmin

Biblical Justice Ministry Center

(800) 222-3872 Ext. 2394; Fax (610) 768-2453

Focus: General Peace & Justice; Women
Mission: To advocate God's justice for all of God's people, especially concerning ecological stewardship, church-state issues, racial justice, women's needs, and child abuse.

Ecology & Racial Justice

(800) 222-3872 Ext. 2410; Fax (610) 768-2453

Focus: Discrimination; Ecology & Environment
Mission: To increase awareness of and commitment to care of creation and racial justice as interconnected priorities, bringing together networks of American Baptist leaders committed to eco-justice.

Economic Justice

(800) 222-3872 Ext. 2382; Fax (610) 768-2453

Focus: Economic Concerns
Mission: To share the biblical mandates regarding economic justice, to enhance existing networks and build new bridges between faith communities advocating for economic justice, and to develop resources to aid those tasks.

Office of Governmental Relations

110 Maryland Ave NE #504, Washington, DC 20002 USA; (202) 544-3400; Fax (202) 544-0277

Focus: Advocacy
Mission: To share views of the ABC/USA with federal governmental decision makers, while encouraging American Baptist participation in the political process. The office maintains a "Faith in Action Network" whose members receive action alerts on issues of concern.

Reconciliation Ministries

(800) 222-3872 Ext. 2451; Fax (610) 768-2453

Focus: Peace & Nonviolence
Mission: To raise awareness and provide resources on peace and justice issues and to be a liaison to the UN. A special focus is on developing opportunities for training in "community conflict transformation."

Aboriginal Rights Coalition—Canada

153 Laurier Ave E 2nd FL, Ottawa, ON K1N 6N8 Canada; (613) 235-9956; Fax (613) 235-1302; http://home.istar.ca/~arc

Focus: Discrimination; Indigenous or Displaced Persons
Mission: ARC works with a partnership of Aboriginal activists and church groups to promote education-action programs seeking full human rights for Aboriginal peoples and for reconciliation between Aboriginal peoples and all levels of the Christian community.

Academy of Guru Granth Studies

6415 Amicable Dr, Arlington, TX 76016 USA; (817) 654-0844; Fax (707) 922-7724; hlal@hsc.unt.edu

Focus: Ecumenical & Interfaith Cooperation
Mission: The Academy, in the Sikh tradi-

tion, promotes kinship of humankind, prohibition on prejudices or injustice, and upholding of human rights, through rekindling the human heart with the Divine Spirit.

Action Coalition for Global Change

55 New Montgomery St #219, San Francisco, CA 94105 USA; (415) 896-2242; Fax (415) 227-4878; http://www.acgc.org

Focus: Ecology & Environment; Economic Concerns; Global Peace & Security
Mission: Believing that positive changes are needed now to ensure survival of life on this planet, the ACGC's goal is to strengthen the effectiveness of their 60 member groups in effecting social and economic justice, restoring the earth's ecosystems, and replacing the war systems.

ACTS for Eco-Justice

LSTC 1100 E 55th St, Chicago, IL 60615 USA; (773) 256-0774; Fax (773) 256-0782

Focus: Ecology & Environment; Societies, Seminaries & Funds
Mission: Seminarians from the Association of Chicago Theological Schools gather for education in eco-justice ministry programs and activities.

ADVANCE—Avoiding Domestic Violence & Affirming Nonviolent Creative Efforts

750 Kelly, York, PA 17404 USA; (717) 848-6238; Fax (717) 852-8600; advance@lutheranscp.org

Focus: Children, Youth & Family; Training & Resources
Mission: ADVANCE helps men who are batterers develop alternative ways of interacting with women, children, and others. Both volunteer/court-ordered sign a contract, attend 26 weekly sessions, and learn to avoid physical abuse, sexual abuse, intimidation, coercion, and threats, as well as minimization, denial, and blaming. Resources are available.

Africa Faith and Justice Network

3035 Fourth St NE, Washington, DC 20017 USA; (202) 832-3412; Fax (202) 832-9051; http://afjn.cua.edu

Focus: Advocacy; Human Rights

Mission: A network of Catholics committed in faith to collaborate in the task of transforming US mentality and policy on Africa by using education and advocacy on behalf of justice for Africa.

African Methodist Episcopal Church—Service and Development Agency

1134 11th St NW #214, Washington, DC 20001 USA; (202) 371-8723; Fax (202) 371-0981; http://www.amenet.org/sada

Focus: Human Rights
Mission: Since 1787, AME has worked for a better quality of life for its people. In 1978 SADA began development and relief projects. Currently, SADA takes education about nutrition and family planning, training for midwives, and distribution of vaccines and food supplements to 72 Haitian communities.

AFSC—American Friends Service Committee

1501 Cherry St, Philadelphia, PA 19102-1479 USA; (215) 241-7030; Fax (215) 241-7282
http://www.afsc.org

Focus: General Peace & Justice; Women
Mission: The AFSC includes people of many faiths committed to social justice, peace, and humanitarian service, based on the Quaker belief in the worth of every person and faith in the power of love to overcome violence and injustice.

International Regions

(215) 241-7000 Ext. 7151; Fax (215) 241-7026;

Focus: Human Rights
Mission: To promote peace, justice, reconciliation, and to support people outside North America in developing their own power and resources through relief and reconstruction, community development, training, and support.

National Community Relations Unit

(215) 241-7000 Ext. 7120; Fax (215) 241-7119;
Focus: Discrimination; Human Rights
Mission: To root out those causes of injustice and violence in US society which lie in poverty, imbalance of wealth, and in exclusion and denial of recognition of rights based on race, gender, class, religion, nationality, and sexual orientation.

Peace Unit

(215) 241-7163; Fax (215) 241-7177
Focus: Peace & Nonviolence
Mission: To seek the abolition of war and fulfillment of human rights by promoting education and organizing in the US on international concerns for peace and justice, the reduction of military spending, and abolishing nuclear weapons worldwide.

Proyecto Campesino

111 NW 3rd Ave, Visalia, CA 93291 USA; (559) 733-4844; Fax (559) 733-2306;

Focus: Human Rights
Mission: To assist farm workers in organizing for economic and political empowerment by promoting citizenship, voting, tenant's rights, and civic action participation among immigrants. The Project assists farm worker rights organizations, provides direct services and referrals to about 3,600 farm-worker families annually.

AIDS National Interfaith Network

1400 I St NW #1220, Washington, DC 20005 USA; (202) 842-0010; Fax (202) 842-3323; http://www.thebody.com

Focus: Health Issues
Mission: ANIN is an organization of HIV/AIDS ministries and faith communities that mobilize people and institutions for education, advocacy for and support of persons affected by HIV/AIDS.

Albert Schweitzer Institute for Humanities

PO Box 550, Wallingford, CT 06492 USA; (203) 697-2744; Fax (203) 697-2748; asih1@aol.com

Focus: Health Issues; Training & Resources
Mission: Founded to perpetuate Albert Schweitzer's philosophy of Reverence for Life, it is committed to activities which provide opportunities for moral discourse and encourages community service, including educational programs for schools, publications, workshops, and special events.

All Faiths Seminary International

7 W 96th St #19B, New York, NY 10025 USA; (212) 866-3795; http://www.interfaith.org/allfaiths

Focus: Societies, Seminaries & Funds
Mission: To follow these guiding principles: 1) to affirm the truth in all faiths and religious paths, 2) to affirm the value of interfaith interactions as enriching awareness of Spirit in the world, and 3) to work together toward a common goal, the spiritual awakening of the world.

Alliance for Democracy

PO Box 683, Lincoln, MA 01773 USA; (781) 259-9395; Fax (781) 259-0404; http://www.afd-online.org

Focus: Economic Concerns
Mission: To free all people of all faiths and creeds from corporate domination of politics, economics, the culture, the environment, and propaganda; and to create a just society with a sustainable, equitable economy.

Alliance for Jewish Renewal

7318 Germantown Ave, Philadelphia, PA 19119 USA; (215) 247-9700; Fax (215) 247-9703; http://www.aleph.org

Focus: General Peace & Justice
Mission: AJR is a resource for those seeking a spiritual path within Judaism that is open to the rewarding work of repairing this world's fragmentation so that it manifests a conscious unity in relation to its creator. Shalom Center, www.shalomctr.org, is a project of AJR.

Alliance for Spiritual Community

24032 Caravel Pl, Laguna Niguel, CA 92677-4252 USA; (949) 661-3087; Fax (949) 496-5535; http://asc-spiritualcommunity.org

Focus: Ecumenical & Interfaith Cooperation
Mission: The Alliance proclaims and affirms the spiritual nature of all communities by sponsoring events that support community; monthly interfaith dialogues, an annual interfaith prayer breakfast, and an annual religious diversity fair.

Alliance for Tolerance & Freedom

PO Box 5096, Lancaster, PA 17606 USA; (717) 581-8292; Fax (717) 581-0347; http://www. geocities.com/CapitolHill/4497

Focus: Discrimination; Religious & Civil Liberty
Mission: The Alliance promotes tolerance, diversity, and equality in religion, society, and politics through awareness, education, and community involvement.

Alliance of Baptists, Inc.

1328 16th St NW, Washington, DC 20036 USA; (202) 745-7609; Fax (202) 745-0023; http://www. AllianceofBaptists.org

Focus: Religious & Civil Liberty
Mission: An alliance of individuals and churches dedicated to historic Baptist principles and freedoms, AOB upholds the freedom of the individual conscience and the local church. It favors cooperation with the larger body of Jesus Christ. AOB also adheres to the principle of a free church in a free state and opposes any effort, either by church or state, to use the other for its own purposes.

Alternative Gifts International

9656 Palomar Tr, Lucerne Valley, CA 92356-2267 USA; (800) 842-2243; Fax (760) 248-2195; http://www.altgifts.org

Focus: Training & Resources
Mission: To send authentic, life-giving gifts to a needy world (gifts that build a partnership with oppressed people in crisis and that protect and preserve the earth's endangered environment) and to nourish and sustain a more equitable and peaceful global community. AGI sponsors an annual "Alternative Gift Market."

Alternatives for Simple Living

5312 Morningside Ave, Sioux City, IA 51106-0857 USA; (800) 821-6153; Fax (712) 274-1402; http://www.SimpleLiving.org

Focus: Peace & Nonviolence; Training & Resources
Mission: Providing resources for 25 years, Alternatives equips people of faith to challenge consumerism, live justly, and celebrate responsibly. Alternatives' most widely read resource is the Christmas booklet, "Whose Birthday Is It, Anyway?"

Alternatives to Violence Project USA

PO Box 300431, Houston, TX 77320-0431 USA; (713) 747-9999; Fax (713) 747-9999; http://www.avpusa.org

Focus: Peace & Nonviolence; Training & Resources
Mission: AVP, an association of community and prison-based groups, seeks to empower people to lead nonviolent lives using the same nonviolent skills and techniques of Mohandas Gandhi and Dr. Martin Luther King, Jr. Experiential workshops in conflict resolution and responses to violence are offered.

AMANI—Society of Justice and Charity

7325 S Luella Ave, Chicago, IL 60649 USA; (773) 375-3911; skalonji@prodigy.net

Focus: Human Rights
Mission: AMANI gives voice to the African Presence in the US, seeks to forge partnerships between African and American peoples, and educates for concrete actions in favor of a full development of the African communities in the US and in Africa.

America—National Catholic Weekly

106 W 56th St, New York, NY 10019 USA; (212) 581-4640; Fax (212) 399-3596; http://www.americapress.org

Focus: Communication
Mission: *America*, edited by US Jesuits, is a Catholic weekly magazine for Catholic and non-Catholics to inform and comment on theological and ecclesiastical subjects, moral and pastoral concerns, issues of economic and social justice, politics, education, and the arts.

American Forum for Jewish-Christian Cooperation

1407 Montford Dr, Harrisburg, PA 17110 USA; (717) 236-0437; Fax (717) 540-1430; http://www.listscape.com/afjcc.htm

Focus: Ecumenical & Interfaith Cooperation
Mission: AFJCC seeks to develop communication and understanding between the Jewish and Christian communities by educating each about their common biblical and moral ground, studying the way this common ground has affected history, and determining mutual action to benefit contemporary society.

American Humanist Association

PO Box 1188, Amherst, NY 14226-7188 USA; (716) 839-5080; Fax (716) 839-5079; http://www.humanist.net

Focus: Religious & Civil Liberty; Training & Resources
Mission: To promote the philosophy of humanism by providing a bi-monthly magazine, books, literature, audio, and videotapes, and by holding seminars and conferences.

American Indian—Alaska Native Lutheran Assn

13007 NE Fremont, Portland, OR 97230 USA; (503) 253-9460; Fax (503) 253-2648; sotorank@aol.com

Focus: Indigenous or Displaced Persons
Mission: The Association, a gathering of indigenous people of North America who are both enrolled tribal members and members of the Lutheran Church, advocates for peace and justice and supports tribal sovereignty.

American Islamic College

640 W Irving Park Rd, Chicago, IL 60613 USA; (773) 281-4700; Fax (773) 281-8552

Focus: Societies, Seminaries & Funds
Mission: The College provides educational programs within an Islamic environment and philosophic orientation. Peace and justice education is included.

American Jewish Committee

165 E 56th St, New York, NY 10022-2746 USA; (212) 751-4000; Fax (212) 319-6156; jbi@ajc.org

Focus: Discrimination; Religious & Civil Liberty; Training & Resources
Mission: Founded in 1906, now in 600 communities, AJC conducts educational programs, combats bigotry, and seeks to protect religious and civil rights.

American Jewish Congress

15 E 84th St, New York, NY 10028 USA; (212) 879-4500; Fax (212) 249-3672; http://www.ajcongress.org

Focus: Discrimination; Religious & Civil Liberty
Mission: AJC works to preserve First Amendment protections of religious liberty, to safeguard the separation of church and state, to oppose any form of discrimination and bigotry, to foster the well-being of the Jewish people, and to secure a just, lasting, and secure peace for the people of Israel.

American Jewish World Service

989 Avenue of the Americas, 10th Fl, New York, NY 10018 USA; (212) 736-2597; Fax (212) 736-3463; http://www.ajws.org

Focus: Human Rights
Mission: To help alleviate human suffering, poverty, hunger, and diseases regardless of race, religion, or nationality. AJWS works with partners worldwide and with local, nation, and nongovernmental organizations to engage in education, community building, health care, agriculture, and income generation.

American Kurdish Information Network

2623 Connecticut Ave NW #1, Washington, DC 20008-1522 USA; (202) 483-6444; Fax (202) 483-6476; http://www.kurdistan.org

Focus: Human Rights
Mission: To foster Kurdish-American understanding and friendship, to hold a mirror to human rights violations and repression of the Kurdish people in the Middle East nations, to be a resource for policy makers, scholars, and students of the region.

American Muslim Council

1212 New York Ave NW #400, Washington, DC 20005 USA; (202) 789-2262; Fax (202) 789-2550; http://www.amconline.org

Focus: Discrimination
Mission: To promote ethical values that enhance the quality of life in North America, to act as a catalyst for American Muslims, to identify and oppose discrimination against Muslims and other minorities, and to serve as a resource for interorganizational and cross-cultural cooperation.

American Scientific Affiliation

Box 668, Ipswich, MA 01938 USA; (978) 356-5656; Fax (978) 356-4375; http://www.asa3.org

Focus: Societies, Seminaries & Funds
Mission: To integrate, communicate, and facilitate properly researched science and biblical theology in service to the church and the scientific community. 7 chapters.

Americans for Religious Liberty

PO Box 6656, Silver Spring, MD 20916 USA; (301) 598-2447; Fax (301) 438-8424; arlinc@erols.com

Focus: Religious & Civil Liberty; Training & Resources
Mission: To defend religious liberty, freedom of conscience, and the principle of church-state separation, ARL opposes vouchers, threats to public schools religious neutrality, and reproductive choice. It sponsors research, publishing, public speaking, litigation, and coalition building.

Americans United for Separation of Church & State

518 C St NE, Washington, DC 20002 USA; (202) 466-3234 Ext. 201; Fax (202) 466-2587 http://www.au.org

Focus: Religious & Civil Liberty
Mission: Since 1947, AU has defended US church-state separation and served as a resource on church-state legislation, the Religious Right, and pertinent legal cases. Director Barry Lynn and 7 of 15 board members hold clergy status. 40 US chapters.

Amnesty International—Interfaith Network for Human Rights

53 W Jackson Blvd #1163, Chicago, IL 60604 USA; (312) 427-2060; Fax (312) 427-2589; http://www.amnestyusa.org/interfaith

Focus: Human Rights
Mission: To mobilize people and communities of faith to take action to stop human rights abuses, to support people of faith who are on the front line of the human rights struggle, and to provide awareness of human rights abuses based on religious belief.

Anglican Church of Canada—EcoJustice Committee

600 Jarvis St, Toronto, ON M4Y 2J6 Canada; (416) 924-9199 Ext. 202; Fax (416) 924-3483; http://www.anglican.ca

Focus: Ecology & Environment; Indigenous or Displaced Persons
Mission: To challenge the attitudes and structures that cause injustice, especially to indigenous people, and other social,

economic and environmental-related justice issues through the 30 Anglican dioceses in Canada.

Anglican Communion Office at the UN

815 2nd Ave, New York, NY 10017 USA; (212) 716-6263; Fax (212) 687-1336; http://www.aco.org/united-nations

Focus: Global Peace & Security
Mission: The Anglican Communion is committed by Christian faith to work for peace on earth and justice among men and women. This office acts for that goal by relating to the work of the United Nations.

Anti-Defamation League

823 UN Plaza, New York, NY 10017 USA; (212) 885-7700; Fax (212) 867-0779; http://www.adl.org

Focus: Discrimination; Religious & Civil Liberty
Mission: The League promotes interfaith and intergroup relations, works against anti-Semitism, counteracts anti-democratic extremism, and seeks to strengthen democratic values and structures. 32 regional offices.

Asia Pacific Center for Justice & Peace

110 Maryland Ave NE #504, Washington, DC 20002 USA; (202) 543-1094; Fax (202) 546-5103; http://www.apcjp.org

Focus: Economic Concerns; Human Rights
Mission: APCJP works for justice and peace with partners in that area by focusing on the policies and actions of the US government, corporations, and international institutions as they impact the people of the Asia Pacific region.

Association for Global New Thought

1565 Maple Ave #204-205, Evanston, IL 60201 USA; (847) 866-9525; Fax (847) 866-9545; http://www.gandhiking.com

Focus: Peace & Nonviolence
Mission: To promote and nurture a spiritual way of life that reveals humankind's oneness and also embodies the principles and practices of cocreation. Its initiatives promote awareness of

nonviolence and peacemaking as a powerful way to heal, transform, and empower earth and its communities.

Association for Religion & Intellectual Life

College of New Rochelle, New Rochelle, NY 10805 USA; (914) 235-1439; Fax (914) 235-1584; http://www.aril.org

Focus: Training & Resources
Mission: A global network of people from various religious traditions, ARIL addresses issues of peace and justice from an interreligious perspective in its journal, conferences, and networking groups on college campuses and local communities across the country.

Association for Rights of Catholics in Church

PO Box 912, Delran, NJ 08075 USA; (609) 461-8960; Fax (609) 921-3924; http://astro.temple.edu/~arcc

Focus: Renewal of Faith Group
Mission: Founded in 1980 by lay and clerical Catholics in the wake of Vatican condemnations of several respected Catholic theologians, ARCC's goal is to institute a collegial and egalitarian understanding of the church in which decision making is shared and accountability realized.

Association of Interfaith Ministers

838 E 218th St, Bronx, NY 10467-5806 USA; (203) 855-0000; Fax (203) 855-1126; http://www.interfaithclergy.org

Focus: Societies, Seminaries & Funds
Mission: AIM is a professional organization of interfaith-oriented and trained clergy providing member support services, education, and a referral service for the public.

Association of Lutheran Older Adults

Valparaiso U, Valparaiso, IN 46383 USA; (800) 930-2562; Fax (219) 464-6824

Focus: Children, Youth & Family
Mission: A national organization, ALOA seeks to ensure that the needs and blessings of the years be understood, shared, and celebrated to the benefit of older adults.

Association of Professors & Researchers in Religious Education

950 Marietta Ave, Lancaster, PA 17603 USA; (717) 393-0654 Ext. 130; http://associations.anderson.edu/appre

Focus: Societies, Seminaries & Funds
Mission: APRRE is a professional organization for educators and researchers from all faiths. Copublishing *The Religious Education Journal,* sponsoring an annual meeting and a conference, its office is at Lancaster Theological Seminary.

Au Sable Institute of Environmental Studies

7526 Sunset Tr NE, Mancelona, MI 49659 USA; (231) 587-8686; Fax (231) 587-5353; http://www.ausable.org

Focus: Societies, Seminaries & Funds
Mission: Serving and promoting Christian earthkeeping through academic programs, research projects, forums, programs for schoolchildren, and information services for Christian churches, denominations, and the wider community, SA works on three continents.

B'nai B'rith

1640 Rhode Island Ave NW, Washington, DC 20036-3278 USA; (202) 857-6536; Fax (202) 857-1099; http://www.bnaibrith.org

Focus: Discrimination; Human Rights
Mission: Working in the UN, EU, national capitals, and local communities, B'nai B'rith supports human rights and opposes discrimination. It is the largest national sponsor of federally funded nonsectarian housing for low-income seniors.

Bahá'í—Office of Public Information

866 UN Plaza #120, New York, NY 10017 USA; (212) 803-2500; Fax (212) 803-2573; http://www.bahai.org

Focus: Ecumenical & Interfaith Cooperation; General Peace & Justice; Women
Mission: Bahá'í seek the oneness of humankind, equality of women and men, racial integration, economic justice, uni-

versal education, and the creation of a world commonwealth of nations. There are 7,228 USA chapters.

Bahá'í Community of Canada

7200 Leslie St, Thornhill, ON L3T 6L8 Canada; (905) 889-8168; Fax (905) 889-8184; http://www.bahai.org

Focus: Ecumenical & Interfaith Cooperation; General Peace & Justice; Women
Mission: Dedicated to equality of men and women, the elimination of discrimination, the harmony and dialogue of science and religion, Bahá'í of Canada view the establishment of a peaceful and just global society as the preeminent challenge facing humanity.

Baptist Joint Comm on Public Affairs—Religious Liberty Council

200 Maryland Ave NE, Washington, DC 20002 USA; (202) 544-4226; Fax (202) 544-2094; http://www.bjcpa.org

Focus: Religious & Civil Liberty
Mission: To protect, uphold, and defend the significant and historical Baptist doctrine of a free church in a free state with explicit commitment to religious liberty.

Baptist Peace Fellowship—NA

4800 Wedgewood Rd, Charlotte, NC 28210 USA; (704) 521-6051; Fax (704) 521-6053; http://www.bpfna.org

Focus: Peace & Nonviolence
Mission: To unite and enable Baptist Christians to work for peace in our warring world, rooted in faith in Jesus Christ.

Benedictine Resource Center—TX

530 Bandera Rd, San Antonio, TX 78228 USA; (210) 735-4988; Fax (210) 735-2615; snmika@texas.net

Focus: Peace & Nonviolence
Mission: To develop a deeper sense of solidarity with all living under oppressive structures and to empower others to use their gifts to become change agents.

Benetvision Publishers

355 E 9th St, Erie, PA 16503-1107 USA; (814) 459-5994; Fax (814) 459-8066 http://www.erie.net/~erie-osb

Focus: Communication; Training & Resources; Women

Mission: Benetvision publishes books, journals, audio and videotapes on contemporary spiritual life addressing issues of women, justice, spirituality, and Benedictinism.

Blueprint for Social Justice— Newsletter

Loyola U Box 907, 7214 St Charles Ave, New Orleans, LA 70118 USA; (504) 861-5380; Fax (504) 861-5833; http://www.loyno.edu/twomey

Focus: Communication
Mission: *The Blueprint,* distributed free of charge nine times annually, is kept brief by focusing on only one social justice topic each month, covering the subject with a variety of authors.

Border Assn for Refugees from Central America, Inc

PO Box 715, Edinburg, TX 78540 USA; (956) 631-7447; Fax (956) 687-9266

Focus: Indigenous or Displaced Persons
Mission: BARCA offers legal orientation, advocacy, and services to an indigent immigrant and refugee community residing, apprehended, or detained in a four-county South Texas area.

Boston Research Center for the 21st Century

396 Harvard St, Cambridge, MA 02138-3924 USA; (617) 491-1090; Fax (617) 491-1169; http://www.brc21.org

Focus: Societies, Seminaries & Funds
Mission: The BRC fosters consultations among scholars, theologians, and activists on common values across cultures and religions. Focal points are human rights, nonviolence, ecological harmony, and economic justice.

Brahma Kumaris World Spiritual Organization

46 S Middle Neck Rd, Great Neck, NY 11021 USA; (516) 773-0971; Fax (516) 773-0976; http://www.bkwsu.com

Focus: Training & Resources; Ecumenical & Interfaith Cooperation
Mission: The Organization carries out a wide range of educational programs for the development of human and spiritual values throughout its 4,000 branches in over 70 countries. It works at all levels

of society for positive change including Raja Yoga meditation.

Brahmi Jain Society

1884 Dorsetshire Rd, Columbus, OH 43229 USA; (614) 899-2678; Fax (614) 899-2678 (Fax dial #14)

Focus: Ecumenical & Interfaith Cooperation; Peace & Nonviolence
Mission: To promote studies of the Jain religion and participate in multifaith dialogues to better the understanding between faiths. The fundamental principle of Jainism is nonviolence (Ahimsa). "Live, let live, and help others to live."

Bread for the World

1100 Wayne Ave #1000, Silver Spring, MD 20910 USA; (301) 608-2400; Fax (301) 608-2401; http://www.bread.org

Focus: Advocacy; Human Rights
Mission: A Christian citizens' movement that seeks justice for the world's hungry people by lobbying our nation's decision makers, BFW advocates changes in public policy to address the root causes of hunger and poverty in the US and overseas.

Brethren Peace Fellowship

PO Box 455, New Windsor, MD 21776 USA; (410) 848-5631; braune@ccpl.carr.org

Focus: Peace & Nonviolence
Mission: The Fellowship sponsors Christian peace education, peace vigils, and support groups for peacemakers.

Brethren—Mennonite Council for Lesbian & Gay Concerns

PO Box 6300, Minneapolis, MN 55406 USA; (612) 722-6906; http://www.webcom.com/bmc

Focus: Discrimination
Mission: To provide support for Brethren and Mennonite gay, lesbian, and bisexual people and their parents, spouses, relatives, and friends by providing accurate information about homosexuality from the social sciences, biblical studies, and theology. 14 US and Canadian chapters.

Bruderhof Communities

Catskill Bruderhof, Elka Park, NY, 12427 USA; (518) 589-5103; http://www.bruderhof.org/

Focus: Peace & Nonviolence
Mission: A movement of families, and single men and women, living in 8 communities in NY, PA, and southern England, BC follow Christ's Sermon on the Mount: brother love and love of enemies, mutual service, nonviolence, and the refusal to bear arms. BC sponsors *Plough* monthly magazine.

Buddhist Churches of America

1710 Octavia St, San Francisco, CA 94109 USA; (415) 776-5600; Fax (415) 771-6293

Focus: Ecumenical & Interfaith Cooperation
Mission: Since 1899, the Buddhist Churches of America have shared peace guided by the text, "Just as the sun does not discriminate, including some and neglecting others, so the compassion of the Amida Buddha be equal toward all sentient beings."

Buddhist Peace Fellowship

PO Box 4650, Berkeley, CA 94704 USA; (510) 655-6169; Fax (510) 655-1369; http://www.bpf.org

Focus: Peace & Nonviolence
Mission: To awaken peace where there is conflict, bring insight to institutionalized ignorance, promote communication and cooperation in the spirit of wisdom, compassion, and harmony. 5000 Buddhist members of many traditions are involved in disarmament work and environmental and human rights.

Buddhist Society for Compassionate Wisdom

1710 W Cornelia Ave, Chicago, IL 60657-1219 USA; (773) 528-8685; Fax (773) 528-9909; http://www.zenbuddhisttemple.org

Focus: Peace & Nonviolence
Mission: Believing that all beings were originally Buddhas, the Society urges that each person train to help realize Buddhahood. Then all can respect and honor everyone as Buddhas through whatever means is available: kindness, friendship, and physical help.

Call to Action

4419 N Kedzie, Chicago, IL 60625 USA; (773) 604-0400; Fax (773) 604-4719; http://www.cta-usa.org

Focus: Renewal of Faith Group; Women
Mission: Laity, religious, priests, and bishops work in the spirit of Vatican II and the US Bishops' "Call to Action" to foster peace, justice, and love in their world, the church, and themselves, holding that God's spirit is at work in the whole church, not just its appointed leaders, and that the entire Catholic Church has the obligation of responding to a needy world. 33 US regional affiliate organizations.

Call to Renewal

2401 15th St NW, Washington, DC 20009 USA; (201) 328-8745; Fax (202) 328-8757; http://www.calltorenewal.com

Focus: Human Rights
Mission: Those Christians who answer "The Call" are from many churches, communities, and agencies who join together to build a faith-based movement to overcome poverty through moral politics that combine spiritual renewal and social responsibility.

Calling Prophets Project

428 College Ave, Richmond, IN 47374 USA; (765) 939-7133; http://www.nonviolence.org/training/calling.htm

Focus: Peace & Nonviolence
Mission: To help young people in the historic peace churches explore their faith and heritage and build skills for justice seeking and nonviolent living.

Campaign for a Fair Minimum Wage

1625 K St #210, Washington, DC 20006 USA; (202) 785-5980; Fax (202) 785-5969; http://www.adaction.org

Focus: Advocacy; Economic Concerns
Mission: This office advocates on behalf of a coalition of 130 public policy, advocacy, and faith organizations supporting an increase in the federal minimum wage.

Campaign for Equity—Restorative Justice

217 High St, Brattleboro, VT 05301 USA; (802) 254-2826; Fax (802) 254-2826; http://www.cerj.org

Focus: Criminal Justice System
Mission: CERJ seeks to build a societal effort for justice reform, foster public awareness and adoption of alternative solutions that exist for crime, and replace problematic justice practices with outreach and public education.

Canada-Asia Working Group

947 Queen St E #213, Toronto, ON M4M 1J9 Canada; (416) 465-8826; Fax (416) 463-5569; cawg@web.net

Focus: Economic Concerns; Human Rights
Mission: An ecumenical coalition of Canadian Churches seeking to understand and practice God's mission for peace, justice, human dignity, and the integrity of creation, CAWG works in solidarity with Asian partners through analysis, advocacy, education, and networking on justice issues.

Canadian Catholic Organization for Development and Peace

5633 Sherbrooke St E, Montreal, QB H1N 1A3 CAN; (514) 257-8710 Ext. 309; Fax (514) 257-8497; http://www.devp.org

Focus: Economic Concerns; Human Rights
Mission: To improve living and working conditions in developing nations, to alert Canadians to the true causes of poverty, and to support initiatives by third world peoples to take control of their lives. Chapters in the 65 Catholic dioceses in Canada, offices in 14 cities.

Canadian Centre for Ecumenism

2065 Sherbrooke St W, Montreal, QC H3H 1G6 Canada; (514) 937-9176; Fax (514) 937-2684; http://www.total.net/~ccocce

Focus: Ecumenical & Interfaith Cooperation
Mission: A resource centre committed to the promotion of Christian unity as well as interfaith relations, its major areas of activity are prayer, sharing of spiritual riches, education, and dialogue.

Canadian Churches Forum for Global Ministries

230 St Clair Ave W, Toronto, ON M4V 1R5 Canada; (416) 924-9351; Fax (416) 924-5356; ccforum@web.net

Focus: Ecumenical & Interfaith Cooperation; Training & Resources
Mission: For 75 years, the Forum has enabled Canadian churches to reflect and work together on global mission, social justice, and interfaith concerns through programs of education, dialogue, and training.

Canadian Coalition for Rights of Children

180 Argyle Ave #322, Ottawa, ON K2P 1B7 Canada; (613) 788-5085; Fax (613) 788-5106; http://www.cfc-efc.ca/ccrc

Focus: Human Rights
Mission: To ensure a collective voice for Canadian organizations concerned with the rights of children as described in the UN Convention on the Rights of the Child and the World Summit for Children Declaration.

Canadian Conference of Catholic Bishops—Social Affairs Commission

90 Parent Ave, Ottawa, ON K1N 7B1 Canada; (613) 241-9461; Fax (613) 241-5087; http://www.cccb.ca

Focus: Societies, Seminaries & Funds
Mission: To assist the bishops and the people of God in proclaiming the Gospel through activities for justice and the transformation of society, the Commission does research, and education and suggests action on a variety of social justice concerns, both national and international.

Canadian Council for Refugees

6839 Drolet #302, Montreal, QC H2S 2T1 Canada; (514) 277-7223; Fax (514) 277-1447; ccr@web.net

Focus: Indigenous or Displaced Persons; Training & Resources
Mission: Committed to the rights, protection, and settlement of refugees and immigrants, CCR fulfills its mission by providing sponsoring conferences, working groups, publications, research, media, and advocacy.

Canadian Council of Christian Charities

1–21 Howard Ave, Elmira, ON N3B 2C9 Canada; (519) 669-5137; Fax (519) 669-3291; http://www.cccc.org

Focus: Societies, Seminaries & Funds
Mission: To serve Christian charitable organizations by providing training in effective administration, setting a God-honouring code of ethics as a governing standard, administering the CCCC Seal for Financial Accountability, providing services as needed, and providing comment to government on legislation affecting charities.

Canadian Council of Christians & Jews

2 Carlton S #820, Toronto, ON M5B 1J3 Canada; (416) 597-9693; Fax (416) 597-9775; http://www.interlog.com/~cccj

Focus: Discrimination; Training & Resources
Mission: CCCJ is an educational organization dedicated to eliminating prejudice and promoting cultural, racial, and religious harmony among the people of Canada.

Canadian Council of Churches— Peace & Justice

3250 Bloor St W, 2nd Fl, Toronto, ON M8X 2Y4 CAN; (416) 232-6070 X2021; Fax (416) 236-4532; http://www.web.net/~ccchurch

Focus: Ecumenical & Interfaith Cooperation; General Peace & Justice
Mission: To act as an agency for conference and consultation for common planning and actions as churches wish to take, to encourage ecumenical understanding and action throughout Canada, and to relate to the World Council of Churches.

Canadian Friends Service Committee

60 Lowther Ave, Toronto, ON M5R 1C7 Canada; (416) 920-5213; Fax (416) 920-5214; http://www.web.net/~cfsc

Focus: Criminal Justice System; Indigenous or Displaced Persons; Peace & Nonviolence
Mission: CFSC, established in 1931, supports action for peace, global justice, solidarity with aboriginal peoples,

reform of the criminal justice system, and other social justice concerns of the Religious Society of Friends (Quakers).

Canadian Lutheran Office for Public Policy

c/o Waterloo Lutheran Seminary, Waterloo, ON N2L 3C5 Canada; (519) 884-1970 Ext. 3907; Fax (519) 725-2434; http://www.wlu.ca/~wwwsem/ice/index/html

Focus: Advocacy
Mission: To provide a public witness for social justice of the Evangelical Lutheran Church in Canada as it works with partner churches to address issues of public policy in Canada and internationally.

Canadian Religious Conference

219 Argyle Ave, Ottawa, ON K2P 2H4 Canada; (613) 236-0824; Fax (613) 236-0825; http://www.crcn.ca/crcn/

Focus: Societies, Seminaries & Funds
Mission: CRC is an association of the leadership of Roman Catholic religious orders of men and women whose mission includes support for the elimination of poverty and oppression, care for the environment, and work for peace.

Catholic Campaign for Human Development

3211 4th St NE, Washington, DC 20017-1194 USA; (202) 541-3210; Fax (202) 541-3329; http://www.nccbuscc.org/cchd

Focus: Human Rights
Mission: The Campaign is the domestic antipoverty, social justice program of the US Catholic bishops. Its mission is to address the root causes of US poverty through promotion and support of community-controlled self-help organizations and through transformative education.

Catholic Central Verein of America

3835 Westminster Pl, St Louis, MO 63108 USA; (314) 371-1653

Focus: Children, Youth & Family
Mission: To awaken in all mankind a consciousness to human dignity and social rights and duties; to protect human life, marriage, the family, and

parental rights and duties. 3 US chapters.

Catholic Charities USA

1731 King St #200, Alexandria, VA 22314 USA; (703) 549-1390; Fax (703) 549-1656; http://www.catholiccharitiesusa.org

Focus: Human Rights
Mission: To provide service for people in need, to advocate for justice in social structures, and to call the entire church and people of goodwill to do the same.

Catholic Conference of Major Superiors of Men's Institutes

8808 Cameron St, Silver Spring, MD 20910 USA; (301) 588-4030; Fax (301) 587-4575; http://www.cmsm.org

Focus: Advocacy
Mission: Advocacy office for the 23,000 Catholic religious priests and brothers seeking to further human rights and economic development.

Catholic Health Association of Canada

1247 Kilborn PL, Ottawa, ON K1H 6K9 Canada; (613) 731-7148; Fax (613) 731-7797; http://www.chac.ca

Focus: Health Issues
Mission: The CHAC is a bilingual national organization committed to advancing a vision of health and healing that encompasses the emotional, spiritual, social, and physical well-being of people.

Catholic Network of Volunteer Service

4121 Harewood Rd NE, Washington, DC 20017 USA; (800) 543-5046; Fax (202) 526-1094; http://www.cnvs.org

Focus: Human Rights; Training & Resources
Mission: CNVS, challenged by the message of the Gospel, promotes and assists volunteers to serve in member programs in the US and throughout the world. CNVS advocates an increased role for all women and men to utilize their gifts in service to the church and the world.

Catholic Organizations for Renewal

18 Ruggles St, Melrose, MA 02176 USA; (781) 665-5657; Fax (781) 665-5066; http://www.cta-usa.org/cor

Focus: Renewal of Faith Group
Mission: COR, a coalition, is a forum of 28 autonomous organizations, whose focus is renewal of the Catholic Church.

Catholic Relief Services

209 W Fayette St, Baltimore, MD 21201 USA; (410) 625-2220; Fax (410) 685-1635; http://www.catholicrelief.org

Focus: Human Rights
Mission: To promote true justice and lasting peace by standing alongside suffering communities in solidarity; sharing talents, resources, and time; and addressing structural causes and systems of poverty.

Catholics Against Capital Punishment

PO Box 3125, Arlington, VA 22203 USA; (301) 652-1125; Fax (301) 652-1125; http://www.igc.org/cacp

Focus: Criminal Justice System
Mission: CACP works to promote better understanding of Catholic Church teachings on the issue of the death penalty by fellow Catholics and others.

Catholics for Free Choice/ Catholics for Contraception

1436 U St NW #301, Washington, DC 20009-3997 USA; (202) 986-6093; Fax (202) 332-7995; http://www.cath4choice.org

Focus: Religious & Civil Liberty; Renewal of Faith Group
Mission: To support sexual and reproductive ethics that are based on justice, are committed to women's well-being, and which affirm the moral capacity of women and men to make sound decisions about their lives. Through discourse, education, and advocacy, CFFC works to infuse these values into public policy, feminist analysis, and Catholic social thinking and teaching.

Center for Action & Contemplation

PO Box 12464, Albuquerque, NM 87195 USA; (505) 242-9588; Fax (505) 242-9518; http://www.rc.net/org/cac/index.html

Focus: Training & Resources
Mission: The Center offers an intensive spiritual formation program, "Radical Grace," internships, workshops and a bimonthly newsletter for individuals, lay and religious, seeking the integration of social justice and prayer.

Center for Global Ethics—Global Dialogue Institute

Temple University, Religion Dept., Philadelphia, PA 19122 USA; (215) 204-7251; Fax (215) 204-4569; http://astro.temple.edu/~dialogue/geth.htm

Focus: Societies, Seminaries & Funds
Mission: To coordinate the work of thinkers, scholars, and activists from around the world who are working to define, implement, and promote policies of responsible global citizenship. The Center seeks recognition of the need to advance the acceptance of a viable and sustainable Global Ethic.

Center for New Community

PO Box 346066, Chicago, IL 60634-6066 USA; (708) 848-0319; Fax (708) 848-0327; http://www.newcomm.org

Focus: Discrimination; Training & Resources
Mission: With the primary goal of working with faith groups using the Center's faith-based, organizing methodology to revitalize both church and community, the Center also educates and trains leaders and organizations to develop effective responses to the white supremacist movement.

Center for Non Violence

PO Box 1058, San Jacinto, CA 92581-1058 USA; (909) 654-5493; Fax (909) 652-0798

Focus: Peace & Nonviolence; Training & Resources
Mission: To promote the conscious practice of nonviolence as a dynamic means of affecting personal change and creating a more just, peaceful, and sustainable world, the Center provides resources for reflection, action, empow-

erment, and leadership development, encouraging all to address social problems by life-affirming, nonviolent means.

Center for Process Studies

1325 N College Ave, Claremont, CA 91711-3154 USA; (800) 626-7821; Fax (909) 621-2760; http://www.ctr4process.org

Focus: Societies, Seminaries & Funds
Mission: To contribute to the development of a new cultural paradigm influenced by a relational worldview. This process, integrating science, religion, ethics, and aesthetics, generates a perspective that includes feminist, ecological, political, economic, and other issues that takes account of issues beyond immediate concern for itself.

Center for Progressive Christianity

99 Brattle St, Cambridge, MA 02138 USA; (617) 441-0928; Fax (617) 441-6201; http://www.tcpc.org

Focus: Training & Resources
Mission: To promote Christian practice and teaching that lead to acceptance of all people, respect for other religious traditions, and upholding of evangelism as an agent of justice and peace. The Center is opposed to exclusive dogma that limits the search for truth and free inquiry. Workshops, conferences, lectures, and resources are offered.

Center for Religion, Ethics, and Social Policy

Anabel Taylor Hall, Cornell U, Ithaca, NY 14853 USA; (607) 255-6202; Fax (607) 255-9985; http://www.sas.cornell.edu/cresp

Focus: Societies, Seminaries & Funds
Mission: CRESP fosters study, dialogue, and action for a just and sustainable society.

Center for Respect of Life & Environment

2100 L St NW, Washington, DC 20037 USA; (202) 778-6133; Fax (202) 778-6138; http://www.crle.org

Focus: Societies, Seminaries & Funds
Mission: To promote the greening of higher and theological education and foster earth ethics to guide sustainable development.

Center for Sexuality and Religion

987 Old Eagle School Rd # 719, Wayne, PA 19087 USA; (610) 995-0341; Fax (610) 995-0364; http://www.ctrsr.org

Focus: Societies, Seminaries & Funds
Mission: A consortium of theologians, sexologists, educators, and health care professionals, the Center assists groups in providing healthy and responsible sexuality education in the context of religious and theological study. The inherent goodness of sexuality, its connection with religion, and the need for continual dialogue between sexual sciences and religious systems are basic to CTRSR.

Center for Study of Religion in Public Life

Trinity College-300 Summit St, Hartford, CT 06106 USA; (860) 297-2353 Ext. 860; Fax (860) 297-5215; http://frontpage.trincoll.edu/csrpl

Focus: Societies, Seminaries & Funds
Mission: To explore challenges posed by religious pluralism and tensions between religious and secular values, and to examine the influence of religion on politics, civic culture, family life, gender roles, and other issues.

Center for the Prevention of Sexual & Domestic Violence

936 N 34th St #200, Seattle, WA 98103 USA; (206) 634-1903; Fax (206) 634-0115; http://www.cpsdv.org

Focus: Training & Resources; Women
Mission: The Center educates the religious community on sexual and domestic violence and sexual abuse by clergy. It also provides training, video resources, and publications.

Center for Women, the Earth, the Divine

114 Rising Ridge Rd, Ridgefield, CT 06877 USA; (203) 438-3867; Fax (203) 438-1970; http://www.CWED.org

Focus: Societies, Seminaries & Funds
Mission: To explore the parallels existing between the imaging/treatment of women and the Earth, and how our images of the Divine are related to those parallels. This is done with Christian, Buddhist, Goddess, Hindu,

indigenous, Jewish, and Muslim traditions. Resources available.

Center of Concern

1225 Otis St NE, Washington, DC 20017 USA; (202) 635-2757 Ext. 110; Fax (202) 832-9494; http://www.coc.org/coc

Focus: General Peace & Justice; Women; Training & Resources
Mission: The Center engages in social analysis, theological reflection, policy advocacy, and public education on issues of peace and justice, rooted in a faith commitment and guided by a global vision. Current programs focus on economic alternatives, peace initiatives, women in society and church, and social theology.

Center on Conscience & War

1830 Connecticut Ave NW, Washington, DC 20009 USA; (202) 483-2220; Fax (202) 483-1246; http://www.nisbco.org

Focus: Peace & Nonviolence; Religious; Civil Liberty; Training & Resources
Mission: Sponsored by 37 different religious groups, the Center seeks to protect the rights of conscientious objectors by advocating for the worldwide recognition of the rights of conscience and religious freedom. Legal counseling and a referral service for military service members are available.

Central Committee for Conscientious Objectors

1515 Cherry St, Philadelphia, PA 19102 USA; (215) 563-8787; Fax (215) 567-2096; http://www.objector.org

Focus: Peace & Nonviolence
Mission: CCCO supports and promotes individual and collective resistance to war and preparations for war. The GI Rights Hotline (800-394-9544) is a free, confidential nationwide hotline for service members who have questions about their rights, need a discharge, etc.

Central Conference of American Rabbis

355 Lexington Ave, New York, NY 10017 USA; (212) 972-3636; http://www.ccarnet.org

Focus: Ecumenical & Interfaith Cooperation; Societies, Seminaries & Funds

Mission: CCAR seeks dialogue and joint action with people of other faiths in the hope that together we can bring peace, freedom, and justice to our world. It works to narrow the gap between the affluent and the poor, to act against discrimination and oppression, to pursue peace, to welcome the stranger, and to protect the earth's biodiversity.

Centre for Social Concern

King's College, 266 Epworth Ave, London, ON N6A 2M3 Canada; (519) 433-3491; Fax (519) 433-0353; bhammond@julian.uwo.ca

Focus: Training & Resources
Mission: To educate around social justice and peace issues from the perspective of Catholic social thought.

Chaplaincy Institute for Arts & Interfaith Ministries

PO Box 7956, Berkeley, CA 94707-0956 USA; (510) 869-5134; Fax (510) 559-1854; http://www.chaplaincyinstitute.org

Focus: Societies, Seminaries & Funds
Mission: To inspire, empower, educate and ordain individuals to a new paradigm of creative interfaith chaplaincy and healing ministry, for work in schools, healthcare facilities and residential treatment centers, hospices, community and correctional facilities.

Chicago Women-Church

2572 W Argyle, Chicago, IL 60625 USA; (773) 728-5533; Fax (773) 784-2498; http://www.chicagowomenchurch.com

Focus: Women
Mission: A sacred circle of powerful and loving women, respecting individual differences, CW-C honors and encourages the spiritual growth in each and is dedicated to the continual exploration of the feminine. CW-C values and encourages risk-taking and freedom in ritual expression.

Children's Defense Fund

25 E St NW, Washington, DC 20001 USA; (202) 628-8787; Fax (202) 662-3540; http://www.childrensdefense.org

Focus: Children, Youth & Family
Mission: The mission of the Children's Defense Fund is to "Leave No Child Behind" and to "Ensure Every Child a Healthy Start, a Head Start, a Fair Start, a Safe Start, and a Moral Start" in life.

Christian Century Weekly

104 S Michigan #700, Chicago, IL 60603 USA; (312) 263-7510; Fax (312) 263-7540; http://www.christiancentury.org

Focus: Communication
Mission: To probe the religious and moral issues of modern culture with the task of appropriating and embodying Christian faith amid the cultural realities of our time: poverty, human rights, economic justice, international relations, national priorities, and popular culture.

Christian Church—Disciples of Christ

130 E Washington St, Indianapolis, IN 46206-1986 USA; (317) 635-3100; Fax (317) 635-3700; http://www.disciples.org

Focus: General Peace & Justice
Mission: We believe God's mission for the church is to be and to share the good news of Jesus Christ, witnessing and serving from our doorsteps "to the ends of the earth." (Acts 1:8)

Christian Ethics Today Magazine

PO Box 670784, Dallas, TX 75367-0784 USA; (972) 404-0050; Fax (972) 404-0070;

Focus: Communication
Mission: To bear witness to the relevance of the Christian gospel in the world today, emphasizing applied Christianity based on Christian experience, biblical truth, theological insight, historical perspective, current research, human needs, and the divine imperative to love God with our whole hearts and our neighbors as ourselves.

Christian Peacemaker Teams

PO Box 6508, Chicago, IL 60680 USA; (312) 455-1199; Fax (312) 432-1213; http://www.prairienet.org/cpt

Focus: Human Rights; Peace & Nonviolence
Mission: CPT is a program of the Mennonite, Quaker, and Church of the Brethren congregations who share a vision of active peacemaking rooted in spirituality. Teams of trained peacemakers participate in nonviolent direct action, symbolic public witness, human rights reporting, and negotiation, often in situations of conflict.

Christian Reformed Churches in Canada

3475 Mainway PO Box 5070, Burlington, ON L7R 3Y8 Canada; (905) 336-2920; Fax (905) 336-8344; http://www.kingsu.ab.ca/~jake/ccrcc.htm

Focus: General Peace & Justice; Women
Mission: To proclaim the good news of Jesus Christ and to be an active representation of God's justice and mercy.

Christian Social Action Magazine

100 Maryland Ave NW, Washington, DC 20002 USA; (202) 488-5621; Fax (202) 488-1617; http://www.umc-gbcs.org

Focus: Communication
Mission: CSA provides in-depth coverage of social issues from a faith-based perspective intended to inform, educate, and motivate readers as they carry out ministries of justice. Published by the UMC.

Christian Support Ministries

5115 S A1A Hwy #201b, Melbourne Beach, FL 32951 USA; (407) 952-0601; Fax—call first; http://www.rmbowman.com/csm

Focus: Peace & Nonviolence; Renewal of Faith Group
Mission: To assist in presenting authentic Christianity as a clear alternative to that of the Christian Coalition and other right-wing Christian groups. CSM seeks to inspire Christians to follow the nonviolent Jesus of Nazareth who clashed with the religious authorities of his day showing inclusivity, compassion, care for the outcasts of society, and unconditional love.

*Christian*New Age Quarterly*

Box 276, Clifton, NJ 07011-0276 USA; http://members.aol.com/CNAQ/ChristianNewAgeQuarterly.html

Focus: Communication
Mission: Devoted to dialog, *Christian*New Age Quarterly* clarifies the differences and the common ground of Christianity and the New Age movement. It seeks to be a lively journal with high-quality writing, sound scholarship, and the sparkle of plain, good fun.

Christians for Peace in El Salvador (CRISPAZ)

319 Camden, San Antonio, TX 78215 USA; ; (210) 222-2018; http://www.crispaz.org

Focus: Human Rights
Mission: A faith-based organization dedicated to standing with the church of the poor and marginalized communities in El Salvador, CRISPAZ strives for peace, justice, and human liberation.

The Christophers Publishing

12 E 48th St, New York, NY 10017 USA; (212) 759-4050;

Fax (212) 838-5073; http://www.christophers.org

Focus: Communication
Mission: To remind people of all faiths and no faith that they are unique and can change the world for the better, TC publishes brochures, books, calendars, videos, and a weekly TV series, *Christopher Closeup.*

Church & Society Magazine

100 Witherspoon St, Louisville, KY 40202-1396 USA; (502) 569-5810; Fax (502) 569-8116; http://www.horeb.pcusa.org/ churchsociety

Focus: Communication
Mission: C&S provides a forum on subjects of social concern to Christians. Each issue is devoted to one subject, exploring the many challenges Christians face in their search for a just society. Published by PC/USA.

Church & State Magazine

518 C St NE, Washington, DC 20002 USA; (202) 466-3234; Fax (202) 466-2587; http://www.au.org

Focus: Communication
Mission: C&S prints news and views of interest to those who support the belief that keeping a wholesome distance between the institutions of government and religion benefits citizens of all religious faiths as well as their government. Published by Americans United for Separation of Church and State.

Church and Labor Concerns—Institute for Mission USA

198 6th St E #604, St Paul, MN 55101-1948 USA; (651) 291-7550; wcstumme@aol.com

Focus: Economic Concerns
Mission: CLC seeks to assist the Lutheran Church ELCA in its outreach mission to working people and the poor, and to work cooperatively with organized labor in the struggle for a greater measure of economic justice.

Church Council on Justice & Corrections

507 Bank St, 2nd fl, Ottawa, ON K2P 1Z5 Canada; (613) 563-1688; Fax (613) 237-6129; ccjc@web.net

Focus: Criminal Justice System
Mission: CCJC, an 11-member Canadian church coalition, promotes a restorative approach to justice with an emphasis on addressing the needs of victims and offenders, mutual respect, healing, individual accountability, community involvement, and crime prevention.

Church Innovations Institute

1456 Branston St, St Paul, MN 55108 USA; (888) 223-7631; Fax (651) 646-3356; http://www.churchinnovations.org

Focus: Training & Resources
Mission: CII sponsors "Growing Healthier Congregations" video workshops for congregations. Not a conflict resolution method, but a way to create space for spiritual discernment over key questions, the process results in a stable structure, enabling a move from conversation to decision and action.

Church of God Peace Fellowship

1826 St James Pl, Anderson, IN 46012 USA; (765) 643-0049; Fax (765) 644-1518; m-dcaldwell@juno.com

Focus: Peace & Nonviolence
Mission: An international community committed to Jesus and his nonviolent way of life, praying and working for peace with justice in all of God's world.

Church of Scientology—Canada

696 Yonge St, Toronto, ON M4Y 2A7 Canada; (416) 925-2145; Fax (416) 925-9471; http://www.scientology.org

Focus: General Peace & Justice; Women
Mission: To work toward a civilization without insanity, without criminals, and without war where the able can prosper, human beings have rights, and where humanity is free to rise to greater heights.

Church of Scientology—USA

6331 Hollywood Blvd. #1200, Los Angeles, CA 90028 USA; (213) 960-3500; Fax (213) 960-3508; http://www.scientology.org

Focus: Criminal Justice System; Religious & Civil Liberty
Mission: To work with like-minded people on education, morals, prison reform, and drug rehabilitation programs.

Church of the Brethren—Washington Office

337 N Carolina Ave SE, Washington, DC 20002 USA; (202) 546-3202; Fax (202) 544-5852; http://www. members.aol.com/washofc/main.html

Focus: Advocacy
Mission: To provide a witness to the government on peace and justice issues, and to assist church members in making their citizenship reflective of their faith.

Church of the Brethren—Witness Office

1451 W Dundee Ave, Elgin, IL 60120 USA; (800) 323-8039; Fax (847) 742-6103; http://www.brethren.org

Focus: Ecology & Environment; Peace & Nonviolence
Mission: To equip Brethren members, congregations, and districts to express their faith in the world around them in the areas of peace and justice, environmental stewardship, and political advocacy.

Church Women United—DC

110 Maryland Ave NE #108, Washington, DC 20002 USA; (202) 544-8747; Fax (202) 544-9133; http://www.churchwomen.org

Focus: Advocacy; Women
Mission: In the nation's Capitol, CWU engages in advocacy, seeking to influence public policy on justice issues, especially those that affect the pauperization of women and children.

Church Women United—NY

475 Riverside Dr #500, New York, NY 10115 USA; (212) 870-2347; Fax (212) 870-2338; http://www.churchwomen.org

Focus: Children, Youth & Family; General Peace & Justice; Women

Mission: Founded in 1941, CWU is a national ecumenical movement of Protestant, Roman Catholic, Orthodox, and other Christian women with a strong commitment to social justice, human rights, civil rights, and the welfare and flourishing of women and children. Local and state units are active in a broad spectrum of community ministries.

Churches' Center for Theology & Public Policy

4500 Massachusetts Ave NW, Washington, DC 20016 USA; (202) 885-8648; Fax (202) 885-8605; http://www.wesleysem.org

Focus: Societies, Seminaries & Funds
Mission: To study the relationship between Christian revelation and critical issues of public policy and to enable the churches to contribute more fruitfully to public dialogue concerning those issues.

Churches for Middle East Peace

110 Maryland Ave NE #108, Washington, DC 20002 USA; (202) 546-8425; Fax (202) 543-7532; http://www.cmep.org

Focus: Advocacy; Human Rights
Mission: CMEP dialogues with US policy and law makers, believing that US policy is crucial to achieving and maintaining peace in the Middle East. Its principal advocacy concerns are the resolution of armed conflicts, human rights, arms transfers, foreign aid, and the unique status of Jerusalem, sacred to Christians, Jews, and Muslims.

Citizen's Budget Campaign—Friends Committee on Natl Legislation

245 Second St NE, Washington, DC 20002 USA; (202) 547-6000; Fax (202) 547-6019; http://www.fcnl.org/pub/fcnl

Focus: Economic Concerns
Mission: Endorsed by 25 faith/interfaith organizations, CBC educates and advocates for increased investment in human and environmental needs, supports cuts in military spending and foreign military assistance, and advocates generation of additional government revenues by increasing corporate and upper income taxes.

Citizens for Tax Justice

1311 L St NW, Washington, DC 20005 USA; (888) 626-2622; Fax (202) 638-3486; http://www.ctj.org

Focus: Economic Concerns
Mission: Since 1979, CTJ has given middle, and lower-income Americans a voice in the crafting of tax policy at the federal, state, and local levels. CTJ promotes progressive tax policies according to the ability to pay principle; those with greater resources should contribute more of their income.

Citizens United for Alternatives to the Death Penalty

PMB 297, 177 US Hwy #1, Tequesta, FL 33469 USA; (800) 973-6548; Fax (561) 743-2500; http://www.cuadp.org

Focus: Criminal Justice System
Mission: To end the death penalty in the United States through public education and tactical grassroots activism among interfaith and interdisciplinary constituencies, believing that morally, socially, and economically, the death penalty is bad public policy.

Clergy & Laity United for Economic Justice

548 S Spring St, Los Angeles, CA 90013 USA; (213) 486-9880 Ext. 103; Fax (213) 486-9886; cluela@earthlink.net

Focus: Economic Concerns
Mission: A gathering of clergy and lay persons from various religious traditions, CLUE promotes living wages as public policy, supports low wage workers seeking better wages and working conditions, and promotes the creation of a strong safety net for the unemployed.

Clergy for Compassion and Harmony

4749 64th St #19, Delta, BC V4K 4W4 Canada; (604) 940-8027; Fax (604) 940-8027

Focus: Ecumenical & Interfaith Cooperation
Mission: An association of clergy from historic religions, CCH's mission is to support fellow clergy through friendship, prayer, worship, theological reflection, and discussion of common

issues and problems faced by the religious communities.

Coalition for Appalachian Ministry

1329 Wears Valley Rd, Townsend, TN 37882 USA; (423) 448-5940; Fax (423) 448-5938; http://www.4cam.cnchost.com

Focus: Human Rights
Mission: The Coalition seeks to make a positive impact wherever the reformed tradition and Appalachian culture come together, networking with church and community, to provide educational and volunteer opportunities.

Coalition for International Criminal Court

c/o WFM/IGP 777 UN Plaza, New York, NY 10017 USA; (212) 687-2176; Fax (212) 599-1332; http://www.iccnow.org

Focus: Global Peace & Security
Mission: This Coalition of more than 800 groups advocates for the creation of an effective and just international Criminal Court. The Coalition brings together human rights, faith, and interfaith groups and international law experts to develop strategies designed to further its creation.

Coalition on the Environment & Jewish Life

443 Park Ave S, 11th Fl, New York, NY 10016 USA; (212) 684-6950 Ext. 210; Fax (212) 686-1353; http://www.coejl.org

Focus: Ecology & Environment; Training & Resources
Mission: COEJL encourages Jewish institutions and individuals to bring the moral passion of Jewish tradition and social action to the issues of environmental stewardship in order to advance social justice, protect future generations, and preserve the integrity of creation.

Coalition to Stop Gun Violence

1000 16th St NW #603, Washington, DC 20036 USA; (202) 530-0340 Ext. 24; Fax (202) 530-0331; http://www.CSGV.org

Focus: Peace & Nonviolence
Mission: Composed of 44 civic, professional, and religious organizations and 120,000 individual members that advo-

cate a ban on the sale and possession of handguns and assault weapons, CSGV engages in a vigorous program of lobbying the US Congress and state legislatures. CSGV maintains a comprehensive library on the gun industry and gun violence research.

Columban Fathers Justice & Peace Office—US

PO Box 29151, Washington, DC 20017-0151 USA; (202) 529-5115; Fax (202) 832-5195; http://www.st.columban.org

Focus: Human Rights
Mission: CFJPO, the research advocacy and educational arm of the Columban Fathers, brings an abiding concern for the poor of the world to the attention of colleagues and constituents.

Committee on Inter-Church and Interfaith Relations

3250 Bloor St W, Etobicoke, ON M8X 2Y4 Canada; (416) 231-5931 Ext. 2016; Fax (416) 232-6002; pwyatt@uccan.org

Focus: Ecumenical & Interfaith Cooperation
Mission: To challenge the church to a vision of ecumenism which includes the whole inhabited world.

Common Ground Network for Life and Choice

1601 Connecticut Ave NW #200, Washington, DC 20009 USA; (202) 265-4300; Fax (202) 232-6718; http://www.searchforcommonground. org

Focus: Peace & Nonviolence; Religious & Civil Liberty
Mission: The Network is a project that brings together those people on the pro-choice and pro-life sides of the abortion debate for dialogue and exploration of common concerns and potential joint actions.

Common Ground, Inc

815 Rosemary Ter, Deerfield, IL 60015 USA; (847) 940-7870; Fax (847) 940-7872; http://www.cg.org

Focus: Ecumenical & Interfaith Cooperation
Mission: Common Ground is a center for inquiry, study, and dialogue focusing on the world's great cultural, philo-

sophical, religious, and spiritual traditions and their implications for every dimension of human experience, believing that all have much to offer to the collective wisdom of the planet.

Common Spirit

PO Box 1037, Lyons, CO 80540 USA; (303) 823-9303; Fax (303) 823-9303 http://www.commonspirit.org

Focus: Ecumenical & Interfaith Cooperation
Mission: Common Spirit seeks to inspire respect, harmony and understanding among all people by honoring their experience of the sacred, and discovering the shared values of different faiths, beliefs, and wisdom traditions.

Commonweal Magazine

475 Riverside Dr #405, New York, NY 10115 USA; (212) 662-4200; Fax (212) 662-4183; http://www. commonwealmagazine.org

Focus: Communication
Mission: An independent magazine, edited by lay Catholics, whose goal is to help create an informed, spiritually grounded, doctrinally sophisticated American Catholic laity.

Congress of National Black Churches

1225 Eye St NW #750, Washington, DC 20005 USA; (202) 371-1091; Fax (202) 371-0908; http://www.cnbc.org

Focus: Children, Youth & Family; Discrimination; Economic Concerns
Mission: A coalition of the eight historic African American denominations, the Congress represents 65,000 churches with 20 million members. CNBC empowers members through collective action, technical assistance, training, and works with federal agencies in the areas of community and economic development, hate crime prevention, social justice, and children and family development.

Consortium on Peace Research, Education and Development

Inst for Conflict Analysis and Resolution, George Mason U., Fairfax, VA 22030-4444 USA; (703) 933-2405; Fax (703) 933-2406; http://www.gmu. edu/departments/ICAR/copred

Focus: Societies, Seminaries & Funds
Mission: COPRED is a community of

500 institutional individual members: educators, activists, and researchers working on alternatives to violence and war. A hub for 300 university peace degree programs, it provides bibliographies, syllabi collections, curriculum services, a speaker's bureau, an annual conference, a quarter journal *Peace and Change*, and a newsletter *The Peace Chronicle*.

Contra Mundum

PO Box 2535, New York, NY 10108-2535 USA; (212) 307-1573; Fax (212) 664-7929; http://www.contramundum.com

Focus: Communication
Mission: A newsletter committed to theological reflection on contemporary activities focusing on the religious establishment, CM summons persons to theological awareness. It originated among clinical pastoral supervisors and counselors.

Cooperative Baptist Fellowship

PO Box 450329, Atlanta, GA 31145-0329 USA; (770) 220-1600; Fax (770) 220-1685; http://www.cbfonline.org

Focus: General Peace & Justice; Women
Mission: To do missions in a world without borders; championing Baptist principles of faith and practice; and affirming diversity, viewing ethnicity, race, and gender as gifts from God.

Council for a Livable World Education Fund

110 Maryland Ave NE #201, Washington, DC 20002 USA; (202) 546-0795; Fax (202) 546-5142; http://www.clw.org/pub/clw/ef/clwef. html

Focus: Global Peace & Security
Mission: To educate the public about international arms control issues: nuclear, biological, and chemical weapons; conventional arms sales and controls; and military budget concerns.

Council for a Parliament of the World's Religions

PO Box 1630, Chicago, IL 60690-1630 USA; (312) 629-2990; Fax (312) 629-2991; http://www.cpwr.org

Focus: Ecumenical & Interfaith Cooperation
Mission: CPWR promotes understanding

and cooperation among faith groups, celebrates their rich diversity, and uses insights of their traditions in meeting the challenges facing the global community. CPWR's 1999 Parliament in Cape Town, SA, was easily "the most extraordinary interreligious gathering ever held." Another is scheduled for 2004.

Council of National Religious AIDS Networks

1400 I St NW #1220, Washington, DC 20005 USA; (202) 842-0010; Fax (202) 842-3323; http://www.anin.org

Focus: Health Issues
Mission: A coalition of the networks of 13 faith groups gathered to work constructively on various AIDS issues.

Council of Societies for Study of Religion

Valparaiso University, Valparaiso, IN 46383-6493 USA; (219) 464-5515; Fax (219) 464-6714; http://www.cssr.org

Focus: Societies, Seminaries & Funds
Mission: CSSR is a federation of learned societies in the field of religious studies, seeking to further scholarship, research, and teaching and concerned with the needs and interests of their members.

Council on American-Islamic Relations

453 New Jersey SE, Washington, DC 20003 USA; (202) 659-2247; Fax (202) 659-2254; http://www.cair-net.org

Focus: Discrimination
Mission: CAIR is a nonprofit, grassroots membership organization dedicated to presenting an Islamic perspective on issues of importance to the American public.

Covenant of the Goddess

PO Box 1226, Berkeley, CA 94701 USA; http://www.cog.org

Focus: Religious & Civil Liberty
Mission: To increase cooperation among Witches and to secure for Witches and covens the legal protection enjoyed by members of other religions.

Creative Transformation Magazine

1325 N College Ave, Claremont, CA 91711-3154 USA; (800) 626-7821 Ext. 288; Fax (909) 621-2760; http://www.ctr4process.org

Focus: Communication
Mission: CT shares "process theology" with faith-based leaders of peace & justice groups. Knowing that God's work is always creative and transformative, leaders are enabled to be co-workers with God by seeking new formulations and more effective ways of action. A publication of the Center for Process Studies at Claremont College.

Crossroads Ministry

425 S Central Pk, Chicago, IL 60624 USA; (773) 638-0166; Fax (773) 638-0167; http://www.home.pacbell. net/rodrigrm/crossroads

Focus: Discrimination
Mission: To educate, train, and organize to dismantle systemic racism and build/institutionalize antiracist multicultural diversity.

Cult Awareness Network

1680 N Vine St #415, Los Angeles, CA 90028 USA; (800) 556-3055; Fax (213) 468-0562; http://www.cultawarenessnetwork.org

Focus: Training & Resources
Mission: To aid the general public, CAW provides counseling and a cult awareness hotline. CAW goals are 1) to provide quality, expert, impartial information, 2) to function as a multidenominational organization promoting respect and tolerance for the beliefs of others, and 3) to promote family unity through development of mutual respect and understanding.

Cultural Survival

96 Mount Auburn St, Cambridge, MA 02138 USA; (617) 441-5400; Fax (617) 441-5417; http://www.cs.org

Focus: Indigenous or Displaced Persons; Training & Resources
Mission: To advocate for the rights, voice, and vision of indigenous peoples using Web site, publications, conferences, and outreach, seeking to draw attention to the issues confronting indigenous peoples and promote appropriate responses.

Development & Peace—Canada

10 St Mary St #420, Toronto, ON M4Y 1P9 Canada; (416) 922-1592; Fax (416) 922-0957; http://www.devp.org

Focus: Economic Concerns; Human Rights
Mission: A Canadian Catholic organization with third world partners, D&P pursues alternatives to unjust social, political, and economic structures that oppress and denigrate the world's poor and disadvantaged. Believing that all Canadians have a responsibility to help, it seeks to educate all about the causes of impoverishment and to mobilize actions for change.

Dignity Canada

Box 2102 Stn D, Ottawa, ON K1P 5W3 Canada; (613) 746-7279; Fax (613) 746-0353; http://www.odyssee.net/~prince/dcd. html

Focus: Discrimination; Renewal of Faith Group
Mission: Dignity Canada is Canada's national organization of gay and lesbian Roman Catholics and their friends. 14 Canadian chapters.

Dignity USA

1500 Massachusetts Ave NW #11, Washington, DC 20005 USA; (800) 877-8797; Fax (202) 429-9808 http://www.dignityusa.org

Focus: Discrimination; Renewal of Faith Group
Mission: Dignity's purpose is to enable g/l/b/t Catholics to reconcile their spirituality and sexuality, proclaim their dignity as gay Catholics, and to work to change the wider church's prejudices against homosexuality. 75 nationwide chapters.

Disciples Advocacy Washington Network—DC

5 Thomas Circle, Washington, DC 20005 USA; (202) 669-8772; Fax (202) 797-0111; dawnccca@aol.com

Focus: Advocacy
Mission: DAWN serves as an informal Washington office for the Christian Church (Disciples of Christ), hosting congressional visits and facilitating communication between Disciples and those who shape our national public policy.

DAWN focuses on issues of racism, violence, and poverty.

Disciples Justice Action Network

4733 S Woodlawn Ave, Chicago, IL 60615 USA; (773) 285-3248; Fax (773) 363-7086; http://www.djan.net

Focus: General Peace & Justice
Mission: DJAN calls socially sensitive Christians to risk for the sake of the Gospel's call to justice. The Network identifies issues, proposes stances, and responds to social crises while building long-term ethical perspectives on justice issues.

Disciples Peace Fellowship

PO Box 1986, Indianapolis, IN 46206 USA; (317) 635-3113; Fax (317) 635-4426; http://www.disciples.org

Focus: Discrimination; Economic Concerns; Peace & Nonviolence
Mission: Since the 1930s, the DPF has seen its mission as keeping alive a passion for peace and justice and welcoming all, regardless of race, gender, ethnicity or sexual orientation. Current foci of their work is opposition to the death penalty, corporate responsibility, and Mexican/Texas border concerns.

Dominicans—Social Justice

1919 S Ashland Ave, Chicago, IL 60608 USA; (312) 226-6161; Fax (312) 226-6119; http://www.op.org/domcentral

Focus: Human Rights
Mission: Dominicans preach, act for peace and justice, and promote corporate actions for justice for the province. They encourage solidarity with the poor and oppressed, act to transform unjust social and economic structures, and educate on issues of peace and justice.

E Pluribus Unum Project

6101 Montrose Rd #200, Rockville, MD 20852 USA; (301) 770-5070; Fax (301) 770-6365; http://www.epu.org

Focus: Training & Resources
Mission: EPU conducts an annual intensive three-week Washington, DC, educational experience for 60 to 100 high school students entering their final year. Those chosen for leadership training, $1/3$ Jewish, $1/3$ Catholic, and $1/3$ Protestant, are enabled to become effective advocates for responsible

social and political change informed by the teachings of religion.

Earth Charter Campaign

Apdo 2323-1002, San Jose, Costa Rico; (506) 256-1611; Fax (506) 225-2197; http://www.earthercharter.org

Focus: Ecology & Environment; Societies, Seminaries & Funds
Mission: Promoting a statement of ethical principles similar to the UN Declaration on Human Rights that will guide the conduct of people and nations toward each other and the Earth to ensure peace, equity, and a sustainable future. Copies are available online in 11 languages.

Earth Ministry

1305 NE 47th St, Seattle, WA 98105-4498 USA; (206) 632-3426; Fax (206) 632-2082; http://www.earthministry.org

Focus: Ecology & Environment
Mission: Seeking to transform through deepening relations with God's creation, EM encourages simplified living, environmental stewardship, justice for all creation, and a worldview which sees creation as a revelation of God.

EarthAction Network

30 Cottage St, Amherst, MA 01002 USA; (413) 549-8118; Fax (413) 549-0544; http://www.earthaction.org

Focus: Ecology & Environment; Training & Resources
Mission: With 1,800 citizen groups in 150 countries, EAN's purpose is to enable all to act simultaneously on critical global issues by producing an Action Kit four times a year which is distributed to those groups to mobilize their members.

EarthSpirit

PO Box 723, Williamsburg, MA 01096 USA; (413) 238-4240; Fax (413) 238-7785; http://www.earth-spirit.com

Focus: Ecology & Environment
Mission: To connect practitioners of earth-centered spiritual paths and indigenous people's faith groups with one another, to educate the public about these practices, and to help build a stronger correspondence between spirituality and the environment on national and global levels.

Ecumenical Coalition for Economic Justice

947 Queen St E #208, Toronto, ON M4M 1J9 Canada; (416) 462-1613; Fax (416) 463-5569; http://www.ecej.org

Focus: Economic Concerns; Women
Mission: The ECEJ, a project of six Canadian Churches (Anglican, Roman Catholic, Lutheran, Presbyterian, Quaker, and United), works for economic justice in Canada and internationally through research, popular education, and political action. Current priorities include global restructuring, valuing women's paid and unpaid work, and economic literacy.

Ecumenical Peace Institute

PO Box 9334, Berkeley, CA 94709 USA; (510) 548-4141; http://www.epicalc.org

Focus: Discrimination; Indigenous or Displaced Persons; Peace & Nonviolence
Mission: The Institute is an interfaith justice and peace education action group that focuses on militarism, racism, political prisoners, and youth and native American concerns.

Ecumenical Program on Central America and the Caribbean

1470 Irving St NW, Washington, DC 20010 USA; (202) 332-0292; Fax (202) 332-1184; http://www.igc.org/epica

Focus: Economic Concerns; Human Rights
Mission: EPICA is an independent, faith-based organization which educates the US public on issues regarding Central America, Mexico, and the Caribbean, combining social analysis, theological reflection, and political advocacy.

Ecumenicon Fellowship

11348 Cherry Hill Rd,#302, Beltsville, MD 20705-3741 USA; (301) 595-7434; http://www.ecumenicon.org

Focus: Ecumenical & Interfaith Cooperation
Mission: A forum to enable those of many faiths to communicate with each other in a nonthreatening, nonproselytizing environment, and effectively celebrate our diversity.

Education as Transformation Project

Wellesley College, Wellesley, MA 02181 USA; (781) 283-2659; Fax (781) 283-3676; http://www. wellesley.edu/RelLife/transformation

Focus: Societies, Seminaries & Funds
Mission: The project seeks to enable a multireligious, multiconstituency dialogue about religion, pluralism, and spirituality in higher education. Helpful resources are available.

Educational Concerns for Hunger

17391 Durrance Rd, Ft Myers, FL 33917-2239 USA; (941) 543-3246; Fax (941) 543-5317; http://www.echonet.org

Focus: Human Rights; Training & Resources
Mission: An ecumenical Christian group which provides practical agricultural information and distributes seed of underexploited food, forage, and reforestation plants to development workers and missionaries for small third world farmers.

Eighth Day Center for Justice

205 W Monroe 2W, Chicago, IL 60606 USA; (312) 641-5151; Fax (312) 641-1250; http://www.claret.org/~8thday

Focus: General Peace & Justice
Mission: In 1974, men and women in Catholic religious communities joined together to work for justice through systemic change. Using research, education, direct action, coalition building, networking, and legislative action, the Center seeks to shift local, national, and international priorities.

ELCA—Evangelical Lutheran Church of America

8765 W Higgins Rd, Chicago, IL 60631 USA; http://www.elca.org

Corporate Social Responsibility

9625 Perry Hwy, Pittsburgh, PA 15237 USA; (412) 367-8222; Fax (412) 369-8840; http://www.elca.org/dcs/corp.html
Focus: Economic Concerns
Mission: To dialogue with business representatives on the social implications of company practices and to affect ELCA investment policy in socially responsible ways.

Division for Church in Society

(773) 380-2710; Fax (773) 380-2707; http://www.elca.org/dcs
Focus: General Peace & Justice
Mission: To enable members of the ELCA to witness to Jesus Christ who frees us to do justice by working for the common good, confronting obstacles to local and global community, and promoting care for creation and for all people according to their needs.

Lutheran Hunger Program

(773) 380-2709; Fax (773) 380-2707; http://www.elca.org/co/hunger
Focus: Human Rights
Mission: In addition to providing relief and development assistance in this and other countries, the ELCA Hunger Program educates to encourage responsible stewardship and advocates policies and actions for social and economic justice with government, business institutions, structures of the church, and its agencies.

Lutheran Office for Governmental Affairs

122 C St NW #125, Washington, DC 20001 USA; (202) 783-7507; Fax (202) 783-7502; http://www.loga.org
Focus: Advocacy
Mission: Faithful to God's call, LOGA represents the ELCA positions in the area of public debate, committed to a prophetic vision which stands with the poor and powerless. LOGA also educates, informs, and enables full involvement of the church in this ministry.

Women (WELCA)

(773) 380-2735; Fax (773) 380-2419
Focus: Human Rights; Women
Mission: WELCA works for peace with justice, united in the belief that all of God's people deserve the opportunity to develop their gifts and their callings, to have adequate food, shelter, and resources to meet their needs and enable them to contribute to the well-being of society.

Endangered Species Coalition

1101 14th Street NW #1400, Washington, DC 20005 USA; (202) 682-9400; Fax (202) 682-1331

Focus: Ecology & Environment
Mission: A network of 450 organizations representing millions of Americans, ESC is dedicated to the preservation and recovery of endangered species. From environmental organizations to religious groups, from science associations to animal welfare societies, the Coalition is made up of groups as varied as the species we seek to protect.

Engaged Zen Foundation

PO Box 700, Ramsey, NJ 07446-0700 USA; (201) 236-0335; Fax (201) 818-5113; http://www.engaged-zen.org

Focus: Criminal Justice System; Training & Resources
Mission: EZF, of the Rinzai Zen Buddhist tradition, publishes a journal for the incarcerated to foster the practice of contemplative meditation in prisons. It is available to all, regardless of their faith.

Environmental Justice Program— The US Catholic Conference

3211 4th St NE, Washington, DC 20017 USA; (202) 541-3160; Fax (202) 541-3339; http://www.nccbuscc.org/sdwp/ejp

Focus: Ecology & Environment
Mission: EJP seeks to educate and motivate Catholics to a deeper respect for God's creation, and to engage parishes in activities aimed at dealing with environmental problems, particularly as they affect the poor.

Episcopal Appalachian Ministries

PO Box 51931, Knoxville, TN 37950-1931 USA; (800) 956-2776; Fax (423) 558-9437; sandy.elledge@ecunet.org

Focus: Human Rights; Training & Resources
Mission: To inspire, nurture, and affirm those who serve the unique needs of the people of Appalachia through advocacy, consciousness-raising, networking, education and other appropriate programs.

Episcopal Church—Peace & Justice Ministries

815 2nd Ave, New York, NY 10017 USA; (800) 334-7626 Ext. 5207; Fax (212) 490-6684; http://www.ecusa.anglican.org

Focus: General Peace & Justice
Mission: To equip Episcopalians to carry out the promise made in their Baptismal Covenant, to strive for peace and justice and respect the dignity of

every human being, PJM provides resources supporting the social policies of the church.

Episcopal Peace & Justice Network for Global Concerns

660 Preston Forest Ctr #398, Dallas, TX 75230 USA; (972) 490-6022; Fax (972) 387-9069; Rekerner@aol.com

Focus: Human Rights; Training & Resources
Mission: The Network seeks to provide Episcopalians with tools, resources, and the opportunity to exchange information in order to work for conditions in which God's peace and justice may take place.

Episcopal Peace Fellowship

PO Box 28156, Washington, DC 20038-8156 USA; (202) 783-3380; Fax (202) 393-3695; http://www.nonviolence.org/epf

Focus: Peace & Nonviolence
Mission: To aid and encourage all Episcopalians to strive for justice and peace among all people and to bear nonviolent witness to Christ's call to peace.

Episcopal Public Policy Network

110 Maryland Ave NE #309, Washington, DC 20002 USA; (202) 547-7300; Fax (202) 547-4457; http://www.ecusa.anglican.org/ppn

Focus: Advocacy
Mission: The EPPN is a nationwide network of Episcopalians who are committed to fulfilling their Baptismal Covenant to "strive for justice and peace," by communicating with their national lawmakers on issues of importance to the mission of the church.

Episcopal Responsible Investment Program

815 2nd Ave, New York, NY 10017 USA; (800) 334-7626; Fax (212) 490-6684; HarryVB@aol.com

Focus: Economic Concerns **Mission:** This program seeks to use the church's resources as a shareholder in corporate structures to effect social change in American corporations.

Episcopal Society for Ministry on Aging

PO Box 3065, Meridian, MS 39303 USA; (601) 485-0311; http://www.esmanet.com

Focus: Children, Youth & Family
Mission: To strengthen God's people for ministry throughout the entire life span.

Equal Exchange, Inc—Interfaith Coffee Project

251 Revere St, Canton, MA 02021 USA; (781) 830-0303 Ext. 231; Fax (781) 830-0282; http://www.equalexchange.com

Focus: Training & Resources
Mission: EE is a worker-owned fair trade organization working with small-scale coffee farmers in Latin America, Africa, and Asia. EE offers congregations fairly traded coffees and teas for use at fellowship hour, for fundraising projects and holiday bazaars, and other events. Call for information.

Equal Partners in Faith

2026 P St NW, Washington, DC 20036 USA; (202) 296-4672 Ext. 14; Fax (202) 296-4673; http://www.us.net/epf

Focus: Religious & Civil Liberty
Mission: A national multiracial, multi-faith network of religious leaders and people of faith committed to equality and diversity. EPF is concerned about the religious right and its manipulation of religion to promote inequality and exclusion.

Erie Benedictines for Peace

345 E 9th St, Erie, PA 16503 USA; (814) 459-7199; Fax (814) 459-8066; benedectine@igc.apc.org

Focus: Peace & Nonviolence; Women
Mission: The Benedictines work for disarmament, ecological stewardship, and social justice in solidarity with the poor and the oppressed, especially women. They seek nonviolent solutions to all conflicts and stand for life—in issues such as land mines, nuclear and conventional weapons, handguns, and the death penalty.

Evangelical Environmental Network

10 E Lancaster Ave, Wynnewood, PA 19096 USA; (610) 645-9392; Fax (610) 649-8090; http://www.esa-online.org/een/

Focus: Ecology & Environment
Mission: World Vision and Evangelicals for Social Action established the EEN to encourage recognition that the care of creation is a part of biblical discipleship.

Evangelical Fellowship of Canada—Social Action Commission

MIP Box 3745, Markham, ON L3R 0Y4 Canada; (905) 479-5885; Fax (905) 479-4742; http://www.efc-canada.com

Focus: General Peace & Justice; Women
Mission: As Canada struggles with a bewildering array of social, moral, and ethical issues, EFC seeks to help Canadian Christians participate using Gospel values. It investigates and responds to issues such as poverty, new reproductive technologies and television violence.

Evangelical Lutheran Coalition for Mission in Appalachia

PO Box 338, Indiana, PA 15701-0338 USA; (724) 463-8422; Fax (724) 463-8422; elcma@twd.net

Focus: Human Rights
Mission: ELCMA, responding to the grace of God in Jesus Christ, exists to enable Appalachian people to come together to plan and implement ministries of outreach, leadership, development, empowerment, and advocacy.

Evangelical Lutheran Women of Canada

302-393 Portage Ave, Winnipeg, MB R3B 3H6 Canada; (204) 984-9163; Fax (204) 984-9162; elwinc@elcic.ca

Focus: General Peace & Justice; Women
Mission: To proclaim the gospel of Jesus Christ, to provide leadership and opportunities for women to develop a sense of self-worth in a changing society, and to work for justice and peace by engaging in congregational and community outreach.

Evangelicals for Middle East Understanding

N Park U-3225 W Foster Ave,
Chicago, IL 60625 USA;
(773) 244-5785; Fax (773) 583-0858;
dwagner@northpark.edu

Focus: Human Rights
Mission: To engage Western
Evangelical Christians in the issues of
peace, justice, and God's Kingdom
work through churches in the Middle
East. EMEU conducts an annual conference in the US, an annual trip to the
Middle East, and occasional regional
symposia in North America.

Evangelicals for Social Action

10 E Lancaster Ave, Wynnewood, PA
19096 USA; (800) 650-6600;
Fax (901) 664-8966;
http://www.esa-online.org

Focus: General Peace & Justice
Mission: ESA is an evangelical voice for
social justice, racial and gender reconciliation, balanced public policy reflection, and cutting-edge cultural analysis.

Exodus World Service

PO Box 620, Itasca, IL 60143-0620
USA; (630) 307-1400; Fax (630) 307-
1430; http://www.e-w-s.org

Focus: Indigenous or Displaced Persons;
Training & Resources
Mission: To mobilize Christian volunteers for service to refugees by providing education, training, and innovative
service projects.

Expanding Humanity's Vision of God

Gordon College, 255 Grapevine Rd,
Wenham, MA 01984 USA;
(878) 927-2306; Fax (978) 524-3752;
herrmann@faith.gordon.edu

Focus: Societies, Seminaries & Funds
Mission: Focusing on recent scientific
discoveries, EHVG seeks to foster an
expanded vision of God about the
nature of the universe and the place of
humans in the world. A program of the
John Templeton Foundation.

Facts for Action Newsletter

6148 NW Wales Rd, Kansas City, MO
64150 USA; (816) 741-5096;
Fax (816) 741-5096 (call first)

Focus: Communication
Mission: To create a collective con-

science against a violent and unjust system, FFA provides up-to-date factual news
for faith-motivated activists. Published by
the Midwest branch of the FOR.

Faith and Politics Institute

110 Maryland Ave NE #306,
Washington, DC 20002 USA;
(202) 546-1299; Fax (202) 546-4025

Focus: Societies, Seminaries & Funds
Mission: The Institute provides occasions
for moral reflection and spiritual community for political leaders, drawing
universal wisdom from a range of religious traditions. Encouraging civility
and respect as essential to democracy,
it works to strengthen US political leadership in order to contribute to healing
the wounds that mark America's
divided citizens.

Federation of Zoroastrian Associations of NA

5750 South Jackson St, Hinsdale, IL
60521 USA; http://www.fezana.org

Focus: General Peace & Justice; Women
Mission: The Association seeks to provide effective leadership to Zoroastrian
members and communities in addressing the critical issues of our times with
wisdom and righteousness.

Fellowship Magazine

PO Box 271, Nyack, NY 10960 USA;
(914) 358-4601; Fax (914) 358-4924;
http://www.nonviolence.org/for/
fellowship

Focus: Communication; Peace &
Nonviolence
Mission: *Fellowship* envisions a world
where differences are respected, conflicts addressed nonviolently, oppressive
structures dismantled, and where people live in harmony with the earth, nurtured by diverse spiritual traditions that
foster compassion and reconciliation.
Sponsored by FOR.

Fellowship of Reconciliation

Spoonstratt 38, 1815 BK Alkmaar,
Netherlands; 31-72-512-3014; Fax 31-
72-512-1102; http://www.ifor.org

Focus: Global Peace & Security; Peace
& Nonviolence
Mission: The world's oldest interfaith
peace and justice organization, since
1915 FOR has educated about and
advocated for projects concerned with
domestic and international peace and

justice, nonviolent alternatives to conflict, and for the rights of conscience. It
has chapters in 40 countries. USA
branch is at www.forusa.org.

Fellowship of Southern Illinois Laity

PO Box 31, Belleville, IL 62222 USA;
(618) 234-4073; Fax (618) 234-4225;
http://www.cta-usa.org

Focus: Renewal of Faith Group
Mission: FOSIL calls for reform in the
Roman Catholic Church: favoring inclusion of women, ending mandatory
celibacy, opening priesthood to women,
and involving the laity in selection of
local bishops. FOSIL opposes censorship of theologians and scholars and
asks that all church employees are
guaranteed fair wages and due
process.

FEZANA Journal

5750 S Jackson St, Hinsdale, IL 60521
USA; (630) 325-5383;
http://www.fezana.org/

Focus: Communication
Mission: *Fezana Journal,* a publication
of the Federation of Zoroastrian
Associations of North America, disseminates inspirational and educational articles about Zoroastrianism (the religion
of the prophet Zoroaster) as well as
news and views of the Zoroastrian community.

Fig Tree—Ecumenical Newspaper

620 N Monroe St, Spokane, WA
99205 USA; (509) 329-1410; Fax
(509) 329-1410; scem245@aol.com

Focus: Communication
Mission: The *Fig Tree* covers religious,
human service, and human interest
news. Its goals are to inform, build
cooperation and understanding,
develop awareness of physical and
spiritual needs, and pool ideas for
action.

Floresta—Healing the Land and Its People

4903 Morena Blvd #1215, San Diego,
CA 92117 USA; (800) 633-5319;
Fax (619) 274-3728;
http://www.floresta.org

Focus: Human Rights; Training &
Resources
Mission: To attack economic problems
in developing countries caused by

deforestation. Floresta brings hope and opportunity to the poor affected by these problems through technically appropriate, business-based programs that lead to self-sufficiency.

Foundation for Interfaith Research & Ministry

701 N Post Oak Rd #330, Houston, TX 77024 USA; (713) 682-5995; Fax (713) 682-0639; firm-hou@neosoft.com

Focus: Societies, Seminaries & Funds
Mission: FIRM sponsors and conducts interfaith and interdisciplinary programs of scholarship, research, education, and service.

Fourth World Movement International

95480 Pierrelaye, France, (301) 336-9489; Fax (301) 336-0092; http://www.atd-fourthworld.org

Focus: Human Rights
Mission: FWM is dedicated to overcoming extreme poverty. Its goal is to partner with families living in chronic poverty and to encourage private citizens and public officials to join the effort. Founded by a Catholic priest in 1957, it is active in 8 European countries, North and Central America, Africa, and Asia. USA office: fourthworld@eros.com.

Franciscan Federation of Brothers and Sisters of US

817 Varnum St NE PO Box 29080, Washington, DC 20017 USA; (202) 529-2334; Fax (202) 529-7016; http://www.franfed.org

Focus: Peace & Nonviolence
Mission: FFBS is an educational leadership training group dedicated to enabling/educating their members to work for peace and justice. A special initiative mandate is to "Close the School of the Americas."

Franciscan Sisters of Mary

1100 Bellevue Ave, St Louis, MO 63117-1883 USA; (314) 768-1827; Fax (314) 768-1880; http://www.fsmonline.org

Focus: Peace & Nonviolence; Women
Mission: "As Franciscan Evangelical Women of the Gospel, we embrace our charism to be the presence of the loving, serving, compassionate, and heal-

ing Jesus. Transformed and energized, we act in loving and respectful relationship with one another and with all of God's creation. From a feminist prophetic stance we promote justice, peace, and nonviolence."

Franciscans International

211 E 43rd St #1100, New York, NY 10017-4707 USA; (212) 490-4624; Fax (212) 857-4977; http://www.franintl.org

Focus: Ecology & Environment; Human Rights; Peace & Nonviolence
Mission: Franciscans International, an NGO at the UN, is designed to engage world leaders in dialogue and collaborative actions regarding care of creation, peacemaking, and concern for the poor.

Freedom for Religions in Germany

1701 20th St NW, Washington, DC 20009 USA; (202) 667-6404; Fax (202) 667-6314; bratschi@juno.com

Focus: Religious & Civil Liberty
Mission: FRG provides a voice and support for religious minorities whose protests are being ignored by the German government.

Freedom of Religion for Everyone Everywhere

411 Cleveland St #170, Clearwater, FL 33755 USA; (727) 449-0109; http://www.communicate-now.com/free

Focus: Religious & Civil Liberty
Mission: To enlist people of faith in promoting "Peace on Earth, Good Will among Men" in fighting persecution and violence, and in promoting peace, unity, and freedom of choice. FREE endorses the UN Charter granting religious freedom to all.

Friends Committee on National Legislation

245 Second St NE, Washington, DC 20002-5795 USA; (202) 547-6000; Fax (202) 547-6019; http://www.fcnl.org

Focus: Advocacy
Mission: Since 1943, the FCNL has endeavored to bring Quaker values to bear on national policy through congressional testimony, Capitol Hill visits, educational activities, publications, and grassroots lobbying.

Friends Committee on Unity with Nature

173-B N Prospect St, Burlington, VT 05401-1607 USA; (802) 658-0308; Fax same (call first); fcun@together.net

Focus: Ecology & Environment
Mission: FCUN has two primary goals: the development of a clear witness on environmental issues among Friends and like-minded people, and the support of informed, spirit-led action with a commitment to a sustainable future.

Friends Committee to Abolish the Death Penalty

1501 Cherry St, Philadelphia, PA 19102 USA; (215) 241-7137; Fax (215) 241-7119; http://www.quaker.org/fcadp

Focus: Criminal Justice System
Mission: A national Quaker organization advocating for the abolition of capital punishment in the US through public education and activism. FCADP fosters communication and support among concerned Friends, promotes anti-death penalty activism, and nurtures the process of victim-victimizer reconciliation.

Friends for a Non-Violent World

Center for P & J 1929 S 5th St, Minneapolis, MN 55454 USA; (612) 321-9787; Fax (612) 321-9788; http://www.fnvw.org

Focus: Peace & Nonviolence
Mission: Through education, example, and experience in nonviolent living, FNVW works to build a world where all people can speak truth to power, practice alternatives to violence, gain strength from community, and act in a spirit of cooperation to work for peace and justice.

Friends Journal

1216 Arch St #2A, Philadelphia, PA 19107 USA; (215) 563-8629; Fax (215) 568-1377; FJSusanCF@aol.com

Focus: Communication
Mission: The *Journal's* mission is to present and explore Quaker viewpoints on peace, justice, and society.

Friends of Religious Humanism Journal

7 Harwood Dr, PO Box 1188, Amherst, NY 14226 USA; (716) 839-1214; Fax (716) 839-5079; http://www.humanist.net/frh

Focus: Communication
Mission: To encourage religious, ethical, and philosophical thought and to provide inspirational and scholarly materials which apply the scientific spirit and methods to the materials of ethics and religion. Publishes *Religious Humanism*, a biannual journal.

From Both Sides of the Ocean

PO Box 428, Bloomington Hills, MI 48303 USA; (248) 858-7215 Ext. 287; Fax (248) 858-8314; jazbag@aol.com

Focus: Communication
Mission: A magazine that shares wisdom between Punjab and the rest of the world.

Fung Loy Kok Institute of Taoism

1060 Bannock St, Denver, CO 80204-4049 USA; (303) 623-5163; Fax (303) 431-6094; http://www.ttcs-co.org/fung_loy_kok.htm

Focus: Training & Resources
Mission: Dedicated to the teaching and practice of Taoism; self-cultivation through chanting, meditation, *chi-kung*, scripture study, internal exercises, and to promote charity for others through community service.

FutureChurch

15800 Montrose Ave, Cleveland, OH 44111-1804 USA; (216) 228-0869; Fax (216) 228-0947; http://www.futurechurch.org

Focus: Renewal of Faith Group; Women
Mission: A coalition of parish-based Catholics concerned about the shortage of priests, FC sponsors two national grassroots organizing efforts, "A Call for National Dialogue on the Future of Priestly Ministry" and "A Call for National Dialogue on Women in Church Leadership."

Gay, Lesbian and Affirming Disciples Alliance (Open & Affirming Program)

PO Box 44400, Indianapolis, IN 46244 USA; http://www.sacredplaces.com/glad

Focus: Discrimination; Renewal of Faith Group
Mission: This program seeks the full inclusion of lesbian, gay, bisexual, and transgender persons in the life and leadership of the church.

Glinodo Center

6270 East Lake Rd, Erie, PA 16511-1533 USA; (814) 899-4584; Fax (814) 899-0253; http://www.erie.net/~glearthf

Focus: Ecology & Environment; Training & Resources
Mission: To enable people to value self, others, and the earth, the Center sponsors a summer camp for aged 6–14 youths, "Spirit of the Seasons" retreats, a creation-centered spirituality program, and an "Earth Force" program for middle schools that links environmental action, civic engagement, and service learning.

Global Awareness Through Experience

912 Market St, LaCrosse, WI 54601 USA; (608) 791-5283; Fax (608) 782-6301; http://www.fspa.org

Focus: Human Rights; Women
Mission: Sponsored by the Franciscan Sisters of Perpetual Adoration, GATE arranges trips abroad to offer learning experiences through immersion in the culture, the faith, the struggles, and the dreams of other peoples.

Global Education Associates

475 Riverside Dr #1848, New York, NY 10115 USA; (212) 870-3290; Fax (212) 870-2729; http://www.globaleduc.org

Focus: General Peace & Justice; Training & Resources
Mission: A partnership of individuals and organizations in 90 countries, GEA works to enable people to understand and respond constructively to the crisis and opportunities of today's interdependent world by emphasizing the development of global ethics, values, and systems. Since 1973, GEA has conducted 2,700 workshops in 90 countries.

Global Health Ministries

7831 Hickory NE, Minneapolis, MN 55432 USA; (612) 586-9590; Fax (612) 586-9591; http://www.ghm.org

Focus: Human Rights
Mission: To support Lutheran medical work in developing countries overseas through recycling medical supplies, recruiting workers, and funding projects.

Global Options

8160 Manitoba St #315, Playa del Rey, CA 90293-8640 USA; (310) 821-1864; Fax (310) 821-1864; http://www.scudh.edu/global_options

Focus: Peace & Nonviolence; Training & Resources
Mission: GO consults on global futures, peace, and intercultural/interreligious synergy. GO also teaches, writes, and offers talks and workshops on those topics.

Global Peace Services USA

PO Box 27922, Washington, DC 20038-7922 USA; (202) 216-9886; Fax (301) 681-7390; http://www.globalpeaceservices.org

Focus: Peace & Nonviolence; Training & Resources
Mission: GPS is a movement to create a professional peace service by promoting education and skills-training for men and women based on a philosophy of active nonviolence.

Global Response—Environmental Action & Education Network

PO Box 7490, Boulder, CO 80306-7490 USA; (303) 444-0306; Fax (303) 449-9794; http://www.globalresponse.org

Focus: Ecology & Environment
Mission: An international letter-writing network in partnership with indigenous, environmental, faith, school, and civic groups and individuals, GR develops "Actions" that describe specific urgent threats to the environment. Members respond with personal letters to the corporations, governments, or organizations having the power and responsibility to make environmentally sound decisions.

Gobind Sadan, USA

PO Box 4980, Syracuse, NY 13221 USA; (315) 449-3000; Fax (314) 449-3030; http://www.gobindsadan.org

Focus: Ecumenical & Interfaith Cooperation
Mission: "Religion is meant to be practical, not theoretical." GS's Sikh

teachings hold that hard work, sharing with others, and recognizing and loving God as the doer and giver of all will result in happiness and blessing and solve the world's problems.

Graymoor Ecumenical & InterReligious Institute

Rte 9 PO Box 300, Garrison, NY 10524-0300 USA; (914) 424-3671; Fax (914) 424-3473

Focus: Ecumenical & Interfaith Cooperation
Mission: To further ecumenical understanding, the Institute sponsors conferences and research, publishes *Ecumenical Trends* newsletter, and sponsors and provides resources for an Annual Week of Prayer for Christian Unity.

Groundwork for a Just World

11224 Kercheval, Detroit, MI 48214-3323 USA; (313) 822-2055; Fax (313) 822-5197; groundwork@aol.com

Focus: General Peace & Justice
Mission: GJW's members, lay and religious Catholics, strive to integrate faith with action for systemic change, and work collaboratively to bring about the justice and peace of God's reign.

Guatemala Accompaniment Project

1830 Connecticut Ave NW, Washington, DC 20009 USA; (202) 265-8713; Fax (202) 265-0042; ncoordgap@igc.org

Focus: Human Rights; Indigenous or Displaced Persons
Mission: Since 1993, GAP has monitored refugee returns from Mexico to Guatemala and has trained human rights monitors to lessen the likelihood the state will carry out violence against their own population. Inquiries are welcomed from US groups and individuals wishing to be human rights monitors.

Guatemala Human Rights Commission/USA

3321 12th St NE, Washington, DC 20017 USA; (202) 529-6599; Fax (202) 526-4611

Focus: Human Rights
Mission: Since 1982 GHRC has monitored the human rights situation in Guatemala, worked in cooperation with

Guatemalan organizations advocating respect for the human rights of all persons, and aided victims/survivors of human rights violations.

Habitat for Humanity International

121 Habitat St, Americus, GA 31709 USA; (800) 422-4828; Fax (912) 924-6541; http://www.habitat.org

Focus: Human Rights
Mission: HHI works in partnership with God and people everywhere to build and renovate houses to provide decent houses in decent communities in which people can live and grow into all that God intended.

Heifer Project International

1015 Louisiana St, Little Rock, AR 72202 USA; (501) 376-6836; Fax (501) 376-8906; http://www.heifer.org

Focus: Training & Resources
Mission: Since 1944, rooted in the Christian tradition, HPI has worked to alleviate hunger and poverty by providing more than 4 million impoverished families a way to become self-reliant through the gift of livestock and training. Each gift multiplies because each family promises to give one of their animal's offspring to another family in need.

Hinduism Today Magazine

107 Kaholalele Rd, Kapaa, HI 96746 USA; (800) 890-1008; Fax (808) 822-4351; http://www.hinduismtoday.org

Focus: Communication; Renewal of Faith Group
Mission: Satguru Sivaya Subramuniyaswami founded *Hinduism Today* in 1979 in order to dispel myths, illusions, and misinformation about Hinduism and to nurture and monitor the ongoing spiritual Hindu renaissance.

Holy Orthodox Catholic Church

407 Donovan Rd, Brushton, NY 12916 USA; (518) 358-4168; Fax (518) 358-9667; http://www.jesusfocus.org

Focus: Renewal of Faith Group
Mission: Works sacramentally to restore a Christ-centered Church, thereby creating the mindset of Christ's love—the one true cause which fulfills all efforts done in His name.

Honor Our Neighbors Origins and Rights

PO Box 694, Bayfield, WI 54814 USA; (715) 779-9595; Fax (715) 779-9598; http://www2.dgsys.com/~honor

Focus: Indigenous or Displaced Persons
Mission: HONOR is a human rights coalition that focuses on American Indian issues. Members, Indian and non-Indian, stand together as allies seeking justice on critical concerns facing indigenous peoples today.

Horizon Interfaith Council TV

31 Buckhurst Cresc, Scarborough, ON M1S 4C3 Canada; (416) 292-8550; Fax (416) 609-1380

Focus: Communication
Mission: HIC fosters religious programming on cable TV in Toronto by distributing available air time among member groups of the council, and providing assistance in planning and producing.

Houston Peace News

PO Box 8763, Houston, TX 77249 USA; (713) 524-2682; HpeaceNews@aol.com

Focus: Communication
Mission: HPN is the alternative newspaper for Houston's peace, justice, and environmental communities. It encourages democratic debate on issues of human dignity and global survival.

Human Quest: The Churchman Magazine

4300 NW 23rd Ave Box 203, Gainesville, FL 32614-7050 USA; (352) 378-3871; Fax (352) 378-3871; chasmagg@aol.com

Focus: Communication
Mission: A monthly journal of religious humanism, HQ is published in the conviction that religious journalism must provide a platform for the free exchange of ideas and opinions, that religion is consonant with the most advanced revelations in every department of knowledge, and that humans are a fraternal world community.

Human Rights Action Service

438 N Skinker Blvd, St Louis, MO 63130 USA; (314) 725-5303; Fax (314) 725-8568; http://www.hras.com

Focus: Advocacy; Human Rights
Mission: Following the UN Universal

Declaration on Human Rights, HRAS provides subscribers monthly with 1) a personalized action letter seeking redress of a human rights violation, 2) a buyer's guide providing consumer information on the labor behind the products, and 3) a media watch with analysis of press coverage of human rights issues.

Iliff School of Theology, Justice & Peace Studies

2201 S University Blvd #I-402, Denver, CO 80210 USA; (303) 765-3191; Fax (303) 777-0164; http://www.iliff.edu

Focus: Societies, Seminaries & Funds
Mission: Students at Iliff School of Theology work together, building upon strong spiritual foundations, to respond to the challenges of race and racism, class and economic exploitation, sexism and militarism.

Imagine a World of Wanted and Nurtured Children

PO Box 1001, San Jacinto, CA 92581 USA; http://adsforchoice.org

Focus: Religious & Civil Liberty; Training & Resources; Women
Mission: To offer a collection of tasteful, educational, illustrated, pro-choice ads, for use by individuals or groups in weekly community newspapers or advertisement circulars without charge. An American Humanist Association project promoting a more civilized world through population growth control and greater nurturing of children.

In the Spirit of Jubilee

294 Haviland Crescent, Saskatoon, SK S0K 1V0 Canada; (306) 373-6233; http://www.lights.com/jubilee

Focus: Economic Concerns
Mission: In the ancient Old Testament Jubilee year, debts were cancelled and slaves set free. Now, in the new century, ISJ is part of the world movement seeking to do that for heavily indebted third-world countries.

Initiative for Religion, Ethics & Human Rights/US Institute of Peace

1200 17th St NW #200, Washington, DC 20036-3011 USA; (202) 457-1700; Fax (202) 429-6063; http://www.usip.org/research/rehr.html

Focus: Societies, Seminaries & Funds
Mission: IREHR explores the significance of religion and ideology, as a source of conflict and a source of peace, giving special attention to the religious aspects of ethnic identity, the close link between nationalism, ideological and religious beliefs, and the human rights tradition as a guarantor of the freedom of conscience.

Institute for First Amendment Studies

PO Box 589, Great Barrington, MA 01230 USA; (413) 274-0012; Fax (413) 274-0245; http://www.ifas.org

Focus: Religious & Civil Liberty; Training & Resources
Mission: IFAS is an educational and research organization dedicated to preserving First Amendment freedoms, with particular emphasis on maintaining the separation between church and state.

Institute for Integrated Social Analysis

811 E 47th St, Kansas City, MO 64110-1631 USA; (816) 753-2057; Fax (816) 753-7741; http://www.seamless-garment.org/iisa.html

Focus: Societies, Seminaries & Funds
Mission: The research arm for the Seamless Garment Network, its purpose is to increase the quantity and quality of research on matters pertaining to the consistent life ethic and the connections between issues of violence, from abortion and euthanasia to the death penalty and war.

Institute for Peace & Justice

4144 Lindell Blvd #408, St Louis, MO 63108 USA; (314) 533-4445; Fax (314) 533-1017; http://members.aol.com/ppjn

Focus: Peace & Nonviolence; Training & Resources
Mission: IPJ creates resources and provides learning experiences in peace education and social justice for schools, religious institutions, families and counselors, focusing on racial and economic injustice, parenting for peace and justice, multicultural education, nonviolent conflict resolution, and integrating spirituality with social justice.

Institute for Religion and Social Change

Box 311, Maryknoll, NY 10545-0311 USA; (914) 941-0783 Ext. 5624; j.chatfield@worldnet.att.net

Focus: General Peace & Justice
Mission: To work together for responsible change.

Institute for Religious Studies

ISER, Ladeira da Glória, 98; Rio de Janeiro; RJ; Brazil 22211 120; Tel. 55 21 285 5271; Fax 55 21 5581381; http://www.iser.org.br

Focus: Ecumenical & Interfaith Cooperation; General Peace & Justice
Mission: Founded in 1970, ISER develops projects in four areas: violence, public safety, and human rights; environment and development; organizations of the civil society; and religion and society.

Institute for World Spirituality

5757 S University Ave, Chicago, IL 60637 USA; (773) 752-5757 Ext. 275; Fax (773) 752-0905; http://www.worldspirit.org

Focus: Ecumenical & Interfaith Cooperation; General Peace & Justice
Mission: Formed to address the urgent need for interreligious cooperation on behalf of the world, IWS facilitates interreligious encounters between people committed to act for social wholeness. Partnerships include a Prison to Community Initiative, an Interreligious Microcredit Initiative, and an Initiative for Environmental Conservation.

Institute of Islamic Information & Education

PO Box 41129, Chicago, IL 60641-0129 USA; (773) 777-7443; Fax (773) 777-7199; http://www.iiie.net

Focus: Societies, Seminaries & Funds
Mission: IIIE, dedicated to the cause of Islam in North America, strives to elevate the image of Islam and Muslims by providing the correct information about Islamic beliefs, history, and civilization from the authentic sources. Inquires are welcomed.

Institute on Religion & Democracy

1521 16th St NW #300, Washington, DC 20036-1466 USA; (202) 986-1440; Fax (202) 986-3159; http://www.ird-renew.org

Focus: Societies, Seminaries & Funds
Mission: Committed to reforming the Church's social and political witness and building and strengthening democracy and religious liberty at home and abroad, the IRD sponsors an Ecumenical Coalition on Women and Society and an International Religious Freedom project.

Inter-Church Action for Development, Relief & Justice

947 Queen St E #205, Toronto, ON M4M 1J9 Canada; (416) 461-3634; Fax (416) 463-5569; http://www.web.net/~icact

Focus: Human Rights
Mission: ICA, an ecumenical witness to Christ's mission of love and justice, responds to emergencies and works worldwide to promote sustainable human development.

Inter-Church Coalition on Africa

129 St Clair Ave W, Toronto, ON M4V 1N5 Canada; (416) 927-1124; Fax (416) 927-7554; http://www.web.net/~iccaf

Focus: Economic Concerns; Human Rights
Mission: A research, education, awareness, and advocacy program on African issues of human rights and the economy, the ICCAF works in solidarity with churches and NGOs to carry out its biblically grounded mission to promote justice in Africa.

Inter-Church Committee for Refugees

129 St Clair Ave W, Toronto, ON M4V 1N9 Canada; (416) 921-9967; Fax (416) 921-3843; http://www.web.net/~iccr

Focus: Indigenous or Displaced Persons
Mission: ICCR, a coalition of ten Canadian church bodies, is mandated to promote an equitable, generous, and compassionate response to refugees. ICCR monitors the world refugee situation and Canadian responses, and develops reports, briefs, and letters to the Canadian government and relevant international forums.

Inter-Church Committee on Human Rights in Latin America

129 St Clair Ave W, Toronto, ON M4V 1N5 Canada; (416) 921-0801; Fax (416) 921-3843; http://www.web.net/~icchrla

Focus: Human Rights
Mission: ICCHRLA's mission is to promote human rights and social justice throughout Mexico, Central and South America in solidarity with both Canadian and Latin American partner churches, human rights groups, and grassroots organizations.

InterAction

1717 Massachusetts Ave NW, Washington, DC 20036 USA; (202) 667-8227; Fax (202) 667-8236; http://www.interaction.org

Focus: Human Rights
Mission: A coalition of 150 faith and secular organizations engaged in international humanitarian efforts, InterAction is the nation's leading advocate for international relief, refugee, and development programs building support for programs that save lives and help poor people help themselves.

Intercommunity Center for Justice & Peace—NY

20 Washington Sq N, New York, NY 10011 USA; (212) 475-6677; Fax (212) 475-6969; icjpny@aol.com

Focus: General Peace & Justice
Mission: A coalition of 40 religious congregations/orders of women and men, the Center has a twofold purpose: 1) to foster the integration of faith and justice in all areas of life, and 2) to effect changes in societal structures toward the realization of a more human, just, and peaceful society.

Intercommunity Justice & Peace Center

215 E 14th St, Cincinnati, OH 41059 USA; (513) 579-8547; Fax (513) 579-0674; http://www.members.aol.com/IJPCCinti/index.html

Focus: General Peace & Justice
Mission: IJPC, a coalition of women and men committed to deepening awareness of justice as integral to faith, collaborates with other concerned groups for stronger public witness and impact on justice. IJPC concerns are human

rights, violence prevention, women's issues, peace, ecology, racial justice, and economic justice.

Interfaith Action for Racial Justice, Inc

325 E 25th St, Baltimore, MD 21218-5303 USA; (410) 889-8333; Fax (410) 889-5719; http://www.bcpl.net/~iarj/Welcome.html

Focus: Discrimination
Mission: IARJ promotes understanding and tolerance among people of diverse backgrounds and traditions and strives to end racism and ethnic prejudice by fostering dialogue, creating community, and engaging in action for justice.

Interfaith Alliance

1012 14th St NW #700, Washington, DC 20005 USA; (202) 639-6370; Fax (202) 639-6375; http://www.tialliance.org

Focus: Religious & Civil Liberty
Mission: TIA promotes the positive role of religion as a healing and constructive force in public life, challenging those who manipulate religion to advance an extreme political agenda. Its goal is to build a revitalized mainstream religious movement based on shared religious values. Clergy-led local Alliances are in 38 states.

Interfaith Center at the Presidio

2107 Van Ness Ave #300, San Francisco, CA 94109 USA; (415) 775-4635; Fax (415) 771-8681; http://www.interfaith-presidio.org

Focus: Ecumenical & Interfaith Cooperation
Mission: The Interfaith Center welcomes and celebrates the diverse spiritual wisdom and faith traditions of the Bay Area.

Interfaith Center for Corporate Responsibility

475 Riverside Dr #550, New York, NY 10115 USA; (212) 870-2296; Fax (212) 870-2023

Focus: Economic Concerns
Mission: A coalition of Christian and Jewish institutional investors holding corporations accountable by sponsoring shareholder resolutions, divesting stock, conducting public hearings, and publishing reports. ICCR challenges nuclear weapons production, foreign military

sales, sweatshops, racism, sexism, tobacco production and marketing, insurance and bank redlining, and environmental destruction.

Interfaith Church of Metaphysics

HCR 1, Box 15, Windyville, MO 65783 USA; (417) 345-8411; Fax (417) 345-6668; http://www.som.org

Focus: Societies, Seminaries & Funds
Mission: The ICM holds that all holy scriptures, when interpreted in the "Universal Language of Mind," describe Universal Laws and offer common instruction for achieving peace and fulfillment. ICM publishes books and offers education for ordained ministers, meditation, and prayer services.

Interfaith Coalition for Immigrant Rights

965 Mission St #514, San Francisco, CA 94103 USA; (415) 227-0388; Fax (415) 543-0442; http://www.igc.org/icir

Focus: Indigenous or Displaced Persons
Mission: ICIR's mission is to call together people of faith to affirm and defend the rights and dignity of all immigrants and refugees by challenging policies, legislation, and attitudes that attack newcomers.

Interfaith Coalition for the Environment

401 Westshire Rd, Baltimore, MD 21229 USA; (410) 747-3811; Fax (410) 328-5208; phamm001@umaryland.edu

Focus: Ecology & Environment
Mission: Clergy and laity, of religious and spiritual traditions who advocate environmental justice, join to encourage individuals and faith groups 1) to explore the connection between their faith and environmental stewardship, 2) to seek equity between all people and communities, 3) to adopt a simpler lifestyle to reduce human impact on the earth, 4) to preserve undeveloped land, and 5) to care for the interdependent web of life.

Interfaith Coalition on Energy

7217 Oak Ave, Melrose Park, PA 19027-3222 USA; (215) 635-1122; Fax (215) 635-1903

Focus: Ecology & Environment
Mission: The Coalition's mission is to inspire congregations to use less energy and to practice environmental stewardship.

Interfaith Community Ministry Network

14727 Rio Pinar, Houston, TX 77095 USA; (888) 529-5254; Fax (281) 463-2144; http://www.neosoft.com/~icmn

Focus: Societies, Seminaries & Funds
Mission: "Bringing Community-Based Ministries Together." The ICMN is a national network of community ministries, ecumenical and interfaith, created to provide a link for mutual support, leadership development, and promotion of community-based, cooperative ministry.

Interfaith Community Partnership of the Chicago Public Schools

125 S Clark St #921, Chicago, IL 60603 USA; (773) 553-2140; Fax (773) 553-2141; revjwilson@ameritech.net

Focus: Children, Youth & Family
Mission: A multicultural interfaith partnership formed in 1996 to assist schools in Chicago in addressing crisis in the schools: student discipline problems, truancy, low attendance, school safety, and student and staff attitude and esteem.

InterFaith Conference of Metropolitan Washington

1419 V St NW, Washington, DC 20009 USA; (202) 234-6300; Fax (202) 234-6303; http://www.interfaith-metrodc.org

Focus: Ecumenical & Interfaith Cooperation; General Peace & Justice
Mission: IFC brings together the Bahá'í, Hindu, Islamic, Jewish, Latter-Day Saints, Protestant, Roman Catholic and Sikh faith communities in the DC region to 1) increase understanding, dialogue, and a sense of community among peoples of diverse faiths from different races and cultures; and 2) address issues of social and economic justice in defense of human dignity.

Interfaith Council of Greater New York

20 Washington Sq N, Yonkers, NY 10019 USA; (212) 627-7099; Fax (212) 627-2939

Focus: General Peace & Justice; Training & Resources
Mission: The ICGNY addresses local and world issues of social and civic concerns, and conveys unifying teachings of faith groups through an interfaith newsletter, an interfaith calendar, and training of people in conflict resolution, peace building, and social harmony.

Interfaith Council of Montreal

2065 Sherbrooke St W, Montreal, QC H3H 1G6 Canada; (514) 937-9176; Fax (514) 937-4986; http://www.total.net/~ccocee

Focus: Ecumenical & Interfaith Cooperation
Mission: To promote communication and relationships between people of various faiths, believing that individuals deepen their own religious commitments as they understand and appreciate other faiths. ICOM sponsors dialogue and public education and responds to events affecting faith communities.

Interfaith Dialogue Association

6264 Grand River Dr NE, Ada, MI 49301-9549 USA; (616) 682-9022; Fax (616) 682-9023; conexus@iserv.net

Focus: Ecumenical & Interfaith Cooperation
Mission: Goals of the IDA are 1) to eliminate prejudice between members of different faith traditions; 2) to advance understanding, harmony, and appreciation among religions; 3) to identify commonalities and differences; and 4) to enhance personal growth and transformation, friendship, and trust. IDA sponsors an annual World Religions Conference.

Interfaith Fairness Coalition of MD

15812 Kerr Rd, Laurel, MD 20707 USA; (301) 776-6891; Fax (301) 776-6891; ekobee@aol.com

Focus: Discrimination
Mission: IFCM encourages members of the religious community to support Maryland's gay, lesbian, bisexual, and transgender community in its efforts to win equal rights under the law and end discrimination based on sexual orientation.

Interfaith Health Program

750 Commerce Dr #301, Decatur, GA
30030 USA; (404) 592-1460;
Fax (404) 592-1462;
http://www.ihpnet.org

Focus: Health Issues
Mission: To encourage faith groups to
improve the individual and collective
health of their members and the communities they serve by integrating the
strengths and resources of the faith community with public health programs,
especially in the area of preventive
medicine.

Interfaith Hunger Appeal

PO Box 1687, Elkhart, IN 46515 USA;
(219) 262-8821;
http://www.ihaglobal.org

Focus: Human Rights
Mission: To promote reconciliation of
the peoples of the earth from hunger
and poverty by providing a US forum
for interfaith cooperation and by alleviating human suffering abroad through
its partner agencies: The American
Jewish Joint Distribution Committee,
Catholic Relief Services, Church World
Service, and Lutheran World Relief.

InterFaith Network—UK

5-7 Tavistock Pl, London, WC1H 9SN
UK; (01) 71 388-0008; Fax (01) 71
387-7968; http://www.interfaith.org.uk

Focus: Ecumenical & Interfaith Cooperation; Societies, Seminaries & Funds
Mission: To build good relations
between the communities of the major
faiths in the UK. The Network links
more than 85 groups including major
faith communities, national and local
interfaith organizations, academic institutions, and bodies concerned with multifaith education.

Interfaith Partnership on the Environment

UNEP/RONA, #Dc2-803, United
Nations, NY 10017 USA;
(212) 963-8039; Fax (212) 963-7341;
http://www.RONA.unep.org

Focus: Ecology & Environment
Mission: IPE works with the United
Nations Environment Programme to promote the first weekend of June each
year as an Environmental Rest Day (formerly called the Environmental
Sabbath). The IPE publishes "Only One

Earth" with up-to-date environmental
information, prayers, and spiritual
reflection.

Interfaith Seminary (East–West)

PO Box 2123, Santa Cruz, CA 95063
USA; (831) 425-3320 or
(831) 464-0985; Fax (831) 464-0985;
http://www.spiritofinterfaith.org

Focus: Societies, Seminaries & Funds
Mission: To honor all spiritual traditions
and teaching, while focusing on training ministers to act as practitioners; to
lead services, act as spiritual counselors, and to minister to broader community needs, via residential and Web
programs.

Interfaith Sexual Trauma Institute

St John's Abbey & University,
Collegeville, MN 56321 USA; (320)
363-3931; Fax (320) 363-3954;
http://www.csbsju.edu/isti

Focus: Children, Youth & Family
Mission: ISTI affirms the goodness of
human sexuality and promotes the prevention of sexual abuse and exploitation through research, education and
publication. ISTI also facilitates healing
of survivors, faith communities, and
offenders, as well as those who care for
them.

Interfaith Theological Seminary

1731 E Allen Road, Tucson, AZ 85719
USA; (520) 319-2070; Fax (520) 319-
2076; http://www.azstarnet.com/
nonprofit/ifts

Focus: Societies, Seminaries & Funds
Mission: Offering a two-year program
of study and training leading to ordination, ITS acknowledges the call many
have to affirm an interfaith spiritual
foundation to their vocation as a lifelong spiritual practice devoted to compassion, peace, and loving-kindness.

Interfaith Voices Against Hunger

29 John St #708, New York, NY
10038-4005 USA; (212) 227-8480;
Fax (212) 385-4330; nyccah@juno.com

Focus: Human Rights
Mission: IFVAH is a coalition of anti-
hunger groups helping New York City's
grassroots network of emergency food
programs work to relieve hunger now,
while seeking long-term solutions to
hunger and an end to the need for
emergency food programs.

Interfaith Voices for Peace & Justice

PO Box 270214, St Louis, MO 63127-
0214 USA; (314) 892-1192;
Fax (314) 892-1255;
http://www.interfaithvoices.org

Focus: Communication
Mission: To provide an accurate listing
of English-speaking faith and interfaith
groups, numbering more than 800, that
work for peace and justice, both hard
copy and at www.interfaithvoices.org,
enabling communication, support, and
cooperation in joint efforts.

Interfaith Working Group

PO Box 11706, Philadelphia, PA
19101 USA; (215) 235-3050;
http://www.iwgonline.org/

Focus: Religious & Civil Liberty
Mission: Believing that portrayal of
social debates as disagreements
between the religious and the irreligious
is not helpful, the IWG's mission is to
inform the public of the diversity of religious opinion by providing a voice for
religious organizations and clergy who
support equal rights for sexual minorities, reproductive freedom, and the separation of church and state.

International Association for Religious Freedom

2 Market St, Oxford, UK OX1 3EF, 44-
01-865-202-744; Fax 865-202-746;
http://www.iarf-religiousfreedom.net
In North America: IARFUSA, 14
Concord Ave., Cambridge, MA
02138; (617) 876-3059

Focus: Societies, Seminaries & Funds
Religious & Civil Liberty
Mission: With NGO status at the UN,
IARF is an international network of
groups and individuals committed to
creating an earth community that protects freedom of religion or belief and
all other fundamental human rights. It
also promotes just and sustainable
development for all the world's peoples.
Offices are world-wide.

International Coalition for Religious Freedom

7777 Leesburg Pike #307N-A, Falls
Church, VA 22043 USA;
(703) 790-1500; Fax (703) 790-5562;
http://www.religiousfreedom.com

Focus: Religious & Civil Liberty
Mission: To defend the religious freedom of all, regardless of creed, gender, or ethnic origin, ICRF works largely through its Web site offering links to tens of organizations working for religious freedom worldwide. Founded in 1983, by the Unification Church community.

International Committee for the Peace Council

2702 International Ln, Madison, WI 53704 USA; (608) 241-2200; Fax (608) 241-2209;
http://www.peacecouncil.org
Focus: Ecumenical & Interfaith Cooperation; Human Rights; Peace & Nonviolence
Mission: In a world where religion is often used to justify division, hatred, and violence, ICPC offers an alternative: the example of religious leaders working effectively together to relieve suffering and make the world whole. The Peace Council works in Mexico, Thailand, Cambodia, Korea, Israel/Palestine, and with the Campaign to Ban Landmines.

International Council of Christians and Jews

475 Park Ave S, 19th Fl, New York, NY 10016 USA; http://www.iccj.org
Focus: Discrimination; Ecumenical & Interfaith Cooperation
Mission: ICCJ serves as the umbrella group of 30 international Jewish-Christian dialogue organizations which are dedicated to fighting bias, bigotry, and racism by promoting understanding and respect among all races, religions, and cultures through advocacy, conflict resolution, and education. The USA organization may be reached at www.nccj.org.

International Institute of Islamic Thought

PO Box 669, Herndon, VA 20172-0669 USA; (703) 471-1133; Fax (703) 471-3922; http://www.iiit.org
Focus: Societies, Seminaries & Funds
Mission: IIIT is dedicated to the revival and reform of Islamic thought and methodology in order to deal more effectively with present challenges, giving divine guidance to the progress of human civilization.

International Interfaith Centre

2 Market St, Oxford, UK OX1 3EF; 44 (0) 1 865 202745;
Fax 44 (0) 1 865 202746;
http://www.interfaith-center.org
Focus: Ecumenical & Interfaith Cooperation
Mission: To support the work of organizations and individuals, seeking to further peaceful relations, respect, and understanding between people with different faith beliefs.

International Religious Liberty Association

12501 Old Columbia Pike, Silver Spring, MD 20904-6600 USA; (301) 680-6680; Fax (301) 680-6695; http://www.irla.org
Focus: Discrimination; Religious & Civil Liberty
Mission: IRLA believes that religious liberty and the elimination of intolerance and discrimination based on religion or belief are essential to promote understanding, peace, and friendship among peoples.

International Service for Peace—SIPAZ

PO Box 2415, Santa Cruz, CA 95063 USA; (408) 425-1257; Fax (408) 425-1257; http://www.nonviolence.org/sipaz/index.html
Focus: Human Rights
Mission: A coalition of peace and faith-based organizations actively seeking to support a dignified, just, and lasting peace in Chiapas, Mexico, through communication, observation, and international presence in the region.

International Shinto Foundation, Inc

777 UN Plaza WCRP-9A, New York, NY 10017 USA; (212) 661-9117; Fax (212) 661-1872;
http://www.shinto.org
Focus: Ecumenical & Interfaith Cooperation
Mission: Among the Foundation's goals is the desire to cooperate with other religious traditions to create a more harmonious world.

International Society of Divine Love

400 Barsana Rd, Austin, TX 78737-9075 USA; (512) 288-7180; Fax (512) 288-0447; http://www.isdl.org
Focus: Training & Resources
Mission: To reveal the eternal knowledge of the Vedas, Gita, and Bhagwatam (Holy Scriptures) to interested souls, and to impart the practical process of divine upliftment, "divine-love-consciousness" based on the ancient path of raganuga bhakti.

InterReligious Coalition on Smoking or Health

110 Maryland Ave NE #507, Washington, DC 20002-5626 USA; (202) 547-7440; Fax (202) 547-7508; wihealth@aol.com
Focus: Health Issues
Mission: Composed of organizations from all faith traditions, the IRCSH is committed to educating religious communities and the public on policy initiatives to control tobacco, focusing on both the executive and legislative branches of federal and state government.

InterReligious Federation for World Peace

4 W 43rd St, New York, NY 10036 USA; (212) 869-6023; Fax (212) 869-6424; http://www.irfwp.org
Focus: Societies, Seminaries & Funds
Mission: This global organization brings together believers and scholars from the many religious traditions of the world to work for world peace.

InterReligious Foundation for Community Organization

402 W 145th St, New York, NY 10031 USA; (212) 926-5757; Fax (212) 926-5842;
http://www.ifconews.org
Focus: Human Rights; Training & Resources
Mission: IFCO is an ecumenical agency whose mission is to assist oppressed people as they struggle for justice, dignity, and self-determination. It conducts programs to enable local churches to address international, domestic, and public policy issues.

Interweave: Unitarian Universalists for Gay, Lesbian, Bisexual & Transgender Concerns

167 Milk St #406, Boston, MA 02215 USA; http://www.interweave.uua.org

Focus: Discrimination
Mission: Interweave is dedicated to the spiritual, political, and social well-being of UU's who are confronting oppression as lesbians, gay men, bisexuals, transgender persons, and their heterosexual allies. Interweave facilitates the celebration of the culture and the lives of its members.

IQRA' International Educational Foundation

7450 Skokie Blvd, Skokie, IL 60077 USA; http://www.iqra.org

Focus: Societies, Seminaries & Funds
Mission: Since 1983, IQRA' has supported the development, writing, and marketing of publications of Islamic educational materials.

Islamic Council of Imams—Canada

Box 72012, 2898 Ellesmere Rd, Scarborough, ON M1E 5G4 Canada; (416) 282-4342; Fax (416) 282-2642

Focus: Societies, Seminaries & Funds
Mission: The Coordinating Council guides the community and explores the response of Islamic religion to various challenges through reflective religious leadership of the Muslim community.

Islamic Society of North America

PO Box 38, Plainfield, IN 46168 USA; (317) 839-8157; Fax (317) 839-1840; http://www.isna.net

Focus: Societies, Seminaries & Funds
Mission: ISNA is an association of Muslim organizations and individuals whose mission is to provide a unified platform of expression for Islam, to develop educational, da'wah, and social services that translate the teachings of the Qur'an and the Sunnah into everyday living, and to enhance Islamic identity in the Society.

Jain Society of Toronto

37 Tuscarora Dr, North York, ON M2H 2K4 Canada; (416) 491-5560; http://www.geocities.com/Heartland/Acres/6123

Focus: Peace & Nonviolence
Mission: Jains practice nonviolence in thought, word and deed. "Mutual assistance to all" and "Ahimsa" (nonviolence) are fundamental Jain principles.

JAINA—Federation of Jain Associations in NA

11820 Triple Crown Rd, Reston, VA 20191-3014 USA; (703) 620-9837; Fax (703) 620-6280; manojdharamsi@juno.com

Focus: Training & Resources
Mission: To promote understanding of the Jain religion and encourage its principles; among them nonviolence, multifaced viewing, limiting possessions, and truthfulness.

Jesuit Social and International Ministries

1616 P St NW #400, Washington, DC 20036-1405 USA; (202) 462-0400; Fax (202) 328-9212; http://www.jesuit.org/advocacy

Focus: General Peace & Justice
Mission: To advocate on behalf of people and communities served by Jesuit-sponsored initiatives.

Jesuit Volunteer Corps

PO Box 3928, Portland, OR 97208 USA; (503) 335-8202; Fax (503) 249-1118; jvcnw@aol.com

Focus: General Peace & Justice
Mission: The JVC enlists women and men as volunteers to work at deepening personal spirituality, serving those in need and working for social justice.

Jewish Council for Public Affairs

443 Park Ave S, New York, NY 10016 USA; (212) 684-6950 Ext. 207; Fax (212) 686-1353; mraffel@thejcpa.org

Focus: Advocacy
Mission: A coalition of 122 local and 13 national agencies dealing with public policy issues that affect the American Jewish Community. Its principal task forces are the "Task Force on Israel and Other International Concerns," the "Task Force on Equal Opportunity and Social Justice," and the "Task Force on Jewish Security and Bill of Rights."

Jewish Currents Magazine

22 E 17th St #601, New York, NY 10003 USA; (212) 924-5740; Fax (212) 924-5740

Focus: Communication
Mission: *Jewish Currents* is a progressive Jewish monthly that reports on Israel and the peace process, Black/Jewish relations, Yiddish literature and culture, labor struggle, and Holocaust resistance and commemoration.

Jewish Fund for Justice

260 Fifth Ave #701, New York, NY 10001 USA; (212) 213-2113; Fax (212) 213-2233; http://www.jfjustice.org

Focus: Societies, Seminaries & Funds
Mission: Built on the historic commitment of the Jewish people to social and economic justice, JFJ has given grants since 1984 to aid low-income Americans in fighting poverty, aided interdenominational efforts, and created materials to educate and involve Jews in social and economic justice.

Jewish Peace Fellowship

PO Box 271, Nyack, NY 10960 USA; (914) 358-4601; Fax (914) 358-4924; http://www.jewishpeacefellowship.org

Focus: Peace & Nonviolence
Mission: Uniting those who believe that Jewish ideals and experiences provide inspiration for a nonviolent commitment to life, JPF aids those who address themselves to the remaking of our society.

Jewish Women International

1828 L St NW #250, Washington, DC 20036 USA; (202) 857-1300; Fax (202) 857-1380; http://www.jewishwomen.org

Focus: Children, Youth & Family; Peace & Nonviolence; Women
Mission: Seeking a safe world for women, children, and families, JWI works to break the cycle of violence by developing emotionally healthy adults, empowering women, and strengthening families. JWI accomplishes its work through direct service, education, advocacy, and the promotion of "best practice" models.

Jews for Racial & Economic Justice

140 W 22nd St #302, New York, NY 10011 USA; (212) 647-8966; Fax (212) 647-7124; jfrej@igc.org

Focus: Economic Concerns; Human Rights; Indigenous or Displaced Persons
Mission: JFREJ strengthens a progressive Jewish voice in debates over NYC's future and activates the Jewish community as partners in the struggle for justice. In coalition with communities of color and labor organizations, JFREJ fights for social programs, fair labor practices, accountable policing, and immigrants rights.

Jobs with Justice

501 3rd St NW, Washington, DC 20001 USA; (202) 434-1106; Fax (202) 434-1477; http://www.jwj.org

Focus: Economic Concerns
Mission: A national campaign for workers' rights that works through coalitions of labor, community, religious, and constituency organizations, Jobs with Justice fights for workers' rights and economic justice.

Jonah House

1301 Moreland Ave, Baltimore, MD 21216 USA; (410) 233-6238; Fax (410) 233-4067; disarmnow@aol.com

Focus: Peace & Nonviolence
Mission: Jonah House is a faith-based, intentional community committed to simple lifestyle, nonviolence, civil resistance to militarism, and plowshares actions.

Journal of Women's Ministries

PO Box 928, Vineland, NJ 10017 USA; (800) 374-9510; Fax (856) 696-2130

Focus: Communication; Women
Mission: The official publication of the Council for Women's Ministries of the Episcopal Church, the *Journal's* purpose is to bring wholeness to the church through personal and corporate transformation.

Jubilee 2000/USA Campaign

222 E Capitol St NE, Washington, DC 20003-1036 USA; (202) 783-3566; Fax (202) 546-4468; http://www.j2000usa.org

Focus: Human Rights
Mission: Jubilee 2000/USA is part of a worldwide movement advocating cancellation of crushing international debt borne by impoverished countries in Africa, Asia, and Latin America.

Kairos 2000/USA

5757 N Sheridan Rd #16A, Chicago, IL 60660 USA; (773) 275-5410; Fax (773) 275-6359; jtelbert@aol.com

Focus: Human Rights
Mission: To discern the "kairos" of our time (a Greek word meaning "a time of both crisis and opportunity") to act and reflect, theologically and politically, locally and globally, on issues of justice. An immediate goal is realization of jubilee justice (Lev. 25) in the new millennium.

Kashi Ashram

11155 Roseland Rd #11, Sebastian, FL 32958 USA; (561) 589-1403 Ext. 106; Fax (561) 589-6686; http://www.kashi.org

Focus: Human Rights
Mission: A community embracing all religions whose members dedicate their lives to serving those who are terminally ill or in need. The KA's teaching, blending Eastern and Western traditions, holds that all paths followed with a pure heart lead to the God within.

KAZI Publications Inc

3023 W Belmont Ave, Chicago, IL 60618 USA; (773) 267-7001; Fax (773) 267-7002; http://www.kazi.org

Focus: Communication
Mission: To educate people, eliminate ignorance, alleviate prejudices, and enhance mutual understanding and cooperation among the followers of the great religions, thereby making the Earth a peaceful abode for everyone. It does this by producing and distributing new Islamic books, reprinting and revising existing literature on Islam, and producing textbooks for schools and colleges.

Kentucky Interreligious Taskforce on Central America

1200 S Shelby St, Louisville, KY 40203 USA; (502) 636-0296; Fax (502) 636-2379; jflynn@igc.apc.org

Focus: Economic Concerns; Human Rights

Mission: KITCA goals are 1) to conscientize Kentucky-area people about injustices in Central America, often caused by US policies; 2) to organize delegations to go to Central America with "Witness for Peace;" and 3) to participate with WFP and others in alleviating the crushing debt on poor countries.

Kirkridge Retreat Center— The Picket & Pray Place

2495 Fox Gap Rd, Bangor, PA 18013 USA; (610) 588-1793; Fax (610) 588-8510; http://www.kirkridge.org

Focus: Peace & Nonviolence; Training & Resources
Mission: In a spirit of ecumenicity, the Center seeks to integrate personal growth and social change with a goal of enabling people of faith to work out peace and justice imperatives in their own lives and in the structure of society.

Koinonia Partners, Inc

1324 Hwy 49 S, Americus, GA 31709 USA; (877) 738-1741; Fax (912) 924-6504; http://www.koinoniapartners.org

Focus: Human Rights; Peace & Nonviolence
Mission: KP is a Christian organization seeking to be a "demonstration plot for the Kingdom of God," committed to nonviolence, peaceful solutions to society's problems, reconciliation among all people, and the empowerment of the poor, the neglected, and the oppressed.

Latin America Working Group

110 Maryland Ave NE Box 15, Washington, DC 20002 USA; (202) 546-7010; Fax (202) 543-7647 http://www.lawg.org

Focus: Human Rights; Peace & Nonviolence
Mission: A coalition of 60 religious, human rights, progressive policy, and development organizations, LAWG strives for US policies that promote peace, justice, and sustainable development in Latin America by providing information to nongovernmental organizations, congressional offices, the media, and concerned citizens.

Leadership Conference of Women Religious

8808 Cameron St, Silver Spring, MD 20910-4113 USA; (301) 588-4955; Fax (301) 587-4575; http://www.lcwr.org

Focus: General Peace & Justice; Societies, Seminaries & Funds
Mission: Consisting of elected leaders in religious orders representing 83,000 Catholic sisters, LCWR develops leadership, promotes collaboration within church and society, and serves as a voice for systemic change.

Leadership Conference on Civil Rights

1629 K St NW #1010, Washington, DC 20006 USA; (202) 466-3311; Fax (202) 466-3435

Focus: Discrimination
Mission: Committed to equal justice and equal opportunity for all Americans of every heritage, LCCR teaches that all citizens are one people, bound together, not by bloodlines, but by our respect for human rights and the Constitution.

Liberty Magazine—7th-Day Adventist

12501 Old Columbia Pike, Silver Spring, MD 20940-6600 USA; Fax (301) 680-6695; http://www.libertymagazine.org

Focus: Communication; Religious & Civil Liberty
Mission: To preserve separation of church and state, with emphasis on the Establishment and Free Exercise clauses of the US Constitution.

Lilith Magazine—Jewish Feminist Quarterly

250 W 57th St #2432, New York, NY 10107-0001 USA; (212) 757-0818; Fax (212) 757-5705; http://www.lilithmag.com

Focus: Communication; Women
Mission: *Lilith* looks at Jewish life through a feminist filter and speaks out on Jewish feminist concerns to the general women's movement.

Loretto Community—Englewood, CO

300 E Hampden Ave #400, Englewood, CO 80110-2661 USA;

(303) 783-0450; Fax (303) 783-0611; http://www.lorettocommunity.org

Focus: General Peace & Justice
Mission: Loretto Sisters, co-members, and volunteers in 36 states and 7 countries, take stands to create a nonviolent world, promote equality and dignity, transform unjust systems, work to heal the earth, educate, minister to the sick and disenfranchised, advocate for women, and seek economic justice.

Latin America—Caribbean Committee
Focus: Human Rights
Mission: LC/LACC works for peace in Latin American and the Caribbean in solidarity with brothers and sisters in those places, following the Gospel's call to work for peace and act for justice.

Loretto Community—St. Louis, MO

590 E Lockwood Ave, St Louis, MO 63119-3279 USA; (314) 962-8112; Fax (314) 962-0400

Earth Network

http://www.lorettocommunity.org/ earthnet.html
Focus: Ecology & Environment
Mission: LEN is dedicated to re-establishing right relationships between the human and the Earth community through programs of education, prayerful reflection, and action designed to make connections between faith and caring for Earth.

Women's Network

Focus: Discrimination; Women
Mission: A network of feminists within the Loretto Community committed to act for the empowerment of women and to work toward reorganizing institutional, personal, and structural relationships based on domination and subordination, LWN affirms the rights of all women, regardless of racial, ethnic, class, age, sexual orientation, or national background.

Loretto Network for NonViolence

2544 Cherry St, Kansas City, MO 64108-2751 USA; (816) 842-5170; Fax (816) 842-3412; dorek@aol.com

Focus: Peace & Nonviolence
Mission: Aware that violence is on the increase in our world and to our world, LNN pledges to learn nonviolence, to teach nonviolence, and to collaborate with others to work for peace.

Lutheran Human Relations Association of America

5233 N 51st Blvd, Milwaukee, WI 53218-3302 USA; (414) 536-0585; Fax (414) 536-0690; lhra@ecunet.org

Focus: Discrimination
Mission: To bring people together to do justice by breaking down hostilities and fears between them, seeking to bridge racial, cultural, gender, age, ability, class, and income gaps, and building human community.

Lutheran Immigration & Refugee Service

390 Park Ave S, New York, NY 10016 USA; (212) 532-6350; Fax (212) 683-1329; http://www.lirs.org

Focus: Indigenous or Displaced Persons
Mission: LIRS protects the rights and well-being of uprooted people in the United States through program and advocacy services carried out by staff and volunteers nationwide.

Lutheran Network for Inclusive Vision

PO Box 16313, San Diego, CA 92176 USA; (619) 283-0171; Fax (619) 283-0751; cwittucm@aol.com

Focus: Discrimination; Renewal of Faith Group
Mission: The Network provides a public roster of church leaders committed to witness to the inclusive Gospel of Jesus Christ by fostering the full inclusion of persons who are gay, lesbian, bisexual, or transgendered in the congregational life and ordained ministry of the ELCA.

Lutheran Peace Fellowship

1710 11th Ave, Seattle, WA 98122-2420 USA; (206) 720-0313; Fax call first; http://www.nonviolence.org/lpf

Focus: Peace & Nonviolence; Training & Resources
Mission: Responding to the gospel call to be peacemakers and justice seekers, LPF has, since 1941, offered a wide range of expertise, encouragement, and resources. It supports discussion/activity in congregations and schools, and participates in regional/national events.

Lutheran Volunteer Corps

1226 Vermont Ave NW, Washington, DC 20005 USA; (202) 387-3222; Fax (202) 667-0037; http://www.lvchome.org

Focus: Peace & Nonviolence
Mission: In response to the Gospel of Jesus Christ, volunteers seek to answer God's call to Shalom by supporting the Church as it works for peace and justice. Each pledges to help the others grow spiritually, affirm diversity in community, live simply, and do justice.

Lutherans Concerned—North America

2466 Sharondale Dr, Atlanta, GA 30305 USA; (404) 266-9615; Fax (404) 266-9615; http://www.lcna.org

Focus: Discrimination; Renewal of Faith Group
Mission: To affirm God's love for all people regardless of sexual orientation. Since 1974, LC has worked to create an inclusive Lutheran Church and to help people reconcile their spirituality and sexuality in a positive way. It works through 38 chapters and 160 "Reconciled in Christ" congregations.

M K Gandhi Institute for Nonviolence

650 E Parkway S, Memphis, TN 38104 USA; (901) 452-2824; Fax (901) 452-2775; http://www.cbu.edu/Gandhi

Focus: Peace & Nonviolence; Training & Resources
Mission: The Institute's goal is to teach and apply the principles of nonviolence as a positive force to prevent violence and resolve personal and public conflicts.

Mahavir World Vision Inc

1884 Dorsetshire Rd, Columbus, OH 43229 USA; (614) 895-3190; Fax (614) 899-2678; http://www.jainspirit.org

Focus: Communication; Peace & Nonviolence
Mission: Seeking to advance the Jain religion's goal of nonviolence, MWV produces films, videos, and other audiovisual materials.

Mainstream Coalition

5250 W 94th Ter #108, Prairie Village, KS 66207 USA; (913) 649-3326; Fax (913) 649-3285; mainstream@birch.net

Focus: Children, Youth & Family; Religious & Civil Liberty
Mission: The Coalition is a group of religious, business, political, and community leaders who have united to counteract the threat to constitutional freedoms by sectarian and political extremists. Its focus is church/state separation and support of public education.

Maple Buddhist Society

9089 Richmond, Brossard, QC J4X 2S1 Canada; (514) 591-8726; Fax (514) 466-8958; chanhuy@prisco.net

Focus: Peace & Nonviolence
Mission: To share Buddhist teachings and practices of peace in the tradition of Zen Master Thich Nhat Hanh.

Margaret Sanger's Supporters

PO Box 324, Huntington, NY 11743 USA; (516) 673-6871; Fax (516) 673-6871; bbaird0322@aol.com

Focus: Religious & Civil Liberty
Mission: To present educational materials about birth control, to publicize the work of Margaret Sanger, the 1972 Baird v Eisenstadt Supreme Court decision legalizing birth control for unmarried persons and the 1993 Roe v Wade decision legalizing abortion rights. MSS seeks to alert the public to the dangers that fundamentalist religionists pose to these freedoms.

Marianist Social Justice Collaborative

4301 Roland Ave, Baltimore, MD 21210-2793 USA; (410) 366-1324; Fax (410) 889-5743; http://www.msjc.net

Focus: Societies, Seminaries & Funds
Mission: To strengthen the combined efforts of lay and religious members of the Marianist Family in educating and acting for social justice.

Maryknoll Office for Global Concerns

PO Box 29132, Washington, DC 20017 USA; (202) 832-1780; Fax (202) 832-5195; http://www.maryknoll.org/GLOBAL/OFFICE/office.htm

Focus: Human Rights
Mission: This Office links the people overseas, whom Maryknoll missioners serve, with US advocacy, justice, and peace education. Maryknoll hopes to raise awareness of justice issues among US Catholics, leading them to see that action for justice, and peace is integral to faith.

Mature Years Magazine

Box 801, Nashville, TN 37202-0801 USA; (615) 749-6292; Fax (615) 749-6512; mcropsey@umpublishing.org

Focus: Children, Youth & Family; Communication
Mission: MY's purpose is to help people understand and use the resources of the Christian faith in dealing with specific opportunities and problems related to aging.

MAZON: A Jewish Response to Hunger

12401 Wilshire Blvd #303, Los Angeles, CA 90025 USA; (310) 442-0020; Fax (310) 442-0030; http://www.mazon.org

Focus: Societies, Seminaries & Funds
Mission: A fundraising and grant-making organization working to prevent and alleviate hunger, Mazon has granted more than $16 million to virtually all aspects of the nation's anti-hunger network.

Mennonite Central Committee—Canada

134 Plaza Dr, Winnipeg, MB R3T 5K9 Canada; (204) 261-6381; Fax (204) 269-9875; http://www.mcc.org

Focus: General Peace & Justice
Mission: MCC Canada seeks to demonstrate God's love by working among people suffering from poverty, conflict, oppression and natural disaster and strives for peace, justice, and dignity of all people by sharing experiences, resources, and faith in Jesus Christ.

Mennonite Central Committee—US

21 S 12th St PO Box 500, Akron, PA 17501-0500 USA; (717) 859-1151; Fax (717) 859-2171; http://www.mcc.org

Focus: General Peace & Justice
Mission: A relief, service, community development, and peace agency, MCC shares God's love through committed women and men who serve others suffering from poverty, conflict, oppression, and natural disaster.

Washington Office

110 Maryland Ave NE #502, Washington, DC 20002 USA; (202) 544-6564; Fax (202) 544-2820; http://www.mcc.org

Focus: Advocacy
Mission: To be a Mennonite and Brethren in Christ presence on Capitol Hill to give and encourage prophetic witness to the way of Christ on matters of US public policy.

Women's Concerns

(717) 859-3889; Fax (717) 859-3875

Focus: Children/Youth/Family; Discrimination; Women
Mission: To encourage mutuality and wholeness in male-female relations and promote awareness and reflection on issues of gender and theology. It produces resources on family violence and sexual abuse and coordinates a network of adult survivors of sexual abuse.

Mennonite Church—Peace & Justice Committee

PO Box 173, Orrville, OH 44667-0173 USA; (330) 683-6844; Fax (330) 683-6844; http://www.MennoLink.org/peace

Focus: Peace & Nonviolence
Mission: MCPJC teaches Christ's way of peacemaking, calls the Church to a renewal of faith, and urges use of the transforming power of God's love in homes, neighborhoods, and the world.

Mennonite Church/Gen Conf—Commission on Home Ministries

722 Main St, Box 347, Newton, KS 67114 USA; (316) 283-5100; Fax (316) 283-0454; http://www2.southwind.net/~gcmc

Focus: General Peace & Justice; Women
Mission: To nurture shalom in the life

and witness of General Conference Mennonite Churches of North America. Literature, programs, and speakers are available.

Methodist Federation for Social Action

212 E Capitol St NE, Washington, DC 20003 USA; (202) 546-8806; Fax (202) 546-6811; http://www.olg.com/mfsa

Focus: General Peace & Justice
Mission: To witness prophetically to the Biblical faith in solidarity with persons who are oppressed, to establish a society based on democratic social-economic principles, to defend civil liberties and human rights, and to work to eliminate war between nations. 35 regional chapters.

Methodists United for Peace with Justice

1500 16th St NW, Washington, DC 20036 USA; (301) 896-0013; Fax (301) 896-0013; mupj@igc.apc.org

Focus: Global Peace & Security; Peace & Nonviolence
Mission: MUPJ seek the abolition of all nuclear weapons, favor shifts in federal budget priorities from excessive military spending to urgent human needs, and support the International Criminal Court.

Metodistas Asociados Representalando la Causa de Hispano-Americanos

PO Box 639, Lakewood, CA 90714-0639 USA; (562) 944-4744; Fax (562) 944-9914

Focus: Discrimination
Mission: MARCH advocates for, supports, and represents Hispanic churches and ministries in the United Methodist Church and seeks elimination of racism and discrimination against Hispanics in society.

Mexican InterFaith Council (Consejo Interreligioso de Mexico)

Luis Inclan 13, Colonia Toriello Guerra, Mexico City DF, 14050 Mexico; (525) 528-7278 (Ignore Spanish msg); Fax same as phone; http://www.latinsynergy.org/

Focus: Ecumenical & Interfaith Cooperation

Mission: CIM, a group of diverse religious communities, works to foster ecumenical and interfaith understanding and tolerance through education and community activities.

Michigan Faith & Resistance Peace Team

1516 Jerome St, Lansing, MI 48912 USA; (517) 484-3178; Fax (517) 484-4219; http://www.traverse.com/nonprofit/peaceteam

Focus: Peace & Nonviolence; Training & Resources
Mission: The Team empowers people of faith to engage in active nonviolent peacemaking by offering nonviolence training and sending violence reduction peace teams to work in areas of conflict, both domestic and international.

Midwest Buddhist Meditation Center

29750 Ryan Rd, Warren, MI 48092-2244 USA; (810) 573-2666; Fax (810) 573-6661; mbmc@hotmail.com

Focus: Ecumenical & Interfaith Cooperation
Mission: To provide meditation retreats, interfaith activities, Buddhist studies, and encourage mutual understanding and action for world peace.

Millennium Institute

1117 N 19th St #900, Arlington, VA 22209-1708 USA; (703) 841-0048; Fax (703) 841-0050; http://www.millenniuminstitute.net

Focus: Human Rights; Societies, Seminaries & Funds, Training & Resources
Mission: The Institute uses systems thinking and the turn of the Millennium to catalyze a redirection of human civilization toward a peaceful, just, and sustainable future. "Studies for the 21st Century" is available. MI sponsors collegiate studies programs at 27 schools.

Ministry of Money

11315 Neelsville Church Rd, Germantown, MD 20876 USA; (301) 428-9560; minmon@erols.com

Focus: Peace & Nonviolence; Training & Resources
Mission: To provide a caring and safe place for persons at any economic level to acknowledge the impact of possessions in their lives, to discern God's will

for their life and their financial resources, and to discover how the joyful liberation of sharing those resources can lead them into the very heart of God.

Mobilization for the Human Family

1325 N College Ave, Claremont, CA 91711 USA; (909) 625-8722; Fax (909) 625-1820; http://www.mobilization.org

Focus: Discrimination
Mission: To be a prophetic presence in the Church and in the world, steadfastly proclaiming the radically inclusive love of God and faithfully working for the inclusion of and justice for ALL God's children, regardless of sexual orientation, gender, age, race, ethnicity, or socio-economic status.

Monastic Interreligious Dialogue

1402 Southern Ave, Beech Grove, IN 46107-1197 USA; (317) 788-7581 X3167; Fax (317) 782-3142; http://www.osb.org/mid

Focus: Societies, Seminaries & Funds
Mission: A leader in the dialogue between Christianity and the great religions of the East, MID sponsors conferences and seminars on East-West dialogue and monastic spirituality, has an intermonastic exchange with Tibetan monks and nuns exiled in India, and has a network of contact people from each US monastery.

More Light Presbyterians

PMB 246 4737 County Rd 101, Minnetonka, MN 55345-2634 USA; http://www.mlp.org

Focus: Discrimination; Renewal of Faith Group
Mission: Seeking to make the Church a true community of hospitality, MLP works for the full participation of lesbian, gay, bisexual, and transgender people of faith in the life, ministry, and witness of the PC/USA.

Mother-to-Mother Ministry

PO Box 1986, Indianapolis, IN 46206 USA; (317) 635-3113; Fax (317) 635-4426; http://www.dis.org

Focus: Training & Resources; Women
Mission: To provide opportunities for women to build intentional friendships across economic and racial barriers in

a ministry of reconciliation that fosters changes in perception, attitudes, and social systems. An ecumenical ministry affiliated with the Christian Church (Disciples of Christ).

Multifaith Action Society

385 Boundary Rd, Vancouver, BC V5K 4S1 Canada; (604) 469-1164; Fax (604) 926-7533; http://www.geocities.com/Athens/Thebes/7594

Focus: Ecumenical & Interfaith Cooperation
Mission: To promote interreligious understanding, provide information and resources on world religions to the community, and encourage people of all religions to dialogue on community issues.

Multifaith Institute

PO Box 39070, Solon, OH 44139 USA; (440) 248-0321; Fax (440) 248-7812; http://www.multifaith.net

Focus: Training & Resources
Mission: MI provides information products and services to interfaith organizations and the public including researching, editing and publishing, library and electronic database resources, and educational materials and programs.

Multifaith Resources

PO Box 128, Wofford Heights, CA 93285 USA; (760) 376-4691; Fax (760) 376-1528; http://www.nonviolence.org/mpf

Focus: Economical & Interfaith Cooperation
Mission: Providing books, the *Multifaith* calendar, and other resources for interreligious understanding.

Muslim Peace Fellowship

PO Box 271, Nyack, NY 10960 USA; (914) 358-4601; Fax (914) 358-4924; http://www.nonviolence.org/mpf

Focus: Peace & Nonviolence
Mission: MPF is a gathering of peace and justice-oriented Muslim of all backgrounds who are dedicated to making the beauty of Islam evident in the world.

Muslim Public Affairs Council

923 National Press Building, Washington, DC 20045 USA; (202) 879-6726; Fax (202) 879-6728; http://www.mpac.org/

Focus: Ecumenical & Interfaith Cooperation
Mission: Since 1988, MPAC has been committed to providing accurate information about Islam and Muslims, making Islamic ethical values available to the American political process, and seeking a positive relationship with other groups to promote shared values of peace, freedom, justice, and dignity for all people.

Muslim World League

PO Box 537, Makkah al-Mukarramah, Saudi Arabia; http://www.arab.net/mwl

Focus: Ecumenical & Interfaith Cooperation
Mission: Since 1962, MWL has represented Muslims worldwide, has been an NGO, and has been a member UNESCO and UNICEF. It defends Islamic causes, refutes false allegations, and seeks to build unity and trust. 32 offices worldwide.

National Association for Evangelicals—Office for Governmental Affairs

1001 Connecticut Ave NW #522, Washington, DC 20036 USA; (202) 789-1011; Fax (202) 842-0392; http://www.nae.net

Focus: Advocacy; General Peace & Justice; Women
Mission: This office, the public policy arm of the NAE, addresses the issues of faith, peace, human rights, and national security simultaneously, believing they are interdependent.

National Association of Ecumenical & Interreligious Staff

86-17 105th St, Richmond Hill, NY 11418 USA; (718) 847-6764; Fax (718) 847-7392; skip@ecunet.org

Focus: Societies, Seminaries & Funds
Mission: Fostering development of colleague relationships, NAEIS empowers its members for effective and faithful ecumenical/interfaith ministry by offering sharing, support, networking, spiritual growth, and experience in racial, ethnic, and faith diversity.

National Black Sisters' Conference US

3027 4th St NE, Washington, DC 20017 USA; (202) 529-9250; Fax (202) 529-9370; nbsc@igc.apc.org

Focus: Discrimination; Women
Mission: The NBSC confronts individual and institutional racism found in society and in the Church, works for the liberation of black people, and witnesses to their unity and mission with prayer, study, fellowship, and cooperative action.

National Campaign for a Peace Tax Fund

2121 Decatur PL NW, Washington, DC 20008 USA; (888) PEACETAX; Fax (202) 986-1007; http://www.nonviolence.org/peacetax

Focus: Advocacy; Peace & Nonviolence
Mission: The NCPTF advocates for legislation enabling conscientious objectors to war to pay their full federal taxes into a fund which could not be used for the military.

National Catholic Conference for Interracial Justice

1200 Varnum St NE, Washington, DC 20017 USA; (202) 529-6480; Fax (202) 526-1262;

Focus: Discrimination; Training & Resources
Mission: NCCIJ seeks to educate, advocate, and facilitate interracial and economic justice relations, to uncover and fight racism wherever it is found, and to promote and carry out model programs of interracial/intercultural communication, collaboration, reconciliation, and celebration.

National Catholic Reporter—Weekly Newspaper

115 E Armour Blvd, Kansas City, MO 64111 USA; (816) 968-2273; Fax (816) 968-2292; http://www.natcath.org

Focus: Communication; Renewal of Faith Group
Mission: Holding a vision of a compassionate and inclusive Catholicism in which God's people pray and work to build a more just and peaceful world, the NCR reports on contemporary faith, social, and political activities from the perspective of treasured Catholic tradition and the "Spirit of Renewal" of Vatican Council II.

National Coalition Against Censorship

275 Seventh Ave, New York, NY 10001 USA; (212) 807-6222; Fax (212) 807-6245; http://www.ncac.org

Focus: Religious & Civil Liberty
Mission: A coalition of 43 national civic and faith groups united by a conviction that freedom of thought, inquiry, and expression must be defended, the NCAC works to educate about the dangers of censorship and how to oppose it.

National Coalition to Abolish Death Penalty

1436 U St NW #104, Washington, DC 20009 USA; (202) 387-3890 Ext. 14; Fax (202) 387-5590; http://www.ncadp.org

Focus: Peace & Nonviolence
Mission: A coalition of organizations and individuals, faith based, civic, and professional, committed to the abolition of capital punishment, the NCADP provides information, advocates for public policy, and supports people and institutions that share rejection of the state's use of homicide as a instrument of social policy.

National Conference for Community & Justice

475 Park Ave S, 19th Fl, New York, NY 10016-6901 USA; (212) 545-1300 Ext. 229; Fax (212) 545-8053; http://www.nccj.org

Focus: Discrimination; Peace & Nonviolence
Mission: NCCJ is a human relations organization dedicated to fighting bias, bigotry, and racism in America by promoting understanding and respect among all races, religions, and cultures through advocacy, conflict resolution, and education. Formerly known as The National Conference of Christians and Jews.

National Conference of Interfaith Families

7 W 96th St #19-B, New York, NY 10025 USA; (212) 866-3795; http://www.interfaith.org

Focus: Ecumenical & Interfaith Cooperation; Training & Resources
Mission: Founded to support and affirm interfaith couples, support their children in understanding and embracing their rich spiritual legacy, and help multifaith

families see their diversity as a source of spiritual wealth. These goals are achieved through the distribution of a children's curriculum, family counseling sessions, group workshops, and seminar series.

National Council of Catholic Women

1275 K St NW #975, Washington, DC 20005 USA; (202) 682-0334; Fax (202) 682-0338; nccw@us.net

Focus: General Peace & Justice; Women
Mission: Founded in 1920, NCCW acts to support, empower, and educate all Catholic women in spirituality, leadership, and service. NCCW serves as a forum for Catholic women to share resources and respond to a variety of social justice issues.

National Council of Jewish Women

53 W 23rd St, 6th Fl, New York, NY 10010 USA; (212) 645-4048; Fax (212) 645-7466; http://www.ncjw.org

Focus: Children, Youth & Family; Women
Mission: The NCJW, inspired by Jewish values, works through a program of research, education, advocacy, and community service seeking to improve the quality of life for women, children, and families and to ensure individual rights and freedoms for all. There are 140 US sections.

National Episcopal AIDS Coalition

1925 K St NW, #220, Washington, DC 20006 USA; (800) 588-6628; Fax (202) 872-1511; http://www.neac.org

Focus: Health Issues
Mission: The National Episcopal AIDS Coalition works collaboratively for effective HIV/AIDS ministry by all levels of the Episcopal Church.

National Farm Worker Ministry

438 N Skinker Blvd, St. Louis, MO 63130 USA; (314) 726-6470; Fax (314) 862-8155; http://www.nfwm.org

Focus: Economic Concerns
Mission: NFWM is a movement within faith communities to support farm workers as they organize to achieve equality, freedom, and justice. After 80 years of ministry with farm workers, NFWM is convinced that union contracts are

the farm workers' best hope for a better life.

National Federation of Interfaith Volunteer Caregivers

One W Armour Blvd #202, Kansas City, MO 64111 USA; (816) 931-5442; http://www.nfivc.org

Focus: Societies, Seminaries & Funds; Training & Resources
Mission: To develop and support Interfaith Volunteer Caregiving Programs in every community so lives and spirits of those who give and receive care may be enriched.

National Interfaith Committee for Worker Justice

1020 W Bryn Mawr, 4th Fl, Chicago, IL 60660 USA; (773) 728-8400; Fax (773) 728-8409; http://www.igc.org/nicwj

Focus: Economic Concerns
Mission: A network of 40 faith and civic groups educating and mobilizing the religious community to become involved with workers' issues as a faith ministry.

National Interfaith Hospitality Network

120 Morris Ave, Summit, NJ 07901 USA; (908) 273-1100; Fax (908) 273-0030; http://www.nihn.org

Focus: Human Rights
Mission: NIHN provides shelter, meals, and comprehensive assistance for homeless families by mobilizing existing community resources: churches and synagogues for overnight shelters, congregations for volunteers, and social service agencies for referrals and day programs.

National Jewish Democratic Council

777 N Capitol St NE #305, Washington, DC 20002 USA; (202) 216-9060; Fax (202) 216-9061 http://www.njdc.org

Focus: Religious & Civil Liberty
Mission: Fighting for continued separation of church and state, public education, and preservation of a woman's right to choose, NJDC stands opposed to the politics of divisiveness and hate and all attempts of religious zealots to impose their values on society.

National Religious Partnership for Environment

1047 Amsterdam Ave, New York, NY 10025 USA; (212) 316-7441; Fax (212) 231-6754; http://www.nrpe.org

Focus: Ecology & Environment
Mission: A coalition of four faith groups and their agencies: United States Catholic Conference, Evangelical Environmental Network, Coalition on the Environment and Jewish Life, and National Council of Churches of Christ, NRPE seeks to protect and restore God's creation.

National Spiritualist Association of Churches

PO Box 217, Lily Dale, NY 14752 USA; (716) 595-2000; Fax (716) 595-2020; http://www.nsac.org

Focus: Religious & Civil Liberty
Mission: The NSAC is a religion, philosophy, and a science that protests any attempt to compel humanity to worship God in any particular or prescribed manner, and protects and encourages Spiritualist teachers and mediums.

National War Tax Resistance Coordinating Committee

PO Box 6512, Ithaca, NY 14851 USA; (800) 269-7464; Fax (607) 277-0593; http://www.nonviolence.org/wtr

Focus: Peace & Nonviolence
Mission: Viewing racism, sexism, homophobia, poverty, economic exploitation, and environmental destruction as integrally linked with militarism, NWTRCC members seek redirection of their tax dollars in order to contribute to the struggle for peace and justice.

National Woman's Christian Temperance Union

1730 Chicago Ave, Evanston, IL 60201-4585 USA; (847) 864-1396; Fax (847) 864-9497; http://www.wctu.org

Focus: Health Issues
Mission: To educate and encourage all people, with the help of God, to choose a way of life without alcohol, illegal drugs, and tobacco.

National Youth Project

221 DD Upadhayaya Marg, New Delhi, 110-002 India; (011) 322-2329

Focus: Children, Youth & Family; Training & Resources
Mission: Inspired by Gandhi and Vinoba Bhave, NYP has, since 1970, conducted camps throughout India to inspire youth and give them experience in choosing a life of service, self-help, self-discipline, harmony with others' religions and languages, and the dignity of manual work.

Native American Rights Fund

1506 Broadway, Boulder, CO 80302 USA; (303) 447-8760; http://www.narf.org

Focus: Advocacy; Indigenous or Displaced Persons
Mission: To provide legal representation for Native American tribes and villages, organizations, and individuals to help untangle the maze of laws impacting their lives, and works to help shape laws that will assure the civil and religious rights of all Native Americans.

NCCC Church World Service

28606 Phillips St, PO Box 968, Elkhart, IN 46515 USA; (219) 264-3102 Ext. 38; Fax (219) 262-0966; http://www.churchworldservice.org

Focus: Human Rights
Mission: To meet basic needs of people in peril, work for justice and dignity with the poor and vulnerable, promote peace and understanding among people of different faiths, races, and nations, and affirm and preserve the diversity and integrity of God's creation.

NCCC Committee on Justice for Children and Their Families

410 Sunset Ln, Glencoe, IL 60022 USA; (847) 835-1410; Fax (847) 835-1452; atuohy@aol.com

Focus: Children, Youth & Family
Mission: CJCF coordinates and strengthens the religious community's efforts to inform and empower churches and religious organizations to respond to children's needs, especially those of vulnerable and impoverished children and their families.

NCCC National Council of Churches of Christ—USA

475 Riverside Dr #852, New York, NY 10115 USA; (212) 870-2048; Fax (212) 870-2030; http://www.ncccusa.org

Focus: Ecumenical & Interfaith Cooperation; General Peace & Justice
Mission: Formed in 1950 and comprising 36 Protestant, Anglican, and Orthodox denominations with nearly 52 million members, NCCC seeks to manifest the group's oneness in Christ, doing together those things which can better be done united. Specialized committees work in 13 peace and justice areas.

Committee on Disabilities

(212) 870-2673; Fax (212) 870-2030; http://www.ncccusa.org/nmu/mce/dis
Focus: Discrimination
Mission: To promote wholeness in Christ's church by seeking the full inclusion and participation of all differently-abled Christians. NCCCD identifies areas of need and gifts, and coordinates ideas and resources which encourage, enable, and challenge.

Eco-Justice Working Group

(212) 870-2385; Fax (212) 870-2265; http://www.webofcreation.org/NCCWorkgrp.html
Focus: Ecology & Environment
Mission: To provide opportunities for NCCC member groups to protect and restore God's creation by sponsoring an Environmental Justice "Covenant Congregation Program," a "Black Church Eco-Justice Program," and an annual "Earth Day."

EcuLink Newsletter

(212) 870-2228; Fax (212) 870-2030
Focus: Communication
Mission: Witnessing to NCCC's common faith, *EcuLink* seeks to further Christian unity and to serve churches and the human family.

Ecumenical Networks

(212) 870-2155; Fax (212) 870-2817
Focus: Ecumenical & Interfaith Cooperation
Mission: Ecumenical Networks serves as the arm of the NCCC that partners with state, local, and regional ecumenical interfaith organizations throughout the United States.

Inclusiveness and Justice

(212) 870-2916; Fax (212) 870-2817
Focus: Discrimination; Women
Mission: To assist in the worldwide struggle of women, the disabled, people of color, and other oppressed peoples in their efforts to obtain relief from physical, political, economic, social, and cultural oppression in order to build a new, just, and humane society.

Interfaith Health Care Initiative

(212) 870-3560; Fax (212) 870-3341; http://www.ncccusa.org/health
Focus: Advocacy; Health Issues
Mission: To support development of denominational and local congregation-based health ministry programs, and educate, organize, and advocate for the NCCC's Universal Health Care Campaign (U2K) endorsed November 1999.

International Justice and Human Rights Program

(212) 870-2377; Fax (212) 870-2055
Focus: Global Peace & Security; Human Rights
Mission: To bring ecumenical partners together to work for global peace, social justice, and common security; to affirm and support economic, social, cultural, civil, and political human rights; and to promote better understanding, human dignity, and tolerance within the global community.

Justice for Women Program

(212) 870-2421; Fax (212) 870-2265 http://www.nccusa.org/nmu/jw.html
Focus: Women
Mission: To bring theology and ethics to a Justice for Women agenda that includes women in prison, prostitution, housing, health, pay equity, welfare, and leadership development.

Mark-Up Newsletter

110 Maryland Ave NE, Washington, DC 20002 USA; (202) 544-2350; Fax (202) 543-1297; ncc_Washington.parti@ecunet.org
Focus: Advocacy; Communication
Mission: A newsletter available to member churches and interested individuals, *Mark-Up* reports on public policy issues confronting Congress when they involve issues addressed by the Gospel of Jesus Christ.

Pillars of Peace

(212) 870-2424; Fax (212) 870-2055
Focus: General Peace & Justice; Training & Resources
Mission: To support the United Nations in its work with seven preconditions to peace in the 21st century, recognizing that peace is rooted in justice. Resources available for congregational use.

Public Education and Literacy

35006 13th Place SW, Federal Way, WA 98023 USA; (253) 661-7620; dbrown7086@aol.com
Focus: Children, Youth & Family
Mission: NCCC's PE&L committee works, in a spirit of ecumenism, to strengthen public school education for all children and to improve literacy among adults nationwide.

Racial Justice Program

(212) 870-2491; Fax (212) 870-2265; http://www.ncccusa.org/nmu/rjp.html
Focus: Discrimination
Mission: To organize, advocate, educate, and coordinate and develop resources to further racial justice.

Urban Initiatives Program

(212) 870-3064; Fax (212) 870-2030; http://www.ncccusa.org/nmu/ui.html
Focus: Discrimination; Human Rights
Mission: Seeking justice for residents of our cities, UIP addresses issues of racism, violence, health care, unemployment, and community development. Its programs include a youth volunteer program, a religious investors initiative, support for universal health care, an antiviolence program model, and a public housing program development model.

NETWORK: A National Catholic Justice Lobby

801 Pennsylvania Ave SE #460, Washington, DC 20003 USA; (202) 547-5556; Fax (202) 547-5510; http://www.networklobby.org

Focus: Advocacy; Human Rights
Mission: NETWORK educates, lobbies, and organizes to influence the formation of federal legislation to promote economic and social justice. A contemporary response to the ministry of Jesus, NETWORK uses Catholic social teaching and life experience of people who are poor as lenses for viewing social reality.

Nevada Desert Experience

46645, Las Vegas, NV 89144-6645 USA; (702) 646-4814; Fax (702) 631-5538; nde@igc.org

Focus: Global Peace & Security
Mission: A faith-based organization, with Franciscan roots, opposed to nuclear weapons testing and nuclear deterrence policy, the NDE leads educational workshops, vigils, prayer services, and protests in Las Vegas and at the Nevada Test Site.

New Call to Peacemaking

21 S 12th St PO Box 500, Akron, PA 17501 USA; (717) 859-1958; Fax (717) 859-1958; jkstoner@ptd.net

Focus: Communication; Peace & Nonviolence
Mission: To promote the vision of nonviolent peacemaking in and beyond the historic peace churches (Friends, Brethren, and Mennonites) through conferences, a newsletter, and books.

New Israel Fund

1625 K St NW #500, Washington, DC 20006 USA; (202) 223-3333; Fax (202) 659-2789; http://www.nif.org

Focus: Societies, Seminaries & Funds
Mission: To strengthen democracy and promote social justice in Israel by supporting Israeli organizations that promote Jewish-Arab equality and coexistence, religious pluralism and tolerance, elevated status of women, closing of social and economic gaps, and environmental justice.

New Seminary

PO Box 20433 Columbus Circle Sta, New York, NY 10023 USA; (212) 582-5577; Fax (212) 247-6038; http://www.newseminary.org

Focus: Societies, Seminaries & Funds
Mission: An institute for the training of Interfaith Ministers who teach counsel and work in the community, the NS respects all paths leading toward a deepening of one's relationship with God and with all of life.

News/Views Newsletter

1700 W Paces Ferry Rd NW, Atlanta, GA 30327 USA; (404) 355-0927; Fax (404) 355-0927; jbpender@juno.com

Focus: Communication
Mission: Reprinting selected articles from mainstream media, N/V is sent 21 times a year to those working for a world free of violence and war, a society with equity and justice for all, and an earth restored and protected. Published by Atlanta Friends Meeting.

NGO Committee on Freedom of Religion or Belief

546 11th St #4A, New York, NY 10009-4976 USA; (212) 674-2412; Fax (212) 808-5480

Focus: Religious & Civil Liberty; Societies, Seminaries & Funds
Mission: Bringing together NGOs affiliated with the UN, NGO-FRB works for freedom of religion or belief as articulated by the UN's "Declaration of Human Rights" (Art. 18) and the "Elimination of All Forms of Intolerance and Discrimination Based on Religion or Belief."

No More Violence

PO Box 406769, Louisville, KY 40204-6769 USA; (888) 757-0607; http://www.nomoreviolence.org

Focus: Peace & Nonviolence; Training & Resources
Mission: To open participants' eyes to the subliminal and overt practices that encourage violence in their own communities, affecting children from the earliest ages, NMV sponsors an educational bus "tour of violence," one of many NMV programs.

NonViolent Alternatives

825 4th St, Brookings, SD 57006 USA; (605) 692-8465;

Focus: Peace & Nonviolence; Training & Resources
Mission: NonViolent Alternatives is a resource and activity center for exploration and experimentation with alternatives to violence.

North American Christian Peace Conference

777 UN Plaza #1, New York, NY 10017-3521 USA; (212) 661-1621; Fax (516) 223-1880; philipoke@earthlink.net

Focus: Global Peace & Security; Human Rights
Mission: Affiliated with the Intl Christian Peace Conference, Prague CZ, NACPC seeks to mobilize Christians, churches, and institutions in the struggle for peace and social justice by promoting racial and economic equality, support for the UN, and an end to US foreign military intervention and embargoes.

North American Coalition for Christianity & Ecology

PO Box 40011, St Paul, MN 55104 USA; (612) 698-0349; Fax (612) 699-7031; http://www.nacce.org

Focus: Ecology & Environment
Mission: Viewing destruction of the Earth as the greatest moral issue of the century, NACCE's mission is to bring Christians into a loving relationship with God's creation, to facilitate formation of regional earthkeeping ministries, and to promote church partnerships with eco-justice groups.

North American Coalition on Religion & Ecology

5 Thomas Circle NW #500, Washington, DC 20005 USA; (202) 462-2591; Fax (202) 462-6534

Focus: Societies, Seminaries & Funds
Mission: To enable the NA religious community to enter into the environmental movement with more understanding and deeper commitment, NACRE uses an interdisciplinary approach whereby scientific disciplines interact with major environmental and ethical concerns.

North American Interfaith Network Newsletter

6264 Erand River Dr, NE, Ada, MI 49301 USA; (616) 682-0922;

Focus: Ecumenical & Interfaith Cooperation; Societies, Seminaries & Funds
Mission: To provide communication and mutual strengthening of interfaith organizations and agencies, and interfaith programs of faith institutions in NA, NAIN affirms and celebrates humanity's diverse and historic spiritual resources, bringing these to bear on contemporary issues.

Numata Center for Buddhist Translation and Research

2620 Warring St, Berkeley, CA 94704 USA; (510) 843-4128; Fax (510) 845-3409; numata @slip.net

Focus: Societies, Seminaries & Funds
Mission: To present the efforts of the Society for the Promotion of Buddhism and the Numata Center and to translate and publish the Taisho Chinese Buddhist canon into English.

Odyssey Network TV

12700 Ventura Blvd, Los Angeles, CA 91604 USA; (818) 755-2400; http://www.odysseychannel.com

Focus: Communication
Mission: A cable television service offering quality, entertaining programming for "today's family," with a commitment to exploring faith and the human condition.

Oikocredit

475 Riverside Dr 16th Fl, New York, NY 10115 USA; (212) 870-2725; Fax (212) 870-2722; http://www.oikocredit.org

Focus: Human Rights; Societies, Seminaries & Funds Women
Mission: To mobilize investment capital in order to provide loans to poor people for business enterprises which operate on principles of justice. Finances originate from those who subscribe to this process as one that liberates, aids economic growth, social justice, self-reliance, and respect for creation.

On Earth Peace Assembly, Inc

PO Box 188, 500 Main St, New Windsor, MD 21776USA; (410) 635-8704; Fax (410) 635-8707; http://www.brethren.org

Focus: Peace & Nonviolence
Mission: Grounded in the Church of the Brethren, the Assembly's purpose is to empower people to discern the things that make for peace, as individuals, within families, in and between nations, and to advocate for peace and justice, seeking the realization of God's will on earth as it is in heaven.

One World Week

PO Box 2555, Reading Berkshire, RG1 4XW UK; 0118-939-4933; http://gn.apc.org/oneworldweek

Focus: Economic Concerns; Human Rights **Mission:** Churches Together in Britain and Ireland offer resources for OWW; the week following the annual 'Week of Prayer for World Peace' each October. Concerned with globalization, poverty, economics, and third world debt, OWW seeks to build a movement of globally aware and active citizens who will make an impact on decision makers locally, nationally, and internationally.

Ontario Consultants on Religious Tolerance

PO Box 27026 Frontenac PO, Kingston, ON K7M 8W5 Canada; (613) 547-6600; Fax (613) 547-6600; http://www.religioustolerance.org

Focus: Communication; Ecumenical & Interfaith Cooperation

Mission: OCRT provides accurate information on a variety of religions, "hot" religious topics, and advocates religious tolerance. Its Web site, containing 850 essays, is the most-visited religious Web site on the Internet, receiving 1 million hits per week.

Ontario Multifaith Council on Spiritual & Religious Care

789 Don Mills Rd #608, Toronto, ON M3C 1T5 Canada; (416) 422-1490; Fax (416) 422-4359; http://www.omc.on.ca

Focus: Societies, Seminaries & Funds
Mission: The Council coordinates the ministry of religious care through chaplaincy services for a wide variety of faith groups in Ontario.

Open Hands Magazine

3801 N Keeler Ave, Chicago, IL 60641 USA; (773) 736-5526; Fax (773) 736-5475

Focus: Communication; Discrimination
Mission: A magazine designed for congregations and individuals seeking to be in ministry with lesbian, bisexual, and gay persons. *Open Hands* is sponsored by groups supporting sexual diversity in the UMC, Disciples, UCC, Lutheran, PCUSA, and ABC/USA .

Other Sheep

319 N 4th St, #902, St Louis, MO 63102 USA; (314) 241-2400; Fax (314) 241-2403; http://www.othersheep.org

Focus: Discrimination; Renewal of Faith Group
Mission: To spiritually enrich and empower gay, lesbian, bisexual, and transgender Christians and their families and friends, helping them reclaim scripture as their own, and whenever possible, to work for justice within their religious tradition.

Parallax Press

PO Box 7355, Berkeley, CA 94707 USA; (510) 525-0101; Fax (510) 525-7129; http://www.parallax.org

Focus: Communication
Mission: A project of the Community of Mindful Living, Parallax is dedicated to publishing books and tapes on socially engaged Buddhism. Parallax means "to change," a word of Western origin to help Western people realize that Buddhism is universal and can positively affect their lives—not just something to study in a museum or a textbook.

Park Ridge Center

211 E Ontario #800, Chicago, IL 60611 USA; (312) 266-2222; Fax (312) 266-6086; http://www.prchfe.org

Focus: Societies, Seminaries & Funds
Mission: To explore and enhance the interaction of health, faith, and ethics through research, education, and consultation to improve the lives of individuals and communities.

Passion Newsletter

6025 N Wolcott Ave #3W, Chicago, IL 60660-2371 USA; (773) 743-1288

Focus: Communication; Discrimination
Mission: A monthly newsletter reflecting on Christian spirituality from a gay perspective, *Passion* offers meditations on scripture; muses on everyday life; reviews books, tapes, and music, and always includes original prayer and reflection questions.

Pastors for Peace

PO Box 408130, Chicago, IL 60640-8130 USA; (773) 271-4817; Fax (773) 271-5269; http://www.ifconews.org

Focus: Human Rights
Mission: As an international network of church and solidarity organizations, PFP sponsors humanitarian aid shipments, study tours, construction brigades, and educational events in Mexico, Central America, and the Caribbean.

Pax Christi USA

532 W 8th St, Erie, PA 16502-1343 USA; (814) 453-4955; Fax (814) 452-4784; http://www.nonviolence.org/pcusa

Focus: Peace & Nonviolence; Training & Resources
Mission: PCUSA works for a more peaceful, just, and sustainable world and promotes the gospel imperative of peacemaking as a priority in the US Catholic Churches. Its members include 550 religious communities, 200 parishes, 140 bishops, and more than 500 local groups coordinated in 18 geographic areas.

Pax World Service

1111 16th St NW #120, Washington, DC 20036 USA; (202) 293-7290; Fax (202) 293-7023; http://www.paxworld.org

Focus: Human Rights
Mission: PWS works for a more just and equitable world by initiating and supporting innovative programs that encourage peacemaking, citizen diplomacy, and sustainable development. PWS cosponsors aid and education tours to Guatemala, Cuba, North Korea, and other countries.

Peace & Freedom Magazine

1213 Race St, Philadelphia, PA 19107 USA; (215) 563-7110; Fax (215) 563-5527; http://www.wilpf.org

Focus: Communication; Peace & Nonviolence
Mission: Published by WILPF-US, its mission is to unite women worldwide who oppose oppression and exploitation. WILPF stands for equality of all people in a world free of racism, sexism, and homophobia, the building of a constructive peace through world disarmament, and the changing of government priorities to meet human needs.

Peace & Justice Resource Center

1710 11th Ave, Seattle, WA 98122-2420 USA; (206) 720-0313; Fax call first; http://www.nonviolence.org/pjrc

Focus: Training & Resources
Mission: The PJRC aids activists by maintaining a large peace and justice reference library with bibliographies, policy analysis, resource guides, presentations and workshop outlines, and a book service with 1,200 recommended titles.

Peace Action

1819 H St NW #420, Washington, DC 20006 USA; (202) 862-9740; Fax (202) 862-9762; http://www.webcom.com/peaceact

Focus: Global Peace & Security; Peace & Nonviolence
Mission: To educate and organize an interfaith citizens' movement with the sustained political power to reverse the arms race, abolish nuclear weapons, and construct a world of peace and justice. An annual voting record for each member of Congress is published.

Peace Brigades International

5 Caledonian Rd, London, N1 9DX, UK; 44-020-7713-0392; Fax 44-020-7837-2290; http://www.igc.org/pbi

Focus: Human Rights
Mission: To send trained volunteer teams to areas of political repression and conflict. PBI offers international accompaniment to threatened human rights defenders and training in nonviolent conflict transformation. 14 affiliate offices.

Peace Resource Center

Pyle Center Box 1183, Wilmington, OH 45177 USA; (937) 382-6661 Ext. 275; Fax (937) 382-7077; http://www.wilmington.edu

Focus: Peace & Nonviolence; Training & Resources
Mission: To insure that the tragedy of Hiroshima and Nagasaki is never repeated, PRC provides peace education resources to schools, churches, peace groups, and individual researchers.

Peace with Justice Week

435 First St, Henderson, KY 42420 USA; (270) 826-0281; paffhaus@paffhaus.net

Focus: General Peace & Justice
Mission: PJW sponsors an annual national gathering of peace and justice activists. Exhibits, concerts, workshops, discussions, worship celebrations, and informal strategy sessions are offered to renew strength for continued striving for social change.

Peaceday Organization

PO Box 565245, Miami, FL 33256 USA; (305) 270-8890; Fax call first; http://www.peaceday.org

Focus: Communication; Peace & Nonviolence
Mission: To educate the general public about alternative conflict resolution and to promote peace with the environment, with each other, and within ourselves. Peaceday provides an online networking site.

Peacework Magazine—AFSC

2161 Massachusetts Ave, Cambridge, MA 02140 USA; (617) 661-6130; Fax (617) 354-2832; http://www.afsc.org/peacewrk

Focus: Communication; Economic Concerns
Mission: *Peacework*, published since 1972, is intended to serve the movements for nonviolent social change by covering social justice and peace issues in a way that links grassroots work with national and international perspectives.

People of Faith Network

85 S Oxford St, Brooklyn, NY 11217 USA; (718) 625-2819; Fax (718) 625-3491; http://www.cloud9.net/~pofn

Focus: Economic Concerns; Religious & Civil Liberty
Mission: A multi-faith coalition, POFN unites congregations, clergy, and activists in campaigns which challenge the growing inequality and mean-spiritedness that are linked to changes wrought by economic globalization. The Network opposes the expansion of apparel sweatshops, public hospital closures, and the influence of the religious right.

Periodica Islamica

22 Jalan Liku, Kuala Lumpur, 59100 Malaysia; [+60-3] 282-5286; Fax [+60-3] 282-1605; http://www.ummah.org.uk/dranees/periodica

Focus: Communication
Mission: *Periodica Islamica*, a quarterly, has gained worldwide recognition as the premiere source of reference for all multidisciplinary discourses on the world of Islam.

Perspectives, a Journal of Reformed Thought

PO Box 470, Ada, MI 49301 USA; (616) 241-2053; Fax (616) 241-2064; boogaart@macatawa.org

Focus: Communication; General Peace & Justice
Mission: *Perspectives'* purpose is to use reformed theology to engage the issues that Christians meet in personal, church, and societal life in ways that contribute to the mission of the Church of Jesus Christ.

Plough Magazine

Spring Valley Bruderhof, Farmington, PA 15437-9506 USA; (800) 521-8011; Fax (724) 329-0914; http://www.plough.com

Focus: Communication
Mission: Knowing faith without deeds is fruitless, the *Plough* is dedicated to all who strive for both, by challenging the assumptions of institutional Christendom, encouraging self-examination, discussion, and nonviolent action. Published by the Bruderhof Communities.

PLURA Fund

3250 Bloor St W, Toronto, ON M8X 2Y4 Canada; (416) 231-7680 Ext. 5046; Fax (416) 232-6005;

Focus: Societies, Seminaries & Funds
Mission: PLURA (Presbyterian, Lutheran, United, Roman Catholic, and Anglican) is a funding program that provides seed money to low-income, self-help groups to attack the root causes of poverty in local Canadian communities.

Pluralism Project

25 Francis Ave,201 Vansberg Hall, Cambridge, MA 02138 USA; (617) 496-2481; Fax (617) 496-2428; http://www.pluralism.org

Focus: Societies, Seminaries & Funds
Mission: PP studies and documents the growing religious diversity in the US with three goals: 1) to document changes taking place by mapping the new religious demography, 2) to study how religious traditions are changing in their new context, and 3) to explore how the US is changing by appropriating the new religious diversity. Harvard University.

Preamble Center

1737 21st St NW, Washington, DC 20009 USA; (202) 265-3263; Fax (202) 234-0981; http://www.preamble.org

Focus: Societies, Seminaries & Funds
Mission: Dedicated to research, education, and advocacy on global economic issues to raise awareness and promote realistic alternatives, the Center works cooperatively with a variety of religious, labor, environmental, student, consumer, and public interest groups in the US and internationally.

Presbyterian Church in Canada

50 Wynford Dr, Toronto, ON M3C 1J7 Canada; http://www.presbyterian.ca

Justice Ministries

(416) 441-1111 Ext. 250; Fax (416) 441-2825;
Focus: General Peace & Justice
Mission: Justice Ministries assist PC/CN members to respond faithfully to the gospel on matters of peace, social justice, and ecology.

World Service and Development

(416) 441-1111 Ext. 245; Fax (416) 441-2825;
Focus: Human Rights
Mission: WSD promotes activities worldwide that restore human dignity, ease the pain of want, promote self-help and development, and encourage community cooperation. Within Canada it works to sensitize and connect Presbyterians to the needs of others.

Presbyterian Church USA

100 Witherspoon St, Louisville, KY 40202 USA; http://www.pcusa.org

Criminal Justice Office

(502) 569-5803; Fax (502) 569-8116 Carol_Davies@pcusa.org
Focus: Criminal Justice System; Training & Resources
Mission: To involve Presbyterians and other people of faith in service or advocacy work with the US criminal justice system, PC/USA CJO publishes a newsletter and study/action resources on restorative justice, death penalty, gun control, victims rights, and other subjects.

Ending Homelessness of Women

6527 200th St SW #104, Lynnwood, WA 98036 USA; (425) 712-1677; Fax (425) 673-0265; http://www.pcusa.org/women
Focus: Human Rights; Women
Mission: To promote understanding of the reality, root causes, and biblical directives relating to homelessness and to provide resources and suggest appropriate responses from church, government, and ecumenical groups. EHW suggests that "Every Church Open One Room in 77 Ways."

Health, Education & Welfare Association

(502) 569-5794; Fax (502) 569-8034;
Focus: Human Rights
Mission: To make the people of the PC/USA more responsive to the needs of the excluded and suffering and to provide resources and support for those involved in social justice and welfare ministries.

Hunger Program

(502) 569-5816; Fax (502) 569-8963; http://www.pcusa.org/hunger
Focus: Human Rights; Women
Mission: To aid communities, churches, and organizations in alleviating hunger and eliminating its causes, using direct aid, development assistance, education, and advocacy.

Peacemaking Program

(800) 338-4987; Fax (800) 392-5788; http://www.horeb.pcusa.org/peacemaking
Focus: Economic Concerns; Peace & Nonviolence
Mission: To gather, educate, and motivate people of faith to engage in God's peacemaking activities in all arenas of life. An annual peacemaking conference offers a myriad of experiences and resources.

Presbyterian Women

(502) 569-5365; http://www.pcusa.org/women
Focus: General Peace & Justice; Women
Mission: PW is committed to support the mission of the church worldwide, to work for justice and peace, and to build an inclusive, caring community of women that strengthens the PC/USA and witnesses to the promise of God's kingdom.

United Nations Office

777 UN Plaza, New York, NY 10017 USA; (212) 697-4568; Fax (212) 986-3002
Focus: Global Peace & Security
Mission: This office supports the UN in its search for a just peace, based on social and economic equality, sustain-

able development, and acceptance of our common humanity. It represent PC/USA at the UN and presents the UN to PC/USA members and departments.

Washington Office

110 Maryland Ave NE, Washington, DC 20002 USA; (202) 543-1126; Fax (202) 543-7755;
Focus: Advocacy; General Peace & Justice
Mission: To equip members to advocate the social witness perspectives of the PC/USA General Assembly in national and state governments by publishing regular updates on civil rights and religious liberties, ecology and environment, global security, health care, hunger and human needs, Latin America, women, and families.

Women's Advocacy Office

(502) 569-5361; http://www.pcusa/women
Focus: Renewal of Faith Group; Women
Mission: To engage in ministries of justice and quality of life on behalf of women, to envision and advocate for a church in which women are full partners, and to promote the theological and liturgical contributions of women.

Presbyterian Peace Fellowship

PO Box 271, Nyack, NY 10960 USA; (914) 358-4601; Fax (914) 358-4924
Focus: Peace & Nonviolence **Mission:** The PPF holds that faith in Jesus Christ calls all the faithful to seek justice, reconciliation, and peace through works of love, and to reject war and violence.

Presbyterians for Restoring Creation

PO Box 2146, Boone, NC 28607 USA; (828) 262-3881; Fax same (call first); bill_knox@pcusa.org
Focus: Ecology & Environment
Mission: A grassroots fellowship of Presbyterians who care about restoring the earth for future generations, PRC works with ecumenical and community groups that also care for the earth.

Primate's World Relief & Development Fund

600 Jarvis St, Toronto, ON M4Y 2J6 Canada; (416) 924-9192; Fax (416) 924-3483; http://www.pwrdf.org

Focus: Societies, Seminaries & Funds
Mission: Through PWRDF, Canadian Anglicans bear witness to God's healing love in a broken world, by supporting others who do development work, responding to emergencies, working to protect refugees, and educating and advocating for change.

Prism Magazine

10 E Lancaster Ave, Wynnewood, PA 19096 USA; (610) 645-9397; Fax (610) 649-8090; http://www.esa-online.org

Focus: Communication
Mission: *Prism*, a bimonthly magazine, seeks to challenge and inform Christians as they strive to integrate the biblical call to spiritual formation, evangelism, and social change.

Prison Fellowship

PO Box 17500, Washington DC, 20041-0500 USA; (703) 478-0100; http://www.prisonfellowship.org

Focus: Criminal Justice System
Mission: Founded in 1976 by Charles Colson shortly after his release from prison with proceeds from his autobiography *Born Again*, PR recruits, trains, and mobilizes volunteers to participate in a broad array of Christian ministries to prisoners, ex-prisoners, victims, and their families. PR promotes biblical standards of justice in the criminal justice system.

Prisoner Visitation & Support

1501 Cherry St, Philadelphia, PA 19102 USA; (215) 241-7117; Fax (215) 241-7227

Focus: Criminal Justice System
Mission: PVS is the only nationwide, interfaith program authorized by the Federal Bureau of Prisons and the Dept. of Defense to visit any prisoner in the federal and military prison systems (not state prisons). More than 260 volunteers visit 75 federal & military prisons across the US.

Progressive National Baptist Convention

601 50th St NE, Washington, DC 20019 USA; (202) 396-0558; Fax (202) 398-4998; http://www.pnbc.org

Focus: Discrimination
Mission: The home and platform of the late Rev Dr Martin Luther King, Jr,

PNBC continues to give voice, leadership, and active support to the struggle for civil and human rights. New generations work for full voter registration, affirmative action against all forms of racism and bigotry, black economic empowerment, and equal educational opportunity.

Project Equality, Inc

7132 Main St, Kansas City, MO 64114-1406 USA; (816) 361-9222; Fax (816) 361-8997; http://www.projectequality.org

Focus: Discrimination
Mission: PE, a national program sponsored by religious, civic, and business groups has two goals: to assist employers to achieve equal employment opportunities for all people and to validate the EEO commitment and patterns of vendors, suppliers, travel providers, and meeting sites for use by the religious and nonprofit communities.

Project Ploughshares

Conrad Grebel College-Inst/Peace & Conflict Study, Waterloo, ON N2L 3G6 Canada; (519) 888-6541; Fax (519) 885-0806; http://www.ploughshares.ca

Focus: Global Peace & Security; Peace & Nonviolence
Mission: PP researches, educates, promotes, and advocates for disarmament and demilitarization, the peaceful resolution of political conflict and the pursuit of security based on equity, justice, and a sustainable environment.

Promoting Enduring Peace, Inc

866 United Nations Plaza #4043, New York, NY 10017 USA; (212) 223-7520; Fax (212) 223-7520; enduringpeace@msn.com

Focus: Global Peace & Security
Mission: A religious and educational organization consisting of faith and secular groups participating in the UN Association of the USA.

Protestants for the Common Good

200 N Michigan Ave #502, Chicago, IL 60601 USA; (312) 223-9544; Fax (312) 726-0425; http://www.protcomgood.org

Focus: General Peace & Justice
Mission: To mobilize people of faith for the common good. Holding that

Christians are called to witness in the political arena, PCG provides resources enabling Christians to relate their faith to current public policies, and urges political action that fosters a community of inclusion, equality, and love.

Quaker United Nations Office

777 UN Plaza, New York, NY 10017 USA; (212) 682-2745; Fax (212) 983-0034; http://www.quno.org

Focus: Advocacy; General Peace & Justice
Mission: QUNO monitors and reports on peace and social justice issues at the United Nations, presents the views of Quaker and other faith organizations to the UN community, and facilitates informal meetings and other contacts in support of UN negotiations.

Quality of Life Group: Dharma Society

306 Joy St, Natchitoches, LA 71457 USA; (318) 354-0854; oep4@cp-tel.net

Focus: Peace & Nonviolence
Mission: QLG recognizes the common aspirations of all living beings as obtaining peace, rest, wholeness, freedom, equanimity, and happiness. It urges creation of universal communities and sanctuaries, and practices and commits to the absolute value of non-force, nonharming, nonaggression, and nonviolence.

Quixote Center

PO Box 5206, Hyattsville, MD 20782-0206 USA; (301) 699-0042; Fax (301) 864-2182; http://www.quixote.org

Catholics Speak Out

http://www.quixote.org/cso;
Focus: Renewal of Faith Group; Women
Mission: Encouraging Catholics to accept responsibility for the life of the church by speaking out on issues of concern, CSO advocates basic justice within the church: women's ordination, married clergy, democratic governance, gay/lesbian rights, change in teaching on contraception, an end to silencing theologians, and an open dialogue on sexual/reproductive issues.

Equal Justice USA

http://www.quixote.org/ej
Focus: Criminal Justice System

Mission: EJ-USA is a grassroots campaign for human rights in the US legal system. Through education and mobilization, the project seeks to expand public opposition to the death penalty and bring into clear focus the racial, economic and political biases active in US courts, prisons, jails, and policing agencies.

Faith Matters, Weekly Broadcast

http://www.quixote.org/cso
Focus: Communication
Mission: Providing insights into religious issues that shape our culture, FM is built on the ideals of dialogue and religious tolerance. Diverse viewpoints are presented on controversial topics, believing that the difficult issues of our time need the wisdom of many voices. Call-ins are welcomed.

Haiti Reborn

http://www.quixote.org/haiti
Focus: Human Rights
Mission: Haiti Reborn is a Catholic social concerns group supporting Haitian literacy, democracy, and grassroots organization.

Priests for Equality

http://www.quixote.org/pfe
Focus: Communication; Renewal of Faith Group; Training & Resources
Mission: An international movement of lay, religious, and clergy seeking full participation of women and men in church and society, PFE challenges sexism and offers an alternative vision that frees and empowers. PFE publishes newly translated "Inclusive Scripture."

Rabbinical Council of America

305 7th Ave, New York, NY 10001-6008 USA; (212) 807-7888; Fax (212) 727-8452; http://www.rabbis.org

Focus: Societies, Seminaries & Funds
Mission: A dynamic professional organization serving 980 Orthodox Rabbis in the US, Canada, Israel, and throughout the world. RCC serves as a spokesman for Orthodoxy on the national and international level, sponsors conferences, disseminates information on timely issues, and defends the interests of the religious Jewish community.

Radio Free Maine

PO Box 2705, Augusta, ME 04338 USA; (207) 622-6629; Fax (207) 622-6629; http://www.radiofreemaine.com

Focus: Communication; General Peace & Justice
Mission: RFM, an independent news agency, provides the peace & justice witness of distinguished people of faith (professors, writers, activists, experts in their fields) not heard on mainstream religious programming. Noted individuals are available on audiotape and VHS videotape.

Rainbow/Push Coalition

930 E 50th St, Chicago, IL 60615 USA; (773) 373-3366 Ext. 247; Fax (773) 373-3571; http://www.rainbowpush.org

Focus: Discrimination; Economic Concerns
Mission: R/PC is a membership organization working toward social, racial, and economic justice by uniting people of diverse ethnic, religious, economic, and political backgrounds to make America's promise of "Liberty and Justice for All" a reality. 40 US chapters.

Ramakrishna-Vivekananda Center—NY

17 E 94th St, New York, NY 10128 USA; (212) 534-9445; Fax (212) 828-1618; http://www.ramakrishna.org

Focus: Ecumenical & Interfaith Cooperation
Mission: The Center, basing its teachings on the Vedanta (Hindu religion and philosophy) teaches that every soul is potentially divine, promotes worship, meditation, unselfish work and philosophical discrimination. It teaches that Truth is universal and that every faith is a valid means for its own followers to realize the Truth.

Random Acts of Kindness Foundation

2530 10th St #6, Berkeley, CA 94710 USA; (800) 660-2811; Fax (510) 845-2142; rakday@aol.com

Focus: Peace & Nonviolence; Training & Resources
Mission: To reverse the tide of anger and violence in today's society through the practice of simple day-to-day kindness shown to fellow humans. RAKF

creates and distributes materials, trains volunteer community coordinators, and counsels individuals and groups to help them design impactful, ongoing, and annual "Random Acts of Kindness" activities.

Religion and Ethics TV Newsweekly

PO Box 245, Little Falls, NJ 07424-0245 USA; (888) 165-7537; Fax (212) 560-6948; http://www.thirteen.org/religion/home.html

Focus: Communication
Mission: Produced by 13/WNET-NY, *R&E Newsweekly* is a $^1/_2$-hour PBS program that goes behind the headlines for a deeper understanding of the religious and ethical challenges facing people of faith. The most-watched PBS public affairs program in nonprimetime, it is aired by 200 PBS stations nationwide and reaches 500,000 listeners weekly.

Religion and Public Education Resource Center

California State University, Chico, Chico, CA 95929 USA; (530) 898-4739; Fax (530) 898-5468; http://www.csuchico.edu/rs/reperc.html

Focus: Religious & Civil Liberty; Training & Resources
Mission: To promote the distinction between school-sponsored practice of religion and the academic study of religion, RPERC provides resources for teaching about religions in public schools in ways that are constitutionally permissible and academically sound.

Religion in American Life, Inc—Invite a Friend Program

2 Queenston PL #200, Princeton, NJ 08540 USA; (609) 921-3639; Fax (609) 921-0551; http://www.rial.org

Focus: Communication; Ecumenical & Interfaith Cooperation
Mission: IAFP is a "user-friendly" program for congregations seeking to enlarge their membership and ministry. As a multifaith program, free public service advertising is available to congregations.

Religious Action Center of Reform Judaism

2027 Massachusetts Ave NW, Washington, DC 20036 USA; (202) 387-2800; Fax (202) 667-9070; http://www.rj.org/rac

Focus: Advocacy; General Peace & Justice; Women
Mission: RAC educates and mobilizes the American Jewish community on legislative and social concerns, serving as an advocate in Congress on issues ranging from Israel, economic justice, and civil rights, to international peace and religious liberty.

Religious Coalition for Reproductive Choice

1025 Vermont Ave NW # 1130, Washington, DC 20005 USA; (202) 628-7700; Fax (202) 628-7716; http://www.rcrc.org

Focus: Advocacy; Religious & Civil Liberty
Mission: Serving as the voice of pro-choice people of faith, RCRC has worked since 1973 to ensure reproductive choice through the moral power of religious communities.

Religious Consultation on Population, Reproductive Health & Ethics

2717 E Hampshire St, Milwaukee, WI 53211 USA; (414) 962-3166; Fax (414) 962-9248; http://www.consultation.org/consultation

Focus: Religious & Civil Liberty; Societies, Seminaries & Funds
Mission: An international network of progressive religious scholars and leaders who bring the moral energies of their faith traditions to the interrelated issues of population, reproductive health, and the empowerment of women, RCPRHE participates in forums, convenes symposia of theologians and religious ethicists, and publishes both scholarly and popular materials.

Religious Education Association

http://rea.home.mindspring.com/rea.htm

Focus: Societies, Seminaries & Funds
Mission: To provide discussion of research and its implications, support for professional development, and to explore appropriate relationships between religion and education, espe-

cially government-sponsored religious education.

Religious Organizing Against the Death Penalty

1501 Cherry St, Philadelphia, PA 19102 USA; (215) 241-7130; Fax (215) 241-7119; pclark@afsc.org

Focus: Criminal Justice System
Mission: A national effort enabling people of faith to become effective advocates for the abolition of capital punishment, ROADP helps religious groups organize, provides religiously based anti-death penalty materials, and plans educational and activist events throughout the US.

Religious Working Group on World Bank & IMF

PO Box 29132, Washington, DC 20017 USA; (202) 832-1780; Fax (202) 832-5195; http://www.religiouswg.org

Focus: Economic Concerns
Mission: Forty groups, whose work is motivated by their faith traditions, insist that public policies be shaped and evaluated according to God's love and justice.

Resource Center for Nonviolence

515 Broadway, Santa Cruz, CA 95060 USA; (408) 423-1626; Fax (408) 423-8716; http://www.rcnv.org

Focus: Peace & Nonviolence; Training & Resources
Mission: RCN teaches nonviolence as a dynamic means of affecting personal change and creating a just, peaceful, and sustainable world, providing resources, leadership development, and individual and group empowerment training.

Resources for Christian Living—Vatican II

200 E Bethany Dr, Allen, TX 75002 USA; (888) 275-4725; Fax (800) 611-0230

Focus: Renewal of Faith Group; Training & Resources
Mission: RCL provides a documentary and other print and multimedia resources that support the spirit and vision of Vatican II.

Risho Kosei-kai

2-11-1 Wada Suginami-ku, Tokyo, 166
Japan; (03) 3380-5185; Fax (03)
3381-9792; http://www.kosei-kai.or.jp

Focus: Ecumenical & Interfaith
Cooperation
Mission: RK is a large international lay
Buddhist organization, which encourages social engagement and interfaith
outreach through regional and international interfaith organizations. RK publishes *Dharma World* magazine.

Rivier College Center for Peace & Social Justice

420 Main St, Nashua, NH 03060
USA; (603) 888-1311 Ext. 8250; Fax
(603) 897-0154; http://www.rivier.edu

Focus: Societies, Seminaries & Funds
Mission: Rivier College offers a Catholic
liberal education for social justice.

Sakyadhita: International Assn of Buddhist Women

1143 Piikoi Pl, Honolulu, HI 96822
USA; (808) 944-6294; Fax (808) 944-
7070; http://www2.hawaii.edu/
~tsomo

Focus: Peace & Nonviolence; Societies,
Seminaries & Funds
Mission: To promote world peace
through Buddha's teachings, to create a
communication network for Buddhist
women, to promote harmony and
understanding among various Buddhist
traditions, and to encourage and educate women as teachers of
Buddhadharma.

Salt of the Earth

205 W Monroe St, Chicago, IL 60606
USA; (312) 236-7782;
Fax (312) 236-8207;
http://www.salt.claretianpubs.org

Focus: Communication; General Peace
& Justice;
Mission: To serve as an electronic
resource for Catholic social justice
teaching, covering the peace and justice issues of our times and providing
online support for parish social ministry.

SBC Ethics & Religious Liberty Commission

901 Commerce St #750, Nashville, TN
37203 USA; (615) 244-2495; Fax
(615) 242-0065; http://www.erlc.com

Focus: General Peace & Justice
Mission: ERLC assists SBC churches in
understanding the moral demands of
the gospel, applying those principles to
moral and social problems and public
policy, and in promoting religious liberty.

Scarboro Missions—Justice & Peace Office

2685 Kingston Rd, Scarborough, ON
M1M 1M4 Canada; (416) 261-7135
X226; Fax (416) 261-0820;
http://www.web.net/~sfms

Focus: Ecumenical & Interfaith
Cooperation; General Peace & Justice
Mission: SM is a Catholic missionary
community whose mission is one of
Crossing Cultures (linking, sharing
experiences), Weaving Justice (working
for justice, peace, and the integrity of
creation), and Bridging Faiths (dialoguing and learning from those of other
faiths).

School of Metaphysics

HCR 1, Box 15, Windyville, MO
65783 USA; (417) 345-8411; Fax
(417) 345-6668; http://www.som.org

Focus: Societies, Seminaries & Funds;
Mission: To promote peace, understanding, and goodwill among all people by
aiding individuals to become spiritually
enlightened.

School of the Americas Watch

PO Box 4566, Washington, DC 20017
USA; (202) 234-3440; Fax (202) 636-
4505; http://www.soaw.org

Focus: Advocacy; Peace & Nonviolence
Mission: To educate legislators and the
public to the negative impact of the
School of the Americas at Fort Benning,
GA. Its activities and graduates, responsible for some of the most horrendous
atrocities in Latin America, are monitored with the goal of forcing its closure.

School Sisters of Notre Dame— Shalom Center

320 E Ripa Ave, St Louis, MO 63125
USA; (314) 544-0455; Fax (314) 544-
6754; genroca@aol.com

Focus: Ecology & Environment; Human
Rights
Mission: To take action leading to reconciliation, solidarity with the
oppressed, the promotion of human dig-

nity, and collaboration with ecological
movements to safeguard the earth.

Schools for Chiapas

1717 Kettner Blvd #125, San Diego,
CA 92101 USA;
(619) 232-2841; Fax (619) 232-0500;
http://www.mexicopeace.org

Focus: Peace & Nonviolence; Training
& Resources
Mission: SFC supports indigenous education and a peaceful resolution to the
war in Chiapas, working through a
monthly e-mail magazine, speakers,
books, and videos, as well as regular
trips to southern Mexico.

Science of Spirituality

Kirpal Ashram Vijay Nagar, Delhi, 110-
009 India; 91-11-7222244;
http://skrm.sos.org

Focus: Ecumenical & Interfaith
Cooperation
Mission: Sawan Kirpal Ruhani Mission's
SOS provides a forum for people to
learn meditation, experience personal
transformation, and bring about inner
and outer peace. It has 1,200 centers
worldwide with western headquarters in
Naperville, IL USA—www.sps.org.
SKRM sponsors major events on spirituality, human unity, and religious fellowship and engages in
national/international interfaith conferences.

Seamless Garment Network, Inc—USA

PO Box 792, Garner, NC 27529 USA;
(716) 442-8497; Fax (716) 442-8497
http://www.seamless-garment.org

Focus: Peace & Nonviolence
Mission: With more than 100 faith
groups committed to the protection of
life, threatened in today's world by war,
abortion, poverty, racism, the arms
race, and the death penalty, SGN holds
these issues are linked under a consistent ethic of life. It challenges those
opposed to any/all of these issues to
maintain a cooperative spirit of peace
and respect.

Search for Common Ground

1601 Connecticut Ave NW #200,
Washington, DC 20009 USA; (202)
265-4300; Fax (202) 232-6718;
http://www.searchforcommonground.org

Focus: Peace & Nonviolence; Training & Resources
Mission: With a vision of transforming how the world deals with conflict, away from adversarial approaches and toward cooperative solutions, SFCG sponsors programs that teach conflict resolution and violence prevention.

SeedHouse

451 Flemridge Ct, Cincinnati, OH 45231-4050 USA; (513) 729-3317; http://www.members.tripod.com/ ~SEEDHOUSE/index.html

Focus: General Peace & Justice
Mission: To facilitate meaningful dialogue and action leading to reconciliation across religious and ethnic boundaries, SH promotes the ideals of biblical justice and compassion in a multitude of venues through conferences, Internet, lectures, and publications.

Seeds of Hope Publisher

602 James, Waco, TX 76706 USA; (254) 755-7745; Fax (254) 753-1909 http://www.seedspublishers.org

Focus: Human Rights; Training & Resources
Mission: Acting on the strong belief that biblical mandates to feed the poor are not optional, SHP affirms, enables, and empowers a variety of responses to the problems of poverty by producing helpful ecumenical resources and periodicals.

Seminary Consortium for Urban Pastoral Education

200 N Michigan Ave #502, Chicago, IL 60601-5909 USA; (312) 726-1200; Fax (312) 726-0425; http://www.scupe.com

Focus: Societies, Seminaries & Funds
Mission: SCUPE develops leaders and provides consultation and educational resources for individuals, educational institutions, churches, and agencies that seek to enhance the spiritual, social, and physical quality of life for those who live in the city.

Sequoia—Interreligious Newsmagazine

1280 Laguna St #10J, San Francisco, CA 94115-4275 USA; (415) 885-6202; Fax (415) 885-6202; rforsberg@aol.com

Focus: Communication; Peace & Nonviolence
Mission: News of religion and society with an emphasis on peacemaking.

SERRV International

500 Main St, Box 365, New Windsor, MD 21776-0365 USA; (800) 723-3712; Fax (410) 635-8774; http://www.serrv.org

Focus: Human Rights; Training & Resources
Mission: SERRV gathers handcrafts made by artisans in 32 developing countries to be sold in more than 3,000 US churches and communities. Thus, workers in developing countries are provided a fair return for their work. A catalog is available.

Sikh Dharma International

RR2 Box 4 Shady Ln, Espanola, NM 87532 USA; (505) 753-5881; Fax (505) 753-5982; http://www.sikhnet.com

Focus: Ecumenical & Interfaith Cooperation; Peace & Nonviolence
Mission: Based on the belief in One Creator of all humanity, SDI reaches out to people of all faiths/cultures, encouraging all to see beyond their differences and to work together for world peace and harmony. The youngest of the world religions, Sikh Dharma offers a unique blend of Eastern and Western wisdom and techniques.

Simon Wiesenthal Center

9760 W Pico Blvd, Los Angeles, CA 90035 USA; (310) 553-9036; Fax (310) 553-4521; http://www.wiesenthal.com

Focus: Discrimination; Peace & Nonviolence
Mission: A center for Holocaust remembrance, for the defense of human rights and the Jewish people, the mission of SWC is to recount the story of the most monumental example of man's inhumanity to man, the Holocaust, and to explore racism and prejudice in the American experience.

Sisters of Charity BVM—Women's Office

1337 W Ohio St, Chicago, IL 60622-6490 USA; (312) 226-7585; Fax (312) 829-8915; rmmeyerwom@aol.com

Focus: Women
Mission: Commitment to systems change through analysis, advocacy, consciousness-raising, education, networking, organizing, and resourcing with regard to women's issues.

Sisters of Mercy of the Americas—Center for Justice & Peace

703 Lexington Ave, Brooklyn, NY 11221 USA; (718) 452-3136; Fax (718) 452-3945; http://www.sistersofmercy.org

Focus: Human Rights
Mission: As a community of Catholic women vowed to serve people who suffer from poverty, sickness, and ignorance, with a special concern for women and children, SMA address human needs through collaborative efforts in education, health care, housing, pastoral, and social services in 25 regional communities.

Sisters of St Joseph of Carondelet

6400 Minnesota, St Louis, MO 63111 USA; (314) 481-8800; Fax (314) 481-2366; http://www.csjsl.org

Focus: General Peace & Justice
Mission: SSJC seek to form loving relationships with ourselves, with God, and with community, church, and society, working toward this mission through ministries of prayer, direct service, consciousness raising, and systemic change.

Sisters Online

5024 Beard Ave S, Minneapolis, MN 55410 USA; (612) 925-0087; http://www.sistersonline.org

Focus: Communication; General Peace & Justice
Mission: Twelve communities of women religious partnered with the growing global movement of women working to create a new social order, Sisters Online offers a Web site for communication, encouragement, and communication.

Snow Lion Publications

PO Box 6483, Ithaca, NY 14851-6483 USA; (800) 950-0313; Fax (607) 273-8508; http://www.snowlionpub.com

Focus: Communication
Mission: Publishing scholarly and trade

books on Tibet, Tibetan culture, Tibetan Buddhism, and His Holiness the Dalai Lama, Snow Lion has become a major force in bringing Tibetan culture and Buddhism to the West.

SocialAction.com—a Web Magazine

56 Kearney Road #B, Needham, MA 02494 USA; (781) 449-9894; Fax (781) 449-9825; http://www.SocialAction.com

Focus: Communication; General Peace & Justice
Mission: Published by Jewish Family & Life, *SocialAction.com* makes helpful resources available to all those working for social justice.

Society for Buddhist-Christian Studies

651 College Ave, Valparaiso U, IN 46383 USA; (219) 464-5515; Fax (219) 464-6714; http://www.cssr.org

Focus: Societies, Seminaries & Funds
Mission: To support comparative study of, and practical interaction between, Buddhism and Christianity, and seek balance with regard to geography, ethnicity, age, sex, denomination or lineage, tradition, and leadership.

Society for Humanistic Judaism

28611 W Twelve Mile Rd, Farmington Hills, MI 48334 USA; (248) 478-7610; Fax (248) 478-3159; http://www.shj.org

Focus: Societies, Seminaries & Funds
Mission: To mobilize individuals to celebrate Jewish identity consistent with a humanistic philosophy of life and to endorse and promote freedom and dignity for all human beings, SHJ organizes Humanistic Jewish congregations, trains rabbis and leaders, and develops resources.

Sojourners Magazine

2401 15th St NW, Washington, DC 20009 USA; (800) 714-7474; Fax (202) 328-8757; http://www.sojourners.com

Focus: Communication; Human Rights
Mission: To proclaim and practice the biblical call to integrate spiritual renewal and social justice, *Sojourners* publishes a bimonthly magazine, supports the DC Sojourners Neighborhood

Center; organizes, teaches, preaches, and advocates.

Soka Gakkai International-USA

606 Wilshire Blvd, Santa Monica, CA 90401 USA; (310) 260-8900; Fax (310) 260-8917; http://www.sgi-usa.org

Focus: Peace & Nonviolence
Mission: A Buddhist organization, SGI's mission is to contribute to peace, culture, and education based on the philosophy of the Buddhism of Nichiren for the development of a humane and peaceful society. "Soka" means value creation, "Gakkai" means society.

Southern Christian Leadership Conference

334 Auburn Ave NE, Atlanta, GA 30312 USA; (404) 522-1420; Fax (404) 527-4333

Focus: Human Rights
Mission: Founded by the late Martin Luther King, Jr, to give moral and spiritual leadership to those involved in the struggle against racial oppression, the Conference now works through education and social work with the poor.

Special Ideas

2900 W Bristol Dr, Bloomington, IN 47404 USA; (800) 326-1197; http://www.special-ideas.com

Focus: Training & Resources
Mission: SI publishes and distributes material for the Bahá'í faith. Some are of a generic nature, thus enabling use by other faith and interfaith groups focusing on similarities in diverse faith groups. Golden Rule–type directives of each of the major faiths are used in postcards, greeting cards, and posters.

Spiritual Eldering Institute

7318 Germantown Ave, Philadelphia, PA 19119 USA; (215) 248-9308; Fax (215) 247-9703; http://www.spiritualeldering.org

Focus: Children, Youth & Family; Training & Resources
Mission: "From Age-ing to Sage-ing," elder retreats, workshops, and spiritual strategies are offered as tools for successful life completion as wise elders.

Spiritual Rx

Trinity Church, Wall St, New York, NY USA; (800) 551-1220; http://www.spiritualrx.com

Focus: Communication
Mission: Spiritual Rx.com is a database of 1,500 reviews of TV programs, feature films, and videos from a spiritual perspective. It allows search by author/director, title, or theme. Reviewers are Frederic & Mary Ann Brussat of Values & Visions Review Service.

St Louis Economic Conversion Project

438 N Skinker Blvd, St Louis, MO 63130 USA; (314) 726-6406; Fax (314) 862-8155; slecp@yahoo.com

Focus: Global Peace & Security
Mission: To provide education and action opportunities with the goal of reducing global, national, and local arms proliferation and the violence caused by weapons trade.

Stand for Children

1834 Connecticut Ave NW, Washington, DC 20009 USA; (800) 663-4032; Fax (202) 234-0217; http://www.stand.org

Focus: Children, Youth & Family
Mission: To raise awareness, change public policy, and offer service initiatives to improve children's lives. The SFC national office encourages and supports chapters with technical assistance, training, and resources.

Strategic Pastoral Action Network

PO Box 98, Rushville, NY 14544 USA; (716) 554-6644; Fax (716) 554-6644; http://www.spanweb.org

Focus: Human Rights; Peace & Nonviolence
Mission: SPAN, a human rights and social justice project, works in areas of struggle in nonviolent ways, using liberation theology and pedagogy of the oppressed.

Student Christian Movement of Canada

310 Danforth Ave, Toronto, ON M4K 1N6 Canada; (416) 463-4312; Fax (416) 466-6854; http://www.web.net/~scmcan

Focus: General Peace & Justice
Mission: SCM exists to manifest progressive social justice in a holistic and educated way through study, exploration of tradition, action, worship, and intentional community.

Summer Peacebuilding Institute

Eastern Mennonite University, Harrisonburg, VA 22802 USA; (540) 432-4490; Fax (540) 432-4449; http://www.emu.edu/ctp/ctp.htm

Focus: Training & Resources
Mission: SPI offers 8-day summer sessions titled "Religion and Conflict: Courses for Religious and Interreligious Peacebuilders."

Tara Meditation Center

1 S 171 Pine Ln, Lombard, IL 60148 USA; (630) 629-9181

Focus: Training & Resources
Mission: Recognizing that all humans have, in their present life, the capacity to reach Buddhahood with no prejudice to race, age, sex, gender, or religion, TMC teaches that the guru (teacher) comes in many forms. People of all faiths are welcomed to learn spiritual development through meditation, martial arts, and yoga.

Taskforce on Churches and Corporate Responsibility

129 St Clair Ave W, N6-N10, Toronto, ON M4V 1N5 Canada; (416) 923-1758; Fax (416) 927-7554; tccr@web.net

Focus: Economic Concerns
Mission: A coalition of major Canadian churches, TCCR has, since 1975, acted to assist its members in influencing Canadian-based corporations and financial institutions to practice socially and environmentally responsible policies.

Temple of Understanding

720 5th Ave, New York, NY 10019 USA; (212) 246-2746; Fax (212) 246-2340; http://www.templeofunderstanding.org

Focus: Ecumenical & Interfaith Cooperation
Mission: Committed to worldwide promotion of interfaith dialogue and education, TOU's purpose is to achieve understanding among the people of the world's religions and beyond.

Ten Days for Global Justice

947 Queen St E #201, Toronto, ON M4M 1J9 Canada; (416) 463-5312; Fax (416) 463-5569; http://www.web.net/~tendays

Focus: General Peace & Justice
Mission: An interchurch/interfaith network of groups working for global justice through education and action, TDGJ challenges dehumanizing and destructive forces and promotes alternative models of society that put people and creation first.

Texas Baptists Committed

PO Box 3330, San Angelo, TX 76902 USA; (915) 659-4102; Fax (915) 655-3603; http://www.Txbc.org

Focus: Religious & Civil Liberty; Renewal of Faith Group
Mission: Dedicated to upholding the historic Baptist principle of separation of church and state.

Thanks-Giving Square

Box 1770, Dallas, TX 75221-1770 USA; (214) 969-1977; Fax (214) 754-0152; http://www.thanksgiving.org

Focus: Ecumenical & Interfaith Cooperation
Mission: To be a place for all people to give thanks to God, to witness, to celebrate, and to promote the value and spirit of thanksgiving for both sacred and secular cultures throughout the world.

The Humanist Magazine

#7 Harwood Drive PO Box 1188, Amherst, NY 14226 USA; (800) 743-6646; Fax (716) 839-5080; http://www.humanist.net

Focus: Communication; Religious & Civil Liberty
Mission: A bimonthly magazine of critical inquiry and social concern published by the American Humanist Association.

The Mastery Foundation

1 Charlton Ct #104, San Francisco, CA 94123 USA; (415) 885-8540; Fax (415) 474-6128; http://www.masteryfoundation.org

Focus: Training & Resources
Mission: TMF is an interfaith lay/clergy group committed to further empower those who minister by offering a four-day course designed to bring a fundamental shifting of thought in what is possible in ministry.

The Other Economic Summit

Holding Green #206E, Cambridge, MA 02138 USA; THWilliamson@igc.apc.org

Focus: Economic Concerns
Mission: An international forum for discussion and advocacy for ideas and practices upon which a more just and sustainable society can be built, TOES's major activity is a forum held in conjunction with the annual G-8 meeting of the world's leading industrial countries.

The Other Side Magazine

300 W Apsley St, Philadelphia, PA 19144 USA; (800) 700-9280; Fax (215) 849-3755; http://www.theotherside.org

Focus: Communication; Peace & Nonviolence
Mission: A bimonthly magazine, TOS advances a healing Christian vision that is biblical and compassionate, intertwining personal spirituality and social transformation. Jesus' radically inclusive message is lifted up, dialogue is encouraged, and community is built.

The Peace Abbey

2 N Main St, Sherborn, MA 01770 USA; (508) 650-3659; Fax (508) 655-5031; http://www.peaceabbey.org

Focus: Training & Resources
Mission: The Peace Abbey is an interfaith retreat center dedicated to the sacred journey of loving the ways others love God, practicing peace through prayer, nonviolence, and social activism.

Theosophical Society in America

PO Box 270, Wheaton, IL 60189 USA; (630) 688-1571; http://www.theosophical. org

Focus: Ecumenical & Interfaith Cooperation
Mission: A worldwide organization devoted to human solidarity, cultural understanding, and self-development, the TSA seeks to bring people together, to reconcile the religions, philosophies, and sciences of both East and West, and to increase awareness of the inner reality inherent in every human being.

Tikkun Magazine

2107 Van Ness Ave #302, San
Francisco, CA 94109 USA;
(415) 575-1200; Fax (415) 575-1434;
http://www.tikkun.org

Focus: Communication; Renewal of
Faith Group
Mission: Written from a Jewish faith perspective, holding that progressive politics demands a new bottom line of
loving and caring, *Tikkun* seeks to bring
spiritual and psychological sensitivity to
political thought, embracing and
respecting all faiths.

Traditional Circle of Indian Elders and Youth

PO Box 1388, Bozeman, MT 59771-
1388 USA; (406) 587-1002;
http://www.mt.net/~aii/

Focus: Societies, Seminaries & Funds
Mission: In cooperation with the
American Indian Institute, TCIE&Y links
traditional leaders of Indian Nations
with Institute personnel to nurture grassroots renewal of traditional values and
lifeways, to ensure the continuity of
Native wisdom, and to bring that wisdom to bear upon the threats to land
and life.

Tricycle: The Buddhist Review

92 Vandam St, New York, NY 10013
USA; (212) 645-1143; Fax (212) 645-
1493; http://www.tricycle.com

Focus: Communication
Mission: *Tricycle*...referring to a "loop,"
is a quarterly journal written from a
Buddhist viewpoint, containing contemporary news, articles, reviews, poetry,
and instruction. The Tricycle Exchange,
its community Web site, is rich in
Dharma materials, a listing of all Zen
Centers nationwide, a newsletter,
Buddhism 101, and travel opportunities.

True Buddha School Chin Yin Buddhist Society

10853-98 St, Edmonton, AL T5H 2P6
Canada; (403) 423-0447;
Fax (403) 426-3230;

Focus: Ecumenical & Interfaith
Cooperation
Mission: With the motto "We are many
faiths, but we are one in the unity of
love," the True Buddha School is active
in ecumenical work in Alberta.

TV-Free America

1611 Connecticut Ave NW #3A,
Washington, DC 20009 USA; (202)
887-0436; Fax (202) 518-5560;
http://www.tvfa.org

Focus: Children, Youth & Family
Mission: Encouraging a dramatic reduction in the amount of TV watched in
order to promote healthier, more peaceful, and more connected lives, families,
and communities, TVFA sponsors an
annual "National TV-Turnoff Week."

UCC—United Church of Christ

700 Prospect Ave, Cleveland, OH
44115 USA; http://www.ucc.org

Board for Homeland Ministries

(216) 736-3273; Fax (216) 736-3263;
stiefr@ucc.org

Focus: General Peace & Justice; Women
Mission: UCC-BHM promotes God's
mission of love and justice for all persons through evangelism, education,
and prophetic action. Committees of the
Board work in specialized areas.

Committee for Racial Justice

(216) 736-2160; Fax (216) 736-2171
Focus: Discrimination
Mission: To provide leadership in mobilizing UCC members to work for racial
justice and reconciliation, both within
the Churches and in society. A monthly
opinion editorial is available for reproduction.

Community Empowerment Ministry

(216) 736-3275; Fax (216) 736-3263
porratam@ucc.org
Focus: Criminal Justice System; Human
Rights; Training & Resources
Mission: To work with national and
local faith-based organizations to eliminate injustice and promote peace and
justice in urban areas.

Family Life/Human Sexuality Ministry

(216) 736-3282; Fax (216) 736-3263
Focus: Children, Youth & Family; Women
Mission: To provide resources and educational opportunities that will assist
UCC churches in providing effective
ministries with families in their churches
and communities.

Health and Welfare Program

(216) 736-3272; Fax (216) 736-3263
Focus: Health Issues; Human Rights
Mission: To educate, nurture, advocate,

and empower the UCC for healthy
holistic ways of living, and to offer
direct services through churches, conferences, and service agencies of the
Church.

Justice & Peace Ministry

(216) 736-2170; Fax (216) 736-3293
Focus: Advocacy; General Peace &
Justice
Mission: To provide members with a
biblical understanding of prophetic ministry and to equip them with the knowledge and skills necessary to shape
social policies in keeping with God's
vision of a just and loving society.

Liberation Ministries

(216) 736-3280
Focus: Discrimination; Human Rights
Mission: To stand in solidarity with
oppressed peoples struggling for human
rights and self-determination.

Racial and Ethnic Concerns

(216) 736-2107; Fax (216) 736-2120
Focus: Discrimination
Mission: To advocate for concerns of
Pacific Islanders, Asian Americans,
Hispanics, American Indians, and Black
Christians.

Women in Church and Society

(216) 736-2150; Fax (216) 736-2156
Focus: Advocacy; Training & Resources;
Women
Mission: To advocate for justice for
women and to provide resources for
church women's groups. Areas of advocacy are violence against women,
reproductive rights, welfare reform, and
elimination of all forms of oppression.

UCC Coalition for Lesbian, Gay, Bisexual & Transgender Concerns

800 Village Way #230, Guilford, CT
06437 USA; (800) 653-0799;
Fax (203) 789-6356;
http://www.coalition.simplenet.com

Focus: Discrimination; Renewal of Faith
Group; Training & Resources
Mission: To provide support, sanctuary,
advocacy and full inclusion for lesbian,
gay, bisexual, and transgender persons, their family and friends in the
United Church of Christ and society. An
Open & Affirming program assists local
congregations with education and
advocacy.

UCC Council for American Indian Ministry

PO Box 412, Excelsior, MN 55331 USA; (612) 474-3532; Fax (612) 474-3532; Armin_Schmidt.parti@ecunet.org

Focus: Indigenous or Displaced Persons; Training & Resources
Mission: To act as a resource to the UCC on issues relating to American Indians.

UCC Network for Environmental & Economic Responsibility

PO Box 220, Pleasant Hill, TN 38578 USA; (931) 277-5467; Fax (931) 277-5593 http://www.Center1.com/NEER1.html

Focus: Ecology & Environment
Mission: To mobilize UCC persons, networks, and resources for a holistic ministry cognizant that the earth and its creatures are interdependent in a vast web of life. God's promise of Shalom is envisioned in ecological as well as sociological terms.

UCC United Church of Christ—DC

110 Maryland Ave NE, Washington, DC 20002 USA; (202) 543-1517; Fax (202) 543-5994

Environmental Issue Group

http://www.ucsusa.org
Focus: Ecology/Environment
Mission: To inform, educate, and advocate for the responsible stewardship of all of God's creation.

Office for Church in Society

http://www.ucc.org/justice/justice.htm
Focus: Advocacy; General Peace & Justice; Women
Mission: As Jesus' ministry was caring and prophetic, Christians are called to continue this ministry by uniting the personal with the systemic and the spiritual with the political in order to care for all of God's creation and change the systems that oppress it.

UMC—United Methodist Church

100 Maryland Ave NE, Washington, DC 20002 USA; http://www.umc-gbcs.org

Children and Welfare

(202) 488-5657; Fax (202) 488-5663; http://www.umc-gbcs.org/mghc.htm
Focus: Children, Youth & Family; Indigenous or Displaced Persons; Religious & Civil Liberty
Mission: To work for God's justice for children, youth, families, and Native Americans as well as impacting church and state policy, religious freedom, bilingual and public education, and welfare reform.

Economic Justice Concerns

(202) 488-5645; Fax (202) 488-5639; http://www.umc-gbcs.org/mgc.htm
Focus: Economic Concerns **Mission:** Holding that the reconciliation that God effected through Christ involves personal, social, and civic righteousness, UMC-EJC seeks to bring all of human life, activities, possessions, resources, community and world relationships into conformity with God's will.

Environmental Justice Concerns

(202) 488-4649; Fax (202) 488-5639; http://www.umc-gbcs.org/mgc.htm
Focus: Ecology & Environment
Mission: UMC-EJ concerns are toxic waste cleanup, clean water and air, endangered species, climate, desertification, biodiversity, forest protection, and children's environmental health.

Health & Wholeness Priorities

(202) 488-5636; Fax (202) 488-5663; http://www.umc-gbcs.org/mghc.htm
Focus: Advocacy; Health Issues
Mission: Concerns are universal health care, managed care, mental health parity, implementation of Children's Health Insurance Program, and monitoring changes to Medicare and Medicaid.

Immigration and Refugee Concerns

(202) 488-5637; Fax (202) 488-5639; http://www.umc-gbcs.org/mgc.htm
Focus: Indigenous or Displaced Persons
Mission: Concerns are immigration benefits, deportation relief, just and safe environment for low-wage immigrant workers, and monitoring abuses in INS detention centers.

Ministry of God's Creation

(202) 488-5650; Fax (202) 488-5639; http://www.umc-gbcs.org/mgc.htm
Focus: Ecology & Environment; Economic Concerns: Women
Mission: To address climate change, science & technology, genetics, corporate responsibility, conditions in China, and Ireland.

Ministry of God's Human Community

(202) 488-5654; Fax (202) 488-5653; http://www.umc-gbcs.org/mghc.htm
Focus: Children, Youth & Family
Mission: To address women's issues, human sexuality, reproductive rights, infant formula, disability rights, population, and social security programs.

Native American International Caucus

616 SW 70th St, Oklahoma City, OK 73139 USA; (405) 634-2005; Fax (405) 634-2181; http://members.aol.com/deer4naic
Focus: Indigenous or Displaced Persons
Mission: To advocate for inclusion of Native Americans in leadership roles within the church, for new Native American ministries, and for tribal sovereignty, tribal and individual Native American rights.

Peace With Justice

(202) 488-5647; Fax (202) 488-5639; http://www.umc-gbcs.org/gbcs007.htm
Focus: Peace & Nonviolence
Mission: To support the Comprehensive Nuclear Test Ban Treaty, the Landmine Ban Treaty, closure of the School of the Americas, and delivery of food and medicine to Cuba.

Restorative & Racial Justice

(202) 488-5658; Fax (202) 488-5663; http://www.umc-gbcs.org/mghc.htm
Focus: Criminal Justice System; Discrimination
Mission: To support hate crimes prevention and gun control, and to oppose capital punishment, violence against women, initiatives to eliminate affirmative action, and legislation for juvenile offenders that focus on punishment rather than prevention.

Seminars on National & International Affairs

(202) 488-5611; Fax (202) 544-0390; http://www.umc-gbcs.org/seminar1.htm
Focus: General Peace & Justice; Training & Resources
Mission: To design and present seminars that examine domestic and international public policy concerns through the lens of the UMC Social Principles and Christian ethical commitments to justice and inclusivity for all people.

United Nations Office

777 UN Plaza, New York, NY 10017

USA; (212) 682-3633; Fax (212) 682-5354; http://www.umc-gbcs.org/unminstr.htm

Focus: Global Peace & Security; Training & Resources

Mission: Providing UMC presence and support at the UN and reporting UN activities to the UMC, UMCUNO also facilitates opportunities for biblical, theological, and ethical reflection on international affairs.

UMC National Federation of Asian Americans

300 27th St, Oakland, CA 94612 USA; (510) 836-0993; Fax (510) 836-0995; nfaaum@earthlink.net

Focus: Discrimination; General Peace & Justice

Mission: To address Asian American issues: racism, leadership development, violence against Asian Americans, equity, conflict resolution, ministry, women, immigration, welfare, bilingual children, and poverty.

UMC Reconciling Congregation Program

3801 N Keeler Ave, Chicago, IL 60641 USA; (773) 736-5526; Fax (773) 736-5475; http://www.rcp.org

Focus: Discrimination; Renewal of Faith Group; Training & Resources

Mission: A network of UMC individuals, congregations, and other ministries that publicly affirm their ministry with all persons, regardless of sexual orientation, inviting other individuals, congregations, and ministries to join with them.

UMC Shalom Ministries

PO Box 66147, Portland, OR 97290 USA; (503) 760-4215; Fax (503) 761-5977; shalommin@uswest.net

Focus: Discrimination

Mission: A ministry of empowerment, education, and advocacy that serves lesbian, gay, and bisexual people, people living on the social or economic edge, people alienated from religion, and churches who want to welcome any of those persons. Sponsored by the Oregon/Idaho Conference.

Union of Orthodox Jewish Congregations—Institute for Public Affairs

11 Broadway, New York, NY 10004 USA; (212) 613-8123; Fax (212) 564-9058; http://www.ou.org/public

Focus: General Peace & Justice

Mission: IPA brings the perspective of Jewish law and tradition to bear on public policy issues confronting American society, thus seeking to fulfill the mission of the UOJC to work for the betterment of the world; "tikkun olam" for all humanity.

Unitarian Universalist Association—UUA

25 Beacon St, Boston, MA 02108 USA; http://www.uua.org

Bisexual, Gay, Lesbian & Transgender Concerns

(617) 742-2100 Ext. 470; Fax (617) 742-0321; http://www.uua.org/obgltc

Focus: Discrimination; Training & Resources

Mission: Guided by a vision of the day when oppression against bisexual, gay, lesbian, or transgender people, whether overt or subtle, will be a thing of the past, this UUA office works for that reality.

Faith in Action—DC

2026 P St NW #3, Washington, DC 20036 USA; (202) 296-4672; Fax (202) 296-4673

Focus: Advocacy; General Peace & Justice

Mission: Works directly with interreligious and secular coalitions to represent the UUA positions in national public policy and legislative issues.

Service Committee

130 Prospect St, Cambridge, MA 02139-1845 USA; (617) 868-6600 Ext. 230; Fax (617) 868-7102 http://www.uusc.org

Focus: General Peace & Justice

Mission: Grounded in UU principles that affirm the worth, dignity, and human rights of every person and the interdependence of all life, UUSC works to advance justice and promote peace throughout the world.

United Nations Office

777 UN Plaza # C-C, New York, NY 10017 USA; (212) 986-5165; Fax (212) 983-5498; http://members.aol.com/uuuno2/index.html

Focus: Global Peace & Security

Mission: Because a UUA priority is "to affirm and promote the goal of a world community with peace, liberty, and justice for all," this office works to strengthen and advance the role of the UN.

Women's Federation

(617) 742-2100; Fax (617) 367-3237; uuwf@uua.org

Focus: Children, Youth & Family; Women

Mission: The Federation works for human rights for all, especially women, promoting quality child care, concern for the family, prevention of violence against women, reproductive rights, action on clergy's sexual misconduct, and aid for the aging.

Unitarian Universalist Council— Canada

55 Eglinton Ave E #705, Toronto, ON M4P 1G8 Canada; (416) 489-4121; Fax (416) 489-9010; http://www.web.net/~cuc

Focus: General Peace & Justice

Mission: The CUC acts to nurture and promote UU goals in Canada by providing support for religious exploration, spiritual growth, and social responsibility. It represents the UU in the larger social and religious environments.

Unitarian Universalist Peace Fellowship

6512 Warren Ave, Edina, MN 55439-1247 USA; (612) 941-3508; Fax (612) 941-3508 (call first); natchison@igc.org

Focus: Peace & Nonviolence

Mission: Guided by a deep commitment to non-violence, UUPF stands opposed to war, defends the freedom of personal conscience, supports conscientious objectors, provides peace education services, and works for government action that will lead to a world of peace and justice.

Unitarian Universalists for a Just Economic Community

1110 Resaca Place #3, Pittsburgh, PA 15212 USA; (412) 321-5260; Fax (412) 321-0513; http://www.pitt.edu/~hirtle/uujec.html

Focus: Economic Concerns; Renewal of Faith Group
Mission: Believing that democracy and economic equity are at great risk in the US, UUJEC engages, educates, and activates Unitarian Universalists to work for economic justice in alliance with labor, community, and other faith-based groups.

United Catholic Church

5115 S A1A Hwy #101, Melbourne Beach, FL 32951 USA; (407) 952-0600; Fax call first; http://www.rmbowman.com/catholic

Focus: Renewal of Faith Group
Mission: To serve as a bridge church providing a basis for future unity between Roman Catholics, Orthodox, and Protestants. With the Catholic liturgy and Quaker social conscience, UCC is an inclusive church.

United Church of Canada—Interfaith Relations

3250 Bloor St W, Etobicoke, ON M8X 2Y4 Canada; (416) 231-7680 Ext. 171; Fax (416) 232-6008; http://www.uccan.org

Focus: Ecumenical & Interfaith Cooperation
Mission: To empower the church to work collaboratively with people of other faith communities to build a culture of nonviolence and respect, while working toward just economic relationships, tolerance, truthfulness, and equal rights and partnerships between men and women.

United Communities of Spirit

PO Box 23346, Santa Barbara, CA 93121 USA; (805) 966-9515; http://origin.org/ucs.cfm

Focus: Communication; Ecumenical & Interfaith Cooperation
Mission: In a world where religious differences are often the cause of tragedy and warfare, UCS provides an online network where people of goodwill from every faith tradition can come together, learn from one another, and develop a

shared understanding that can inspire and uplift the world.

United for a Fair Economy

37 Temple Pl, 5th fl, Boston, MA 02211 USA; (617) 423-2148 Ext. 18; Fax (617) 423-0191; http://www.stw.org

Focus: Economic Concerns; Training & Resources
Mission: Working with civic, labor, and religious groups, UFE organizes support for a fairer US economy by focusing attention on US economic inequality and its implications for American life and labor. UFE provides educational resources, trains grassroot groups, and supports legislative action to reduce inequality.

United Lodge of Theosophists

245 East 33rd St, Los Angeles, CA 90007 USA; (213) 748-7244; http://www.ult.org

Focus: Ecumenical & Interfaith Cooperation
Mission: To disseminate the fundamental principles of the Philosophy of Theosophy, and the exemplification in practice of those principles, through a truer realization of the SELF and a profound conviction of Universal Brotherhood.

United Methodist Appalachian Development Committee

108 E Franklin St, PO Box 2231, Hagerstown, MD 21741 USA; (301) 791-7355; Fax (301) 791-7355; umadc@aol.com

Focus: Human Rights
Mission: To enhance ministry in the Appalachian region by addressing issues and communicating concerns through networking, interpreting, resourcing, and advocacy.

United Muslim Women of Canada

PO Box 55050, Knottwood RPO, Edmonton, AB T6K 4C5 Canada; (403) 461-7746; Fax (403) 450-2724; sdevjee@hotmail.com

Focus: Women
Mission: To meet the political, social, religious, and educational needs of Muslim women. UMWC is affiliated with Islamic Humanitarian Service.

United Nations Assn of the US

801 2nd Ave, New York, NY 10017 USA; (212) 907-1300 Ext. 325; Fax (212) 682-9185; http://www.unausa.org

Focus: Global Peace & Security
Mission: A coalition of more than 100 organizations including 40 faith groups, since 1949 the UNA-US has supported the attempts of the UN to prevent conflict, promote economic and social development, and preserve the environment.

United Religions Initiative

PO Box 29242, San Francisco, CA 94129 USA; (415) 561-2300; Fax (415) 561-2313; http://www.united-religions.org

Focus: Ecumenical & Interfaith Cooperation
Mission: A bridge-building organization, not a religion, URI promotes enduring, daily interfaith cooperation, an end to religiously motivated violence and a culture of peace, justice, and healing for the Earth and all living beings.

United Synagogues of Conservative Judaism—Social Action & Public Policy

155 5th Ave, New York, NY 10010 USA; (212) 533-7800 Ext. 2601; Fax (212) 353-9439; http://www.uscj.org

Focus: General Peace & Justice
Mission: The concerns of USCJ-SAPP are homelessness, hunger, reproductive choice, anti-Semitism, universal health care, domestic violence, cults, and the environment.

Universal Fellowship of Metropolitan Community Churches

8704 Santa Monica Blvd, 2nd Fl, W Hollywood, CA 90069 USA; (310) 360-8640; Fax (310) 360-8680; http://www.ufmcc.com

Focus: Discrimination
Mission: A Christian Church, the UFMCC reaches to and beyond the gay and lesbian communities, proclaiming Christian liberation, inclusivity, and community, social action, and justice. It seeks and celebrates the integration of spirituality and sexuality.

Universal Health Care Action Network

2800 Euclid Ave #520, Cleveland, OH 44115-2418 USA; (800) 634-4442; Fax (216) 241-8423; http://www.uhcan.org

Focus: Health Issues
Mission: A network of faith-based and secular organizations and individuals, UHCAN works for universal health care by activating, uniting, and strengthening local grassroots activists across the US.

Universal Pantheist Society

PO Box 265, Big Pine, CA 93513 USA; http://www.pantheist.net/society

Focus: Ecology & Environment
Mission: UPS seeks to motivate humankind to take action to protect and restore the earth, advocating a revision of social attitudes away from anthropocentrism and toward reverence for the earth.

Urantia Book Readers Online Network

609 de la Vina, #28, Santa Barbara, CA 93101 USA; (805) 963-1258; Fax (805) 963-0975; http://origin.org/ub.cfm

Focus: Ecumenical & Interfaith Cooperation; General Peace & Justice
Mission: UBRON's goal is to spread the "benign virus of love across the globe," by fostering spiritual living and supporting activities promoting awareness that all humankind is part of the same family.

US Catholic Conference

3211 4th St NE, Washington, DC 20017-1194 USA

Migration and Refugee Services

(202) 541-3169; Fax (202) 722-8755
Focus: Indigenous or Displaced Persons
Mission: To provide program support and coordination for a network of over 100 diocesan refugee resettlement offices, acting as an agency of the American Catholic Bishops.

Social Development & World Peace

3211 4th St NE, Washington, DC 20017-1194 USA; (202) 541-3195; Fax (202) 541-3339; http://www. nccbuscc.org/sdwp
Focus: General Peace & Justice
Mission: To support 185 US Diocesan

offices as they seek to apply the Church's social teaching to domestic and international issues, to advocate effectively for the poor and vulnerable, and act effectively in defense of human life, human dignity, and human rights.

US Catholic Magazine

205 W Monroe St, Chicago, IL 60606 USA; (312) 236-7782; Fax (312) 236-8207; http://www.uscatholic.org

Focus: Communication
Mission: A monthly forum for lay Catholics published by Claretian Missionaries, the USC celebrates tradition, yet embraces the spirit of Vatican II reform and rejuvenation.

Virtual Religion Index

Dept of Religion Loree 140, Rutgers U, New Brunswick, NJ 08901 USA; (732) 932-9641; Fax (732) 932-1271; http://religion.rutgers.edu.vri/index.html

Focus: Communication; Training & Resources
Mission: A comprehensive, current, and well-organized collection of resources on religion classified in 20 categories; from Ancient Near East Studies to Psychology of Religion on an easy-to-use Web site. Provided by Rutgers U—School of Religion.

Vision TV

80 Bond St, Toronto, ON M5B 1X2 Canada; (416) 368-3194; Fax (416) 368-9774; http://www.visiontv.ca

Focus: Communication; General Peace & Justice
Mission: VTV, "entertainment with insight," presents two programming streams: Cornerstone & Mosaic. Each is a forum for views and ideas on faith, ethics, values, and life's biggest questions.

Voices for Survival

100 E Adams Ave, Kirkwood, MO 63122 USA; (314) 965-4608; Fax (314) 965-3861; http://www. artsci. wustl.edu/~ejhadley/pop/voices.html

Focus: Ecology & Environment
Mission: An interfaith coalition, VFS calls people of faith to take responsibility for preserving and restoring the created order, reacting to overpopulation and overconsumption.

Voices in the Wilderness

1460 W Carmen Ave, Chicago, IL 60640 USA; (773) 784-8065; Fax (773) 784-8837; kkelly@igc.apc.org

Focus: Human Rights
Mission: VIW solicits and transports needed medical supplies to the people of Iraq in deliberate violation of the US/UN economic sanctions against Iraq.

War Tax Resisters Penalty Fund

Box 25, N Manchester, IN 46962 USA; (219) 982-2971

Focus: Peace & Nonviolence
Mission: WTRPF provides financial support for conscientious war tax resisters who have had interest and penalties levied by the IRS.

Washington Institute for Jewish Leadership & Values

6101 Montrose Rd #200, Rockville, MD 20852 USA; (301) 770-5070; Fax (301) 770-6365; http://www.wijlv.org

Focus: Societies, Seminaries & Funds
Mission: WIJLV seeks renewal of American Jewish life through study, social justice, and civic engagement, offering programs providing motivation and skills to advocate and serve.

Washington Office on Africa

212 E Capitol St, Washington, DC 20003 USA; (202) 547-7503; Fax (202) 547-7505; http://www.woaafrica.org

Focus: Advocacy; Human Rights
Mission: To educate faith communities and the public by advocating an American policy toward Africa that is just, sensitive to the integrity of Africa, and concerned with human development, human rights, and the common good.

Washington Office on Latin America

1630 Connecticut Ave NW 2nd fl, Washington, DC 20009 USA; (202) 797-2171; Fax (202) 797-2172; http://www.wola.org

Focus: Economic Concerns; Human Rights
Mission: Founded in 1974 by a coalition of religious and civic leaders, WOLA promotes human rights, democracy, and social and economic justice

in Latin America and the Caribbean. It facilitates dialogue, monitors the impact of NGO and government policies and programs, and promotes alternatives through reporting, education, training, and advocacy.

Web of Creation

LSTC 1100 E 55th St, Chicago, IL 60615 USA; (773) 256-0774; Fax (773) 256-0782; http://www.webofcreation.org

Focus: Communication; Ecology & Environment
Mission: By providing an informative Web site, the WOC offers eco-justice resources to faith-based communities for use in worship, education, care of buildings and grounds, personal lifestyle, public ministry, and advocacy.

Wingspan

100 N Oxford, St Paul, MN 55104-6540 USA; (651) 224-3371; Fax (651) 224-6228; http://www.cyberword.com/spr

Focus: Discrimination; Renewal of Faith Group
Mission: To advance the quality of life and growth in Christian faith for gay men, lesbian women, bisexual and transgender persons, their families and friends in ELCA congregations, local synods, and churchwide.

Wisdom Publications

199 Elm St, Somerville, MA 02144 USA; (617) 776-7416; Fax (617) 776-7841; http://www.widompubs.org

Focus: Communication
Mission: A leading publisher of books on Buddhism, Tibet, and the Tibetan culture including books by His Holiness, the Dalai Lama.

Witness for Peace

1229 15th St NW, Washington, DC 20005 USA; (202) 588-1471; Fax (202) 588-1472; http://www.witnessforpeace.org

Focus: Peace & Nonviolence
Mission: WFP is a national organization promoting just alternatives to US policies that contribute to poverty and oppression in Latin America and the Caribbean, acting as people of faith dedicated to principles of nonviolence.

Witness Magazine

HC35 Box 647, Tenants Harbor, ME 04860 USA; (207) 372-6396; Fax (207) 372-6297; http://www.thewitness.org

Focus: Communication
Mission: Advocating since 1917 for those denied systemic power and celebrating those who have found ways to live humanly, *Witness* is committed to brevity for the sake of readers who find little time to read, but can enjoy an idea, a poem, or a piece. Its roots are Episcopalian.

Women Against Military Madness

310 E 38th St #225, Minneapolis, MN 55409 USA; (612) 827-5364; Fax (612) 827-6433; http://www.worldwidewamm.org

Focus: Global Peace & Security; Peace & Nonviolence
Mission: Working in solidarity with faith and civic groups, WAMM's goal is to dismantle systems of militarism and global oppression and replace them with a system of social equality, self-determination, and justice.

Women Vision International

6405 Metcalf Bldg 3 #509, Overland Park, KS 66202 USA; (913) 432-2883; Fax (913) 432-2873; http://www.womenvision.org

Focus: Women
Mission: WVI is an organization of women working together in harmony with the Higher Spirit to improve the quality of life for women and children throughout the world by empowering women to be economically self-sufficient.

Women's Alliance for Theology, Ethics and Ritual

8035 13th St, Silver Spring, MD 20910 USA; (301) 589-2509; Fax (301) 589-3150; http://www.hers.com/water

Focus: General Peace & Justice; Women
Mission: WATER is a feminist religious educational center building a network of justice-seeking people through attention to religiously based social change.

Women's Interchurch Council of Canada

394 Bloor St W #201, Toronto, ON M5S 1X4 Canada; (416) 929-5184; Fax (416) 929-4064; http://www.wicc.org

Focus: Ecumenical & Interfaith Cooperation; General Peace & Justice; Women
Mission: WICC encourages Christian women to work ecumenically, share spirituality, organize, and take action together for social justice and human rights.

Women's International League for Peace & Freedom

1213 Race St, Philadelphia, PA 19107 USA; (215) 563-7110; Fax (215) 563-5527; http://www.wilpf.org

Focus: Economic Concerns; Global Peace & Security; Peace & Nonviolence
Mission: Since 1915, the men and women of WILPF have worked internationally seeking fundamental change in areas ranging from arms control and disarmament, to economic and political relations, based on the premise of fair sharing of resources among/within nations and equal rights for all.

Women's Ordination Conference

PO Box 2693, Fairfax, VA 22031 USA; (703) 352-1006; Fax (703) 352-5181; http://www.womensordination.org

Focus: Renewal of Faith Group
Mission: WOC seeks ordination of women as priests and bishops into a renewed priestly ministry in the Roman Catholic Church. To this end WOC works for justice and equality for women, elimination of domination and discrimination, and affirmation of women's talents, gifts, and calls to ministry.

Women-Church Convergence

2572 W Argyle, Chicago, IL 60625-2604 USA; (773) 784-2498; Fax (773) 784-2498

Focus: Renewal of Faith Group
Mission: W-CC is a coalition of 33 autonomous Catholic-rooted organizations/groups raising a feminist voice and committed to an ekklesia of women which is participative, egalitarian, and self-governing.

Won Buddhism of America

143-42 Cherry Ave, Flushing, NY 11355 USA; (718) 762-4103; Fax (718) 353-5382 http://www.wonbuddhism.org

Focus: Ecumenical & Interfaith Cooperation
Mission: To find what a person has within, round and perfect like "Irwon" (Korean word for "circle"), to cultivate and utilize it perfectly and fairly in one's body and mind. WBA does not exclude other faiths or views because the symbol of Irwon points to the sameness of the enlightened mind of all Buddhas and saints.

Woodstock Theological Center

37th &, Washington, DC 20057 USA; (202) 687-3532; Fax (202) 687-5835;

Focus: Societies, Seminaries & Funds
Mission: The Center engages in theological and ethical reflection on topics of social, economic, business, scientific, cultural, religious, and political importance, using as guide the mission of the Society of Jesus.

Working Group on Refugee Resettlement

1339 King St W #3, Toronto, ON M6K 1H2 Canada; (416) 588-1612; Fax (416) 588-1702;

Focus: Indigenous or Displaced Persons
Mission: WGRR's mission is to challenge and enable churches to support and resettle refugees.

World Alliance of Young Men's Christian Associations—YMCA

12 Clos Belmont, 1208 Geneva, Switzerland; 41-22-849-5100; Fax 41-22-849-5110; http://www.ymca.int

Focus: General Peace & Justice
Mission: A worldwide Christian movement seeking to share the Christian ideal of building a human community of justice with love, peace, and reconciliation enabling fullness of life for all creation, the YMCA is present in 120 countries, and has 14,000 local associations and approximately 30 million members. Web site has complete directory.

World Alliance of Young Women's Christian Associations—YWCA

16 Ancienne Rt CH-1218 Grand Saconnex, Geneva, Switzerland; 41-22-929-6040; Fax 41-22-929-6044; http://www.worldywca.org

Focus: Ecology & Environment; Peace & Nonviolence; Women
Mission: WYWCA unites 25 million women in 100 countries through 95 national YWCAs, promotes fair and equal participation in society, works for social and economic justice, and mobilizes women's collective power for action on women's rights, human rights, peace, and the integrity of the environment. All WYWCA work is based on Christian ecumenical principles, welcoming women of all faiths.

World Assembly of Muslim Youth

PO Box 8096, Falls Church, VA 22041 USA; (703) 916-0924; Fax (703) 916-0925; http://www.wamy.com

Focus: Training & Resources
Mission: WAMY is the first International Islamic Organization dealing specifically with youth affairs embracing over 450 Islamic youth/student organizations on five continents. International office is PO Box 10845 Riyadh, Saudi Arabia 11443.

World Conference on Religion & Peace International

777 UN Plaza, New York, NY 10017 USA; (212) 687-2163; Fax (212) 983-0566; http://www.wcrp.org

Focus: Ecumenical & Interfaith Cooperation; General Peace & Justice
Mission: WCRP engages in peace initiatives throughout the world on a multireligious basis, promoting religious tolerance, conflict resolution, disarmament, sustainable development, welfare of children and youth, care for refugees/displaced persons, and environmental projects.

World Congress of Faiths

2 Market St, Oxford, OX1 3EF UK; 44 (0) 1 865-202751; Fax 44 (0) 1865 202746; http://www.interfaith-center.org/oxford/wcf

Focus: Ecumenical & Interfaith Cooperation
Mission: Believing that understanding

between people of different religions is important for good community relations, for moral and spiritual renewal, and for world peace, the WCF arranges conferences, meetings, retreats, publications, and group travel that provide occasion to learn what others believe, how they pray, meditate, and worship.

World Council of Churches

PO Box 2100, 1211 Geneva 2, Switzerland; 41-22-791-6111; Fax 41-22-791-0361; http://www.wcc-coe.org

Focus: Communication; Ecumenical & Interfaith Cooperation; General Peace & Justice
Mission: Inaugurated in 1948, the WCC is a fellowship of churches, now 330, in more that 100 countries in all continents from virtually all Christian traditions. The Roman Catholic Church is not a member church but works cooperatively. Its Commissions are actively seeking peace/justice. Its Web site contains links to 200 church/ecumenical groups worldwide, 27 World Christian bodies and 18 National Council offices.

World Council of Muslim Women Foundation

PO Box 128, Seba Beach, AL T0E 2B0 Canada; (403) 439-5088; Fax (403) 439-5088; wcomwf@connect.ab.ca

Focus: Peace & Nonviolence; Women
Mission: The Foundation is a global organization dedicated to the education and safety of women and to a peaceful environment through out the world.

World Faiths Development Dialogue

33-37 Stockmore St, Oxford, OX4 1JT UK; (44) 186 579-0011; Fax (44) 186 579-0011; http://www.wfdd.org.uk

Focus: Economic Concerns; Societies, Seminaries & Funds
Mission: Seeking equity among the world's peoples, WFDD explores the meaning of development from the standpoint of religious and cultural values and promotes interfaith dialogue regarding the actions and policies of the World Bank.

World Fellowship of Buddhists

616 Benjasiri Park Soi 24 Sukhumvit Rd, Bangkok, 10110 Thailand; (662) 661-1284-89; Fax (662) 661-0555; http://www.buddhanet.net/wfb.htm

Focus: Human Rights
Mission: To stimulate and promote active practice of the principles of Buddhism, and to assist in organizing and maintaining institutions for humanitarian services, without becoming involved in political activity.

World InterFaith Education Assn

154 University Ave #200, Toronto, ON M5H 3Z4 Canada; (416) 340-6630; Fax (416) 591-7911; http://www.web.net/~wifeaont

Focus: Ecumenical & Interfaith Cooperation; Training & Resources
Mission: WIFEA promotes programs offering knowledge about diverse beliefs, faiths, and spiritual traditions and teaches the skills necessary to nurture values of mutual understanding, respect, and cooperation among those groups.

World Muslim Congress

8944 Kirkham, Indianapolis, IN 46260 USA; (317) 844-3646; Fax (317) 872-5150; http://www.islam-usa.com

Focus: Ecumenical & Interfaith Cooperation
Mission: The Congress seeks to promote interfaith understanding, to educate non-Muslims about Islam, to inform on political developments, and to foster peace.

World Peace Prayer Society

800 3rd Ave, 37th Fl, New York, NY 10022 USA; (212) 755-4755; Fax (212) 935-1389; http://www.worldpeace.org

Focus: Peace & Nonviolence
Mission: Since 1955, WPPS has been dedicated to creating peace through a simple prayer, "May Peace Prevail on Earth." Through World Peace Prayer Ceremonies, the Peace Pole Project, and the Peace Pals program for young people, supporters carry the universal message of peace to communities on every continent.

World Peacemakers Inc

11427 Scottsbury Terr Ave NW, Germantown, MD 20876 USA; (301) 916-0442; Fax (301) 916-5335; http://www.nonviolence.org/worldpeacemakers

Focus: Peace & Nonviolence
Mission: With the goal of abolishing all violence and war, WPI works to establish and sustain small peace and justice groups, believing that small gatherings of people, conscious of the action of the Holy Spirit in their lives, are a strong force for peace.

World Sabbath of Religious Reconciliation

50750 Van Buren, Plymouth, MI 48170 USA; (734) 459-7319; http://members.aol.com/revrodrev/index.html

Focus: Ecumenical & Interfaith Cooperation; Peace & Nonviolence
Mission: To build recognition for an annual interfaith holy day, the 4th Saturday of January, to proclaim to the world that "religious wars" are caused by revenge, ambition, and greed, not by religious faith.

World Tibet Day

11155 Roseland Rd, Sebastian, FL 32958 USA; (561) 388-0699; http://www.worldtibetday.com

Focus: Human Rights
Mission: To build support for Tibetan human rights and to assist in preserving their culture, WTD sponsors an annual day of remembrance, requesting worldwide participation through houses of worship of any and all faiths.

World Vision Inc

34834 Weyerhaeuser Way S, Federal Way, WA 98001 USA; (888) 511-6598; http://www.worldvision.org

Focus: Human Rights
Mission: An international Christian humanitarian organization serving the world's poor and displaced, WVI provides programs that help save lives, bring hope, and restore dignity, without regard to religious beliefs, gender, or ethnic background.

Yearbook of American & Canadian Churches

475 Riverside Dr #880, New York, NY 10115-0050 USA; (212) 870-2031; Fax (212) 870-2817; http://www.ncc-cusa.org

Focus: Communication; Ecumenical & Interfaith Cooperation
Mission: The single best source of information about the status of North American churches and related organizations, the *Yearbook* contains 3,000 entries, statistics, and directories. Published annually by the NCCC.

Yoga Journal

2054 University Ave #600, Berkeley, CA 94704 USA; (510) 841-9200; Fax (510) 644-3101; http://www.yogajournal.com

Focus: Communication
Mission: Published bimonthly since 1975, *Yoga Journal* is dedicated to communicating the qualities of being that yoga exemplifies: peace, integrity, clarity, and compassion. It is America's leading magazine on yoga, holistic healing, and conscious living.

Zygon Center for Religion and Science

1100 E 55th St, Chicago, IL 60615-5199 USA; (773) 256-0670; Fax (773) 256-0682; http://www.zygoncenter.org

Focus: Societies, Seminaries & Funds
Mission: Dedicated to relating religious traditions and the best scientific knowledge to gain insight into origins, nature, and destiny of humans and their environment, ZCRS's goal is a world in which love, justice, and responsible patterns of living prevail.

Index of Organizations in the Directory by Area of Focus

1. GENERAL PEACE & JUSTICE
Groups working in four or more areas are listed here (but not in all specific areas).
ABC/USA—Biblical Justice Ministry Center
AFSC—American Friends Service Committee
Alliance for Jewish Renewal
Bahá'í—Office of Public Information
Bahá'í Community of Canada
Canadian Council of Churches—Peace & Justice
Center of Concern
Christian Church—Disciples of Christ
Christian Reformed Churches in Canada
Church of Scientology—Canada
Church Women United—NY
Cooperative Baptist Fellowship
Disciples Justice Action Network
Eighth Day Center for Justice
ELCA—Division for Church in Society
Episcopal Church—Peace & Justice Ministries
Evangelical Fellowship of Canada—Social Action
    Commission
Evangelical Lutheran Women of Canada
Evangelicals for Social Action
Federation of Zoroastrian Associations of NA
Global Education Associates
Groundwork for a Just World
Institute for Religion and Social Change
Institute for Religious Studies
Institute for World Spirituality
Intercommunity Center for Justice & Peace—NY
Intercommunity Justice & Peace Center
InterFaith Conference of Metropolitan Washington
Interfaith Council of Greater New York
Jesuit Social and International Ministries
Jesuit Volunteer Corps
Leadership Conference of Women Religious
Loretto Community
Mennonite Central Committee—Canada
Mennonite Central Committee—US
Mennonite Church Commission on Home Ministries
Methodist Federation for Social Action
National Association for Evangelicals—Ofc for
    Governmental Affairs
National Council of Catholic Women
NCCC National Council of Churches of Christ—USA
Peace with Justice Week

Perspectives, a Journal of Reformed Thought
Presbyterian Church in Canada—Justice Ministries
Presbyterian Church USA—Presbyterian Women
Presbyterian Church USA—Washington Office
Protestants for the Common Good
Quaker United Nations Office
Radio Free Maine
Religious Action Center of Reform Judaism
Salt of the Earth
SBC Ethics & Religious Liberty Commission
Scarboro Missions—Justice & Peace Office
SeedHouse
Sisters of St Joseph of Carondelet
Sisters Online
SocialAction.com—a Web Magazine
Student Christian Movement of Canada
Ten Days for Global Justice
UCC—Board for Homeland Ministries
UCC—Justice & Peace Ministry
UCC—DC Office for Church in Society
UMC—National Federation of Asian Americans
UMC—Seminars on National & International Affairs
Union of Orthodox Jewish Congregations
UU Council—Canada
UUA—Faith in Action—DC
UUA Service Committee
United Synagogues of Conservative Judaism
Urantia Book Readers Online Network
US Catholic Conference—Social Development & World
    Peace
Vision TV
Women's Alliance for Theology, Ethics and Ritual
Women's Interchurch Council of Canada
World Alliance of Young Men's Christian Associates
World Conference on Religion & Peace International
World Council of Churches

2. ADVOCACY
Groups that advocate for their cause(s) to civic leaders or governmental officials as a primary goal
20/20 Vision
50 Years Is Enough: Network US for Global Economic
    Justice
ABC/USA—Office of Governmental Relations
Africa Faith and Justice Network
Bread for the World

Campaign for a Fair Minimum Wage
Canadian Lutheran Office for Public Policy
Catholic Conference of Superiors of Men's Institutues
Church of the Brethren—Washington Office
Church Women United—DC
Churches for Middle East Peace
Disciples Advocacy Washington Network—DC
ELCA Lutheran Office for, Governmental Affairs
Episcopal Public Policy Network
Friends Committee on National Legislation
Human Rights Action Service
Jewish Council for Public Affairs
Mennonite Central Committee—Washington Office
Nat. Assn. for Evangelicals—Governmental Affairs
National Campaign for a Peace Tax Fund
Native American Rights Fund
NCCC—Interfaith Health Care Initiative
NCCC—*Mark-Up* Newsletter
NETWORK: A National Catholic Justice Lobby
Presbyterian Church USA—Washington Office
Quaker United Nations Office
Religious Action Center of Reform Judaism
Religious Coalition for Reproductive Choice
School of the Americas Watch
UCC—DC Office for Church in Society
UCC—Justice & Peace Ministry
UCC—Women in Church and Society
UMC—Health & Wholeness Priorities
Unitarian Universalist Faith in Action—DC
Washington Office on Africa

3. CHILDREN, YOUTH & FAMILY
Aging, child care, child or spouse abuse, family planning, influence of TV, parenting, and/or quality and special education

ADVANCE—Avoiding Domestic Violence, Affirming Nonviolent Creative Efforts
Assn. of Lutheran Older Adults
Catholic Central Verein of America
Children's Defense Fund
Church Women United—NY
Congress of National Black Churches
Episcopal Society for Ministry on Aging
Interfaith Community Partnership of the Chicago Public Schools
Interfaith Sexual Trauma Institute
Jewish Women International
Mainstream Coalition
Mature Years Magazine
Mennonite Central Committee—Women's Concerns
National Council of Jewish Women
National Youth Project

NCCC Committee on Justice for Children and their Families
NCCC—Public Education and Literacy
Spiritual Eldering Institute
Stand for Children
TV-Free America
UCC—Family Life/Human Sexuality Ministry
UMC—Children and Welfare
UMC—Ministry of God's Human Community
Unitarian Universalist Women's Federation
World Alliance of YMCAs
World Alliance of YWCAs

4. COMMUNICATION
Groups which use books, magazines, radio, TV, or the Internet as their primary tool for sharing their message

America—National Catholic Weekly
Benetvision Publishers
Blueprint for Social Justice—Newsletter
Christian Century Weekly
Christian Ethics Today Magazine
Christian Social Action Magazine—UMC
Christian New* Age Quarterly
The Christophers Publishing
Church & Society Magazine PC/USA
Church & State Magazine
Commonweal Magazine
Contra Mundum Newsletteer
Creative Transformation Magazine
Facts for Action Newsletter
Fellowship Magazine
Fezana Journal
Fig Tree—Ecumenical Newspaper
Friends Journal
Friends of Religious Humanism Journal
From Both Sides of the Ocean Magazine
Hinduism Today Magazine
Horizon Interfaith Council TV
Houston Peace NEWS
Human Quest: The Churchman Magazine
Interfaith Voices for Peace & Justice – Online
Jewish Currents Magazine
Journal of Women's Ministries
KAZI Publications Inc
Liberty Magazine
Lilith Magazine—Jewish Feminist Quarterly
Mahavir World Vision Inc
Mature Years Magazine
National Catholic Reporter—Newspaper
NCCC Eculink Newsletter
NCCC Mark-Up Newsletter
New Call to Peacemaking Newsletter

News/Views Newsletter
Odyssey Network TV
Ontario Consultants on Religious Tolerance—Online
Open Hands Magazine
Parallax Press
Passion Newsletter
Peace & Freedom Magazine
Peaceday Organization—Online
Peacework Magazine
Periodica IslamIca—a Quarterly
Perspectives, a Journal of Reformed Thought
Plough Magazine
Prism Magazine
Quixote Center—*Faith Matters*, Weekly Broadcast
Quixote Center—Priests for Equality Publishing
Radio Free Maine
Religion and Ethics TV Newsweekly
Religion in American Life, Inc—Invite a Friend Program
Salt of the Earth Online
Sequoia—Interreligious Newsmagazine
Sisters Online
Snow Lion Publications
SocialAction.com—a Web Magazine
Sojourners Magazine
Spiritual Rx Online
The Humanist Magazine
The Other Side Magazine
Tikkun Magazine
Tricycle: The Buddhist Review
United Communities of Spirit Online
US Catholic Magazine
Virtual Religion Index Online
Vision TV
Web of Creation Online
Wisdom Publications
Witness Magazine
World Council of Churches Online
Yearbook of American/Canadian Churches
Yoga Journal

5. CRIMINAL JUSTICE SYSTEM
Crime prevention, death penalty, juvenile offenders, prison visitation, rehabilitation, sentencing reform and/or victim rights
Campaign for Equity—Restorative Justice
Canadian Friends Service Committee
Catholics Against Capital Punishment
Church Council on Justice & Corrections
Church of Scientology—USA
Citizens United for Alternatives to the Death Penalty
Engaged Zen Foundation
Friends Committee to Abolish the Death Penalty

Presbyterian Church USA—Criminal Justice Office
Prison Fellowship
Prisoner Visitation & Support
Quixote Center—Equal Justice USA
Religious Organizing Against the Death Penalty
UCC—Community Empowerment Ministry
UMC—Restorative & Racial Justice

6. DISCRIMINATION
Based on age, disability, ethnicity, gender, income, race, religion, and/or sexual orientation
ABC/USA Association of Welcoming & Affirming
    Baptists
ABC/USA Ecology & Racial Justice
Aboriginal Rights Coalition—Canada
AFSC—National Community Relations Unit
Alliance for Tolerance & Freedom
American Jewish Committee
American Jewish Congress
American Muslim Council
Anti-Defamation League
B'nai B'rith
Brethren—Mennonite Council for Lesbian & Gay
    Concerns
Canadian Council of Christians & Jews
Center for New Community
Congress of National Black Churches
Council on American-Islamic Relations
Crossroads Ministry
Dignity Canada
Dignity USA
Disciples Peace Fellowship
Ecumenical Peace Institute
Gay, Lesbian and Affirming Disciples Alliance
Interfaith Action for Racial Justice, Inc
Interfaith Fairness Coalition of MD
International Council of Christians and Jews
International Religious Liberty Association
Interweave: UU for Gay, Lesbian & Bisexual Concerns
Leadership Conference on Civil Rights
Loretto Community—Women's Network
Lutheran Human Relations Assn of America
Lutheran Network for Inclusive Vision
Lutherans Concerned—North America
Mennonite Central Committee—Women's Concerns
Metodistas Asociados Representalando la Causa de
    Hispano-Americanos
Mobilization for the Human Family
More Light Presbyterians
National Black Sisters Conference
National Catholic Conference for Interracial Justice
National Conference for Community & Justice

NCCC—Committee on Disabilities
NCCC—Inclusiveness and Justice
NCCC—Racial Justice Program
NCCC—Urban Initiatives Program
Open Hands Magazine
Other Sheep
Passion Newsletter
Progressive National Baptist Convention
Project Equality, Inc
Rainbow/Push Coalition
Simon Wiesenthal Center
UCC Coalition for Lesbian, Gay, & Bisexual Concerns
UCC—Committee for Racial Justice
UCC—Liberation Ministries
UCC—Racial and Ethnic Concerns
UMC—National Federation of Asian Americans
UMC—Reconciling Congregation Program
UMC—Restorative & Racial Justice
UMC—Shalom Ministries
UU Bisexual, Gay, Lesbian & Transgender Concerns
Universal Fellowship of Metropolitan Community Churches
Wingspan

7. ECOLOGY & ENVIRONMENT
Clean air and water, deforestation, endangered species, energy conservation, global warming and/or nuclear wastes

20/20 Vision
ABC/USA—Ecology & Racial Justice
Action Coalition for Global Change
ACTS for Eco-Justice
Anglican Church of Canada—EcoJustice Committee
Church of the Brethren—Witness Office
Coalition on the Environment & Jewish Life
Earth Charter Campaign
Earth Ministry
EarthAction Network
EarthSpirit
Endangered Species Coalition
Environmental Justice Program—US Catholic Conference
Evangelical Environmental Network
Franciscans International
Friends Committee on Unity with Nature
Glinodo Center
Global Response—Environmental Action & Education Network
Interfaith Coalition for the Environment
Interfaith Coalition on Energy
Interfaith Partnership on the Environment
Loretto Community—Earth Network
National Religious Partnership for Environment

NCCC—Eco-Justice Working Group
NA Coalition for Christianity & Ecology
Presbyterians for Restoring Creation
School Sisters of Notre Dame—Shalom Center
UCC DC Environmental Issue Group
UCC Network for Environmental & Economic Responsibility
UMC—Environmental Justice Concerns
UMC—Ministry of God's Creation
Universal Pantheist Society
Voices for Survival
Web of Creation

8. ECONOMIC CONCERNS
Ramifications of globalization: International Monetary Fund, nation, and multination, corporations, salary inequities, World Bank, and World Trade Organization; also minimum/living wage, rural/farming concerns, progressive taxation, and/or workers rights

50 Years Is Enough: US Network for Global Economic Justice
ABC/USA—Economic Justice
Action Coalition for Global Change
Alliance for Democracy
Asia Pacific Center for Justice & Peace
Campaign for a Fair Minimum Wage
Canada-Asia Working Group
Canadian Catholic Organization for Development and Peace
Church and Labor Concerns—Institute for Mission USA
Citizen's Budget Campaign
Citizens for Tax Justice
Clergy & Laity United for Economic Justice
Congress of National Black Churches
Development & Peace—Canada
Disciples Peace Fellowship
Ecumenical Coalition for Economic Justice
Ecumenical Program on Central America & Caribbean
ELCA—Corporate Social Responsibility
Episcopal Responsible Investment Program
In the Spirit of Jubilee
Inter-Church Coalition on Africa
Interfaith Center for Corporate Responsibility
Jews for Racial & Economic Justice
Jobs with Justice
Kentucky Interreligious Taskforce on Central America
National Farm Worker Ministry
National Interfaith Committee for Worker Justice
One World Week
Peacework Magazine—AFSC
People of Faith Network
Presbyterian Church USA—Peacemaking Program

Rainbow/Push Coalition
Religious Working Group on World Bank & IMF
Taskforce on Churches & Corporate Responsibility
The Other Economic Summit
UMC—Economic Justice Concerns
UMC—Ministry of God's Creation
UU for a Just Economic Community
United for a Fair Economy
Washington Office on Latin America
Women's International League for Peace & Freedom
World Faiths Development Dialogue

9. ECUMENICAL INTERFAITH COOPERATION
Groups for which learning, sharing, and creating relationships with those of other denominations or faiths is a primary goal
Academy of Guru Granth Studies
Alliance for Spiritual Community
American Forum for Jewish-Christian Cooperation
Bahá'í—Office of Public Information
Bahá'í Community of Canada
Brahma Kumaris World Spiritual Organizations
Brahmi Jain Society
Buddhist Churches of America
Call to Renewal
Canadian Centre for Ecumenism
Canadian Churches Forum for Global Ministries
Canadian Council of Churches—Peace & Justice
Central Conference of American Rabbis
Clergy for Compassion and Harmony
Committee on Inter-Church & Interfaith Relations
Common Ground, Inc
Common Spirit
Council for a Parliament of the World's Religions
Ecumenicon Fellowship
Gobind Sadan, USA
Graymoor Ecumenical & InterReligious Institute
Institute for Religious Studies
Institute for World Spirituality
Interfaith Center at the Presidio
InterFaith Conference of Metropolitan Washington
Interfaith Council of Montreal
Interfaith Dialogue Association
Interfaith Network—UK
Interfaith Seminary (East-West)
International Committee for the Peace Council
International Council of Christians and Jews
International Interfaith Centre
International Shinto Foundation, Inc
Mexican InterFaith Council
Midwest Buddhist Meditation Center
Multifaith Action Society

Multifaith Resources
Muslim Public Affairs Council
Muslim World League
National Conference of Interfaith Families
NCCC Ecumenical Networks
NCCC National Council of Churches of Christ—USA
North American Interfaith Network
Ontario Consultants on Religious Tolerance
Ramakrishna-Vivekananda Center—NY
Religion in American Life, Inc—Invite a Friend Program
Risho Kosei-kai
Scarboro Missions—Justice & Peace Office
Science of Spirituality
Sikh Dharma International
Temple of Understanding
Thanks-Giving Square
Theosophical Society in America
True Buddha School Chin Yin Buddhist Society
United Church of Canada—Interfaith Relations
United Communities of Spirit
United Lodge of Theosophists
United Religions Initiative
Urantia Book Readers Online Network
Women's Interchurch Council of Canada
Won Buddhism of America
World Conference on Religion & Peace International
World Congress of Faiths
World Council of Churches—International Office
World InterFaith Education Assn
World Muslim Congress
World Sabbath of Religious Reconciliation
Yearbook of American & Canadian Churches

10. GLOBAL PEACE & SECURITY
Armaments: biological, chemical, conventional, and nuclear, their control, manufacture, sale, testing, and waste; also, landmines, overpopulation, work of the United Nations, and/or US foreign military intervention
Action Coalition for Global Change
Anglican Communion Office at the UN
Coalition for International Criminal Court
Council for a Livable World Education Fund
Fellowship of Reconciliation
Methodists United for Peace with Justice
NCCC—International Justice and Human Rights Program
Nevada Desert Experience
North American Christian Peace Conference
Peace Action
Presbyterian Church USA—United Nations Office
Project Ploughshares
Promoting Enduring Peace, Inc
St Louis Economic Conversion Project

UMC—United Nations Office
UUA—United Nations Office
United Nations Assn of the US
Women Against Military Madness
Women's International League for Peace & Freedom

11. HEALTH ISSUES
Alcohol, drug and tobacco use, HIV/AIDS, holistic health, and/or universal health care
AIDS National Interfaith Network
Albert Schweitzer Institute for Humanities
Catholic Health Association of Canada
Council of National Religious AIDS Networks
Interfaith Health Program
InterReligious Coalition on Smoking or Health
National Episcopal AIDS Coalition
National Woman's Christian Temperance Union
NCCC—Interfaith Health Care Initiative
UCC—Health and Welfare Program
UMC—Health & Wholeness Priorities
Universal Health Care Action Network

12. HUMAN RIGHTS
Health care, housing, hunger, living wage, political repression, poverty, sweatshops, third world debt, US embargoes, vocational and job training, voting rights, and/or welfare reform
Africa Faith and Justice Network
AME—Service and Development Agency
AFSC—International Regions
AFSC—National Community Relations Unit
AFSC—Proyecto Campesino
AMANI—Society of Justice and Charity
American Jewish World Service
American Kurdish Information Network
Amnesty International—Interfaith Network for Human Rights
Asia Pacific Center for Justice & Peace
B'nai B'rith
Bread for the World
Call to Renewal
Canada-Asia Working Group
Canadian Catholic Organization for Development and Peace
Canadian Coalition for Rights of Children
Catholic Campaign for Human Development
Catholic Charities USA
Catholic Network of Volunteer Service
Catholic Relief Services
Christian Peacemaker Teams
Christians for Peace in El Salvador
Churches for Middle East Peace

Coalition for Appalachian Ministry
Columban Fathers Justice & Peace Office—US
Development & Peace—Canada
Dominicans—Social Justice
Ecumenical Program on Central America & the Caribbean
Educational Concerns for Hunger
ELCA—Women (WELCA)
ELCA—Lutheran Hunger Program
Episcopal Appalachian Ministries
Episcopal Peace & Justice Network for Global Concerns
Evangelical Lutheran Coalition for Mission in Appalachia
Evangelicals for Middle East Understanding
Floresta—Healing the Land and Its People
Fourth World Movement International
Franciscans International
Global Awareness Through Experience
Global Health Ministries
Guatemala Accompaniment Project
Guatemala Human Rights Commission/USA
Habitat for Humanity International
Human Rights Action Service
Inter-Church Action for Development, Relief & Justice
Inter-Church Coalition on Africa
Inter-Church Committee on Human Rights in Latin America
InterAction
Interfaith Hunger Appeal
Interfaith Voices Against Hunger
International Committee for the Peace Council
International Service for Peace
InterReligious Foundation for Community Organization
Jews for Racial & Economic Justice
Jubilee 2000/USA Campaign
Kairos 2000/USA
Kashi Ashram
Kentucky Interreligious Taskforce on Central America
Koinonia Partners, Inc
Latin America Working Group
Loretto Community—Latin America–Caribbean Committee
Maryknoll Office for Global Concerns
Millennium Institute
National Interfaith Hospitality Network
NCCC Church World Service
NCCC—International Justice & Human Rights Program
NCCC—Urban Initiatives Program
NETWORK: A National Catholic Justice Lobby
North American Christian Peace Conference
Oikocredit
One World Week

Pastors for Peace
Pax World Service
Peace Brigades International
Presbyterian Church in Canada—World Service and
    Development
PC/USA—Ending Homelessness of Women
PC/USA—Health, Education & Welfare Association
PC/USA—Hunger Program
Quixote Center—Haiti Reborn
School Sisters of Notre Dame—Shalom Center
Seeds of Hope Publisher
SERRV International
Sisters of Mercy of the Americas—Ctr for Justice &
    Peace
Sojourners Magazine
Southern Christian Leadership Conference
Strategic Pastoral Action Network
UCC—Community Empowerment Ministry
UCC—Health and Welfare Program
UCC—Liberation Ministries
United Methodist Appalachian Development Committee
Voices in the Wilderness
Washington Office on Africa
Washington Office on Latin America
World Fellowship of Buddhists
World Tibet Day
World Vision Inc

13. INDIGENOUS OR DISPLACED PERSONS
Needs and rights of aboriginals, immigrants, indigenous peoples and/or refugees
Aboriginal Rights Coalition—Canada
American Indian—Alaska Native Lutheran Assn
Anglican Church of Canada—EcoJustice Committee
Border Assn for Refugees from Central America, Inc
Canadian Council for Refugees
Canadian Friends Service Committee
Cultural Survival
Ecumenical Peace Institute
Exodus World Service
Guatemala Accompaniment Project
Honor Our Neighbors Origins and Rights
Inter-Church Committee for Refugees
Interfaith Coalition for Immigrant Rights
Jews for Racial & Economic Justice
Lutheran Immigration & Refugee Service
Native American Rights Fund
UCC Council for American Indian Ministry
UMC—Children and Welfare
UMC—Immigration and Refugee Concerns
UMC—Native American International Caucus
US Catholic Conference—Migration and Refugee Services

Working Group on Refugee Resettlement

14. PEACE & NONVIOLENCE
Conflict resolution, death penalty, disarmament, International Criminal Court, militarism, nonviolence, Nuclear Test Ban Treaty, School of the Americas, simple lifestyle, and/or US budget priorities
20/20 Vision
ABC/USA—Reconciliation Ministries
AFSC—Peace Unit
Alternatives for Simple Living
Alternatives to Violence Project USA
Association for Global New Thought
Baptist Peace Fellowship of North America
Benedictine Resource Center—TX
Brahmi Jain Society
Brethren Peace Fellowship
Bruderhof Communities
Buddhist Peace Fellowship
Buddhist Society for Compassionate Wisdom
Calling Prophets Project
Canadian Friends Service Committee
Center for Non Violence
Center on Conscience & War
Central Committee for Conscientious Objectors
Christian Peacemaker Teams
Christian Support Ministries
Church of God Peace Fellowship
Church of the Brethren—Witness Office
Coalition to Stop Gun Violence
Common Ground Network for Life and Choice
Disciples Peace Fellowship
Ecumenical Peace Institute
Episcopal Peace Fellowship
Erie Benedictines for Peace
Fellowship Magazine
Fellowship of Reconciliation
Franciscan Federation of Brothers and Sisters of US
Franciscan Sisters of Mary
Franciscans International
Friends for a Non-Violent World
Global Options
Global Peace Services USA
Institute for Peace & Justice
International Committee for the Peace Council
Jain Society of Toronto
Jewish Peace Fellowship
Jewish Women International
Jonah House
Kirkridge Retreat Center—The Picket & Pray Place
Koinonia Partners, Inc
Latin America Working Group

Loretto Network for NonViolence
Lutheran Peace Fellowship
Lutheran Volunteer Corps
M K Gandhi Institute for Nonviolence
Mahavir World Vision Inc
Maple Buddhist Society
Mennonite Church—Peace & Justice Committee
Methodists United for Peace with Justice
Michigan Faith & Resistance Peace Team
Ministry of Money
Muslim Peace Fellowship
National Campaign for a Peace Tax Fund
National Coalition to Abolish Death Penalty
National Conference for Community & Justice
National War Tax Resistance Coordinating Committee
New Call to Peacemaking
No More Violence
NonViolent Alternatives
On Earth Peace Assembly, Inc
Pax Christi USA
Peace & Freedom Magazine
Peace Action
Peace Resource Center
Peaceday Organization
Presbyterian Church USA—Peacemaking Program
Presbyterian Peace Fellowship
Project Ploughshares
Quality of Life Group: Dharma Society
Random Acts of Kindness Foundation
Resource Center for Nonviolence
Sakyadhita: International Assn of Buddhist Women
School of the Americas Watch
Schools for Chiapas
Seamless Garment Network, Inc—USA
Search for Common Ground
Sequoia—Interreligious Newsmagazine
Sikh Dharma International
Simon Wiesenthal Center
Soka Gakkai International-USA
Strategic Pastoral Action Network
The Other Side Magazine
UMC—Peace With Justice
Unitarian Universalist Peace Fellowship
War Tax Resisters Penalty Fund
Witness for Peace
Women Against Military Madness
Women's International League for Peace & Freedom
World Council of Muslim Women Foundation
World Peace Prayer Society
World Peacemakers Inc
World Sabbath of Religious Reconciliation
World Alliance of YMCAs

World Alliance of YWCAs

15. RELIGIOUS & CIVIL LIBERTY
First Amendment rights, religious freedom, separation of church and state; also censorship, prayer in public schools, reproductive choice, and/or school vouchers
Alliance for Tolerance & Freedom
Alliance of Baptists, Inc
American Humanist Association
American Jewish Committee
American Jewish Congress
Americans for Religious Liberty
Americans United for Separation of Church & State
Anti-Defamation League
Baptist Joint Comm on Public Affairs
Catholics for Free Choice/Catholics for Contraception
Center on Conscience & War
Church of Scientology—USA
Common Ground Network for Life and Choice
Covenant of the Goddess
Equal Partners in Faith
Freedom for Religions in Germany
Freedom of Religion for Everyone Everywhere
The Humanist Magazine
Imagine a World of Wanted and Nurtured Children
Institute for First Amendment Studies
Interfaith Alliance
Interfaith Working Group
International Coalition for Religious Freedom
International Religious Liberty Association
Liberty Magazine
Mainstream Coalition
Margaret Sanger's Supporters
National Coalition Against Censorship
National Jewish Democratic Council
National Spiritualist Association of Churches
NGO Committee on Freedom of Religion or Belief
People of Faith Network
Religion and Public Education Resource Center
Religious Coalition for Reproductive Choice
Religious Consultation on Population, Reproductive
    Health & Ethics
Texas Baptists Committed
UMC—Children and Welfare

16. RENEWAL OF FAITH GROUP
Seeking change in organizational leadership, practices, and/or policy
ABC/USA Assn of Welcoming & Affirming Baptists
Association for Rights of Catholics in Church
Call to Action
Catholic Organizations for Renewal

Catholics for Free Choice/Catholics for Contraception
Christian Support Ministries
Dignity Canada
Dignity USA
Fellowship of Southern Illinois Laity
FutureChurch
Gay, Lesbian and Affirming Disciples Alliance
Hinduism Today Magazine
Holy Orthodox Catholic Church
Lutheran Network for Inclusive Vision
Lutherans Concerned—North America
More Light Presbyterians
National Catholic Reporter—Weekly Newspaper
Other Sheep
PC/USA—Women's Advocacy Office
Quixote Center—Catholics Speak Out
Quixote Center—Priests for Equality
Resources for Christian Living—Vatican II
Texas Baptists Committed
TIKKUN Magazine
UCC Coalition for Lesbian, Gay, Bisexual & Transgender Concerns
UUA for a Just Economic Community
United Catholic Church
UMC—Reconciling Congregation Program
Wingspan
Women's Ordination Conference
Women-Church Convergence

17. SOCIETIES, SEMINARIES & FUNDS
Advisory groups, foundations, funds, graduate education, and theological seminaries; also leadership, occupational, and professional societies or networks
AAAS Dialogue on Science, Ethics & Religion
ACTS for Eco-Justice
All Faiths Seminary International
American Islamic College
American Scientific Affiliation
Assn of Interfaith Ministers
Assn of Professors & Researchers in Religious Education
Au Sable Institute of Environmental Studies
Boston Research Center for the 21st Century
Canadian Conference of Catholic Bishops
Canadian Council of Christian Charities
Canadian Religious Conference
Center for Global Ethics—Global Dialogue Institute
Center for Process Studies
Center for Religion, Ethics, and Social Policy
Center for Respect of Life & Environment
Center for Sexuality and Religion
Center for Study of Religion in Public Life
Center for Women, the Earth, the Divine

Central Conference of American Rabbis
Chaplaincy Institute for Arts & Interfaith Ministries
Churches' Center for Theology & Public Policy
Consortium on Peace Research, Education & Development
Council of Societies for Study of Religion
Earth Charter Campaign
Education as Transformation Project
Expanding Humanity's Vision of God
Faith and Politics Institute
Foundation for Interfaith Research & Ministry
Iliff School of Theology Justice & Peace Studies
Initiative for Religion, Ethics & Human Rights
Institute for Integrated Social Analysis
Institute of Islamic Information & Education
Institute on Religion & Democracy
Interfaith Church of Metaphysics
Interfaith Community Ministry Network
Interfaith Network—UK
Interfaith Seminary
Interfaith Theological Seminary
International Association for Religious Freedom
International Institute of Islamic Thought
InterReligious Federation for World Peace
IQRA' International Educational Foundation
Islamic Council of Imams—Canada
Islamic Society of North America
Jewish Fund for Justice
Leadership Conference of Women Religious
Marianist Social Justice Collaborative
MAZON: A Jewish Response to Hunger
Millennium Institute
Monastic Interreligious Dialogue
National Association of Ecumenical & Interreligious Staff
National Federation of Interfaith Volunteer Caregivers
New Israel Fund
New Seminary
NGO Committee on Freedom of Religion or Belief
North American Coalition on Religion & Ecology
North American Interfaith Network
Numata Center for Buddhist Translation and Research
Ontario Multifaith Council on Spiritual & Religious Care
Park Ridge Center
PLURA Fund
Pluralism Project
Preamble Center
Primate's World Relief & Development Fund
Rabbinical Council of America
Religious Consultation on Population, Reproductive Health & Ethics
Religious Education Association
Rivier College Center for Peace & Social Justice

Sakyadhita: International Assn of Buddhist Women
School of Metaphysics
Seminary Consortium for Urban Pastoral Education
Society for Buddhist-Christian Studies
Society for Humanistic Judaism
Traditional Circle of Indian Elders and Youth
Washington Institute for Jewish Leadership & Values
Woodstock Theological Center
World Faiths Development Dialogue
Zygon Center for Religion and Science

18. TRAINING & RESOURCES
Groups offering training or resources for others' use as a primary goal

ADVANCE—Avoiding Domestic Violence & Affirming
    Nonviolent Creative Efforts
Albert Schweitzer Institute for Humanities
Alternative Gifts International
Alternatives to Violence Project USA
American Humanist Association
Americans for Religious Liberty
Association for Religion & Intellectual Life
Benetvision Publishers
Brahma Kumaris World Spiritual Organization
Canadian Churches Forum for Global Ministries
Canadian Council for Refugees
Canadian Council of Christians & Jews
Catholic Network of Volunteer Service
Center for Action & Contemplation
Center for New Community
Center for Non Violence
Center for Progressive Christianity
Center for the Prevention of Sexual & Domestic Violence
Center of Concern
Center on Conscience & War
Centre for Social Concern
Church Innovations Institute
Coalition on the Environment & Jewish Life
Cult Awareness Network
Cultural Survival
E Pluribus Unum Project
EarthAction Network
Educational Concerns for Hunger
Engaged Zen Foundation
Episcopal Appalachian Ministries
Episcopal Peace & Justice Network for Global Concerns
Equal Exchange, Inc—Interfaith Coffee Project
Exodus World Service
Floresta—Healing the Land and Its People
Fung Loy Kok Institute of Taoism
Glinodo Center
Global Education Associates

Global Peace Services USA
Heifer Project International
Institute for First Amendment Studies
Institute for Peace & Justice
Interfaith Council of Greater New York
International Society of Divine Love
InterReligious Foundation for Community Organization
JAINA Federation
Kirkridge Retreat Center—The Picket & Pray Place
Lutheran Peace Fellowship
M K Gandhi Institute for Nonviolence
The Mastery Foundation
Michigan Faith & Resistance Peace Team
Ministry of Money
Mother-to-Mother Ministry
Multifaith Institute
NCCC—Pillars of Peace
National Catholic Conference for Interracial Justice
National Conference of Interfaith Families
National Federation of Interfaith Volunteer Caregivers
National Youth Project
No More Violence
NonViolent Alternatives
Pax Christi USA
The Peace Abbey
Peace & Justice Resource Center
Peace Resource Center
Presbyterian Church USA—Criminal Justice Office
Quixote Center—Priests for Equality
Random Acts of Kindness Foundation
Religion and Public Education Resource Center
Resource Center for Nonviolence
Resources for Christian Living—Vatican II
Schools for Chiapas
Search for Common Ground
Seeds of Hope Publisher
SERRV International
Special Ideas
Spiritual Eldering Institute
Summer Peacebuilding Institute
Tara Meditation Center
UCC Coalition for Lesbian, Gay & Bisexual Concerns
UCC—Community Empowerment Ministry
UCC—Women in Church and Society
UCC Council for American Indian Ministry
UMC—Reconciling Congregation Program
UMC—Seminars on National & International Affairs
UMC—United Nations Office
UUA Bisexual, Gay, Lesbian & Transgender Concerns
United for a Fair Economy
Virtual Religion Index
World Assembly of Muslim Youth

World InterFaith Education Assn

19. WOMEN
Abuse, education, employment and job training, equal rights, health care, housing, incarceration, language, poverty and/or reproductive control

ABC/USA—Biblical Justice Ministry Center
AFSC—American Friends Service Commission
Bahá'í—Office of Public Information
Bahá'í Community of Canada
Benetvision Publishers
Call to Action
Center for the Prevention of Sexual & Domestic Violence
Center of Concern
Chicago Women-Church
Christian Reformed Churches in Canada
Church Women United
Cooperative Baptist Fellowship
Ecumenical Coalition for Economic Justice
Evangelical Fellowship of Canada—Social Action Commission
ELCA—Women (WELCA)
Evangelical Lutheran Women of Canada
Federation of Zoroastrian Associations of NA
Franciscan Sisters of Mary
Global Awareness through Experience
Imagine a World of Wanted and Nurtured Children
Jewish Women International
Journal of Women's Ministries
Lilith Magazine—Jewish Feminist Quarterly
Loretto Community—Women's Network
Mennonite Central Committee—Women's Concerns
Mother-to-Mother Ministry
National Association for Evangelicals—Ofc for Governmental Affairs
National Black Sisters' Conference US
National Council of Catholic Women
National Council of Jewish Women
NCCC—Justice for Women Program, Inclusiveness and Justice
Oikocredit
PC/USA—Ending Homelessness of Women
PC/USA—Hunger Program
PC/USA—Women's Advocacy Office
PC/USA—Presbyterian Women
Quixote Center—Catholics Speak Out
Religious Action Center of Reform Judaism
Sisters of Charity BVM—Women's Office
UCC Board for Homeland Ministries
UCC Family Life/Human Sexuality Ministry
UCC Office for Church in Society

UCC—Women in Church and Society
UMC Ministry of God's Human Community
Unitarian Universalist Women's Federation
United Muslim Women of Canada
Women's Alliance for Theology, Ethics, and Ritual
Women's Interchurch Council of Canada
Women Vision International
World Council of Muslim Women Foundation
World Alliance of YWCAs

INDEX

A

`Abdu'l-Bahá (Abbas Effendi), 6–8, 281, 315
Abdullah II, 156
abortion, 314–15
Absolute, the, 252, 253
Abu-Baker, 300
Adam's sin, 24, 25
advaita, 252, 253
Adventist family, 24
advocacy, organizations focusing on, 420–21
Africa, 3; history and culture, 3; Zulu traditional religion of Southern, 5
African American Judaism, 33
African slaves, 73, 75
African (traditional) religion(s), 3–5; from within, 3–4; concept of, 3; defined, 4; prayers and religious expression, 4–5. *See also* Islam
afterlife. *See* Hereafter
Agamas (Further Scriptures), 50–51
agriculture, 192, 193
ahimsa, 82, 83, 221
AIDS, 96, 202
al-Attas, Syed Muhammad Naquib, 73
Ali, 70
Allah, 66, 67, 69, 75, 76
Anekantavada, 82
angels, 69, 119
animism, 42, 117
Ansari of Herat, 290
anthroposophy, 98–99
anti-Semitism, 212–16; temples firebombed, 212–14
appeal, 264
Arcane School, 99–100
Arial, 47
Arjan, Guru, 95, 96
Armenians, 21
arts, the, 195–97
Ashoka, 273
Association of Interfaith Ministers (AIM), 148, 159
Association of Religious NGOs, 154
Astasajasrika, 12
atheism, 25, 61
Atman (Self), 55, 56, 252, 253
atman (self), 251, 252
atonement, 87
at-one-ment, 29
attunement, 29
Augustine, St., 274
Aulakh, Gurmit Singh, 334
Aurobindo, Sri, 100–101; evolutionary philosophy, 100–101
Australian Aboriginals, 47

autonomy, false, 18
awakening process, dual, 349–50
awareness, 252
Axial Age, 238–39; Second, 239, 240

B

Báb, the (Alí-Muhammad), 6
Bahadur, Guru Tegh, 95
Bahá'í, 6–8, 172, 237, 254, 281, 315; response to challenges facing humanity, 8–10; view of challenges facing humanity, 8–9
Bahá'u'lláh (Mirzá Husayn-`Alí), 6–10
Bailey, Alice A., 99, 100
balance, 114; cultural and ecological, 53, 114. *See also* harmony
Bancroft, Anne, 338
Baptism, 24, 330
baptism, 21, 23
Berry, Thomas, 30, 274
Berry, Wendell, 286–87
Besant, Annie, 102
Bethge, Everhard, 352
Beversluis, Joel, 206, 207
Bhakti Yoga, 57, 59
Bible, 20, 22, 25. *See also* New Testament; Old Testament
Biblical contradictions, 24
Black Elk, 46, 288, 289
Blavatsky, H. P., 102–4
Bodhidharma, 17
Bodhisattva, 13, 14
body-mind dualism, 251
Bohm, David, 126–27
Boissière, Robert, 45
Bonney, Charles, 129
Book of Mormon, 25
Brahman, 41, 50–52, 55, 252, 253
Braybrooke, Marcus, 127–28, 147, 151–52, 156, 163, 171, 173, 232
Britain, 150
British Israel Movement, 24
brotherhood, 68, 102, 103. *See also* harmony; *Ummah*
Buddha (Siddartha Gautama), 11–14, 350
Buddhism, 11–15, 237–38, 350; and denial of self, 251; and other religions, 40, 41; Tibetan, 239 (*see also* Dalai Lama); women and, 338
Buddhist-Christian dialogue, 132, 154, 156
Buddhist experience in North America, 15–17
Buddhist prayers and quotations, 172, 255, 280, 296, 315
Buddhist *sutras*, 40
Buffalo, White, 46
Burger, Julian, 42–43, 45

C

Cairo Declaration on Population and Development, 313–15
"Call to Our Guiding Institutions, A," 183–85, 188–201, 204, 207, 241; broadening the base support for, 207–8; Preamble, 189; rationale, 185–88
Calvin, John, 22, 25
Calvinism, 25, 112
Cape Town, 167. *See also* Parliaments of the World's Religions
caste system, 95
Catholic Church, 23, 26, 132
Catholicism, 20–22, 255
causality, 13
"Celebration of the Earth," 295
Center for World Thanksgiving, 148
Ceric, Mustafa, 209
Chaffee, Paul, 155
Ch'an (meditation), 40
Chang Tzu, 37, 105
change, 37, 261; principles of, 38. *See also* transformation
charity, 69, 74
chi, 106
children, 181; organizations focusing on, 421; recognizing the rights of, 340–41; religious and spiritual responsibilities regarding, 342; responsibilities of governments and international organizations to, 341–42; society's responsibility to, 341
China, 14, 273; Buddhism in, 40 *(see also* Tibet)
chosen people, 72
Christ: body of, 34; return/second coming of, 24, 110. *See also* Jesus Christ; savior
Christian ethics, 27
Christian family tree, 21–26
Christian missionaries and evangelism, 330
Christian mysticism, 253
Christian Science-Metaphysical family, 26
Christian Way, 28
Christianity, 172, 237–38, 280, 296–97, 315–16; African American, 32–34; Anglican, 255; call for evangelical renewal, 34–36; and the challenges facing humanity, 26–28; dialogue with other religions, 88, 132, 135, 154, 156–57; enriching theological traditions, 29–31; ethical guidance in, 28–29; interfaith relations, 20; origins and beliefs, 18–20. *See also specific denominations*
Christians, 72
Chu Hsi, 39, 41
Church, function of, 24
Church of Jesus Christ of Latter-Day Saints, 24, 25
CIM. *See* Mexican InterFaith Council
Circle, 34
Civil Rights movement, 33, 203–5
civil society, organizations of, 200–201
civilization. *See* society
Cobb, John, 31
codependent origination, 16. *See also* dependent origination
Cohen, Michael, 292
commerce, 193
commitment, 263–64
Communal Family, 26
communalism, 133
communication, 64; nonviolent, 223; organizations focusing on, 421–22

communion(s), 27–28, 30, 242
communism, 15
community *vs.* individual interests, 322
community(ies), 264; emphasis on, 16; global, 16, 125; living in, 239; of religions, x–xi, 1, 123–25, 231, 237–38; sense of, 124
compassion, 243. *See also* charity; poverty
confession, 22
Conficius, 37, 40
conflict resolution, 64, 65
Confucianism, 37–39, 172; integration with other traditions, 40–41; in the world today, 39–40
Congregation B'nai Israel, 212
consciousness, 251; Earth-life and the locus of, 294; mystical dimension, 250–51, 253; transformation of, 181–82
Consejo Interreligioso Disease Mexico (CIM; Mexican InterFaith Council), 142–43, 152
Consultation of the Environment and Jewish Life, 153
contingent genesis, 11–13
"Contributions by Religions to the Culture of Peace, The," 263–64
conversion: religious, 33, 322, 330–31; spiritual, 30
cooperation and collaboration, 73; among diverse religions, 52–53, 160–61
Coptic churches of Egypt and Ethiopia, 22
cosmic life, 4
Council for a Parliament of the World's Religions (CPWR), 149, 163, 172–73, 182–85, 189, 204
covenant ethics, 29
covenant theological tradition, 29
Craft, the. *See* Wicca
Crazy Horse, 46
creation, 4; concerning acts of initiative and, 353
Creator: God the, 32, 33; thankfulness to, 48–49
criminal justice system, organizations focusing on, 422
cross, 29
Crossing-Makers *(Tirthankaras),* 80–81

D

Dalai Lama, 15, 128, 182, 204, 209, 274, 315, 330
death, 44
"Declaration of a Global Ethic," 172–82
"Declaration of Human Responsibilities for Peace and Sustainable Development ," 269–72
Declaration of the Sacred Earth Gathering, 309
Declaration on the Elimination of All Forms of Intolerance and of Discrimination Based on Religion and Belief, 218–20
Deep-Dialogue: areas in which it operates, 141, 150; ground rules for personal and communal, 138–41
Deganawida (Peacemaker), 46
democracy, 307–8
dependent origination, 11. *See also* codependent origination
Dharma, 54
Dhyani Ywagoo, 46–47
dialogue, defined, 138
"Dialogue-Decalogue: Ground Rules for Interreligious, Interideological Dialogue," 127, 138–41
directives, universal/irrevocable, 178–82, 186
discipleship, 99
discipline, 56
disciplined practice, 137–38

discrimination: eliminating, 217–20; organizations focusing on, 422–23; against religious minorities, 133
diversity: building a community in, 187; religious, 71, 112–13
Divine, 114–16, 253. *See also* God, within self
"Do unto others…". *See* Golden Rule
Downey, Michael, 233
Drum, 34
Dzogchen, 252

E

Earth, 42–45, 117, 237, 240; Mother, 34; new scientific paradigm and new mythology of the, 292–94; as our home, 304; overconsumption and the, 317; people as stewards *vs.* pirates of the, 293–94; prayers, scriptures, and reflections in celebration of the, 295–303; preserving and cherishing the, 282–83; as self-regulating organism, 292–93. *See also* Nature
Earth Community, 274, 276, 277
Earth Council and Earth Charter, 303–8
Earth-life, 294
Earth religions, 114, 237
Eastern Liturgical tradition, 21
Eastern Orthodox tradition, 20, 21, 256–57
Eckhart, Meister, 291
eco-feminism, 117, 237
ecological balance and harmony, 53, 114, 242
ecological integrity, 305–6
ecology and eco-justice, 28–31, 64, 168, 194, 237, 240, 260; organizations focusing on, 423. *See also* environment
Economic and Social Council (ECOSOC) of the United Nations, 278
economic concerns: organizations focusing on, 423–24. *See also* poverty
economic growth and development, 64
economic justice, 8, 306–7
economic life of indigenous people, 44
economic order, commitment to culture of, 179, 186
economics, nonviolent, 222–23
Ecozoic Age, 240
"ecumenical," defined, 146
education, 39, 41, 194–95; about overconsumption, 318–19; nonviolent, 224; religion and, 314; universal, 8–9, 63, 194, 203
EDUCATION as *Transformation* Project, 234
egoism, 177–78
Elder Brother, 46
Elements, Five, 106
emptiness *(sunyata),* 13
enlightenment, 13
entropy, and the Earth, 293
environment, 29, 94, 114–15, 153, 168, 260; Bahá'í reflections on the, 295–96; and development, 9; organizations focusing on the, 423. *See also* ecology and eco-justice
environmental concerns, 96, 266, 267; and challenges ahead, 304–5; the global situation, 304; and the way forward, 308
environmental crisis, 283, 309; spiritual dimensions, 283–90; urgency of a Jewish response to the, 311–12
environmental destruction, 31, 317
equality: for all human beings, 71, 120, 140, 177–78 *(see also* racism; women); of all life, 48; gender, 95–96; moral, 63

eucharist, 22
evangelical Christianity, 34–36; mature, 30
Evangelical Declaration on the Care of Creation, An, 310
Evangelical Environment Network (EEN), 153, 310
Evangelical Lutheran Church in America (ELCA), 215–16
Evangelicals for Social Action (ESA), 310
evangelism, 330
evangelistic methods, door-to-door, 25
exclusivist position, 134–35, 231, 232, 239
extremism, 132, 134. *See also* fundamentalism

F

Fai, Ghulam Nabi, 332
faith, 22, 25, 27, 29, 58, 69; organizations focusing on renewal of, 427–28
family(ies), 264; organizations focusing on, 421; regulation of the, 39
fasting. *See* Sawn
feast, 7
Federation of Zoroastrianism Associations of North America (FEZANA), 121
Fellowship of Reconciliation (FOR), 149–50
feminine, Divine, 115
feminism, 30, 117, 237
"fitting," 29
Fitzpatrick, Karen, 233–34
Folk Shinto, 89
Forman, Robert, 234
Four Noble Truths, 12, 13
"Fourth World," 42
Francis of Assisi, St., 297
Free-Church family, European, 23
freedoms, 322. *See also* human rights
Friends. *See* Quakers
fundamentalism, 134, 169. *See also* extremism
funds, organizations focusing on, 428–29
future: choosing our, xi; visions of the, xi

G

Gaia hypothesis, 291–94
Gandhi, Mahatma, 44, 128, 221–23, 239, 243, 311
Gandhi, Virchand Raghavji, 84
gender: and the Divine, 115. *See also* women
gender equality, 95–96
General Anthroposophical Society, 98
genocide, 118
"Gifts of Service to the World," 183
Global Dialogue Institute (GDI), 150
global ethic, 133, 134, 166, 241; declaration of a, 174–82; defined, 176–77; intention, 177; as necessary for new global order, 176–77; principles, 175–82; quest for a, 125, 168, 171–74 (see also Parliaments of the World's Religions); toward a, 174–82
Global Ethic Foundation, 173
global responsibility, 178
global spirituality(ies), 235, 237–38; toward a, 236–37
God, 4, 51, 71, 93, 119; approaches to, 57–58; belief *vs.* non-belief in, 251–52; concept of, 16; messengers of, 6–8; oneness of, 7, 52; path(s) to, 52, 100; within self, 57, 58; union with, 50–51, 59, 251, 253. *See also* Allah; Brahman; *specific religions*

God-consciousness, 5
"God Is Dead," 61
God-Love, 18–20
God the Creator, 32, 33
Goddess, 115–16
goddesses, 50, 89, 117. *See also* Kali
Godhead, 252
gods, 50. *See also* kami
Goethe, Johann Wolfgang von, 353
Golden Rule, 172–73, 177
Gomez-Ibanez, Daniel, 334
Gospel of Christ, 35
government, 39, 63, 191–92; education, religion, and, 314; nonviolent, 223–24
grace, 22–24, 30, 71–72, 76
grassroots model, 157–59
gratitude, 297, 303
Gregorios, Paulos Mâr, 205–6
Gualtiere, Judi, 234
Gupta, Lina, 338–39
Guru Granth Sahib, 92–95
gurus, 92, 93, 95

H

Hadith, 68
Hajj (pilgrimage), 69
Hammarskjold, Dag, 353
Hare Krishna Movement, 59
harmony, 3; with all people and things, 45; among religions, 9; cultural and ecological, 53, 114, 242; peace and, 58; visions of, 202–5
Harvard University, 153–54
healing, 303. *See also* medicine
health issues, organizations focusing on, 425
heart: rectifying of the, 39; toward a universal civilization with a, 273–77
Heathen, 117. *See also* Wicca
Hell, 24
Hereafter, eternal life of, 69
Hildegard of Bingen, 296–97
Hinayana, 14
Hindu community: response to challenges facing humanity, 55–56
Hindu myths, 54
Hindu sub-traditions *(sampradayas),* 52
Hinduism, 33–34, 50, 172, 227, 252, 256, 273, 280, 316; approaches to interfaith dialogue and cooperation, 52–53, 55; main sources of religious knowledge, 50–51; women, Kali, and, 338–39. *See also* religious freedom; Yoga
3HO (Healthy, Happy, Holy Organization), 94
holiness, 23
Holocaust, 321
Holy Spirit, 20, 23
honesty: in interfaith dialogue, 139. *See also* truthfulness
Honore, Pierre, 45
hope, 349
Hopi prophecies, 46
Huang Te-Hui, 41
Huarta, Willaru, 47
human rights, 33–34, 260, 270; caring and, 94; current challenge regarding, 324–25; faith in, 320–25; organizations focusing on, 425–26; religious support for, 321–22; in the 20th century, 321; understandings of the nature of, 322. *See also* rights; Universal Declaration of Human Rights
human rights abuses, 331–35
human rights enforcement, 323
human rights struggle: nonviolence and the, 323
humanism, 60–61; and democratic society, 63–64; ethics, 62; and humanity as a whole, 65; and the individual, 62–63; and religion, 61–62; types of, 61; and world community, 64
Humanist Manifesto II, 60–65
humanistic culture, 238
Hunbatz Men, 47–48
hunger. *See* poverty
Hutterite community, 26
hymns, 34, 51–53, 56

I

I-Ching, 40, 41, 106
I-Kuan-Tao (Integrated Tao), 41
Id al-Adha, 70, 71
Id al-Fitr, 70–71
idealists, 38–39
Ijma, 68
Ijtihad, 68
imminent return of savior. *See* return of savior
immortality, 24
impersonalism, 252
incense, 34
Independent Fundamentalist families, 24
India, 33–34, 132–33, 227, 332–34
Indian Sikhs, 94–95
indifferentism, 130
indigenous peoples, 42–45, 243; organizations focusing on, 426. *See also* native traditions
individual *vs.* community interests, 322
individual(s): in community, 4; preciousness and integrity of, 62
individualism, 16
industry, 193
intelligence, 62
Inter-Religious Federation for World Peace (IRFWP), 109, 152, 226, 312–13
InterAction Council, 344
interconnectedness, x, 17, 38, 39, 48, 231, 241
interdependence: sense of, 242; spiritual, 243
"interfaith": definitions of, 146, 159. *See also* "interreligious"
interfaith activities, types of, 146–47
Interfaith Alliance, 150
Interfaith Center of New York, 229
Interfaith Conference, Metropolitan Washington, D.C. (ICMW), 164
interfaith cooperation, ecumenical: organizations focusing on, 424
interfaith dialogue, 9, 55, 126–27; assumptions in, 231; bilateral conversations, 132; difficulties to be addressed in, 135–36; future of, 228; history, 126–27, 131; labels and, 134; and listening to other disciplines, 135; misuse, 133; new agenda, 127–28, 133–37; points of similarity/agreement found in, 137–38; religious institutions engaging in, 132; types of, 126; widening the circle of, 134–35. *See also* Parliaments of the World's Religions; World's

Parliament of Religions
Interfaith Dialogue Association (IDA), 146, 157–59
interfaith dialogue organizations, 159; forming, 157; goals, 158–59; practical ideas for, 158; programs, 158; young adult and youth, 162–65
interfaith Internet links, 360–62
Interfaith Ministers vs. Interfaith Clergy, 159
interfaith movement, 147–48; assumptions in, 231; evangelism, conversion, and the, 330–31; growth, 170; as illusion/wishful thinking, 136–37; new agenda, 171; problems, 147; strategies and tasks, 124–25; in 20th century, 129–37; what is emerging in the, 123–24; what still needs to be done, 133. See also community(ies), of religions
InterFaith Network for the United Kingdom, 146, 150
interfaith networking and Internet communications, 356–57
interfaith organizations, 130–31; need to be together, 136–37; problems, 147; sampling of, 148–57; types, 146–47. See also specific organizations
interfaith understanding, practical importance of, 132–33
Interfaith Voices for Peace and Justice (Internet forum), 206
Interfaith Youth Corps, 162, 163
International Association for Religious Freedom (IARF), 130, 136, 147, 151, 164, 170, 171, 279, 320, 323–25
International Conference on Population and Development, 312–13
International Council of Christians and Jews (ICCJ), 136, 151
International Covenant on Civil and Political Rights, 217–18
International Decade for a Culture of Peace and Nonviolence for the Children of the World (2001-2010), 150
International Federation for World Peace, 109
International Interfaith Centre (IIC), 136, 151, 173
international intergovernmental organizations, 198–200
International Jewish Committee on Inter-Religious Consultations, 132
International Religious Youth Organizations' Seminar (IRYOS), 164–65
International Society for Krishna Consciousness (ISKCON), 59
International Year of Thanksgiving (2000), 148
International Year of Tolerance (1995), 262
Internet: online congress of the world religions, 356–57
"interreligious": defined, 146. See also "interfaith"
Interreligious Assembly of the Vatican, 211–12
interreligious cooperation, 314
interreligious dialogue, role of love in, 348
"Interspiritual Age, The" (Teasdale), 235
interspiritual wisdom, 235, 238, 240
intra-religious dialogue, 135
intuitive approach, 41
Islam, 66, 78, 173, 238, 256, 281, 316; beliefs and observances, 68–69; contemporary movements, 70; feasts and festivals, 70–71; historical establishment, 66–68; in North America, 73–75; and other religious traditions, 71–75, 78, 132, 134; Pillars, 69; and religious conversion, 33, 322; schools of law, 69; theological schools and schisms, 69–70; in the world today, 76–78. See also Muslims
Isma'iliyah, 70
Ithna 'Ash'ariyyah (Twelvers), 70

J

Jain declaration on nature, 310–11
Jainism, 79–84, 173, 210, 281; code of conduct, 82

Japan. See Shinto
Jehovah's Witnesses, 24, 25
Jesus Christ, 285; and Christianity, 19–21, 25, 27–30, 32, 110–11; crucifixion, 29; resurrection, 29
Jewish-Christian dialogue, 88, 132, 135, 156, 215–16
Jews, 72. See also anti-Semitism
jihad, verbal, 77
Jinas, 80
Joe, Jennie, 334–35
John Paul II, Pope, 134, 155, 160–61, 209
Johnson, Thomas M., 332–33
Johnston, Carol, 31
journalism. See media
Judaism, 33, 85–87, 238, 254–55, 280, 316; converts to, 33; and interfaith dialogue, 88
justice, 73, 259–60; organizations focusing on, 420, 422; a witness to, 243

K

Kali, 338–39
kami (deities), 89–90
karma, 12, 51
karuna, 252
Kashmir, 332
Kathrada, Ahmed, 203
Kenney, Jim, 183
Khawarij (secessionists), 70
King, Ursula, 337–38
klesa (afflictors), 12–13
Knitter, Paul, 134
knowledge: attaining, 48; completion of, 39
"knowledge self," 39
Kocherry, Thomas, 333
Kogi, 47
Kollek, Teddy, 134
Korea, 14
Krishnamurti, 163
Kriya Yoga, 59
Kuftaro, Sheikh Ahmad, 316
Kukulcan, 45–48
Küng, Hans, 134, 136, 159, 172, 173, 239, 274, 320

L

labor, 193
Ladjamaya, 332
Lakota Sioux, 46
language: limitations, 253–4; problem of, 232–33; universal auxiliary, 9
Lao Tzu, 105–7, 280, 302
Latter-Day Saints family, 25
Leopold, Aldo, 287
Liberal family, 25
liberation, 51, 52, 56, 346
life, 48; all life as equal, 48; commitment to culture of respect for, 178, 186; nature of, 3; purpose(s)/goal(s) of, 51, 54, 57; respect and care for the community of, 305; reverence for all, 241–42; stages in, 51, 54; threat to, 3
love, 6, 253, 296, 350; for all human beings, 27, 40; nonviolence and, 221–22; towards the dialogue of, 348–49
Lovelock, James, 291–93
Luther, Martin, 215, 216

Lutheran Church, 22; and Judaism, 215–16
Lutheran World Federation, 216
Lyons, Oren, 301, 316

M

magic, 115
Mahavira, 310
Mahayana, 14
Makkan Muslims, 67
Mandela, Nelson, 182, 203, 205
marriage, 44, 181
Massignon, Louis, 348
materialism, 53, 285–87
Mayan prophecy, 47–48
Mbiti, J. S., 4
Mbon, Friday M., 338
media, 195–97, 210, 277
medicine, 197–98, 249; alternative, 117; preventive, 55
Medicine person, 117
meditation, 40, 55, 56, 93, 253, 351–52. *See also* Yoga
Mennonites, 24
Merton, Thomas, 124
messenger-prophets, 71, 72
metaphysical traditions, 26
Methodist Episcopal Church, 23
Methodists, 213
Mexican InterFaith Council (Consejo Interreligioso Disease
     Mexico–CIM), 142–43, 152
Mexico, 152; proposed ethics code among religions in,
     142–45
military, 135
Miller, William, 24
ministers: female, 26; interfaith, 148
minority voices, listening to, 135
Monastic Inter-religious Dialogue (MID), 152–53, 275
monasticism, 26
Monophysites, 21
Moon, Hak Ja Han, 109, 110
Moon, Sun Myung, 109, 110, 152, 164
moral capacity and commitment, 241
moral equality, 63
"moral self," 39
Moravian Church, 22, 23
More, Thomas, 274
Mormonism, 25
Mother, 101, 115
Msimang, Afrika, 182
Muhammad, Prophet (SAAWS), 66–69, 71
Muhammad al-Muntazar, 70
Muller, Robert, 317, 351
multifaith organizations, defined, 146
Munsterites, 26
Muslim-Christian dialogue, 132, 156–57
Muslims, 6, 66, 227, 238
mutual recognition, 15
mystical consciousness, varieties and categories of, 251–53
mystical dimension of consciousness, 250–51
mystical experience *vs.* mystical process, 251
mystical perception, 252
mysticism, 87; universal understanding of, 250–53

N

Nagarjuna, 13–14
Nanak, Guru, 92, 95–96
National Conference for Community and Justice (NCCJ), 147,
     151
National Conference of Christians and Jews, 171
National Council of Churches, 147, 279
National Council of the Churches of Christ, 147, 153
National Religious Partnership for the Environment (NRPE),
     153, 282
National Youth Project, 165
Native American-Christian worship, 34
Native American Free Exercise of Religion Act (NAFERA), 336
Native American spirituality, 48–49, 173, 254, 280, 316–17
Native American tribes, 46, 254
native traditions, first peoples and, 42–49
Nature, 43, 114; Jain declaration on, 310–11; respect for all
     creation of, 120. *See also* Earth
Nature religions, 117. *See also* Wicca
Nature spirituality, 117. *See also* Wicca
Nature spirituality terms, 117–18
Nazi Germany, 321
Neo-Confucianism, 38–39, 41
Nestorians, 21
networking, 351, 356–57
new age, 239
New Testament, 20, 26
New Thought, 26
Next Generation, 163
Nhat Hanh, Thich, 289–90, 352
Nigeria, 285–86
nirvana, 12, 251
niyama dhammas (five laws), 16–17
no-self, 251
Non-Governmental Committee on Freedom of Religion and
     Belief, 328–29
Non-Governmental Liaizon Service (NGLS), United Nations,
     278
nongovernmental organizations (NGOs), 269, 278–79, 325;
     religiously based, 269, 278–79
nonviolence, 237; deep, 241–42; democracy, peace, and,
     307–8; and the human rights struggle, 323; organizations
     focusing on, 150, 426–27; prophetic, 210–11; suggestions
     for implementing, 221–22; as supreme religion, 81, 82;
     universal declaration of, 216–17. *See also* Jainism
nonviolent response to conflict, 210
nonviolent social change in the Gandhian tradition, 221–24
North American Board for East-West Dialogue. *See* Monastic
     Inter-religious Dialogue
North American Interfaith Network (NAIN), 153, 154, 164
North American prophecies, 46–47
nuclear weapons, threat of, 228–29; moral call to eliminate
     the, 229–30

O

Office on Inter-Religious Relations, 132
Old Religion. *See* Wicca
Old Testament, 22, 28–29
Old Testament laws, 24. *See also* Sabbath

Om, 52
Omar, Sheikh Ahmed Tijani Ben, 333
"open-gate policy," 169
openness, 139
Oral Tradition, 20
organizational development, 234
organizational effectiveness and efficiency, 38
original sin, denial of, 25, 112
overconsumption: as mounting catastrophe, 317–18; strategies for ending, 318–19
Oxlaj, Don Alejandro, 48

P

Pa Qua (eight trigrams), 106
pacifism, 24
Pagans. See Wicca
Pakistan, 227, 332
Palmer, Parker, 234
pantheism, 117
Papau New Guinea, 44
Paradise: remembrances of, 273–74. *See also* society, ideal
Parliament Assembly, 183
Parliaments of the World's Religions, 166–67; of 1993, 127–28, 166, 184–85, 239–40, 331–35; of 1999, 166, 182–83, 202–6; of 2004, 205; as conspiracy *vs.* CoNexus, 166–67, 202; disasters, wisdom, and new alliances, 168; experiences of the heart, 168–69; impact, 166; lessons on unity and diversity from, 167–68; and "opening the gates," 169–70; opposition to, 166, 202; programs and themes, 182–83, 203–5; and religious change, 170–71; social agenda, 207; suggestions to strengthen and broaden, 205–8; underlying Western presupposition, 206–7; vis-à-vis a universal society, 274–75; vision and legacy, 171
Patel, Ebrahim, 162, 163
patriotism, 8
Paul, Saint, 288, 350
peace, 44, 58, 73, 83, 152, 153, 260, 263; among religions, 239, 240; commitment to culture of nonviolence, 178, 186; democracy, nonviolence, and, 307–8; nonviolence and the culture of, 275; organizations focusing on, 420, 424–26; prayers, scriptures, and reflections on, 280–81, 283; reorientation towards, 272; role of religions in promoting a culture of, 262–64; seeking a culture of, 259–60; seeking the true meaning of, 269–70; through religion, 131. *See also* nonviolence
Peace Council, 153
peace failure, causes of, 266
Pentecostals, 23
People of the Way, 28
Perfect Wisdom of the Buddhas, 12
perfection and sinlessness, 23
personalism, 251
Pietist-Methodist churches, 22–23
Plan, 99, 100
Plato, 274
pluralism, 153–54, 231, 232; in the subject and "object" of mystical experience, 251–52
political conflict: interreligious, 209–10. *See also* war

politics, nonviolent, 223–24
polytheism, 117
Pontifical Council for Inter-Religious Dialogue, 132
Pontifical Council on Interfaith Relations, 147
population and development, debate on issues of, 312–13
poverty, 8, 26, 28, 29, 69, 157, 179, 222, 350–51. *See also* economic concerns
prayer, 74, 119, 427; action and, 352
prayers, 69; for peace, 131
predestination, 23, 112
Presbyterian Church, 22
Project Global 2000 (PG2000), 265
promiscuity, 314
prophecies, ancient, 45–48
prophets, 69, 71, 72. *See also specific individuals*
Protestantism, 20, 257

Q

Q'ero, 47
Quakers, 24
Quechua Incan prophecies, 47
Quetzalcoatl, 45–48
Qur'an, 66, 68, 72, 73

R

racial unity, 8, 72, 73
racism, 32–33, 63–64, 167, 203, 332, 334. *See also* genocide
Raja Yoga, 57
Rajchandra, Shrimad, 311
Ramage, David, 128
Ramakrishna, 58
Rasor, Stephen C., 233
Raspberry, William, 233
rationalists, 38–39
rationality, 41, 55
reason, 20, 25, 30, 62
Reconstructionism, Jewish, 87
Reformation, 112. *See also* Protestantism
reincarnation, 51, 59
Religion and World Order Program, 269
religion(s): call to, 189–91; cosmology, 116, 244–49; defined, 233; essence, 57; goal, 3; nature of, 142; oneness of all, 7, 41; spiritual interdependence among, 241
religious beliefs, willingness to consider the incompleteness of one's, 126
religious consensus, 135
religious dialogue. *See* interfaith dialogue
religious experience, acceptance of variety in, 53, 55
religious fanatics, pity on, 226–28
religious freedom, 322–23, 329–30; organizations focusing on, 427. *See also* human rights
religious identity, question of, 232
religious intolerance, 133, 209; eliminating, 217–20
religious leaders, 131
religious life, ambiguities of, 27
religious minorities: discrimination against, 133; and religious freedom, 322–23
religious networks, role of, 267–69

religious oppression, 329. *See also* religious freedom
Religious Youth Service (RYS), 164
resource depletion, 317–18
responsibility: religious, 264; universal, 272, 274, 305
return of savior, 24, 45
revelation, 25, 69
rights, 48, 63; children's, 340–41; individual, 54; women's, 181, 187. *See also* Civil Rights movement; human rights
rites, 4, 5
rituals, 119–20
Rockefeller, Steven C., 124
Romelus, Willie, 332
Rose, Jonathan, 152
Rta, 55
Russell, Charles Taze, 24, 25

S

Sabbath, 22, 24, 28
saccidananda, 252
sacramental tradition, 30
Sacramento, temples firebombed in, 212–14
sacraments, 21, 22. *See also* specific sacraments
sacred community, 240–41, 354
Sacred Earth Gathering, 309
saints, 22
Sakyamuni. *See* Buddha
Salat, 69
salvation, 13, 22, 24, 25, 51, 52, 61, 110; quest for, 3
Samphell, Norbu, 333
samsara, 13, 338
sannyasa, universal order of, 276
sarvodaya, 349–50
Satan, 110
savior, 119. *See also* Christ; Jesus Christ
Sawn (fasting), 69, 74
Schuman, Bruce, 154
Schuon, Frithjof, 250
Schweitzer, Albert, 221
science(s), 197–98, 227; limitations, 313
Seattle, Chief, 286, 288, 316
secularism, 227, 314
segregation, racial, 32, 33
Self, 50, 55, 56
self, 38, 251
self-critical, being healthily, 140–41
self-discipline, 39
self-interest, beyond the borders of, 260–61
self-knowledge, mature, 242
Self-Realization Fellowship (SRF)/Yogoda Satsanga Society of India, 59
self-responsibility, 178, 181–82
selfishness, 177–78
selfless service, 243
selflessness, 16, 40, 56
seminaries: organizations focusing on, 428–29
separation from God-Love, 18
service, 94
Seventh Day Adventists, 24
sexes, commitment to partnership between the, 181, 187
sexism, 64, 181, 187
sexual education, 314

sexuality and sexual morality, 62–63, 181, 338
Shahadah, 69
shalom, vision of, 29
shamanism, 117–18
Sherman, E. B., 84
Shi'ah, 68–70
Shinto, 89–90, 281; challenges facing, 90; and interfaith dialogue and cooperation, 90; types of, 89; in the world today, 90–91
Shinto myths, 89
Shiva, 52
Shoghi Effendi, 7, 8
shunyata, 252
Sigal, Phillip, 157
Sikhism, 92, 173, 257, 281; beliefs, 92–95; and interfaith dialogue, 95, 237; responses to social problems, 95–96; service to humanity, 96–97
Sikhs, 334
simplicity of life, 242–43
sin, 18–19; Adam's, 24, 25; original, 25, 112
Singh, Guru Gobind, 92, 93
Singh, Karan, 316
sinlessness, perfection and, 23
slavery, 32, 33
Smartas, 52
Smith, Joseph, 25
social justice, 26–27, 29, 32–34, 37, 58, 63–64, 192, 306–7, 350–51; striving for, 188. *See also* specific issues
social networks, 39, 54
social problems, 53–54. *See also* specific problems
social programs, and spirituality, 233
social service, 39, 96–97, 183, 350–51
society, ideal, 25–26, 39, 40, 275–77
Society for Buddhist-Christian Studies, 136, 154
solidarity, 29; commitment to culture of, 179, 186; and service, 188; spiritual, 242
Solle, Dorothy, 349
Song, Choan-Seng, 136–37
soul, denial of, 251
South Africa, 203–4
South American prophecies, 47
Spayde, Jon, 235
spells, casting, 116
Spirit as Sacred, 234–35
spiritual experience and development, 234
spiritual grounding, seeking, 188
spiritual growth, personal, 58
spiritual movements, listening to, 135
spiritual mysteries, 45–46, 297
spiritual philosophies, 98–104
spiritual practice, 242
spiritual relationships, 233
spiritual renaissance, need for a, 235
spirituality(ies), 31; call to, 189–91; exploring, 235; global, 125; meaning and nature of, 48, 233–34, 236, 241; of new civilization, 276; patterns in the way people use the term, 234; religion and, 233, 250–51, 268; universal understanding of, 250–53
Steiner, Rudolf, 98, 99
submission, 71
suffering (*dukha*), 12

sufficiency, 29, 30
Sufi Sheikh, golden words of a, 75–76
Sufism *(Tasawwuf)*, 71
Sunnah, 68
Sunni Muslims, 68–70
"suspension of belief," 126
sustainability, commitment to, 187–88, 319
Suter, Keith, 278
Suzuki Roshi, Shunryu, 17
Swedenborg, Emmanuel, 26
Swedish Evangelical Church, 22, 23
Swidler, Leonard, 126, 127, 150, 172, 173
Swing, William E., 162
syncretism, 130
Syrian churches, 22

T

Taborites, 26
Taiwan, 41
Tanchuma, Midrash, 316
tantras, 14
Tao Te Ching, 105
Tao (Truth/Great Ultimate), 37–39, 41
Taoism, 14, 41, 105–7, 280; in the world today, 108
Tathagatananda, 316
Teasdale, Brother Wayne, 125, 235, 354
technology, 64, 120, 227, 317, 318
Tecumseh, 49
Temple of Understanding (ToU), 130, 154, 229, 279
Ten Commandments, 18. *See also* directives
Thanksgiving World Assembly, 148–49
theism *vs.* nontheism, 251–52
Theosophical Society, 101–3
theosophy, 101–2; and primary challenges and issues facing humanity, 103–4; in the world today, 102–3
thought, sincerity of, 39
Tibet, 14–15, 243
tolerance: commitment to culture of, 180; religious *(see* interfaith dialogue; religious experience, acceptance of variety in)
tongues, speaking in, 23
"Towards a Global Ethic: An Initial Declaration," 173–86, 189–92, 197, 198, 200, 241
traditionalists, welcomed in interfaith dialogue, 134
Transcendence, 71
Transcendentalism, 25
transformation: of consciousness, 181–82; cultural, 239; individual/personal, 38, 41, 347–48; social, 38–41, 318–19; visions of, 202–5
transpersonalism, 252
transportation, 64
transubstantiation, 22
trinitheism, 25
Trinity, 25, 112; Hindu, 52
trust, and interfaith dialogue, 139–40
truth, 41, 82, 345–46. *See also Tao*
truth claims, 232; conflicting, 231
truthfulness, commitment to life of, 180, 186–87
Tsele, Molefe, 334

U

Ultimate Reality, 137, 189, 231, 241
Ummah, 68, 70, 76–77, 238
unification, 41
Unification Church, 109–10
Unit for Dialogue with People of Living Faiths, 132
Unitarian Universalist Association (UUA), 112, 113
Unitarian Universalist Church, 112–13
unitarianism, 25
Unitarians in Romania, 322–23
United Communities of Spirit, 154
United Nations (UN), 148, 243, 265; NGOs affiliated with, 278; peacekeeping function, 209. *See also specific covenants and declarations*
United Nations Charter, 265, 266
United Nations Conference on Population and Development, 312–13
United Nations Convention on the Rights of the Child, 340–43
United Nations Educational, Scientific, and Cultural Organization (UNESCO), 224, 262–63, 269, 275
United Nations Environment Programme (UNEP), 269, 295, 315
United Nations Rio Earth Summit (UNCED), 295, 309
United Religions Initiative (URI), 154–55, 162
unity: of the family, 271–72; of humankind, 8, 45, 50, 71, 75; of the world, 271
Unity Church of Christianity, 26
Universal Declaration of Human Responsibilities, 343–44
Universal Declaration of Human Rights, 143, 176, 217, 320–22, 325–28, 340, 344
universal spirituality, 231; elements of a, 241–43
universalism, 25, 88, 231. *See also* Unitarian Universalist Church
universe, sacred story of the, 244–49
Upanishads, 50
utopian society. *See* society, ideal

V

Values Caucus, 154
Vatican Council, Second, 239
Vedanta, 57–58
Vedantists, 237
Vedas (Scriptures), 50, 52, 59
vegetarianism, 82
violence, 64, 178, 212–14, 227–28; science, nature *vs.* nurture, and, 224–26; Seville statement on, 224–26. *See also* war
virtue, 19–20, 73, 105–6
Vision TV, 155
vision(s): of challenge, harmony, and transformation, 202–5; forging new, 243–44; of the world, 185–86, 189–91, 193–200
Vivekananda, Swami, 58, 132, 226, 227
"Voices of the Dispossessed," 331–35

W

Waitaha nation, 47
Waldorf schools, 98–99

Walton, Joni, 233
war, 44, 224–25; and human rights abuses, 331–32; incompatibility of religion and, 216–17. *See also* genocide; nuclear weapons; political conflict
Wartenberg-Potter, Barbel Von, 336
wealth, 26; sharing, 69
Whitney, Diana, 234–35
Wicca, 114–16, 118
wisdom tradition, 29–30
Witches, 118. *See also* Wicca
witnessing, religious: cross-fertilization from, 330
women: commitment to partnership between men and, 181, 187; emancipation, 8; equal rights for, 181, 187; faith, strength, and, 58; organizations focusing on, 430; religion and, 314, 337–40. *See also* gender equality
Women in the World's Religions (King), 337–38
Women's Federation for World Peace, 109
Woodson, Robert L., Sr., 233
world, response to those who despair about the state of the, 347–48
World Conference on Religion and Peace (WCRP), 91, 131, 146, 155–56, 164, 165, 170, 269, 279
World Congress of Faiths (WCF), 130, 136, 156, 171, 173
World Council of Churches (WCC), 321; Office on Inter-Religious Relations, 132, 156–57
World Council of Faiths, 136
World Faiths Development Dialogue (WFDD), 157
world federal system, 9
World Muslim League, 132
world order: religion and, 264–69
World Summit for Children, 343
World's Parliament of Religions (1893), 57, 58, 84, 112–13, 205–6, 232; impact, 166; objectives, 128–29; and study of the world's religions, 130
WorldWide Church of God, 24
worship, 69

Y

Year of Interreligious Understanding and Cooperation (1993), 133–34, 151, 170
Yin and Yang, 37, 38, 40, 105
Yoga, 56–57; approaches to, 57, 59; in the West, 57
Yoga-Sutras (Patanjali), 56–57
Yogananda, Paramahansa, 59
Yogoda Satsanga Society of India, 59
Yoruba practices, 4
Ywagoo, 46–47

Z

Zakat, 69, 74
Zarathushtra, 119
Zaydiyah, 70
Zen, 14, 17, 40
Zoroastrianism, 119–20, 173, 255, 281; beliefs, 119; contributions to Western thought, 121; as a minority religion, 120; sources of religious knowledge, 119; in the world today, 120–21
Zulu, 5

ACKNOWLEDGMENTS

Among the great rewards of shaping this *Sourcebook* is the interaction by the Editor with authors and organizations who offer welcome inspiration and fellowship. The numerous contributors to this book have generously provided essays, articles, permissions, insights, and information. By participating in the creation of this book, they have also validated my purpose in compiling their materials: documenting the existence of—and potential for—Earth's emerging community of religions.

At the same time, because the *Sourcebook* is a wide-ranging collection of beliefs, interpretations, critiques, and visionary statements, no individuals or organizations presented in it should be construed as endorsing any specific contents of this book other than what they have written.

The Editor, Joel Beversluis, bears all responsibility for the selection of the materials and for remaining errors in interpretation or presentation. Corrections, new information, and suggestions may be sent to the Editor at CoNexus Press, 6264 Grand River Dr. NE, Ada, MI 49301 USA.

Many of these articles and documents were first published in this book, either in this edition or earlier ones. In some cases, copyright notices and sources are printed with the articles, as requested. In other cases, we offer our grateful appreciation to the following sources for use of copyrighted and previously printed materials:

American Humanist Association. "Humanist Manifesto II." First printed in Volume 33, Number 5, September/October 1973, *The Humanist.* Reprinted with permission.

Association of Interfaith Ministers. "A Definition of Terms" copyright © 1998 AIM. Used with permission.

College Theology Society. "The Cosmology of Religions." by Thomas Berry, in *College Theology Annual Volume,* #34, edited by Dr. Paul Knitter. Used with permission.

CoNexus Press. "The Interfaith Movement in the 20th Century" from *Faith and Interfaith in a Global Age,* copyright © Marcus Braybrooke, 1998. Used with permission.

Council for a Parliament of the World's Religions. "Towards a Global Ethic (An Initial Declaration)", copyright © 1993; and "A Call to Our Guiding Institutions," copyright© 1999. Used with permission. Copyright for the materials published in the 1993

edition of *A Sourcebook for the Community of Religions* was transferred to Joel Beversluis in 1999.

Fellowship Press. "The Golden Words of a Sufi Sheikh," copyright © 1981 Fellowship Press, 5820 Overbrook Avenue, Philadelphia, PA 19131. Used with permission.

Fox, Selena. "A Guide to Nature Spirituality Terms," copyright © 1994 Selena Fox. Used with permission.

GAIA Books Ltd. *The Gaia Atlas of First Peoples* by Julian Burger. A Gaia Original, copyright © 1990 Gaia Books Ltd., 66 Charlotte Street, London W1P 1LR UK. Published in the US by Doubleday/Anchor. Used with permission.

Global Dialogue Institute, "The Deep-Dialogue Decalogue," copyright © 1998 Dr. Leonard Swidler. Used with Permission.

Global Education Associates. "Religion and World Order," by Patricia Mische, copyright © 1994.